SAT/PSAT Quick Review

This review sheet contains useful information about preparing for the SAT and PSAT. Be sure to read the book and take the practice tests before referring to this sheet. Review the information included on this review sheet prior to entering the testing center, paying close attention to the areas where you feel you need the most review. This sheet should not be used as a substitute for actual preparation; it is simply a review of important information presented in detail elsewhere in this book.

GENERAL TEST-TAKING STRATEGIES

1. Relax.
   - ▶ Don't panic if you are having a hard time answering the questions! You do not have to answer all the questions correctly to get a good score.
   - ▶ Take a few moments to relax if you get stressed during the test. Put your pencil down, close your eyes, take some deep breaths, and stop testing. When you get back to the test, you will feel better.

2. Do the easy stuff first.
   - ▶ You don't have to do the questions from each section in order. Skip the hard ones and come back to them later.
   - ▶ Keep moving so that you don't waste valuable time. If you get stuck on a question, move on!

3. Manage the grid.
   - ▶ Do not go to your answer sheet after each question. Mark your answers in the book, and then transfer them every one to two pages. Pay attention to question numbers, especially if you skip a question. Your score depends on what is filled in on your answer sheet.

4. You own the test booklet.
   - ▶ Do the math! Draw pictures to help you figure out problems and use the space available to write down your calculations.
   - ▶ Circle your answer choices, cross out answers you eliminate, and mark questions that you need to come back to later. If you cannot eliminate an answer choice, but think that it might work, underline it.
   - ▶ Make notes and marks in the margins of the reading passages as needed.

5. Be aware of time.
   - ▶ Pace yourself. You learned in practice which questions you should focus on and which questions you should skip and come back to later if you have the time.
   - ▶ Time yourself with a watch. Do not rely on the proctor's official time announcements.
   - ▶ You have only a limited amount of time. Read and work actively through the test.
   - ▶ Stay focused. Ignore the things going on around you that you cannot control.
   - ▶ Check over your answers if you have time remaining.

6. Guessing.
   - ▶ Remember the "guessing penalty!"
   - ▶ *Never* guess at random; make educated guesses only.
   - ▶ Eliminate answer choices that you know are wrong. The more you can eliminate, the better your chance of getting the question right.
   - ▶ It is better to leave some questions blank.

7. Changing your mind.
   - ▶ Do not second-guess yourself. Your first answer choice is more likely to be correct. If you're not completely comfortable with your first choice, place a question mark next to your answer and come back to it later if you have time.
   - ▶ Only change your answer when you are sure that it's wrong.

D1609628

CRITICAL READING STRATEGIES

PSAT and SAT Critical Reading sections include Reading Comprehension questions and Sentence Completion questions. The following are specific strategies for each of the sections.

READING COMPREHENSION

1. Read the questions first, making notes on the passage when the questions refer to specific lines or words. Do not try to memorize—just get an idea of what you should be looking for.

2. Read each passage for topic, scope, and purpose. Then skim for structure. Try to isolate one topic word or sentence for each paragraph. The details will still be there when you need them. Don't spend precious time trying to "learn" them.

3. Do not stop on unfamiliar words the first time through. You might not need to know the meaning of a word to answer the questions. Remember that you will be rereading most of the passage as you work on the questions.

4. Read the question and the answer choices before making a selection. Answer the questions carefully, referring back to the passage as needed.

5. Try to predict an answer before looking at the answer choices. If an answer choice matches your prediction, it is most likely correct.

6. Paraphrase when you need to. Putting the question into your own words makes it easier to answer.

7. You do not have to do the questions in order. Skip the hard ones, circle them in your test booklet, and come back to them later if you have time.

SENTENCE COMPLETION

1. Use the Latin roots, prefixes, and suffixes to figure out what hard words mean. Look for "cognates" from French, Spanish, or Italian if you recognize them.

2. Let the context of the sentence guide you and use context clues when needed to figure out the meaning of words

3. Try to look for "clue" words and phrases in the sentence that might suggest a contrast or comparison.

4. When you think that you have the correct answer, read the entire sentence to yourself, using your choice(s) in the blank(s). If it makes sense, mark your answer.

WRITING SKILLS STRATEGIES

Both the PSAT and SAT Writing Skills sections include Identifying Sentence Error questions, Improving Sentences questions, and Improving Paragraphs questions. The SAT includes an Essay writing task as well. The following are specific strategies for each of the sections.

IDENTIFYING SENTENCE ERRORS

1. You do not have to do the questions in order. Skip the hard ones, circle them in your test booklet, and come back to them later if you have time.

2. Carefully read the questions and look for obvious errors.

3. If you cannot find an error, mark answer choice E.

4. Trust what you know about basic grammar. If you struggle with one of the underlined portions as you read the sentence, that portion is most likely the one that contains the error.

IMPROVING SENTENCES

1. The underlined portion of the sentence might need to be revised. When reading the sentence, pay attention to the underlined portion.

2. If the underlined portion seems correct as it is within the sentence, mark choice (A) on your answer sheet.

3. If the underlined portion does not seem correct, try to predict the correct answer. If an answer choice matches your prediction, it is most likely correct.

4. If your predicted answer does not match any of the answer choices, determine which of the selections is the most clear and simple.

IMPROVING PARAGRAPHS

1. Quickly read over the entire passage, focusing on its general meaning.

2. The purpose of this section is for you to revise the given passage. Expect to notice several errors as you are reading.

3. Make sure that all of your answer choices fit within the overall context of the passage.

4. Remember that you are looking for ways to improve the paragraph, but you will not necessarily need to add further details to clarify the paragraph. Simply answer the questions that are asked.

SAT ESSAY

1. You will have 25 minutes to complete this section. Use your time wisely.

2. Carefully read the prompt. Remember that an essay written off the topic will receive a score of 0.

3. Spend 10–15 minutes planning your essay. Create an outline to keep you on track.

4. Remember, there is no correct position; choose the position that you can most strongly support.

EXAM✓PREP

SAT/PSAT

Steven W. Dulan
Advantage Education

SAT/PSAT Exam Prep

International Standard Book Number: 0-7897-3615-2

Printed in the United States of America

First Printing: December 2006

09 08 07 06   4 3 2 1

Trademarks

Warning and Disclaimer

Bulk Sales

Que Publishing offers excellent discounts on this book when ordered in quantity for bulk purchases or special sales. For more information, please contact

U.S. Corporate and Government Sales
1-800-382-3419
corpsales@pearsontechgroup.com

For sales outside the U.S., please contact

International Sales
international@pearsoned.com

Library of Congress CIP Data is available upon request.

PUBLISHER
Paul Boger

ACQUISITIONS EDITOR
Betsy Brown

DEVELOPMENT EDITOR
Rick Kughen

MANAGING EDITOR
Patrick Kanouse

PROJECT EDITOR
Seth Kerney

COPY EDITOR
Kevin Kent

INDEXER
Ken Johnson

PROOFREADER
Chrissy White

TECHNICAL EDITORS
Molly Forster

Dan Powroznik

PUBLISHING COORDINATOR
Vanessa Evans

BOOK DESIGNER
Gary Adair

PAGE LAYOUT
Bronkella Publishing LLC

Contents at a Glance

Table of Contents

Chapter 6:
SAT/PSAT Quantitative

Part III: Content Area Review

Chapter 7:
Quantitative Review

About the Author

Steven W. Dulan, J.D., has been involved with PSAT and SAT preparation since 1989 when, as a former U.S. Army Infantry Sergeant and undergraduate student at Michigan State University, Steve became a PSAT and SAT instructor. He has been helping students to prepare for success on the PSAT and SAT and other standardized exams ever since. Steve has scored in the 99th percentile on every standardized test he has ever taken.

After graduating from Michigan State University, Steve attended the Thomas M. Cooley Law School on a full Honors Scholarship. While attending law school, Steve continued to teach standardized test prep classes (including ACT, SAT, PSAT, GRE, GMAT, and LSAT) an average of 30 hours each week and tutored some of his fellow law students in a variety of subjects and in essay exam writing techniques. Steve has also served as an instructor at Baker University, Cleary University, Lansing Community College, the Ohio State University-Real Estate Institute, and the Thomas M. Cooley Law School. His guest lecturer credits include Michigan State University, University of Michigan, Detroit College of Law, Marquette University, Texas Technical University, University of Miami, and Wright State University.

Thousands of students have benefited from Steve's instruction, coaching, and admissions consulting and have entered the colleges of their choice. Steve's students have gained admission to some of the most prestigious institutions of higher learning in the world and have received numerous scholarships and fellowships of their own. Since 1997, Steve has served as the president of Advantage Education® (www.AdvantageEd.com), a company dedicated to providing effective and affordable test prep education in a variety of settings, including one-on-one tutoring via the Internet worldwide using its Personal Distance Learning® system. The information and techniques included in this book are the result of Steve's experiences with test preparation students at all levels over many years.

Acknowledgments

I would like to acknowledge the outstanding contribution of the faculty and staff of Advantage Education. Your hard work and dedication have made this endeavor a success. You are not only the smartest, but also the best.

Special thanks must be given to the following Advantage Education faculty and staff members:

Lisa DiLiberti for her thoughtful critique; Lauren Johnson for her critical editing eye; Matt Mathison for his math expertise; Ryan Particka for his attention to detail; Andrew Sanford for his eloquence; and Kim So for her patience in checking everyone's work.

Most importantly, I would like to acknowledge the single biggest contributor to this work: my wife, colleague, co-author, editor, typist, employee, boss, and friend, Amy Dulan. None of this would have been possible without you.

We Want to Hear from You!

As the reader of this book, *you* are our most important critic and commentator. We value your opinion and want to know what we're doing right, what we could do better, what areas you'd like to see us publish in, and any other words of wisdom you're willing to pass our way.

As an acquisitions editor for Que Publishing, I welcome your comments. You can email or write me directly to let me know what you did or didn't like about this book—as well as what we can do to make our books better.

Please note that I cannot help you with technical problems related to the topic of this book. We do have a User Services group, however, where I will forward specific technical questions related to the book.

When you write, please be sure to include this book's title and author as well as your name, email address, and phone number. I will carefully review your comments and share them with the author and editors who worked on the book.

Email: scorehigher@pearsoned.com

Mail: Betsy Brown
Acquisitions Editor
Que Publishing
800 East 96th Street
Indianapolis, IN 46240 USA

If you would like to contact the author directly, please send an email to sat@AdvantageEd.com.

Reader Services

Visit our website and register this book at www.examcram.com/register for convenient access to any updates, downloads, or errata that might be available for this book.

PART I

Introduction to the SAT/PSAT

CHAPTER ONE

Overview of the Tests

Each year, more than one million students take the SAT Reasoning Test to gain entrance into the colleges of their choice. The SAT is a standardized test designed to measure your critical thinking skills and to assess your ability to apply knowledge and logic when solving problems. Your SAT score will be evaluated along with your high school grade point average, involvement in school and extracurricular activities, letters of recommendation, and college application essay. While the SAT is just one factor that is examined during the admissions process, it is essential that you maximize your SAT score so that you can remain competitive among the many other applicants.

About the SAT

There is a company called The College Board that decides exactly what is going to be on your SAT Reasoning Test. These experts consult with classroom teachers at the high school and college level. They look at high school and college courses, and they consult with educators and specialized psychologists called *psychometricians* (measurers of the mind), who know a lot about the human brain and how it behaves under a variety of conditions.

Another entity, the non-profit organization Educational Testing Service (ETS), develops and administers the SAT in conjunction with The College Board. You will most likely see the initials ETS on your registration materials, test-admission ticket, and score report.

The SAT requires you to answer questions related to Critical Reading, Writing, and Math that are intended to assess your general readiness for college and to show college admissions professionals whether you will perform successfully in college. Visit www.sat.org for more information.

The SAT is not a direct measure of your abilities. It is not an IQ test. The SAT is certainly not a measure of your value as a person, nor is it a measure of your natural, inborn ability. If it were, we wouldn't have had the successes that we have had in raising past students' scores on SAT exams.

The SAT actually measures a predictable set of skills and some specific knowledge. It is "trainable," meaning that you can do better on your SAT if you put the time into learning the knowledge and perfecting the skills that are tested.

Structure of the SAT

The SAT Reasoning Test includes a total of 170 questions (not counting the variable section), plus one Essay assignment. You are given 3 hours and 45 minutes to complete the test. Your actual SAT will include a variable section in Critical Reading, Writing, or Math, which will not count toward your score. This additional 25-minute section tries out new questions for future versions of the SAT and helps ensure that scores are comparable from one test administration to the next. This is a process called *norming*.

Table 1.1 shows a breakdown of the question types, number of each question type, and time allotted for each section.

Table 1.1 SAT Structure

Critical Reading	
67 total questions	Two 25-minute sections
	One 20-minute section
Content	**Number of questions**
Sentence completion	19
Passage-based reading	48
Mathematics	
54 total questions	Two 25-minute sections
	One 20-minute section
Content	**Number of questions**
Multiple choice	44
Student produced response	10
Writing Skills	
49 total questions	Two 25-minute sections
	One 10-minute section
Content	**Number of questions**
Identifying sentence errors	18
Improving sentences	25
Improving paragraphs	6
Essay	1

About the PSAT

The PSAT is a standardized test that provides firsthand practice for the SAT. It is also used to qualify you for the National Merit Scholarship Corporation (NMSC) scholarship programs. In fact, the full name of the test is Preliminary SAT/National Merit Scholarship Qualifying Test (PSAT/NMSQT).

The National Merit Scholarship® is administered by the National Merit Scholarship Corporation and recognizes the top 50,000 scorers out of more than one million students who take the test each year. To qualify, you must take the test during your third year of high school (usually called your junior year). Approximately 16,000 of the top 50,000 are named as Semi-Finalists. The remaining students are sent Letters of Commendation. About 15,000 out of the 16,000 become Finalists by qualifying based on academic standards. Approximately 8,200 of the Finalists actually receive Merit Scholarship® awards, which are valued at a minimum of $2,500.

In some cases, these scholarships amount to full scholarships, which can be renewed for up to 4 years of college. Each year, about 1,600 of the top 50,000 who are not Finalists are awarded Special Scholarships of varying amounts. Detailed information about these scholarships can be found online at www.nationalmerit.org.

The PSAT is administered by high school officials in October each year. Students typically take the PSAT during either their sophomore or junior years, but only the scores that you achieve during your junior year are used for scholarship qualifying purposes.

Structure of the PSAT

The PSAT includes a total of 125 questions of the same type as those that appear on the SAT—Critical Reading, Writing, and Math. However, the PSAT does not include an Essay assignment or third-year math questions. You are given approximately 2 hours and 30 minutes to complete the PSAT.

Table 1.2 shows a breakdown of the question types, number of each question type, and time allotted for each section.

Table 1.2   PSAT Structure

Critical Reading	
48 total questions	Two 25-minute sections
Content	**Number of questions**
Sentence completion	13
Passage-based reading	35
Mathematics	
38 total questions	Two 25-minute sections
Content	**Number of questions**
Multiple choice	28
Student produced response	10
Writing Skills	
39 total questions	One 30-minute section
Content	**Number of questions**
Identifying sentence errors	14
Improving sentences	20
Improving paragraphs	5

Differences Between the PSAT and the SAT

Because the PSAT is considered a practice SAT, this book focuses primarily on SAT preparation. Rest assured that all of the skills and strategies outlined in this book will apply to each test.

Following are the major difference between the PSAT and the SAT:

1. The SAT includes an Essay section, whereas the PSAT does not.

2. The SAT quantitative questions test third-year math concepts, whereas the PSAT quantitative questions do not.

3. The SAT includes 170 total questions, whereas the PSAT includes 125 total questions.

What's Next?

The next chapter will include information on how to register for the SAT, what to expect at the testing center, and how the SAT is scored. We will also provide a review of the policies governing test takers with disabilities.

The chapters in Part II of this book will give you the strategies that you need to successfully tackle the questions on your SAT, and the simulated tests contained in Part IV provide you with material on which to practice and hone your test-taking skills.

Plan to take one full-length test about one week prior to the actual SAT. Read the explanations for the questions that you missed, and review the content-specific chapters as necessary. Remember, practice as much as you can under realistic testing conditions to maximize your SAT score.

CHAPTER TWO

Taking the Tests

Ideally, you will be reading this book at least 3 to 4 weeks before you take your actual PSAT or SAT exam. If that is not the case, you can still benefit from this book. You should look at Chapter 4, "Strategies for Success," first and then work through at least some of the practice questions. Even just a few hours of study and practice can have a positive impact on your test score.

If you have enough time between now and your actual PSAT or SAT exam (at least 3 weeks, preferably), you should work through this entire book. Some of the material is meant to be used as realistic practice material to get you ready for the whole experience of taking a PSAT or SAT exam.

As you work through the simulated tests in Part IV, you should be aware that they are not actual exams. They are reasonably accurate simulations written by experienced experts. They contain basically the same mix of question types as a real SAT. If you work through all of the material provided, you can rest assured that there won't be any surprises on test day.

Generally, students tend to score a little better on each successive practice test. However, both PSAT and SAT exams are sensitive to individual conditions such as fatigue and stress. Therefore, the time of day that you take your practice exams, your environment, and other things that might be going on in your life can have an impact on your scores. Don't get worried if you see some score fluctuation because of a bad day or because the practice test revealed weaknesses in your knowledge or skills. Simply use the information that you gather to help you improve.

In our experience, the students who see the largest increases in their scores are the ones who put in consistent effort over several weeks. Try to keep your frustration to a minimum if you are struggling, and try to keep from becoming overconfident when everything is going your way.

You will improve with practice. Decide when you are going to take the SAT and allow enough time to work through all of the material in this book before your test date.

Registering for the SAT

You have to register for the SAT in advance. You can't just show up on test day with a #2 pencil and expect to be given a test. The best source of information for everything regarding the SAT is, not surprisingly, the SAT website: www.sat.org. The preferred method of registration is online, where you will create your own personal account.

There is also a strong chance that a pre-college counselor at your school has an SAT Registration Book, which includes all the information that you need for your registration, including how to register and pay your fees by mail.

Stand-by registration is available for an additional fee at most testing locations. You are not guaranteed a seat, so your best bet is to register online well in advance of the registration deadline.

Scoring the SAT

You receive one point for each of the questions that you answer correctly on the SAT. If you answer a multiple choice question incorrectly, an extra ¼ point will be deducted. You will receive zero points for questions that are left blank. Because of this scoring system, we recommend that you do not guess at random on the SAT. Follow the strategies included in this book to learn how to make educated guesses when necessary.

Scores from each of the three sections of the SAT—Critical Reading, Writing, and Math—are reported on a scale from 200 to 800, with additional subscores reported for the essay. These essay subscores range from 2 to 12 and are discussed further in Chapter 5, "SAT/PSAT Verbal Sections." The multiple-choice writing questions also receive a subscore that is measured on a 20-to-80 scale. Visit www.sat.org for more detailed information on scores and score reports.

What Your SAT Scores Mean to Schools

Most colleges and universities use SAT scores as an admissions tool because SAT scores are a reliable measure of an individual's performance at the college level and because SAT scores provide a consistent means by which to evaluate applicants. Admissions professionals also take into account an applicant's grade point average, personal interviews, and letters of recommendation. However, because each of these methods of evaluation is variable and subjective, admissions departments need a standardized tool to provide a more objective measure of academic success.

A Note on Scoring the Practice Tests in This Book

The practice tests in this book are created by experts to simulate the question types, difficulty level, and content areas that you will find on your real SAT. The scoring worksheets included for each test are guides to computing approximate scores. Actual SAT exams are scored with scales that are unique to each test form. Do not get overly worried about your practice test scores; your goal should be to learn something from every practice experience and to get used to the format and types of questions on the SAT.

Scoring the PSAT

Like the SAT, the PSAT penalizes you for marking an answer incorrectly on your answer sheet. For each question you answer correctly, one point is awarded, but for each question that you answer incorrectly, ¼ point is deducted.

Score reports are mailed directly to school principals in December of each year. For more information on PSAT scores, visit www.psat.org.

Test Takers with Disabilities

The College Board provides additional information for test takers with disabilities that includes guidelines for documenting disabilities, suggestions for test takers, and the necessary forms required to obtain special accommodations. For test takers with documented disabilities, these accommodations might include:

▶ Additional or extended testing time and breaks

▶ Allowance of medical devices and/or special computer equipment in the testing center

▶ A reader, a sign language interpreter, and/or recording devices

▶ Small group settings

Accommodation requests must be made in advance and by following the guidelines set forth in *Instructions for Completing the Student Eligibility Form*, available as a download at www.collegeboard.com. Documentation review could take as long as 6 weeks, so be sure to submit all of the required forms and information several months prior to your desired test date.

What's Next?

The Diagnostic Test—a full length simulated SAT—in Chapter 3 should be your next step. It will help you to focus on areas of strength and weakness in your knowledge base and skill set. Once you've assessed your current readiness for the SAT, focus on the remaining chapters in the book to help you to maximize your PSAT and SAT scores.

PART II
Preparing for the SAT/PSAT

CHAPTER THREE

Diagnostic Test with Answers and Explanations

This chapter will assist you in evaluating your current readiness for both the SAT and the PSAT. Make an honest effort to answer each question and then review the explanations that follow. Don't worry if you are unable to answer many or most of the questions at this point. The rest of the book contains information and resources to help you to maximize your SAT and PSAT scores.

This simulated test is designed to mimic an actual SAT test. Remember that the PSAT tests the same concepts, but with fewer sections.

There are nine separate sections on this test, including:

- ▶ One 25-minute Essay
- ▶ Five other 25-minute Verbal and Math Sections
- ▶ Two 20-minute Verbal and Math Sections
- ▶ One 10-minute Verbal Section

Work on only one section at a time, and make every attempt to complete each section in the time allowed for that particular section. Carefully mark only one answer on your answer sheet for each question. Remember that you can and should write on the test itself to help you to correctly answer the questions.

Tear out the Answer Sheets on pages 14 – 19 before you start the test.

Begin your essay on this page. If you need more space, continue on the next page. Do not write outside of the essay box.

Continuation of ESSAY Section 1 from previous page. Write below only if you need more space.

Start with number 1 for each new section. If a section has fewer questions than answer spaces, leave the extra answer spaces blank. Be sure to erase any errors or stray marks completely.

SECTION 2

1 Ⓐ Ⓑ Ⓒ Ⓓ Ⓔ	11 Ⓐ Ⓑ Ⓒ Ⓓ Ⓔ	21 Ⓐ Ⓑ Ⓒ Ⓓ Ⓔ	31 Ⓐ Ⓑ Ⓒ Ⓓ Ⓔ
2 Ⓐ Ⓑ Ⓒ Ⓓ Ⓔ	12 Ⓐ Ⓑ Ⓒ Ⓓ Ⓔ	22 Ⓐ Ⓑ Ⓒ Ⓓ Ⓔ	32 Ⓐ Ⓑ Ⓒ Ⓓ Ⓔ
3 Ⓐ Ⓑ Ⓒ Ⓓ Ⓔ	13 Ⓐ Ⓑ Ⓒ Ⓓ Ⓔ	23 Ⓐ Ⓑ Ⓒ Ⓓ Ⓔ	33 Ⓐ Ⓑ Ⓒ Ⓓ Ⓔ
4 Ⓐ Ⓑ Ⓒ Ⓓ Ⓔ	14 Ⓐ Ⓑ Ⓒ Ⓓ Ⓔ	24 Ⓐ Ⓑ Ⓒ Ⓓ Ⓔ	34 Ⓐ Ⓑ Ⓒ Ⓓ Ⓔ
5 Ⓐ Ⓑ Ⓒ Ⓓ Ⓔ	15 Ⓐ Ⓑ Ⓒ Ⓓ Ⓔ	25 Ⓐ Ⓑ Ⓒ Ⓓ Ⓔ	35 Ⓐ Ⓑ Ⓒ Ⓓ Ⓔ
6 Ⓐ Ⓑ Ⓒ Ⓓ Ⓔ	16 Ⓐ Ⓑ Ⓒ Ⓓ Ⓔ	26 Ⓐ Ⓑ Ⓒ Ⓓ Ⓔ	36 Ⓐ Ⓑ Ⓒ Ⓓ Ⓔ
7 Ⓐ Ⓑ Ⓒ Ⓓ Ⓔ	17 Ⓐ Ⓑ Ⓒ Ⓓ Ⓔ	27 Ⓐ Ⓑ Ⓒ Ⓓ Ⓔ	37 Ⓐ Ⓑ Ⓒ Ⓓ Ⓔ
8 Ⓐ Ⓑ Ⓒ Ⓓ Ⓔ	18 Ⓐ Ⓑ Ⓒ Ⓓ Ⓔ	28 Ⓐ Ⓑ Ⓒ Ⓓ Ⓔ	38 Ⓐ Ⓑ Ⓒ Ⓓ Ⓔ
9 Ⓐ Ⓑ Ⓒ Ⓓ Ⓔ	19 Ⓐ Ⓑ Ⓒ Ⓓ Ⓔ	29 Ⓐ Ⓑ Ⓒ Ⓓ Ⓔ	39 Ⓐ Ⓑ Ⓒ Ⓓ Ⓔ
10 Ⓐ Ⓑ Ⓒ Ⓓ Ⓔ	20 Ⓐ Ⓑ Ⓒ Ⓓ Ⓔ	30 Ⓐ Ⓑ Ⓒ Ⓓ Ⓔ	40 Ⓐ Ⓑ Ⓒ Ⓓ Ⓔ

SECTION 3

1 Ⓐ Ⓑ Ⓒ Ⓓ Ⓔ	11 Ⓐ Ⓑ Ⓒ Ⓓ Ⓔ	21 Ⓐ Ⓑ Ⓒ Ⓓ Ⓔ	31 Ⓐ Ⓑ Ⓒ Ⓓ Ⓔ
2 Ⓐ Ⓑ Ⓒ Ⓓ Ⓔ	12 Ⓐ Ⓑ Ⓒ Ⓓ Ⓔ	22 Ⓐ Ⓑ Ⓒ Ⓓ Ⓔ	32 Ⓐ Ⓑ Ⓒ Ⓓ Ⓔ
3 Ⓐ Ⓑ Ⓒ Ⓓ Ⓔ	13 Ⓐ Ⓑ Ⓒ Ⓓ Ⓔ	23 Ⓐ Ⓑ Ⓒ Ⓓ Ⓔ	33 Ⓐ Ⓑ Ⓒ Ⓓ Ⓔ
4 Ⓐ Ⓑ Ⓒ Ⓓ Ⓔ	14 Ⓐ Ⓑ Ⓒ Ⓓ Ⓔ	24 Ⓐ Ⓑ Ⓒ Ⓓ Ⓔ	34 Ⓐ Ⓑ Ⓒ Ⓓ Ⓔ
5 Ⓐ Ⓑ Ⓒ Ⓓ Ⓔ	15 Ⓐ Ⓑ Ⓒ Ⓓ Ⓔ	25 Ⓐ Ⓑ Ⓒ Ⓓ Ⓔ	35 Ⓐ Ⓑ Ⓒ Ⓓ Ⓔ
6 Ⓐ Ⓑ Ⓒ Ⓓ Ⓔ	16 Ⓐ Ⓑ Ⓒ Ⓓ Ⓔ	26 Ⓐ Ⓑ Ⓒ Ⓓ Ⓔ	36 Ⓐ Ⓑ Ⓒ Ⓓ Ⓔ
7 Ⓐ Ⓑ Ⓒ Ⓓ Ⓔ	17 Ⓐ Ⓑ Ⓒ Ⓓ Ⓔ	27 Ⓐ Ⓑ Ⓒ Ⓓ Ⓔ	37 Ⓐ Ⓑ Ⓒ Ⓓ Ⓔ
8 Ⓐ Ⓑ Ⓒ Ⓓ Ⓔ	18 Ⓐ Ⓑ Ⓒ Ⓓ Ⓔ	28 Ⓐ Ⓑ Ⓒ Ⓓ Ⓔ	38 Ⓐ Ⓑ Ⓒ Ⓓ Ⓔ
9 Ⓐ Ⓑ Ⓒ Ⓓ Ⓔ	19 Ⓐ Ⓑ Ⓒ Ⓓ Ⓔ	29 Ⓐ Ⓑ Ⓒ Ⓓ Ⓔ	39 Ⓐ Ⓑ Ⓒ Ⓓ Ⓔ
10 Ⓐ Ⓑ Ⓒ Ⓓ Ⓔ	20 Ⓐ Ⓑ Ⓒ Ⓓ Ⓔ	30 Ⓐ Ⓑ Ⓒ Ⓓ Ⓔ	40 Ⓐ Ⓑ Ⓒ Ⓓ Ⓔ

CAUTION Use the answer spaces in the grids below for Section 2 or Section 3 only if you are told to do so in your test book.

Student-Produced Responses ONLY ANSWERS ENTERED IN THE CIRCLES IN EACH GRID WILL BE SCORED. YOU WILL NOT RECEIVE CREDIT FOR ANYTHING WRITTEN IN THE BOXES ABOVE THE CIRCLES.

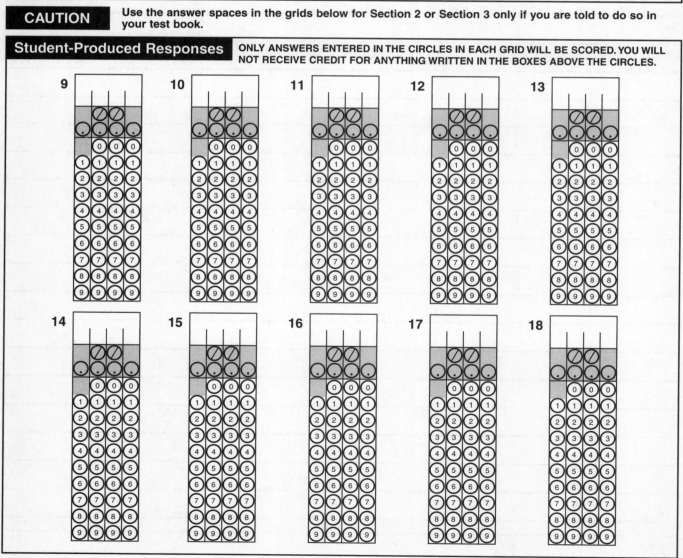

Start with number 1 for each new section. If a section has fewer questions than answer spaces, leave the extra answer spaces blank. Be sure to erase any errors or stray marks completely.

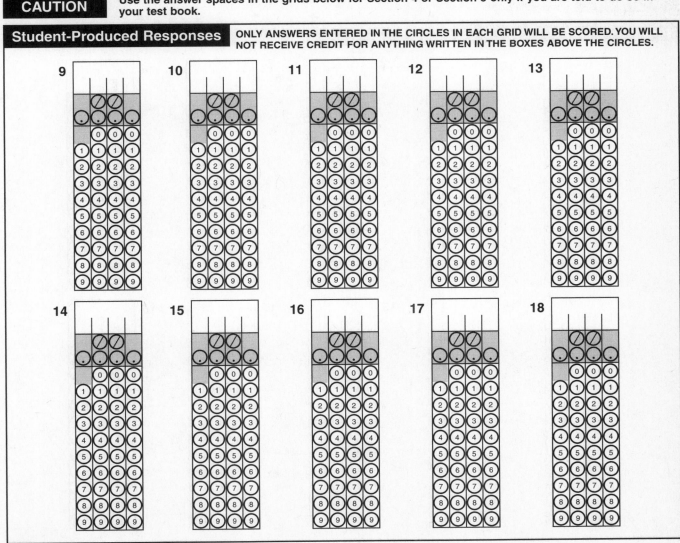

CAUTION Use the answer spaces in the grids below for Section 4 or Section 5 only if you are told to do so in your test book.

Student-Produced Responses ONLY ANSWERS ENTERED IN THE CIRCLES IN EACH GRID WILL BE SCORED. YOU WILL NOT RECEIVE CREDIT FOR ANYTHING WRITTEN IN THE BOXES ABOVE THE CIRCLES.

Start with number 1 for each new section. If a section has fewer questions than answer spaces, leave the extra answer spaces blank. Be sure to erase any errors or stray marks completely.

SECTION 6

1 Ⓐ Ⓑ Ⓒ Ⓓ Ⓔ   11 Ⓐ Ⓑ Ⓒ Ⓓ Ⓔ   21 Ⓐ Ⓑ Ⓒ Ⓓ Ⓔ   31 Ⓐ Ⓑ Ⓒ Ⓓ Ⓔ
2 Ⓐ Ⓑ Ⓒ Ⓓ Ⓔ   12 Ⓐ Ⓑ Ⓒ Ⓓ Ⓔ   22 Ⓐ Ⓑ Ⓒ Ⓓ Ⓔ   32 Ⓐ Ⓑ Ⓒ Ⓓ Ⓔ
3 Ⓐ Ⓑ Ⓒ Ⓓ Ⓔ   13 Ⓐ Ⓑ Ⓒ Ⓓ Ⓔ   23 Ⓐ Ⓑ Ⓒ Ⓓ Ⓔ   33 Ⓐ Ⓑ Ⓒ Ⓓ Ⓔ
4 Ⓐ Ⓑ Ⓒ Ⓓ Ⓔ   14 Ⓐ Ⓑ Ⓒ Ⓓ Ⓔ   24 Ⓐ Ⓑ Ⓒ Ⓓ Ⓔ   34 Ⓐ Ⓑ Ⓒ Ⓓ Ⓔ
5 Ⓐ Ⓑ Ⓒ Ⓓ Ⓔ   15 Ⓐ Ⓑ Ⓒ Ⓓ Ⓔ   25 Ⓐ Ⓑ Ⓒ Ⓓ Ⓔ   35 Ⓐ Ⓑ Ⓒ Ⓓ Ⓔ
6 Ⓐ Ⓑ Ⓒ Ⓓ Ⓔ   16 Ⓐ Ⓑ Ⓒ Ⓓ Ⓔ   26 Ⓐ Ⓑ Ⓒ Ⓓ Ⓔ   36 Ⓐ Ⓑ Ⓒ Ⓓ Ⓔ
7 Ⓐ Ⓑ Ⓒ Ⓓ Ⓔ   17 Ⓐ Ⓑ Ⓒ Ⓓ Ⓔ   27 Ⓐ Ⓑ Ⓒ Ⓓ Ⓔ   37 Ⓐ Ⓑ Ⓒ Ⓓ Ⓔ
8 Ⓐ Ⓑ Ⓒ Ⓓ Ⓔ   18 Ⓐ Ⓑ Ⓒ Ⓓ Ⓔ   28 Ⓐ Ⓑ Ⓒ Ⓓ Ⓔ   38 Ⓐ Ⓑ Ⓒ Ⓓ Ⓔ
9 Ⓐ Ⓑ Ⓒ Ⓓ Ⓔ   19 Ⓐ Ⓑ Ⓒ Ⓓ Ⓔ   29 Ⓐ Ⓑ Ⓒ Ⓓ Ⓔ   39 Ⓐ Ⓑ Ⓒ Ⓓ Ⓔ
10 Ⓐ Ⓑ Ⓒ Ⓓ Ⓔ   20 Ⓐ Ⓑ Ⓒ Ⓓ Ⓔ   30 Ⓐ Ⓑ Ⓒ Ⓓ Ⓔ   40 Ⓐ Ⓑ Ⓒ Ⓓ Ⓔ

SECTION 7

1 Ⓐ Ⓑ Ⓒ Ⓓ Ⓔ   11 Ⓐ Ⓑ Ⓒ Ⓓ Ⓔ   21 Ⓐ Ⓑ Ⓒ Ⓓ Ⓔ   31 Ⓐ Ⓑ Ⓒ Ⓓ Ⓔ
2 Ⓐ Ⓑ Ⓒ Ⓓ Ⓔ   12 Ⓐ Ⓑ Ⓒ Ⓓ Ⓔ   22 Ⓐ Ⓑ Ⓒ Ⓓ Ⓔ   32 Ⓐ Ⓑ Ⓒ Ⓓ Ⓔ
3 Ⓐ Ⓑ Ⓒ Ⓓ Ⓔ   13 Ⓐ Ⓑ Ⓒ Ⓓ Ⓔ   23 Ⓐ Ⓑ Ⓒ Ⓓ Ⓔ   33 Ⓐ Ⓑ Ⓒ Ⓓ Ⓔ
4 Ⓐ Ⓑ Ⓒ Ⓓ Ⓔ   14 Ⓐ Ⓑ Ⓒ Ⓓ Ⓔ   24 Ⓐ Ⓑ Ⓒ Ⓓ Ⓔ   34 Ⓐ Ⓑ Ⓒ Ⓓ Ⓔ
5 Ⓐ Ⓑ Ⓒ Ⓓ Ⓔ   15 Ⓐ Ⓑ Ⓒ Ⓓ Ⓔ   25 Ⓐ Ⓑ Ⓒ Ⓓ Ⓔ   35 Ⓐ Ⓑ Ⓒ Ⓓ Ⓔ
6 Ⓐ Ⓑ Ⓒ Ⓓ Ⓔ   16 Ⓐ Ⓑ Ⓒ Ⓓ Ⓔ   26 Ⓐ Ⓑ Ⓒ Ⓓ Ⓔ   36 Ⓐ Ⓑ Ⓒ Ⓓ Ⓔ
7 Ⓐ Ⓑ Ⓒ Ⓓ Ⓔ   17 Ⓐ Ⓑ Ⓒ Ⓓ Ⓔ   27 Ⓐ Ⓑ Ⓒ Ⓓ Ⓔ   37 Ⓐ Ⓑ Ⓒ Ⓓ Ⓔ
8 Ⓐ Ⓑ Ⓒ Ⓓ Ⓔ   18 Ⓐ Ⓑ Ⓒ Ⓓ Ⓔ   28 Ⓐ Ⓑ Ⓒ Ⓓ Ⓔ   38 Ⓐ Ⓑ Ⓒ Ⓓ Ⓔ
9 Ⓐ Ⓑ Ⓒ Ⓓ Ⓔ   19 Ⓐ Ⓑ Ⓒ Ⓓ Ⓔ   29 Ⓐ Ⓑ Ⓒ Ⓓ Ⓔ   39 Ⓐ Ⓑ Ⓒ Ⓓ Ⓔ
10 Ⓐ Ⓑ Ⓒ Ⓓ Ⓔ   20 Ⓐ Ⓑ Ⓒ Ⓓ Ⓔ   30 Ⓐ Ⓑ Ⓒ Ⓓ Ⓔ   40 Ⓐ Ⓑ Ⓒ Ⓓ Ⓔ

CAUTION   Use the answer spaces in the grids below for Section 6 or Section 7 only if you are told to do so in your test book.

Student-Produced Responses   ONLY ANSWERS ENTERED IN THE CIRCLES IN EACH GRID WILL BE SCORED. YOU WILL NOT RECEIVE CREDIT FOR ANYTHING WRITTEN IN THE BOXES ABOVE THE CIRCLES.

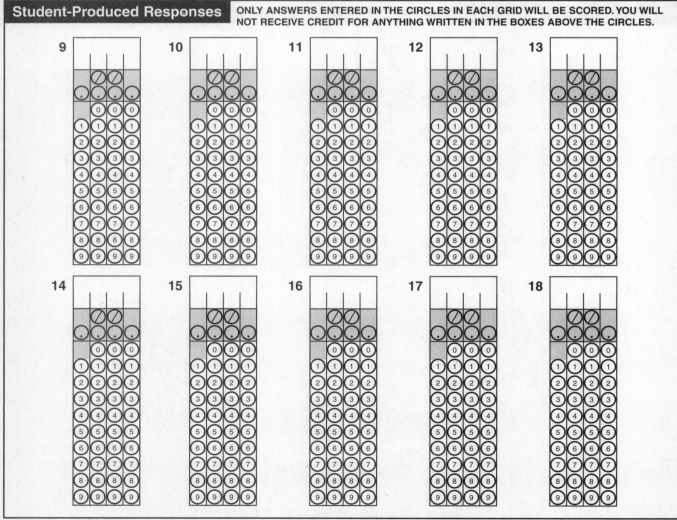

Start with number 1 for each new section. If a section has fewer questions than answer spaces, leave the extra answer spaces blank. Be sure to erase any errors or stray marks completely.

SECTION 8

1 Ⓐ Ⓑ Ⓒ Ⓓ Ⓔ	11 Ⓐ Ⓑ Ⓒ Ⓓ Ⓔ	21 Ⓐ Ⓑ Ⓒ Ⓓ Ⓔ	31 Ⓐ Ⓑ Ⓒ Ⓓ Ⓔ
2 Ⓐ Ⓑ Ⓒ Ⓓ Ⓔ	12 Ⓐ Ⓑ Ⓒ Ⓓ Ⓔ	22 Ⓐ Ⓑ Ⓒ Ⓓ Ⓔ	32 Ⓐ Ⓑ Ⓒ Ⓓ Ⓔ
3 Ⓐ Ⓑ Ⓒ Ⓓ Ⓔ	13 Ⓐ Ⓑ Ⓒ Ⓓ Ⓔ	23 Ⓐ Ⓑ Ⓒ Ⓓ Ⓔ	33 Ⓐ Ⓑ Ⓒ Ⓓ Ⓔ
4 Ⓐ Ⓑ Ⓒ Ⓓ Ⓔ	14 Ⓐ Ⓑ Ⓒ Ⓓ Ⓔ	24 Ⓐ Ⓑ Ⓒ Ⓓ Ⓔ	34 Ⓐ Ⓑ Ⓒ Ⓓ Ⓔ
5 Ⓐ Ⓑ Ⓒ Ⓓ Ⓔ	15 Ⓐ Ⓑ Ⓒ Ⓓ Ⓔ	25 Ⓐ Ⓑ Ⓒ Ⓓ Ⓔ	35 Ⓐ Ⓑ Ⓒ Ⓓ Ⓔ
6 Ⓐ Ⓑ Ⓒ Ⓓ Ⓔ	16 Ⓐ Ⓑ Ⓒ Ⓓ Ⓔ	26 Ⓐ Ⓑ Ⓒ Ⓓ Ⓔ	36 Ⓐ Ⓑ Ⓒ Ⓓ Ⓔ
7 Ⓐ Ⓑ Ⓒ Ⓓ Ⓔ	17 Ⓐ Ⓑ Ⓒ Ⓓ Ⓔ	27 Ⓐ Ⓑ Ⓒ Ⓓ Ⓔ	37 Ⓐ Ⓑ Ⓒ Ⓓ Ⓔ
8 Ⓐ Ⓑ Ⓒ Ⓓ Ⓔ	18 Ⓐ Ⓑ Ⓒ Ⓓ Ⓔ	28 Ⓐ Ⓑ Ⓒ Ⓓ Ⓔ	38 Ⓐ Ⓑ Ⓒ Ⓓ Ⓔ
9 Ⓐ Ⓑ Ⓒ Ⓓ Ⓔ	19 Ⓐ Ⓑ Ⓒ Ⓓ Ⓔ	29 Ⓐ Ⓑ Ⓒ Ⓓ Ⓔ	39 Ⓐ Ⓑ Ⓒ Ⓓ Ⓔ
10 Ⓐ Ⓑ Ⓒ Ⓓ Ⓔ	20 Ⓐ Ⓑ Ⓒ Ⓓ Ⓔ	30 Ⓐ Ⓑ Ⓒ Ⓓ Ⓔ	40 Ⓐ Ⓑ Ⓒ Ⓓ Ⓔ

SECTION 9

1 Ⓐ Ⓑ Ⓒ Ⓓ Ⓔ	11 Ⓐ Ⓑ Ⓒ Ⓓ Ⓔ	21 Ⓐ Ⓑ Ⓒ Ⓓ Ⓔ	31 Ⓐ Ⓑ Ⓒ Ⓓ Ⓔ
2 Ⓐ Ⓑ Ⓒ Ⓓ Ⓔ	12 Ⓐ Ⓑ Ⓒ Ⓓ Ⓔ	22 Ⓐ Ⓑ Ⓒ Ⓓ Ⓔ	32 Ⓐ Ⓑ Ⓒ Ⓓ Ⓔ
3 Ⓐ Ⓑ Ⓒ Ⓓ Ⓔ	13 Ⓐ Ⓑ Ⓒ Ⓓ Ⓔ	23 Ⓐ Ⓑ Ⓒ Ⓓ Ⓔ	33 Ⓐ Ⓑ Ⓒ Ⓓ Ⓔ
4 Ⓐ Ⓑ Ⓒ Ⓓ Ⓔ	14 Ⓐ Ⓑ Ⓒ Ⓓ Ⓔ	24 Ⓐ Ⓑ Ⓒ Ⓓ Ⓔ	34 Ⓐ Ⓑ Ⓒ Ⓓ Ⓔ
5 Ⓐ Ⓑ Ⓒ Ⓓ Ⓔ	15 Ⓐ Ⓑ Ⓒ Ⓓ Ⓔ	25 Ⓐ Ⓑ Ⓒ Ⓓ Ⓔ	35 Ⓐ Ⓑ Ⓒ Ⓓ Ⓔ
6 Ⓐ Ⓑ Ⓒ Ⓓ Ⓔ	16 Ⓐ Ⓑ Ⓒ Ⓓ Ⓔ	26 Ⓐ Ⓑ Ⓒ Ⓓ Ⓔ	36 Ⓐ Ⓑ Ⓒ Ⓓ Ⓔ
7 Ⓐ Ⓑ Ⓒ Ⓓ Ⓔ	17 Ⓐ Ⓑ Ⓒ Ⓓ Ⓔ	27 Ⓐ Ⓑ Ⓒ Ⓓ Ⓔ	37 Ⓐ Ⓑ Ⓒ Ⓓ Ⓔ
8 Ⓐ Ⓑ Ⓒ Ⓓ Ⓔ	18 Ⓐ Ⓑ Ⓒ Ⓓ Ⓔ	28 Ⓐ Ⓑ Ⓒ Ⓓ Ⓔ	38 Ⓐ Ⓑ Ⓒ Ⓓ Ⓔ
9 Ⓐ Ⓑ Ⓒ Ⓓ Ⓔ	19 Ⓐ Ⓑ Ⓒ Ⓓ Ⓔ	29 Ⓐ Ⓑ Ⓒ Ⓓ Ⓔ	39 Ⓐ Ⓑ Ⓒ Ⓓ Ⓔ
10 Ⓐ Ⓑ Ⓒ Ⓓ Ⓔ	20 Ⓐ Ⓑ Ⓒ Ⓓ Ⓔ	30 Ⓐ Ⓑ Ⓒ Ⓓ Ⓔ	40 Ⓐ Ⓑ Ⓒ Ⓓ Ⓔ

ESSAY
Time—25 minutes

You have 25 minutes to write an essay based on the topic presented below. Do not write on another topic. Your essay should be written on the lined pages provided. For the best results, write on every line and keep your handwriting to a reasonable, legible size. Be sure to fully develop your point of view, present your ideas clearly and logically, and use the English language precisely.

Think carefully about the following issue and assignment:

> Space was once regarded as the final frontier, but to some degree we have achieved the technology necessary to explore this vast realm of the unknown. We have landed on the moon, assembled an orbiting space station, placed telescopes into orbit, and are currently sending probes to distant planets. Nevertheless, we still lack the means to send manned expeditions to places beyond our moon. Do you think that further space exploration is a worthy and necessary goal for scientific research?

Assignment: Plan and write an essay in which you develop your point of view on this topic. Support your position with reasoning and solid examples taken from your personal experience, observations, reading, or studies.

WRITE YOUR ESSAY ON PAGES 14 AND 15.

**If you finish writing before your time is called, check your work on this section only.
Do not turn to any other section in the test.**

SECTION 2
Time—25 minutes
20 Questions

Directions: Solve each problem and determine which is the best of the answer choices given. Fill in the corresponding circle on your answer sheet. Use any available space to solve the problems.

Notes

1. The use of a calculator is permitted.
2. All numbers are real numbers.
3. Figures that accompany problems in this test are intended to provide information useful in solving the problems. They are drawn as accurately as possible EXCEPT when it is stated in a specific problem that the figure is not drawn to scale. All figures lie in a plane unless otherwise indicated.
4. Unless otherwise specified, the domain of any function f is assumed to be the set of all real numbers x for which $f(x)$ is a real number.

Reference Information

    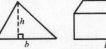

$A = \Pi r^2$ $A = lw$ $A = \frac{1}{2}bh$ $V = lwh$ $V = \Pi r^2 h$ $c^2 = a^2 + b^2$ Special Right Triangles
$C = 2\Pi r$

The number of degrees of arc in a circle is 360.
The sum of the measures in degrees of the angles of a triangle is 180.

1. If $3a + 5 = 14$, what is the value of $2a - 4$?

(A) 2
(B) 6
(C) 8
(D) 19
(E) 21

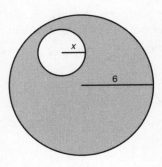

2. In the figure above, a small circle, with radius x, is inside a larger circle, with radius 6. What is the area, in terms of x, of the shaded region?

(A) $6\pi - 2\pi x$
(B) $6\pi - \pi x^2$
(C) $12\pi - 2\pi x$
(D) $36\pi - 2\pi x$
(E) $36\pi - \pi x^2$

GO ON TO THE NEXT PAGE

3. There are 6 sections of seats in a theater. Each contains at least 120 seats but not more than 180 seats. Which of the following could be the number of seats in this theater?

   (A) 300
   (B) 360
   (C) 721
   (D) 1,081
   (E) 1,800

4. If $2^{2y} = 8^{y-1}$, what is the value of y?

   (A) -3
   (B) -1
   (C) 0
   (D) 3
   (E) 4

5. In the xy-plane, point P is at (2, 3), point R is at (8, 3), and point S is at (8, 6). What is the area of triangle PRS?

   (A) 4.5
   (B) 9
   (C) 13.5
   (D) 18
   (E) 27

6. If $a + b = 20$ and $a > 7$, then which of the following must be true?

   (A) $b > 0$
   (B) $b = 7$
   (C) $b = 13$
   (D) $b < 13$
   (E) $a < 20$

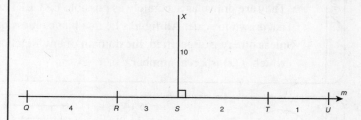

7. In the figure above, XS is perpendicular to m. Which of the following line segments has the greatest length?

   (A) XQ
   (B) XR
   (C) XS
   (D) XT
   (E) XU

8. If 4 more than 2 times a certain number is 3 less than the number, what is the number?

   (A) -7
   (B) 4
   (C) 6
   (D) 10
   (E) 13

GO ON TO THE NEXT PAGE

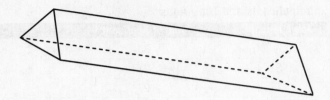

9. The three-dimensional figure represented above consists of rectangular and triangular faces. Each triangular face has area $7p$, and each rectangular face has area $4v$. What is the total surface area of the figure, in terms of p and v?

   (A) $7p + 4v$
   (B) $14p + 8v$
   (C) $14p + 12v$
   (D) $14p + 16v$
   (E) $28p + 28v$

10. The average (arithmetic mean) of the test scores of 9 students is s. In terms of s, what is the sum of the test scores?

   (A) $9s$

   (B) $\dfrac{s}{9}$

   (C) $9 + s$

   (D) $\dfrac{9}{s}$

   (E) $9 - s$

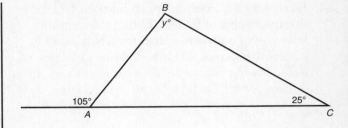

11. In triangle ABC above, what is the value of y?

   (A) $25°$
   (B) $50°$
   (C) $60°$
   (D) $75°$
   (E) $80°$

12. How many integers greater than 15 and less than 25 are each the product of exactly two different numbers, both of which are prime?

   (A) 0
   (B) 2
   (C) 3
   (D) 5
   (E) 9

13. How many more degrees of arc are there in $\frac{1}{3}$ of a circle than in $\frac{1}{4}$ of a circle?

   (A) $30°$
   (B) $60°$
   (C) $90°$
   (D) $120°$
   (E) $210°$

GO ON TO THE NEXT PAGE

14. During a sale, a customer can buy one CD for r dollars. Each additional CD that the customer buys costs s dollars less than the first CD. (The cost of the second CD is $r - s$ dollars.) Which of the following represents the customer's cost, in dollars, for n CDs bought during this sale?

(A)　$r + n(r - s)$

(B)　$r + (n - 1)(r - s)$

(C)　$n(r - s)$

(D)　$r + \dfrac{(r - s)}{n}$

(E)　$\dfrac{r + (r - s)}{n}$

15. Let the operation $\oplus$ be defined by $x \oplus y = \dfrac{(x - y)}{(x + y)}$ for all numbers x and y, where $x \neq y$. If $2 \oplus 3 = 2 \oplus z$, what is the value of z?

(A)　-3

(B)　$1\frac{1}{3}$

(C)　$1\frac{1}{2}$

(D)　3

(E)　5

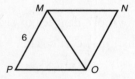

Note: Figure not drawn to scale.

16. If the five line segments in the figure above are all congruent, what is the length of PN (not shown)?

(A)　$2\sqrt{3}$

(B)　6

(C)　$6\sqrt{3}$

(D)　12

(E)　36

Job Applicants and Their Ages

Job Applicant	Age of Applicant
R	35
S	21
T	27
U	u
V	38
X	29
Y	25

17. The table above shows the age of seven job applicants designated R through Y. If the median age of these applicants is 29, then the age of applicant U could be any of the following EXCEPT

(A)　28

(B)　30

(C)　37

(D)　39

(E)　42

18. If p is the greatest prime factor of 42 and r is the greatest prime factor of 90, what is the value of $p - r$?

(A)　0

(B)　2

(C)　5

(D)　7

(E)　13

GO ON TO THE NEXT PAGE

19. Rectangle *WXYZ* lies in the standard *xy* plane so that its sides are <u>not</u> parallel to the axes. What is the product of the slopes of all four sides of rectangle *WXYZ*?

(A) -2
(B) -1
(C) 0
(D) 1
(E) 2

20. There are 40 more boys than girls enrolled in the summer art program. If there are *g* girls enrolled, then, in terms of *g*, what percent of those enrolled are girls?

(A) $\dfrac{g}{g + 40}$%

(B) $\dfrac{g}{2g + 40}$%

(C) $\dfrac{g}{100(2g + 40)}$%

(D) $\dfrac{100g}{g + 40}$%

(E) $\dfrac{100g}{2g + 40}$%

STOP

**If you finish before your time is up, check your work on this section only.
You may not turn to any other section in the test.**

SECTION 3
Time—25 minutes
24 Questions

Directions: For each of the questions in this section, choose the best answer and fill in the corresponding circle on your answer sheet.

Each sentence that follows has either one or two blanks. Each blank indicates that a word has been omitted from the sentence. Beneath each sentence are five words or sets of words. Select the word or set of words that, when inserted into the sentence in place of the blank(s), best fits the context of the sentence as a whole.

1. The issue of establishing a dress code at the high school has caused so much ------- among the teachers that several have threatened to resign.

   (A) apathy
   (B) ambiguity
   (C) hostility
   (D) civility
   (E) regard

2. A wave of ------- swept over the group of students; they could not believe what the professor was saying.

   (A) corruption
   (B) aversion
   (C) indifference
   (D) incredulity
   (E) conviction

3. In light of ------- reports from the investigative teams, Tom decided to discontinue his search for the misappropriated funds.

   (A) ambivalent
   (B) beneficial
   (C) cordial
   (D) diligent
   (E) keen

4. Many people ------- the ballet for its grace and tranquility; others ------- it for the same reasons.

   (A) despise . . abhor
   (B) enumerate . . disavow
   (C) cherish . . savor
   (D) condemn . . revile
   (E) relish . . spurn

5. As an ardent ------- of standardized test preparation, Andrew had a ------- of supporters at the education conference established to promote the test preparation industry.

   (A) critic . . multitude
   (B) proponent . . myriad
   (C) advocate . . lack
   (D) opponent . . plethora
   (E) foe . . crowd

GO ON TO THE NEXT PAGE

Each of the passages that follow is accompanied by several questions based on the content of the passage. Answer the questions based on what is either stated or implied in each passage. Be sure to read any introductory material that is provided.

Questions 6–9 are based on the following passages.

Passage 1

The presence of numerous asteroids, meteors, and comets in space virtually guarantees that some of these celestial bodies will impact the earth, perhaps with catastrophic

Line
5 consequences. Recent studies have shown that the risk from cosmic impact is directly proportional to the size of the projectile; the greatest risk is associated with objects large enough to perturb the Earth's climate on a global scale by

10 sending large quantities of dust into the upper atmosphere. Such an impact event could lead to decreased temperatures around the globe, resulting in massive reduction of food production and a possible breakdown of society.

15 Therefore, it is imperative that we continue extensive research into the detection of asteroids, meteors, and comets before they become a threat to our planet.

Passage 2

Although there is scientific evidence to suggest that the earth has been bombarded with cosmic objects in the past, there is little

Line
  recent proof that any large celestial body will
5 impact the earth with enough force to alter the face of the planet as we know it. Hundreds, perhaps thousands, of small asteroids and other space debris enter the Earth's atmosphere daily. Because they burn up long before they reach

10 the Earth's surface, they pose no risk. Even though the consequences of a larger object impacting the Earth would be potentially devastating, the likelihood that such an impact will occur is remote because of the rarity of

15 such objects traveling through space.

6. In lines 5–11, the author of Passage 1 mentions activities that suggest asteroids

(A) will never reach a size that poses any danger to life on the earth

(B) could impact the Earth with enough force to change the global climate

(C) do not typically enter the earth's upper atmosphere

(D) are not as easily detected as comets and meteors

(E) present a problem that can ultimately be overcome with enough research

7. The author of Passage 2 would most likely respond to the last sentence of Passage 1 by

(A) suggesting that additional research will provide definitive proof that a large celestial body cannot impact the Earth

(B) observing that global climatic conditions are often affected by cosmic impacts

(C) arguing that the mere presence of asteroids, meteors, and comets in space does not guarantee a catastrophic impact event

(D) questioning the validity of any research conducted into the potential risk to the Earth from cosmic impacts

(E) noting that the Earth's atmosphere prevents large celestial bodies from reaching the surface

8. The two passages differ in their views on cosmic impact events in that Passage 1 states that impacts

(A) are rare because space debris burns up in the Earth's atmosphere before hitting the ground

(B) will break down society

(C) require minimal research

(D) could send dust into the earth's atmosphere, resulting in a global climate change

(E) pose risks only to the environment

GO ON TO THE NEXT PAGE

9. Which generalization about cosmic impact events is supported by both passages?

(A) A large object hitting the surface would possibly be devastating.

(B) Space debris burns up before it hits the surface of the earth.

(C) Cosmic impact events are unavoidable, but research into them should continue.

(D) There is little recent proof that any large celestial body will impact the Earth with enough force to alter the face of the planet as we know it.

(E) A cosmic impact event would heat the Earth's atmosphere to an unbearable temperature.

GO ON TO THE NEXT PAGE

Questions 10–15 are based on the following passage.

The following is an adaptation of Joseph Conrad's "The Heart of Darkness," © 1899.

The *Nellie*, a cruising ship, swung to her anchor without a flutter of the sails, and was at rest. The tide had come in, the wind was nearly calm, and being bound down the river, the only
Line
5   thing for it was to come to and wait for the turn of the tide.

The Director of Companies was our captain and our host. We four affectionately watched his back as he stood in the bows
10   looking toward the sea. On the whole river there was nothing that looked half so nautical. He resembled a pilot, which to a sailor is trustworthiness personified. It was difficult to realize his work was not out there in the
15   luminous estuary, but behind him, within the brooding gloom.

Between us there was, as I have already said somewhere, the bond of the sea. Besides holding our hearts together through long
20   periods of separation, it had the effect of making us tolerant of each other's stories—and even convictions. The Lawyer—the best of old fellows—had, because of his many years and many virtues, the only cushion on deck, and
25   was lying on the only rug. The Accountant had brought out already a box of dominoes, and was toying architecturally with the pieces. Marlow sat cross-legged, leaning against the mast. He had sunken cheeks, a yellow
30   complexion, a straight back, and, with his arms dropped, the palms of his hands outwards, resembled an idol. The Director, satisfied the anchor had good hold, made his way forward and sat down amongst us. We exchanged a few
35   words lazily. Afterwards there was silence on board the yacht. For some reason or another we did not begin that game of dominoes. We felt meditative, and fit for nothing but placid staring.
40   "And this also," said Marlow suddenly, "has been one of the dark places of the earth." He was the only man of us who still "followed the sea." The stories of seamen have a direct

simplicity, the whole meaning of which lies
45   within the shell of a cracked nut. But Marlow was not typical, and to him the meaning of an episode was not inside like a kernel but outside, enveloping the tale. The worst that could be said of him was that he did not represent his
50   class—always the same. In their unchanging surroundings, the foreign shores, the foreign faces glide past, veiled not by a sense of mystery but by a slightly disdainful ignorance; for there is nothing mysterious to a sailor unless it be the
55   sea itself, which is the mistress of his existence and as inscrutable as destiny.

His remark did not seem at all surprising. It was just like Marlow. It was accepted in silence. No one took the trouble to grunt even;
60   and presently he said, very slow—"I was thinking of very old times, when the Romans first came here, nineteen hundred years ago." And at last, in its curved and imperceptible fall, the sun sank low, and from glowing white
65   changed to a dull red without rays and without heat, as if about to go out suddenly, stricken to death by the touch of that gloom brooding over a crowd of men.

10. In creating an impression of the Director of Companies, the author makes use of

(A) foreshadowing
(B) allusions
(C) metaphorical language
(D) imagery
(E) contrast

11. In line 15, "luminous" most nearly means

(A) dangerous
(B) respected
(C) bright
(D) beautiful
(E) dark

GO ON TO THE NEXT PAGE ➡

12. Lines 18–22 suggest that the narrator

(A) regards his fellow sailors with benevolence

(B) is concerned that he has been at sea too long

(C) believes that the upcoming journey will be unbearable

(D) is unable to appreciate the bleakness of the situation

(E) eagerly awaits the stories told by his fellow sailors

13. In lines 38–39, the author includes the detail of "and fit for nothing but placid staring" primarily to emphasize the

(A) bleak ambiance of the scene

(B) listlessness of the sailors

(C) loneliness of the scene

(D) camaraderie among the sailors

(E) joviality of the scene

14. In line 63, "imperceptible" most nearly means

(A) curved

(B) brooding

(C) unchanging

(D) disdainful

(E) undetectable

15. The passage suggests that Marlow's main short-coming is that

(A) he is extremely lazy

(B) he has complete disregard for those around him

(C) he appears unaware of the effect he has on his shipmates

(D) he is a terrible storyteller

(E) he lacks the skills necessary to being a good sailor

GO ON TO THE NEXT PAGE

Questions 16–24 are based on the following passage.

The following passage discusses the "readjustment" policy, which was designed to assist Native Americans.

During the mid-twentieth century the United States began a policy toward Native Americans called "readjustment." This policy
Line
5 stemmed from the rise of the civil rights movement. Because of the movement, there was greater awareness that all Americans needed to be able exercise the rights guaranteed by the United States Constitution. Readjustment recognized that life on reservations prevented
10 Native Americans from exercising those rights. Reservations created segregation that caused just as much damage as racially segregated schools, still prevalent throughout the nation during the period. The readjustment move-
15 ment advocated the end of the federal government's involvement in Native American affairs and encouraged the assimilation of Native Americans into mainstream American society. The belief was that if it were beneficial for
20 African-American children to be placed in schools with white children, it was also beneficial for Native Americans to become integrated into white society. The policy, however, failed to recognize the emergence of a new genera-
25 tion of Native American leadership and efforts to develop tribal institutions and reaffirm tribal identity. The new leadership did not desire assimilation but instead wanted more segregation. The Native American community was
30 vying to reassert its distinct identity and separate itself from mainstream America.

These two trends began to clash as the federal government began pushing tribal communities to accept readjustment. The
35 government suggested to tribal leadership that it would be in their best interest to own property and pay taxes on it like other landowners. The federal government attempted to encourage this by reassuring tribal leadership that after the
40 tribes owned the property, the federal government would not restrict their ability to sell their property. The government offered to give the tribes the land without charge. In addition, the government attempted to sweeten the deal by
45 offering a lump sum payment to help cover the costs associated with land ownership.

Native American leadership reacted negatively to the offers of land ownership. They believed that land ownership would cause reser-
50 vation lands to recede, and that land ownership and the resulting taxation would create new financial burdens, foreclosures, and subsequent tax sales of property. Furthermore, they believed that individual ownership of land—
55 even if the land was not involuntarily sold— would eventually lead to the loss of Native American lands as individual land owners were enticed to sell their land. Native American leadership saw individual land ownership as a sure
60 route to the destruction of Native American community and culture.

Instead, the leadership desired to improve tribal living and encourage more Native Americans to stay on reservations. The leader-
65 ship lobbied for the passage of the Native American Community Act, which created a federal fund to build and support schools in tribal communities. It also aimed to create more job opportunities on Native American
70 lands. In fact, tribal leaders used the special sovereign status enjoyed by native territory to entice new business ventures—including casinos. With greater education levels and increased funding to pay for community
75 improvements, Native American leadership hoped to convince Native Americans to reject assimilation into mainstream America.

16. According to the passage, the "readjustment" policy encouraged Native Americans to

   (A) readjust to past cultural practices
   (B) reject assimilation
   (C) sell property and live on reservations
   (D) own property and send their children to schools with white students
   (E) learn the ways of the white world

17. In line 15, "advocated" most nearly means

   (A) rejected
   (B) disapproved
   (C) illustrated
   (D) transformed
   (E) supported

GO ON TO THE NEXT PAGE

18. The statements in line 19–23 ("The belief was that if it were beneficial for African-American children to be placed in schools with white children, it was also beneficial for Native Americans to become integrated into white society.") suggest that

    (A) the government classified all minorities in the same way
    (B) the readjustment policy led to additional segregation
    (C) African-American children did not attend school with Native American children
    (D) only white children attended school prior to the mid-twentieth century
    (E) assimilation was not suitable for Native Americans

19. According to the passage, what is one of the ways in which the federal government tried to entice Native Americans to accept readjustment?

    (A) offering low prices for land
    (B) giving them land free of charge
    (C) placing slight restrictions on selling land
    (D) demonstrating the benefits of public schools
    (E) creating cultural preservation programs

20. According to the passage, what is one reason the Native Americans criticized the readjustment policy?

    (A) They believed that it would lead to a decrease in reservation lands.
    (B) They thought that assimilation was a better solution.
    (C) They wanted to own property.
    (D) They wanted to avoid taxation.
    (E) They thought that it would lead to the Native American Community Act.

21. In line 54–55, the author uses the words "even if the land was not involuntarily sold" to

    (A) detail various types of land sales in the United States
    (B) express concern regarding the likely results of the readjustment policy
    (C) further show that Native Americans were bound to lose in the deal
    (D) examine the readjustment policy's effect on the federal government
    (E) offer a suggestion for improvement to the readjustment policy

22. The author uses the phrase "sweeten the deal" (line 44) primarily to

    (A) emphasize the importance of owning property in the United States
    (B) criticize the Native American's reluctance to own property
    (C) indicate that the government was unwilling to offer any concessions
    (D) emphasize the government's desire that the tribes own their land
    (E) demonstrate the willingness of the tribes to sell their land to the government

23. Which of the following is NOT one of the things that Native American leadership tried to do?

    (A) encourage Native Americans to stay on reservations
    (B) alter the requirements of the education system
    (C) entice new business onto the reservations
    (D) lobby for the passage of the Native American Community Act
    (E) create more job opportunities for Native Americans

24. The author develops the fourth paragraph (lines 61–76) by presenting

    (A) a common opinion and the reasons it was held
    (B) a thesis followed by explanatory details
    (C) various sides of a specific issue
    (D) an argument and refutations against that argument
    (E) a hypothesis and its potential consequences

STOP

If you finish before your time is up, check your work on this section only.
You may not turn to any other section in the test.

SECTION 4
Time—25 minutes
18 Questions

Directions: This section includes two types of questions. For Questions 1–8, solve each problem and determine which is the best of the answer choices given. Fill in the corresponding circle on your answer sheet. Use any available space to solve the problems. For Questions 9–18, solve each problem and fill in your answer on the answer sheet.

Notes

1. The use of a calculator is permitted.
2. All numbers are real numbers.
3. Figures that accompany problems in this test are intended to provide information useful in solving the problems. They are drawn as accurately as possible EXCEPT when it is stated in a specific problem that the figure is not drawn to scale. All figures lie in a plane unless otherwise indicated.
4. Unless otherwise specified, the domain of any function f is assumed to be the set of all real numbers x for which $f(x)$ is a real number.

Reference Information

$A = \Pi r^2$
$C = 2\Pi r$

$A = lw$

$A = \frac{1}{2}bh$

$V = lwh$

$V = \Pi r^2 h$

$c^2 = a^2 + b^2$

Special Right Triangles

The number of degrees of arc in a circle is 360.
The sum of the measures in degrees of the angles of a triangle is 180.

1. What number, when used in place of ♣ above, makes the statement true?

(A) 1
(B) 2
(C) 3
(D) 6
(E) 9

2. X, Y, and Z are points on a line in that order. If $XY = 5$ and $YZ = 21$ more than XY, what does XZ equal?

(A) 5
(B) 15
(C) 16
(D) 26
(E) 31

GO ON TO THE NEXT PAGE

3. If $6 = 2a$, then $3a + 13 =$

(A) 4
(B) 22
(C) 26
(D) 31
(E) 49

Question 4 refers to the following graph.

**NUMBER OF BOOKS SOLD AT THE BOOKWORM
(FROM 2001-2006)**

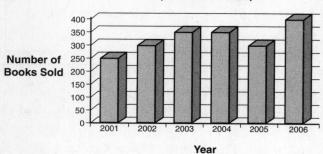

Year

4. During which year did sales at the Bookworm increase the most over the previous year?

(A) 2001
(B) 2002
(C) 2003
(D) 2005
(E) 2006

5. The average (arithmetic mean) of c and d is 12, and the average of c, d, and e is 10. What is the value of e?

(A) 6
(B) 10
(C) 12
(D) 18
(E) 2

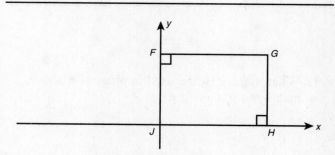

6. On the number line above, m, n, o, p, q, r, and s are coordinates of the indicated points. Which of the following is closest in value to $|n - p|$?

(A) m
(B) n
(C) o
(D) p
(E) s

7. If $x = \frac{1}{2}$, what is the value of $\frac{8}{x} + \frac{4}{(x - 1)}$?

(A) -8
(B) 0
(C) 8
(D) 16
(E) 24

Note: Figure not drawn to scale.

8. In figure above, $JF = JH$ and the coordinates of G are $(k, 8)$. What is the value of k?

(A) -8
(B) -4
(C) -1
(D) 0
(E) 8

GO ON TO THE NEXT PAGE

Directions: For Student-Produced Response questions 9-18, use the grids at the bottom of the answer sheet page on which you have answered questions 1-8.

Each of the remaining 10 questions requires you to solve the problem and enter your answer by marking the circles in the special grid, as shown in the examples below. You may use any available space for scratchwork.

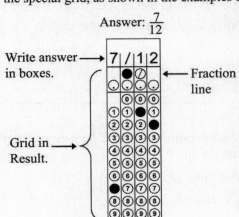

Answer: $\frac{7}{12}$

Write answer in boxes.

Fraction line

Grid in Result.

Answer: 2.5

Decimal point

Answer: 201
Either position is correct.

Note: You may start your answers in any column, space permitting. Columns not needed should be left blank.

- Mark no more than one circle in any column.

- Because the answer sheet will be machine-scored, **you will receive credit only if the circles are filled in correctly**.

- Although not required, it is suggested that you write your answer in the boxes at the top of the columns to help you fill in the circles accurately.

- Some problems may have more than one correct answer. In such cases, grid only one answer.

- No question has a negative answer.

- **Mixed numbers** such as $3\frac{1}{2}$ must be gridded as 3.5 or 7/2. (If [3 1 / 2] is gridded, it will be interpreted as $\frac{31}{2}$, not $3\frac{1}{2}$.)

Decimal Answers: If you obtain a decimal answer with more digits than the grid can accomodate, it may be either rounded or truncated, but it must fill the entire grid. enter the most accurate value the grid will accommodate. For example, if you obtain an answer such as 0.6666..., you should record your result as .666 or .667. **A less accurate value such as .66 or .67 will be scored as incorrect.**

Acceptable ways to grid $\frac{2}{3}$ are:

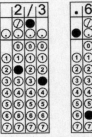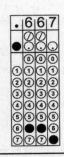

9. When the positive <u>even</u> integer c is increased by 5 and then quadrupled, the result is between 44 and 65. What is one possible value of c?

10. The perimeter of a rectangular plot of land is 110 meters. If the length of one side of the plot is 35 meters, what is the area of the plot, in square meters?

GO ON TO THE NEXT PAGE

11. A salesperson's monthly gross pay is $3,000 plus 30% of the dollar amount of her sales. If her gross pay for one month was $4,500, what was the dollar amount of her sales for that month?

12. If $5(3x - 2y)(y + 5) = 280$ and $3x - 2y = 8$, what is the value of $4x - y$?

13. In a rectangular coordinate system, the center of a circle has coordinates (-4, -2), and the circle touches the x-axis at one point only. What is the diameter of the circle?

14. What is the greatest three-digit integer that has a factor of 32?

15. Matt wants to cut a circular pie into wedge-shaped pieces. The tip of each piece is at the center of the pie, and the angle at the tip is at least 40° and at most 50°. What is one possible number of whole pieces into which the pie can be cut?

16. Let the operations Φ and Ξ be defined for all real numbers a and b as follows:

$a \, \Phi \, b = 3ab + 3b$

$a \, \Xi \, b = 9a + 2b$

If $3 \, \Phi \, 2y = 6 \, \Xi \, 3y$, what is the value of y?

17. What is the slope of a line that passes through the origin and the point (5, 1)?

18. Kara drives to work in the morning using the highway but returns home from work using back roads because of traffic. Both routes are equal in distance. She averages 75 miles per hour going to work and 50 miles per hour returning home from work. Her total commute time to and from work is 60 minutes. How many miles does Kara drive to work in the morning?

S T O P

**If you finish before your time is up, check your work on this section only.
You may not turn to any other section in the test.**

SECTION 5
Time—25 minutes
35 Questions

Directions: For each question, select the best answer from among the choices listed. Fill in the corresponding circle on your answer sheet.

The following questions test the correct and effective use of standard written English in expressing an idea. Part of each sentence (or the entire sentence) is underlined. Following each sentence are five different ways of phrasing the underlined portion. Answer choice A repeats the original phrasing. If you think that the original phrasing is best, select answer choice A. Otherwise, select from the remaining four choices. Your selection should result in the most effective, clear sentence, free from awkwardness or ambiguity.

1. Burdened with a backpack and an armful of books, Kim's search for a place to sit was desperate.

   (A) Kim's search for a place to sit was desperate
   (B) Kim desperately searched for a place to sit
   (C) Kim's desperate search was for a place to sit
   (D) a place to sit was what Kim desperately searched for
   (E) a place to sit for which Kim desperately searched

2. Last year, more students from neighboring states visited the university than local students.

   (A) local students
   (B) in comparison to local students
   (C) local ones
   (D) did local students
   (E) local student's did

3. Despite her popularity, the actress failed to win the coveted award.

   (A) Despite her popularity
   (B) Despite her being popular
   (C) Her popularity, despite it
   (D) Her being popular, despite it
   (E) In spite of her being popular

4. During the snowstorm, a truck carrying crates of oranges overturned, thereby spilling oranges into the road and so traffic was blocked.

   (A) thereby spilling oranges into the road and so traffic was blocked
   (B) spilling oranges into the road and blocking traffic
   (C) which then spilled oranges into the road and so blocked traffic
   (D) so oranges were spilled and the road was blocked to traffic
   (E) by which traffic was blocked due to the spilling of oranges

5. Griffiths, a large printing company, recently acquired Redi-Print, it was a small, family-owned business.

   (A) Redi-Print, it was a
   (B) Redi-Print, being a
   (C) Redi-Print, a
   (D) Redi-Print; it being a
   (E) Redi-Print; for it was a

6. The study of archeology often requires fieldwork where they can observe an artifact within the context of its natural surroundings.

   (A) where they
   (B) about which they
   (C) and so the archeologist
   (D) during which the archeologist
   (E) so they

GO ON TO THE NEXT PAGE

7. Lacking a solid foundation, <u>the construction crew could not yet begin work on remodeling the house</u>.

   (A) the construction crew could not yet begin work on remodeling the house
   (B) the house could not yet be remodeled by the construction crew
   (C) remodeling could not be started on the house by the construction crew
   (D) work on remodeling the house could not begin by the construction crew
   (E) work by the construction crew to remodel the house could not begin

8. It is a common misconception that scientists are <u>too absorbed in their work</u> to have fun.

   (A) too absorbed in their work
   (B) too absorbed working
   (C) absorbed too much working
   (D) in its work too absorbed
   (E) in working too absorbed

9. <u>Although the Grand Canyon is better known than Antelope Canyon, thousands of tourists still visit Antelope Canyon annually.</u>

   (A) Although the Grand Canyon is better known than Antelope Canyon, thousands of tourists still visit Antelope Canyon annually.
   (B) The Grand Canyon, being better known than Antelope Canyon, even though it is visited by thousands of tourists annually.
   (C) Although not as well known as the Grand Canyon, thousands of tourists, they still visit Antelope Canyon annually.
   (D) It being less well known than the Grand Canyon, Antelope Canyon is still visited by thousands of annual tourists.
   (E) Thousands of tourists still annually visit Antelope Canyon, although Antelope Canyon is not better known than the Grand Canyon.

10. After scoring ten home runs in the first inning, the baseball players thought that <u>they would have ensured a victory</u>.

    (A) they would have ensured a victory
    (B) they had ensured victory
    (C) they will ensure their victory
    (D) a victory will be ensured
    (E) a victory they would ensure

11. Jordan became fascinated with Impressionist <u>paintings, he</u> attended a special viewing of several of Monet's works.

    (A) paintings, he
    (B) paintings, therefore, he
    (C) paintings; instead, he
    (D) paintings; while
    (E) paintings; in fact, he

GO ON TO THE NEXT PAGE

The following questions test your ability to recognize grammar and usage errors in standard written English. Each sentence contains either a single error or no error at all. Refer to the underlined, lettered portions of each sentence. If the sentence contains no error, select answer choice E. If the sentence contains an error, select the one underlined and lettered portion (A, B, C, or D) that is incorrect.

12. Studies <u>show</u> that <u>taking</u> notes when listening
A   B

<u>with a speaker</u> <u>greatly</u> increases the chance
C   D

of remembering what was said. <u>No error</u>.
E

13. The Beaufort Wind Scale <u>rates</u> wind strength
A

<u>on a scale</u> of zero to twelve, <u>from being</u> calm
B   C

to hurricane <u>level</u>. <u>No error</u>.
D   E

14. It is always <u>important</u> to <u>work with</u> a college
A   B

<u>advisor</u> when <u>determining</u> which credits to
C   D

transfer. <u>No error</u>.
E

15. Large <u>volcanic eruptions</u> can <u>affect</u> the weather
A   B

for years due to the <u>creation</u> of clouds from
C

<u>volcanic debris</u>. <u>No error</u>.
D   E

16. People <u>which</u> have advanced computer skills <u>are</u>
A   B

commonly selected for employment <u>over</u>
C

applicants who <u>lack</u> these skills. <u>No error</u>.
D   E

17. In baseball, a pitcher <u>could balk</u>, <u>at which point</u>
A   B

all base runners <u>would advance</u> to the <u>next base</u>.
C   D

<u>No error</u>.
E

18. In <u>his book</u>, *The Human Side of Enterprise*,
A

Douglas McGregor <u>explains</u> his X and Y
B

<u>theory</u> <u>in regards</u> the world of work. <u>No error</u>.
C   D   E

19. The Sugar Act, <u>passed</u> in 1764, was <u>Parliaments</u>
A   B

first law <u>drafted</u> to <u>raise</u> tax money from
C   D

the colonies. <u>No error</u>.
E

20. Thomas <u>Paine's</u> pamphlet, <u>*Common Sense*</u>, is a
A   B

<u>moving plea</u> for <u>independence</u>. <u>No error</u>.
C   D   E

21. As heating and cooling <u>costs</u> continue to <u>rise</u>,
A   B

shopping malls <u>are</u> giving <u>away</u> to smaller
C   D

outdoor strip malls. <u>No error</u>.
E

GO ON TO THE NEXT PAGE ⟩

22. The Flatiron Mountains in <u>eastern Colorado</u> can
                                     A

be easily <u>distinguishing</u> from many <u>miles away</u>,
               B   C

even though they are <u>part</u> of the Rocky
                         D

Mountain chain. <u>No error</u>.
                   E

23. Louisa was <u>nervous about</u> her first art show
                 A

<u>opening</u>; she had <u>invited</u> many friends who
    B   C

<u>never</u> seen her paintings. <u>No error</u>.
    D   E

24. Martha was delighted when <u>her</u> and her sister
                 A

<u>took</u> a sewing class together and <u>made</u> a quilt
  B   C

for <u>their mother</u>. <u>No error</u>.
        D   E

25. People who <u>rent</u> moving trucks are often
           A

<u>unaware</u> of the <u>importance</u> of <u>even</u> distributing
  B   C   D

the weight of the articles inside the truck.
<u>No error</u>.
  E

26. <u>In baseball</u>, a pinch hitter may take the place of a
    A

scheduled <u>batter,</u> but the batter who
         B

<u>is replaced</u> forfeits <u>his chance</u> to bat again
   C   D

during the game. <u>No error</u>.
            E

27. The children <u>laughing</u> uproariously <u>as they</u>
      A   B

watched the prairie dogs first <u>scamper</u> about,
                    C

and then sit up <u>on their</u> hind legs. <u>No error</u>.
           D   E

28. The Stamp Act of 1765 taxed <u>reading materials</u>
                    A

such as newspapers and <u>pamphlets</u>, and was <u>met</u>
                 B   C

with <u>many organized</u> protests from the colonists.
    D

<u>No error</u>.
  E

29. When helping someone to <u>buy</u> or sell a home, a
            A

good real estate broker <u>must be willing</u> and able
                B

<u>in answering</u> all questions about the <u>process</u>.
   C   D

<u>No error</u>.
  E

GO ON TO THE NEXT PAGE

Directions: The following passage is a rough draft of a student essay. Some parts of the passage need to be rewritten to improve the essay.

Read the passage and select the best answer for each question that follows. Some questions ask you to improve the structure or word choice of specific sentences or parts of sentences, while others ask you to consider the organization and development of the essay. Follow the requirements of standard written English.

Questions 30–35 are based on the following passage.

(1)Portion control is crucial in the effort to achieve and maintain weight loss. (2)Studies have clearly shown that food portions in stores and restaurants have really had recent increases in years. (3)So, we should be careful when we shop to pay attention to labels and ask our servers to bring us half-portions at restaurants. (4)It is easy to fool yourself into thinking that you've had "one" portion of something at a single meal. (5)In reality, that portion might be 25–200% larger than it needs to be to satisfy hunger and nutritional requirements.

(6)People should become more aware of the portion size in order not to become obese. (7)Also, if we continue not to exercise, we will most likely not achieve our desired weight loss. (8)A combination of diet and exercise is the key to a healthy lifestyle many people are not aware that they must do both. (9)Most of the scientific studies conducted indicate that we would all be more healthy if we ate less and exercised more. (10)This type of behavior would make sure that people who are currently obese, or who want to avoid it, will be able to accomplish their goal.

30. In context, which of the following most logically replaces "have really had recent increases in years" in Sentence 2 (reproduced below)?

Studies have clearly shown that food portions in stores and restaurants have really had recent increases in years.

(A) have undergone great increases in years
(B) have recently in years greatly increased
(C) have greatly increased in recent years
(D) have had great and recent increases in years
(E) have shown, in recent years, great increases

31. In context, which is the best version of Sentence 5 (reproduced below)?

When in reality, that portion might be 25–200% larger than it needs to be to satisfy hunger and nutritional requirements.

(A) (As it is now)
(B) That portion, in reality, might be 25–200% larger to satisfy hunger and nutritional requirements than it needs to be.
(C) That portion might, in reality be 25–200% larger than to satisfy hunger and nutritional requirements.
(D) That portion might, in reality, be 25–200% larger to satisfy hunger and nutritional requirements, than it needs to be.
(E) That, in reality, the portion might be 25–200% larger than to satisfy hunger and nutritional requirements it needs to be.

32. In context, which of the following revisions is necessary in Sentence 6 (reproduced below)?

People should become more aware of their portion size in order not to become obese.

(A) Insert "even more" after "in order not to"
(B) Change "people" to "they"
(C) Delete "the" after "aware of"
(D) Change "aware" to "in tune"
(E) Delete "size" after "portion"

GO ON TO THE NEXT PAGE

33. In context, what is the best way to deal with Sentence 7 (reproduced below)?

Also, if we continue not to exercise, we will most likely not achieve our desired weight loss.

   (A)   Leave it as it is.
   (B)   Place it after Sentence 8.
   (C)   Change "Also" to "On the contrary"
   (D)   Insert "due to watching portion size" at the end of the sentence.
   (E)   Use "therefore" at the end of Sentence 7 to link it with Sentence 8.

34. Which is the best way to deal with Sentence 8 (reproduced below)?

A combination of diet and exercise is the key to a healthy lifestyle many people are not aware that they must do both.

   (A)   Insert the phrase "In addition" at the beginning.
   (B)   Insert a period after "lifestyle" and begin a new sentence with "Many"
   (C)   Delete it; the point has already been made.
   (D)   Move it to the end of Paragraph 2 (after Sentence 10).
   (E)   Insert a comma after "lifestyle" and delete the word "many"

35. Which of the following is the best version of the underlined portion of Sentence 10 (reproduced below)?

This type of behavior would make sure that people who are currently obese, or who <u>want to avoid it</u>, will be able to accomplish their goal.

   (A)   (As it is now)
   (B)   desiring to avoid it
   (C)   avoiding obesity
   (D)   want to avoid obesity
   (E)   want an avoidance of it

STOP

**If you finish before your time is up, check your work on this section only.
You may not turn to any other section in the test.**

SECTION 6
Time—25 minutes
24 Questions

Directions: For each of the questions in this section, choose the best answer and fill in the corresponding circle on your answer sheet.

Each sentence that follows has either one or two blanks. Each blank indicates that a word has been omitted from the sentence. Following each sentence are five words or sets of words. Select the word or set of words that, when inserted into the sentence in place of the blank(s), best fits the context of the sentence as a whole.

1. Even though they tended to be ------- toward each other in private, Dr. Mathison and Dr. Clemens maintained an ------- demeanor whenever they appeared together in public.

   (A) malicious . . amiable
   (B) absurd . . enigmatic
   (C) lenient . . aristocratic
   (D) cordial . . honest
   (E) spiteful . . coherent

2. Despite all of the advertisements ------- the new product, its first quarter sales were -------.

   (A) criticizing . . protracted
   (B) praising . . extraordinary
   (C) lauding . . abysmal
   (D) abrogating . . profound
   (E) censuring . . marred

3. One theory ------- that the organisms have a common ancestor.

   (A) alienates
   (B) deplores
   (C) postulates
   (D) correlates
   (E) transposes

4. His ----- for learning history should prove to be ----- during his studies to become a history teacher.

   (A) disdain . . useful
   (B) penchant . . practical
   (C) dislike . . exceptional
   (D) affinity . . futile
   (E) appreciation . . gratuitous

5. The politician was -------; she refused to change her crooked ways even after being indicted for corruption.

   (A) adept
   (B) curable
   (C) candid
   (D) melancholy
   (E) incorrigible

6. The prime minister, considered one of his country's greatest -------, was notorious for his ability to ------- his countrymen during the war.

   (A) orators . . inspire
   (B) aviators . . restrict
   (C) generals . . depict
   (D) writers . . discount
   (E) politicians . . loathe

7. Teaching evolution in schools, still a rather ------- issue, has been a topic of debate for years.

   (A) ephemeral
   (B) settled
   (C) abbreviated
   (D) contentious
   (E) inexplicable

8. We felt ------- once the committee issued its report that ------- our actions.

   (A) angered . . supported
   (B) abused . . endorsed
   (C) vindicated . . authenticated
   (D) helpless . . applauded
   (E) ignorant . . dignified

GO ON TO THE NEXT PAGE

Each passage below is followed by several questions based on the content of the passage. Answer the questions based on what is either stated or implied in each passage. Be sure to read any introductory material that is provided.

Questions 9–10 are based on the following passage.

Thousands of years ago, royalty of diverse cultures were often buried in extremely lavish tombs that they themselves commissioned in
Line preparation for their inevitable deaths. About
5   2,200 years ago, a Chinese emperor named Qin Shihuang had such a tomb prepared.

At the age of 13, Qin Shihuang had succeeded his father as emperor. The boy was very aggressive and ambitious. He assumed full
10   power at the age of 22 by ridding himself of his rival, a man who had controlled the throne while Qin Shihuang was a minor. Qin Shihuang's goal was to unify and subjugate all of the Chinese states using his formidable polit-
15   ical, economic, and military strength.

Despite an ongoing quest for immortality, Qin Shihuang died at the age of 49 while traveling. Although he has been dead for centuries, historians can continue to learn of his life by
20   studying the artifacts found in the extravagant tomb in which he was laid to rest.

9. Based on information in the passage, Qin Shihuang can best be described as

(A) benevolent
(B) modest
(C) spontaneous
(D) insightful
(E) ruthless

10. In line 13, "subjugate" most nearly means

(A) liberate
(B) coordinate
(C) conquer
(D) redeem
(E) conserve

Questions 11–12 are based on the following passage.

Warren Buffet is widely regarded as one of the world's best investors. One of the few things that investors can control is how much
Line they pay for shares in a business. Since Buffet
5   always invests with a margin of safety, he focuses on stock trading at a discount and always considers the company's intrinsic worth. To him, stocks do an emotional dance full of jumps and dives. As Buffet watches the dance,
10   he picks up good dancers who have slipped and fallen. Dancers who join his troupe have a way of becoming stronger and more graceful than anyone had expected.

11. The author most likely refers to the "margin of safety" in line 5 to

(A) indicate that Buffet thinks the stock market is a safe place to invest money
(B) explain Buffet's value-driven investing philosophy
(C) demonstrate that buying stocks on margin is very risky
(D) suggest that Buffet buys high-priced stocks of companies in established industries
(E) imply that Buffet thinks investing in the stock market is similar to gambling

12. In lines 6–7, the author's point about Buffet's investing philosophy is primarily developed through the use of

(A) foreshadowing
(B) irony
(C) stereotype
(D) metaphor
(E) repetition

GO ON TO THE NEXT PAGE ⟩

Questions 13–24 are based on the following passages.

Following are two fictional accounts of modern-day refugees coming to America. The first describes a man and his son leaving Cuba, and the second describes two "Lost Boys" of Sudan. Both are based on true accounts. Consider the relationship between the two situations.

Passage 1

Pedro had heard his mother and father whispering each night now for over a week. He was sure they thought that he and his siblings *Line* were asleep, but in a two-room wooden shack it
5 was difficult to keep even subdued voices unheard. As Pedro drifted in and out of sleep, he occasionally heard phrases such as, "how many others?" and "what about the money?" In a quiet yet angry tone, he even heard his mother
10 once harshly whisper, "But what will become of us?" As the oldest son, Pedro always felt a strong sense of responsibility and duty to his family of seven. Now that he was 18, he felt somehow that he should be in on whatever it was that his
15 parents were so fervently discussing in secret.

Pedro found out soon enough what the clandestine conversations were about when, the next evening, his parents put the other children to bed and took Pedro outside to talk to him. The
20 plan, explained to him in hushed voices, was that he and his father would leave the next day for a boat trip to America. It would be a long, arduous journey. They would never return to their home-land of Cuba. But this was their only chance to
25 escape poverty and make a life for themselves. It would be nearly impossible to get permission to leave the country, so they would depart covertly in 24 hours along with 15 other men on a small boat equipped only with oars. A motor would be
30 a dead give-away to those looking for escapees. Anyone attempting to flee the country would be dealt with harshly by the authorities. Upon hearing the plan, Pedro swallowed his fear, looked his father in the eye, and nodded.

35 If all went well, the group could reach American soil in about 3 days. There was no way of knowing whether the attempted escape would be successful; the men would simply have to take their chances. Pedro's Uncle Max had sent some
40 money to help them pay for food and other supplies. Max would open his home to them and help them to find jobs if they made it to Florida.

These activities would be conducted quietly and secretly, however, as the refugees could be threat-
45 ened with deportation at any point.

Pedro's father desperately hoped that in a year or so he would be able to send for the rest of the family and they could all live together in freedom. Pedro had heard many horror stories
50 of others in their small town attempting similar escapes, but he knew that now was not the time to give voice to those fears.

Passage 2

Michael and Paul had been close friends for the past 10 years, since they were each about 8
55 years old. Their parents had been victims of a long and terrible civil war, and their sisters had been taken into captivity long ago. Only boys like Michael and Paul, who once lived quiet lives tending their families' sheep, had been let go, to
60 literally run from their war-torn country of Sudan in hopes of finding a new life somewhere else. In total, approximately 10,000 boys and young men had left Sudan in this way, most of them without food and water or shelter from the
65 elements. The boys had no idea where they were going, but many ended up crossing Sudan's border into neighboring Ethiopia. Unfortunately, many of them perished along the way.

For several years, Ethiopia provided crude
70 camps for Paul and Michael and the others. While the conditions were far from ideal, the boys at least had some food and limited water and were free from the blasts of bombs and the constant fear that the explosions instilled in them.
75 Paul and Michael managed to make the best of their stay in the camps, despite the bleakness of their situation. Unfortunately, the Ethiopian government shut down these camps for "Lost Boys" in 1992, and once again Paul and Michael
80 were let go on foot, only to return to Sudan.

Although Paul and Michael had no real idea whether they were the oldest members of the group they both had taken on leadership roles, perhaps because of their tremendous
85 heights and deep voices. One evening, as the group was resting for the night, a stranger approached the band of boys and asked to speak to one of the older boys. The younger boys

GO ON TO THE NEXT PAGE

directed the stranger to Paul and Michael, who
90 were then told to take the small band of
refugees and head toward Kenya, where help
would be waiting.
        After walking again for more than a year,
the "Lost Boys" entered Kenya, an African
95 country that offered aid to thousands of
refugees from the entire continent. Michael and
Paul were two of the lucky ones; more than half
of the 26,000 "lost boys" had succumbed to the
harsh conditions they had been forced to
100 endure during their long trek. In Kenya, the
boys once again found the basic necessities as
well as protection from the many dangers and
hardships they had faced over the years. One
day, as Paul and Michael were settling into their
105 new Kenyan life, they were called to a meeting
of all the older boys. The announcement was
made that several thousand boys would have the
opportunity to go to America where they would
be assisted by many generous people in
110 pursuing their education and finding jobs.
Though Paul and Michael were unsure of what
the future would hold, they remained optimistic, knowing that if chosen, they would go
together to this new land of great promise.

13. In lines 1–11, the description of the conversations
being held between Pedro's parents is primarily
intended to illustrate

(A) the difficulty of keeping secrets with seven
    children in such a small home
(B) the anger Pedro's mother felt regarding the
    topic of secretive conversation
(C) the furtive nature of what was being discussed
(D) the sense of obligation that Pedro felt
    regarding his siblings
(E) the relationship between Pedro and his family

14. In lines 5–7, the author refers to "boys like
Michael and Paul, who once lived quiet lives
tending their families' sheep" primarily to

(A) illustrate the harsh contrast between the boys
    lives pre- and post-civil war
(B) provide background information about the
    boys and their childhoods
(C) use a specific example to help establish the
    main point of the sentence
(D) indicate that the boys continued to work for
    their families after the civil war began
(E) explicate how Michael and Paul's friendship
    came to be

15. Which of the following is true regarding both
passages?

(A) The boys in both passages felt optimistic
    about the opportunities that awaited them
    in America.
(B) The boys had to be very cautious upon
    arrival in America for threat of deportation.
(C) The boys in both stories were illicitly fleeing
    their home countries.
(D) The boys in both stories were not fully
    confident as to whether they would reach
    America.
(E) The families of the boys in both stories
    hoped to eventually join them in America.

16. The word "fervently" in line 15 most nearly means

(A) hastily
(B) impulsively
(C) warily
(D) nonchalantly
(E) anxiously

17. The author's statements about the escape mechanism in lines 25–30 ("It would be nearly...
escapees") of Passage 1 suggests that the men

(A) disconnected the motor from their boat to
    remain inconspicuous
(B) could lawfully leave the country while oper-
    ating a manually controlled boat
(C) were too poverty-stricken to be able to
    afford a motor boat, which would help
    them flee the authorities if need be
(D) required at least 17 men to row the boat
    quickly enough to escape Cuba and the
    Cuban government
(E) took every precaution to be discreet in their
    escape from Cuba to avoid apprehension

GO ON TO THE NEXT PAGE ⇒

18. In line 27, the fact that the group of boys are named the "Lost Boys" is significant because the name

(A) emphasizes the fact that the boys were in unfamiliar surroundings with boys they did not know

(B) serves as a prophecy of the year-long journey the boys were about to embark on to reach Kenya

(C) reinforces the fact that the boys could not escape their constant fear for their own well-being

(D) reflects the fact that the boys had first been stripped of their homes and families and had now been forced from their place of refuge

(E) reiterates the desolation of the internment camp conditions

19. The passages can both be best described as

(A) social commentaries that recount why some refugees are welcomed into America, while others are extradited

(B) stories of individuals inspiring groups of people to seek a better life

(C) illustrations of the plight of present-day refugees from selected countries

(D) introductions into conventional lives of Cuban and Sudanese youth

(E) allegories that exemplify triumph over tragedy

20. The word "crude" in line 69 most closely means

(A) offensive
(B) lacking sophistication
(C) blunt
(D) ideal conditions
(E) deprived

21. In line 97, the author refers to Paul and Michael as the "lucky ones" primarily because they

(A) found refuge in Kenya, where they were provided with provisions and security

(B) suffered through the trek to Kenya but endured the harsh conditions

(C) were some of the eldest in the group, thus their potential to be chosen to go to American was very high

(D) traveled for approximately one year from Sudan to Kenya with the band of thousands of other boys

(E) were assured continuing education and employment upon arrival in America

22. Which statement most appropriately describes a distinction between the passages?

(A) Passage 1 emphasizes the significance of finding employment, while Passage 2 does not.

(B) Passage 1 fails to discuss the importance of the family unit, while Passage 2 does not.

(C) Passage 1 depicts a sense of hopelessness whereas Passage 2 does not.

(D) Passage 1 is centered around the living conditions of refugees, whereas Passage 2 is not.

(E) Passage 1 does not center around danger in the lives of its characters, whereas Passage 2 does.

23. When Paul and Michael become aware that they may be going to America, the author implies that they feel

(A) cautiously encouraged
(B) overwhelmingly jubilant
(C) exceedingly pleased
(D) moderately sullen
(E) emotionally distraught

24. When Pedro was informed of the plan to escape to America, he conducted himself most like someone who

(A) is in command of his emotions
(B) is fearless in the face of danger
(C) wants to please his parents
(D) acts arrogant and aggressive
(E) had no desire to leave his home

STOP

If you finish before your time is up, check your work on this section only.
You may not turn to any other section in the test.

SECTION 7
Time—20 minutes
16 Questions

Directions: Solve each problem and determine which is the best of the answer choices given. Fill in the corresponding circle on your answer sheet. Use any available space to solve the problems.

Reference Information

$A = \Pi r^2$
$C = 2\Pi r$ $A = lw$ $A = \frac{1}{2}bh$ $V = lwh$ $V = \Pi r^2 h$ $c^2 = a^2 + b^2$ Special Right Triangles

The number of degrees of arc in a circle is 360.
The sum of the measures in degrees of the angles of a triangle is 180.

1. If $x + z = 12$ and $y - z = 3$, then $x + y =$

   (A) 4
   (B) 9
   (C) 15
   (D) 18
   (E) 36

2. If $n(4a + b) = 54$ and $na = 9$, what is the value of nb?

   (A) 9
   (B) 18
   (C) 27
   (D) 36
   (E) 45

GO ON TO THE NEXT PAGE

3. R, S, and T are points on a line in that order. If $RS = 12$ and $ST = 13$ more than RS, what does RT equal?

   (A) 12
   (B) 25
   (C) 37
   (D) 40
   (E) 50

4. One circle has a radius of 2, and another circle has a radius of 4. What is the ratio of the area of the larger circle to the area of the smaller circle?

   (A) 1:4
   (B) 1:2
   (C) 2:3
   (D) 2:1
   (E) 4:1

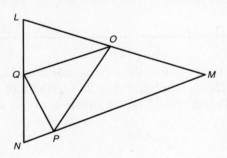

Note: Figure not drawn to scale.

5. In the figure above, $LM = MN$. If the measure of angle LMN is 40° and the measure of angle LOQ is 30°, what is the measure of angle LQO?

   (A) 15°
   (B) 25°
   (C) 40°
   (D) 65°
   (E) 80°

6. If $\frac{3x}{2y} = \frac{8}{6}$, what is the value of $\frac{4x}{6y}$?

   (A) $\frac{3}{4}$
   (B) $\frac{3}{2}$
   (C) $\frac{2}{3}$
   (D) $\frac{1}{3}$
   (E) $\frac{2}{9}$

7. If $|4 - 3x| < 5$, which of the following is a possible value of x?

   (A) 2
   (B) 3
   (C) 4
   (D) 5
   (E) 6

8. What is the remainder when 8^3 is divided by 11?

   (A) 9
   (B) 8
   (C) 7
   (D) 6
   (E) 5

GO ON TO THE NEXT PAGE ⟩

9. If *abcd* = 36 and *abde* = 0, which of the following must be true?

(A) $a > 0$
(B) $b > 0$
(C) $c = 0$
(D) $d = 0$
(E) $e = 0$

10. During the basketball game, the away team scored one seventh of its points in the first quarter, one fourth of its points in the second quarter, 23 points in the third quarter, and the remaining points in the fourth quarter. If the away team scored a total of 56 points, how many points did the away team score in the fourth quarter?

(A) 8
(B) 11
(C) 12
(D) 20
(E) 3

11. If $3^{8x} = 81^{3x-2}$, what is the value of *x*?

(A) -2
(B) 0
(C) 2
(D) 3
(E) 4

12. If $0 < n < 1$, which of the following gives the correct ordering of $4n$, n^2, $\sqrt{n}$, and n?

(A) $4n < \sqrt{n} < n^2 < n$
(B) $4n < n < n^2 < \sqrt{n}$
(C) $n^2 < \sqrt{n} < n < 4n$
(D) $n^2 < n < \sqrt{n} < 4n$
(E) $n^2 < 4n < \sqrt{n} < n$

13. If *a*, *b*, *c*, and *d* are four nonzero numbers, then all of the following proportions are equivalent EXCEPT

(A) $\frac{a}{b} = \frac{c}{d}$
(B) $\frac{a}{c} = \frac{b}{d}$
(C) $\frac{c}{a} = \frac{d}{b}$
(D) $\frac{bc}{ad} = \frac{1}{1}$
(E) $\frac{b}{c} = \frac{a}{d}$

14. In the *xy*-plane, the equation of line *l* is $2y = 3x + 7$. If line *m* is parallel to line *l*, which of the following could be the equation of line *m*?

(A) $y = 6x - 14$

(B) $y = 3x + 14$

(C) $y = \frac{3}{2x} + 2$

(D) $y = -\frac{3}{2x} + 2$

(E) $y = -\frac{3}{2x} - \frac{7}{2}$

GO ON TO THE NEXT PAGE ⇨

15. The greatest integer of a set of consecutive even integers is 12. If the sum of these integers is 40, how many integers are in this set?

(A)　5
(B)　6
(C)　12
(D)　20
(E)　40

16. Set F has f members, Set G has g members, and Set H has h members. Set K consists of all members that are in either set F or set G or set H with the exception of the c common members ($c > 0$). Set K also consists of d members that are not in set F or set G or set H. Which of the following represents the number of members in set K?

(A)　$f + g + h - c + d$
(B)　$f + g + h + c + d$
(C)　$f + g + h - 3c + d$
(D)　$f + g + h + 3c + d$
(E)　$f + g + h - 3c$

STOP

If you finish before your time is up, check your work on this section only.
You may not turn to any other section in the test.

SECTION 8
Time—20 minutes
19 Questions

Directions: For each of the questions in this section, choose the best answer and fill in the corresponding circle on your answer sheet.

Each sentence that follows has either one or two blanks. Each blank indicates that a word has been omitted from the sentence. Following each sentence are five words or sets of words. Select the word or set of words that, when inserted into the sentence in place of the blank(s), best fits the context of the sentence as a whole.

1. As we traveled to college for the first time, the family car was ------- with books, clothing, appliances, and other necessities.

   (A) keen
   (B) indigent
   (C) acute
   (D) plausible
   (E) laden

2. The teacher had the ------- job of leading an extremely unruly class.

   (A) alluring
   (B) indiscreet
   (C) opulent
   (D) onerous
   (E) indecisive

3. Although Justin is often characterized as ------- when people first meet him, he is known by his close friends as ------- because of his willingness to help at a moment's notice.

   (A) gregarious . . inconsiderate
   (B) friendly . . rude
   (C) accepting . . close-minded
   (D) helpful . . inhospitable
   (E) abrasive . . caring

4. By reducing business taxes, the new mayor is hoping to ------- the flow of commerce away from the city and encourage ------- in the downtown area.

   (A) increase . . leniency
   (B) arrest . . revival
   (C) diminish . . decline
   (D) enhance . . growth
   (E) boost . . initiative

5. By handing out pamphlets on a busy street corner, members of the organization were able to effectively ------- their message.

   (A) relegate
   (B) develop
   (C) verbalize
   (D) promulgate
   (E) mitigate

6. While exploring the vast Louisiana Territory, Lewis and Clark often ------- the help of indigenous peoples; without it, the explorers ------- would have been lost.

   (A) enlisted . . indubitably
   (B) received . . auspiciously
   (C) refused . . seemingly
   (D) requested . . incredibly
   (E) preferred . . magnificently

GO ON TO THE NEXT PAGE

The passage that follows is accompanied by several questions based on the content of the passage. Answer the questions based on what is either stated or implied in the passage. Be sure to read any introductory material that is provided.

Questions 7–19 are based on the following passage.

The following passage is an adaptation from a report about the neurological disorder called synesthesia.

Thousands, perhaps even millions, of people around the world are afflicted with a neurological condition called *synesthesia*. The
Line word *synesthesia* comes from the Greek words
5 *syn*, which means "together," and *aisthesis*, which means "perception or sensation." Those affected by the disorder experience an involuntary, simultaneous joining of two senses; for example, some synesthetes—people with
10 *synesthesia*—perceive words or numbers as colors. These people might visualize the number "4" as red, or the letter "a" as blue when they hear or read numbers or words. Researchers do not know the causes of *synes-*
15 *thesia*, nor do they fully understand the mechanisms of the disorder. However, some scientists believe that *synesthesia* results from crossed connections in the brain; synapses that are traditionally associated with one sensory system
20 have somehow crossed over into another sensory system, which leads to a juxtaposition of two, typically unrelated senses.

Another theory postulates that *synesthesia* results from a perception breakdown.
25 Researchers espouse the idea that, up until about 4 months of age, infants experience undifferentiated sensory stimuli; most sounds also result in visual and tactile sensations. As infants continue to develop, the sensory process
30 becomes modularized. *Synesthesia* occurs when this differentiation of the senses is incomplete.

Synesthetic perceptions are idiosyncratic and are as varied as the perceivers themselves. Theoretically, the number of types of *synesthesia*
35 is bound only by the sensory pairings themselves, such as the color/auditory pairing mentioned previously. Researchers estimate that there could be as many as 35 different

broad pairings—sound/touch, taste/hearing,
40 and so on—each characterized by many permutations and unique features. Indeed the variations could be endless, with each synesthete perceiving a slightly different color or sensation, for example. Although the perceptions
45 vary among individuals, according to Dr. Richard Cytowic, a leading *synesthesia* expert, no matter what senses are joined in a given *synesthete*, the lifelong inter-sensory associations of the synesthetes remain stable. In other
50 words, if the word "horse" is dark green, it is always perceived as such by the individual.

Despite the potential diversity in the manifestation of *synesthesia*, the actual known number of people with the disorder is relatively
55 small. This is due, in part, to the probability that many people have the condition but do not realize what it is. Most synesthetes are of normal or above normal intelligence and show no outward signs of an aberrant mental condi-
60 tion. In addition, standard neurological exams indicate no difference between a synesthete's brain activity and the brain activity of a so-called non-synesthete. As a result, most people with *synesthesia* do not know that what they are
65 experiencing is any different from what their friends and family are perceiving. It is also quite common for a synesthete, once he or she realizes any anomaly, to remain silent for fear of being shunned or misunderstood.

70 Currently, there is no officially established criterion or method for diagnosing *synesthesia*; researchers customarily must rely on an individual recognizing his or her perceptual differences and then seeking answers from medical
75 or psychological professionals.

GO ON TO THE NEXT PAGE

7. The passage can primarily be described as

   (A) a personal account leading to a universal theory
   (B) a commentary on a particular phenomenon
   (C) an introduction to a firmly established ideal
   (D) a story of how one individual inspired others
   (E) an illustration of a recent scientific discovery

8. In line 21, "juxtaposition" most nearly means

   (A) positioning close together
   (B) crossing over
   (C) disconnecting two closely related things
   (D) associating based on tradition
   (E) breaking down

9. On the basis of the information in the passage, which statement most accurately describes the relationship between synesthetes and normal sensory development?

   (A) Synesthetes usually experience shifts in sensory perception throughout their life-times.
   (B) Normal sensory development occurs prior to sensory modularization in synesthetes.
   (C) Most individuals who undergo normal sensory development are of below average intelligence.
   (D) Normal sensory development is likely interrupted at a relatively early age in synesthetes.
   (E) Individuals who undergo the type of perception breakdown that leads to synesthesia are far more likely to display outward signs of aberrant mental conditions than are those who experience normal sensory development.

10. The purpose of the second paragraph (lines 23–31) is to

    (A) present a basis for questioning the existence of synesthesia
    (B) advance an alternative explanation for a certain neurological condition
    (C) question the motives of synesthetes who seek treatment
    (D) develop a general theory from evidence of a specific condition
    (E) argue that synesthesia results from cross-firing synapses

11. The author uses the term "idiosyncratic" (line 32) to

    (A) convey the difficulty of diagnosing *synesthesia*
    (B) contrast normal sensory development with abnormal sensory development
    (C) evoke a sense of mystery regarding synesthetic perceptions
    (D) suggest that synesthetic perceptions are unique to the perceiver
    (E) defend one expert's opinion regarding sensory pairings in synesthetes

12. The sentence in lines 37–41 is best described as

    (A) a criticism
    (B) a decision
    (C) an assertion
    (D) an ideology
    (E) a concession

13. The mention of Dr. Richard Cytowic (lines 44–49) serves to

    (A) illustrate the difficulty of describing *synesthesia*
    (B) expand on the idea that *synesthesia* cannot be cured
    (C) weaken the theory regarding perception breakdown
    (D) strengthen the contention that synesthetic perceptions are durable
    (E) demonstrate that most physicians know very little about *synesthesia*

14. Lines 52–55 primarily encourage readers to view *synesthesia* as

    (A) a condition that is relatively unknown
    (B) a disorder that might be difficult to diagnose
    (C) a source of controversy within the scientific community
    (D) a condition that affects a small number of people worldwide
    (E) a well-researched medical phenomenon

GO ON TO THE NEXT PAGE ⇒

15. Which of the following statements regarding *synesthesia* is false?

    (A) The majority of synesthetes are, in all probability, oblivious to their condition.
    (B) The severity of *synesthesia* fluctuates throughout an individual's lifetime.
    (C) Synesthetes show few perceptible symptoms of their disease.
    (D) Extensive research done by scientists has ascertained the cause of *synesthesia*.
    (E) Synesthetes most often must perform self-diagnosis to pinpoint their problem.

16. Why does the author use the phrase "standard neurological exams" in line 60?

    (A) To dispel the notion that synesthetes undergo normal sensory development
    (B) To illustrate the point that synesthetes often suffer from aberrant mental conditions
    (C) To establish the fact that regular medical testing shows no difference between synesthetes and non-synesthetes
    (D) To suggest that synesthetes are often subjected to unwarranted medical tests in order to diagnose their condition
    (E) To emphasize the differences between synesthetes and non-synesthetes

17. The word "anomaly" in line 68 most nearly means

    (A) irregularity
    (B) disease
    (C) dilemma
    (D) hindrance
    (E) deficiency

18. On the basis of the information in the last paragraph, it can be inferred that *synesthesia* would most likely be correctly diagnosed in which of the following situations?

    (A) An infant of 4 months of age experiences undifferentiated sensory stimuli.
    (B) An infant of 4 months of age suffers a head trauma resulting in synaptic damage.
    (C) An adult remains silent for fear of the consequences of seeking professional advice.
    (D) An adult comes to realize that he cannot recognize many of his own family members.
    (E) An adult contacts a university psychology department inquiring about perceptual differences between members of her family.

19. The main point of the passage is to

    (A) describe a medical condition that might be difficult to recognize even though it is clearly defined
    (B) propose a radical new treatment for a medical condition that was once thought untreatable
    (C) question the accuracy of the current definition of a well-known medical condition
    (D) reject one explanation of a complex phenomenon in favor of another
    (E) admit several weaknesses in the current theoretical approach to a complex medical condition

STOP

If you finish before your time is up, check your work on this section only.
You may not turn to any other section in the test.

SECTION 9
Time—10 minutes
14 Questions

Directions: For each question, select the best answer from among the choices listed. Fill in the corresponding circle on your answer sheet.

The following questions test the correct and effective use of standard written English in expressing an idea. Part of each sentence (or the entire sentence) is underlined. Following each sentence are five different ways of phrasing the underlined portion. Answer choice A repeats the original phrasing. If you think that the original phrasing is best, select answer choice A. Otherwise, select from the remaining four choices. Your selection should result in the most effective, clear sentence, free from awkwardness or ambiguity.

1. American novelist Willa Cather drew much of her material from <u>her own experiences while living in Nebraska in the late 1800s</u>.

   (A) her own experiences while living in Nebraska in the late 1800s
   (B) living in Nebraska with her own experiences in the late 1800s
   (C) her experiences from her own living in Nebraska in the late 1800s
   (D) her own experiences from living, in the late 1800s, in Nebraska
   (E) her own experiences in the late 1800s of living in Nebraska

2. Coffee beans can be either dry-processed or wet-processed, <u>which is depending upon the water supply of the area</u> where the coffee plants are growing.

   (A) which is depending upon the water supply of the area
   (B) which, depending upon the water supply of the area
   (C) depending on the water supply of the area
   (D) which, depends upon the water supply of the area
   (E) and it is dependent upon the area's water supply

3. As the pilot was landing the <u>plane, and he saw that the runway</u> wasn't clear, and he immediately pulled the jet upward.

   (A) plane, and he saw that the runway
   (B) plane, he saw that the runway
   (C) plane; therefore, he saw that the runway
   (D) plane and then he saw that the runway
   (E) plane: and he saw that the runway

4. Wolfgang Mozart's music was of the Classical style and included symphonies, operas, concertos, <u>as well as that of chamber music</u>.

   (A) as well as that of chamber music
   (B) including that of chamber musics
   (C) and including chamber music
   (D) and chamber music
   (E) as well as chamber musics

5. The blades of early ice skates were made of oxen or reindeer bones that were first ground down <u>and then they would be polished</u>.

   (A) and then they would be polished
   (B) and then they are polished
   (C) and then they are to be polished
   (D) and then polished
   (E) and next they would be polished

6. The city of Las Vegas has grown exponentially in the last decade, <u>which this has created</u> a huge impact on the road system.

   (A) which this has created
   (B) this is creating
   (C) creating
   (D) which has been creating
   (E) this has created

GO ON TO THE NEXT PAGE ⇒

7. Molds that grow outdoors <u>are important with the breaking down of</u> dead organic matter, such as tree limbs and fallen leaves.

   (A) are important with the breaking down of
   (B) are important in the breakdown of
   (C) break down importantly
   (D) are important with the breaking down
   (E) are important by breaking down

8. Many people find that eating healthy foods, exercising regularly, and getting plenty of sleep <u>all have a positive impact on their lives</u>.

   (A) all have a positive impact on their lives
   (B) all has a positive impact on their life
   (C) impact his or her life in a positive way
   (D) impacts their life positively
   (E) impact positively upon their lives

9. At most major airports, several transportation <u>systems, including</u> shuttle buses, underground trains, and conveyor belts, are available to move airline passengers from one terminal to another.

   (A) systems, including
   (B) systems, thereby including
   (C) systems; including
   (D) systems; which are including
   (E) systems these include

10. Suzanne was startled awake when <u>she could hear a loud noise from the outside of her window</u>.

    (A) she could hear a loud noise from the outside of her window
    (B) she heard a loud noise from outside her window
    (C) from the outside of her window she heard a loud noise
    (D) she heard a noise that was loud from the outside of her window
    (E) a loud noise from outside her window she heard

11. Scientists estimate that the Cambrian period lasted 570 million years, during which time <u>most of the world's land masses were</u> in the Southern Hemisphere.

    (A) most of the world's land masses were
    (B) most all of the world's land masses were
    (C) the world's land masses, most of which, were
    (D) almost all of the worlds land masses were
    (E) the worlds land masses are

12. No sooner had Michael arrived on campus <u>so his mother began</u> calling him repeatedly.

    (A) so his mother began
    (B) than his mother began
    (C) but his mother had began
    (D) but he was called by his mother
    (E) then he was called by his mother

13. As I entered the gymnasium, my coach <u>while turning to me to say</u> that the team was counting on me to guarantee a win.

    (A) while turning to me to say
    (B) will turn and say to me
    (C) turns to me and is saying
    (D) turns and also says to me
    (E) turned to me and said

14. In 1994, during her final performance at the Olympic games, the figure skater <u>had fallen twice</u>.

    (A) had fallen twice
    (B) twice had fallen
    (C) fell twice
    (D) falls twice
    (E) has fell twice

STOP

If you finish before your time is up, check your work on this section only.
You may not turn to any other section in the test.

SAT Diagnostic Test Answer Key

Section 1

Because grading the essay is subjective, we've chosen not to include any "graded" essays here. Your best bet is to have someone you trust, such as your personal tutor, read your essays and give you an honest critique. Make the grading criteria mentioned in Chapter 5 available to whomever grades your essays. If you plan on grading your own essays, review the grading criteria and be as honest as possible regarding the structure, development, organization, technique, and appropriateness of your writing. Focus on your weak areas and continue to practice in order to improve your writing skills.

Section 2

1. A	16. C
2. E	17. A
3. C	18. B
4. D	19. D
5. B	20. E
6. D	
7. A	
8. A	
9. C	
10. A	
11. E	
12. D	
13. A	
14. A	
15. D	

Section 3

1. C	16. D
2. D	17. E
3. A	18. A
4. E	19. B
5. B	20. A
6. B	21. C
7. C	22. D
8. D	23. B
9. A	24. B
10. D	
11. C	
12. A	
13. B	
14. E	
15. C	

Section 4

Multiple Choice

1. C
2. E
3. B
4. E
5. A
6. C
7. C
8. E

Student Produced Response

9. 8 or 10
10. 700
11. 5000
12. 14
13. 4
14. 992
15. 8 or 9
16. 3
17. .2 or $\frac{1}{5}$
18. 30

Section 5

1. B
2. D
3. A
4. B
5. C
6. D
7. B
8. A
9. A
10. B
11. E
12. C
13. C
14. E
15. E
16. A
17. E
18. D
19. B
20. E
21. D
22. B
23. D
24. A
25. D
26. E
27. A
28. E
29. C
30. C
31. A
32. C
33. A
34. B
35. D

Section 6

1. A	17. E
2. C	18. D
3. C	19. C
4. B	20. B
5. E	21. B
6. A	22. C
7. D	23. A
8. C	24. A
9. E	
10. C	
11. B	
12. D	
13. C	
14. A	
15. D	
16. E	

Section 7

1. C
2. B
3. C
4. E
5. E
6. A
7. A
8. D
9. E
10. B
11. C
12. D
13. E
14. C
15. A
16. C

Section 8

1. E
2. D
3. E
4. B
5. D
6. A
7. B
8. A
9. D
10. B
11. D
12. C
13. D
14. B
15. B
16. C
17. A
18. E
19. A

Section 9

1. A
2. C
3. B
4. D
5. D
6. C
7. B
8. A
9. A
10. B
11. A
12. B
13. E
14. C

Scoring Your Simulated SAT Exam

Check your responses with the Answer Key. Fill in the blanks below and do the calculations to get your math, critical reading, and writing raw scores. Use the tables on the next pages find your scaled scores.

Remember that this is a simulated test and that the score should only be used to estimate your score on the actual SAT.

Get Your Math Raw Score:

	Number Correct	**Number Incorrect**
Section 2:	_____	_____
Section 4:		
(#1 – #8)	_____	_____
(#9 – #18)	_____	
Section 7:	_____	_____
Totals:	_____	_____

Divide the total Number Incorrect by 4 and subtract the result from the total Number Correct. This is your Raw Score: _____

Round Raw Score to the nearest whole number. Use Table 1 to find Scaled Score range.

Math Scaled Score Range: _____ - _____

Get Your Critical Reading Raw Score:

	Number Correct	**Number Incorrect**
Section 3:	_____	_____
Section 6:	_____	_____
Section 8:	_____	_____
Totals:	_____	_____

Divide the total Number Incorrect by 4 and subtract the result from the total Number Correct. This is your Raw Score: _____

Round Raw Score to the nearest whole number. Use Table 2 to find Scaled Score range.

Critical Reading Scaled Score Range: _____ - _____

Get Your Writing Raw Score:

	Number Correct	Number Incorrect
Section 5:	_____	_____
Section 9:	_____	_____
Totals:	_____	_____

Divide the total Number Incorrect by 4 and subtract the result from the total Number Correct. This is your Raw Score: _____

Round Raw Score to the nearest whole number. Use Table 3 to find Scaled Score range.

Writing Score Range: _____ - _____

Note that your Writing Score assumes an Essay score of 4. If you believe that your Essay warrants a score of 5 or 6, your Writing Score would increase by an average of 30 to 50 points. Likewise, if your Essay is in the 1 to 3 range, your Writing Score would decrease by an average of 30 to 50 points.

Get Your Composite Score:

To calculate your Composite Score Range, simply add the 3 sub-score ranges (Math, Critical Reading, and Writing).

Composite Score Range: _____ - _____

Table 1   Math Score Conversion

Raw Score	Scaled Score	Raw Score	Scaled Score
54	800	23	460-520
53	750-800	22	450-510
52	720-800	21	440-500
51	700-780	20	430-490
50	690-770	19	430-490
49	680-740	18	420-480
48	670-730	17	410-470
47	660-720	16	400-460
46	640-700	15	400-460
45	630-690	14	390-450
44	620-680	13	380-440
43	620-680	12	360-440
42	610-670	11	350-430
41	600-660	10	340-420
40	580-660	9	330-430
39	570-650	8	320-420
38	560-640	7	310-410
37	550-630	6	290-390
36	550-630	5	280-380
35	540-620	4	270-370
34	530-610	3	260-360
33	520-600	2	240-340
32	520-600	1	230-330
31	520-580	0	210-310
30	510-570	-1	200-290
29	500-560	-2	200-270
28	490-550	-3	200-250
27	490-550	-4	200-230
26	480-540	-5	200-210
25	470-530	-6 and below	200
24	460-520		

Table 2   Critical Reading Score Conversion

Raw Score	Scaled Score	Raw Score	Scaled Score
67	800	30	470-530
66	770-800	29	470-530
65	740-800	28	460-520
64	720-800	27	450-510
63	700-800	26	450-510
62	690-790	25	440-500
61	670-770	24	440-500
60	660-760	23	430-490
59	660-740	22	420-480
58	650-730	21	420-480
57	640-720	20	410-470
56	630-710	19	400-460
55	630-710	18	400-460
54	620-700	17	390-450
53	610-690	16	380-440
52	600-680	15	380-440
51	610-670	14	370-430
50	600-660	13	360-420
49	590-650	12	350-410
48	580-640	11	350-410
47	580-640	10	340-400
46	570-630	9	330-390
45	560-620	8	310-390
44	560-620	7	300-380
43	550-610	6	290-370
42	550-610	5	270-370
41	540-600	4	260-360
40	530-590	3	250-350
39	530-590	2	230-330
38	520-580	1	220-320
37	510-570	0	200-290
36	510-570	-1	200-290
35	500-560	-2	200-270
34	500-560	-3	200-250
33	490-550	-4	200-230
32	480-540	-5	200-210
31	480-540	-6 and below	200

Table 3   Writing Score Conversion

Raw Score	Scaled Score	Raw Score	Scaled Score
49	750-800	21	460-590
48	720-800	20	460-580
47	700-800	19	450-580
46	680-800	18	440-570
45	670-800	17	430-560
44	660-790	16	420-550
43	640-780	15	410-540
42	630-770	14	400-530
41	620-760	13	390-520
40	620-750	12	390-510
39	610-740	11	380-510
38	600-730	10	370-500
37	590-720	9	360-490
36	580-720	8	350-480
35	570-710	7	340-470
34	570-700	6	330-460
33	560-690	5	320-460
32	550-680	4	320-450
31	540-670	3	310-440
30	530-660	2	300-430
29	520-650	1	280-410
28	520-650	0	270-410
27	510-640	-1	250-390
26	500-630	-2	240-370
25	490-620	-3	240-360
24	480-610	-4	220-340
23	470-600	-5	200-320
22	460-590	-6 and below	200

Answer Key and Explanations

Section 1

Because grading the essay is subjective, we've chosen not to include any "graded" essays here. Your best bet is to have someone you trust, such as your personal tutor, read your essays and give you an honest critique. Make the grading criteria mentioned in Chapter 5 available to whomever grades your essays. If you plan on grading your own essays, review the grading criteria and be as honest as possible regarding the structure, development, organization, technique, and appropriateness of your writing. Focus on your weak areas and continue to practice to improve your writing skills.

Section 2

1. **The correct answer is A.** The first step in answering this question is to solve the first equation for a:

   $3a + 5 = 14$

   $3a = 9$

   $a = 3$

   Next, substitute 3 for a in the second equation:

   $2(3) - 4$

   $6 - 4 = 2$

2. **The correct answer is E.** The area of a circle is π times the radius^2 (πr^2). Therefore, the area of the larger circle is 36π. The area of the smaller circle is πx^2. To find the area of the shaded region, simply subtract the area of the smaller circle from that of the larger one: $36\pi - \pi x^2$.

3. **The correct answer is C.** To solve this problem, determine the minimum and maximum number of seats that could be in the theater. The minimum is 6×120, or 720, and the maximum is 6×180, or 1,080. The only number among the answer choices that is between these two numbers is 721.

4. **The correct answer is D.** To solve this problem, you must first recognize that $8 = 2^3$. Substitute 2^3 for 8 and apply the correct rules of exponents as follows:

   $2^{2y} = (2^3)^{y-1}$

   $2^{2y} = 2^{3y-3}$

   Now because the base is the same (2), you can set the exponents equal to each other and solve for y:

   $2y = 3y - 3$

   $-y = -3$

   $y = 3$

5. **The correct answer is B.** The area of a triangle is $\frac{1}{2}$ (base)(height). To solve this problem it might be helpful to draw a diagram, as shown below:

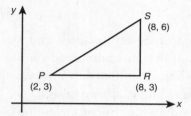

The line segment PR is 6 units long, and it is the base of the right triangle. The line segment RS is 3 units long, and it is the height of the right triangle. Using this information, the area of triangle PRS is $\frac{1}{2}$ (6)(3), or 9.

6. **The correct answer is D.** To answer this question, first solve for b: $b = 20 - a$. Because a must be greater than 7, b must be less than 13. The remaining answer choices are incorrect because either they do not *have* to be true (they simply *could* be true), or they invalidate the equation.

7. **The correct answer is A.** To solve this problem, you need to use Pythagorean Theorem because line segments XQ, XR, XT, and XU will each be the hypotenuse of a right triangle. Because QS is the longest line segment shown (7 units), it will also be the longest possible side of a right triangle. Therefore, the hypotenuse of this particular right triangle will be the longest of all of the line segments. The hypotenuse of this triangle is XQ.

8. **The correct answer is A.** To solve this problem, use the variable x as the "certain number." Next, set up an equation. The left side of the equation will be four more than two times the number, or $2x + 4$. The problem says that this value is 3 less than the number. Therefore, $2x + 4 = x - 3$. Solve this equation as follows:

$2x + 4 = x - 3$

$2x - x = -3 - 4$

$x = -7$

9. **The correct answer is C.** To solve this problem, first count the number of triangular faces and the number of rectangular faces that make up the three-dimensional figure. There are two triangular faces and three rectangular faces. Surface area is the sum of the areas of each of the faces. The area of each triangular face is given as $7p$, and the area of each rectangular face is given as $4v$. So the surface area is $7p(2) + 4v(3)$, or $14p + 12v$, answer choice C.

10. **The correct answer is A.** To solve this problem, let x be the sum of the test scores. Given that the number of scores is 9 and the average is s, you can form the equation $s = \frac{x}{9}$. This is equivalent to $x = 9s$, answer choice A.

11. **The correct answer is E.** To solve this problem, remember that the sum of interior angles in a triangle is 180°, and a straight line contains 180°. Because the outside angle at point A on the horizontal line is 105°, the complimentary angle must be 180° − 105°, or 75°. The triangle has 180° total, so 180° − 75° − 25° = 80°, which is the value of y.

12. **The correct answer is D.** A prime number is a number whose only factors are 1 and itself. Make a list of the integers between 15 and 25, as follows:

    16, 17, 18, 19, 20, 21, 22, 23, 24

    Next, check to see which of the numbers can be divided only by 1 and itself, or which have two other prime factors. The three prime numbers are 17, 19, and 23, and the two non-prime numbers with prime factors are 21 (7×3) and 22 (11×2).

13. **The correct answer is A.** There are 360° in a circle, which means that $\frac{1}{3}$ of a circle contains $\frac{360°}{3}$, or 120°, and $\frac{1}{4}$ of a circle contains $\frac{360°}{4}$, or 90°. The difference between 120° and 90° is 30°.

14. **The correct answer is A.** To solve this problem, start with one CD, r. Next, multiply the remaining number of CDs, n, by the cost of each of the remaining CDs, $(r - s)$, to get $n(r - s)$. Now, add the cost of the first CD, r, as follows: $r + n(r - s)$.

15. **The correct answer is D.** In this "defining a new operation" problem, simply substitute the given values into the operation. Find the value of $2 \oplus 3$, according to the definition of $x \oplus y$. Because $x \oplus y = \frac{(x - y)}{(x + y)}$, $2 \oplus 3 = \frac{(2 - 3)}{(2 + 3)}$, or $-\frac{1}{5}$. Now, substitute $-\frac{1}{5}$ for $2 \oplus 3$ in the second equation: $-\frac{1}{5} = \frac{(2 - z)}{(2 + z)}$. Cross multiply and solve for z:

    $5(2 - z) = -1(2 + z)$

    $10 - 5z = -2 - z$

    $-5z = -12 - z$

    $-4z = -12$

    $z = 3$

16. **The correct answer is C.** To solve this problem, first draw a perpendicular bisector from point P to the midpoint of line MN and then use the Pythagorean Theorem to calculate the length of the bisector. You are given that the measure of both PM and MN is 6 (all of the line segments are congruent.) This means that half the length of MN must be 3. Perform the following calculations:

    $a^2 + 3^2 = 6^2$

    $a^2 = 36 - 9$

    $a = \sqrt{27}$, which can be reduced to $3\sqrt{3}$.

    The length of PN, then, is $2(3\sqrt{3}.)$, or $6\sqrt{3}$.

17. **The correct answer is A.** In an odd set of values, the median is the middle value when the values are in order of least to greatest. In an even set of values, the median is the average of the two middle values when the values are in order of least to greatest. Because this is a set with an odd number of values, the median will be the middle value. Put the values in order, at first excluding u: 21, 25, 27, 29, 35, 38. Because you are given that 29 is the median, or middle value, u must come after 29 and, therefore, be a value greater than 29.

18. **The correct answer is B.** To solve this problem, first make a list of the factors of 42 and another list of the factors of 90.

Factors of 42:	Factors of 90:
42:1	90:1
21:2	45:2
14:3	30:3
7:6	18:5
	15:6
	10:9

    Remember that a prime number is one that is only divisible by 1 and itself. The greatest prime factor of 42 (p) is 7, and the greatest prime factor of 90 (r) is 5. Therefore the value of $p - r = 7 - 5$, or 2.

19. **The correct answer is D.** Because the figure is a rectangle, each of the adjacent sides is perpendicular to each other. Perpendicular lines have slopes that are negative reciprocals of each other, meaning that the product of their slopes is -1. Because there are four lines and four perpendicular angles, the product of the slopes is $(-1) \times (-1) \times (-1) \times (-1)$, which equals 1.

20. **The correct answer is E.** The first step in solving this problem is to calculate the total number of boys and girls in the program. You are given that there are 40 more boys than girls enrolled in the summer art program. Set the number of girls equal to g. Therefore, the number of boys enrolled is equal to $g + 40$, and the total number of students is $g + g + 40$, or $2g + 40$. To find the percentage of girls enrolled, simply divide the total number of students ($2g + 40$) by the number of girls (g), and multiply by 100 as follows:

$$100 \frac{g}{2g + 40} \%$$

Section 3

1. **The best answer is C.** The context of the sentence implies that there was discord among the teachers over the dress-code issue. The word "hostility" refers to "unfriendliness and feeling or showing ill-will," so it is the most appropriate word to insert into the blank. "Civility" and "regard" refer to "courteous and respectful behavior," which would not cause teachers to threaten to resign. Answer choice A is incorrect because "apathy" refers to a "lack of feeling or emotion," and answer choice B is incorrect because "ambiguity" refers to "doubtfulness or uncertainty."

2. **The best answer is D.** The information following the semicolon offers a definition for the word that best fits in the blank. "Incredulity" refers to "doubt" or disbelief," so it is the most appropriate word to insert into the blank. Answer choices A, B, C, and E do not mean "doubt" or "disbelief."

3. **The best answer is A.** The context of the sentence indicates that the reports Tom received led to his decision to discontinue his search. Therefore, the reports could not have included information that was helpful to Tom. "Ambivalence" often refers to "uncertainty" or "lack of clarity." This type of information would not be helpful. Answer choice B is incorrect because it suggests that the information was helpful. Answer choice C is incorrect, because "cordial" means "friendly," which does not appropriately describe reports. Answer choice D is incorrect because "diligent" is an adjective that would better describe the investigators; a report is not "diligent." "Keen" means "sharp," which does not fit the context of the sentence, so eliminate answer choice E.

4. **The best answer is E.** The context of the sentence suggests that the words that best fit the blanks will be antonyms; many people feel one way about ballet, while others feel a different way. "Relish" means "to have a strong appreciation for," whereas "despise" indicates a "strong dislike." Answer choices A, B, C, and D contain word pairs that are either synonyms or do not fit the context of the sentence.

5. **The best answer is B.** According to the sentence, Andrew had supporters at the education conference, which was designed to promote the test preparation industry. This suggests that Andrew agreed with and supported standardized test preparation. Therefore, you can eliminate answer choices A, D, and E because the first word in each pair is not appropriate for the first blank in the sentence. The word "proponent" refers to someone who "supports" or "advocates" something. "Myriad" means "a vast number," which best fits the context of the sentence. It does not make sense that Andrew would "lack" supporters, so answer choice C is incorrect.

6. **The best answer is B.** The author of Passage 1 states that "the greatest risk is associated with objects large enough to perturb the Earth's climate on a global scale by sending large quantities of dust into the upper atmosphere." This best supports answer choice B. Answer choice A contradicts statements made in the passage, so it is incorrect. The other answer choices are not supported by the passage.

7. **The best answer is C.** The author of Passage 2 states, "hundreds, perhaps thousands, of small asteroids and other space debris enter the Earth's atmosphere daily. Because they burn up long before they reach the earth's surface, they pose no risk." This suggests that the author of Passage 2 believes that the author of Passage 1 is overreaching in his or her statement regarding researching the detection of asteroids, meteors, and comets. The other answer choices are not supported by the passage.

8. **The best answer is D.** The author of Passage 1 states, "the greatest risk is associated with objects large enough to perturb the Earth's climate on a global scale by sending large quantities of dust into the upper atmosphere. Such an impact event could lead to decreased temperatures around the globe." Passage 2 makes no such claim.

9. **The best answer is A.** The author of Passage 1 details the devastating effects that would come from a cosmic impact event, and the author of Passage 2 states that "the consequences of a larger object impacting the Earth would be potentially devastating." The remaining answer choices could be supported by one or the other of the passages, but not both.

10. **The best answer is D.** The author writes, "We four affectionately watched his back as he stood in the bows looking toward the sea. On the whole river there was nothing that looked half so nautical. He resembled a pilot, which to a sailor is trustworthiness personified." This imagery helps the reader create an impression of the character being described.

11. **The best answer is C.** The word "luminous" means "full of light, or bright." The passage contrasts the "luminous estuary" with the "brooding gloom," so you could have eliminated answer choice E.

12. **The best answer is A.** The passage states, "We four affectionately watched his back…," and "The Lawyer—the best of old fellows—…," which suggests that the narrator held good feelings toward his fellow sailors. These statements and the general tone of the passage best support answer choice A because "benevolence" refers to a "disposition to do good."

13. **The best answer is B.** The context of the passage indicates that the sailors were very relaxed and probably somewhat tired. "Listless" means "lacking energy," and "placid" means "calm or quiet." The passage does not suggest that the scene was "bleak," only that the sailors were very relaxed, so eliminate answer choice A. Likewise, the passage suggests that the sailors were not lonely because of the bond that they shared, so eliminate answer choice C. Answer choices D and E are not emphasized by the use of the phrase "placid staring."

14. **The best answer is E.** The word "imperceptible" means "impossible or difficult to perceive," which best matches answer choice E. The other answer choices are words that appear in the passage but do not have the same meaning as "imperceptible."

15. **The best answer is C.** According to the passage, Marlow was not typical in his storytelling—his stories tended to be long and complicated—but continued to tell stories regardless. The passage goes on to say that the men accepted Marlow's comment "…in silence. No one took the trouble to grunt even," which suggests that the men had grown used to his long stories. Because the passage indicates a sense of resignation among the men in regard to Marlow's behavior, it is likely that this behavior has been going on for some time and that Marlow is completely unaware of his effect on his shipmates. The other answer choices are not supported by the passage.

16. **The best answer is D.** The passage states, "The belief was that if it was beneficial for African-American children to be placed in schools with white children, it was also beneficial for Native Americans to become integrated into white society" and "…the government suggested to tribal leadership that it would be in their best interest to own their property and pay taxes on it like other landowners." This best supports answer choice D.

17. **The best answer is E.** The government was striving to integrate Native Americans into mainstream society to end their involvement in Native American affairs. Thus, the federal government *supported* the new readjustment policy. Answer choices A and B are incorrect because they imply that the government did not encourage the readjustment of Native Americans. The readjustment movement did not "illustrate" the end of the federal government's involvement; rather, it caused the federal government to be more involved in trying to push readjustment onto the Native Americans.

18. **The best answer is A.** In saying that if African Americans should be placed in schools with white children, Native Americans should, too, the government is not differentiating between African Americans and Native Americans and ignoring any possible differences between the two groups. The other answer choices are not supported by the passage.

19. **The best answer is B.** The author states, "the government offered to give the tribes the land without charge." The passage explicitly states that there would be no cost for the land and no restrictions on selling it. The passage does not mention the benefits of public schooling or cultural preservation programs.

20. **The best answer is A.** According to the passage, the Native Americans "…believed that land ownership would cause reservation lands to recede." Answer choice D appears to be correct, but the Native Americans were not trying to avoid taxation. As stated in the passage, they were simply worried about the increased financial burden that taxes would cause: "It was their belief that land ownership and the resulting taxation would create new financial burdens, foreclosures, and subsequent tax sales of property." The other answer choices are not supported by the passage.

21. **The best answer is C.** The phrase further illustrates that the Native Americans will eventually lose their land, regardless of how it is sold. While many Native Americans wanted to keep their land, Native Americans would still lose land when "individual land owners were enticed to sell their land." The other answer choices are not supported by the passage.

22. **The best answer is D.** The phrase "sweeten the deal" serves to emphasize the government's desire to do whatever it took to convince the Native Americans to own their land. By offering the tribes the land for no charge and offering funds to cover the costs associated with land ownership, the government was doing everything in its power to persuade the Native Americans to own their land. While the government said that it would be in the best interest of the tribes, the government clearly wanted the tribes to be in possession of tribal land. The other answer choices are not supported by the passage.

23. **The best answer is B.** In the last paragraph, the author mentions everything that Native American leadership tried to do, including encouraging Native Americans to stay on reservations, enticing new business, lobbying for the passage of the Native American Community Act, and creating more job opportunities for Native Americans. The last paragraph does not include any information about altering the requirements of the education system.

24. **The best answer is B.** The main idea of the fourth paragraph lies in its first sentence, informing the reader that Native American leadership strove to encourage Native Americans to stay on reservations. The rest of the paragraph outlines how the Native American leadership planned to increase incentives for their people to remain on reservations. This best supports answer choice B.

Section 4

1. **The correct answer is C.** The best way to solve this problem is to replace the unknown symbol with the variable x and solve for x as follows:

$$\frac{9 - x}{3} = 2$$

$$9 - x = 6$$

$$-x = -3$$

$$x = 3$$

2. **The correct answer is E.** To solve, add the length of XY to the length of YZ. You are given that the length of XY is 5 and that the length of YZ is 21 more than XY. Therefore, the length of YZ is 5 + 21, or 26, and the length of XZ is 5 + 26, or 31.

3. **The correct answer is B.** To answer this question, first solve for a in the first equation: $6 = 2a$, so $a = 3$. Now, substitute 3 for a in the second equation: $3(3) + 13 = 9 + 13 = 22$.

4. **The correct answer is E.** To answer this question, look closely at the data represented in the graph. According to the graph, there were 300 books sold in 2005 and 400 books sold in 2006. This increase of 100 is the greatest increase in books sold from one year to the next.

5. **The correct answer is A.** To solve this problem, first recognize that, if the average of c and d is 12, then $c + \frac{d}{2} = 12$, and $c + d = 24$. Also, if the average of c, d, and e is 10, then $\frac{(c + d + e)}{3} = 10$, and $c + d + e = 30$. Therefore, $24 + e = 30$, so e must equal $30 - 24$, or 6.

6. **The correct answer is C.** The absolute value of any number is always positive. Eliminate answer choice A because it is negative ($m = -1$). Because n is close to 0.6 on the number line shown, and p is close to 1.75 on the number line shown, the difference between n and p is close to -1.15 on the number line shown. Therefore, the absolute value of $n - p$ is 1.15; this corresponds to o on the number line.

7. **The correct answer is C.** To solve this problem, substitute $\frac{1}{2}$ for x and simplify. Remember that when you divide by a fraction, you should multiply by the reciprocal of that fraction, as follows:

$$\frac{8}{\frac{1}{2}} = 8 \times 2, \text{ or } 16$$

$$\frac{4}{(\frac{1}{2} - 1)} = \frac{4}{-\frac{1}{2}}$$

$$\frac{4}{-\frac{1}{2}} = 4 \times -2, \text{ or } -8$$

$$16 + -8 = 8$$

8. **The correct answer is E.** To solve this problem, first recognize that the figure is a square ($JF = HG$). Therefore, the x-coordinate must be the same number of units as the y-coordinate. Because the y-coordinate is 8, the x-coordinate, k, must also be 8. If you did not realize that the figure was a square, you could at least have eliminated answer choices A, B, and C because point G is in Quadrant I, and the x-coordinate (k) must be positive. Likewise, you can eliminate answer choice D because coordinate k cannot have a value of 0.

9. **The correct answer is 8 or 10.** The first step in solving this problem is to determine the equation involving c: $(c + 5) \times 4$, or $4(c + 5)$. Next, set up an inequality: $44 < 4(c + 5) < 65$. Now, expand the middle term: $44 < 4c + 20 < 65$. Finally, isolate the c-term and solve for c:

$24 < 4c < 45$

$6 < c < 11.25$

Because you are given that c is a positive even integer, the two possible values are 8 and 10.

10. **The correct answer is 700.** The perimeter, P, of a rectangle is equal to $l + l + w + w$. Perform the following operations:

$110 = 35 + 35 + 2w$

$110 = 70 + 2w$

$40 = 2w$ and $w = 20$

The area of a rectangle is equal to $l \times w$; so $35 \times 20 = 700$.

11. **The correct answer is 5000.** To solve this problem, first subtract the fixed amount ($3,000) from the salesperson's gross pay ($4,500): $4,500 – $3,000 = $1,500. You are given that this amount is equivalent to 30% of the dollar amount of her sales. Set her sales equal to x, set up a proportion, and solve for x:

$\frac{1500}{x} = \frac{30}{100}$ (remember that 30% equals 30 over 100)

$30x = 150,000$

$x = 5,000$

12. **The correct answer is 14.** To solve this problem, first notice that both equations share the term $(3x – 2y)$. Rearrange the first equation, as follows, to isolate $(3x – 2y)$: $(3x – 2y) = \frac{280}{[5(y + 5)]}$. Because you are given that $(3x – 2y) = 8$, you can set $\frac{280}{[5(y + 5)]} = 8$. Now, cross multiply and solve for y, as follows:

$280 = 40y + 200$

$80 = 40y$

$y = 2$

Substitute 2 for y into $(3x – 2y) = 8$ and solve for x:

$3x – 4 = 8$

$x = 4$

Finally, substitute 2 for y and 4 for x in the last equation and solve:

$4x – y = 4(4) – 2$, or 14

13. **The correct answer is 4.** If the center of the circle is at (-4, -2) and the circle only touches the x-axis at one point, then it must touch at the point (-4, 0). The radius of the circle is the change in y-coordinates, or -2. That means that the diameter of the circle is -2(-2), or 4.

14. **The correct answer is 992.** According to the question stem, you are looking for a three-digit integer, which means that it must be less than 1,000. The number must also be divisible both by 2 and 8 because 2 and 8 are factors of 32. Because 1,000 is divisible by 8, first try 8 less than 1,000 (the next lowest number divisible by both 8 and 4), or 992. Because 992 is divisible by both 8 and 2, it must be the greatest three-digit integer that is divisible by, or has a factor of, 32.

15. **The correct answer is 8 or 9.** To solve this problem, remember that a circle contains 360°. If the tip of one piece of pie is at least 40°, there can be 360 ÷ 40, or 9 pieces. Likewise, if the tip is at most 50°, there can be 360 ÷ 50, or 7.2 pieces. Because the question asks for the number of whole pieces, Matt can cut the pie into either 8 or 9 whole pieces.

16. **The correct answer is 3.** You are given that $a \Phi b = 3ab + 3b$. Therefore, $3 \Phi 2y$ means that $a = 3$ and $b = 2y$. Substitute those values into the first newly defined operation and solve:

    $3(3)(2y) + 3(2y) = 24y$

    Next, you are given that $a \Xi b = 9a + 2b$. Therefore, $6 \Xi 3y$ means that $a = 6$ and $b = 3y$. Substitute those values into the second newly defined operation and solve:

    $9(6) + 2(3y) = 54 + 6y$

    Now, set these values equal to each other and solve for y:

    $34y = 54 + 6y$

    $18y = 54$

    $y = 3$

17. **The correct answer is .2 or $\frac{1}{5}$.** To find the slope of a line, divide the change in y-values by the change in x-values. The origin is at point (0, 0), so the change in y-values is $1 - 0$, or 1, and the change in x-values is $5 - 0$, or 5. Therefore, the slope of this line is $\frac{1}{5}$.

18. **The correct answer is 30.** Let x be the number of miles Kara drives each way. Then

    $$\frac{(x \text{ miles})}{(75 \text{ miles/hour})} + \frac{(x \text{ miles})}{(50 \text{ miles/hour})} = 60 \text{ minutes, or 1 hour.}$$

    The lowest common factor of 75 and 50 is 150, so 150 will be the lowest common denominator.

    Therefore, $\frac{(2x \text{ miles})}{(150 \text{ miles/hour})} + \frac{(3x \text{ miles})}{(150 \text{ miles/hour})} = 1 \text{ hour.}$

    Add the fractions and solve for x, as follows:

    $$\frac{(5x \text{ miles})}{(150 \text{ miles/hour})} = 1 \text{ hour}$$

    $5x = 150$

    $x = 30$

Section 5

1. **The best answer is B.** The replacement for the underlined portion that most clearly indicates that Kim was burdened by her backpack and books and needed to find a place to sit is "Kim desperately searched for a place to sit." Eliminate answer choices D and E, which suggest that a place to sit was burdened with a backpack and an armful of books. Answer choices A and C are awkward.

2. **The best answer is D.** The sentence as it is written compares the university with local students. To correctly compare the students from neighboring states who visited the university with the local students who visited the university, it is necessary to include the verb "did." While answer choice E correctly includes the verb "did," it incorrectly includes the possessive "student's."

3. **The best answer is A.** This sentence is best as it is written. It effectively expresses the idea and is free from ambiguity. Answer choices B, C, D, and E are awkward and unclear.

4. **The best answer is B.** The only choice that clearly and effectively conveys the intended idea is the simple phrase "spilling oranges onto the road and blocking traffic." In addition, this selection maintains parallelism between the verb forms in the sentence. The other answer choices are awkward.

5. **The best answer is C.** The sentence as it is written is a run-on sentence. In addition, the pronoun "it" is ambiguous because it does not refer to a clear antecedent. By eliminating the phrase "it was," the sentence is clear and concise and free from errors in grammar. The other answer choices are grammatically incorrect.

6. **The best answer is D.** In the sentence as it is written, the pronoun "they" is ambiguous and somewhat confusing. By indicating *who*—the archeologist—can observe the artifact, the sentence becomes clear and concise. Although answer choice C mentions the archeologist, the phrase "and so" is out of place, and the sentence lacks clarity.

7. **The best answer is B.** The sentence as it is written suggests that the construction crew lacked a solid foundation, which is not the intention of the sentence. The modifying phrase "Lacking a solid foundation" must refer directly to "the house." Only answer choice B places the modifier directly before the object it is intended to modify.

8. **The best answer is A.** This sentence is best as it is written. It effectively expresses the idea and is free from ambiguity. Answer choices B, C, D, and E are awkward and unclear.

9. **The best answer is A.** This sentence is best as it is written. It effectively expresses the idea and is free from ambiguity. Answer choices B, C, D, and E are awkward and unclear.

10. **The best answer is B.** Answer choice B maintains parallel verb form and is clear and concise. The other answer choices do not use the correct verb tense and are awkwardly constructed.

11. **The best answer is E.** This sentence includes two related, independent clauses that need to be separated by either a semicolon or a comma followed by a coordinating conjunction. Answer choices A and B can be eliminated; the comma is not followed by a coordinating conjunction. Answer choice C is incorrect because it implies a contrast that does not exist between the two clauses. Answer choice D is incorrect because replacing "he" with "while" creates an awkward and incomplete sentence. Answer choice E properly uses a semicolon and remains clear and concise.

12. **The best answer is C.** This question tests the proper use of idiom, or the common usage of the language. A speaker is not listened "with;" a speaker is listened "to." The other underlined portions are correct and appropriate.

13. **The best answer is C.** It is not necessary to include the verb "being" in this sentence; the sentence simply compares a calm wind to a hurricane level wind. By including the verb "being," the sentence incorrectly compares an action, "being calm," to a noun, "hurricane level."

14. **The best answer is E.** This sentence does not contain any errors. It is appropriate to use the word "important," and it is idiomatic to use the phrase "work with." An "advisor" is a person, so the word is correctly being used as a noun, and the participle "determining" is used correctly in this sentence.

15. **The best answer is E.** This sentence does not contain any errors. The verb "affect" is correctly used in this sentence to indicate an action. Likewise, the other underlined words and phrases are correct and appropriate.

16. **The best answer is A.** When referring to the noun "people," it is correct to use the pronoun "who." "Which" is used only to refer to things. The other underlined portions are correct and appropriate.

17. **The best answer is E.** This sentence does not contain any errors. All of the verb forms match in tense and function.

18. **The best answer is D.** It is not correct to simply say "in regards." The proper phrase is "in regards to." The sentence would be equally as effective if the word "regarding" were used in place of the phrase "in regards."

19. **The best answer is B.** The sentence indicates that "Parliament" possesses something—the first law—so the possessive, apostrophe "s," must be used.

20. **The best answer is E.** This sentence does not contain any errors. It is correct to use the possessive "Paine's" because the sentence discusses *his* pamphlet. Likewise, the other underlined portions are correct and appropriate.

21. **The best answer is D.** To be idiomatic, the sentence should read "giving way," which is generally understood to mean "yielding to." It is correct to use the plural "costs" because the subject is plural—"heating and cooling." Likewise, the present tense forms of "rise" and "are" are appropriate within the context of the sentence.

22. **The best answer is B.** The participle form "distinguishing" is not appropriate to this sentence; the word should be "distinguished" to best fit with the helping verbs "can be." The other underlined portions are correct and appropriate.

23. **The best answer is D.** To maintain parallelism within the sentence, you must include the helping verb "had" before the verb phrase "never seen." The other underlined portions are correct and appropriate.

24. **The best answer is A.** In this sentence, it is necessary to use the subject form of the pronoun "she" rather than the object form of the pronoun "her." The other underlined portions are correct and appropriate.

25. **The best answer is D.** In this sentence, the word "even" is being used as an adverb to describe how the weight must be distributed. Therefore, you must add "-ly." The other underlined portions are correct and appropriate.

26. **The best answer is E.** This sentence does not contain any errors. It is appropriate to begin the sentence with the prepositional phrase, "In baseball." Likewise, because the sentence indicates that there is only one batter, it is appropriate to use the singular verb form "is" and the singular pronoun "his."

27. **The best answer is A.** In this sentence, the participle "laughing" is not correct. You must use the past tense verb "laughed" to match the past tense verb "watched" to describe the actions of the children. The other underlined portions are correct and appropriate.

28. **The best answer is E.** This sentence does not contain any errors. The plural nouns "reading materials" and "pamphlets" match the plural noun "newspapers." Because the sentence is written in the past tense, as evidenced by the verb "taxed," all of the verb forms match as well.

29. **The best answer is C.** To maintain parallelism within this sentence, the verb forms must match. Therefore, the verb form "in answering" should be changed to "to answer," which matches the earlier verb form "to buy or sell." The other underlined portions are correct and appropriate.

30. **The best answer is C.** The selection that most clearly and effectively conveys the idea is "have greatly increased in recent years." This choice appropriately modifies the verb "increased" with the adverb "greatly" and appropriately uses the adjective "recent" to modify the noun "years." The other answer choices are awkwardly constructed.

31. **The best answer is A.** The sentence is best as it is written. The current version of the sentence is clear and concise and free from grammatical errors. The other answer choices are awkwardly constructed.

32. **The best answer is C.** The best way to revise this sentence is to delete the word "the" before "portion size." The context of the passage suggests that people must be more aware of portion sizes in general, and not one specific "portion size," as "the" indicates.

33. **The best answer is A.** There is nothing wrong with the structure or placement of Sentence 7. Moving it would disrupt the flow of the paragraph. Adding to it or changing it in any way would decrease the clarity. Linking it with Sentence 8 would create a long, awkward, run-on sentence.

34. **The best answer is B.** As it is written, Sentence 8 is a run-on sentence. The best way to revise it would be to break it into two complete sentences. It is an important part of the paragraph, so deleting it would not be appropriate. Likewise, the remaining selections do not appropriately address the fact that it is a run-on sentence.

35. **The best answer is D.** As it is written, the sentence contains an ambiguous pronoun; the pronoun "it" does not clearly refer to a specific antecedent. You should restate the noun in order to maintain clarity within the sentence. While answer choice C includes the noun "obesity," it lacks a verb.

Section 6

1. **The best answer is A.** The phrase "even though" indicates that the words in the blanks will contradict each other. The context suggests that the two doctors behave differently toward each other in private than they do in public. "Malicious" means "deliberately harmful, or spiteful," whereas "amiable" means "friendly and agreeable." Answer choice B is incorrect because "absurd" does not contradict "enigmatic," which means "puzzling." Answer choices C and D are incorrect because the word pairs do not indicate contradiction. Likewise, although "spiteful" might have been a good choice for the first blank, "coherent," which means "logical or orderly," does not contradict "spiteful" and would not have worked in the second blank.

2. **The best answer is C.** The word "despite" indicates that two clauses of the sentence will contradict each other. "Lauding" means "praising and glorifying," and "abysmal" means "very bad." Answer choices B and E are incorrect because the word pairs do not indicate contradiction. Answer choice A is incorrect because advertisements would not "criticize" or "express disproval" of the product, and first quarter sales could not be "protracted" or "prolonged" because the first quarter is a specific time period. Answer choice D is incorrect because "abrogating" means "ending or abolishing," and advertisements would not end the new product.

3. **The best answer is C.** To "postulate" is "to suggest a theory or idea as a basic principle." Answer choice A is incorrect because to "alienate" is to "cause to become unfriendly or differentiated." "Deplore" means "to say or think that something is very bad." "Correlates" suggests a relationship which is not present in this statement. To "transpose" is to "put into a different order."

4. **The best answer is B.** To have a penchant for something means to have a fondness for it. A fondness for history would be practical or helpful for future studies in the field. Answer choices A and C are incorrect because anyone having "disdain" (hate) or "dislike" for history would certainly not study to become a history teacher. While "affinity" means "liking," "futile" means "having no useful result." An "appreciation" for history would not be "gratuitous" or "without cause or unnecessary" during studies.

5. **The best answer is E.** "Incorrigible" means "impossible to change or reform," which fits the context of the sentence about a politician who refused to change her ways. If the politician was "curable," she would change her crooked ways; thus, answer choice B is incorrect. Answer choices A, C, and D do not fit the context of the sentence.

6. **The best answer is A.** As a good orator, or public speaker, a leader could become well known for inspiring his or her countrymen. An aviator, or pilot, would not restrict, or limit, his countrymen. If the prime minister was a general, it is unreasonable that he would be known for his ability to "depict" or "illustrate" his countrymen. If the prime minister was a writer, it is illogical that he would become well known for "discounting" his countrymen or deciding that they were not worth attention. As a politician, it is not logical that he would be known for his ability to "loathe" or "hate" his countrymen.

7. **The best answer is D.** Because "contentious" means "controversial," it fits well in a sentence that refers to debate on an issue. Answer choices A and C both imply that the issue was fleeting and short, not a topic of debate for years. "Settled" implies that the topic was one that has been "established," not debated. "Inexplicable" means "unable to be explained" and does not make sense in the context of the sentence.

8. **The best answer is C.** "Vindicated" means "cleared of suspicion or doubt," and "authenticated" means "proved to be genuine." The rest of the answer choices are contradictory in nature and do not fit the context of the sentence.

9. **The best answer is E.** The context of the passage suggests that Qin Shihuang was powerful and controlling. The passage states that Qin Shihuang gained control as the emperor by "…ridding himself of his rival…" In addition, the passage states that his goal was to "…subjugate all of the Chinese states…," which means that he wanted to "conquer and enslave" the people of his empire. This best supports answer choice E, "ruthless," which means "without mercy or compassion."

10. **The best answer is C.** The word "subjugate" means to "conquer or enslave." This best fits the context of the passage; the remaining answer choices have a more positive connotation, which is not appropriate to the context of the passage.

11. **The best answer is B.** The passage states that Buffet "…focuses on stock trading at a discount, and always considers the company's intrinsic worth," which suggests that he is concerned about the value of a stock. This best supports answer choice B. Answer choices A and C might be correct statements, but they are not supported by information in the passage. Answer choice D directly contradicts information in the passage.

12. **The best answer is D.** A metaphor is a figure of speech in which one object is likened to another by speaking of it as if it were that other object. In this passage, stocks are referred to as dancers, and the actions of the stock market are likened to those of a dance.

13. **The best answer is C.** "Furtive" means "secretive." As stated in the passage, Pedro wanted to be let in on the matter "…his parents were so fervently discussing in secret." The author used this language most likely to emphasize the importance of keeping the contents of the discussion a secret. The other answer choices are not supported by the passage.

14. **The best answer is A.** Once the civil war began in Sudan, the boys spent years in makeshift camps and traveling on foot to their next destination, with no real direction and no solid place to call home. Before the war, they spent their time tending sheep. This fact highlights the sharp contrast between their lives before and after the civil war began. While this fact does provide background information about the boys and their childhoods, it is not the primary purpose of including this detail in the passage.

15. **The best answer is D.** The boys in both stories had doubts as to whether they would reach America. In Passage 1, Pedro was afraid he would not reach America because of detainment by the authorities and a somewhat crude mode of transportation. In Passage 2, Michael and Paul were not sure that they would be among the boys chosen to go to America. The other answer choices refer to one or the other of the passages but not to both.

16. **The best answer is E.** According to the passage, Pedro's parents discussed the matter "fervently" over the course of several days; thus, "hastily" and "impulsively" can both be eliminated. If his parents were discussing the matter "nonchalantly," they would be discussing it "casually," not in secret at night after the children were in bed. "Anxiously" best fits the context of the passage.

17. **The best answer is E.** The passage states that "It would be nearly impossible to get permission to leave the country, so they would depart covertly in 24 hours along with 15 other men on a small boat equipped only with oars. A motor would be a dead giveaway to those looking for escapees. Anyone attempting to flee the country would be dealt with harshly by the authorities." This suggests that Pedro and his fellow travelers would use a rowboat instead of a motorboat to remain discreet and avoid detection.

18. **The best answer is D.** All of the boys in the Ethiopian camps were in situations similar to Michael and Paul's. Once these Ethiopian camps were shut down, the boys were left to find their own way to Sudan and provide completely for themselves. This is best reflected in answer choice D.

19. **The best answer is C.** Both passages discuss refugees from different countries and provide information regarding the difficulty that some people face in attempting to escape poverty, war, and so on. The other answer choices are not supported by the passages.

20. **The best answer is B.** The passage describes the camps that the boys stayed in as "crude" and further describes the camps as having conditions that were "far from ideal." The phrase "lacking sophistication" most clearly describes the conditions of the camps in which the boys were forced to stay.

21. **The best answer is B.** The passage states that "Michael and Paul were two of the lucky ones; more than half of the 26,000 'lost boys' had succumbed to the harsh conditions they had been forced to endure during their long trek." This best supports answer choice B. Answer choice A is incorrect because the boys did not find refuge in Kenya until later in their journey. Likewise, the other answer choices are not supported by this particular statement in the passage.

22. **The best answer is C.** Passage 1 includes statements such as "They would never return to their homeland…" and "Anyone attempting to flee the country would be dealt with harshly by the authorities." This passage also indicates that, even if Pedro and his father made it to Florida, they would still be pursued by government authorities and would have to continue to be cautious. Passage 2, on the other hand, includes more positive statements, such as "Paul and Michael managed to make the best of their internment in the camps…," and "…several thousand boys would have the opportunity to go to America where they would be assisted by many generous people in pursuing their education and finding a job." The overall tone of Passage 2 is more hopeful than that of Passage 1.

23. **The best answer is A.** The passage states that "Though Paul and Michael were unsure of what the future would hold, they remained optimistic, knowing that if chosen, they would go together to this new land of great promise." This suggests that they were hopeful that America would provide them with more opportunities than they had previously had but were still uncertain about their future, which best supports answer choice A.

24. **The best answer is A.** The passage states that "Upon hearing the plan, Pedro swallowed his fear, looked his father in the eye and nodded." This best supports the idea that Pedro knew how to control his fear and self-doubt. Despite the hardships of the journey, Pedro appeared determined to be strong. The other answer choices are not supported by the passage.

Section 7

1. **The correct answer is C.** To answer this question, solve the first equation for x and solve the second equation for y, as follows:

   $x + z = 12$

   $x = 12 - z$

   $y - z = 3$

   $y = 3 + z$

   Now simply add these values:

   $12 - z + 3 + z = 15$

2. **The correct answer is B**. To solve this problem, apply the Distributive Property, as follows:

   $n(4a + by) = 54$ is equivalent to $4na + nb = 54$

   You are given that $na = 9$, so substitute 9 for na and solve for nb as follows:

   $4(9) + ab = 54$

   $36 + ab = 54$

   $ab = 18$

3. **The correct answer is C.** To solve this problem, first calculate the length of ST. You are given that $RS = 12$, and ST is 13 more than RS. Therefore, $ST = 12 + 13$, or 25. Now add the length of RS to the length of ST:

   $12(RS) + 25(ST) = 37$

4. **The correct answer is E.** The formula for the area of a circle is πr^2, so the area of the smaller circle is $\pi(2)^2$, or 4π, and the area of the larger circle is $\pi(4)^2$, or 16π. Thus, the ratio of the area of the larger circle to the area of the smaller circle is 16:4, or 4:1.

5. **The correct answer is E.** You are given that $LM = MN$, which means that angle N = angle L. Angle M (LMN) is given as 40°, so angles N and L must each be 70° (180° − 40° = 140°, and 140° ÷ 2 = 70°). Because angle LOQ is 30°, angle LQO must be be 80° (180° − 70° − 30° = 80°).

6. **The correct answer is A.** To solve this problem, set the values in the numerators equal to each other and the values in the denominators equal to each other as follows:

If $\frac{4x}{3y} = \frac{8}{6}$, then $4x = 8$ and $3y = 6$

Now you can solve for x and y:

$4x = 8$, so $x = 2$

$3y = 6$, so $y = 2$

Substitute 2 for x and 2 for y into $\frac{9x}{12y}$ to get $\frac{(9 \times 2)}{(12 \times 2)}$, or $\frac{18}{24}$. Reduce this fraction by dividing both the numerator and the denominator by 6 to get $\frac{3}{4}$.

7. **The correct answer is A.** This problem tests your knowledge of absolute values and inequalities. $|\,4 - 3x\,| < 5$ can be written as two separate inequalities: $4 - 3x < 5$ AND $4 - 3x > -5$. Because the original inequality was a "less than," the word in between the two new inequalities must be AND. Solve both inequalities as follows:

$4 - 3x < 5$

$-3x < 1$

$-x < \frac{1}{3}$

When you multiply both sides of an inequality by a negative number, you must reverse the inequality sign.

$x > \frac{1}{3}$

Now move onto the next inequality.

$4 - 3x > -5$

$3x > -9$

$x < 3$

Only 2, answer choice A, is less than 3 and greater than $-\frac{1}{3}$.

8. **The correct answer is D.** To solve this problem, first remember that "8^3 divided by 11" is another way of saying $\frac{(8 \times 8 \times 8)}{11}$, or $\frac{512}{11}$. You could use your calculator to get 46.5454 (repeating), but because you're looking for a remainder, long division is more accurate:

$$\sqrt{512}$$

$$\begin{array}{r} 46 \\ 11\overline{)512} \\ -44 \\ \hline 72 \\ -66 \\ \hline 6 \end{array}$$

Therefore, the remainder is 6 when 8^3 is divided by 11.

9. **The correct answer is E.** Because $abcd = 36$, none of these variables can equal 0. If one of them did equal 0, their product would also be 0. Thus, eliminate answer choices C and D. If a and b were both negative, a times b would still be positive, and therefore, you can eliminate answer choices A and B. Because $abde = 0$ and a, b, and d cannot equal 0, e must equal 0.

10. **The correct answer is B.** Given that the total number of points scored is 56, you can determine how many points were scored in each of the quarters. In the first quarter, one seventh of the points were scored, which means that $56 \div 7$, or 8 points were scored in the first quarter. In the second quarter, one fourth of the points were scored, which means that $56 \div 4$, or 14 points were scored in the second quarter. In the third quarter, 23 points were scored. In the fourth quarter, then, the team scored $56 - 8 - 14 - 23$, or 11 points.

11. **The correct answer is C.** Because 81 can be rewritten as 3^4, you can rewrite the equation as $3^{8x} = 3^{4(3x-2)}$. Now you can set the exponents equal to each other and solve for x, as follows:

    $8x = 12x - 8$

    $-4x = -8$

    $x = 2$

12. **The correct answer is D.** Because n is a positive fraction (less than 1 but greater than 0), you should be able to conclude two things: (1) $4n$ is greater than n, and (2) n^2 is less than n. Given this information, only answer choices C and D are possible solutions. Now you must determine if n is greater than or less than $\sqrt{n}$. Because n can be any positive fraction less than 1, choose $\frac{1}{4}$ for the value of n. You know that $\frac{1}{4}$ is $\frac{1}{2}$ because $\frac{1}{2}^2 = \frac{1}{4}$. You also know that $\frac{1}{2} > \frac{1}{4}$, so $\sqrt{n} > n$, and answer choice D is correct.

13. **The correct answer is E.** To solve this problem, you should recognize that the first step will be to cross-multiply the proportions. Work through each answer choice; the one that is NOT equivalent to the others will be the correct choice.

    Answer choice A: $\frac{a}{b} = \frac{c}{d}$; $ad = bc$

    Answer choice B: $\frac{a}{c} = \frac{b}{d}$; $ad = cb$. This proportion is equivalent to the proportion in answer choice A, so eliminate answer choices A and B.

    Answer choice C: $\frac{c}{a} = \frac{d}{b}$; $cb = ad$. This proportion is equivalent to the proportions in answer choices A and B, so eliminate answer choice C.

    Answer choice D: $\frac{bc}{ad} = \frac{1}{1}$; $bc = ad$. This proportion is equivalent to the proportions in answer choices A, B, and C, so eliminate answer choice D.

    Answer choice E: $\frac{b}{c} = \frac{a}{d}$; $bd = ca$. This proportion is NOT equivalent to any of the proportions in the other answer choices. Therefore, it is the correct answer.

14. **The correct answer is C.** Because line m is parallel to line l, the lines will have the same slope. First put the equation of line l in the standard form ($y = mx + b$):

$$2y = 3x + 7$$

$$y = \frac{3}{2x} + \frac{7}{2}$$

This means that the slope of both lines is $\frac{3}{2}$. Only answer choice C includes an equation of a line with a slope of $\frac{3}{2}$.

15. **The correct answer is A.** The easiest way to solve this problem is to start with 12 and add each preceding even integer until you get to a sum of 40, and then count the terms:

$12 + 10 + 8 + 6 + 4 = 22$. There are 5 terms.

16. **The correct answer is C.** Set K will have the members from Set F (f), plus the members from Set G (g), plus the members from Set H (h), minus the common members of Set F, Set G, and Set H ($3c$), plus the additional members (d). Thus, Set K includes $f + g + h - 3c + d$.

Section 8

1. **The best answer is E.** The word "laden" means "weighed down" or "burdened," which best fits the context of the sentence. The other answer choices contain words that are not appropriate.

2. **The best answer is D.** The context of the sentence indicates that the teacher's job was likely difficult. "Onerous" means "troublesome or burdensome," which best fits the context of the sentence. The other answer choices contain words that are not appropriate.

3. **The best answer is E.** The sentence begins with the word "although," which suggests a contrast between how people often characterize Justin and how Justin is characterized by his friends. In addition, the second word should have a meaning that corresponds to Justin's willingness to help at a moment's notice. Therefore, you can eliminate answer choices A, B, C, and D because they contain words that do not make sense if inserted into the second blank.

4. **The best answer is B.** The sentence indicates that the mayor hopes to encourage something in the downtown area, which, based on the context, would be something related to commerce. It is unlikely that the mayor would hope to encourage "decline," so eliminate answer choice C. It is also unlikely that the mayor would hope to "increase," "enhance," or "boost" the flow of commerce away from the city, so eliminate answer choices A, D, and E. This leaves you with answer choice B, which makes the most sense when you insert the words into the blanks.

5. **The best answer is D.** Handing out pamphlets is a way to spread a message. A synonym of spread is "promulgate," which specifically means "to announce publicly." If members of the organization wished to "verbalize" a message, the members would most likely talk to people, as opposed to handing out pamphlets.

6. **The best answer is A.** The context of the sentence indicates that Lewis and Clark needed the help of indigenous peoples; therefore, you can eliminate answer choice C because it would insert the word "refused" in the first blank. The word "indubitably" means "apparent or unquestionable," which best fits the context of the sentence.

7. **The best answer is B.** The focus of the passage is a review of the condition called *synesthesia*. A "commentary" is generally an explanation or illustration of something. The passage is not a personal account, so eliminate answer choice A. Likewise, it is neither an inspirational story nor an illustration of a recent scientific discovery—the passage does not indicate when *synesthesia* was discovered; eliminate answer choices D and E. The condition of *synesthesia* is not a firmly established ideal, so answer choice C is incorrect.

8. **The best answer is A.** The word "juxtaposition" refers to "the state of being placed side by side." The passage indicates that different synapses are somehow crossed, resulting in two unrelated senses somehow occurring together. The other answer choices are not supported by the passage.

9. **The best answer is D.** According to the passage, some researchers believe that synesthesia is caused by a "perception breakdown" that occurs as an infant develops. This breakdown results in an incomplete separation of the senses, most likely at a relatively early stage in the development process. Answer choice A is incorrect because it directly contradicts information in the passage. Answer choice B is incorrect because the passage indicates that synesthetes do not experience normal sensory development. Answer choices C and E are not supported by the passage.

10. **The best answer is B.** The second paragraph begins with the word "Another," which indicates that some additional or alternative information, in this case a theory regarding the cause of synesthesia, is being presented. This best supports answer choice B. Answer choice E is discussed in the first paragraph; the remaining answer choices are not supported by details in the second paragraph.

11. **The best answer is D.** The term "idiosyncratic" refers to something that is "peculiar to an individual or group." The author uses this term to illustrate the uniqueness of synesthetic perceptions—most synesthetes perceive things in a way that is unique unto themselves. The other answer choices are not supported by the passage.

12. **The best answer is C.** The sentence referenced in the question stem states, "Researchers estimate that there could be as many as 35 different broad pairings—sound/touch, taste/hearing, and so on—each characterized by many permutations and unique features." This is an assertion, or declaration, made by researchers regarding one aspect of *synesthesia*. The remaining answer choices do not accurately describe the sentence given in the question stem.

13. **The best answer is D.** According to the passage, Dr. Cytowic's research indicates that synesthetes endure "life-long inter-sensory associations," which serves to strengthen the idea that synesthetic perceptions are durable. The other answer choices are not supported by the passage.

14. **The best answer is B.** The passage states that, "Despite the potential diversity in the manifestation of *synesthesia*, the actual known number of people with the disorder is relatively small." This statement encourages the readers to view *synesthesia* as a disorder that might be difficult to diagnose. In addition, the passage also indicates that many people are not aware that they have *synesthesia*, so it is unlikely that these people will ever be properly diagnosed. The other answer choices are not supported by the passage.

15. **The best answer is B.** The passage states that "Although the perceptions vary among individuals, according to Dr. Richard Cytowic, a leading *synesthesia* expert, no matter what senses are joined in a given *synesthete*, the lifelong inter-sensory associations of the synesthetes remain stable. In other words, if the word "horse" is dark green, it is always perceived as such by the individual." Therefore, it is unlikely that the severity of synesthesia fluctuates throughout an individual's lifetime.

16. **The best answer is C.** The author most likely uses the phrase "standard neurological exams" to show that standard, or regular, testing shows no difference between the brain of a synesthete and the brain of a non-synesthete. The passage stresses the point that synesthetes are typically normal in every other way. The remaining answer choices are not supported by the passage.

17. **The best answer is A.** The word "anomaly" refers to something that is "out of the ordinary." In the passage, it indicates that altered sensory perceptions, such as those associated with *synesthesia*, are not normal. The other answer choices do not mean the same thing as "anomaly."

18. **The best answer is E.** The last paragraph states that "…researchers customarily must rely on an individual recognizing that he or she perceives things differently than the rest of the world and seeking some answers from medical or psychological professionals." Therefore, it is likely that a correct diagnosis would be made only if an adult contacted researchers to discuss perceptual differences he or she might have noticed between members of the family.

19. **The best answer is A.** The passage focuses primarily on describing synesthesia and provides details regarding what synesthesia is and how the disorder is manifested. However, the passage also clearly indicates that, despite being easily defined, synesthesia can be difficult to recognize because most synesthetes do not know that they are afflicted with the disorder. The remaining answer choices are not supported by the passage.

Section 9

1. **The best answer is A.** This sentence is best as it is written. It effectively expresses the idea and is free from ambiguity. Answer choices B, C, D, and E are awkward and unclear.

2. **The best answer is C.** In the sentence as it is written, the phrase "which is" is unnecessary; it creates awkward phrasing. It would also be correct to say "which is dependent upon," or "which depends upon," but those are not among the answer choices. Answer choice D includes an extraneous comma after "which," so it is incorrect.

3. **The best answer is B.** It is not necessary to include the conjunction "and" in the underlined portion because the conjunction appears correctly later in the sentence. The pilot did two things: he saw that the runway wasn't clear, and he immediately pulled the jet upward. Likewise, it is not necessary to include any other transitional language at that point in the sentence.

4. **The best answer is D.** To maintain parallelism within the list of types of music, you should simply conclude the list with "and chamber music." Answer choices B and E are incorrect because, in addition to being awkward, they include the word "musics," which is not correct. The plural of "music" is "music."

5. **The best answer is D.** The underlined portion of the sentence does not match in tense with the rest of the sentence. The sentence is written in the past tense, but the underlined portion uses the future tense "would be." The other answer choices also include incorrect verb tense.

6. **The best answer is C.** The sentence as it is written is awkward. It would be correct to either change the verb form to "creating," as in answer choice C, or to delete the word "this" from the underlined portion. Answer choices B and E are incorrect because they create comma splices.

7. **The best answer is B.** The sentence as it is written is awkward and contains an error in idiom. The compound word "breakdown" is more effective than the phrase "breaking down" in expressing the action taking place in the sentence. The other answer choices are awkward in their use of the prepositions "with" and "by" after "important."

8. **The best answer is A.** This sentence is best as it is written. It effectively expresses the idea and is free from ambiguity. Answer choices B, C, D, and E are awkward and unclear.

9. **The best answer is A.** This sentence is best as it is written. It effectively expresses the idea and is free from ambiguity. Answer choices B, C, D, and E are awkward and unclear.

10. **The best answer is B.** The simple past tense "heard" is necessary to form a correct tense chain with the verb phrase "was startled." Only answer choice B correctly uses the word "heard" while also using the active voice and avoiding awkward construction.

11. **The best answer is A.** This sentence is best as it is written. It effectively expresses the idea and is free from ambiguity. Answer choices B, C, D, and E are awkward and unclear.

12. **The best answer is B.** The context of the sentence indicates that first one thing happened and then another thing happened. To best express this chronology of events, the word "than" should be used. You should also have recognized the idiom that has this pattern: "No sooner had… than…" Answer choices D and E create redundancy when inserted into the sentence.

13. **The best answer is E.** The sentence describes an event that occurred in the past. The verb phrase "is turning to me" describes an event that is occurring at that moment. The correct verb phrase is "turned to me," which is consistent with the tense of the sentence and maintains parallelism.

14. **The best answer is C.** The verb in the underlined portion should indicate an action that has already taken place. Therefore, you should use the simple past tense verb "fell." It is not correct to use the helping verb "has" with the past tense verb "fell," so answer choice E is incorrect.

CHAPTER FOUR

Strategies for Success

Now that you've assessed your strengths and weaknesses, it's time to take a look at some general test-taking strategies that should help you approach the PSAT and SAT with confidence. We'll start by discussing the importance of acquiring the skills necessary to maximize your test scores and finish with some tips on how to handle stress before, during, and after the tests. Additional chapters in the book include strategies and techniques specific to each of the PSAT and SAT sections.

EXAM/PREP Study TIP

Practice sufficiently to avoid "concentration errors" and to recognize the gaps in your knowledge.

Sometimes when you look back over a practice test that you took, you can tell right away why you got a particular question wrong. We have heard many students call these errors "stupid mistakes." We suggest that you refer to these errors as "concentration errors." Everyone makes them from time to time, and you should not get overly upset or concerned when they occur. There is a good chance that your focus will be much better on the real test as long as you train yourself properly using this book. You should note the difference between those concentration errors and any questions that you get wrong because of a lack of understanding or holes in your knowledge base. If you have the time, it is probably worth reading the explanations for any of the questions that were at all difficult for you. Sometimes students get questions correct but for the wrong reasons, or because they simply guessed correctly. While you are practicing, you should mark any questions that you want to recheck and be sure to read the explanations for those questions.

KSA (Knowledge, Skills, Abilities)

Cognitive psychologists, the ones who study learning and thinking, use the letters KSA to refer to the basic components of human performance in all human activities, from academics to athletics, playing music to playing games. The letters stand for Knowledge, Skills, and Abilities. As mentioned previously, both the PSAT and the SAT measure a specific set of skills that can be improved through study and practice. You probably already understand this because you are reading this book. In fact, many thousands of students over the years have successfully raised their PSAT and SAT scores through study and practice.

Learning Factual Information Versus Acquiring Skills

The human brain stores and retrieves factual knowledge a little differently from the way it acquires and executes skills. Knowledge can generally be learned quickly and is fairly durable, even when you are under stress. You learn factual information by studying, and you acquire skills through practice. There is some overlap between these actions; you will learn while you practice, and vice versa. In fact, research shows that repetition is important for both information storage and skills acquisition.

You must use repetition to acquire and improve skills: knowing *about* a skill, or understanding how the skill should be executed, is not the same as actually *having* that skill. For example, you might be told *about* a skill such as driving a car with a standard transmission, playing the piano, or typing on a computer keyboard. You might have a great teacher, have wonderful learning tools, and pay attention very carefully. You might *understand* everything perfectly. But the first few times you actually attempt the skill, you will probably make some mistakes. In fact, you will probably experience some frustration because of the gap between your understanding of the skill and your actual ability to perform the skill.

Perfecting skills takes practice. When skills are repeated so many times that they can't be further improved, psychologists use the term "perfectly internalized skills," which means that the skills are executed automatically, without any conscious thought. You need repetition to create the pathways in your brain that control your skills. Therefore, you shouldn't be satisfied with simply reading this book and then saying to yourself, "I get it." You will not reach your full SAT scoring potential unless you put in sufficient time practicing as well as understanding and learning.

Practicing to Internalize Skills

We hope that you will internalize the skills you need for top performance on the PSAT and SAT so that you don't have to spend time and energy figuring out what to do during the introduction to the exam. We are hoping you will be well into each section while some of your less-prepared classmates are still reading the directions and trying to figure out exactly what they are supposed to be doing. We suggest that you practice sufficiently so you develop your test-taking skills and, specifically, good PSAT/SAT-taking skills. While you practice, you should distinguish between practice that is meant to serve as a learning experience and practice that is meant to be a realistic simulation of what will happen on your actual test.

EXAM✔**PREP**
Study**TIP**

It is important to note that you should not attempt any timed practice tests when you are mentally or physically exhausted. This will add unwanted stress to an already stressful situation. You must be realistic about how you spend your time and energy during the preparation process.

During practice that is meant for learning, it is okay to "cheat." You should feel free to disregard the time limits and just think about how the questions are put together; you can stop to look at the explanations in the back of the book. It is even okay to talk to others about what you are learning during your "learning practice." However, you also need to do some simulated testing practice, where you time yourself carefully and try to control as many variables in your environment as you can. Some research shows that you will have an easier time executing your skills and remembering information when the environment you are testing in is similar to the environment where you studied and practiced.

There is a psychological term, *cognitive endurance*, which refers to your ability to perform difficult mental tasks over an extended period of time. Just as with your physical endurance, you can build up your cognitive endurance through training. As you prepare yourself for the PSAT or SAT, you should start off with shorter practice sessions and work up to the point where you can easily do a 25-minute section with no noticeable fatigue. Then work up to two sections, then three such sections without a break. That is the longest you will have to work on test day without a break.

Now let's explore the skills and strategies important to ensuring your success on the SAT.

Do the Easy Stuff First

You will have to get familiar with the format of each section of the PSAT and SAT so that you can recognize passages and questions that are likely to give you trouble. We suggest that you "bypass pockets of resistance" and go around those trouble spots rather than through them. It is a much better use of your time and energy to pick up all of the correct answers that you can early on, and then go back and work on the tougher questions that you actually have a legitimate shot at answering correctly. Learn to recognize the question types that are likely to give you trouble and be sure not to get goaded into a fight with them.

The writers of the PSAT and the SAT have built traps into the exams. There will be some time-consuming questions early in each section that are meant to lure you into wasting time that would be better spent answering some more reasonable questions.

All of the questions on a PSAT and an SAT test are weighted exactly equally to one another. Some of the questions are harder than others. Don't get sucked into a battle with a hard question while still other, probably less difficult questions are waiting for you later in the section. Most likely you will encounter some questions that you are probably going to get wrong on test day. So when you see those questions, don't be surprised. Just recognize them and work on the easier material first. If time permits, you can always come back and work on the challenging problems in the final minutes before the proctor calls, "Time!"

We give specific suggestions in each chapter regarding which question types you should probably skip. You'll also develop "likes and dislikes" while practicing, meaning you will know that certain question types are always going to be tough for you. By test day you will have done enough timed practice that you will also develop a "feel" for how long you should be spending on each question. Be flexible. Even if a question is of a type that you can usually answer easily, do not spend more time than you should on it. You always have time to come back if you leave a question too soon. However, once you waste a second of time, you cannot get it back.

Stay "On Point"

It is important to note that most incorrect PSAT/SAT answers are incorrect because they are irrelevant. This applies to all of the different question types on all of the various sections. If you get very good at spotting answer choices that are outside the scope of the stimulus passage, for example, you'll go a long way toward improving your score.

EXAM✓PREP
StudyTIP

Because what is easy for some is not necessarily easy for others, be sure to do enough practice to quickly recognize the question types that will be easy for you. Answer those questions first; then go back and work on the more difficult questions if time allows.

This can be more difficult than it sounds because some of the irrelevant choices will use terms and ideas from the stimulus. A good way to check relevance is to ask yourself "so what?" when evaluating the answer choices.

When your training is finished, you will be able to do this type of analysis on most of the questions and answer choices that you encounter on your test. You will be able to quickly and efficiently eliminate all of the answer choices that are irrelevant, or not "on point."

Manage the Answer Grid

EXAM/PREP
StudyTIP

Circle your answers in the test booklet before you transfer them to the answer sheet. This will help you to keep track of your intended answer as you check your work.

You should be certain to avoid the common mistake of marking the answer to each question on your answer document as you finish the question. In other words, you should NOT go to your answer sheet after each question. This is dangerous and wastes time. It is dangerous because you run an increased risk of marking your answer grid incorrectly and perhaps not catching your error on time. It wastes time because you have to find your place on the answer sheet and then find your place back in the test booklet. The amount of time that is "wasted" is not large as you mark each question. But it adds up over the course of an entire test section and could cost you the amount of time you need to answer a few more questions correctly.

Instead, you should first mark your answers in the test booklet and transfer your answers from the test booklet to the answer sheet in groups. Doing this after each passage on the Reading Comprehension section is an obvious idea and has the added benefit of helping you to clear your head between passages so that it is easier to concentrate on the passage at hand. On any of the sections, filling in circles on your answer sheet can be a good activity to keep you busy when you simply need a break to clear your head.

There is a dangerous, and dishonest, strategy that we have heard of from past students. Apparently, some so-called PSAT/SAT prep experts are telling students to just put a little pencil dot in the circles on the answer sheet and then come back to fill them in later. Specifically, some students are taught to do this on the sections where they have trouble finishing on time. Then they are told to come back to the section later and fill in the circles while they are supposed to be working on another section. The idea is dangerous because the directions for the test clearly state that a test taker is not to work on any other section than the one being timed by the proctor. This rule means that you may NOT go back to fill in the circles that you marked with a dot.

> **NOTE**
>
> Some students worry if they notice strings of the same answer on their answer sheets. This does not necessarily indicate a problem. While analyzing actual, released SAT exams, we counted strings of up to four questions long all marked with the same answer choice on the answer sheet, and all were correct. You should not be too concerned even if you find a string of four answer choices that are all the same.

Use the Test Booklet

The PSAT and SAT test booklets are meant to be used by one test-taker only. You will not have any scratch paper on test day. You are expected to do all note-taking and figuring on the booklet itself. Generally, no one ever bothers to look at the test booklet because you cannot receive credit for anything that is written there. Your score comes only from the answers that you mark on the answer sheet. Therefore, you should feel comfortable in marking up the passages or drawing diagrams to help you to stay focused on relevant information.

Guess Wisely

Remember that you face a guessing penalty on both the PSAT and the SAT. This means that you should never make a random guess; if you do not know the answer and have no hope of figuring it out, you should leave the circle on your answer document for that question blank. Later chapters will provide more information on how to employ the process of elimination to increase your chances of answering a question correctly. A good rule of thumb is that if you can eliminate at least one answer as being clearly incorrect, then you should guess from among the remaining answer choices. You are now making an educated guess, as opposed to a random guess.

It's a good idea to add a symbol or two to the common repertoire to help distinguish between the answer choices that you eliminate and those that could be correct. For example, when you eliminate an answer choice, make a mark through the letter so that you no longer consider it a viable choice, as shown below:

(A)
(B)
(C)
(D)
(E)

The suggestion just mentioned is fairly common. If you think that an answer choice *may* be correct, but want to consider the remaining choices before you make your final decision, underline the answer choice, or place a check next to it:

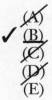

(A)
(B)
(C)
(D)
(E)

After you've decided on your final answer, circle it for later transfer to the answer sheet:

If you have eliminated one or more of the answer choices and still don't feel comfortable guessing among those that remain, place a large **X** next to the question, leave the circle empty on your answer sheet, and come back to the question later if you have time. Try to budget your time so that you have at least a minute or two left at the end of each section to locate the questions you've marked with an **X**; because you will be making an educated guess, select one of the answer choices you did not already eliminate and fill in the corresponding circle on your answer sheet.

You also need to find out whether you are an answer-changer or not. Meaning, if you change an answer, are you more likely to change it *to* the correct answer or *from* the correct answer? You can learn this about yourself only by doing practice exams and paying attention to your tendencies.

CAUTION

Remember that you cannot skip back and forth between sections on either the PSAT or the SAT. In other words, if you are supposed to be working on Section 4, you cannot look back at any previous sections, nor can you look ahead to the upcoming sections.

Manage Stress

In college, stress arises from sources such as family expectations, fear of failure, heavy workload, competition, and difficult subjects. The PSAT and the SAT are designed to create similar stresses. The psychometricians (specialized psychologists who study the measurement of the mind) who contribute to the design of standardized tests, use artificial stressors to test how you will respond to the stress of college. In other words, they are actually trying to create a certain level of stress in you.

The main stressor is the time limit. The time limits are set on the SAT so that most students cannot finish all of the questions in the time allowed. Use the specific strategies mentioned in Chapter 5, "PSAT/SAT Verbal Section," and Chapter 6, "PSAT/SAT Quantitative Section," to help you select as many correct answers as possible in the time allowed. Also be sure to read Chapter 7, "Quantitative Review," and Chapter 8, "Verbal Review," for a complete review of the concepts and subject matter tested on the PSAT and SAT.

Another stressor is the element of surprise that is present for most test takers. Remember, if you practice enough, there should be no surprises on test day.

Relax to Succeed

Probably the worst thing that can happen to a test-taker is to panic. Research shows very predictable results when a person panics. When you panic, you can usually identify a specific set of easily recognizable symptoms: sweating, shortness of breath, muscle tension, increased pulse rate, tunnel vision, nausea, lightheadedness, and, in rare cases, even loss of consciousness. These symptoms are the results of chemical changes in the brain brought on by some stimulus. The stimulus does not have to be external. Therefore, we can panic ourselves just by thinking about certain things.

The stress chemical in your body called *epinephrine*, more commonly known as *adrenalin*, brings on these symptoms. Adrenalin changes the priorities in your brain activity. It moves blood and electrical energy away from some parts of the brain and to others. Specifically, it increases brain activity in the areas that control your body and decreases blood flow to the parts of your brain that are involved in complex thinking. Therefore, panic makes a person stronger and faster—and also less able to perform the type of thinking that is important on the SAT. It is not a bad thing to have a small amount of adrenalin in your bloodstream because of a healthy amount of excitement about your exam. But you should be careful not to panic before or during your test.

You can control your adrenalin levels by minimizing the unknown factors in the testing process. The biggest stress-inducing questions are:

► "What do the test-writers expect?"

► "Am I ready?"

► "How will I do on test day?"

If you spend your time and energy studying and practicing under realistic conditions before test day, you have a much better chance of controlling your adrenalin levels and handling the exam with no panic.

The goals of your preparation should be to learn about the test, acquire the skills that are being measured by the test, and learn about yourself and how you respond to the different parts of the test. You should also consider which question types you will try on test day and which ones you will give an educated guess. You need to be familiar with the material that is tested on each section of your test. As you work through this book, make an assessment of the best use of your time and energy. Concentrate on the areas that will give you the highest score in the amount of time that you have until you take the PSAT or SAT. This will give you a feeling of confidence on test day even when you are facing very challenging questions.

Specific Relaxation Techniques

The following sections present various ways to help you be as relaxed and confident as possible on test day:

Be Prepared

The more prepared you feel, the less likely it is that you'll be stressed on test day. Study and practice consistently during the time between now and your test day. Be organized. Have your supplies and lucky testing clothes ready in advance. Make a practice trip to the test center before your test day.

Know Yourself

Get to know your strengths and weaknesses on the PSAT and SAT and the things that help you to relax. Some test-takers like to have a slightly anxious feeling to help them focus. Others folks do best when they are so relaxed that they are almost asleep. You will learn about yourself through practice.

Rest

The better rested you are, the better things seem. As you get fatigued, you are more likely to look on the dark side of things and worry more, which hurts your test scores.

Eat Right

Sugar is bad for stress and brain function in general. Consuming refined sugar creates biological stress that has an impact on your brain chemistry. Keep it to a minimum for several days before your test. If you are actually addicted to caffeine, (you can tell that you are if you get headaches when you skip a day), get your normal amount. Don't forget to eat regularly while you're preparing for the PSAT or SAT. It's not a good idea to skip meals simply because you are experiencing some additional stress. It is also important to eat something before you take the test. An empty stomach might be distracting and uncomfortable on test day.

Breathe

If you feel yourself tensing up, slow down and take deeper breaths. This will relax you and get more oxygen to your brain so that you can think more clearly.

Take Breaks

You cannot stay sharply focused on your test for the whole time in the testing center. You are certainly going to have distracting thoughts or times when you just can't process all the information. When this happens, close your eyes, clear your mind, and then start back on your test. This process should take only a minute or so. You could pray, meditate, or just visualize a place or person that helps you relax. Try thinking of something fun that you have planned to do after your test.

Have a Plan of Attack

Know how you are going to work through each part of the exam. You have no time to create a plan of attack on test day. Practice enough that you internalize the skills you need to do your best on each section, and you won't have to stop to think about what to do next.

Be Aware of Time

You should time yourself on test day. You should time yourself on some of your practice exams. Remember, all that matters during the test is your test. All of life's other issues will have to be dealt with after your test is finished. You might find this attitude easier to attain if you lose track of what time it is in the "outside world."

A Note on Music

Some types of music increase measured brain stress and interfere with clear thinking. Specifically, some rock, hip-hop, and dance rhythms, while great for certain occasions, can have detrimental effects on certain types of brain waves that have been measured in labs. Other music seems to help to organize brain waves and create a relaxed state that is conducive to learning and skills acquisition.

The Impact of Mozart

A great debate rages among scientists and educators about a study that was done some years ago that seemed to show that listening to Mozart made students temporarily more intelligent. While not everyone agrees that it helps, no one has ever seriously argued that it hurts. So, get yourself a Mozart CD and listen to it before practice and before your real test. It might help. In the worst-case scenario, you will have listened to some good music and maybe broadened your horizons a bit. You cannot listen to music *during* your actual test, so do not listen to it during your practice tests.

What to Expect on Test Day

If you work through the material in this book and do some additional practice on released PSAT and SAT items, you should be more than adequately prepared for the test. Use the following tips to help the entire testing process go smoothly:

Do a Dry Run

Make sure that you know how long it will take to get to the testing center, where you will park, alternative routes, and so on. If you are testing in a place that is new to you, try to get into the building between now and test day so that you can absorb the sounds and smells, find out where the bathrooms and snack machines are, and so on.

Wake Up Early

You generally have to be at the testing center by 8:00 a.m. Set two alarms if you have to. Leave yourself plenty of time to get fully awake before you have to run out the door.

EXAM/**PREP**
Study**TIP**

We suggest that you use an analog (dial-faced) watch. You can turn the hands on your watch back from noon to allow enough time for the section that you are working on.

For example, you should set your watch to 11:35 for each 25 minute section—that way you know exactly how much time you have remaining for that section.

Dress for Success

Wear loose, comfortable clothes in layers so that you can adjust to the temperature. Remember your watch. There might not be a clock in your testing room.

Fuel Up

Eat something without too much sugar in it on the morning of your test. Get your normal dose of caffeine, if any. (Test day is not the time to "try coffee" for the first time!)

Bring Supplies

Bring your driver's license (or passport), your admission ticket, several sharpened number 2 pencils, erasers, a timepiece, and your approved calculator. If you need them, bring your glasses or contact lenses. You won't be able to eat or drink while the test is in progress, but you can bring a snack for the break time.

Warm Up Your Brain

Read a newspaper or something similar or review some practice material so that the PSAT or SAT isn't the first thing you read on test day. If you review any test material, make sure that it is something that you have worked through before and focus on the part of the test that you tend to be best at. This is certainly the time to accentuate the positive.

Plan a Mini-Vacation

Most students find it easier to concentrate on their test preparation and on their PSAT or SAT if they have a plan for some fun right after the test. Plan something that you can look forward to as a reward for all the hard work and energy that you're putting into preparing for and taking the test.

What's Next?

Chapters 5 and 6 in this book focus on the specific sections of the PSAT and SAT: Critical Reading, Writing Skills, and Quantitative Skills. Read these chapters carefully, note the particular strategies and techniques, and answer the practice questions included at the end of each chapter. Chapters 7 and 8 include in-depth reviews of the quantitative (math) and verbal concepts that are tested on the PSAT and SAT. The full-length simulated Practice SAT Tests can be found directly following these chapters in Part IV. Plan to take a full-length test approximately one week prior to your actual PSAT or SAT. Read the explanations for the questions that you missed, and review Chapters 4 through 8 as necessary. Remember, practice as much as you can under realistic testing conditions to maximize your PSAT and SAT scores.

CHAPTER FIVE

SAT/PSAT Verbal

The SAT/PSAT Verbal Sections include questions that test your Critical Reading and Writing skills. You will be required to answer multiple-choice questions and write an essay based on a specific prompt. The Verbal Sections contain the following question types: Sentence Completion and Passage-Based Reading (Critical Reading skills); Identifying Sentence Errors; Improving Sentences and Paragraphs; and Essay Writing (Writing skills).

Critical Reading Sections

The Critical Reading Sections are designed to measure the skills required to carefully read and understand sentences and passages written in standard written English. The complexity and content of these sections are comparable to the subject matter you will encounter during your freshman year of college.

The sections include Sentence Completion questions and Passage-Based Reading questions. A total of 48 multiple-choice questions will test your Critical Reading skills on the PSAT, while the SAT includes a total of 67 such questions. In this chapter, we'll give you useful strategies and techniques, an overview of the question types, and a breakdown of the critical reading skills that will be tested. At the end of the chapter, you will find some sample practice questions and explanations.

Sentence Completion

A strong vocabulary is the cornerstone of critical reading. The best way to develop a large and varied vocabulary is by reading. In addition to reading more, you might want to review the vocabulary list included as Appendix A, "SAT/PSAT Vocabulary List," at the end of this book.

The PSAT and SAT include both vocabulary in context and logic-based Sentence Completion questions that are designed to test your grasp of the English language. There will be a total of 13 Sentence Completion questions on the PSAT and 19 on the SAT, each consisting of a sentence with either one or two blanks and five answer choices from which to select the appropriate word or words to put into those blanks. You should select the best possible answer.

You will probably not recognize every word that appears in the PSAT or SAT Sentence Completion sections. If you don't know the meaning of a particular word, don't panic. You can use context clues to eliminate answer choices that clearly do not fit the meaning of the sentence. You should also consider related words, prefixes, and suffixes during the process of elimination. If you can narrow the answer choices down to three or four possible candidates (in other words, eliminate at least one answer choice), it is in your best interest to make an educated guess.

Anatomy of an SAT and PSAT Sentence Completion Question

Before we get to the strategies, we want you to understand what a Sentence Completion question looks like. Consider the following:

Sentence { 1. Despite Jordan's ------- efforts, the team still suffered a ------- loss.

Answer Choices {
    (A) complicated . . modest

    (B) daring . . beneficial

    (C) generous . . constructive

    (D) heroic . . devastating

    (E) selfish . . desperate

These are easily recognizable questions that generally appear first in the Critical Reading sections. You will be presented with several Sentence Completion questions at the beginning of the section, followed by the Passage-Based Reading questions. The strategies covered next will help you to effectively tackle the Sentence Completion questions on your PSAT or SAT.

General Strategies for SAT and PSAT Sentence Completion Questions

EXAM/PREP
Study**TIP**

As you read the sentence, try to fill in the blank(s) with a word (or words) that makes sense based on the context of the sentence. The context refers to the intended meaning of the sentence, so pay attention to what the sentence is about.

PSAT and SAT Sentence Completion questions usually test the standard meaning of a word. Pay attention to the logic of the sentence. Try to predict a word to insert in the blank or blanks as you read the sentence and then look for your word or a *synonym* of your word among the answer choices. A *synonym* is a word that has the same meaning as another word. You should also look for *antonyms*, which are words that have the opposite meaning of your predicted word. If you locate any words among the answer choices that have a meaning opposite to the word that you would like to insert in the blank, eliminate those answer choices.

It often helps to use Latin roots, prefixes, and suffixes to figure out what hard words mean. Look for *cognates* from French, Spanish, or Italian (the modern version of Latin) if you recognize them. A *cognate* is a word that means the same or nearly the same thing in more than one language. For example, the word *amigo*, which means friend in Spanish, the word *ami*, which means friend in French, and the word *amicable*, which means friendly in English, all come from the Latin root word for friend, *amicus*. These words are considered cognates.

Let the context of the sentences guide you. Make sure that you understand what's going on in the sentence and pay attention to introductory and transitional words and phrases in each sentence that might suggest a continuation, contrast, or comparison. Figure 5.1 shows a table of commonly used introductory and transitional words and phrases.

WORDS OR PHRASES THAT SUGGEST CONTINUATION	WORDS OR PHRASES THAT SUGGEST CONCLUSION
Furthermore Moreover In addition	Therefore Thus In other words

WORDS OR PHRASES THAT SUGGEST COMPARISON	WORDS OR PHRASES THAT SUGGEST CONTRAST	WORDS OR PHRASES THAT SUGGEST EVIDENCE
Likewise Similarly Just as Like	But Whereas Although Despite However	Because Since As a result of Due to

FIGURE 5.1 Commonly used introductory and transitional words and phrases.

If the question requires you to fill in two blanks, focus on one blank at a time. You can start with either the first or the second blank. Remember that if one word in the answer choice doesn't fit within the context of the sentence, you can eliminate the entire answer choice. Work on both blanks together only if you have not been able to eliminate all of the incorrect answers. When you think that you have the correct answer, read the entire sentence silently to yourself, using your choice(s) in the blank(s). If the sentence makes sense, mark your answer.

EXAM PREP Study TIP

Remember that the difficulty level generally increases as you move through the Sentence Completion questions. Move quickly through the less difficult questions and skip those that give you trouble the first time through. Mark them on your test booklet and come back to them later if you have time.

Practice Sentence Completion Questions

Directions: Each sentence that follows has either one or two blanks. Each blank indicates that a word has been omitted from the sentence. Beneath each sentence are five words or sets of words. Select the word or set of words that, when inserted into the sentence in place of the blank(s), best fits the context of the sentence as a whole.

1. As we traveled to college for the first time, the family car was ------- with books, clothing, appliances, and other necessities.

   (A) keen

   (B) indigent

   (C) barren

   (D) pallid

   (E) laden

The best answer is E. The word "laden" means "weighed down with a heavy load," which best fits the description in this sentence of the family car. The other words do not fit the context of the sentence.

2. Although the scientist's recommendations may have been -------, the students had trouble following his ------- presentation and were, therefore, against his proposal.

   (A) plausible . . organized

   (B) absurd . . intricate

   (C) realistic . . convoluted

   (D) judicious . . dynamic

   (E) ubiquitous . . empirical

The best answer is C. The word "although" suggests a conflict between the words that best fit in the blanks. Because the students were against the scientist's proposal, it makes sense that the word in the second blank would have a somewhat negative connotation. Answer choice C best fits the context of the sentence; even though the students thought the recommendations were realistic, the presentation was so hard to follow that the students did not support the scientist's proposal. None of the other answer choices fit the context of the sentence.

3. Running a marathon is an ------- task, taking months of both physical and mental preparation and training before actually running a grueling 26.2 miles.

   (A) arduous

   (B) ambiguous

   (C) involuntary

   (D) eloquent

   (E) overt

The best answer is A. The context of the sentence indicates that running a marathon is quite challenging and takes a lot of preparation. "Arduous" means "difficult or demanding great effort," which best fits the context of the sentence.

4. The fear inspired by the media's coverage of unprovoked shark attacks is ------- ; there are actually more fatalities each year from lightning strikes than from shark attacks.

   (A) pompous

   (B) amplified

   (C) candid

   (D) subdued

   (E) veritable

The best answer is B. The part of the sentence that follows the semicolon provides information about the best word to insert in the blank. Because more fatalities result from lightning strikes than from shark attacks, any fear inspired by the media's coverage regarding shark attacks is probably exaggerated. "Amplified" means to "increase or exaggerate," so it is the best fit for the blank. The other answer choices do not fit the context of the sentence.

5. The American Civil War began after the Confederate States of America seceded from the Union, in essence dividing the United States into two ------- countries.

   (A) concordant

   (B) allied

   (C) distinct

   (D) banded

   (E) united

The best answer is C. After the Civil War, the United States was divided into two, "distinct" or "separate" entities. All of the other answer choices suggest that the United States was somehow joined or brought together, which does not fit the context of the sentence.

Passage-Based Reading

There are a total of 35 Passage-Based Reading questions on the PSAT and 48 on the SAT designed to test how well you understand information presented in the passages. Each passage ranges from about 100 words up to about 800 words in length and discusses subjects in the areas of humanities, social studies, natural sciences, and literary fiction. You might be tested on one longer passage or be asked to consider two shorter, related passages. In either case, the passage or passages will be followed by a series of questions, each with five answer choices. You should select the best possible answer for each question.

The Passage-Based Reading sections are not meant to test your knowledge about a particular subject. You should answer all the questions based only on the information presented in the passage or passages, not on any prior knowledge that you might have of the subject. You might be asked to draw a conclusion (inference), but you should only do so based on what the writer's words actually say or imply.

Anatomy of an SAT and PSAT Passage-Based Reading (Reading Comprehension) Question

Before we get to the strategies, we want you to understand what a Passage-Based Reading question looks like. Consider the following:

Passage

Scientists know very little about the eating habits of our ancestors who lived over two and a half million years ago. To solve this problem, scientists have started examining chimpanzees' hunting behavior and diet to find clues about our own prehistoric past. It is not difficult to determine why studying chimpanzees might be beneficial. Modern humans and chimpanzees are actually very closely related.

Experts believe that chimpanzees share about 98.5% of our DNA sequence. If this is true, humans are more closely related to chimpanzees than to any other animal species.

Question Stem

1. The main purpose of the passage is to

Answer Choices

(A) explore biological and physiological similarities between humans and chimpanzees

(B) examine the hunting behavior and diet of chimpanzees and compare it to human activity

(C) discuss the health benefits of eating and hunting meat while simultaneously predicting the effect of this behavior on chimpanzee offspring

(D) bring attention to the pioneering research of Dr. Jane Goodall in Tanzania

(E) educate the public on the impact that tool use had on early human societies

General Strategies for SAT and PSAT Passage-Based Reading (Reading Comprehension) Questions

EXAM✓PREP
StudyTIP

Because this is a timed exam, you *cannot* read the passages slowly and carefully. Practice the strategies in this section to increase your reading speed and improve your comprehension.

Probably the biggest mistake that you could make is to read these passages as though you are studying for a high school exam. The open-book aspect of Passage-Based Reading means that you should read in a way that helps your brain to work through the information efficiently. You should not read slowly and carefully as though you will have to remember the information for a long period of time. You should read loosely and only dwell on information that you are sure is important because you need it to answer a question.

This type of reading should be very goal-oriented. If the information you are looking at does not help to answer a question that the test writers find important, you should not linger over it. The best scores on this section are usually earned by students who have two key skills: paraphrasing and skimming. These skills are discussed in more detail later. Following are some specific strategies to apply to the Passage-Based Reading questions of the PSAT and SAT:

▶ Read the Question Stems First

▶ Determine the Main Idea

- ▶ Skim the Passage

- ▶ Paraphrase the Questions

- ▶ Predict an Answer

- ▶ Use the Process of Elimination

- ▶ Apply Logic

- ▶ Read and Answer the Questions

Read the Question Stems First

The single most powerful strategy for tackling this section is to read the question stems first. The question stems are the prompts, or *stimuli*, that appear before the five answer choices. Don't read the answer choices before you read the passage. Most of the answer choices are wrong and, in fact, are referred to by testing professionals as "distractors." If you read them before you read the passage, you will be much more likely to get confused. The questions themselves, though, might contain useful information. You might find that the questions refer to specific names or terms repeatedly. You will find other questions that contain references to the line numbers that are printed down the left side of the passage. These can be very useful in focusing your attention and energy on the parts of the passage that are likely to lead to correct answers to questions.

NOTE

When you read a question that contains a line reference, locate those lines in the passage and make a note in the margin so that you know where to begin to find the answer to the question.

Determine the Main Idea

As you begin to read the passage, your first step should be to determine the main idea. This technique can help you to answer the "big picture" questions and assist you in locating information necessary to answer the other question types (discussed later in this chapter). The main idea has the following three components:

- ▶ Topic (What is the passage about?)

- ▶ Scope (What aspect of the topic does the passage focus on?)

- ▶ Purpose (Why did the author write the passage?)

If you can answer these three questions, you understand the main idea. Consider the following scenarios:

1. *The world's tropical rain forests are being decimated at an alarming rate. Each day, thousands of acres of trees are destroyed in both developing and industrial countries. Nearly half of the world's species of plants and animals will be eliminated or severely threatened over the next 25 years because of this rapid deforestation. Clearly, it is imperative that something be done to curtail this rampant destruction of the rainforests.*

2. *Tropical rain forests are crucial to the health and welfare of the planet. Experts indicate that over 20% of the world's oxygen is produced by the Amazon rain forests alone. In addition, more than half of the world's estimated 10 million species of plants, animals, and insects live in the tropical rain forests. These plants and animals of the rain forest provide us with food, fuel, wood, shelter, jobs, and medicines. Indigenous humans also inhabit the tropical rain forests.*

EXAM/PREP StudyTIP

Too often, test takers confuse topic with the main idea. The topic of the passage only answers the question, "What is the passage about?" If that is all you notice, you are missing some very important information.

Practice reading for the Topic, Scope, and Purpose to get the full picture.

The *topic* of both passages is tropical rain forests. However, the *scope* of each passage is very different. The first passage discusses destruction of the tropical rain forests, whereas the second passage introduces the diversity of the rain forests and indicates why the rain forests are important. The *purpose* of the first passage is a call to action, while the second passage is primarily informative.

The introductory paragraph of the reading passage often indicates the topic or topics being discussed, the author's point of view, and exactly what the author is trying to prove. Read a little more slowly at the beginning of the passage until you get a grip on the three components of the main idea, and then you can shift into higher gear and skim the rest of the passage.

Skim the Passage

Don't use context clues the first time that you skim through a passage. When you come to a word or phrase that is unfamiliar, just read past it. You usually have time to come back if you need to. But often you won't need to bother figuring out exactly what that one word or phrase means in order to answer the bulk of the questions that follow the passage. If you waste some of your precious time, you'll never get it back. With perseverance and practice, you will start to get comfortable with a less than perfect understanding of the passage.

EXAM/PREP StudyTIP

You should not rely on any prior knowledge you might have about a particular topic. The questions are about information that is stated or implied in the passage, not information that you might recall about the topic being discussed.

The goal with skimming is to get a general understanding of the structure of the passage. This is key so that you can find pertinent facts when you refer to the passage as you answer questions.

You should also pay close attention to paragraph breaks. While reading through paragraphs follow these tips to help you gather information more effectively:

▸ Try to determine the subtopic for each paragraph quickly.

▸ Focus on the general content of each paragraph.

▸ Determine the purpose of each paragraph.

NOTE

The first sentence is not always the topic sentence. Don't believe those people who say that you can read the first and last sentence of each paragraph and skip the rest of the sentences completely. You are better off skimming over all of the words even if you end up forgetting most of what you read almost immediately.

Remember that you can write in your test booklet. So, when you see a topic word, circle it. If you can sum up a paragraph in a word or two, jot it down in the margin. Remember that the idea at this stage is not to waste time. Keep moving through the material.

In addition, you should read actively throughout the passages. That is, think about things such as the tone and the purpose of the passage. This technique will help you to stay focused on the material and, ultimately, will allow you to select the best answer to the questions.

Paraphrase the Questions

Once you have found the information in the passage that will provide the answer you are looking for, try to answer the question in your mind. Put the question in your own words so that it makes more sense to you. Do this before you look at the answer choices. Remember that four out of every five answer choices are incorrect. Not only are they incorrect, but also they were written by experts to confuse you. They are less likely to confuse you if you have a clear idea of an answer before you read the answer choices. It often helps to consciously simplify as you read. Try using the phrase, "So what they are really saying is…." This technique works for question stems and answer choices, as well as for the passages.

Predict an Answer

Try to predict an answer for the question, and then skim the choices presented and look for your answer. You might have to be a little flexible to recognize it. Your answer might be there dressed up in different words. If you can recognize a paraphrase of your predicted answer, choose it. Mark the question in your test booklet if you are unsure. Use a mark that will be easy to spot when you are looking back through the test. For example, circle or put a star next to the question number. Whatever symbol you decide to use, be consistent so that the mark always means the same thing every time you use it. Remember that you can always come back to the question later if you have time.

EXAM/PREP
StudyTIP

The most complicated answer choice is not always correct. The correct or best choice is the one that responds to the question based on information and ideas that appear in the passage.

Use the Process of Elimination

Elimination is the process that most test takers use for all the questions that they answer. It is reliable but slow. It is useful to you as a backup strategy for the questions for which either you cannot predict an answer or your prediction is not listed as a choice.

The process of elimination is a good tool. It just shouldn't be the only tool in your box. It can be hard to break the habit of always applying the process of elimination. You have developed this habit because you have been given too much time on most exams that you have taken. Teachers tend to allow long periods of time for exams for a couple of different reasons. The first is that teachers have to allow enough time for even the slower students to have a fair chance to answer questions. The second is that testing time for students is often break time for the instructor. He or she might be able to catch up on paper work during the time that students are testing. These factors tend to lead to students who get used to a leisurely pace on exams.

Apply Logic

It is important that you know the difference between information that is stated directly in the passage and *assumptions* and *inferences*. You might be asked questions based on factual information found in the reading passages. The reading passages might also include information about which you will be asked to make an inference.

An *inference* is a conclusion based on what is stated in the passage. You can infer something about a person, place, or thing by reasoning through the descriptive language contained in the reading passage. In other words, the author's language *implies* that something is probably true.

An *assumption*, on the other hand, is unstated evidence. It is the missing link in an author's argument. Following is a classic example of a conclusion based on stated evidence and unstated evidence (assumption):

Socrates is a man.

Therefore, Socrates is mortal.

Because you are given that Socrates is a man, the conclusion that Socrates is mortal *must* be based on the assumption that men are mortal.

Socrates is a man. (Stated evidence)

Men are mortal. (Unstated evidence)

Therefore, Socrates is mortal. (Conclusion)

Some of the evidence is not stated, but the final conclusion leads you to the existence of that missing evidence, or assumption.

Read and Answer the Questions

Follow these tips as you read and answer the Reading Comprehension questions:

▶ Start at the beginning of each group of questions. Read the first question and make sure that you understand it. Go back to the part of the passage that will probably contain the answer to your question. Some of the questions on the PSAT and SAT ask you to draw conclusions based on the information that you read. However, even these questions should be answered based on the information in the passage. There will always be some strong hints, or evidence, that will lead you to an answer.

▶ Some of the questions contain references to specific lines of the passage. The trick in those cases is to read a little before and a little after the specific line that is mentioned. At least read the entire sentence that contains the line that is referenced.

On the other hand, some of the questions don't really tell you where to look for the answer, or they are about the passage as a whole. In those cases, think about what you learned about the passage while you were skimming it. Note the subtopics for the paragraphs, and let them guide you to the part of the passage that contains the information for which you are looking.

► One of the important skills rewarded by the PSAT and the SAT is the ability to sift through text and find the word or concept for which you are looking. This skill improves with practice.

► Remember that the most complicated-sounding choice is not always correct. Too many SAT takers have cost themselves points over the years by applying the following flawed logic: "If I can't understand it, it must be correct because this is a hard test!" The correct choice is the one that responds to the question based on information and ideas that appear in the passage.

► Don't be afraid to refer back to the passage repeatedly, and don't be reluctant to skip around within the question group that accompanies each of the passages. In fact, many students report success with a strategy of actually skipping back and forth between passages. This plan won't work for everyone. It probably would just create confusion for most test takers. But if you feel comfortable with it after trying it on practice tests, we can't think of any reason not to do it on test day.

► Finally, be careful always to consider all of the choices before you select your answer, even if your predicted answer is among the choices. The difference between the best answer and the second best answer is sometimes very subtle.

NOTE

It is possible for an answer choice to be both true *and* wrong. The answer that you choose must respond correctly to the question being asked. Simply being true is not enough to make an answer correct. The best answer will always be supported by details, inference, or tone.

Passage-Based Reading Question Types

Following is a list of the types of questions you are likely to encounter on the PSAT and SAT Passage-Based Reading (Reading Comprehension) sections. We have also included specific approaches to each question type. You will begin to recognize the different question types as you work through the sample questions and practice exams.

Main Idea/Point of View

These questions might ask about the main idea of the passage as a whole or about a specific paragraph. They also ask about the author's point of view, or perspective, and the intended audience.

Strategy: Answer these questions according to your understanding of the three components of the main idea mentioned previously (topic, scope, and purpose). It is also worth noting that the incorrect choices are usually either too broad or too narrow. You should eliminate both the answer choices that focus on a specific part of the passage and the answer choices that are too general and could describe other passages besides the one on which you are working.

Specific Detail

These questions can be as basic as asking you about some fact that is easily found by referring to a part of the passage. Often, they are a bit more difficult because they ask you to interpret the information that is referred to.

Strategy: Refer to the passage to find the answer to these questions. Use line or paragraph references in the questions if they are given. Sometimes the answer choices are paraphrased, so don't just choose the answers that contain words that appeared in the passage. Make sure that the choice you select is responsive to the question being asked.

Conclusion/Inference

These questions require the test taker to put together information in the passage and use it as evidence for a conclusion. You will have to find language in the passage that will cause you to arrive at the inference that the question demands. (To *infer* is to draw a conclusion based on information in the passage.)

Strategy: Although you have to do a bit of thinking for these questions, you should be able to find very strong evidence for your answers. If you find yourself creating a long chain of reasoning and including information from outside the passage when "selling" the answer to yourself, stop and reconsider. The PSAT and the SAT reward short, strong connections between the evidence in the passage and the answer that is credited.

Extrapolation

These questions ask you to go beyond the passage itself and find answers that are probably true based on what you know from the passage. They can be based on the author's tone or on detailed information in the passage.

Strategy: You need to be sensitive to any clues about the author's tone or attitude and any clues about how the characters in the passage feel. Eliminate any choices that are outside the scope of the passage. As with the inference questions mentioned previously, both the PSAT and the SAT reward short, strong connections between the passage and the correct answers.

Vocabulary in Context

These questions ask what a specific word or phrase means from the passage. The context of the passage should lead you to an educated guess even if you don't know the specific word being asked about.

Strategy: The best way to answer these questions is the simplest way; just read the answer choices back into the sentence mentioned in the question stem and choose the one that changes the meaning of the sentence the least.

Practice Passage-Based Reading Questions

Directions: The passage below is followed by several questions based on the content of the passage. Answer the questions based on what is either stated or implied in each passage.

The human body's defense mechanisms are truly remarkable. When injured, the human body immediately begins to repair itself; when attacked by germs, it increases production of white blood cells to defend itself and fight back against the germs. And, throughout life, the brain and heart never take a break. With an ever-expanding understanding of how
(5) the body keeps itself healthy, modern medicine attempts to work with this predictable machine, supplementing the natural defenses where possible. Unfortunately, the machine occasionally malfunctions, and the very cells designed to protect the body instead attack its allies. For example, leukocytes (white blood cells) occasionally increase for no apparent reason, fighting not against germs, but healthy blood cells; this is commonly referred to as
(10) *leukemia*. Although certainly not a desired disease, doctors have made tremendous progress in successfully curing leukemia. Such is not the case for Huntington's Disease (HD).

HD is a devastating, degenerative brain disorder for which there is no effective treatment or cure. The disease results from genetically programmed degeneration of brain cells, called *neurons*, in certain areas of the brain. This degeneration causes uncontrolled move-
(15) ments, loss of intellectual faculties, and emotional disturbance. Early symptoms of HD may affect cognitive ability or mobility and include depression, mood swings, forgetfulness, irritability, involuntary twitching, and lack of coordination. As the disease progresses, concentration and short-term memory diminish, and involuntary movements of the head, trunk, and limbs increase. Walking, speaking, and swallowing abilities deteriorate. Eventually, HD
(20) sufferers become unable to care for themselves and are totally dependent upon others. Death follows from complications such as choking, infection, or heart failure.

HD is a familial disease, passed from parent to child through a mutation in a normal gene. Each child of an HD parent has a 50-50 chance of inheriting the HD gene. If a child does not inherit the HD gene, he or she will not develop the disease and cannot
(25) pass it to subsequent generations. A person who inherits the HD gene will sooner or later develop the disease. Whether one child inherits the gene has no bearing on whether others will or will not inherit the gene. The rate of disease progression and the age of onset vary from person to person. A genetic test, coupled with a complete medical history and neurological and laboratory tests, help physicians diagnose HD. Pre-symptomatic
(30) testing is available for individuals who are at risk for carrying the HD gene. The test cannot predict when symptoms will begin, and, in the absence of a cure, some individuals "at risk" elect not to take the test.

Named for Dr. George Huntington, who first described this hereditary disorder in 1872, HD is now recognized as one of the more common genetic disorders. More than a
(35) quarter of a million Americans have HD or are "at risk" of inheriting the disease from an affected parent. Because there is no known way to stop or reverse the course of HD, researchers are continuing to study the HD gene with an eye toward understanding how it causes disease in the human body. In the meantime, physicians prescribe a number of medications to help control emotional and movement problems associated with HD.

1. As it is used the in the first paragraph, the word "machine" most nearly means

   (A) the aggregate of human bodily functions

   (B) a selection of medical devices

   (C) the team of doctors assigned to research HD

   (D) the primary complication that arises from HD

   (E) a cell's natural defense against disease

The best answer is A. The passage indicates that the routine, predictable functions of the human body can be likened to a machine. The other choices are not supported by the context of the passage.

2. According to the passage, the symptoms of HD begin when

   (A) white blood cells multiply too quickly

   (B) leukocytes attack other cells

   (C) brain cells are rejuvenated

   (D) neurons break down and eventually die

   (E) the body begins to repair itself

The best answer is D. According to the passage, HD is the result of the degeneration of neurons (a type of brain cell). White blood cells (leukocytes) are mentioned in the opening paragraph in relation to leukemia, not HD. The other answer choices are not supported by the passage.

3. According to the passage, all of the following are examples of symptoms of Huntington's Disease EXCEPT

   (A) difficulty swallowing

   (B) forgetfulness

   (C) frequent rashes

   (D) involuntary twitching

   (E) heart failure

The best answer is C. The passage does not mention "frequent rashes" among the symptoms of HD. However, each of the remaining answer choices is stated explicitly in the passage.

4. Which statement best summarizes the main idea of the passage?

    (A) Huntington's Disease is a life-altering disorder that is relatively easy to diagnose but for which there is no cure.

    (B) Huntington's Disease afflicts only those people whose family members also suffer from the disorder.

    (C) Huntington's Disease can be diagnosed with a genetic test.

    (D) The human body has not yet developed effective defenses against all diseases.

    (E) Symptoms of Huntington's Disease are very debilitating.

The best answer is A. The passage describes HD and provides details regarding the debilitating symptoms. According to the passage, no cure for the disease exists. This information best supports answer choice A. Answer choices C and E, while supported by the passage, do not fully encompass the focus of the passage in its entirety.

5. It can be inferred from the passage that some individuals who might be at risk for Huntington's Disease choose not to be tested for the disease because

    (A) the test itself is risky

    (B) they prefer not to know in advance whether they have a crippling disease for which there is no cure

    (C) they are not aware that such a test exists

    (D) the symptoms of Huntington's Disease will likely occur much earlier in people who are tested for the disease

    (E) they do not want their family members to contract Huntington's Disease

The best answer is B. The passage states that "Pre-symptomatic testing is available for individuals who are at risk for carrying the HD gene. The test cannot predict when symptoms will begin, and, in the absence of a cure, some individuals 'at risk' elect not to take the test." This best supports answer choice B.

Writing Skills Section

The Writing Skills Section is designed to measure your ability to understand and interpret standard written English. The section will require you to identify sentence errors, improve sentences, and improve paragraphs. A total of 39 multiple-choice questions on the PSAT and 49 on the SAT will test your basic English and grammar skills. These questions will also assess your ability to make choices about the effectiveness and clarity of a word, phrase, sentence, or paragraph.

In this chapter, we'll give you useful strategies and techniques for effectively answering these questions, in addition to a breakdown of the writing skills that will be tested. Refer to Chapter 8, "Verbal Review," for an overview of some basic rules of grammar. At the end of this chapter, you will find some sample practice questions and explanations.

Improving Sentences

This section tests your ability to write clear, effective sentences, which is an important skill to develop as you write at the high school and college levels. Typically, each Writing Skills section will begin with several Improving Sentences questions, followed by the Identifying Sentence Errors and Improving Paragraphs questions.

Anatomy of an SAT and PSAT Improving Sentences Question

Before we get to the strategies, we want you to understand what an Improving Sentences question looks like. Consider the following:

Sentence

1. My comments are first, that the decision is unfair, and second, <u>the timing of it is unfortunate</u>.

Answer Choices

   (A) the timing of it is unfortunate

   (B) that the timing is unfortunate of it

   (C) the unfortunate timing

   (D) that its timing is unfortunate

   (E) unfortunately for the timing

Your job is to decide whether the underlined portion of the sentence clearly and effectively expresses the intended idea or if it can be improved in some way.

General Strategies for SAT and PSAT Improving Sentences Questions

Follow these strategies to select the best answers on the Improving Sentences section:

▶ The portion of the sentence that is underlined might need to be revised. When reading the sentence, pay attention to the underlined portion. If the underlined portion makes the sentence awkward, or contains errors in standard written English, it will need to be revised.

▶ If the underlined portion seems correct within the sentence as it is, mark (A) on your answer sheet. The test is designed to assess your ability to improve sentences, which also includes recognizing when a sentence is best as it is written.

▶ If the underlined portion does not seem correct, try to predict the correct answer. If an answer choice matches your predicted answer, it is most likely correct.

▶ If your predicted answer does not match any of the answer choices, determine which of the selections is the most clear and simple. Read the sentence again, replacing the underlined portion with the answer choices in order from (B)–(E). Remember that answer choice (A) will always be a repeat of the original underlined portion.

▶ Sub-vocalize (read "aloud silently" to yourself) to allow your brain to "hear" the sentence with each of the answer choices inserted. Your brain might automatically make the necessary improvement or recognize the best version of the sentence.

Practice Improving Sentences Questions

Directions: The following questions test the correct and effective use of standard written English in expressing an idea. Part of each sentence (or the entire sentence) is underlined. Beneath each sentence are five different ways of phrasing the under-lined portion. Answer choice A repeats the original phrasing. If you think that the original phrasing is best, select answer choice A. Otherwise, select from the remaining four choices. Your selection should result in the most effective, clear sentence, free from awkwardness or ambiguity.

1. According to a study by the National Foundation for Youth Athletics, parents are enrolling about five million children in soccer programs each year, a number almost <u>equivalent to the enrollment of</u> the nation's basketball programs.

   (A) equivalent to the enrollment of

   (B) as many as the enrollment of

   (C) as many as are enrolled in

   (D) equivalent to the number of children enrolled in

   (E) almost equal to those children who are enrolled in

The best answer is D. For this sentence to be correct, the two elements being compared in the sentence must be parallel. Therefore, the underlined portion should be "equivalent to the number of children enrolled in" to parallel the "number" of children being enrolled in soccer programs each year.

2. In a recent poll, only 24% of the public favor a leader who is <u>as liberal or is even more liberal than</u> the current leader.

   (A) as liberal or is even more liberal than

   (B) as liberal a leader as is

   (C) at least as liberal as being

   (D) a leader as liberal or more liberal than is

   (E) a leader that is more liberal, or at least as liberal as,

The best answer is B. Although the sentence as it is written is not necessarily incorrect, it is awkward and wordy. By replacing the underlined portion with answer choice B, you create a succinct sentence that clearly conveys the intended idea. The remaining answer choices are awkward and wordy; answer choice E also refers to a person, the leader, with the pronoun "that" instead of the correct pronoun "who."

3. Amanda took voice lessons last year, <u>and she has been singing in the choir ever since</u>.

   (A) and she has been singing in the choir ever since

   (B) and since then on she has been singing in the choir

   (C) when ever since she sings in the choir

   (D) she has been singing in the choir since then

   (E) and she sings in the choir since then

The best answer is A. The sentence is best as written. It clearly and effectively conveys the intended meaning and is grammatically correct. The remaining answer choices are awkward and wordy.

4. <u>From 1999 to 2002 sales of new cars decreased as more pre-owned cars entered the market.</u>

   (A) From 1999 to 2002 sales of new cars decreased as more pre-owned cars entered the market.

   (B) As more pre-owned cars entered the market, from 1999 to 2002 sales of new cars decreased.

   (C) Occurring between 1999 and 2002, sales of new cars decreased and more pre-owned cars entered the market.

   (D) More pre-owned cars entered the market between 1999 and 2002, the sales of new cars decreased.

   (E) Decreased as more pre-owned cars entered the market the sales of new cars from 1999 to 2002.

The best answer is A. The sentence is best as written. It clearly and effectively conveys the intended meaning and is grammatically correct. The remaining answer choices are awkwardly constructed.

5. Unlike <u>Beethoven's timeless music that endured</u> through the decades, the "Ballad Babes" were a one-hit wonder whose music was soon forgotten.

   (A) Beethoven's timeless music that endured

   (B) Beethoven and his timeless music, enduring

   (C) the timeless music of Beethoven that has endured

   (D) Beethoven, whose timeless music endured

   (E) Beethoven and his timeless music which endured

The best answer is D. The sentence as it is written incorrectly compares Beethoven's music, which is a thing, to the "Ballad Babes," who are people. Only answer choice D correctly compares Beethoven with the "Ballad Babes."

Identifying Sentence Errors

As you write more in high school and college, the ability to recognize mistakes in sentences will become very important. Good writers can express ideas clearly by correctly applying the rules of grammar and selecting the most appropriate words and phrases.

Anatomy of an SAT and PSAT Identifying Sentence Errors Question

Before we get to the strategies, we want you to understand what an Identifying Sentence Errors question looks like. Consider the following:

1. The <u>popularity of</u> her new album, <u>which</u> earned the pop star a gold
        A   B

   record, <u>are proof</u> that with the right sound and image, an unknown
            C

   artist <u>can become</u> a worldwide success overnight. <u>No error</u>
            D   E

Sentence

It is your job to determine which, if any, of the underlined portions are incorrect, and mark the corresponding letter on your answer sheet.

General Strategies for SAT and PSAT Identifying Sentence Errors Questions

When you encounter a possible error, mentally "rewrite" the sentence and correct the underlined portion that contains the error. If you can't find an error, the correct answer may be (E), which is No Error. This answer choice is correct nearly as often as any of the other answer choices.

The Identifying Sentence Errors questions of the PSAT and SAT are tricky, in that you must select the answer choice that contains a mistake. Following are some simple strategies to apply as you work through this type of question:

▶ Read each sentence carefully. Many errors are obvious, and if you can spot them right away, you will be able to move quickly through this section.

▶ Read aloud as you practice and learn to "sub-vocalize," or read to yourself. Remember that if your brain can "hear" an error, it is more likely to recognize it.

▶ Learn to look for common mistakes and correct them automatically as you read the sentence. Chapter 8 includes a list of words that are commonly misused. Review the list so that you can avoid making these mistakes and recognize them when you see them.

▶ Look over answer choices (A)–(D) as you read the sentence to see if something in the sentence needs to be changed. Remember to trust what you know about basic grammar. If you struggle with one of the underlined portions as you read the sentence, that portion is most likely the one that contains the error.

▶ If the sentence seems correct as it is, mark (E) on your answer sheet. The test is designed to assess your ability to recognize mistakes, which also includes recognizing when there is *not* a mistake.

▶ Look for common problems, such as redundancy, misplaced modifiers, faulty parallelism, ambiguous pronouns, and disagreement between the subject and the verb. Be sure that the answer choice you select does not contain any of these errors, which are further discussed in Chapter 8, "Verbal Review."

Practice Identifying Sentence Errors Questions

Directions: The following questions test your ability to recognize grammar and usage errors in standard written English. Each sentence contains either a single error or no error at all. Refer to the underlined, lettered portions of each sentence. If the sentence contains no error, select answer choice E. If the sentence contains an error, select the one underlined and lettered portion (A, B, C, or D) that is incorrect.

1. After watching the presenter <u>stutter uncomfortably</u> and frantically <u>search for</u> his
                                              A   B

<u>place in his</u> notes, Staci realized the <u>important of</u> being well prepared. <u>No error</u>
     C   D   E

The best answer is D. In this sentence, "important" should be replaced with "importance" because to be grammatically correct, the sentence requires a noun, not an adjective. "Stutter" agrees with the singular noun "presenter," and the adverb "uncomfortably" effectively modifies the past tense verb "stuttered." "For" is an appropriate preposition to use after "search." "Place in his" properly refers to the singular noun, "presenter," and successfully expresses a reference of location in the sentence.

2. As summer approached, the students <u>grew</u> <u>increasingly</u> unruly, forcing Miss
                                          A   B

Kern <u>to be more</u> <u>stricter</u> with her punishments. <u>No error</u>.
         C   D   E

The best answer is D. The comparative "more" must be followed by the verb "strict." It would also be correct to simply say "stricter." The past progressive verb "grew" correctly refers to an event that occurred in the past along with another event. "Increasingly" correctly modifies "grew." "To be" correctly refers to the verb tense of the sentence and the singular proper noun "Miss Kern."

3. Every year at my company's strategic planning meeting, no matter how <u>patient</u> I
                                                                                    A

    <u>wait as others</u> share <u>their views</u>, someone <u>always interrupts</u> me as soon as I open
       B   C   D

    my mouth. <u>No error</u>.
              E

The best answer is A. The adjective "patient" should modify the verb "wait" and express the manner in which the "wait" is performed; therefore, "patient" would be best expressed as "patiently." The phrase "wait as others" correctly refers to the pronoun "I," and the phrase "their views" correctly refers to the plural "others" at the meeting. "Always" is an appropriate adverb to express the frequency of an event, and "interrupts" agrees with the singular noun "someone."

4. The tough job market <u>has forced</u> numerous college graduates <u>to make a decision</u>
                  A   B

    between <u>attempts to enter</u> the workforce <u>and</u> attending graduate school. <u>No error</u>.
                  C   D   E

The best answer is C. To maintain parallel construction, the phrase "attempts to enter" should be replaced with "attempting to enter" to correctly parallel the phrase "attending graduate school." The verb phrase "has forced" correctly refers to the singular noun "market" and parallels the verb tense of the sentence. "To make a decision" is an appropriate phrase. The conjunction "and" is used appropriately with "between."

5. <u>Most experts</u> in the medical field <u>find it difficult</u> to determine <u>which factor</u>
   A   B   C

    contributes more to obesity: lifestyle choices <u>or</u> heredity. <u>No error</u>.
                                   D   E

The best answer is E. This sentence contains no errors. The superlative "most" effectively modifies the noun "experts." The verb "find" is in the correct verb tense, and the adverb "difficult" appropriately modifies the verb phrase "to determine." The pronoun "which" is used correctly to identify one of only two choices. The conjunction "or" is effectively used between "lifestyle choices" and "heredity."

Improving Paragraphs

The Improving Paragraphs section of the PSAT and SAT requires you to use all of your skills in writing and revising, as you will be asked to read a rough draft of a student essay and make improvements to the writing style and writing strategies. It will be necessary to recognize and eliminate redundant material, understand the tone of the essay, and make sure that the ideas are expressed clearly and succinctly. This section is also designed to test issues related to the organization of ideas within an essay, the most logical order of sentences and paragraphs, and the relevance of statements made within the context of the essay.

Anatomy of an SAT and PSAT Improving Paragraphs Question

Before we get to the strategies, we want you to understand what an Improving Paragraphs question looks like. Consider the following:

Paragraph

(1) Our society creates leaders and followers and many people give directions while some people are constantly following orders. **(2)** Once you become a follower you lose your sense of identity and take upon the personality that people want you to take on. **(3)** Voice is one of the most important representations of who you are and what you stand for. **(4)** Ben strips his partner Gus of his identity, controlling the actions and thought of Gus. **(5)** In Harold Pinter's *The Dumb Waiter*, Gus is a representation of the dumb waiter, he is constantly being manipulated by others to carry out directions and has no real voice of his own.

Question

1. Which of the following revisions would create a more concise version of Sentence 1 (reproduced below) while best retaining the sentence's original meaning?

   Our society creates leaders and followers, and many people give directions while some people are constantly following orders.

Answer Choices

(A) Delete the word "people" after "some."

(B) Change "some people are constantly following orders" to "some people follow orders."

(C) Change "many people give directions" to "many people are giving directions."

(D) Change "while some people are constantly following orders" to "while some people constantly follow."

(E) Change the word "leaders" to "masters."

General Strategies for SAT and PSAT Improving Paragraphs Questions

Effective practice for this section of the SAT and PSAT will include writing rough drafts of essays and revising the structure and placement of sentences within the essays until the essays are in their final form. Apply the rules of standard written English to your writing. Be certain that your essays are logical and organized so that the purpose and message are clear to the reader.

Following are some simple strategies to apply as you work through the Improving Paragraphs questions:

▶ Quickly read over the entire essay, focusing on its general meaning. You will need to have a feel for the essay's organization and style to correctly answer many of the questions.

▶ The purpose of this section is for you to revise the given essay. Because the essay is a rough draft, expect to notice several errors as you are reading. The questions will not address every error, so don't linger on these mistakes as you read the essay.

▶ Make sure that all of your answer choices fit within the overall context of the essay. If a statement is not relevant to the main idea of the essay or a particular paragraph, it should not be added.

▶ It is your job to select the best choice; other options might be satisfactory, but one will always be better than the others. Focus on the style, organization, and tone of the essay when making your selections. Eliminate the answer choices that will definitely not work and select the best from those that remain.

▶ Typically, the best way to improve your writing is to simplify it. An awkwardly constructed or wordy sentence will not clearly express an idea. It's a good idea to select the answer choice that is the most simple.

Practice Improving Paragraphs Questions

Directions: The following passage is a rough draft of a student essay. Some parts of the passage need to be rewritten in order to improve the essay.

Read the passage and select the best answer for each question that follows. Some questions ask you to improve the structure or word choice of specific sentences or parts of sentences, while others ask you to consider the organization and development of the essay. Follow the requirements of standard written English.

(1)Many forms of music find their roots in the United States, thanks in largely part to the nation's rich ethnic diversity. (2)It is ragtime that is one form of American music. (3)Characterized both by its distinctive African-American syncopation and conservative European classical structure, ragtime in its heyday from 1900 to 1918 was music enjoyed by everyone.

(4)Ragtime grew from the marches and jigs popular in northern black communities of the late nineteenth century. (5)Historians consider 1897 the beginning of mature ragtime. (6)A "rag" can have varied instrumentation; but usually it was written for piano. (7)Ragtime songs have a vocal part, but much of the music made the piano center stage. (8)Predating recorded music, ragtime was distributed almost exclusively as sheet music, which was in turn performed by amateur pianists in homes and cafés around the country. (9)For this reason, many establish ragtime to be a form of classical music. (10)Public performances by ragtime composers were in short supply, though hotly demanded. (11)One alternative to seeing a great performance was to hear the piece on a player piano, since the composers' play normally provided the template for the piano rolls that customers had to feed into the instrument. (12)The first celebrated ragtime hit was Scott Joplin's *Maple Leaf Rag*, published in 1899. (13)America was enthralled by this sophisticated composition.

1. In context, which of the following revisions is necessary in Sentence 1 (reproduced below)?

   Many forms of music find their roots in the United States, thanks in largely part to the nation's rich ethnic diversity.

   (A) Delete "ethnic."

   (B) Change "largely" to "large."

   (C) Change "find their roots" to "finding their roots."

   (D) Delete "in the United States."

   (E) Insert "and kinds" after "forms."

The best answer is B. The word "largely" is an adverb and should be used to modify a verb. As it's used in the sentence, it is incorrectly modifying the noun "part." Therefore, the adverb "largely" should be changed to the adjective "large." Deleting the phrases "ethnic" and "in the United States" would alter the meaning of the sentence, so answer choices A and D are incorrect. Changing the verb "find" to the participle "finding" would create a run-on sentence, so answer choice C is incorrect. Inserting the phrase "and kinds" would create redundancy, so answer choice E is incorrect.

2. In context, what is the best version of Sentence 4 (reproduced below)?

   Ragtime grew from the marches and jigs popular in northern black communities of the late nineteenth century.

   (A) (As it is now)

   (B) Ragtime, having grown popularly from the marches and jigs in northern black communities, late in the nineteenth century.

   (C) The type of music called ragtime grew from the popularity of nineteenth century marches and jigs in northern black communities.

   (D) Growing popular from the marches and jigs of the northern black communities, ragtime grew from the late nineteenth century.

   (E) Ragtime, popular in the late nineteenth century, grew from the marches and jigs that were in the northern black communities.

The best answer is A. The sentence as it is written clearly and simply conveys the intended meaning. It is appropriate to the context of the paragraph and does not require any alteration. The other answer choices are awkwardly constructed and do not best fit the context of the paragraph.

3. What is the best way to deal with Sentence 9 (reproduced below)?

   For this reason, many establish ragtime to be a form of classical music.

   (A) Leave it as it is.

   (B) Delete it.

   (C) Change "establish" to "consider."

   (D) Change "this reason" to "that."

   (E) Change "to be a form" to "in that it is a form."

The best answer is C. The word "establish" appears out of place in the sentence because "establish" is generally used to mean "set up or bring about," which is not appropriate to the context. It makes more sense that people would "consider" or "form an opinion" that ragtime is a type of classical music, based on information presented in the paragraph. The sentence adds relevant information to the paragraph, so it should not be deleted. The remaining answer choices create additional problems with the sentence and, therefore, are not appropriate.

4. What should be done with Sentence 12 (reproduced below)?

   The first celebrated ragtime hit was Scott Joplin's Maple Leaf Rag, *published in 1899.*

   (A) Leave it as it is.

   (B) Delete it.

   (C) Insert "Therefore," at the beginning.

   (D) Move it to the beginning of a new paragraph.

   (E) Add "that rocketed him to fame" at the end.

The best answer is D. Sentence 12 introduces a new topic—namely, Scott Joplin's contribution to the growing popularity of ragtime music. It is most appropriate to begin a new paragraph with this sentence.

5. Which of the following is best to add after Sentence 13 as a concluding sentence?

   (A) Scott Joplin also wrote many other songs, but none were as popular as *Maple Leaf Rag*.

   (B) As a result of Joplin's influence, ragtime was on its way to becoming a favorite among twentieth century music-lovers.

   (C) Americans also began listening to other types of music at the beginning of the twentieth century.

   (D) Therefore, because of its growing popularity, the *Maple Leaf Rag* earned Scott Joplin a place in musical history.

   (E) In conclusion, ragtime was thoroughly enjoyed by all Americans.

The best answer is B. A good concluding sentence refers back to the main topic of the essay, providing a link from the information contained in the last paragraph to the information presented earlier in the essay. Answer choice B does this best. Answer choices A and D are too narrow; they focus only on Scott Joplin. Answer choices C and E are too broad; they do not effectively connect Scott Joplin and his music to the popularity of ragtime music.

Essay Section

The Essay Section is always the first section on the SAT. As we pointed out in the Introduction, you have 25 minutes to plan and write your essay. You will be given a prompt, which requires you to consider a particular issue, and an assignment, which generally asks your opinion about the issue. The PSAT does not include an Essay Section.

The SAT Essay Section does not require any specialized knowledge on your part. You are not tested on what you might know about a particular subject. Instead, you are given an opportunity to demonstrate your ability to reason clearly and write coherently and concisely. College admissions people are looking for logical reasoning, clarity, organization, writing mechanics, and proper usage of the language. You are expected to think clearly and critically about the issue and create a thoughtful, well-reasoned essay supporting your position.

Responding to the Essay Prompt

There is never a "correct" answer. Your task is simply to write a good essay from whatever perspective you choose. Draw from your own observations, experience, and education for relevant supporting examples.

In addition, how *well* you write is much more important than how *much* you write. You should write enough to clearly support your position within the allotted time.

Many responses are possible to any issue prompt. You might agree or disagree in part or in whole. You might attack the underlying assumptions in the statement that is given. You might indicate that the statement you are writing about has only limited applicability in certain situations. You should use at least one example to support your position. You might choose to use more than one example, and that is fine as long as the examples you select are relevant and you stay focused on your main idea. Do not create fictional examples and try to pass them off as factual. It is okay to use hypothetical situations in your discussion if that is appropriate. Just be sure to let your readers know that the situations are hypothetical.

The issues are carefully chosen so that they aren't biased toward any college major or profession. However, luck is a bit of a factor on this section of the SAT. If you are presented with an issue that you know something about, you will probably feel more comfortable writing about it. But be careful to respond to the issue presented and the assignment given. Don't answer a question that wasn't asked just because you happen to know something about the subject matter.

EXAM/**PREP**
Study**TIP**

Avoid being too familiar, colloquial, or humorous in your response. Also do not take any chances with vocabulary. If you are at all unsure of the meaning of a word, DO NOT use it in your essay. If you are wrong, you'll end up sounding foolish or even offensive to your readers.

> **NOTE**
>
> Be sure to explain the connection between the examples that you are using and your conclusion. Don't assume that the reader will agree with your viewpoint regarding the significance of a given fact.

The four categories of information that should be included in your essay are as follows:

- ▶ Positive for your position
- ▶ Negative for your position
- ▶ Positive for the other side
- ▶ Negative for the other side

An effective essay uses facts from all four categories. You can think of your side as "correct" and the other side as "incorrect." When you write a paragraph that is focused on the "correct" side of the issue, you should mention at least one aspect of your choice that might be seen as a negative by some people. Your essay is much more persuasive if you do not ignore potential problems with your side of the debate. Of course, you should be sure to mention plenty of positive information to overcome the potential downside that you are admitting to.

The same technique can be applied to the part of your essay where you discuss the opposition's position. You should admit that the other side of the debate has at least one strong point. Then, follow up with enough discussion of the pitfalls associated with the other side of the argument so that your side ends up looking like the clear winner.

This is known as *dealing with potential counterarguments*, and it is the most effective way of presenting a persuasive written argument. To do this properly requires certain transition words. Following are four basic categories of transition words, along with some sample words:

- ▶ **Contrast**—But, however, on the other hand, conversely, although
- ▶ **Similarity**—Likewise, similarly, furthermore, moreover
- ▶ **Evidence**—Since, because, in light of, first, second, third
- ▶ **Conclusion**—Therefore, thus, as a result, so, it follows that, in conclusion

Writing Strategies and Techniques

As noted earlier in this book, humans acquire skills through practice. Because the Writing section is a test of your writing skills, you should practice writing under test-like conditions. The best way to make sure that you are on track is to have someone with writing experience, someone you trust (such as your personal tutor), give you specific feedback on your practice essays. You should have someone else read and critique your essays because writers tend to develop blind spots when reviewing their own essays.

EXAM/PREP
Study**TIP**

It is always a good idea to get a fresh set of eyes to review your work. It will not take long for an experienced reader to give you valuable feedback.

If you are critiquing your own essays, put them away for a week or so after you write them and then take them out for another review. You might find errors and lapses in logic that were not evident to you as you were writing. Be aware that this process will significantly increase the amount of time required for your overall preparation, so be sure to plan accordingly.

> **NOTE**
>
> Make sure that you understand what is presented before you begin writing. Remember that off-topic responses are not acceptable and will receive a score of 0.

SAT test-takers often make broad, general statements in their essays without giving any specific support. Make sure that you provide clear, simple examples of the general statements that you make and that your evaluations are logical and well supported.

When you start to write your essay, remember that those who read it will consider it as a first draft. Your essay will not be perfect; it should be an example of the best writing you can produce under the time constraints and testing conditions. Be sure to take a few minutes before the end of the time period to read over your essay, correcting any mistakes in grammar, usage, punctuation, and spelling. Make any corrections and revisions neatly so that the reader is not distracted by extraneous marks on the page.

The practice tests included later in this book contain additional essay prompts.

Following are the steps you should follow when writing your essays. To write the best essay that you can in the time allowed, these steps should be performed one at a time.

1. **Carefully read the prompt.**

   It's okay to read it over more than once to be certain that you understand what you are reading. You must know what the task is before you begin. Rushing through this step can cost valuable points and make some of your hard work worthless.

2. **Plan your essay.**

   Your essay should start out with a clear statement of your position on the issue or a clear evaluation of the strength of the argument. The outline that you create does not have to include complete sentences. It does have to include the ideas that you will put into your final draft. You need to be sure that you have a clear picture of where you are going and how you will get there before you start to write on the answer document.

3. **Write your essay in the space provided.**

   Remember that college admissions professionals will only look at what you've written in the lined space provided. Be sure to save time to review your work to make necessary corrections or improvements.

Scoring the Essay

The SAT essay is scored holistically, which means that the entire essay is considered as a whole. Each essay is read by two qualified readers who determine a score based on their overall impressions. These readers are predominantly high school teachers and college professors, who have undergone intensive training in the holistic scoring method.

To ensure fairness and accuracy, the two readers independently evaluate each essay. The readers do not know who you are or how you scored on other sections of the SAT. Each reader assigns your essay a score of 1 to 6, based on the following scoring guidelines:

6: Outstanding—An essay earning a score of 6 demonstrates effective and consistent mastery of the writing task. A typical essay has no major spelling, grammar, and usage errors, although there may be a few minor ones. Language use is accurate, and variation among sentences is meaningful. Ideas follow one another smoothly to develop a stance on an issue that is supported with critical analysis using appropriate evidence and examples.

5: Effective—An essay earning a score of 5 shows reasonable mastery of the writing task. It is generally well written but has occasional errors or breaks in effectiveness. Like an essay of score 6, the point of view is well reasoned and demonstrates sound critical thinking by the use of appropriate evidence and examples. The argument progresses but less coherently than in a 6 essay. Sentences are varied, though some superficially. The essay is generally free of spelling, grammar, and usage errors.

4: Competent—An essay earning a score of 4 shows adequate fulfillment of the writing task. Portions of it may be of poor quality, although it generally develops a point of view and supports it with correct examples. Progression of the argument is limited, as is variety in sentence structure. There are some errors in spelling, grammar, and usage.

3: Inadequate—An essay earning a score of 3 does not sufficiently address the writing task. It develops a point of view on the issue but may inadequately or irregularly support it with evidence and examples. Its organization is unfocused and may be partially disjointed. Some words may be inappropriate or weak choices, and sentences may be dull and patterned. There are significant errors in spelling, grammar, and usage.

2: Seriously Limited—An essay earning a score of 2 is seriously lacking. It is flawed in one or several basic ways. It may develop a vague or weak point of view on the issue or support a good stance with incorrect or weak examples and evidence. It may be poorly organized, lacking unity of ideas. It displays little skill in language use with limited vocabulary or poor word choice. Some errors in spelling, grammar, usage, and sentence structure are so serious that the argument is obscured.

1: Fundamentally Lacking—An essay earning a score of 1 is fundamentally flawed. It adheres very little or not at all to the writing task. It may establish no clear point of view on the issue or provide no evidence to support one. It is difficult to read because of grave errors in focus, organization, vocabulary, and sentence structure. Mistakes in spelling, grammar, and usage obstruct meaning.

An essay that is not written in response to the assignment given will receive a score of 0.

Practice Essay Prompt with Sample Essays

Directions: You have 25 minutes to write an essay based on the topic presented below. Do not write on another topic. Your essay should be written on the lined pages provided. For the best results, write on every line, and keep your handwriting to a reasonable, legible size. Be sure to fully develop your point of view, present your ideas clearly and logically, and use the English language precisely.

Think carefully about the following issue and assignment:

> According to some, morality is a relative concept; what is "good" for one person might not be "good" for another. Generally though, there are certain accepted moral beliefs within a society. A general rule of thumb is the adage, "treat others as you would want to be treated"—not everyone believes this, but society must have some overarching value system.

Assignment: Is morality constant, or can it be relative for any given society? Plan and write an essay in which you develop your point of view on this issue. Support your position with reasoning and examples taken from your reading, studies, experiences, or observations.

Sample Essay 1

The following essay would receive a score of 5 or 6. It is well-developed and uses appropriate examples to effectively demonstrate the author's point of view. In addition, the author explores the possibility of alternate viewpoints. The essay is focused, coherent, and lacks any major grammatical errors.

Morality fosters the peaceful relations between people in a society. While some morals seem to be ubiquitous—prohibition of rape and murder, for example—others are highly variable, and therefore could be considered relative. What is objectionable to one may be insignificant, or even positive, to the another.

Children are first exposed to the moral framework of their community by their parents. Certain actions are strongly reinforced as necessarily good or bad. The youngest children are not expected to weigh a moral decision, which for an adult may be mired in the grey area of the black-and-white standard. For example, a child finds a wallet stuffed with cash lying on the sidewalk. His mother explains that somewhere a stranger is missing his wallet, so the "right" thing to do is to mail it back to him. On one hand, the mother strives to raise an upright citizen in her son, but a darker truth reveals that the woman may not have been so certain about what to do with the wallet, but took the moral high ground to save face before her son. Were she alone, she may have taken the wallet in its entirety or perhaps just the money. Adults are prone to such moral dilemmas.

An obvious problem arises from the question of moral uniformity: it seems impossible that all members of a society could hold the same moral beliefs. After all, plenty of people of every race and creed find trouble with neighbors, friends, family, and the law. Are they immoral? If yes, did they choose to violate a moral they once held or did the change come unprovoked? It seems logical that one's morals develop over a lifetime, just as one's speech and thought patterns change. The reason for this development, I assert, is the persistent tug-of-war between self-interest and empathy. Every person on Earth has unique degrees and manifestations of each of those forces. On any given day, either side could win over the other, making morality a fluid construction in each individual's mind.

Sample Essay 2

The following essay would receive a score of 3 or 4. It is fairly well-organized and somewhat develops the author's point of view. However, it fails to provide adequate evidence to fully support the main idea, does not address any possible alternate viewpoints, and contains several distracting grammatical errors.

I believe that morality is constant, and that what is considered good in one society will be considered good in every society.

For example, most modern societies have laws against murder, because everyone believes that murder is morally wrong. While some people do commit murder, they still know it is not the right thing to do. If people were allowed to go around and kill whoever they wanted then morality would decline. Therefore, morality is not something that is relative from society to society there are certain beliefs that are universal.

Another one is the law against stealing. Some countries have harsh rules against stealing, and will even cut off the hand of the person who steals. And some other countries will make you pay a fine or go to jail if you steal something. This proves that morals are the same across societies because everyone gets punished for not being moral and for breaking society's laws.

In conclusion, I believe that morality is constant and the same for any given society, and that it is a good idea to "treat others as you would want to be treated" no matter where you live.

Sample Essay 3

The following essay would receive a score of 1 or 2. It demonstrates weak critical thinking and fails to support the author's claim. The ideas presented are vague and disorganized. Furthermore, the essay contains many severe errors in grammar, sentence structure, and spelling.

Morality is constant in every society even if you don't see it all the time. I believe that people are generally moral and that it doesn't depend on the situation. But some people are more moral than other people are, so accepted moral beleifs could be different.

Some examples might be to brake the law, that is imoral. Most people know that braking the law is wrong, so they don't do it and other people don't know the difference between rite and wrong. Therefore, this type of society would not have constant morals.

The saying to "treat others the way you would want to be treated" should be obeyed in all societys. The morals should apply to all people, and therefore are contstant.

What's Next

Be sure to write several practice essays between now and test day under timed conditions. Read Chapter 8, "Verbal Review," for insight into writing according to the rules of standard written English.

CHAPTER SIX

SAT/PSAT Quantitative

The SAT and PSAT Quantitative sections are designed to test your ability to reason mathematically, to understand basic math terminology, and to recall basic mathematic formulas and principles. You should be able to solve problems and apply relevant mathematics concepts in arithmetic, algebra, geometry, and data analysis.

The SAT and PSAT Quantitative sections include multiple choice questions, each with five answer choices (A–E), as well as student-produced response questions, for which you are not provided any answer choices. All questions cover the content discussed in Chapter 7, "SAT/PSAT Math Review."

EXAM/PREP
StudyTIP

Be sure to practice the strategies and techniques covered in this chapter on the simulated tests found in Part IV of this book.

Multiple Choice

As we just mentioned, each multiple choice question includes five answer choices (A–E). The answer choices correspond to the circles on your answer sheet. You can use an approved calculator to assist you in answering any of the multiple choice questions, but none of the questions actually require the use of a calculator.

> **NOTE**
>
> Please visit www.sat.org for a list of approved calculators. Generally, calculators with memory and print functions are not allowed. The list of approved calculators is periodically updated, so check the website a couple of weeks before your test.

You will not receive credit for anything that you write in your test booklet, but you should work through the problems in the available space so that you can check your work. Be sure to do enough practice to determine just how much space you need to solve various problems. You can use whatever space is available in the section on which you are working, but you cannot move to another section in search of blank space to solve your math problems.

As mentioned earlier, if you don't know the answer to a question, mark it in your test booklet and come back to it later if you have time. If you are able to eliminate answer choices, cross them off in your test booklet. Make an educated guess if you are able to eliminate at least one answer choice. Remember that you get one point for each correct answer and zero points for answers that are left blank. If you answer a question incorrectly, you lose an additional fraction of a point.

Multiple choice questions will include answer choices in the Roman numeral format. Always take each Roman numeral as a true or false statement: Does it answer the question or not? As you evaluate each of the Roman numerals, eliminate answer choices based on whether the answer choices include the Roman numeral. This process might allow you to arrive at the correct answer without looking at every Roman numeral statement.

Consider the following example:

1. If x and y are both positive even integers, which of the following must be even?

   I. x^y

   II. $(x + 1)^y$

   III. $x^{(y + 1)}$

   (A) I only

   (B) II only

   (C) I and II only

   (D) I and III only

   (E) II and III only

Anatomy of an SAT and PSAT Multiple Choice Quantitative Question

Before we get to the strategies, we want you to understand what a Multiple Choice question looks like. Consider the following:

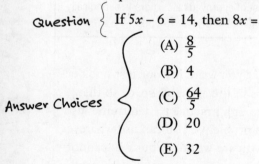

Question { If $5x - 6 = 14$, then $8x =$

   (A) $\frac{8}{5}$

   (B) 4

Answer Choices { (C) $\frac{64}{5}$

   (D) 20

   (E) 32

General Strategies for SAT and PSAT Multiple Choice Quantitative Questions

Remember these general strategies when approaching SAT/PSAT *quantitative*, or math, questions.

Draw Pictures

It really helps sometimes to visualize the problem. This strategy should not take a lot of time and can prevent careless errors. Sometimes you are given a figure or a table that you can work with; sometimes you just have to make your own. Consider the following example:

> The greatest number of diagonals that can be drawn from one vertex of a regular eight-sided polygon is
>
> (A) 1
> (B) 2
> (C) 3
> (D) 4
> (E) 5

The correct answer is E. To solve this problem, draw a diagram like the one that follows:

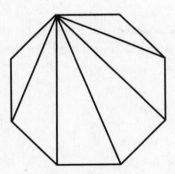

As you can see, if you draw an octagon (eight-sided polygon), you can only make five diagonals from one vertex.

Apply Logic

Even though you can use a calculator, most of the actual calculations are fairly simple. In fact, the SAT test writers are just as likely to test your logical reasoning ability or your ability to follow directions as they are to test your ability to plug numbers into an equation. Consider the following example:

If $b - c = 2$, and $a + c = 16$, then $a + b =$

(A) 8

(B) 14

(C) 16

(D) 18

(E) 32

The correct answer is D. To solve this problem, first recognize that $(b - c) + (a + c) = a + b$. This is true because the c values cancel each other out, leaving you with $b + a$, which is equivalent to $a + b$. Therefore, $a + b$ must equal 2 + 16, or 18.

Answer the Question That You Are Asked

If the problem requires three steps to reach a solution and you completed only two of the steps, it is likely that the answer you arrived at will be one of the choices. However, it will not be the correct choice! Consider the following example:

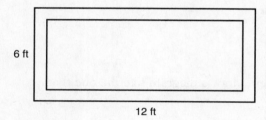

The rectangular garden shown in the figure above has a stone border 2 feet in width on all sides. What is the area, in square feet, of that portion of the garden that excludes the border?

(A) 4

(B) 16

(C) 40

(D) 56

(E) 72

The correct answer is B. This problem is asking for the area of the middle portion of the garden. To solve this problem, perform the following calculations, and remember that the border goes around the entire garden. First, subtract the border width from the length of the garden:

$12 - 2(2) = 8$

Next, subtract the border width from the width of the garden:

$6 - 2(2) = 2$

The area (length × width) of the portion of the garden that excludes the border is 8 × 2, or 16.

If you accounted for only the border along one length and one width of the garden, you would have gotten answer choice C. Answer choice D is the area of the border around the garden. Answer choice E is the area of the entire garden, including the stone border.

Don't Quit Early

Reason your way through the problem so that it makes sense. Keep in mind, though, that these questions do not usually involve intensive calculations or complicated manipulations. Consider the following example:

If $0 < pr < 1$, then which of the following CANNOT be true?

(A) $p < 0$ and $r < 0$

(B) $p < -1$ and $r < 0$

(C) $p < -1$ and $r < -1$

(D) $p < 1$ and $r < 1$

(E) $p < 1$ and $r > 0$

The correct answer is C. At first glance, you might think that you don't have enough information to solve this problem. However, if you recognize that pr must be a positive fraction because it lies between 0 and 1, you can work your way through the answer choices and eliminate those that could be true:

▶ Answer choice A: If both p and r were less than 0, their product would be positive. It's possible for pr to be a positive fraction because both p and r could be negative fractions, so eliminate answer choice A.

▶ Answer choice B: If p were -1 and r were also a negative number, their product would be positive. It's possible for pr to be a positive fraction because r could be a negative fraction, so eliminate answer choice B.

▶ Answer choice C: If both p and r were less than -1, then pr would be greater than 1. This statement cannot be true, and answer choice C is correct.

▶ Answer choice D: If both p and r were less than 1, their product could be positive. It's possible for pr to be a positive fraction because both p and r could be negative fractions, so eliminate answer choice D.

▶ Answer choice E: If p were less than 1, p could be a positive fraction. If r were greater than 0, it would be a positive number, and it's possible for pr to be a positive fraction; eliminate answer choice E.

Check the Choices

Take a quick look at the answer choices as you read the problem for the first time. They can provide valuable clues about how to proceed. For example, many answer choices will be in either ascending or descending order. If the question asks you for the least possible value, try the smallest answer choice first. If it does not correctly answer the question, work through the rest of the answer choices from smallest to largest. Remember that one of them is the correct choice. Consider the following example:

If x is an integer and $y = 7x + 11$, what is the greatest value of x for which y is less than 50?

(A) 7

(B) 6

(C) 5

(D) 4

(E) 3

The correct answer is C. Because the question asks for the greatest value of x, start with answer choice A and use the process of elimination to find the correct answer.

▸ Answer choice A: $y = 7(7) + 11 = 60$. This is not less than 50, so eliminate answer choice A.

▸ Answer choice B: $y = 7(6) + 11 = 53$. This is not less than 50, so eliminate answer choice B.

▸ Answer choice C: $y = 7(5) + 11 = 46$. Because 5 is the greatest of the remaining answer choices and the result is less than 50, answer choice C must be correct.

Pick Numbers for the Variables

You can sometimes simplify your work on a given problem by using actual numbers as "stand-ins" for variables. This strategy works when you have variables in the question and the same variables in the answer choices. You can simplify the answer choices by substituting actual numbers for the variables. Pick numbers that are easy to work with and that meet the parameters of the information given in the question. If you use this strategy, remember that numbers on the PSAT and SAT can be either positive or negative and are sometimes whole numbers and sometimes fractions. You should also be careful not to use 1 or 0 as your "stand-ins" because they can create "identities," which can lead to more than one seemingly correct answer choice.

In addition, it is sometimes necessary to try more than one number to see if the result always correctly responds to the question. If the numbers that you pick work for more than one answer choice, pick different numbers and try again, focusing on the remaining answer choices. Consider the following examples:

1. If x and y are both positive even integers, which of the following must be even?

   I. x^y

   II. $(x + 1)^y$

   III. $x^{(y + 1)}$

   (A) I only

   (B) II only

   (C) I and II only

   (D) I and III only

   (E) II and III only

The correct answer is D. The question states that both x and y are positive even integers. Therefore, you can pick any positive even integer and substitute that value for x and y in each of the Roman numeral choices, as follows:

▶ Roman Numeral I: $2^2 = 4$, which is even; $4^2 = 16$, which is also even. Any positive even integer raised to another positive even integer will result in an even number; therefore, Roman numeral I correctly answers the question. At this point, you could safely eliminate any answer choices that do not contain Roman Numeral I.

▶ Roman Numeral II: $(2 + 1)^2 = 3^2 = 9$, which is odd; $(4 + 1)^2 = 5^2 = 25$, which is also odd. When you add 1 to a positive even integer and raise the sum to a positive even integer, the result will be odd; therefore, Roman numeral II does not correctly answer the question. At this point, you could safely eliminate any remaining answer choices that contain Roman numeral II.

▶ Roman Numeral III: $2^{(2 + 1)} = 2^3 = 8$, which is even; $4^{(2 + 1)} = 4^3 = 64$, which is also even. Any positive even integer raised to an odd power will result in an even number; therefore, Roman numeral III correctly answers the question, and you can eliminate any remaining answer choices that do not contain Roman numeral III.

2. If a and b are positive consecutive odd integers, where $b > a$, which of the following is equal to $b^2 - a^2$?

   (A) $2a$

   (B) $4a$

   (C) $2a + 2$

   (D) $2a + 4$

   (E) $4a + 4$

The correct answer is E. You are given that both a and b are positive consecutive odd integers and that b is greater than a. Pick two numbers that fit the criteria: $a = 3$ and $b = 5$. Now, substitute these numbers into $b^2 - a^2$: $5^2 = 25$ and $3^2 = 9$; therefore, $b^2 - a^2 = 16$. Now, plug the value that you selected for a into the answer choices until one of them yields 16, as follows:

▶ $2(3) = 6$; eliminate answer choice A.

▶ $4(3) = 12$; eliminate answer choice B.

▶ $2(3) + 2 = 8$; eliminate answer choice C.

▶ $2(3) + 4 = 10$; eliminate answer choice D.

▶ $4(3) + 4 = 16$; answer choice E is correct.

Read the Questions Carefully

When you are looking at ratio problems, for example, note whether the question is giving a part-to-part ratio or a part-to-whole ratio, or both. The ratio of girls to boys in a class is a part-to-part ratio. The ratio of girls to students in a class is a part-to-whole ratio. Consider the following example:

> There are two types of candy in a bowl, chocolate and caramel. If the ratio of the number of pieces of chocolate candy to the total number of pieces of candy is $\frac{2}{3}$, each of the following could be the total number of pieces of candy, EXCEPT

> (A) 6

> (B) 12

> (C) 15

> (D) 20

> (E) 30

The correct answer is D. To solve this equation, you must realize that if the number of total candies is expressed in thirds, the total number of candies must be divisible by 3. The number 20 does not break evenly into thirds. However, every other answer choice *does* break evenly into thirds. This is a part-to-whole ratio.

Student-Produced Response

One of the PSAT and SAT quantitative (math) sections includes 10 student-produced response, or grid-in, questions. These questions also cover the content discussed in Chapter 7. The only real difference between multiple choice questions and grid-in questions is that the latter do not include any answer choices. You must work out the problems in the space provided in your test booklet and fill in the circles on a special part of the answer sheet. You can use a calculator to assist you in answering any of the math questions, but none of the questions actually require the use of a calculator.

You will not receive credit for anything that you write in your test booklet, but you should work through the problems in the available space so that you can check your work. As mentioned earlier, if you don't know the answer to a question, mark it in your test booklet and come back to it later if you have time. Each correct answer is worth one point; you will not be penalized for marking an incorrect answer in this section, so it is to your advantage to fill in an answer, even if you're not sure it's correct. It is a good idea to practice with the answer sheet, or grid, on the next page. Tear it out and use it as you work through the student-produced response questions that follow. Only the answers that you actually put in the grid will be scored. The grid has four places and can accommodate only positive numbers and zero. As long as your answer is filled in completely, you can start in any column on the grid. The grid includes both decimal points and fraction lines, so you can grid your answer as either a decimal or a fraction. If your answer is zero, be sure to grid it in column 2, 3, or 4. Carefully read and understand the directions for this section (see Figure 6.1).

Directions: For Student-Produced Response questions 9-18, use the grids at the bottom of the answer sheet page on which you have answered questions 1-8.

Each of the remaining 10 questions requires you to solve the problem and enter your answer by marking the circles in the special grid, as shown in the examples below. You may use any available space for scratchwork.

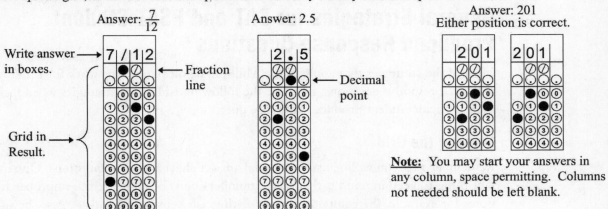

Note: You may start your answers in any column, space permitting. Columns not needed should be left blank.

- Mark no more than one circle in any column.

- Because the answer sheet will be machine-scored, **you will receive credit only if the circles are filled in correctly**.

- Although not required, it is suggested that you write your answer in the boxes at the top of the columns to help you fill in the circles accurately.

- Some problems may have more than one correct answer. In such cases, grid only one answer.

- No question has a negative answer.

- **Mixed numbers** such as $3\frac{1}{2}$ must be gridded as 3.5 or 7/2. (If $3\,1\,/\,2$ is gridded, it will be interpreted as $\frac{31}{2}$, not $3\frac{1}{2}$.)

Decimal Answers: If you obtain a decimal answer with more digits than the grid can accomodate, it may be either rounded or truncated, but it must fill the entire grid. enter the most accurate value the grid will accommodate. For example, if you obtain an answer such as 0.6666..., you should record your result as .666 or .667. **A less accurate value such as .66 or .67 will be scored as incorrect.**

Acceptable ways to grid $\frac{2}{3}$ are:

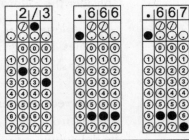

FIGURE 6.1 Directions for student-produced response questions.

Some student-produced response questions ask you for more than one answer. These questions might ask something such as, "What is one possible value of x?" You can fill in any one of the possible correct answers to the question.

General Strategies for SAT and PSAT Student Produced Response Questions

Most of the strategies that apply to the Multiple Choice questions work for the student-produced response questions, too. Use the following additional strategies when tackling more difficult student produced response question:

Manage the Grid

Remember that you will be using a special answer sheet for these questions. One important thing to keep in mind is that mixed numbers must be converted to improper fractions; for example, the computer cannot distinguish between $1\frac{2}{5}$ and $\frac{12}{5}$. Also, be sure that you have accurately recorded your answers on the grid, as only what appears on the answer sheet will be scored.

Double-Check your Answers

Because you do not have any answer choices to guide you, be very careful when performing the necessary calculations. Be sure to accurately set up the problems and write out each step so as not make any careless errors.

Consider the following examples:

1. A salesperson's monthly gross pay is $3,000 plus 30% of the dollar amount of her sales. If her gross pay for one month was $4,500, what was the dollar amount of her sales for that month?

The correct answer is 5,000. To solve this problem, first subtract the fixed amount ($3,000) from the gross pay ($4,500): $4,500 – $3,000 = $1,500. This amount is 30% of the dollar amount of her sales, so her sales must equal $1,500 ÷ .30, which is $5,000.

2. In the (x, y) coordinate system, the center of a circle has coordinates (3, 8), and the circle touches the y-axis at one point only. What is the diameter of the circle?

The correct answer is 6. If the center of the circle is at (3, 8) and the circle only touches the y-axis at one point, then it must touch at the point (0, 8). The radius of the circle is the change in the x-coordinate, or 3. Therefore, the diameter of the circle is 2(3), or 6.

3. Each of 11 people has a blank card on which they have written a positive integer. If the average (arithmetic mean) of these integers is 23, what is the greatest possible integer that could be on one of the cards?

The correct answer is 243. If the average of the 11 numbers is 23, then the sum of the 11 numbers must be 11×23, or 253. Say that 10 of the cards have a 1 written on them (the smallest positive integer); the largest possible number on the eleventh card, then, would be $253 - 10$, or 243.

What's Next

If you require a review of basic math concepts, be sure to read Chapter 7, "Quantitative Review," before you tackle the practice exams in Part IV.

PART III
Content Area Review

CHAPTER SEVEN

Quantitative Review

The SAT and PSAT Quantitative questions are designed to measure your basic mathematical skills, as well as your ability to reason mathematically. You should be able to solve problems and apply relevant mathematical concepts in arithmetic, algebra, geometry, and data analysis. As you've already seen, the Quantitative section includes both multiple choice and student-produced response questions. Each question type was covered previously in Chapter 6, "SAT/PSAT Quantitative."

This chapter serves as a review of the mathematical concepts tested on the PSAT and SAT. Familiarize yourself with the basic mathematical concepts included here and be able to apply them to a variety of math problems.

Numbers and Operations

The Quantitative sections require you to add, subtract, multiply, and divide whole numbers, fractions, and decimals. When performing these operations, be sure to keep track of negative signs and line up decimal points to eliminate careless mistakes. Following is a review of the arithmetic concepts generally tested on the PSAT and the SAT.

These questions might involve basic arithmetic and operations involving decimals, factoring, percents, ratios, proportions, sequences, number sets, number lines, absolute value, and prime numbers.

The Properties of Integers

The following are properties of integers commonly tested on both the PSAT and the SAT.

- ▶ Integers include both positive and negative whole numbers.
- ▶ Zero is considered an integer.
- ▶ Consecutive integers follow one another and differ by 1. For example, 6, 7, 8, and 9 are consecutive integers.
- ▶ The value of a number does not change when multiplied by 1. For example, $13 \times 1 = 13$.

Real Numbers

The following are properties of real numbers commonly tested on both the PSAT and the SAT.

▶ All real numbers correspond to points on the number line, as shown in Figure 7.1:

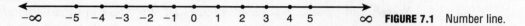

FIGURE 7.1 Number line.

▶ All real numbers except zero are either positive or negative. On a number line, such as that shown in Figure 7.1, numbers that correspond to points to the right of zero are positive, and numbers that correspond to points to the left of zero are negative. Fractions can also be represented on the number line.

▶ For any two numbers on the number line, the number to the left is always less than the number to the right.

▶ Ordering is the process of arranging numbers from smallest to greatest or from greatest to smallest. The symbol > represents "greater than," and the symbol < represents "less than." To represent "greater than or equal to," use the symbol ≥; to represent "less than or equal to," use the symbol ≤.

▶ If any number n lies between 0 and any positive number x on the number line, then $0 < n < x$; in other words, n is greater than 0 but less than x. If n is any number on the number line between 0 and any positive number x, including 0 and x, then $0 \leq n \leq x$, which means that n is greater than or equal to 0, or less than or equal to x.

▶ If any number n lies between 0 and any negative number x on the number line, then $-x < n < 0$; in other words, n is greater than $-x$ but less than 0. If n is any number on the number line between 0 and any negative number x, including 0 and $-x$, then $-x \leq n \leq 0$, which means that n is greater than or equal to $-x$, or less than or equal to 0.

Order of Operations (*PEMDAS*)

Following is a description of the correct order in which to perform mathematical operations. The acronym *PEMDAS* stands for *p*arentheses, *e*xponents, *m*ultiplication, *d*ivision, *a*ddition, *s*ubtraction. It should help you to remember to do the operations in the correct order, as follows:

P—First, do the operations within the *parentheses*, if any.

E—Next, do the *exponents*, if any.

M—Next, do the *multiplication*, in order from left to right.

D—Next, do the *division*, in order from left to right.

A—Next, do the *addition*, in order from left to right.

S—Finally, do the *subtraction*, in order from left to right.

For example, $\dfrac{2(4+1)^2 \times 3}{5} - 7$ would be solved in the following order:

$\dfrac{2(5)^2 \times 3}{5} - 7 =$

$\dfrac{2(25) \times 3}{5} - 7 =$

$\dfrac{50 \times 3}{5} - 7 =$

$\dfrac{150}{5} - 7 =$

$30 - 7 = 23$

Decimals

The following are properties of decimals that are commonly tested on both the PSAT and the SAT.

▶ *Place value* refers to the value of a digit in a number relative to its position. Starting from the left of the decimal point, the values of the digits are ones, tens, hundreds, and so on. Starting to the right of the decimal point, the values of the digits are tenths, hundredths, thousandths, and so on.

▶ When adding and subtracting decimals, be sure to line up the decimal points.

For example:

$$
\begin{array}{r}
236.78 \\
+113.21 \\
\hline
349.99
\end{array}
\qquad
\begin{array}{r}
78.90 \\
-23.42 \\
\hline
55.48
\end{array}
$$

▶ When multiplying decimals, it is not necessary to line up the decimal points. Simply multiply the numbers, then count the total number of places to the right of the decimal points in the decimals being multiplied to determine placement of the decimal point in the product.

For example:

$$
\begin{array}{r}
173.248 \\
\times 0.35 \\
\hline
60.63680
\end{array}
$$

▶ When dividing decimals, first move the decimal point in the divisor to the right until the divisor becomes an integer. Then move the decimal point in the dividend the same number of places.

For example:

$58.345 \div 3.21 = 5834.5 \div 321.$

(The decimal point was moved two places to the right.)

You can then perform the long division with the decimal point in the correct place in the quotient, as shown in the following:

```
          18.17
      _____
321 )  5834.50
      −321
      _____
       2624
      −2568
      _____
        565
       −321
       _____
        2440
       −2247
       _____
         193
```

and so on

Fractions, Rational Numbers, and Scientific Notation

The following are properties of fractions and rational numbers that are commonly tested on both the PSAT and the SAT.

▶ The *reciprocal* of any number, n, is expressed as 1 over n, or $\frac{1}{n}$. The product of a number and its reciprocal is always 1. For example, the reciprocal of 3 is $\frac{1}{3}$, and $3 \times \frac{1}{3} = \frac{3}{3}$, which is equivalent to 1. By the same token, the reciprocal of $\frac{1}{3}$ is $\frac{3}{1}$, or 3.

▶ To change any fraction to a decimal, divide the numerator by the denominator. For example, $\frac{3}{4}$ is equivalent to $3 \div 4$, or 0.75.

▶ Multiplying and dividing both the numerator and the denominator of a fraction by the same non-zero number results in an equivalent fraction. For example, $\frac{1}{4} \times \frac{3}{3} = \frac{3}{12}$, which can be reduced to $\frac{1}{4}$. This is true because whenever the numerator and the denominator are the same, the value of the fraction is 1; $\frac{3}{3} = 1$.

▶ When adding and subtracting like fractions, add or subtract the numerators and write the sum or difference over the denominator. So, $\frac{1}{8} + \frac{2}{8} = \frac{3}{8}$, and $\frac{4}{7} - \frac{2}{7} = \frac{2}{7}$.

▶ To simplify a fraction, find a common factor of both the numerator and the denominator. For example, $\frac{12}{15}$ can be simplified into $\frac{4}{5}$ by dividing both the numerator and the denominator by the common factor 3.

▶ To convert a *mixed* number to an *improper* fraction, multiply the whole number by the denominator in the fraction, add the result to the numerator, and place that value over the original denominator. For example, $3\frac{2}{5}$ is equivalent to $(3 \times 5) + 2$ over 5, or $\frac{17}{5}$.

▶ When multiplying fractions, multiply the numerators to get the numerator of the product, and multiply the denominators to get the denominator of the product. For example, $\frac{3}{5} \times \frac{7}{8} = \frac{21}{40}$.

▶ When dividing fractions, multiply the first fraction by the reciprocal of the second fraction. For example, $\frac{1}{3} \div \frac{1}{4} = \frac{1}{3} \times \frac{4}{1}$, which equals $\frac{4}{3}$, or $1\frac{1}{3}$.

▶ A *rational number* is a fraction whose numerator and denominator are both integers with a denominator that does not equal 0.

▶ When numbers are very large or very small, they are often expressed using *scientific notation*. Scientific notation is indicated by setting a positive number, *N*, equal to a number less than 10, then multiplying that number by 10 raised to an integer. The integer depends on the number of places to the left or right that the decimal was moved. For example, 667,000,000 written in scientific notation would be 6.67×10^8 because the decimal was moved eight places to the left; 0.0000000298 written in scientific notation would be 2.98×10^{-8} because the decimal was moved 8 places to the right.

Number Sets

The following are properties of number sets that are commonly tested on both the PSAT and the SAT.

▶ A *set* is a collection of numbers. The numbers are elements or members of the set. For example: {2, 4, 6, 8} is the set of positive, even integers less than 10 and greater than 0.

▶ The *union* of two sets includes all of the elements in each set. For example: if Set A = {2, 4, 6, 8} and Set B = {1, 3, 5, 7, 9}, then {1, 2, 3, 4, 5, 6, 7, 8, 9} is the union of Set A and Set B.

▶ The *intersection* of two sets identifies the common elements of two sets. For example: if Set A = {1, 2, 3, 4} and Set B = {2, 4, 6, 8}, then {2, 4} is the intersection of Set A and Set B.

Ratio, Proportion, and Percent

The following are properties of ratios, proportions, and percents that are commonly tested on both the PSAT and the SAT.

▶ A *ratio* expresses a mathematical comparison between two quantities. A ratio of 1 to 5, for example, is written as either $\frac{1}{5}$ or 1:5.

▶ When working with ratios, be sure to differentiate between part-part and part-whole ratios. For example, if two components of a recipe are being compared to each other, it is a part-part ratio (2 cups of flour:1 cup of sugar). On the other hand, if one group of students is being compared to the entire class, it is a part-whole ratio (13 girls:27 students).

▶ A *proportion* indicates that one ratio is equal to another ratio. For example, $\frac{1}{5} = \frac{x}{20}$ is a proportion.

▶ A *percent* is a fraction whose denominator is 100. The fraction $\frac{25}{100}$ is equal to 25%. To calculate the percent that one number is of another number, set up a ratio, as shown in the following example:

What percent of 40 is 5?

5 is to 40 as x is to 100

$$\frac{5}{40} = \frac{x}{100}$$

Cross-multiply and solve for x:

$$40x = 500$$
$$x = \frac{500}{40} = 12.5$$

5 is 12.5% of 40

▶ If a price is discounted by p percent, then the discounted price is $(100 - p)$ percent of the original price.

Squares and Square Roots

The following are properties of squares and square roots that are commonly tested on both the PSAT and the SAT.

▶ *Squaring* a negative number yields a positive result. For example, $-2^2 = 4$.

▶ The *square root* of a number, n, is written as $\sqrt{n}$, or the non-negative value a that fulfills the expression $a^2 = n$. For example, "the square root of 5" is expressed as $\sqrt{5}$, and $(\sqrt{5})^2 = 5$. A square root is always a positive number.

▶ A number is considered a perfect square when the square root of that number is a whole number. The polynomial $a^2 \pm 2ab + b^2$ is also a perfect square because the solution set is $(a \pm b)^2$.

NOTE

The polynomial $a^2 \pm 2ab + b^2$ is considered a perfect square binomial because it has two variables, a and b, and because its square root is either $(a + b)^2$ or $(a - b)^2$.

Arithmetic and Geometric Sequences

The following are properties of arithmetic and geometric sequences that are commonly tested on both the PSAT and the SAT.

▶ An *arithmetic sequence* is one in which the difference between one term and the next is the same. To find the nth term, use the formula $a_n = a_1 + (n - 1)d$, where d is the common difference.

▶ A *geometric sequence* is one in which the ratio between two terms is constant. For example, $\frac{1}{2}$, 1, 2, 4, 8… is a geometric sequence where 2 is the constant ratio. To find the nth term, use the formula $a_n = a_1(r)^{n-1}$, where r is the constant ratio.

Factors and Multiples

The following are properties of factors and multiples that are commonly tested on both the PSAT and the SAT.

▶ A *prime number* is any number that can be divided only by itself and 1. That is, 1 and the number itself are the only factors of a prime number. For example: 2, 3, 5, 7, and 11 are prime numbers. (Note that 2 is the only even prime number because all other even numbers can be divided by 2.)

▶ *Factors* are all of the numbers that divide evenly into one number. For example: 1, 2, 4, and 8 are all factors of 8.

▶ *Common factors* include all of the factors that two or more numbers share. For example: 1, 2, 4, and 8 are all factors of 8, and 1, 2, 3, and 6 are all factors of 6. Therefore, 8 and 6 have common factors of 1 and 2.

▶ The *greatest common factor* (GCF) is the largest number that divides evenly into any two or more numbers. For example: 1, 2, 4, and 8 are all factors of 8, and 1, 2, 3, and 6 are all factors of 6. Therefore, the Greatest Common Factor of 8 and 6 is 2.

▶ A number is a *multiple* of another number if it can be expressed as the product of that number and a second number. For example: $2 \times 3 = 6$, so 6 is a multiple of both 2 and 3.

▶ *Common multiples* include all of the multiples that two or more numbers share. For example:

Multiples of 3 include: $3 \times 4 = 12$; $3 \times 8 = 24$; $3 \times 12 = 36$.

Multiples of 4 include: $4 \times 3 = 12$; $4 \times 6 = 24$; $4 \times 9 = 36$.

Therefore, 12, 24, and 36 are all common multiples of both 3 and 4.

▶ The *least common multiple* (LCM) is the smallest number that any two or more numbers divide evenly into. For example, the common multiples of 3 and 4 are 12, 24, and 36; 12 is the smallest multiple, and is, therefore, the least common multiple of 3 and 4.

▶ The Commutative Property of Multiplication is expressed as $a \times b = b \times a$, or $ab = ba$. For example: $2 \times 3 = 3 \times 2$. This property also applies to addition.

▶ The Distributive Property of Multiplication is expressed as $a(b + c) = ab + ac$. For example: $x(x + 3) = x^2 + 3x$.

▶ The Associative Property of Multiplication can be expressed as $(a \times b) \times c = a \times (b \times c)$. For example, $(2 \times 3) \times 4 = 2 \times (3 \times 4)$, in that they both equal 24. This property also applies to addition.

Mean, Median, and Mode

The following are properties of mean, median, and mode that are commonly tested on both the PSAT and the SAT.

▶ The arithmetic *mean* is equivalent to the average of a series of numbers. Calculate the average by dividing the sum of all of the numbers in the series by the total count of numbers in the series. For example: a student received scores of 80%, 85%, and 90% on three math tests. The average score received by the student on those tests is 80 + 85 + 90 divided by 3, or 255 ÷ 3, which is 85.

▶ The *median* is the middle value of a series of numbers when those numbers are in either ascending or descending order. In the series (2, 4, 6, 8, 10) the median is 6. To find the median in an even set of data, find the average of the middle two numbers. In the series (3, 4, 5, 6) the median is 4.5.

▶ The *mode* is the number that appears most frequently in a series of numbers. In the series (2, 3, 4, 5, 6, 3, 7) the mode is 3, because 3 appears twice in the series and the other numbers each appear only once in the series.

Probability and Outcomes

Following are properties of probability and outcomes that are commonly tested on both the PSAT and the SAT.

▶ *Probability* refers to the likelihood that an event will occur. For example, Jeff has three striped and four solid ties in his closet; therefore, he has a total of seven ties in his closet. He has three chances to grab a striped tie out of the seven total ties because he has three striped ties. So, the likelihood of Jeff grabbing a striped tie is 3 out of 7, which can also be expressed as 3:7, or $\frac{3}{7}$.

▶ Two specific events are considered independent if the *outcome* of one event has no effect on the outcome of the other event. For example, if you toss a coin, there is a 1 in 2, or $\frac{1}{2}$, chance that it will land on either heads or tails. If you toss the coin again, the outcome will be the same. To find the probability of two or more independent events occurring together, multiply the outcomes of the individual events. For example, the probability that both coin-tosses will result in heads is $\frac{1}{2} \times \frac{1}{2}$, or $\frac{1}{4}$.

Absolute Value

Absolute value describes the distance of a number on the number line from 0, without considering which direction from 0 the number lies (see Figure 7.2). Therefore, absolute value is always positive. For example, consider the distance from -10 to 0 on the number line and the distance from 0 to 10 on the number line—both distances equal 10 units.

FIGURE 7.2 Absolute value.

▶ The absolute value is indicated by enclosing a number within two vertical lines:

| –3 | = 3, and | 3 | = 3

Algebra and Functions

The PSAT and SAT Quantitative sections require you to calculate specific relationships between values. Following is a review of the algebraic concepts generally tested on both the PSAT and the SAT.

These questions might involve factoring, rules of exponents, solving equations and inequalities, solving linear and quadratic equations, setting up equations to solve word problems, and working with functions.

Factoring

The following are properties of factoring that are commonly tested on both the PSAT and the SAT.

▶ The standard form of a simple quadratic expression is $ax^2 + bx + c$, where a, b, and c are whole numbers. $2x^2 + 4x + 4$ is a simple quadratic equation.

▶ To add or subtract *polynomials* (expressions consisting of more than two terms), simply combine like terms. For example: $(2x^2 + 4x + 4) + (3x^2 + 5x + 16) = 5x^2 + 9x + 20$.

▶ To multiply polynomials, use the distributive property, expressed as $a(b + c) = ab + ac$. Also, remember the *FOIL* Method: multiply the *f*irst terms, then the *o*utside terms, then the *i*nside terms, then the *l*ast terms. For example:

Distributive Property: $2x(4x + 4) = 8x^2 + 8x$

FOIL Method: $(x + 2)(x – 2) = x^2 – 2x + 2x – 4$, or $x^2 – 4$.

F (multiply the first terms): $(x)(x) =$

O (multiply the outside terms): $-2x$

I (multiply the inside terms): $2x$

L (multiply the last terms): $2 \times 2 = 4$

Now add the like terms, as follows:

$x^2 + (-2x) + (2x) + 4$. The x terms cancel each other, so the expression when simplified is $x^2 + 4$.

▶ You might be required to find the factors or solution sets of certain simple quadratic expressions. A factor or solution set takes the form ($x \pm$ some number). Simple quadratic expressions usually have two of these factors or solution sets. For example, the solution sets of $x^2 – 4$ are $(x + 2)$ and $(x – 2)$.

EXAM **PREP**
Study**TIP**

The FOIL method works only with binomials, such as $(a + b)(c + d)$.

- To find the common factor, simply look for the element that two expressions have in common. For example: $x^2 + 3x = x(x + 3)$; the common factor is x.

- You might be required to find the difference of two squares. For example: $a^2 - b^2 = (a + b)(a - b)$.

- It might be easier in some instances to apply the quadratic formula to find the solution sets for a quadratic equation. The quadratic formula is a general solution of the standard form of the quadratic equation, $ax^2 + bx + c = 0$.

Given any quadratic equation with the form $ax^2 + bx + c = 0$, where a, b, and c are constants, the solution(s) for x is(are) given by

$$\frac{-b \pm \sqrt{(b^2 - 4ac)}}{2a}$$

So, to find the solutions of the equation $x^2 + 5x - 14 = 0$, simply plug the values for a, b, and c into the quadratic formula and solve for x, as follows:

$$\frac{-5 \pm \sqrt{(5^2 - 4(1)(-14))}}{2(1)}$$

$$\frac{-5 \pm \sqrt{(25 + 56)}}{2}$$

$$\frac{-5 \pm \sqrt{(81)}}{2}$$

$$x = \frac{-5 \pm 9}{2}$$

$$x = \frac{-5 + 9}{2} \quad \text{or} \quad x = \frac{-5 - 9}{2}$$

$$x = \frac{4}{2} \quad \text{or} \quad x = -\frac{14}{2}$$

$$x = 2 \quad \text{or} \quad x = -7$$

Exponents

The following are properties of exponents that are commonly tested on both the PSAT and the SAT.

- $a^m \times a^n = a^{(m+n)}$

When multiplying the same base number raised to any power, add the exponents. For example: $3^2 \times 3^4 = 3^6$. Likewise, $3^6 = 3^2 \times 3^4$; $3^6 = 3^1 \times 3^5$, and $3^6 = 3^3 \times 3^3$.

- $(a^m)^n = a^{mn}$

  When raising an exponential expression to a power, multiply the exponent and power. For example: $(3^2)^4 = 3^8$. Likewise, $3^8 = (3^2)^4$; $3^8 = (3^4)^2$; $3^8 = (3^1)^8$; and $3^8 = (3^8)^1$.

- $(ab)^m = a^m \times b^m$

  When multiplying two different base numbers and raising the product to a power, the product is equivalent to raising each number to the power and multiplying the exponential expressions. For example: $(3 \times 2)^2 = 3^2 \times 2^2$, which equals 9×4, or 36. Likewise, $3^2 \times 2^2 = (3 \times 2)^2$, or 6^2, which equals 36.

- $(\frac{a}{b})^m = \frac{a^m}{b^m}$

  When dividing two different base numbers and raising the quotient to a power, the quotient is equivalent to raising each number to the power and dividing the exponential expressions. For example: $(\frac{2}{3})^2 = \frac{2^2}{3^2}$, or $\frac{4}{9}$.

- $a^0 = 1$, when $a \neq 0$

  When you raise any number to the power of 0, the result is always 1.

- $a^{-m} = \frac{1}{a^m}$, when $a \neq 0$

  When you raise a number to a negative power, the result is equivalent to 1 over the number raised to the same positive power. For example: $3^{-2} = \frac{1}{3^2}$, or $\frac{1}{9}$.

Inequalities

The following are properties of inequalities that are commonly tested on both the PSAT and the SAT.

- *Inequalities* can usually be worked with in the same way equations are worked with. For example, to solve for x in the inequality $2x > 8$, simply divide both sides by 2 to get $x > 4$.

- When an inequality is multiplied by a negative number, you must switch the sign.

  For example, follow these steps to solve for x in the inequality $-2x + 2 < 6$:

  $-2x + 2 < 6$

  $-2x < 4$

  $-x < 2$

  $x > -2$

Word Problems

The following are concepts that are commonly tested in word problems (story problems) on both the PSAT and the SAT.

- ▶ When solving word problems, translate the verbal statements into algebraic expressions. For example:

    - ▶ "greater than," "more than," and "sum of" mean addition (+)

    - ▶ "less than," "fewer than," and "difference" mean subtraction (−)

    - ▶ "of" and "by" mean multiplication (×)

    - ▶ "per" means division (÷)

- ▶ Distance = rate × time. So if you know that Jordan travels 50 miles per hour (rate), you can calculate how long (time) it would take him to travel 100 miles (distance) as follows:

    $$100 = 50 \times \text{time}$$
    $$\frac{100}{50} = \text{time}$$
    $$2 = \text{time}$$

- ▶ To calculate simple annual interest, multiply the principal × interest rate × time. For example, if you invest $10,000 at 6.0% for 1 year, you would earn $10,000 × .06 × 1, or $600, in interest during that year.

- ▶ If interest is compounded, interest must be computed on the principal as well as on interest that has already been earned.

- ▶ Apply logic and critical thinking to more easily solve word problems.

Functions

The following are properties of functions that are commonly tested on both the PSAT and the SAT.

- ▶ A *function* is a set of ordered pairs where no two of the ordered pairs has the same x-value. In a function, each input (x-value) has exactly one output (y-value). An example of this relationship would be $y = x^2$. Here, y is a function of x because for any value of x, there is exactly one value of y. However, x is not a function of y because for certain values of y, there is more than one value of x. The *domain* of a function refers to the x-values, while the *range* of a function refers to the y-values. If the values in the domain corresponded to more than one value in the range, the relation is not a function. For example: $f(x) = 2x + 3$. If $x = 3$, then $f(x) = 9$. For every x, there is only one $f(x)$, or y.

Geometry

The Quantitative section requires you to work with geometric figures and understand the (x, y) coordinate plane. Following is a review of the geometry concepts generally tested on both the PSAT and the SAT.

These questions might involve parallel and perpendicular lines, triangles, rectangles and other polygons, circles, area, perimeter, volume, and angle measure in degrees.

Coordinate Geometry

The following are properties of coordinate geometry that are commonly tested on both the PSAT and the SAT.

▸ The (x, y) *coordinate plane* is defined by two axes at right angles to each other. The horizontal axis is the x-axis, and the vertical axis is the y-axis.

▸ The *origin* is the point $(0, 0)$, where the two axes intersect, as shown in Figure 7.3.

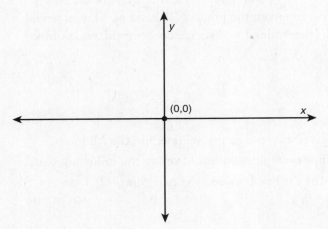

FIGURE 7.3 Origin.

▸ The *slope* of a line is calculated by taking the change in y-coordinates divided by the change in x-coordinates from two given points on a line. The formula for slope is $m = \dfrac{(y_2 - y_1)}{(x_2 - x_1)}$ where (x_1, y_1) and (x_2, y_2) are the two given points. For example, the slope of a line that contains the points $(3, 6)$ and $(2, 5)$ is equivalent to $\dfrac{(6 - 5)}{(3 - 2)}$, or $\dfrac{1}{1}$, which equals 1.

▸ A positive slope means the graph of the line goes up and to the right. A negative slope means the graph of the line goes down and to the right. A horizontal line has a slope of 0, while a vertical line has an undefined slope because it never crosses the y-axis, as seen in Figure 7.4.

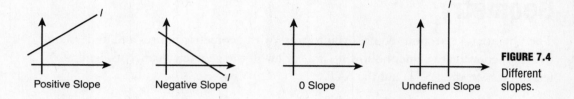

FIGURE 7.4
Different slopes.

Positive Slope   Negative Slope   0 Slope   Undefined Slope

▶ The *slope-intercept* (standard) form of the equation of a line is $y = mx + b$, where m is the slope of the line and b is the y-intercept (that is, the point at which the graph of the line crosses the y-axis).

▶ Two lines are parallel if and only if they have the same slope. For example, the two lines with equations $2y = 6x + 7$ and $y = 3x - 14$ have the same slope (3).

▶ Two lines are perpendicular if and only if the slope of one of the lines is the negative reciprocal of the slope of the other line. In other words, if line a has a slope of 2, and line b has a slope of $-\frac{1}{2}$, the two lines are perpendicular.

▶ To find the distance between two points in the (x, y) coordinate plane, use the Distance Formula $\sqrt{(x_2 - x_1)^2 + (y_2 - y_1)^2}$, where (x_1, y_1) and (x_2, y_2) are the two given points. For example, if you are given the points (2, 3) and (4, 5), you would set up the following equation to determine the distance between the two points:

$\sqrt{(4 - 2)^2 + (5 - 3)^2} =$

$\sqrt{2^2 + 2^2} =$

$\sqrt{8} = 2\sqrt{2}$

▶ To find the midpoint of a line given two points on the line, use the Midpoint Formula $(\frac{[x_1 + x_2]}{2}, \frac{[y_1 + y_2]}{2})$. For example, you would set up the following equation to determine the midpoint of the line between the two points (2, 3) and (4, 5):

$\frac{(2 + 4)}{2} =$

$\frac{6}{2} = 3$; the x-value of the midpoint is 3.

$\frac{(3 + 5)}{2} =$

$\frac{8}{2} = 4$; the y-value of the midpoint is 4.

Therefore, the midpoint of the line between the points (2, 3) and (4, 5) is (3, 4).

▶ A *translation* slides an object in the coordinate plane to the left or right or up or down. The object retains its shape and size and faces in the same direction, as shown in Figure 7.5 where the triangle in the first graph is translated 4 units down in the second graph.

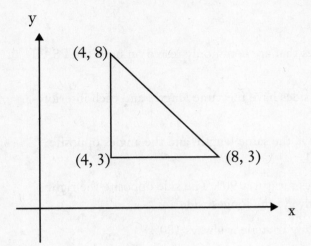

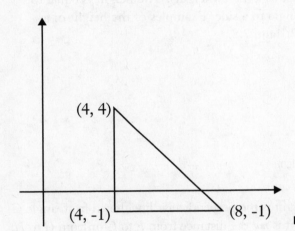

FIGURE 7.5 Translation.

► A *reflection* flips an object in the coordinate plane over either the *x*-axis or the *y*-axis. When a reflection occurs across the *x*-axis, the *x*-coordinate remains the same, but the *y*-coordinate is transformed into its opposite. When a reflection occurs across the *y*-axis, the *y*-coordinate remains the same, but the x-coordinate is transformed into its opposite. The object retains its shape and size. Figure 7.6 shows a triangle that has been reflected across the *y*-axis.

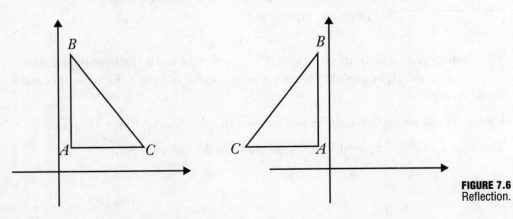

FIGURE 7.6
Reflection.

Triangles

The following are properties of triangles that are commonly tested on both the PSAT and the SAT.

▶ In an *equilateral* triangle, all three sides have the same length, and each interior angle measures 60°.

▶ In an *isosceles* triangle, two sides have the same length, and the angles opposite those sides are congruent, or equal.

▶ In a *right* triangle, one of the angles measures 90°. The side opposite the right angle is the hypotenuse, and it is always the longest side.

▶ The sum of the interior angles in any triangle is always 180°.

▶ The perimeter (P) of a triangle is the sum of the lengths of the sides.

▶ The area (A) of a triangle is equivalent to $\frac{1}{2}$(base)(height). The height is equal to the perpendicular distance from an angle to a side. Examples of the height of a given triangle are shown in Figures 7.7 and 7.8.

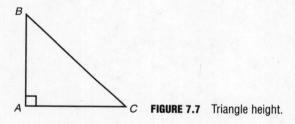

FIGURE 7.7   Triangle height.

▶ In triangle *FGH* in Figure 7.8, the height is the perpendicular line drawn from angle *G* to the midpoint of side *FH*. The height is *not* the distance from *F* to *G* or from *G* to *H*. Triangle *ABC* in Figure 7.7 is a right triangle, so the height is equivalent to side *AB*.

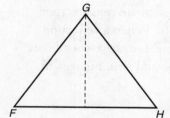

FIGURE 7.8   Triangle height.

▶ The Pythagorean Theorem states that $c^2 = a^2 + b^2$, where *c* is the hypotenuse (the side opposite the right angle) of a right triangle and *a* and *b* are the two other sides of the triangle.

▶ Figure 7.9 shows angle measures and side lengths for Special Right Triangles.

▶ The sides of a 3-4-5 Special Right Triangle have the ratio 3:4:5.

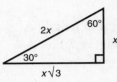
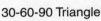

30-60-90 Triangle

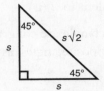

45-45-90 Triangle   **FIGURE 7.9**   Special right triangles.

Quadrilaterals, Lines, and Angles

The following are properties of quadrilaterals, lines, and angles that are commonly tested on both the PSAT and the SAT. A *quadrilateral* is any four-sided object.

▶ In a *parallelogram*, the opposite sides are of equal length, and the opposite angles are equal, as shown in Figure 7.10.

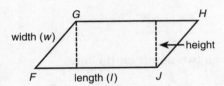

FIGURE 7.10   Parallelogram.

You can write the following equations for a parallelogram:

$GH = FJ$

$GF = HJ$

$\angle F = \angle H$

$\angle G = \angle J$

▶ The area (A) of a parallelogram is equivalent to (base)(height). The height is equal to the perpendicular distance from an angle to a side. In the parallelogram shown in Figure 7.10, the height is the distance from the angle G to the bottom side, or base, or the distance from angle J to the top side, or base. The height is *not* the distance from G to F or the distance from H to J.

▶ A *rectangle* is a polygon, or multisided figure, with four sides (two sets of congruent, or equal, sides) and four right angles, as shown in Figure 7.11. All rectangles are parallelograms.

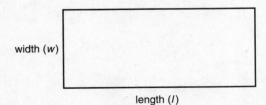

FIGURE 7.11   Rectangle.

▶ The sum of the angles in a rectangle is always 360°, because a rectangle contains four 90° angles.

▶ The perimeter (P) of both a parallelogram and a rectangle is equivalent to $2l + 2w$, where l is the length and w is the width.

▶ The area (*A*) of a rectangle is equivalent to (*l*)(*w*).

▶ The lengths of the diagonals of a rectangle are congruent, or equal in length. A diagonal is a straight line between opposite angles, as shown in Figure 7.12.

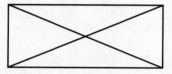

FIGURE 7.12 Diagonals of a rectangle.

▶ A *square* is a special rectangle where all four sides are of equal length. All squares are rectangles.

▶ The length of the diagonals of a square is equivalent to the length of one side times √2. So, for example, a square with a side length of *x* would have diagonals equal to *x*√2.

▶ A *line* is generally understood as a straight line.

▶ A *line segment* is the part of a line that lies between two points on the line.

▶ Two distinct lines are said to be *parallel* if they lie in the same plane and do not intersect.

▶ Two distinct lines are said to be *perpendicular* if their intersection creates right angles.

▶ When two parallel lines are cut by a *transversal*, each parallel line has four angles surrounding the intersection that are matched in measure and position with a counterpart at the other parallel line. The vertical (opposite) angles are congruent, and the adjacent angles are supplementary (they total 180°). See Figure 7.13.

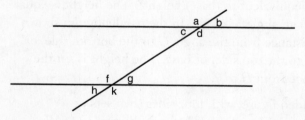

FIGURE 7.13 Parallel lines cut by a transversal.

Vertical angles: $a = d = f = k$

Vertical angles: $b = c = g = h$

Supplementary angles: $a + b = 180°$

Supplementary angles: $c + d = 180°$

Supplementary angles: $f + g = 180°$

Supplementary angles: $h + k = 180°$

▶ An *acute* angle is any angle less than 90°.

▶ An *obtuse* angle is any angle that is greater than 90° and less than 180°.

▶ A *right* angle is an angle that measures exactly 90°.

Other Polygons

The following are properties of other polygons (multisided objects) that are commonly tested on both the PSAT and the SAT.

▶ A *pentagon* is a five-sided figure, as shown in Figure 7.14.

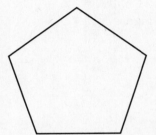

FIGURE 7.14   Pentagon.

▶ The sum of the interior angles of a pentagon is $(5 - 2)(180°)$, or $540°$.

▶ A *hexagon* is a six-sided figure, as shown in Figure 7.15.

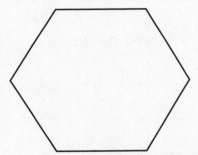

FIGURE 7.15   Hexagon.

▶ The sum of the interior angles of a hexagon is $(6 - 2)(180°)$, or $720°$.

▶ An *octagon* is an eight-sided figure, as shown in Figure 7.16.

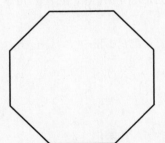

FIGURE 7.16   Octagon.

▶ The sum of the interior angles of a octagon is $(8 - 2)(180°)$, or $1,080°$.

Circles

The following are properties of circles that are commonly tested on both the PSAT and the SAT.

▶ The *radius* (*r*) of a circle is the distance from the center of the circle to any point on the circle.

▶ The *diameter* (*d*) of a circle is twice the radius, as shown in Figure 7.17.

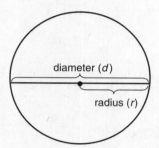

diameter (*d*)

radius (*r*)

FIGURE 7.17   Circle.

▶ The *area* (*A*) of a circle is equivalent to πr^2. So the area of a circle with a radius of 3 is $3^2\pi$, or 9π.

▶ The *circumference* (*C*) of a circle is equivalent to $2\pi r$ or πd. So the circumference of a circle with a radius of 3 is $2(3)\pi$, or 6π.

▶ The equation of a circle centered at the point (*h*, *k*) is $(x - h)^2 + (y - k)^2 = r^2$, where *r* is the radius of the circle.

▶ The complete arc of a circle has 360°.

▶ A *tangent* to a circle is a line that touches the circle at exactly one point.

Three-Dimensional Figures

The following are properties of three-dimensional figures that are commonly tested on both the PSAT and the SAT.

▶ The formula for the volume (*V*) of a rectangular solid is $V = lwh$, where *l* = length, *w* = width, and *h* = height (see Figure 7.18).

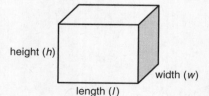

height (*h*)

width (*w*)

length (*l*)

FIGURE 7.18   Rectangular solid.

▶ The surface area of a rectangular solid is the sum of the area (*l* × *w*) of the six faces of the solid. Think of each face as a square or a rectangle.

▶ The formula for the surface area of a rectangular solid is $A = 2(wl + lh + wh)$, where l = length, w = width, and h = height.

Special Symbols

Special symbols are sometimes defined in the PSAT and SAT Quantitative sections. Read the definition carefully and evaluate the mathematical expressions given in the question. For example:

Let $a \clubsuit b = \frac{1}{ab}$. What is the value of $2 \clubsuit 3$?

To solve, simply substitute the numbers given in the problem for a and b.

$2 \clubsuit 3 = \frac{1}{(2)(3)} = \frac{1}{6}$

Data Interpretation

Some of the information presented in the PSAT and SAT Quantitative sections will be in the form of charts, tables, and graphs.

▶ Carefully read the labels on the tables, charts, or graphs.

▶ Make sure that you understand the relationships between the data represented in the tables, charts, or graphs before you answer the question.

▶ For example, in the pie graph shown in Figure 7.19, you should recognize that Miscellaneous funding, $x\%$, is less than 50% and less than 20% of the Total funding. A question might ask you to calculate the value of x as a percentage, and you might be able to quickly eliminate some incorrect answer choices. You should also remember that there are 360° in a circle because a question might ask you to calculate the value of x as the number of degrees it represents on the graph.

Sources of School Funding, 1997

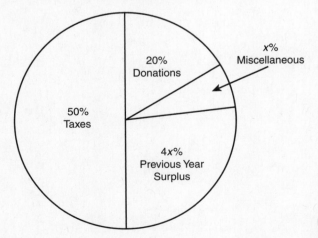

FIGURE 7.19 Sample pie graph.

Internalize the Rules

As you work through the simulated practice tests in Part IV, refer to this chapter as needed to review any math concepts with which you continue to struggle.

In our experience, test takers who internalize the basic math concepts perform better on the PSAT and SAT. When you can quickly recognize the concept that is being tested with a particular question, you can approach that question with confidence.

CHAPTER EIGHT

Verbal Review

Each of the question types on the PSAT and SAT Critical Reading Sections—Reading Comprehension and Sentence Completion—and the PSAT and SAT Writing Sections—Improving Sentences, Identifying Sentence Errors, and Improving Paragraphs—requires a basic understanding of the rules that govern standard written English. You should also rely on the conventions of standard written English when writing the SAT Essay. This chapter provides an overview of the rules of grammar that are most commonly tested on both the PSAT and the SAT.

Subject-Verb Agreement

A well-constructed sentence contains a subject and a verb and expresses a complete thought. The *subject* is who or what the sentence is about. The *verb* tells you either what the subject is doing or what is being done to the subject. The subject and verb must agree—that is, they must share the same person, number, voice, and tense. Some complex sentences on the SAT might try to conceal the subject, making proper subject-verb agreement more of a challenge.

▶ **Person**—A verb must have the same person as the subject.

1. First person: *I am* eating lunch.

2. Second person: *You are* eating lunch.

3. Third person: *She is* eating lunch.

▶ **Number**—A singular subject requires a singular verb.

1. The *earth is* round.

2. *One* of the boys *has* a dog.

3. *Everyone thinks* that I will win.

> **NOTE**
>
> Several indefinite pronouns are considered singular and must be paired with a singular verb. Following is a list of those tricky pronouns: each, either, neither, one, everybody, everyone, nobody, everything, someone, and somebody.

A plural subject requires a plural verb.

1. The *girls are* waiting for the bus.

2. *Patricia and Janet enjoy* suspense novels.

EXAM/PREP
Study**TIP**

When the agent is unknown, reword passive voice using the pronoun *someone*. For example:

1. The cake was eaten. (Passive voice)

2. Someone ate the cake. (Active voice)

▶ **Voice**—*Voice* defines whether the subject performs the action of the verb or receives the action of the verb. The active voice is usually the preferred mode of writing. *Active voice* means that the subject is acting, as in the following sentence:

1. The *dog licked* my brother.

   Passive voice means that the subject is being acted upon, as in the following sentence:

2. *My brother was licked* by the dog.

▶ **Tense**—Verb *tense* provides you with information about when the action took place. Actions take place in the present, in the past, or in the future, as shown in the following:

1. *Present Tense*—The action is taking place now: *Robin works* at the mall after school.

2. *Present Perfect Tense*—The action started in the past and is occurring over time: *Robin has worked* at the mall for the last two years.

3. *Past Tense*—The action happened in the past: *Robin worked* at the mall last year.

4. *Past Perfect Tense*—The action took place before another specified action in the past: *Robin had worked* at the mall before taking a job at the theater.

5. *Future Tense*—The action will happen in the future: *Robin will work* at the mall this year.

6. *Future Perfect Tense*—The action takes place in the past relative to a time in the future: *Robin will have worked* at the mall for two years as of next week.

Nouns and Pronouns

The English language contains two forms of nouns:

▶ *Proper nouns*, which name a specific person, place, or object.

▶ *Common nouns*, which name a non-specific person, place, or object.

Proper nouns begin with an uppercase letter, and common nouns do not. *Pronouns* take the place of either a proper or a common noun. Generally, a pronoun begins with an uppercase letter only if the pronoun begins a sentence. The one notable exception is the personal pronoun *I*, which is always capitalized. You should be able to determine and correctly apply pronoun case, as follows:

▶ **Nominative case** (renames the noun)—I, you, he, she, it, they, we

For example: *Mandy* recently graduated from college; *she* now has a degree in nursing.

▶ **Possessive case** (shows possession)—my, mine, our, ours, your, yours, his, hers, its, their, theirs

For example: This is *my* plane ticket.

▶ **Objective case** (acts as a direct or indirect object)—me, us, you, him, her, it, them

For example: The monkey made faces at *him* through the bars of the cage.

In addition, you should be able to distinguish between *personal*, *relative*, and *indefinite* pronouns.

Personal Pronouns

Personal pronouns identify a specific person or thing.

Use the *nominative* case of a personal pronoun with a compound subject. If the subject consists of one or more nouns, it is a compound subject.

1. Alan and *I* worked together on the project.

2. *She* and Pamela have been friends for a long time.

Use the nominative case of a personal pronoun with the verb form *to be*. The verb *to be* in the present tense is expressed as follows:

1. I am—*I am* running for class president.

2. He/she/it is—*He is* going to challenge my bid for class president.

3. You/they/we are—*You are* going to vote for me, right?

The verb *to be* for the past tense is expressed as follows:

1. I was—*I was* going to see the movie until Steve told me how it ended.

2. He/she/it was—*She was* in such a hurry that she forgot to pack her toothbrush.

3. You/they/we were—*We were* unable to attend the ceremony.

Use the *nominative* case for pronouns that are the subject of an incomplete clause. Completing the clause can lead you to the correct pronoun case.

1. No one in the classroom was as surprised as *I*. (was)

2. He worked longer today than *she*. (worked)

Use a *possessive* pronoun before a gerund. A *gerund is* a verb ending in –ing, which functions as a noun.

1. *Her* singing has often been admired.

2. The class was shocked by *his* studying for the exam.

Use the *objective* case when the pronoun is the object of a verb.

1. A large dog chased *me* down the road.

2. The teacher gave *them* a passing grade.

Use the *objective* case when the pronoun is the object of a preposition. A *preposition* is a word such as "from" or "before" that establishes a relationship between an object and some other part of the sentence, often expressing a location in place or time.

1. Matt received the greatest support from *you* and *me*.

2. The paper fluttered to the ground before *him*.

Relative Pronouns

Relative pronouns are used to identify people, places, and objects in general. The relative pronouns who, whom, and whose refer to people. The relative pronouns which, what, and that refer to places and objects.

> **NOTE**
>
> Remember that people, such as teachers, students, lawyers, and so on, should be identified by the pronoun *who*, not by the pronoun *that*.

Indefinite Pronouns

Indefinite pronouns represent an indefinite number of persons, places, or things. Following are some examples of indefinite pronouns:

1. *Everyone* gather around the campfire!

2. There will be a prize for *each* of the children.

3. *One* of my sisters always volunteers to drive me to school.

Pronoun Consistency

Be sure to maintain consistency in pronoun person and number. It is not grammatically correct to use the plural pronoun "their" to represent neutral gender. This is an example of a major difference between standard written English and the vernacular English that we ordinarily use when speaking. Consider the following:

A small child should always be with *his or her* parent or guardian.

NOT:

A small child should always be with *their* parent of guardian.

Misleading and Ambiguous Pronouns

A pronoun should be placed so that it clearly refers to a specific noun. One of the errors that the PSAT and SAT commonly test is a pronoun with an unclear antecedent (the noun that the pronoun is intended to replace). Following are examples of misleading or ambiguous pronouns, along with corrected sentences:

1. **Misleading pronoun**—Despite the controversy surrounding the candidates, the committee made *their* decision very quickly.

   In this sentence, the plural pronoun *their* incorrectly refers to the singular noun *committee*. To correct this sentence, replace *their* with *its*.

2. **Misleading pronoun**—*Several* of the group elected to return home following the decision.

   In this sentence the plural pronoun *several* refers to the singular noun *group*. To correct this sentence, add the plural noun *members* after the plural pronoun *several*.

In addition, a pronoun should be placed so that it clearly refers to a specific noun. If it does not, it is known as an *ambiguous pronoun*. See the following examples:

1. **Ambiguous pronoun**—Matt and Phil left rehearsal early to get *his* guitar repaired.

   In this sentence, it is unclear whose guitar is getting repaired.

   Correct sentence—Matt and Phil left rehearsal early to get *Phil's* guitar repaired.

2. **Ambiguous pronoun**—Some foods are dangerous for your pets, so *they* should be placed out of reach.

   In this sentence, it is unclear what should be placed out of reach: the potentially dangerous foods or your pets.

   Correct sentence—Some foods are dangerous for your pets; *these foods* should be placed out of reach.

Verbs and Verb Forms

A *verb* describes the action that is taking place in the sentence. All verbs have four principle forms:

▶ **Simple present**—I *write*.

▶ **Simple past**—I *wrote*.

▶ **Present participle**—I am *writing*.

▶ **Past participle**—I have *written*.

Simple Past Versus Past Participle

The *simple past* and *past participle* forms of verbs can sometimes be confusing. Most past tenses are formed by adding –ed to the word, as shown in the examples that follow:

1. **Present tense**—We *move* often.

2. **Past tense**—We *moved* again this year.

Some verbs have special past tense forms, as shown in the examples that follow:

1. **Present tense**—I *see* my best friend every day.

2. **Simple past tense**—I *saw* my best friend yesterday.

3. **Present tense**—My little sister *eats* her breakfast quickly.

4. **Simple past tense**—My little sister *ate* her breakfast quickly.

Remember that the past participle includes *has*, *had*, or *have*, the so-called "helping verbs," as shown in the examples that follow:

1. **Past participle**—I *had seen* my best friend the day before.

2. **Past participle**—My little sister *has eaten* her breakfast quickly.

Parallel Construction

Parallel construction, or *parallelism*, allows a writer to show order and clarity in a sentence or a paragraph by putting grammatical elements that have the same function in the same form. Parallelism creates a recognizable pattern within a sentence and adds unity, force, clarity, and balance to writing. All words, phrases, and clauses used in parallel construction must share the same grammatical form. We have included some examples of sentences that include faulty parallelism, followed by revised versions of each sentence:

1. **Faulty parallel construction**—Patricia enjoyed *running* and *to ride horses*.

   In this sentence, the verb forms do not match. The first of the two verb forms is a participle (running), and the second verb form is in the infinitive form (to ride).

   Correct sentence—Patricia enjoyed *running* and *horseback riding*.

2. **Faulty parallel construction**—The *distance* from Los Angeles to Detroit is greater than Detroit to Windsor, Canada.

   In this sentence, two unlike things are being compared: *distance* and *location*.

   Correct sentence—The *distance* from Los Angeles to Detroit is greater than the *distance* from Detroit to Windsor, Canada.

EXAM✓**PREP**
Study**TIP**

The PSAT and the SAT reward active language. Therefore, you should generally use the simple past tense in your writing because it is more direct.

At any rate, be sure to maintain consistent verb form throughout a sentence.

Run-on Sentences

A *run-on sentence* is a sentence that is composed of more than one main idea and does not use proper punctuation or connectors. Following are examples of run-on sentences along with suggested corrections:

1. **Run-on sentence**—Janet is an actress she often appears in major network television shows.

   Correct sentence—Janet is an actress *who* often appears in major network television shows.

2. **Run-on sentence**—My nephew loves to play football, you can find him on the practice field almost every day.

   Correct sentence—My nephew loves to play football. *You* can find him on the practice field almost every day.

Run-on sentences are often created by substituting a comma for a semicolon or a period, as shown in Sentence 2 above. This is called a *comma splice*, and it is incorrect.

Sentence Fragments/Incomplete Sentences

A *sentence fragment* is a *dependent clause*, which typically functions as part of a complete sentence and cannot stand alone. Sentence fragments are sometimes punctuated as if they were complete sentences. Following are examples of sentence fragments along with suggested corrections:

1. **Sentence fragment**—My car is difficult to start in the *winter. Because* of the cold weather.

   Correct sentence—My car is difficult to start in the *winter because* of the cold weather.

2. **Sentence fragment**—Colorado State University offers a variety of *courses. Such* as Psychology, Biology, Physics, and Music.

   Correct sentence—Colorado State University offers a variety of *courses, such as* Psychology, Biology, Physics, and Music.

Incomplete sentences often include a main clause that lacks a verb, as shown in the examples that follow:

1. **Incomplete sentence**—Yesterday, the *winning* float in the parade.

   The sentence as it is written is incomplete; the word *winning* is a participle and is being used as an adjective to describe the float. The sentence should be revised so that the winning float either performs an action or has an action performed upon it.

   Revised sentence—Yesterday, the *winning* float in the parade *was displayed* on campus.

2. **Incomplete sentence**—The *releasing* of personal information by many school districts to third parties.

The sentence as it is written is incomplete; the word *releasing* is being used as a noun in this sentence. The sentence should be revised so that the subject, *many school districts*, is actually performing an action.

Revised sentence—Many school districts *prohibit the releasing* of personal information to third parties.

Misplaced Modifiers

A sentence must contain at least one main clause. A complex sentence may contain more than one main clause, as well as one or more *relative clauses*. *Relative clauses* follow the nouns that they modify. To maintain clarity within a sentence, it is important to place a relative clause near the object that it modifies. A *modifier* is a word, phrase, or clause that modifies, or changes, the meaning of another word or part of the sentence. Often, a modifier helps explain or describe who, when, where, why, how, and to what extent. Misplaced modifiers can inadvertently change the meaning of the sentence.

We have included some examples of sentences that contain misplaced modifiers, followed by revised versions of each sentence:

1. **Misplaced modifier**—Cassie had trouble deciding which college to attend *at first*.

The meaning of this sentence is obscured by the placement of the modifying clause, at first. It is unlikely that the writer intended to suggest that Cassie was going to attend more than one college.

Correct sentence—*At first*, Cassie had trouble deciding which college to attend.

2. **Misplaced modifier**—As *a teacher*, *the school board* hired Mrs. Smith to coach our team.

This sentence as it is written suggests that the school board, and not Mrs. Smith, is a teacher.

Correct sentence—The school board hired *Mrs. Smith*, *a teacher*, to coach our team.

> **NOTE**
>
> Make sure that each sentence is clear in that you know exactly "who" is doing "what," "how" something happens, and so on.

Punctuation

Although punctuation is not tested directly on either the PSAT or the SAT, we have included some basic punctuation rules here to help you understand the relationship between proper punctuation and effective writing.

A properly punctuated sentence will help the reader understand the organization of the writer's ideas. You might be tested indirectly on the following forms of punctuation:

- ► Commas
- ► Apostrophes
- ► Colons and semicolons
- ► Parentheses and dashes
- ► Periods, question marks, and exclamation points

Commas

A *comma* is used to indicate a separation of ideas or of elements within a sentence.

- ► **Use a comma with a coordinating conjunction**—A coordinating conjunction connects words, phrases, or clauses that are of equal importance in the sentence. Use a comma to separate such main clauses within a sentence. Consider the following:

  1. Jenny sings in the choir, *and* she plays the guitar in a rock band.

  2. Amanda enjoys her job, *but* she is looking forward to her vacation.

  3. I will either study mathematics, *or* I will study chemistry.

  4. Jordan will be playing football this year, *for* he made the team.

  5. Frank earned a promotion, *so* we decided to celebrate.

  6. I just completed my work-out, *yet* I'm not tired.

- ► **Use a comma to separate elements that introduce and modify a sentence**—Modifiers should be set off from the rest of the sentence with a comma, as shown here:

  1. *Yesterday*, I painted the entire garage.

  2. *Before deciding on a major at college*, Rana discussed her options with her parents.

- ► **Use commas before and after a parenthetical expression**—A parenthetical expression is a phrase that is inserted into the writer's train of thought. Parenthetical expressions are most often set off using commas. Consider the following:

  1. Stephanie's decision, *in my opinion*, was not in her best interest.

  2. The new park, *of course*, is a popular tourist destination.

▶ **Use a comma to set off an appositive**—An appositive is a noun or phrase that renames the noun that precedes it. Consider the following:

1. My brother, *a well-respected scientist*, made an important discovery.

2. Mr. Smith, *the 5th grade math teacher*, was a favorite among the students.

▶ **Use commas to set off interjections**—An interjection is a word or phrase that generally expresses some emotion, as in the following examples:

1. *Well*, it's about time that you got here!

2. *Say*, did you pass your history test?

▶ **Use commas to separate coordinate adjectives**—If two adjectives modify a noun in the same way, they are called coordinate adjectives. Consider the following:

1. We walked the *long, dusty* road to the abandoned farm.

2. My cousin ordered a *unique, signed* copy of her favorite book.

Coordinate adjectives can be joined with and, as shown here:

1. We walked the *long and dusty* road to the abandoned farm.

2. My cousin ordered a *unique and signed* copy of her favorite book.

▶ **Use commas to set off nonrestrictive phrases**—A nonrestrictive phrase can be omitted from the sentence without changing the meaning of the sentence. Nonrestrictive clauses are useful because they serve to further describe the nouns that they follow. Consider the following:

1. My sister's dog, *a brown and white terrier*, barks at me whenever I visit.

2. Katie celebrated her birthday, *which was in June*, with a party and a chocolate cake.

▶ **Use a comma to separate items in a list or series**—Generally, when a list contains three or more items, each item should be set off with a comma, as shown next:

1. Jill decided to purchase *a leash, a collar, and a water dish* for her dog.

2. Skippy *packed his suitcase, put on his jacket*, and *left the house*.

3. Please bring the following items to camp: *pillow, blanket, toothbrush, and other personal hygiene products*.

▶ **Use commas in dates, addresses, place names, numbers, and quotations—**
Commas generally separate a quotation from its source. Consider the following:

1. Mary is leaving for Jamaica on *January 7, 2004*.

2. The Library of Congress is located at 101 Independence *Avenue, Washington, D.C.*

3. Annual tuition is currently *$42,500*.

4. "My sister is a nurse," *Becky* said proudly.

Apostrophes

An *apostrophe* is used to form possessives of nouns, to show the omission of letters, and to indicate plurals of letters and numbers.

▶ **Singular possession—**Add an apostrophe and an "s" to form the possessive of singular nouns, plural nouns, or indefinite pronouns that do not end in "s." Consider the following:

1. My friend**'s** house is at the end of the street.

2. The Women**'s** Society meets every Thursday at the high school.

3. Someone**'s** bicycle is leaning against the building.

▶ **Plural possession—**Add an apostrophe to form the possessive of plural nouns ending in "s," as shown here:

1. The horse**s'** stalls were filled with straw.

2. I did not enjoy the brother**s'** rendition of my favorite song.

▶ **Joint possession—**Add an apostrophe to the last noun to indicate joint possession, as shown here:

1. Frank and Ruth**'s** anniversary is in September.

2. Jill and Mandy**'s** class schedules are identical.

▶ **Contractions—**Add an apostrophe to indicate contractions, as shown here:

1. It's raining outside again.

2. We're running against each other in the election.

3. If you're going to the movie with me, we should leave now.

4. My cousin should've taken the bus.

Colons and Semicolons

A colon is used before a list or after an independent clause that is followed by information that directly modifies or adds to the clause. An independent clause can stand alone as a complete sentence.

A semicolon is used to join closely related independent clauses when a coordinate conjunction is not used, with conjunctive adverbs to join main clauses, to separate items in a series that contains commas, and to separate coordinate clauses when they are joined by transitional words or phrases.

- **Lists**—Use a colon before a list, as shown here:

  1. We are required to bring the following items to camp: a sleeping bag, a pillow, an alarm clock, clothes, and personal care items.

- **Direct modifiers**—Use a colon after an independent clause that is followed by information that directly modifies or adds to the clause. Consider the following:

  1. Jennifer encountered a problem that she had not anticipated: a broken Internet link.

  2. My sister suggested a great location: the park down the street from our house.

- **Independent clauses**—Use a semicolon to join closely related independent clauses when a coordinate conjunction is not used. Consider the following:

  1. Jane starts a new job today; she is very excited.

  2. I don't understand the directions; my teacher must explain them to me.

Use a semicolon with conjunctive adverbs to join independent clauses, as shown next:

  1. Skippy is interested in taking the class; however, it does not fit in his schedule.

  2. My brother is very tall; in fact, he is the tallest person in our family.

- **Series**—Use a semicolon to separate items which contain commas and are arranged in series, as shown here:

  1. The art museum contained some beautiful, old oil paintings; bronze, plaster, and marble statues; and recently completed, modern art pieces.

  2. My first meal at college consisted of cold, dry toast; runny, undercooked eggs; and very strong, acidic coffee.

- ▸ **Coordinate clauses**—Use a semicolon to separate coordinate clauses when they are joined by transitional words or phrases. When a sentence contains more than one clause, each of which is considered to be equally as important as the other, the clauses are called *coordinate* clauses. They are typically joined by a coordinating conjunction, such as and or but. When the coordinating conjunction is not used, a semicolon should be, as shown here:

    1. My sister and I enjoyed the play; afterwards, we stopped for an ice cream cone.

    2. Betty often misplaces her keys; perhaps she should get a key locator.

Parentheses and Dashes

Parentheses are used to enclose supplemental information that is not essential to the meaning of the sentence. *Dashes* are used to place special emphasis on a certain word or phrase within a sentence. Consider the following:

Parentheses

1. In addition to serving as Class Treasurer (during her Junior year), she was also a National Merit Scholar.

2. Alan visited the Football Hall of Fame (with his family) during his summer vacation.

Dashes

1. Dr. Evans—a noted scientist and educator—spoke at our commencement ceremony.

2. The Homecoming float—cobbled together with wire and nails—teetered dangerously down the street.

End Punctuation

Periods, question marks, and exclamation points are considered *end punctuation* and should be used at the end of a sentence.

Use a *period* to end most sentences, use a *question mark* to end a direct question, and use an *exclamation point* to end an emphatic statement.

Idiom

Idiom refers to the common or everyday usage of a word or phrase. For instance, idiom tells us which preposition goes with which verb—we sit across *from* someone, not across *with* someone. Idiom is part of standard written English and must be considered when making corrections to or improving sentences on the PSAT and the SAT.

We have included a short list of common idiomatic expressions, or *colloquialisms*, as they might be used in a sentence:

1. Mary thought that the test was *a piece of cake*.

   The phrase *piece of cake* typically signifies the relative ease of a task.

2. During our winter break, my friends and I *hit the slopes*.

   The phrase *hit the slopes* is generally used to indicate snow skiing.

3. My father insisted that I put my *nose to the grindstone* next semester.

   The phrase *nose to the grindstone* suggests that one is working hard.

4. Throughout the summer I lived a *stone's throw* from a popular beach.

   The phrase *stone's throw* generally indicates a short distance.

5. Sandy is often too *bogged down* with her studies to spend time with her friends. The phrase *bogged down* is most often used to mean overwhelmed.

It is important to note that there is a difference between idiom, jargon, and slang. Avoid using *jargon*—specialized or technical language—in your essays because the readers might not know what it means. An otherwise well-written essay might not receive a good score if the reader is confused by unfamiliar terminology.

Likewise, it is not appropriate to use *slang*—informal figures of speech—because slang often becomes quickly outdated and can be very regionalized, which means that some parts of the country use spoken English in ways that other parts of the country do not.

Study TIP

Do not use slang or jargon in your essay. The essay readers might not understand what you are trying to say and could award you fewer points as a result.

Rhetoric

Rhetoric refers to the effective and persuasive use of language. Rhetorical skills, then, refer to your ability to make choices about the effectiveness and clarity of a word, phrase, sentence, or paragraph. Both the PSAT and the SAT Writing Sections test your rhetorical skills by asking you to improve sentences and paragraphs. Good writing involves effective word choice as well as clear and unambiguous expression. The best-written sentences are relevant based on the context of the paragraph, avoid redundancy, and clearly and simply express the intended idea.

Commonly Misused Words

Although thousands of different word usage errors could appear on the PSAT or the SAT, the tests repeatedly include commonly misused words. We've included a list of some of these words here, along with definitions and examples of the proper use of each word.

Accept, Except

Accept is a verb that means "to agree to receive something."

Example: I could not pay for my purchases with a credit card because the store would only *accept* cash.

Except is either a preposition that means "other than, or but," or a verb meaning "to omit or leave out."

Example: *Except* for a B+ in history, Andrea received all As on her report card.

Affect, Effect

Affect is usually a verb meaning "to influence."

Example: Fortunately, Sam's sore ankle did not *affect* her performance in the game.

Effect is usually a noun used to "indicate or achieve a result." Effect is also sometimes used as a transitive verb meaning "to bring into existence," but it is generally not used in this way on the SAT.

Example: Studies have shown that too much exercise can have a negative *effect* on a person's health.

Among, Between

Among is used with more than two items.

Example: Jackie's performance last night was the best *among* all of the actors in the play.

Between is usually used with two items.

Example: Simon could not decide *between* the two puppies at the pound, so he adopted them both.

Assure, Insure, Ensure

Assure means "to convince" or "to guarantee" and usually takes a direct object.

Example: If we leave 2 hours early, I *assure* you that we will arrive at the concert on time.

Insure means "to guard against loss."

Example: Before he could leave for his trip, Steve had to *insure* his car against theft.

Ensure means "to make certain."

Example: Our company goes to great lengths to *ensure* that every product that leaves the warehouse is of the highest quality.

Compare to, Compare with

Compare to means "assert a likeness."

Example: The only way to describe her eyes is to *compare* them *to* the color of the sky.

Compare with means "analyze for similarities and differences."

Example: For her final project, Susan had to *compare* bike riding *with* other aerobic activities and report her findings.

Complement, Compliment

Complement implies "something that completes or adds to" something else.

Example: My favorite place to dine is on the terrace; the breathtaking views are the ideal *complement* to a romantic dinner.

A *compliment* is "flattery or praise."

Example: Larry was thrilled when the award-winning author *complimented* him on his writing style.

Farther, Further

Farther refers to distance.

Example: At baseball camp, Jackson learned that with the correct stance and technique, he could throw the ball *farther* this year than he could last year.

Further indicates "additional degree, time, or quantity."

Example: I enjoyed the book to a certain degree, but I felt that the author should have provided *further* details about the characters.

Fewer, Less

Fewer refers to units or individuals that can be counted.

Example: Trish received all the credit, even though she worked *fewer* hours on the project than did the other members of the group.

Less refers to mass or bulk that can't be counted.

Example: When it comes to reading, Mike is *less* inclined to read for pleasure than is Cassie.

Imply, Infer

Imply means "to suggest."

Example: His sister did not mean to *imply* that he was incorrect.

Infer means "to deduce," "to guess," or "to conclude."

Example: The professor's *inference* was correct concerning the identity of the student.

Its, It's

Its is the possessive form of "it."

Example: In the summer, my family enjoys drinking white tea for *its* refreshing, light flavor.

It's is the contraction of "it is."

Example: Fortunately for the runners, *it's* a sunny day.

Lay, Lie

Lay means "to put" or "to place" and requires a direct object to complete its meaning.

Example: To protect your floor or carpet, you should always *lay* newspaper or a sheet on the ground before you begin to paint a room.

Lie means "to recline, rest, or stay," or "to take a position of rest." This verb cannot take a direct object. The past tense of lie is lay, so use extra caution if you see these words on the SAT.

Example: On sunny days, our lazy cat will *lie* on the porch and bask in the warmth of the sunlight.

Example: Yesterday, our lazy cat *lay* in the sun for most of the afternoon.

Like, Such As

Like should be used to indicate similarity.

Example: Andrea and Carol were very close, *like* two peas in a pod.

Such as should be used to indicate an example or examples.

Example: Composers *such as* Mozart and Bach are among my favorites.

Number, Amount

Number should be used when the items can be counted.

Example: The *number* of students enrolled at Hill College has increased during the last 5 years.

Amount should be used to denote quantity.

Example: A small *amount* of rain has fallen so far this year.

Precede, Proceed

Precede means "to go before."

Example: When I go to an expensive restaurant, I expect a salad course to *precede* the main course.

Proceed means "to move forward."

Example: As a result of failed negotiations, the labor union announced its plan to *proceed* with a nationwide strike.

Principal, Principle

Principal is a noun meaning "the head of a school or an organization."

Example: A high school *principal* is responsible not only for the educational progress of his students but also for their emotional well-being.

Principal can also mean "a sum of money."

Example: I hope to see a 30% return on my *principal* investment within the first two years.

Principal can also be used as an adjective to mean "first" or "leading."

Example: Our *principal* concern is the welfare of our customers, not the generation of profits.

Principle is a noun meaning "a basic truth or law."

Example: A study of basic physics will include Newton's *principle* that every action has an opposite and equal reaction.

Set, Sit

The verb *set* takes an object.

Example: I *set* the bowl of pretzels in the middle of the table so that everyone could reach it.

The verb *sit* does not take an object.

Example: When I dine alone, I always *sit* by the window so that I can watch all the people who pass by the restaurant.

Than, Then

Than is a conjunction used in comparison.

Example: Roberta made fewer mistakes during her presentation *than* she thought she would make.

Then is an adverb denoting time.

Example: Mandy updated her resume *then* applied for the job.

That, Which

That introduces an essential clause in a sentence. Commas generally should not be used before the word *that*.

Example: I usually take the long route because the main highway *that* runs through town is always so busy.

Which is best used to introduce a clause containing nonessential and descriptive information. Commas are required before the word *which* if it is used in this way. *Which* can also be used to introduce an essential clause to avoid repeating the word *that* in the sentence.

Example: The purpose of the Civil Rights Act of 1991, *which* amended the original Civil Rights Act of 1964, was to strengthen and improve federal civil-rights laws.

Example: I gave Michael that book *which* I thought he might like.

There, Their, They're

There is an adverb specifying location.

Example: Many people love to visit a big city, but few of them could ever live *there*.

Their is a possessive pronoun.

Example: More employers are offering new benefits to *their* employees, such as daycare services and flexible scheduling.

They're is a contraction of "they are."

Example: *They're* hoping to reach a decision by the end of the day.

To, Too

To has many different uses in the English language, including the indication of direction and comparison. It is also used as an infinitive in verb phrases.

Example: Mary is driving *to* the beach tomorrow.

Example: Janet's painting is superior *to* Alan's painting.

Example: I try *to* run three miles every day.

Too generally means "in addition" or "more than enough."

Example: It is important that we consider Kevin's opinion, *too*.

Example: Yesterday, I ran *too* far and injured my foot.

Whether, If

Whether should be used when listing alternatives.

Example: Traci could not decide *whether* to order the fish or the chicken.

If should be used when referring to a future possibility.

Example: *If* Traci orders the fish, she will be served more quickly.

Your, You're

Your is a possessive pronoun.

Example: Sunscreen protects *your* skin from sun damage.

You're is a contraction of "you are."

Example: When *you're* at the beach, always remember to wear sunscreen.

Internalize the Rules

Now that you have reviewed the grammar and punctuation rules included in this chapter, you might decide to focus on improving your own speaking and writing where applicable. We've found that if you can internalize the rules and can simply recognize correct English by its "sound," you will do better on the tests. You should practice using proper English in your daily life to supplement the practice testing that you'll do; this will pay off in ways far beyond an improved PSAT or SAT score.

PART IV

Practicing for the SAT and PSAT

CHAPTER NINE

Practice Test 1 with Answers and Explanations

There are nine separate sections on this simulated test, including:

- One 25-minute Essay
- Five other 25-minute Verbal and Math Sections
- Two 20-minute Verbal and Math Sections
- One 10-minute Verbal Section

Work on only one section at a time and make every attempt to complete each section in the time allowed for that particular section. Carefully mark only one answer on your answer sheet for each question. Remember that you can and should write on the test itself to help you to correctly answer the questions.

Tear out pages 192–197 before you begin the test.

Begin your essay on this page. If you need more space, continue on the next page. Do not write outside of the essay box.

Start with number 1 for each new section. If a section has fewer questions than answer spaces, leave the extra answer spaces blank. Be sure to erase any errors or stray marks completely.

SECTION 2

1 Ⓐ Ⓑ Ⓒ Ⓓ Ⓔ	11 Ⓐ Ⓑ Ⓒ Ⓓ Ⓔ	21 Ⓐ Ⓑ Ⓒ Ⓓ Ⓔ	31 Ⓐ Ⓑ Ⓒ Ⓓ Ⓔ
2 Ⓐ Ⓑ Ⓒ Ⓓ Ⓔ	12 Ⓐ Ⓑ Ⓒ Ⓓ Ⓔ	22 Ⓐ Ⓑ Ⓒ Ⓓ Ⓔ	32 Ⓐ Ⓑ Ⓒ Ⓓ Ⓔ
3 Ⓐ Ⓑ Ⓒ Ⓓ Ⓔ	13 Ⓐ Ⓑ Ⓒ Ⓓ Ⓔ	23 Ⓐ Ⓑ Ⓒ Ⓓ Ⓔ	33 Ⓐ Ⓑ Ⓒ Ⓓ Ⓔ
4 Ⓐ Ⓑ Ⓒ Ⓓ Ⓔ	14 Ⓐ Ⓑ Ⓒ Ⓓ Ⓔ	24 Ⓐ Ⓑ Ⓒ Ⓓ Ⓔ	34 Ⓐ Ⓑ Ⓒ Ⓓ Ⓔ
5 Ⓐ Ⓑ Ⓒ Ⓓ Ⓔ	15 Ⓐ Ⓑ Ⓒ Ⓓ Ⓔ	25 Ⓐ Ⓑ Ⓒ Ⓓ Ⓔ	35 Ⓐ Ⓑ Ⓒ Ⓓ Ⓔ
6 Ⓐ Ⓑ Ⓒ Ⓓ Ⓔ	16 Ⓐ Ⓑ Ⓒ Ⓓ Ⓔ	26 Ⓐ Ⓑ Ⓒ Ⓓ Ⓔ	36 Ⓐ Ⓑ Ⓒ Ⓓ Ⓔ
7 Ⓐ Ⓑ Ⓒ Ⓓ Ⓔ	17 Ⓐ Ⓑ Ⓒ Ⓓ Ⓔ	27 Ⓐ Ⓑ Ⓒ Ⓓ Ⓔ	37 Ⓐ Ⓑ Ⓒ Ⓓ Ⓔ
8 Ⓐ Ⓑ Ⓒ Ⓓ Ⓔ	18 Ⓐ Ⓑ Ⓒ Ⓓ Ⓔ	28 Ⓐ Ⓑ Ⓒ Ⓓ Ⓔ	38 Ⓐ Ⓑ Ⓒ Ⓓ Ⓔ
9 Ⓐ Ⓑ Ⓒ Ⓓ Ⓔ	19 Ⓐ Ⓑ Ⓒ Ⓓ Ⓔ	29 Ⓐ Ⓑ Ⓒ Ⓓ Ⓔ	39 Ⓐ Ⓑ Ⓒ Ⓓ Ⓔ
10 Ⓐ Ⓑ Ⓒ Ⓓ Ⓔ	20 Ⓐ Ⓑ Ⓒ Ⓓ Ⓔ	30 Ⓐ Ⓑ Ⓒ Ⓓ Ⓔ	40 Ⓐ Ⓑ Ⓒ Ⓓ Ⓔ

SECTION 3

1 Ⓐ Ⓑ Ⓒ Ⓓ Ⓔ	11 Ⓐ Ⓑ Ⓒ Ⓓ Ⓔ	21 Ⓐ Ⓑ Ⓒ Ⓓ Ⓔ	31 Ⓐ Ⓑ Ⓒ Ⓓ Ⓔ
2 Ⓐ Ⓑ Ⓒ Ⓓ Ⓔ	12 Ⓐ Ⓑ Ⓒ Ⓓ Ⓔ	22 Ⓐ Ⓑ Ⓒ Ⓓ Ⓔ	32 Ⓐ Ⓑ Ⓒ Ⓓ Ⓔ
3 Ⓐ Ⓑ Ⓒ Ⓓ Ⓔ	13 Ⓐ Ⓑ Ⓒ Ⓓ Ⓔ	23 Ⓐ Ⓑ Ⓒ Ⓓ Ⓔ	33 Ⓐ Ⓑ Ⓒ Ⓓ Ⓔ
4 Ⓐ Ⓑ Ⓒ Ⓓ Ⓔ	14 Ⓐ Ⓑ Ⓒ Ⓓ Ⓔ	24 Ⓐ Ⓑ Ⓒ Ⓓ Ⓔ	34 Ⓐ Ⓑ Ⓒ Ⓓ Ⓔ
5 Ⓐ Ⓑ Ⓒ Ⓓ Ⓔ	15 Ⓐ Ⓑ Ⓒ Ⓓ Ⓔ	25 Ⓐ Ⓑ Ⓒ Ⓓ Ⓔ	35 Ⓐ Ⓑ Ⓒ Ⓓ Ⓔ
6 Ⓐ Ⓑ Ⓒ Ⓓ Ⓔ	16 Ⓐ Ⓑ Ⓒ Ⓓ Ⓔ	26 Ⓐ Ⓑ Ⓒ Ⓓ Ⓔ	36 Ⓐ Ⓑ Ⓒ Ⓓ Ⓔ
7 Ⓐ Ⓑ Ⓒ Ⓓ Ⓔ	17 Ⓐ Ⓑ Ⓒ Ⓓ Ⓔ	27 Ⓐ Ⓑ Ⓒ Ⓓ Ⓔ	37 Ⓐ Ⓑ Ⓒ Ⓓ Ⓔ
8 Ⓐ Ⓑ Ⓒ Ⓓ Ⓔ	18 Ⓐ Ⓑ Ⓒ Ⓓ Ⓔ	28 Ⓐ Ⓑ Ⓒ Ⓓ Ⓔ	38 Ⓐ Ⓑ Ⓒ Ⓓ Ⓔ
9 Ⓐ Ⓑ Ⓒ Ⓓ Ⓔ	19 Ⓐ Ⓑ Ⓒ Ⓓ Ⓔ	29 Ⓐ Ⓑ Ⓒ Ⓓ Ⓔ	39 Ⓐ Ⓑ Ⓒ Ⓓ Ⓔ
10 Ⓐ Ⓑ Ⓒ Ⓓ Ⓔ	20 Ⓐ Ⓑ Ⓒ Ⓓ Ⓔ	30 Ⓐ Ⓑ Ⓒ Ⓓ Ⓔ	40 Ⓐ Ⓑ Ⓒ Ⓓ Ⓔ

CAUTION Use the answer spaces in the grids below for Section 2 or Section 3 only if you are told to do so in your test book.

Student-Produced Responses

ONLY ANSWERS ENTERED IN THE CIRCLES IN EACH GRID WILL BE SCORED. YOU WILL NOT RECEIVE CREDIT FOR ANYTHING WRITTEN IN THE BOXES ABOVE THE CIRCLES.

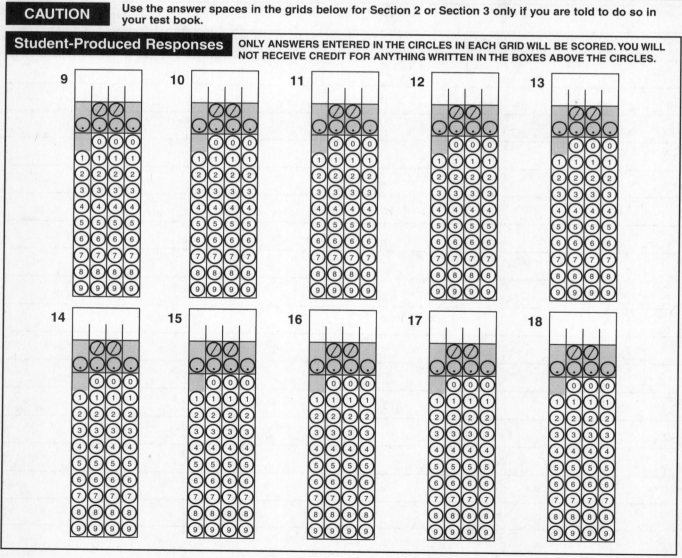

Start with number 1 for each new section. If a section has fewer questions than answer spaces, leave the extra answer spaces blank. Be sure to erase any errors or stray marks completely.

SECTION 4

1 Ⓐ Ⓑ Ⓒ Ⓓ Ⓔ	11 Ⓐ Ⓑ Ⓒ Ⓓ Ⓔ	21 Ⓐ Ⓑ Ⓒ Ⓓ Ⓔ	31 Ⓐ Ⓑ Ⓒ Ⓓ Ⓔ
2 Ⓐ Ⓑ Ⓒ Ⓓ Ⓔ	12 Ⓐ Ⓑ Ⓒ Ⓓ Ⓔ	22 Ⓐ Ⓑ Ⓒ Ⓓ Ⓔ	32 Ⓐ Ⓑ Ⓒ Ⓓ Ⓔ
3 Ⓐ Ⓑ Ⓒ Ⓓ Ⓔ	13 Ⓐ Ⓑ Ⓒ Ⓓ Ⓔ	23 Ⓐ Ⓑ Ⓒ Ⓓ Ⓔ	33 Ⓐ Ⓑ Ⓒ Ⓓ Ⓔ
4 Ⓐ Ⓑ Ⓒ Ⓓ Ⓔ	14 Ⓐ Ⓑ Ⓒ Ⓓ Ⓔ	24 Ⓐ Ⓑ Ⓒ Ⓓ Ⓔ	34 Ⓐ Ⓑ Ⓒ Ⓓ Ⓔ
5 Ⓐ Ⓑ Ⓒ Ⓓ Ⓔ	15 Ⓐ Ⓑ Ⓒ Ⓓ Ⓔ	25 Ⓐ Ⓑ Ⓒ Ⓓ Ⓔ	35 Ⓐ Ⓑ Ⓒ Ⓓ Ⓔ
6 Ⓐ Ⓑ Ⓒ Ⓓ Ⓔ	16 Ⓐ Ⓑ Ⓒ Ⓓ Ⓔ	26 Ⓐ Ⓑ Ⓒ Ⓓ Ⓔ	36 Ⓐ Ⓑ Ⓒ Ⓓ Ⓔ
7 Ⓐ Ⓑ Ⓒ Ⓓ Ⓔ	17 Ⓐ Ⓑ Ⓒ Ⓓ Ⓔ	27 Ⓐ Ⓑ Ⓒ Ⓓ Ⓔ	37 Ⓐ Ⓑ Ⓒ Ⓓ Ⓔ
8 Ⓐ Ⓑ Ⓒ Ⓓ Ⓔ	18 Ⓐ Ⓑ Ⓒ Ⓓ Ⓔ	28 Ⓐ Ⓑ Ⓒ Ⓓ Ⓔ	38 Ⓐ Ⓑ Ⓒ Ⓓ Ⓔ
9 Ⓐ Ⓑ Ⓒ Ⓓ Ⓔ	19 Ⓐ Ⓑ Ⓒ Ⓓ Ⓔ	29 Ⓐ Ⓑ Ⓒ Ⓓ Ⓔ	39 Ⓐ Ⓑ Ⓒ Ⓓ Ⓔ
10 Ⓐ Ⓑ Ⓒ Ⓓ Ⓔ	20 Ⓐ Ⓑ Ⓒ Ⓓ Ⓔ	30 Ⓐ Ⓑ Ⓒ Ⓓ Ⓔ	40 Ⓐ Ⓑ Ⓒ Ⓓ Ⓔ

SECTION 5

1 Ⓐ Ⓑ Ⓒ Ⓓ Ⓔ	11 Ⓐ Ⓑ Ⓒ Ⓓ Ⓔ	21 Ⓐ Ⓑ Ⓒ Ⓓ Ⓔ	31 Ⓐ Ⓑ Ⓒ Ⓓ Ⓔ
2 Ⓐ Ⓑ Ⓒ Ⓓ Ⓔ	12 Ⓐ Ⓑ Ⓒ Ⓓ Ⓔ	22 Ⓐ Ⓑ Ⓒ Ⓓ Ⓔ	32 Ⓐ Ⓑ Ⓒ Ⓓ Ⓔ
3 Ⓐ Ⓑ Ⓒ Ⓓ Ⓔ	13 Ⓐ Ⓑ Ⓒ Ⓓ Ⓔ	23 Ⓐ Ⓑ Ⓒ Ⓓ Ⓔ	33 Ⓐ Ⓑ Ⓒ Ⓓ Ⓔ
4 Ⓐ Ⓑ Ⓒ Ⓓ Ⓔ	14 Ⓐ Ⓑ Ⓒ Ⓓ Ⓔ	24 Ⓐ Ⓑ Ⓒ Ⓓ Ⓔ	34 Ⓐ Ⓑ Ⓒ Ⓓ Ⓔ
5 Ⓐ Ⓑ Ⓒ Ⓓ Ⓔ	15 Ⓐ Ⓑ Ⓒ Ⓓ Ⓔ	25 Ⓐ Ⓑ Ⓒ Ⓓ Ⓔ	35 Ⓐ Ⓑ Ⓒ Ⓓ Ⓔ
6 Ⓐ Ⓑ Ⓒ Ⓓ Ⓔ	16 Ⓐ Ⓑ Ⓒ Ⓓ Ⓔ	26 Ⓐ Ⓑ Ⓒ Ⓓ Ⓔ	36 Ⓐ Ⓑ Ⓒ Ⓓ Ⓔ
7 Ⓐ Ⓑ Ⓒ Ⓓ Ⓔ	17 Ⓐ Ⓑ Ⓒ Ⓓ Ⓔ	27 Ⓐ Ⓑ Ⓒ Ⓓ Ⓔ	37 Ⓐ Ⓑ Ⓒ Ⓓ Ⓔ
8 Ⓐ Ⓑ Ⓒ Ⓓ Ⓔ	18 Ⓐ Ⓑ Ⓒ Ⓓ Ⓔ	28 Ⓐ Ⓑ Ⓒ Ⓓ Ⓔ	38 Ⓐ Ⓑ Ⓒ Ⓓ Ⓔ
9 Ⓐ Ⓑ Ⓒ Ⓓ Ⓔ	19 Ⓐ Ⓑ Ⓒ Ⓓ Ⓔ	29 Ⓐ Ⓑ Ⓒ Ⓓ Ⓔ	39 Ⓐ Ⓑ Ⓒ Ⓓ Ⓔ
10 Ⓐ Ⓑ Ⓒ Ⓓ Ⓔ	20 Ⓐ Ⓑ Ⓒ Ⓓ Ⓔ	30 Ⓐ Ⓑ Ⓒ Ⓓ Ⓔ	40 Ⓐ Ⓑ Ⓒ Ⓓ Ⓔ

CAUTION Use the answer spaces in the grids below for Section 4 or Section 5 only if you are told to do so in your test book.

Student-Produced Responses ONLY ANSWERS ENTERED IN THE CIRCLES IN EACH GRID WILL BE SCORED. YOU WILL NOT RECEIVE CREDIT FOR ANYTHING WRITTEN IN THE BOXES ABOVE THE CIRCLES.

9   10   11   12   13

14   15   16   17   18

Start with number 1 for each new section. If a section has fewer questions than answer spaces, leave the extra answer spaces blank. Be sure to erase any errors or stray marks completely.

SECTION 6

1 Ⓐ Ⓑ Ⓒ Ⓓ Ⓔ	11 Ⓐ Ⓑ Ⓒ Ⓓ Ⓔ	21 Ⓐ Ⓑ Ⓒ Ⓓ Ⓔ	31 Ⓐ Ⓑ Ⓒ Ⓓ Ⓔ
2 Ⓐ Ⓑ Ⓒ Ⓓ Ⓔ	12 Ⓐ Ⓑ Ⓒ Ⓓ Ⓔ	22 Ⓐ Ⓑ Ⓒ Ⓓ Ⓔ	32 Ⓐ Ⓑ Ⓒ Ⓓ Ⓔ
3 Ⓐ Ⓑ Ⓒ Ⓓ Ⓔ	13 Ⓐ Ⓑ Ⓒ Ⓓ Ⓔ	23 Ⓐ Ⓑ Ⓒ Ⓓ Ⓔ	33 Ⓐ Ⓑ Ⓒ Ⓓ Ⓔ
4 Ⓐ Ⓑ Ⓒ Ⓓ Ⓔ	14 Ⓐ Ⓑ Ⓒ Ⓓ Ⓔ	24 Ⓐ Ⓑ Ⓒ Ⓓ Ⓔ	34 Ⓐ Ⓑ Ⓒ Ⓓ Ⓔ
5 Ⓐ Ⓑ Ⓒ Ⓓ Ⓔ	15 Ⓐ Ⓑ Ⓒ Ⓓ Ⓔ	25 Ⓐ Ⓑ Ⓒ Ⓓ Ⓔ	35 Ⓐ Ⓑ Ⓒ Ⓓ Ⓔ
6 Ⓐ Ⓑ Ⓒ Ⓓ Ⓔ	16 Ⓐ Ⓑ Ⓒ Ⓓ Ⓔ	26 Ⓐ Ⓑ Ⓒ Ⓓ Ⓔ	36 Ⓐ Ⓑ Ⓒ Ⓓ Ⓔ
7 Ⓐ Ⓑ Ⓒ Ⓓ Ⓔ	17 Ⓐ Ⓑ Ⓒ Ⓓ Ⓔ	27 Ⓐ Ⓑ Ⓒ Ⓓ Ⓔ	37 Ⓐ Ⓑ Ⓒ Ⓓ Ⓔ
8 Ⓐ Ⓑ Ⓒ Ⓓ Ⓔ	18 Ⓐ Ⓑ Ⓒ Ⓓ Ⓔ	28 Ⓐ Ⓑ Ⓒ Ⓓ Ⓔ	38 Ⓐ Ⓑ Ⓒ Ⓓ Ⓔ
9 Ⓐ Ⓑ Ⓒ Ⓓ Ⓔ	19 Ⓐ Ⓑ Ⓒ Ⓓ Ⓔ	29 Ⓐ Ⓑ Ⓒ Ⓓ Ⓔ	39 Ⓐ Ⓑ Ⓒ Ⓓ Ⓔ
10 Ⓐ Ⓑ Ⓒ Ⓓ Ⓔ	20 Ⓐ Ⓑ Ⓒ Ⓓ Ⓔ	30 Ⓐ Ⓑ Ⓒ Ⓓ Ⓔ	40 Ⓐ Ⓑ Ⓒ Ⓓ Ⓔ

SECTION 7

1 Ⓐ Ⓑ Ⓒ Ⓓ Ⓔ	11 Ⓐ Ⓑ Ⓒ Ⓓ Ⓔ	21 Ⓐ Ⓑ Ⓒ Ⓓ Ⓔ	31 Ⓐ Ⓑ Ⓒ Ⓓ Ⓔ
2 Ⓐ Ⓑ Ⓒ Ⓓ Ⓔ	12 Ⓐ Ⓑ Ⓒ Ⓓ Ⓔ	22 Ⓐ Ⓑ Ⓒ Ⓓ Ⓔ	32 Ⓐ Ⓑ Ⓒ Ⓓ Ⓔ
3 Ⓐ Ⓑ Ⓒ Ⓓ Ⓔ	13 Ⓐ Ⓑ Ⓒ Ⓓ Ⓔ	23 Ⓐ Ⓑ Ⓒ Ⓓ Ⓔ	33 Ⓐ Ⓑ Ⓒ Ⓓ Ⓔ
4 Ⓐ Ⓑ Ⓒ Ⓓ Ⓔ	14 Ⓐ Ⓑ Ⓒ Ⓓ Ⓔ	24 Ⓐ Ⓑ Ⓒ Ⓓ Ⓔ	34 Ⓐ Ⓑ Ⓒ Ⓓ Ⓔ
5 Ⓐ Ⓑ Ⓒ Ⓓ Ⓔ	15 Ⓐ Ⓑ Ⓒ Ⓓ Ⓔ	25 Ⓐ Ⓑ Ⓒ Ⓓ Ⓔ	35 Ⓐ Ⓑ Ⓒ Ⓓ Ⓔ
6 Ⓐ Ⓑ Ⓒ Ⓓ Ⓔ	16 Ⓐ Ⓑ Ⓒ Ⓓ Ⓔ	26 Ⓐ Ⓑ Ⓒ Ⓓ Ⓔ	36 Ⓐ Ⓑ Ⓒ Ⓓ Ⓔ
7 Ⓐ Ⓑ Ⓒ Ⓓ Ⓔ	17 Ⓐ Ⓑ Ⓒ Ⓓ Ⓔ	27 Ⓐ Ⓑ Ⓒ Ⓓ Ⓔ	37 Ⓐ Ⓑ Ⓒ Ⓓ Ⓔ
8 Ⓐ Ⓑ Ⓒ Ⓓ Ⓔ	18 Ⓐ Ⓑ Ⓒ Ⓓ Ⓔ	28 Ⓐ Ⓑ Ⓒ Ⓓ Ⓔ	38 Ⓐ Ⓑ Ⓒ Ⓓ Ⓔ
9 Ⓐ Ⓑ Ⓒ Ⓓ Ⓔ	19 Ⓐ Ⓑ Ⓒ Ⓓ Ⓔ	29 Ⓐ Ⓑ Ⓒ Ⓓ Ⓔ	39 Ⓐ Ⓑ Ⓒ Ⓓ Ⓔ
10 Ⓐ Ⓑ Ⓒ Ⓓ Ⓔ	20 Ⓐ Ⓑ Ⓒ Ⓓ Ⓔ	30 Ⓐ Ⓑ Ⓒ Ⓓ Ⓔ	40 Ⓐ Ⓑ Ⓒ Ⓓ Ⓔ

CAUTION Use the answer spaces in the grids below for Section 6 or Section 7 only if you are told to do so in your test book.

Student-Produced Responses ONLY ANSWERS ENTERED IN THE CIRCLES IN EACH GRID WILL BE SCORED. YOU WILL NOT RECEIVE CREDIT FOR ANYTHING WRITTEN IN THE BOXES ABOVE THE CIRCLES.

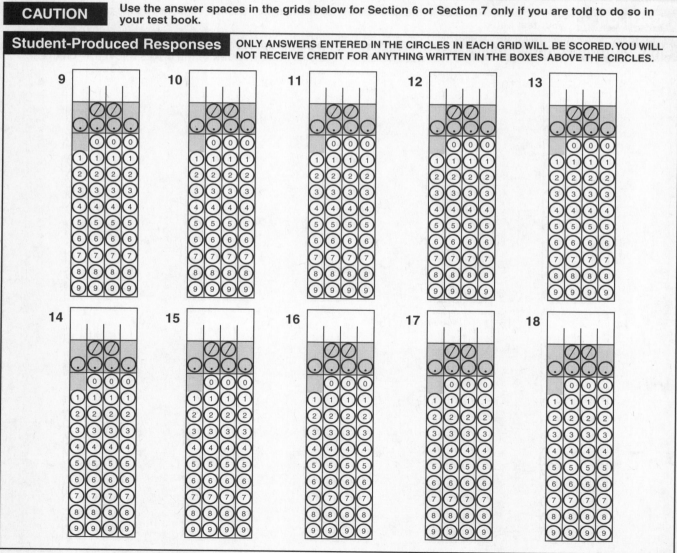

Start with number 1 for each new section. If a section has fewer questions than answer spaces, leave the extra answer spaces blank. Be sure to erase any errors or stray marks completely.

SECTION 8

1 Ⓐ Ⓑ Ⓒ Ⓓ Ⓔ	11 Ⓐ Ⓑ Ⓒ Ⓓ Ⓔ	21 Ⓐ Ⓑ Ⓒ Ⓓ Ⓔ	31 Ⓐ Ⓑ Ⓒ Ⓓ Ⓔ
2 Ⓐ Ⓑ Ⓒ Ⓓ Ⓔ	12 Ⓐ Ⓑ Ⓒ Ⓓ Ⓔ	22 Ⓐ Ⓑ Ⓒ Ⓓ Ⓔ	32 Ⓐ Ⓑ Ⓒ Ⓓ Ⓔ
3 Ⓐ Ⓑ Ⓒ Ⓓ Ⓔ	13 Ⓐ Ⓑ Ⓒ Ⓓ Ⓔ	23 Ⓐ Ⓑ Ⓒ Ⓓ Ⓔ	33 Ⓐ Ⓑ Ⓒ Ⓓ Ⓔ
4 Ⓐ Ⓑ Ⓒ Ⓓ Ⓔ	14 Ⓐ Ⓑ Ⓒ Ⓓ Ⓔ	24 Ⓐ Ⓑ Ⓒ Ⓓ Ⓔ	34 Ⓐ Ⓑ Ⓒ Ⓓ Ⓔ
5 Ⓐ Ⓑ Ⓒ Ⓓ Ⓔ	15 Ⓐ Ⓑ Ⓒ Ⓓ Ⓔ	25 Ⓐ Ⓑ Ⓒ Ⓓ Ⓔ	35 Ⓐ Ⓑ Ⓒ Ⓓ Ⓔ
6 Ⓐ Ⓑ Ⓒ Ⓓ Ⓔ	16 Ⓐ Ⓑ Ⓒ Ⓓ Ⓔ	26 Ⓐ Ⓑ Ⓒ Ⓓ Ⓔ	36 Ⓐ Ⓑ Ⓒ Ⓓ Ⓔ
7 Ⓐ Ⓑ Ⓒ Ⓓ Ⓔ	17 Ⓐ Ⓑ Ⓒ Ⓓ Ⓔ	27 Ⓐ Ⓑ Ⓒ Ⓓ Ⓔ	37 Ⓐ Ⓑ Ⓒ Ⓓ Ⓔ
8 Ⓐ Ⓑ Ⓒ Ⓓ Ⓔ	18 Ⓐ Ⓑ Ⓒ Ⓓ Ⓔ	28 Ⓐ Ⓑ Ⓒ Ⓓ Ⓔ	38 Ⓐ Ⓑ Ⓒ Ⓓ Ⓔ
9 Ⓐ Ⓑ Ⓒ Ⓓ Ⓔ	19 Ⓐ Ⓑ Ⓒ Ⓓ Ⓔ	29 Ⓐ Ⓑ Ⓒ Ⓓ Ⓔ	39 Ⓐ Ⓑ Ⓒ Ⓓ Ⓔ
10 Ⓐ Ⓑ Ⓒ Ⓓ Ⓔ	20 Ⓐ Ⓑ Ⓒ Ⓓ Ⓔ	30 Ⓐ Ⓑ Ⓒ Ⓓ Ⓔ	40 Ⓐ Ⓑ Ⓒ Ⓓ Ⓔ

SECTION 9

1 Ⓐ Ⓑ Ⓒ Ⓓ Ⓔ	11 Ⓐ Ⓑ Ⓒ Ⓓ Ⓔ	21 Ⓐ Ⓑ Ⓒ Ⓓ Ⓔ	31 Ⓐ Ⓑ Ⓒ Ⓓ Ⓔ
2 Ⓐ Ⓑ Ⓒ Ⓓ Ⓔ	12 Ⓐ Ⓑ Ⓒ Ⓓ Ⓔ	22 Ⓐ Ⓑ Ⓒ Ⓓ Ⓔ	32 Ⓐ Ⓑ Ⓒ Ⓓ Ⓔ
3 Ⓐ Ⓑ Ⓒ Ⓓ Ⓔ	13 Ⓐ Ⓑ Ⓒ Ⓓ Ⓔ	23 Ⓐ Ⓑ Ⓒ Ⓓ Ⓔ	33 Ⓐ Ⓑ Ⓒ Ⓓ Ⓔ
4 Ⓐ Ⓑ Ⓒ Ⓓ Ⓔ	14 Ⓐ Ⓑ Ⓒ Ⓓ Ⓔ	24 Ⓐ Ⓑ Ⓒ Ⓓ Ⓔ	34 Ⓐ Ⓑ Ⓒ Ⓓ Ⓔ
5 Ⓐ Ⓑ Ⓒ Ⓓ Ⓔ	15 Ⓐ Ⓑ Ⓒ Ⓓ Ⓔ	25 Ⓐ Ⓑ Ⓒ Ⓓ Ⓔ	35 Ⓐ Ⓑ Ⓒ Ⓓ Ⓔ
6 Ⓐ Ⓑ Ⓒ Ⓓ Ⓔ	16 Ⓐ Ⓑ Ⓒ Ⓓ Ⓔ	26 Ⓐ Ⓑ Ⓒ Ⓓ Ⓔ	36 Ⓐ Ⓑ Ⓒ Ⓓ Ⓔ
7 Ⓐ Ⓑ Ⓒ Ⓓ Ⓔ	17 Ⓐ Ⓑ Ⓒ Ⓓ Ⓔ	27 Ⓐ Ⓑ Ⓒ Ⓓ Ⓔ	37 Ⓐ Ⓑ Ⓒ Ⓓ Ⓔ
8 Ⓐ Ⓑ Ⓒ Ⓓ Ⓔ	18 Ⓐ Ⓑ Ⓒ Ⓓ Ⓔ	28 Ⓐ Ⓑ Ⓒ Ⓓ Ⓔ	38 Ⓐ Ⓑ Ⓒ Ⓓ Ⓔ
9 Ⓐ Ⓑ Ⓒ Ⓓ Ⓔ	19 Ⓐ Ⓑ Ⓒ Ⓓ Ⓔ	29 Ⓐ Ⓑ Ⓒ Ⓓ Ⓔ	39 Ⓐ Ⓑ Ⓒ Ⓓ Ⓔ
10 Ⓐ Ⓑ Ⓒ Ⓓ Ⓔ	20 Ⓐ Ⓑ Ⓒ Ⓓ Ⓔ	30 Ⓐ Ⓑ Ⓒ Ⓓ Ⓔ	40 Ⓐ Ⓑ Ⓒ Ⓓ Ⓔ

ESSAY
Time—25 minutes

You have 25 minutes to write an essay based on the topic presented below. Do not write on another topic. Your essay should be written on the lined pages provided. For the best results, write on every line and keep your handwriting to a reasonable, legible size. Be sure to fully develop your point of view, present your ideas clearly and logically, and use the English language precisely.

Think carefully about the following issue and assignment:

> The old saying, "it's not what you know, but who you know" is an increasingly applicable statement. With the current job market, it is ever more difficult for qualified applicants to stand out. Often, a corporation receives several hundred résumés for a single position. Given the challenge of sorting through them all, it might become a question of whose references are the best. Many argue that such a mentality reduces the job search to a game and that credentials are only marginally important in many fields because the majority of candidates are equally qualified.

Assignment: Are references really more important than credentials for success in the workplace? Plan and write an essay in which you develop your point of view on this topic. Support your position with reasoning and solid examples taken from your personal experience, observations, reading, or studies.

WRITE YOUR ESSAY ON PAGES 192 AND 193.

If you finish writing before your time is called, check your work on this section only. Do not turn to any other section in the test.

SECTION 2
Time—25 minutes
24 Questions

Directions: For each of the questions in this section, choose the best answer and fill in the corresponding circle on your answer sheet.

Each sentence that follows has either one or two blanks. Each blank indicates that a word has been omitted from the sentence. Following each sentence are five words or sets of words. Select the word or set of words that, when inserted into the sentence in place of the blank(s), best fits the context of the sentence as a whole.

1. Because the employee's motives were found to be -------, no disciplinary action will be taken against him for the mistake.

    (A) absurd
    (B) gratuitous
    (C) improvised
    (D) benign
    (E) inevitable

2. The burglar chose to enter by the least ------- window because both doors were ------- by closed-circuit cameras.

    (A) crucial . . inspected
    (B) overt . . transmitted
    (C) translucent . . corroborated
    (D) penetrable . . neglected
    (E) conspicuous . . observed

3. Jennifer loves roses for the ------- appeal of their petals and leaves, but I am most ------- by their olfactory properties.

    (A) aesthetic . . enthralled
    (B) acrid . . interested
    (C) nurturing . . persuaded
    (D) visual . . displeased
    (E) tacit . . disenchanted

4. Police will tell you that strange behavior escalates on nights when a full moon occurs; therefore, many officers insist that the moon holds powers of -------.

    (A) contradiction
    (B) entrancement
    (C) enlightenment
    (D) prostration
    (E) debilitation

5. Many students in our history class were irritated when the professor ------- the focus of the lecture to share his own personal opinions.

    (A) adhered to
    (B) responded to
    (C) strayed from
    (D) drew upon
    (E) argued with

6. When Jonathan reached camp, he walked with a ------- stride, evidence of his long day on horse-back.

    (A) carefree
    (B) fervent
    (C) forceful
    (D) labored
    (E) balanced

7. Paris, France, is ------- into small governmental units, each having its own city hall and local autonomy; this system allows for the most effective communication with the citizens.

    (A) envisioned
    (B) cordoned
    (C) organized
    (D) marooned
    (E) circumscribed

GO ON TO THE NEXT PAGE

8. Christine will never visit that hair stylist again
   after what ------- during her last appointment;
   her hair was a mess!

   (A) exclaimed
   (B) arrived
   (C) transpired
   (D) burgeoned
   (E) imploded

Each passage that follows is accompanied by several questions based on the content of the passage. Answer the questions based on what is either stated or implied in each passage. Be sure to read any introductory material that is provided.

Questions 1–12 are based on the following passages.

Passage 1

Generations of Americans have been enthralled with fad diets. We have struggled to maintain low-fat, low-carbohydrate, sugar-free, and liquid-only diets. We obsess over calorie
Line
5 counting and restricting certain "bad" foods. Indulgence is off-limits, so we enlist the aid of diet pills, the food pyramid, and countless other devices. Diets range from respectable to dubious and even dangerous. Losing weight the
10 disciplined way seems to have fallen out of fashion. Many people in the U.S. will probably never achieve a healthy lifestyle, one in which they eat a variety of healthy foods, moderate their food intake, and exercise regularly.

Passage 2

15 Following fad diets has led to healthier lifestyles for some Americans, but these diets often prove unsustainable. The main problem is the tendency to gain back the lost weight after regressing to old eating habits. The good
20 news, however, is that as more research is conducted and more diets are shown to fail, a growing number of people are realizing that dieting is not the key to long-term weight loss. It is becoming increasingly hard to ignore the
25 evidence that a lifestyle of sensible eating and exercise is the path to health. Perhaps we are on the cusp of an exciting new era of health and vitality.

9. The author of Passage 1 would most likely assert which of the following about "indulgence" (line 6)?

  (A) Diet pills are an effective means to avoid indulgence.

  (B) Indulgence is not something healthy people experience.

  (C) Indulgence is a dangerous vice incompatible with weight loss.

  (D) The wholesale condemnation of it is unnaturally restrictive.

  (E) The food pyramid permits it in various cases.

10. The author of Passage 2 would most likely respond to the last sentence in Passage 1 by

  (A) arguing that the effectiveness of dieting is declining, so fewer people are adhering to strict diets

  (B) suggesting that better diets exist to stimulate sustained weight loss

  (C) observing that increased awareness of the disadvantages of dieting is actually reforming people's lifestyle decisions

  (D) questioning whether the public will ever be able to avoid falling for illegitimate diets

  (E) noting that while diets persist, people are following them for shorter periods of time

11. The two passages differ in their views of eating habits in that Passage 1 states that

  (A) a healthy lifestyle is easy to achieve

  (B) fad diets are an inevitable part of American culture

  (C) diets establish eating habits for long-term health

  (D) while eating habits improve, exercise continues to stagnate

  (E) dangerous eating habits will expose fad diets

GO ON TO THE NEXT PAGE

12. Which generalization about lifestyle is supported by both passages?

   (A) Diets provide a solid framework for a healthy lifestyle.

   (B) A healthy lifestyle forbids indulgence.

   (C) Healthy lifestyles are elusive for everyone.

   (D) Disciplined eating and exercise are the keys to a healthy lifestyle.

   (E) The healthy lifestyle of the future will rely solely on regular caloric management.

GO ON TO THE NEXT PAGE ⟶

Questions 13–24 are based on the following passage.

The following passage examines the issue of climatic changes on the Earth.

While some of the media is often quick to paint a picture of global warming as the cause of the next ice age, the question remains as to whether the phenomenon actually exists and whether it poses any real danger to mankind. The research of Accu-Weather, the world's leading commercial forecaster, suggests that there has been a .45-degree Celsius increase in temperature over the last century. Satellite data conflicts with this statement, indicating that a moderate cooling has occurred over the past 18 years. This data is thought to be the more germane of the two as it is not affected by the urban heat island effect in major cities, which could alter the readings of ground-based thermometers used by Accu-Weather.

Because much of the gas thought to contribute to global warming (CO_2) is water vapor released by natural processes, it is hard to say whether humans are responsible for any perceived change in global temperature. Even if we are responsible, any small change in temperature is unlikely to have the catastrophic repercussions that some of the media likes to foretell. The ice caps will not melt as the result of a relatively small increase in temperature; the likely impacts of such climate change are warmer oceans and an expansion of vegetation—at one point in history, the Vikings were able to farm the now icy continent of Greenland as a result of higher temperatures.

While many politicians decry presently acceptable levels of CO_2 emissions, many scientists are unconvinced that it is necessary to change CO_2 levels. In fact, a massive reduction in the amount of CO_2 released by the major industrialized nations might not have an effect on the perceived warming. Drastically limiting the use of fossil fuels would instead raise energy costs worldwide and impair industrial progress within modernized nations. Although perhaps a shift away from fossil fuels is forthcoming (they will eventually run out), a sudden, forced decrease in their use, as proposed by some international coalitions, is not the answer. It would instead be far more beneficial to the planet to increase reforestation efforts and attempt to limit the clear-cutting of valuable rainforest lands. Every green plant on earth serves as a carbon-sink, releasing oxygen while consuming CO_2. The oceans serve the same purpose. Holding off destruction in the tropics would be just as effective in decreasing greenhouse-gas emissions worldwide as would a dramatic decrease in fossil fuel use. In addition, biomass could potentially be converted into materials to replace cement, steel, and plastic, which take large amounts of energy to create and do little to store energy themselves.

Even making these changes, no one can be sure that the apparent global warming trend will change. There are indeed sustainable practices that we can adopt to improve our situation worldwide, but beyond that, it may best be left in Mother Nature's hands.

13. In line 13, "germane" most nearly means

(A) conflicting
(B) convincing
(C) carefully prepared
(D) dissentious
(E) relevant

14. The reference to "urban heat island effect" (lines 13–14) is used to

(A) suggest that cities appear cooler in satellite data than they actually are
(B) debunk ground-level temperature data in climate analysis
(C) establish the link between cities and greenhouse-gas emissions
(D) argue that cities disproportionately produce greenhouse gases
(E) criticize satellite data for misrepresenting city temperatures

GO ON TO THE NEXT PAGE

15. In line 23, the reference to "the media" emphasizes the

(A) public concern over the global warming
trend
(B) intense debate over global warming
(C) tendency to sensationalize the problems of
global warming
(D) the impendence of major changes to the
Earth from global warming
(E) the multitude of problems emerging from
increased greenhouse-gas emissions

16. The phrase "catastrophic repercussions" (lines
23–34) refers to

(A) industrial greenhouse-gas emissions
(B) rising average temperatures worldwide
(C) farming once frozen land
(D) abundant greenhouse-gas emissions from
nature
(E) deleterious changes to Earth's natural
systems

17. The "expansion of vegetation" referred to in
lines 27–28 most directly supports the claim that

(A) people would benefit from increased plant
growth because of global warming
(B) greater biomass upsets the delicate balance
of atmospheric gases
(C) melting ice caps will cause sea levels to rise
(D) Vikings once farmed Greenland during a
warm period on Earth
(E) the Earth has a deficit of plant life

18. In lines 31–34, the author portrays the "many
scientists" as

(A) reflective
(B) dissenting
(C) demeaning
(D) objectionable
(E) conciliatory

19. Lines 34–37 ("In fact…perceived warming.")
describe a

(A) theory
(B) characteristic
(C) criterion
(D) conclusion
(E) premise

20. The two sentences that begin with "Although
perhaps …" in lines 40–44 serve to express

(A) a proposal
(B) an incentive
(C) an alternative
(D) a perception
(E) a technique

21. The "international coalitions" mentioned in line
44 most likely refer to

(A) industrial firms in similar sectors
(B) friendly governments
(C) groups united by a common ethic
(D) a spirit of compromise between industry
and consumer
(E) competitors to the fossil-fuel industry

22. The biomass reference in line 55 serve to support

(A) the claim that increased plant life because of
global warming is beneficial to humans
(B) the unforeseen effect of global warming on
carbon sequestration
(C) the theory that slowing deforestation is a
better means to combat global warming
(D) the denial of fossil fuels' role in greenhouse-gas emissions
(E) the image of the Earth as a vibrant and
healthy ecosystem

GO ON TO THE NEXT PAGE

23. The passage suggests that "sustainable practices" (lines 61–62)

    (A)   would solve global warming

    (B)   have only limited possibility to mitigate climate change

    (C)   are unlikely to be adopted by people world-wide

    (D)   would become economical if more people adopted them

    (E)   spring from questionable research

24. In line 64, "Mother Nature's hands" refers to the

    (A)   bounty of the Earth

    (B)   international coalitions' use of fossil fuels

    (C)   role of chance

    (D)   immutable forces of nature

    (E)   depths of the Earth

STOP

**If you finish before your time is up, check your work on this section only.
You may not turn to any other section in the test.**

SECTION 3
Time—25 minutes
20 Questions

Directions: Solve each problem and determine which is the best of the answer choices given. Fill in the corresponding circle on your answer sheet. Use any available space to solve the problems.

Reference Information

$A = \Pi r^2$
$C = 2\Pi r$ $A = lw$ $A = \frac{1}{2}bh$ $V = lwh$ $V = \Pi r^2 h$ $c^2 = a^2 + b^2$ Special Right Triangles

The number of degrees of arc in a circle is 360.
The sum of the measures in degrees of the angles of a triangle is 180.

---

1. If $(x - 4) + 4 = 17$, what is the value of x?

(A) 25
(B) 21
(C) 17
(D) 13
(E) 9

3. If $3a + b = 7$, what is the value of $5a + 2b$?

(A) $4 + 10a$
(B) $7 - 3a$
(C) $14 - a$
(D) $21 + 2a$
(E) $25 - a$

2. Which of the following numbers has the digit 5 in the thousandths place?

(A) 5,000.00
(B) 50.0
(C) 0.05
(D) 0.005
(E) 0.0005

GO ON TO THE NEXT PAGE

4. Mandy and Jordan each bought some notebooks and a three-ring binder. Mandy paid $5.85 for 3 notebooks and 1 binder. Jordan paid $4.65 for 2 notebooks and 1 binder. What is the price of one of the notebooks?

   (A) $2.70
   (B) $2.25
   (C) $1.80
   (D) $1.20
   (E) $0.75

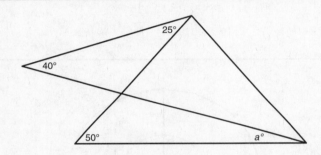

5. In the figure above, what is the value of *a*?

   (A) 15
   (B) 25
   (C) 30
   (D) 45
   (E) 115

6. If $3^{x-1} = 243$, what is the value of *x*?

   (A) -4
   (B) 1
   (C) 3
   (D) 5
   (E) 6

7. What percent of 5 is 7?

   (A) 14%
   (B) 35%
   (C) 71%
   (D) 140%
   (E) 157%

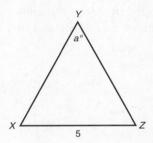

Note: Figure not drawn to scale.

8. In the figure above, *XY* = *YZ*. If *a* = 40°, then *XY* =

   (A) 9.5
   (B) 8.75
   (C) 7.75
   (D) 6.25
   (E) 5.50

9. What is the slope of a line that passes through the origin and the point (-6, 2)?

   (A) 3
   (B) $\frac{1}{3}$
   (C) $-\frac{1}{3}$
   (D) -3
   (E) -6

GO ON TO THE NEXT PAGE

10. The length of a rectangle is 3 times the width. If the area of the rectangle is 48, what is the length?

(A) 16
(B) 12
(C) 9
(D) 6
(E) 4

11. If x is divided by 7, the remainder is 4. What is the remainder if $2x$ is divided by 7?

(A) 1
(B) 4
(C) 5
(D) 7
(E) 8

12. Gary has turtles, cats, and birds for pets. The number of birds he has is four more than the number of turtles, and the number of cats is two times the number of birds. Of the following, which could be the total number of Gary's pets?

(A) 14
(B) 18
(C) 20
(D) 22
(E) 26

13. If g is an integer, which of the following could NOT equal $\sqrt{g^2}$?

(A) 0
(B) 1
(C) 4
(D) $\sqrt{8}$
(E) $\sqrt{9}$

14. Set A contains five consecutive integers. Set B contains all integers that result from adding 4 to each of the integers in Set A and also contains all integers that result from subtracting 4 from each of the integers in Set A. How many more integers are there in Set B than in Set A?

(A) 8
(B) 6
(C) 5
(D) 1
(E) 0

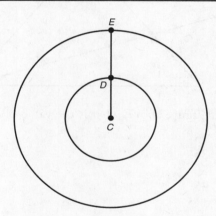

15. In the figure above, both circles have their centers at point C, and point D lies on segment CE. If $CD = 3$ and $DE = 5$, what is the ratio of the area of the larger circle to the area of the smaller circle?

(A) 3:1
(B) 5:3
(C) 8:3
(D) 25:9
(E) 64:9

GO ON TO THE NEXT PAGE

16. If x is a positive integer and $\frac{7x + 6}{5x} = \frac{4}{5}$, then $x = ?$

(A) 5
(B) 4
(C) 3
(D) 2
(E) 1

Multiply x by 3.

Add 4 to this product.

Divide this sum by 2.

17. Which of the following is the result obtained by performing the operations described above?

(A) $\frac{3x}{2}$

(B) $\frac{3x + 4}{2}$

(C) $\frac{3(x + 4)}{2}$

(D) $\frac{3}{2}x$

(E) $12x$

---

18. If $r \times s \times t = 56$, where r, s, and t are integers and $r > s > t$, what is the greatest possible value of r?

(A) 1
(B) 7
(C) 8
(D) 14
(E) 28

19. If a and b are integers and $a + b = 3a + 6$, which of the following must be true?

I. a is even
II. b is even
III. $a^2 = b^2$

(A) I only
(B) II only
(C) I and II only
(D) II and III only
(E) I and III only

---

20. In a certain music store, CDs were put on display and assigned prices for May. Each month after that, the price was 20% less than the price for the previous month. If the price of a CD was d dollars in May, what was the price in August?

(A) $0.2d$
(B) $0.3d$
(C) $0.512d$
(D) $0.64d$
(E) $0.8d$

S T O P

If you finish before your time is up, check your work on this section only.
You may not turn to any other section in the test.

SECTION 4
Time—25 minutes
24 Questions

Directions: For each of the questions in this section, choose the best answer and fill in the corresponding circle on your answer sheet.

Each sentence that follows has either one or two blanks. Each blank indicates that a word has been omitted from the sentence. Following each sentence are five words or sets of words. Select the word or set of words that, when inserted into the sentence in place of the blank(s), best fits the context of the sentence as a whole.

---

1. The frown on his face ------- that he was growing increasingly impatient with the slow-moving traffic.

   (A) surmised
   (B) comprehended
   (C) gratified
   (D) denoted
   (E) implemented

2. Whenever John arrived late to school, he entered by the back door to ------- the ------- glances of Principal Warner.

   (A) alleviate . . curious
   (B) avoid . . cutting
   (C) delay . . conciliatory
   (D) escape . . compassionate
   (E) elicit . . comprehensive

3. Squirrels spend much time in summer and fall hoarding nuts and storing them for ------- in the winter.

   (A) incorporation
   (B) rejection
   (C) consumption
   (D) distraction
   (E) preparation

4. My mother and I started quilting a few years ago as a ------- to salvage many old items of clothing that might previously have been -------.

   (A) method . . valuable
   (B) way . . expensive
   (C) means . . discarded
   (D) product . . useful
   (E) system . . mediocre

5. The air in a room with several houseplants can be more ------- with oxygen than a room without plants.

   (A) ripe
   (B) lean
   (C) saturated
   (D) replaced
   (E) improved

GO ON TO THE NEXT PAGE

Each passage that follows is accompanied by several questions based on the content of the passage. Answer the questions based on what is either stated or implied in each passage. Be sure to read any introductory material that is provided.

Questions 6–7 are based on the following passage.

In Rembrandt's day, many of his fellow painters portrayed their characters much like the idealized gods of Greek and Roman mythology. Rembrandt differed by painting

Line
5 people in a more realistic and humble manner. He used himself, his family members, and even beggars as models. He viewed these people as being just as worthy of being immortalized in art as mythological figures. He also fittingly

10 enhanced his work by the use of *chiaroscuro*, a technique where light striking the figures dramatically contrasts with a dark background. As a man, Rembrandt emulated his paintings and remained true to his singular artistic vision

15 while casting his own light on the darkness of conformity.

6. Why does the author specifically use the word "fittingly" in line 9 to describe how Rembrandt employed the use of *chiaroscuro*?

(A) The author wants to imply that Rembrandt had the courage to use the innovative technique of *chiaroscuro*.

(B) The author wants to show that because Rembrandt viewed common people as worthy of being immortalized, then it is appropriate that he would illuminate them in his paintings.

(C) The author wants to depict Rembrandt as someone who remained humble despite being an accomplished painter.

(D) The author wants to illustrate that while Rembrandt was a talented artist, he was ignorant about Greek and Roman mythology.

(E) The author wants to demonstrate that Rembrandt is still well-known and respected today.

7. According to the information in this passage, Rembrandt's philosophy of art would probably be most analogous to the philosophy of which of these other artists?

(A) A sculptor who obsesses about her work so much that she often neglects to sleep.

(B) A painter who exclusively depicts scenes from Greek and Roman mythology.

(C) A musician who pays homage to fellow songwriters by composing music with elements of other songwriters' works.

(D) A photographer who develops her film with light striking the figures that contrasts dramatically with a dark background.

(E) An architect who focuses on simple designs when the trend in architecture is towards ornate structures.

GO ON TO THE NEXT PAGE ⟶

Questions 8–9 are based on the following passage.

Wally felt like one of the many overstuffed envelopes Ruth had sent to him during
the long war. Now that he was reunited with
his wife, he couldn't contain the secret any
Line
5   longer! He just barely got the words out of his
mouth that he had been diligently saving all of
his pay for a down payment on a new home,
when Ruth unexpectedly starting laughing.
"I've got a secret, too," she said, taking him by
10 the hand. He followed her into the kitchen,
where she pulled a wrinkly old bag out of the
cupboard. From this unassuming bag, she
produced a huge wad of cash, and exclaimed,
"We can buy a really big house now!"

8. The comparison in line 1–3 of Wally to
   an overstuffed envelope is

   (A) an analogy
   (B) hyperbole
   (C) a simile
   (D) a metaphor
   (E) personification

9. What can the reader infer from Ruth's exclamation in line 14, "We can buy a really big house
   now"?

   (A) That Ruth is somewhat materialistic
   (B) That Ruth had also been saving money for
       a down payment
   (C) That Ruth was happy that Wally was home
   (D) That Ruth felt that her secret was better
       than Wally's secret
   (E) That Ruth is terrible at keeping secrets

GO ON TO THE NEXT PAGE

Questions 10–18 are based on the following passage.

In this passage, the origin and meaning of the Chinese zodiac are discussed.

Everyday one takes for granted the ease of finding out what date it is. Most people in the world today follow the Gregorian calendar, which

Line
5   is based on the solar cycle and keeps track of approximately 365.24 days each year. This has not always been the case, however. In ancient China, the calendar was based on the lunar cycle and consisted of years represented by a cycle of 12 animals. Although it was essentially precise in the

10 long run, each year had a varying number of days.

The origins of the 12 animals are deeply mythological, with the story being passed down for countless generations. A common telling of the tale includes a celebration to honor the Jade

15 Emperor, with all the animals expected to pay tribute to him on the night of the new year. The first 12 to arrive would be held in high esteem.

To reach the Emperor's Palace, the animals first had to cross a rushing river. The rat arrived

20 first through his cunning, climbing atop the ox, who was a much stronger swimmer than the rat. The ox received second place, followed shortly thereafter by the tiger, the strength of both allowing them to finish quickly. The rabbit came

25 next, his agility displayed in jumps from stone to stone across the river. Next came the mighty and majestic dragon, who flew across the river; when asked why he was not first, he replied that he needed to make rain for the people of Earth and

30 was thus delayed. His kindness earned him the fifth place in the cycle. During the dragon's explanation there was a galloping sound, signaling the arrival of the horse. Suddenly, though, hidden coiled around the leg of the horse, appeared the

35 snake, nearly as cunning as the rat, who darted in front of the horse, taking sixth place. The horse came in seventh just as a raft reached the shore with three more animals. The sheep (eighth), the monkey (ninth), and the rooster (tenth) had

40 worked together to build a raft and traverse the river using their combined efforts. For this feat they were rewarded in the order that they stepped off of the raft. Next to arrive was the dog,

who was met with questioning looks. Supposedly

45 the best swimmer, the dog was late because he took a bath in the refreshing waters of the river. His vanity nearly cost him the race. Last was the lazy pig, who stopped on the other side of the river for a feast before attempting to cross and

50 was so weighed down by his meal that he arrived only moments before the Emperor declared the race finished.

Missing from this list of animals is the cat. Sadly, he was also a victim of the rat's cunning;

55 the day prior to the race the rat informed the cat that he would awaken him before the race began, so as to allow the cat to rest and save his strength for it. The day of the race arrived and the cat continued to sleep while the rat took his spot atop

60 the ox. When the cat awoke, the race was finished, and he has since hated the rat for what he did.

Beyond the 12-year distinctions that the animals of the Zodiac lend to the calendar, there

65 is an additional 10-year overlay of five elements: water, wood, fire, metal, and earth. Each of these elements occurs 2 years in a row, in balance with the Yang and Yin (governing forces of all things). Even-numbered years are Yang, and odd-

70 numbered years are Yin. When all factors are combined, the result is a 60-year repeating calendar, the current cycle of which began in 1984.

Still today, the Chinese New Year is cele-

75 brated, and the calendar is followed to a certain degree by many. There are great astrological purposes to the Zodiac, the common belief being that the animal who governs the time of a person's birth will influence his or her person-

80 ality for life. Whether that is true is up for debate; the calendar already seems suitably ornate without the additional layer of complexity.

GO ON TO THE NEXT PAGE

10. Which statement best summarizes the description of the Gregorian and ancient Chinese calendars in lines 2–10?

    (A) Solar calendars are more precise than lunar calendars.
    (B) The Gregorian calendar is ubiquitous, but not because it is the superior model.
    (C) The ancient Chinese calendar has unique advantages over the Gregorian one.
    (D) The two calendars are suitably precise, but each has unique characteristics.
    (E) Animals representing years simplified the process of counting days.

11. Lines 11–13 ("The origins...countless generations") suggest that the author

    (A) questions the truth of the story
    (B) reveres the wisdom of the story
    (C) cannot trace the story to its beginning
    (D) admires Chinese culture
    (E) is very knowledgeable about Chinese mythology

12. The central contrast between the second paragraph (lines 11–17) and the third (lines 18–52) is best described in which terms?

    (A) The second paragraph offers a hypothesis that the third paragraph supports with evidence.
    (B) The third paragraph elaborates on the conclusion drawn in the second paragraph.
    (C) The second paragraph defines a problem that the third paragraph analyzes.
    (D) The second paragraph introduces a narrative that the third paragraph recounts.
    (E) The second paragraph describes a concept that the third paragraph defames.

13. In lines 26–31, the author portrays the dragon as

    (A) benevolent
    (B) mediocre
    (C) maladroit
    (D) self-assured
    (E) vain

14. In describing the ways that the animals cross the river the author illustrates all of the following virtues EXCEPT

    (A) chastity
    (B) industriousness
    (C) teamwork
    (D) dexterity
    (E) altruism

15. The story of the finishing order of the animals serves as

    (A) a theory explaining why the ancient calendar uses a 12-year scheme
    (B) the myth of the creation of time
    (C) the impetus for the creation of a cyclic calendar
    (D) an explanation for the arrangement of the animals in the calendar
    (E) a rebuttal to the praises of the Gregorian calendar

16. The two sentences that begin with "Beyond the 12-year distinctions..." in lines 62–67 serve to express the

    (A) results of attempting to simplify such a complex idea as time
    (B) theories of the spiritual significance of any given day
    (C) criticism over the complexity of the Chinese calendar
    (D) perceptions of the Chinese calendar as a complex spiritual instrument for measuring days
    (E) techniques some Chinese people use to distinguish individual days over many years

GO ON TO THE NEXT PAGE

17. In lines 72–80, the author portrays the astrology of the Chinese zodiac as

    (A) frivolous yet fetching
    (B) complex and drab
    (C) common but opaque
    (D) delusive and spurious
    (E) amusing but vague

18. The passage serves mainly to

    (A) explain how the ancient Chinese calendar is better than the Gregorian calendar
    (B) assert that the Chinese calendar's mythic foundation stands up to modern standards of precision
    (C) correct misconceptions about the significance of the ancient Chinese calendar
    (D) entertain the reader with a humorous anecdote
    (E) expose the reader to a subject few people know about in detail

GO ON TO THE NEXT PAGE

Questions 19–24 are based on the following passage.

This passage explores the similarities between humans and our close genetic relatives, chimpanzees.

Scientists know very little about the eating habits of our ancestors from over two and a half million years ago. To solve this problem, scientists have started examining chimpanzees' hunting behavior and diet to find clues about our own prehistoric past.

Studying chimpanzees might be beneficial because modern humans and chimpanzees are very similar genetically. Experts believe that chimpanzees share about 98.5% of the human DNA sequence. If this is true, humans are more closely related to chimpanzees than to any other animal species.

In the early 1960s, English primatologist Dr. Jane Goodall began studying chimpanzees in Tanzania. Before that time, scientists believed that chimpanzees were strict vegetarians. It was Goodall who first reported that meat was a natural part of the chimpanzee diet. In fact, Goodall discovered that chimpanzees are actually very proficient hunters. Individual chimpanzees have been known to hunt and eat more than 150 small animals each year. Some of the chimpanzees' favorite prey are the feral pig, various small antelope species, and the colobus monkey, a dietary staple. In one notable study, the red colobus monkey accounted for more than 80% of the animals eaten by one group of chimpanzees.

Despite these findings, scientists still maintain that chimpanzees are mostly fruit-eating creatures. In fact, meat composes only about 3% of the chimpanzee diet. This is substantially less than the quantity of meat consumed by the average human. Studies show that chimpanzees do most of their hunting in the dry months of August and September. During the dry season, food shortages in the forest cause chimpanzees' body weight to drop.

Consequently, chimpanzees supplement their diets with meat. During the height of the dry season, the estimated meat intake is about 65 grams per day per adult chimpanzee. This is comparable to the quantity of meat eaten by humans who forage when other food sources are scarce. Chimpanzees' eating habits also closely resemble those of the early human hunter-gatherers.

Humans and chimpanzees are the only members of the Great Ape family that hunt and eat meat on a regular basis. However, like chimpanzees, humans are not truly carnivorous creatures. In fact, most ancient humans ate a diet composed primarily of plants, and even modern humans are considered omnivores because they eat fruits, vegetables, and meat.

Most people assume that food choices are based solely on nutritional costs and benefits. Although it is clear that the hunting habits of chimpanzees are guided mostly by nutritional needs, some aspects of chimpanzee behavior are not well explained by nutrition alone. Researchers suggest that chimpanzees might hunt for social gain. For example, a male might try to demonstrate his competence to other males by killing prey. Chimpanzees might use meat as a political tool to punish rivals and reward friends. A study also shows that female chimpanzees that receive large portions of meat after a hunt have healthier and stronger offspring. This indicates that there might be reproductive benefits to eating meat as well.

The information that scientists have been able to gather regarding chimpanzee hunting behavior is shedding some light on the eating habits of our evolutionary ancestors. Further investigation is needed, however, to provide stronger evidence regarding this aspect of human prehistory.

GO ON TO THE NEXT PAGE

19. The primary purpose of the passage is to

    (A) persuade the reader to believe the chimpanzee research findings
    (B) interpret the chimpanzee research findings
    (C) explain the common ancestry of the chimpanzee and human
    (D) introduce a significant link between humans and chimpanzees
    (E) defend meat as biologically necessary for humans

20. The passage states that "chimpanzees...DNA sequence" (lines 9–10) to suggest that

    (A) findings from chimpanzee research indicate humans are not a separate species
    (B) humans and chimpanzees share many physical traits
    (C) humans and chimpanzees are not related
    (D) findings from research involving chimpanzees may hold true for humans
    (E) human-subject research techniques work well for chimpanzee-subject research

21. The author refers to chimpanzees as "actually very proficient hunters" (lines 20–21) to make the point that

    (A) chimpanzees were long believed to be carnivores
    (B) chimpanzees eat a lot of meat
    (C) chimpanzees eat meat for many important reasons
    (D) chimpanzees are less aggressive than many people think
    (E) chimpanzees were poorly observed prior to Goodall

22. In context, the word "maintain" (line 31) most nearly means

    (A) assert
    (B) stay
    (C) repair
    (D) conceal
    (E) endure

23. In line 52, the phrase "truly carnivorous" suggests

    (A) heightened violence
    (B) larger meals
    (C) occasional hunting
    (D) speed and agility
    (E) meat dependence

24. What parallel between chimpanzees and humans does the passage reveal?

    (A) Chimpanzees are the evolutionary ancestors of humans.
    (B) Human DNA is so akin to chimpanzee DNA that the species share certain habits.
    (C) Both require meat for survival.
    (D) Both consume less meat in the dryer months than during the rest of the year.
    (E) Both use meat for political gain.

STOP

If you finish before your time is up, check your work on this section only.
You may not turn to any other section in the test.

SECTION 5
Time—25 minutes
18 Questions

Directions: This section includes two types of questions. For questions 1–8, solve each problem and determine which is the best of the answer choices given. Fill in the corresponding circle on your answer sheet. Use any available space to solve the problems. For questions 9–18, solve each problem and fill in your answer on the answer sheet.

Notes

1. The use of a calculator is permitted.
2. All numbers are real numbers.
3. Figures that accompany problems in this test are intended to provide information useful in solving the problems. They are drawn as accurately as possible EXCEPT when it is stated in a specific problem that the figure is not drawn to scale. All figures lie in a plane unless otherwise indicated.
4. Unless otherwise specified, the domain of any function f is assumed to be the set of all real numbers x for which $f(x)$ is a real number.

Reference Information

$A = \Pi r^2$
$C = 2\Pi r$ $A = lw$ $A = \frac{1}{2}bh$ $V = lwh$ $V = \Pi r^2 h$ $c^2 = a^2 + b^2$ **Special Right Triangles**

The number of degrees of arc in a circle is 360.
The sum of the measures in degrees of the angles of a triangle is 180.

1. If $a^3 = b^2$ and $a = 4$, which could be a value of b?

   (A) -16
   (B) -4
   (C) 8
   (D) 16
   (E) 64

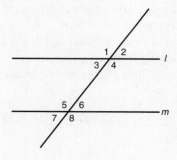

2. In the figure above, if l is parallel to m, then which pair of angles is supplementary?

   (A) 1 and 4
   (B) 2 and 3
   (C) 4 and 5
   (D) 2 and 5
   (E) 5 and 8

GO ON TO THE NEXT PAGE

Voter Registration of Eligible Voters in Garden City

	Registered	Unregistered	Total
Men			31,000
Women	26,000		
Total	45,000		66,000

3. The table above, describing the Garden City voter registration information, is partially filled in. Based on the information in the table, how many eligible male voters are NOT registered to vote?

(A) 9,000
(B) 12,000
(C) 19,000
(D) 21,000
(E) 35,000

4. The German club raked leaves to raise money for a future trip. The rakes used cost a total of $45.00, and they charged $5.00 per lawn raked. The net amount raised, A, in dollars, is given by the function $A(l) = 5l - 45$, where l is the number of lawns raked. If the club raised a net amount of $125.00, how many lawns were raked?

(A) 25
(B) 29
(C) 34
(D) 39
(E) 45

5. If $mn = k$ and $k = x^2n$, and $nk \neq 0$, which of the following is equal to m?

(A) 1

(B) $\frac{1}{x}$

(C) $\sqrt{x}$

(D) x

(E) x^2

6. There are two types of candy in a bowl, chocolate and caramel. If the ratio of the number of pieces of chocolate candy to the number of pieces of candy is 2:3, each of the following could be the total number of pieces of candy EXCEPT

(A) 6
(B) 12
(C) 15
(D) 20
(E) 30

7. If $32\sqrt{32} = a\sqrt{b}$, where a and b are positive integers and $a > b$, which of the following could be the value of ab?

(A) 64
(B) 128
(C) 256
(D) 512
(E) 1,024

8. What is the area of a circle that has a circumference of $\frac{3}{4}\pi$?

(A) $\frac{3}{64}\pi$

(B) $\frac{9}{8}\pi$

(C) $\frac{3}{4}\pi$

(D) $\frac{9}{16}\pi$

(E) $\frac{9}{64}\pi$

GO ON TO THE NEXT PAGE

Directions: For Student-Produced Response questions 9-18, use the grids at the bottom of the answer sheet page on which you have answered questions 1-8.

Each of the remaining 10 questions requires you to solve the problem and enter your answer by marking the circles in the special grid, as shown in the examples below. You may use any available space for scratchwork.

Answer: $\frac{7}{12}$

Write answer in boxes. → Fraction line

Grid in Result. →

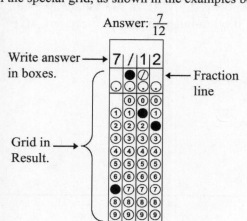

Answer: 2.5

← Decimal point

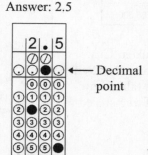

Answer: 201
Either position is correct.

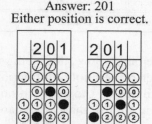

Note: You may start your answers in any column, space permitting. Columns not needed should be left blank.

• Mark no more than one circle in any column.

• Because the answer sheet will be machine-scored, **you will receive credit only if the circles are filled in correctly**.

• Although not required, it is suggested that you write your answer in the boxes at the top of the columns to help you fill in the circles accurately.

• Some problems may have more than one correct answer. In such cases, grid only one answer.

• No question has a negative answer.

• **Mixed numbers** such as $3\frac{1}{2}$ must be gridded as 3.5 or 7/2. (If ▣ is gridded, it will be

interpreted as $\frac{31}{2}$, not $3\frac{1}{2}$.)

Decimal Answers: If you obtain a decimal answer with more digits than the grid can accomodate, it may be either rounded or truncated, but it must fill the entire grid. enter the most accurate value the grid will accommodate. For example, if you obtain an answer such as 0.6666..., you should record your result as .666 or .667. **A less accurate value such as .66 or .67 will be scored as incorrect.**

Acceptable ways to grid $\frac{2}{3}$ are:

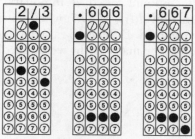

9. If $r^3 = 38$, what is the value of $3r^3$?

10. What is the coordinate of the point on a number line that is exactly halfway between 47 and 64?

11. A certain triangle has two angles that have the same measure. If the lengths of two of the sides of the triangle are 10 and 15, what is the <u>greatest</u> possible value for the perimeter of the triangle?

GO ON TO THE NEXT PAGE ➡

12. If $x^2 - y^2 = 45$ and $x + y = 9$, what is the value of x?

16. Let the function g be defined by $g(x) = 10 + \frac{x^2}{9}$. If $g(3k) = 7k$, what is one possible value of k?

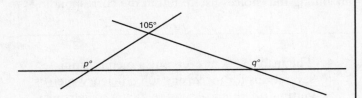

13. In the figure above, what is the sum of p and q?

17. The average (arithmetic mean) of the test scores of a class of n students is 76, and the average of the test scores of a class of p students is 90. When the scores of both classes are combined, the average score is 84. What is the value of $\frac{n}{p}$?

$$(n, 2n, \ldots)$$

14. The first term in the sequence above is n, and each term after the first is twice the preceding term. If the sum of the first 5 terms is 279, what is the value of n?

18. If $3(2x - 3y)(x + 3) = 162$ and $2x - 3y = 9$, what is the value of $2x + y$?

15. The length of a rectangle is 5 inches longer than its width. If the perimeter of the rectangle is 38 inches, what is the width, in inches?

STOP

**If you finish before your time is up, check your work on this section only.
You may not turn to any other section in the test.**

SECTION 6
Time—25 minutes
35 Questions

Directions: For each question, select the best answer from among the choices listed. Fill in the corresponding circle on your answer sheet.

The following questions test the correct and effective use of standard written English in expressing an idea. Part of each sentence (or the entire sentence) is underlined. Following each sentence are five different ways of phrasing the underlined portion. Answer choice A repeats the original phrasing. If you think that the original phrasing is best, select answer choice A. Otherwise, select from the remaining four choices. Your selection should result in the most effective, clear sentence, free from awkwardness or ambiguity.

1. The first motor convoy to travel across the country did so in 1919 and consisting of 81 United States Army vehicles.

   (A) did so in 1919 and consisting of
   (B) had done so in 1919 and consisted of
   (C) did so in 1919 and consisted of
   (D) did so in 1919 and had consisted of
   (E) had did so in 1919, consisting of

2. There is actually a "utensil diet," which advocates limited use of the spoon, fork, and knife to reducing the amount of food consumed at a meal.

   (A) to reducing the amount of food consumed
   (B) by reduction of the amount of food consumed
   (C) that will lead to reducing the amount of food consumed
   (D) to reduce the amount of food consumed
   (E) that reducing the food and amount consumed

3. Caroline nodded off during the movie, which eventually had caused her to drop her bowl of popcorn.

   (A) movie, which eventually had caused her
   (B) movie and which eventually this caused her
   (C) movie, eventually this caused her
   (D) movie; eventually causing her
   (E) movie, which eventually caused her

4. The manager sent everyone a memo listing several tips for increasing job efficiency such as getting rid of clutter and reducing socializing with coworkers.

   (A) for increasing job efficiency such as
   (B) for increasing job efficiency, such as
   (C) that might lead to the increasing of job efficiency, such as
   (D) increasing the efficiency on the job such as
   (E) that would increase job efficiency such as

5. The first step in the Scientific Method is to define the problem, which can sometimes be the more difficult step of all.

   (A) more difficult step
   (B) step with the most difficulty
   (C) far more difficult step
   (D) step that is the more difficult
   (E) most difficult step

6. Outdoor plant material should always be purchased with keeping in mind your growing zone.

   (A) with keeping in mind your growing zone
   (B) while your growing zone is kept in mind
   (C) with keeping your growing zone in your mind
   (D) while keeping in your mind your growing zone
   (E) with your growing zone in mind

GO ON TO THE NEXT PAGE →

7. <u>Storms are often heavier</u> east of a major city because of urban heat colliding with cooler rural temperatures.

   (A)   Storms are often heavier
   (B)   Often, heavier storms are
   (C)   Storms are heavier often
   (D)   Heavier storms are often
   (E)   Heavier storms, often are

8. Learning to identify the constellations can be a satisfying hobby, <u>particularly if they live</u> in an area of mostly clear skies.

   (A)   particularly if they live
   (B)   while living particularly
   (C)   particularly if you live
   (D)   particularly while they live
   (E)   in particular if you live

9. There is a simple way to discern a moth from <u>a butterfly; the antennae</u> of a moth are pointed or feathered, while a butterfly's are club-shaped.

   (A)   a butterfly; the antennae
   (B)   a butterfly: while the antennae
   (C)   a butterfly, for example the antennae
   (D)   a butterfly—because the antennae
   (E)   a butterfly whereas the antennae

10. The acrobat appeared to slip as she grabbed <u>the swing therefore the crowd gave out</u> a loud gasp.

   (A)   the swing therefore the crowd gave out
   (B)   the swing and the crowd had given out
   (C)   the swing, and the crowd has given out
   (D)   the swing, and the crowd gave out
   (E)   the swing, therefore giving out the crowd

11. Attempting to remove two feet of snow from your driveway, <u>even if you use a high-powered snow blower</u>, can be a daunting task.

   (A)   even if you use a high-powered snow blower
   (B)   using a snow blower of high power
   (C)   having a snow blower with high power
   (D)   even if you use a snow blower having high power
   (E)   with a powerfully high snow blower that you use

GO ON TO THE NEXT PAGE →

The following questions test your ability to recognize grammar and usage errors in standard written English. Each sentence contains either a single error or no error at all. Refer to the underlined, lettered portions of each sentence. If the sentence contains no error, select answer choice E. If the sentence contains an error, select the one underlined and lettered portion (A, B, C, or D) that is incorrect.

12. Early <u>inhabitants</u> of Iowa were mound builders
            A
<u>who</u> lived <u>peaceful</u> on the fertile <u>plains</u>.
  B   C   D
<u>No error</u>.
  E

13. I <u>found</u> my statistics lecture <u>to be very</u>
        A   B
<u>confusing</u>, especially the 20-minute
  C
<u>discussing statistical</u> variation. <u>No error</u>.
        D   E

14. President James K. Polk <u>was</u> the first president
                              A
<u>who presiding</u> over the <u>entire country</u>
      B   C
from the Atlantic to the Pacific <u>Ocean</u>. <u>No error</u>.
                                    D   E

15. Negotiation <u>can be</u> a tricky process, but the
                  A
<u>basic</u> rules of negotiation <u>is</u> quite <u>simple</u>
  B   C   D
and universal. <u>No error</u>.
                    E

16. It is <u>commonly known</u> that during <u>a house fire</u>,
              A   B
the <u>biggest</u> danger is often <u>smoke not</u> flames.
      C   D
<u>No error</u>.
  E

17. Thomas Jefferson was very <u>wisely</u> when he
                                A
<u>advised</u> to never <u>spend</u> your money
  B   C
before you actually <u>have</u> it. <u>No error</u>.
                        D   E

18. Although he died in 1965, <u>artist</u> Carl Rakeman
                                A
<u>will have captured</u> the history of American road-
      B
building <u>through</u> his many <u>paintings</u>. <u>No error</u>.
            C   D   E

19. The <u>seemingly</u> innocent and passive <u>appearance</u>
            A   B
of a hockey goalie is in direct <u>contrast to</u> the
                                    C
goalie's dangerous and sometimes violent <u>job</u>.
                                            D
<u>No error</u>.
  E

20. In 1805, Sir Francis Beaufort <u>developing</u> a
                                    A
marine scale to <u>aid</u> in estimating <u>observable</u>
                  B   C
wind strength <u>on</u> the ocean. <u>No error</u>.
                  D   E

GO ON TO THE NEXT PAGE

21. It is startling to <u>realize</u> that the movement of
                        A

    electrical charges <u>within</u> a lightning bolt
                        B

    <u>generate</u> a temperature <u>of up to</u> 30,000 degrees
    C   D

    Fahrenheit. <u>No error</u>.
                 E

22. Dave <u>noticed</u> that even though he <u>put</u> a log on
         A   B

    the fireplace every hour <u>during the night</u>, the
                              C

    cabin <u>was still</u> cold in the morning. <u>No error</u>.
          D   E

23. During the <u>San Francisco earthquake</u> of 1906,
               A

    <u>either</u> the new city hall nor the Fairmont Hotel
    B

    <u>were</u> left <u>standing</u>. <u>No error</u>.
    C   D   E

24. Jose <u>told</u> his mother that the wind <u>was blowing</u>
         A   B

    <u>too</u> hard for <u>him</u> and his sister to keep raking.
    C   D

    <u>No error</u>.
    E

25. Lily <u>was likely</u> to <u>failing</u> the exam since she
         A   B

    <u>had not studied</u> the night <u>before</u>. <u>No error</u>.
    C   D   E

26. Early <u>American's</u> colonists <u>could not have</u> won
          A   B

    the Revolutionary War without the <u>aid</u> of
                                       C

    soldiers, supplies, and financial <u>support</u> from the
                                       D

    French. <u>No error</u>.
             E

27. <u>Many</u> of the dogs at the animal shelter
    A

    <u>were older</u>, which probably made <u>it</u> more
    B   C

    difficult for them to be <u>adopted</u>. <u>No error</u>.
                             D   E

28. There <u>appear</u> to be a link between chewing gum
          A

    and having a good memory, as <u>shown</u> in a study
                                  B

    <u>conducted</u> at an <u>English</u> university. <u>No error</u>.
    C   D   E

29. Prior to the <u>invention</u> of the telescope in the
                 A

    seventeenth century, only the five planets that
    <u>are visible</u> to the <u>naked</u> eye <u>have been</u> identified.
    B   C   D

    <u>No error</u>.
    E

GO ON TO THE NEXT PAGE ⇨

Directions: The following passage is a rough draft of a student essay. Some parts of the passage need to be rewritten to improve the essay.

Read the passage and select the best answer for each question that follows. Some questions ask you to improve the structure or word choice of specific sentences or parts of sentences, while others ask you to consider the organization and development of the essay. Follow the requirements of standard written English.

Questions 30–35 are based on the following passage.

(1)Ocean currents start from south of the equator. (2)Ultimately, they can have a huge impact on weather patterns all the way to the North Pole. (3)Probably the best known ocean currents are the El Nino and La Nina. (4)Both of these tropical Pacific Ocean currents are influencing of producing global heat waves, flooding and droughts. (5)Changes in ocean currents, including temperature and flow, tend to occur in 20- to 30-year cycles.

(6)Beginning in the late 1990s, two other ocean current patterns, known as the PDO and the AMO, became more active. (7)Their flows have gone up in speed and the water temperatures have also risen. (8)Again, these changes have brought unusual levels of precipitation to land, primarily to the North American continent. (9)The greenhouse effect relates to the impact that man has on the environment. (10)Ocean currents also have an effect on the frequency and strength of tropical storms and hurricanes.

(11)Weather patterns are also influenced by man-made objects such as modes of transportation and buildings. (12)This is known as the *greenhouse effect*, and much controversy has developed in determining its degrees of impact on the weather. (13)However, there is no doubt that the heat that radiates from a major city changes the air around it. (14)These urban heat islands emit warm air during the day which reduces the rainfall in those areas. (15)The ultimate hope is that man and nature begin to develop a more symbiotic relationship.

30. Of the following, which is the best way to revise and combine Sentences 1 and 2 (reproduced below)?

Ocean currents start from south of the equator. Ultimately they can have a huge impact on weather patterns all the way to the North Pole.

(A) Ultimately, ocean currents starting from south of the equator can have a huge impact all the way to the North Pole on their weather patterns.

(B) Ocean currents, ultimately, can have a huge impact up to the North Pole's weather patterns.

(C) Ocean currents from south of the equator can have a huge impact on weather patterns extending to the North Pole.

(D) From south of the equator to the North Pole, ocean currents can have a huge impact on weather patterns.

(E) The weather patterns that start south of the equator and go to the North Pole are hugely impacted by ocean currents.

31. Of the following, which is the best way to phrase Sentence 4 (reproduced below)?

Both of these tropical Pacific Ocean currents are influencing of producing global heat waves, flooding and droughts.

(A) (As it is now)

(B) Both of these tropical currents from the Pacific Ocean are influencing and producing global heat waves, flooding, and droughts.

(C) These tropical Pacific Ocean currents, both of them, are producing global heat waves, flooding, and droughts.

(D) Global heat waves, flooding, and droughts are all being produced from both of these tropical currents coming from the Pacific Ocean.

(E) Both of these tropical currents from the Pacific Ocean are influential in producing global heat waves, flooding, and droughts.

GO ON TO THE NEXT PAGE

32. In Sentence 7, the phrase "gone up" is best replaced by

    (A) arisen
    (B) increased
    (C) speeded up
    (D) jumped up
    (E) taken off

33. Which of the following sentences should be omitted to improve the unity of the second paragraph?

    (A) Sentence 6
    (B) Sentence 7
    (C) Sentence 8
    (D) Sentence 9
    (E) Sentence 10

34. In context, which of the following is the best way to phrase the underlined portion of Sentence 12 (reproduced below)?

    This is known as the greenhouse effect, *and much controversy has developed in determining its degrees of impact on* the weather.

    (A) (As it is now)
    (B) the degrees of its impact to
    (C) to what degree it impacts
    (D) to how much of a degree it impacts
    (E) the degree of its impact on

35. A strategy that the writer uses within the third paragraph is to

    (A) create a sense of foreboding regarding the essay's topic
    (B) refer back to the beginning of the essay to make a point
    (C) use humor to reinforce the essay's topic
    (D) motivate the reader to take action
    (E) introduce a new element of the essay's main topic

STOP

**If you finish before your time is up, check your work on this section only.
You may not turn to any other section in the test.**

SECTION 7
Time—20 minutes
19 Questions

Directions: For each of the questions in this section, choose the best answer and fill in the corresponding circle on your answer sheet.

Each sentence that follows has either one or two blanks. Each blank indicates that a word has been omitted from the sentence. Following each sentence are five words or sets of words. Select the word or set of words that, when inserted into the sentence in place of the blank(s), best fits the context of the sentence as a whole.

1. As ------- a phenomenon as forest fires are popularly believed to be, some plant species rely on them for efficient ------- of seedpods.

   (A) malicious . . consumption
   (B) destructive . . insertion
   (C) violent . . replication
   (D) ruinous . . dispersion
   (E) auspicious . . germination

2. Some food critics are appallingly pretentious, ------- praise from those establishments that ignore the formalities of classical cuisine.

   (A) withholding
   (B) removing
   (C) inciting
   (D) receiving
   (E) earning

3. The foundation of a Bachelor of Arts degree is in the liberal studies, which are meant to ------- the intellectual interests of the student.

   (A) rectify
   (B) broaden
   (C) deprive
   (D) parse
   (E) identify

4. Despite the large amount of money that the Mauros spent on their luxury cruise vacation, the food was disappointingly -------, and the entertainment options were very -------.

   (A) bountiful . . scarce
   (B) unsavory . . limited
   (C) delicious . . offbeat
   (D) tasteless . . copious
   (E) meager . . local

5. Cases of Bovine Spongiform Encephalopathy, commonly called BSE or "mad cow disease," threaten to ------- in the future, ------- an acute danger to the world beef supply.

   (A) augment . . averting
   (B) decline . . curtailing
   (C) disappear . . eliminating
   (D) swell . . posing
   (E) accrue . . dispelling

6. Snow may fall in areas with above-freezing temperatures near the ground, provided that the precipitation originates under atmospheric conditions ------- ice crystal formation.

   (A) prohibitive to
   (B) restrictive of
   (C) adverse for
   (D) absent of
   (E) conducive to

GO ON TO THE NEXT PAGE

The two passages that follow are accompanied by several questions based on the content of the passage. Answer the questions based on what is either stated or implied in each passage. Be sure to read any introductory material that is provided.

Questions 7—19 are based on the following passages.

The author of Passage 1 describes a misadventure aboard a sailboat. In Passage 2, a different author describes shopping for a powerboat.

Passage 1

Pictures and postcards of the Caribbean do not lie; the water there shines with every shade of aquamarine, from pale pastel green to deep emerald and navy. The ocean hypnotizes
Line
5   with its glassy vastness. A spell is set upon the soul, and a euphoric swell rises to push up the corners of the mouth.

My good friends and I sailed blissfully from one cay to another. We boating novices
10   were in charge of spotting the light areas of the seafloor that signaled dangerous reefs. Ocean reefs have the potential to rupture the hull of any sailboat that passes over them, so while the electronic depth sounder is an indispensable
15   tool, it is always helpful to spot a reef ahead of time.

Tacking when sailing is often a harrowing experience for those onboard. All at once, our smooth trip turned into complete pandemo-
20   nium as the captain at the wheel began yelling directions to his first mate who quickly began struggling with the sails and rigging. Generally, the wind continued offering resistance. This made the first mate's struggle more demanding
25   and outright frightening to the guests. This mad yelling and steering, along with the raucous flapping of the sails, went on for several minutes before all was right again and the boat settled in to its new course. Following
30   this hair-raising event, the captain and first mate acknowledged each other with congratulatory smiles. We passengers, however, were still recovering from our terror and wondering to ourselves, "Was all that supposed to happen?
35   And they think this is fun?"

As we headed back toward the marina, the unpredictable wind not only slowed but stopped, and soon, too, did the boat. After several patient minutes, the ship's crew grudg-
40   ingly turned on the trolling motor. Unfortunately, the motor wouldn't start, so we lay adrift at sea, no land in sight, just waiting. It was late afternoon when I began to work on the panic that was rising in my throat. Eventually,
45   the ship's captain got the engine running, and we slowly trolled back to our cozy slip. The sails were up, and the little motor hummed along. From the shore, we may have looked as if we were actually sailing. I know better now
50   and admit I was thrilled to see that the beautiful wind-powered craft could run on a motor in a pinch.

Passage 2

It isn't so much the potential speed of a powerboat that attracts me. Perhaps it's like
55   choosing a car over a horse. Certainly a car can break down at any time, but it seems that a person has a bit more control over a motorized vehicle than one powered by nature. This was the premise I operated under when I began
60   talking about purchasing a boat for my lakefront vacation home. As far as boats go, there are just so many options, and it's important to weigh them all before making such a big decision.

Often, when making a decision, it helps to
65   examine the unfavorable aspects as well as the positive ones. This is called the "process of elimination," which has proven very helpful in my boat discussions. For example, I don't want a boat that is too large either to tow or launch
70   into the water. However, the boat needs to be large enough to accommodate my growing family, preferably able to sleep six people. It also needs to be big enough to be capable of staving off a sudden storm or high winds that
75   often present themselves on a large lake. I don't want a sailboat but rather a vessel that relies on a large motor. I would be sure to keep a small

GO ON TO THE NEXT PAGE →

229

motor and a spare propeller on hand in case of breakdown. I also know that I don't want a
80 fishing boat or a speedboat. My dream craft needs to have a full cabin with dining space, a galley, beds, and a bathroom.

Price is a limiting factor in my boat purchase decision. This probably becomes the
85 most difficult obstacle because it restricts me to finding a used boat rather than a new one. When purchasing a used boat, it is important to know what questions to ask the seller: "How old can a boat be before I should question its
90 seaworthiness? How many are too many engine hours?" Because I have never owned a boat before, feeling well informed is a challenge. I have very little idea of what to inquire about, so the danger is buying a watercraft only to spend
95 more in repairs than I would have spent on a brand new boat.

Until I seal the deal, I have decided to continue researching options online and in the classifieds. There are always people hauling
100 their beloved watercraft to curbside with big "FOR SALE" signs attached, so maybe I'll get lucky on the road to the lake. First, though, I have a list of questions to prepare.

7. The authors of both passages agree that

(A) boating is one of the more favorable summer pastimes
(B) every watercraft should have a main motor and a backup engine
(C) boaters should be licensed in order to operate a boat of any kind
(D) there is not much difference between one type of boat and another
(E) boating at the mercy of the wind can be an arduous experience

8. The narrator of Passage 1 uses the phrase "push up…mouth" (lines 6–7) to

(A) point out the subtle terror of an empty sea
(B) suggest disapproval of the harsh marine environment
(C) indicate that the narrator is new to life at sea
(D) express approval for leisure time at sea
(E) show boredom from the monotonous pattern of waves

9. In line 18, the author of Passage 1 uses the phrase "All at once" to indicate

(A) a change in the purpose of the story
(B) how well the boat's crew worked together as a team
(C) a change in the events of the story
(D) a flashback in time
(E) an interjection of emotion into the story

10. In line 23, "resistance" most nearly means

(A) uprising
(B) denial
(C) impedance
(D) conflict
(E) steadiness

11. The questions in lines 34–35 chiefly serve to

(A) illustrate the emotions of the passengers on board the boat
(B) argue in opposition to sailing on the ocean
(C) bring dialogue into the story
(D) develop the characters in the story
(E) demonstrate the skills of the boat's captain and first mate

12. The author of Passage 1 mentions that "It was late afternoon" in order to

(A) tell the story in chronological order
(B) develop the emotions of the narrator
(C) foreshadow the next part of the story
(D) relate the narration back to an earlier time
(E) assure the reader that everything was working out

13. In line 54, "attracts" most nearly means

(A) focuses on
(B) magnetizes
(C) invites
(D) appeals to
(E) charms

GO ON TO THE NEXT PAGE

14. In lines 54–59, the narrator's basic objection to the sailboat is that

(A) its non-motorized design makes it slow
(B) it requires extensive knowledge of rigging and management of the sails
(C) it cannot be operated by one person
(D) it might be impossible to control in certain weather conditions
(E) it is made from wood, which is prone to rotting

15. In lines 66–67, "process of elimination" emphasizes that which of the following is particularly important when making a decision?

(A) knowing ahead of time which characteristics are unacceptable
(B) taking time to examine the unique merits of only the positive options
(C) paying attention to instinctual reactions
(D) purging all options with negative factors
(E) comparing only the positive aspects of each option and ignoring the negative aspects

16. The questions in lines 88–89, ("How old…too many?") primarily draw attention to

(A) the lack of knowledge the author has about boats
(B) the importance of taking time before making a big decision
(C) how easy it is to make a decision by weighing pros and cons
(D) the necessity of keeping an open mind when purchasing a boat
(E) the various ways to find information on a given subject

17. Both passages base their arguments on the unstated assumption that

(A) a motorized water craft is preferable over one without an engine
(B) sailboats are not as safe as powerboats
(C) purchasing a used boat often brings regrets
(D) boat safety should be learned before a boat is purchased
(E) safe boating requires skill and knowledge

18. The author of Passage 2 would most likely respond to lines 32–35 in Passage 1 ("We passengers, however…this is fun?'") by

(A) claiming that the author of Passage 1 is weak for being terrified by the tack
(B) arguing that the excitement of sailing comes from frantic maneuvers
(C) pointing out that sailing has increased its safety record steadily over time
(D) asserting that controlled power boating is favorable to hectic sailing
(E) suggesting the author of Passage 1 take firm hold of the gunwale in future turbulent moments

19. Both passages suggest that boating

(A) is an easy hobby to pursue
(B) can motivate people to pursue other outdoor activities
(C) is more appealing to children than to adults
(D) demands preparedness to ensure safety
(E) is rarely a comfortable leisure activity

STOP

If you finish before your time is up, check your work on this section only.
You may not turn to any other section in the test.

SECTION 8
Time—20 minutes
16 Questions

Directions: Solve each problem and determine which is the best of the answer choices given. Fill in the corresponding circle on your answer sheet. Use any available space to solve the problems.

Notes

1. The use of a calculator is permitted.
2. All numbers are real numbers.
3. Figures that accompany problems in this test are intended to provide information useful in solving the problems. They are drawn as accurately as possible EXCEPT when it is stated in a specific problem that the figure is not drawn to scale. All figures lie in a plane unless otherwise indicated.
4. Unless otherwise specified, the domain of any function f is assumed to be the set of all real numbers x for which $f(x)$ is a real number.

Reference Information

$A = \Pi r^2$
$C = 2\Pi r$　　　$A = lw$　　　$A = \frac{1}{2}bh$　　　$V = lwh$　　　$V = \Pi r^2 h$　　　$c^2 = a^2 + b^2$　　　**Special Right Triangles**

The number of degrees of arc in a circle is 360.
The sum of the measures in degrees of the angles of a triangle is 180.

1. If an object travels at 4 feet per minute, how many feet does it travel in three quarters of an hour?

　(A)　2

　(B)　3

　(C)　$4\frac{3}{4}$

　(D)　180

　(E)　300

2. Allayne bought a bird from a pet store that sells only parakeets and finches. Which of the following must be true?

　(A)　The bird is a finch.
　(B)　The bird is a parakeet.
　(C)　The bird is not a canary.
　(D)　The bird is not a blue parakeet.
　(E)　The bird is not a Zebra finch.

GO ON TO THE NEXT PAGE

3. Carrie spends $4.65 for lunch at work each day. She wants to estimate the amount she will spend for lunch during the month of July, which has 21 work days. Which of the following will give her the best estimate?

   (A) $4.00 × 20
   (B) $4.50 × 20
   (C) $4.00 × 25
   (D) $4.50 × 25
   (E) $4.00 × 30

Table of Conversions			
Number of Ounces	1	5	9
Number of Grains	437.5	2,187.5	n

4. What is the value of *n* in the table above?

   (A) 48.6
   (B) 3,500.0
   (C) 3,937.5
   (D) 4,375.0
   (E) 8,750.0

5. The product of two integers is between 137 and 149. Which of the following CANNOT be one of the integers?

   (A) 15
   (B) 13
   (C) 11
   (D) 10
   (E) 7

COIN COLLECTIONS	
Number of Coins	Number of Coins Collectors
100	1
95	3
90	3
85	4
80	2
75	1
70	2
65	0
60	2

6. At a recent coin collection exhibit, 18 coin collectors brought their collections for viewing. The number of coins each collector brought is shown in the table above. Ryan, who was the only collector not able to attend the exhibit, would have brought 75 coins. Had he been able to attend, what would have been the median number of coins?

   (A) 90
   (B) 87.5
   (C) 85
   (D) 82.5
   (E) 80

Set M = {14, 15, 16, 17, 18, 19, 20}

Set R = {16, 17, 18, 19, 20, 21, 22}

7. Sets M and R are shown above. How many numbers in set M are also in set R?

   (A) Three
   (B) Four
   (C) Five
   (D) Six
   (E) Seven

GO ON TO THE NEXT PAGE ⇨

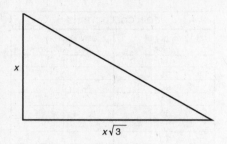

8. In the figure above, the perimeter of the triangle is $12 + 4\sqrt{3}$. What is the value of x?

(A) 2
(B) 4
(C) 6
(D) 8
(E) 12

9. On a map, $\frac{1}{4}$ inch represents 12 miles. If a road is 66 miles long, what is its length, in inches, on the map?

(A) $5\frac{1}{2}$
(B) $5\frac{1}{8}$
(C) $1\frac{1}{2}$
(D) $1\frac{3}{8}$
(E) $\frac{7}{8}$

10. If $n^x \times n^8 = n^{24}$ and $(n^6)^y = n^{18}$, what is the value of $x + y$?

(A) 7
(B) 9
(C) 12
(D) 21
(E) 28

11. If the volume of a cube is 64, what is the shortest distance from the center of the cube to the base of the cube?

(A) 2
(B) 4
(C) $2\sqrt{4}$
(D) $\sqrt{32}$
(E) 16

12. What is the area of the triangle in the figure below?

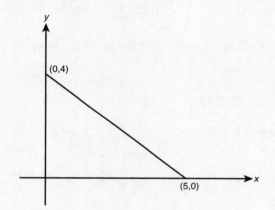

(A) 4.5
(B) 9.0
(C) 10.0
(D) 12.5
(E) 20.0

GO ON TO THE NEXT PAGE

13. How many three-digit numbers have the hundreds digit equal to 8 and the units digit equal to 2?

   (A) 200
   (B) 190
   (C) 20
   (D) 19
   (E) 10

14. If $\frac{x}{5} = x^2$, the value of x can be which of the following?

   I. $-\frac{1}{5}$
   II. $\frac{1}{5}$
   III. 1

   (A) I only
   (B) II only
   (C) III only
   (D) I and III only
   (E) I, II, and III

15. The price of flavored syrup is d dollars for 20 ounces, and each ounce makes b bottles of soda pop. In terms of d and b, what is the dollar cost of the flavored syrup required to make 1 bottle of soda pop?

   (A) $20db$

   (B) $\frac{20d}{b}$

   (C) $\frac{d}{20b}$

   (D) $\frac{db}{20}$

   (E) $\frac{20b}{c}$

16. A shoe store charges $39 for a certain type of sneaker. This price is 30% more than the amount it costs the shoe store to buy one pair of these sneakers. At an end-of-the-year sale, sales associates can obtain any remaining sneakers at 20% off the shoe store's cost. How much would it cost an employee to purchase a pair of sneakers of this type at this sale?

   (A) $31.20
   (B) $25.00
   (C) $24.00
   (D) $21.84
   (E) $19.50

S T O P

**If you finish before your time is up, check your work on this section only.
You may not turn to any other section in the test.**

SECTION 9
Time—10 minutes
14 Questions

Directions: For each question, select the best answer from among the choices listed. Fill in the corresponding circle on your answer sheet.

The following questions test the correct and effective use of standard written English in expressing an idea. Part of each sentence (or the entire sentence) is underlined. Following each sentence are five different ways of phrasing the underlined portion. Answer choice A repeats the original phrasing. If you think that the original phrasing is best, select answer choice A. Otherwise, select from the remaining four choices. Your selection should result in the most effective, clear sentence, free from awkwardness or ambiguity.

1. <u>Although the Mackinaw Bridge in Michigan is better known than the Henry Hudson Bridge in New York, the architect of both bridges, David B. Steinman, preferred the Henry Hudson Bridge.</u>

   (A) Although the Mackinaw Bridge in Michigan is better known than the Henry Hudson Bridge in New York, the architect of both bridges, David B. Steinman, preferred the Henry Hudson Bridge.
   (B) Although not as well known as the Mackinaw Bridge, David B. Steinman, the architect of both bridges, preferred the Henry Hudson Bridge.
   (C) Although more people know about Michigan's Mackinaw Bridge than of the Henry Hudson Bridge in New York, David B. Steinman, in being the architect for both, preferred the latter.
   (D) The Mackinaw Bridge in Michigan being better known that the Henry Hudson Bridge in New York, the architect of both, David B. Steinman, preferred the latter.
   (E) The architect of both the Mackinaw Bridge and the Henry Hudson Bridge was David B. Steinman, he preferred the Henry Hudson Bridge.

2. In recent years, more tourists from China visited museums in France than <u>Italy</u>.

   (A) Italy
   (B) in Italy
   (C) compared to Italy's
   (D) Italy did
   (E) Italian ones

3. <u>Alan Shepard, the first American astronaut to fly in space, doing that</u> just weeks after the Russian astronaut Yuri Gagarin orbited Earth and became the first human in space.

   (A) Alan Shepard, the first American astronaut to fly in space, doing that
   (B) Alan Shepard was the first American astronaut flying in space, accomplishing it
   (C) Alan Shepard became the first American astronaut to fly in space, accomplishing this feat
   (D) Alan Shepard, becoming the first American astronaut flying in space, did it
   (E) Alan Shepard the first American astronaut to fly in space, and who did so

4. Carbon-14 dating reveals that the bones found in South Africa are nearly 3,000 years <u>as old as any of their supposed</u> Arab ancestors.

   (A) as old as any of their supposed
   (B) older than any of their supposed
   (C) as older as they supposed
   (D) any older than their supposed
   (E) older as their supposedly

GO ON TO THE NEXT PAGE ▷

5. <u>Before having been widely harvested for its</u> ivory tusks in the twentieth century, African elephants were plentiful throughout the savannahs of Africa.

(A) Before having been widely harvested for it
(B) Until being widely harvested for its
(C) Until they were widely harvested for their
(D) Before they have been widely hunted for their
(E) Up to them being widely hunted for their

6. Jeff obtained his Connecticut real estate license last year, <u>where, ever since, he sells real estate</u>.

(A) where, ever since, he sells real estate
(B) and selling real estate there ever since
(C) whereas he has been selling real estate in Connecticut since then
(D) and has been selling real estate in Connecticut ever since
(E) since that time he has sold real estate there

7. Since 1992, when the livestock depression began, the number of acres overseen by certified ranch-management companies <u>have grown from 22 million to nearly 37 million, an area that is about Maine's size</u>.

(A) have grown from 22 million to nearly 37 million, an area that is about Maine's size
(B) have grown from 22 million to nearly 37 million, about the size of Maine
(C) has grown from 22 million to nearly 37 million, an area about the size of Maine
(D) has grown from 22 million up to nearly 37 million, an area about the size of Maine
(E) has grown from 22 million up to nearly 37 million, about Maine's size

8. <u>The marathon's finish line having been reached</u>, the exhausted runners collapsed into chairs and began guzzling water.

(A) The marathon's finish line having been reached
(B) When having reached that marathon's finish line
(C) When they reached the marathon's finish line
(D) At the marathon's finish line, when they reached it
(E) The finish line of the marathon being reached

9. Albert Einstein, deemed one of the most influential scientists of the twentieth <u>century, won the Nobel Prize in Physics in 1921 for his explanation of the photoelectric effect</u>.

(A) century, won the Nobel Prize in Physics in 1921 for his explanation of the photoelectric effect
(B) century, his explanation of the photoelectric effect bringing him the Nobel Prize in Physics in 1921
(C) century, winning the Nobel Prize in Physics in 1921 for his explanation of the photoelectric effect
(D) century, winning the Nobel Prize in Physics, which he won in 1921 for his explanation of the photoelectric effect
(E) century, and he won the Nobel Prize in Physics in 1921 for his explanation of the photoelectric effect

10. <u>As a result of the school's new policy, early dismissal from class on Fridays is no longer allowed.</u>

(A) As a result of the school's new policy, early dismissal from class on Fridays is no longer allowed.
(B) The school's new policy results in their no longer being able to allow them early dismissal from class on Fridays.
(C) One result of the school's new policy are that early dismissal from class on Fridays is no longer possible.
(D) One result of the school's new policy is that early dismissal from class on Fridays can no longer be allowed.
(E) As one result of their new policy, the school can no longer allow early dismissal from class on Fridays.

GO ON TO THE NEXT PAGE

11. Some studies indicate that even after two decades, adult men and women still experience some of the effects of a traumatic incident <u>occurring when an adolescent</u>.

   (A) occurring when an adolescent
   (B) occurring when adolescents
   (C) that occurred when a adolescent
   (D) that occurred when they were adolescents
   (E) that has occurred as each was an adolescent

12. <u>The artist, who takes the observer on a visual expedition through his native land, skillfully</u> combining creativity and imagination with true-to-life details that make his home unique.

   (A) The artist, who takes the observer on a visual expedition through his native land, skillfully
   (B) The artist, taking the observer on a visual expedition through his native land, skillfully
   (C) The artists takes the observer on a visual expedition through his native land, skillfully
   (D) The observer is taken on a visual expedition through the artist's native land by skillfully
   (E) The observer is taken on a visual expedition through his native land by the artist who is skillfully

13. Because the production company failed to properly advertise its upcoming play, <u>their attendance on opening night, being very low, was not surprising</u>.

   (A) their attendance on opening night, being very low, was not surprising
   (B) this lowered, not surprisingly, their attendance on opening night
   (C) not to anyone's surprise their attendance was very low on opening night
   (D) attendance on opening night was, not surprisingly, very low
   (E) the very low attendance was not to anyone's surprise on opening night

14. Lacking information about electricity use, families tend to overestimate the amount of energy used by <u>equipment, such as computers, that are noticeable and must be turned on and off and underestimate that</u> used by inconspicuous equipment, such as air purifiers.

   (A) equipment, such as computers, that are noticeable and must be turned on and off and underestimate that
   (B) noticeable equipment, such as computers, that must be turned on and off, and underestimate the amount
   (C) equipment, such as computers, that is noticeable and must be turned on and off and underestimate it when the amount
   (D) equipment, such as computers, that are noticeable and must be turned on and off and underestimate when
   (E) noticeable equipment, such as computers, that must be turned on and off and underestimate it when

STOP

**If you finish before your time is up, check your work on this section only.
You may not turn to any other section in the test.**

Practice Test 1 Answer Key

Section 1

Because grading the essay is subjective, we've chosen not to include any "graded" essays here. Your best bet is to have someone you trust, such as your personal tutor, read your essays and give you an honest critique. Make the grading criteria mentioned in Chapter 5 available to whomever grades your essays. If you plan on grading your own essays, review the grading criteria and be as honest as possible regarding the structure, development, organization, technique, and appropriateness of your writing. Focus on your weak areas and continue to practice in order to improve your writing skills.

Section 2

1. D	18. A
2. E	19. B
3. A	20. C
4. B	21. C
5. C	22. C
6. D	23. B
7. C	24. D
8. C	
9. D	
10. C	
11. B	
12. D	
13. B	
14. E	
15. C	
16. E	
17. A	

Section 3

1. C	18. E
2. D	19. C
3. C	20. C
4. D	
5. A	
6. E	
7. D	
8. B	
9. C	
10. B	
11. A	
12. C	
13. D	
14. C	
15. E	
16. D	
17. B	

Section 4

1. D

2. B

3. C

4. C

5. C

6. B

7. E

8. C

9. B

10. D

11. C

12. D

13. A

14. A

15. D

16. D

17. C

18. E

19. D

20. D

21. E

22. A

23. E

24. B

Section 5

Multiple Choice

1. C

2. D

3. B

4. C

5. E

6. D

7. C

8. E

Student Produced Response

9. 114

10. 55.5

11. 40

12. 7

13. 285

14. 9

15. 7

16. 2 or 5

17. $\frac{3}{4}$ or .75

18. 5

Section 6

1. C	26. A
2. D	27. E
3. E	28. A
4. B	29. D
5. E	30. C
6. E	31. E
7. A	32. B
8. C	33. D
9. A	34. C
10. D	35. E
11. A	
12. C	
13. C	
14. B	
15. C	
16. D	
17. A	
18. B	
19. E	
20. A	
21. C	
22. E	
23. B	
24. D	
25. B	

Section 7

1. D
2. A
3. B
4. B
5. D
6. E
7. E
8. D
9. C
10. C
11. A
12. B
13. D
14. D
15. A
16. A
17. E
18. D
19. D

Section 8

1. D
2. C
3. C
4. C
5. A
6. C
7. C
8. B
9. D
10. D
11. A
12. C
13. E
14. B
15. C
16. C

Section 9

1. A
2. B
3. C
4. B
5. C
6. D
7. C
8. C
9. A
10. A
11. D
12. C
13. D
14. B

Scoring Practice Test 1

Check your responses with the Answer Key. Fill in the blanks below and do the calculations to get your math, critical reading, and writing raw scores. Use the tables on the next pages find your scaled scores.

Remember that this is a simulated test and that the score should only be used to estimate your score on the actual SAT.

Get Your Math Raw Score:

	Number Correct	**Number Incorrect**
Section 3:	_____	_____
Section 5:		
(#1 – #8)	_____	_____
(#9 – #18)	_____	
Section 8:	_____	_____
Totals:	_____	_____

Divide the total Number Incorrect by 4 and subtract the result from the total Number Correct. This is your Raw Score: _____

Round Raw Score to the nearest whole number. Use Table 1 to find Scaled Score range.

Math Scaled Score Range: _____ - _____

Get Your Critical Reading Raw Score:

	Number Correct	**Number Incorrect**
Section 2:	_____	_____
Section 4:	_____	_____
Section 7:	_____	_____
Totals:	_____	_____

Divide the total Number Incorrect by 4 and subtract the result from the total Number Correct. This is your Raw Score: _____

Round Raw Score to the nearest whole number. Use Table 2 to find Scaled Score range.

Critical Reading Scaled Score Range: _____ - _____

Get Your Writing Raw Score:

	Number Correct	Number Incorrect
Section 6:	_____	_____
Section 9:	_____	_____
Totals:	_____	_____

Divide the total Number Incorrect by 4 and subtract the result from the total Number Correct. This is your Raw Score: _____

Round Raw Score to the nearest whole number. Use Table 3 to find Scaled Score range.

Writing Score Range: _____ - _____

Note that your Writing Score assumes an Essay score of 4. If you believe that your Essay warrants a score of 5 or 6, your Writing Score would increase by an average of 30 to 50 points. Likewise, if your Essay is in the 1 to 3 range, your Writing Score would decrease by an average of 30 to 50 points.

Get Your Composite Score:

To calculate your Composite Score Range, simply add the 3 sub-score ranges (Math, Critical Reading, and Writing).

Composite Score Range: _____ - _____

Table 1 Math Score Conversion

Raw Score	Scaled Score	Raw Score	Scaled Score
54	800	23	460-520
53	750-800	22	450-510
52	720-800	21	440-500
51	700-780	20	430-490
50	690-770	19	430-490
49	680-740	18	420-480
48	670-730	17	410-470
47	660-720	16	400-460
46	640-700	15	400-460
45	630-690	14	390-450
44	620-680	13	380-440
43	620-680	12	360-440
42	610-670	11	350-430
41	600-660	10	340-420
40	580-660	9	330-430
39	570-650	8	320-420
38	560-640	7	310-410
37	550-630	6	290-390
36	550-630	5	280-380
35	540-620	4	270-370
34	530-610	3	260-360
33	520-600	2	240-340
32	520-600	1	230-330
31	520-580	0	210-310
30	510-570	-1	200-290
29	500-560	-2	200-270
28	490-550	-3	200-250
27	490-550	-4	200-230
26	480-540	-5	200-210
25	470-530	-6 and below	200
24	460-520		

Table 2 Critical Reading Score Conversion

Raw Score	Scaled Score	Raw Score	Scaled Score
67	800	30	470-530
66	770-800	29	470-530
65	740-800	28	460-520
64	720-800	27	450-510
63	700-800	26	450-510
62	690-790	25	440-500
61	670-770	24	440-500
60	660-760	23	430-490
59	660-740	22	420-480
58	650-730	21	420-480
57	640-720	20	410-470
56	630-710	19	400-460
55	630-710	18	400-460
54	620-700	17	390-450
53	610-690	16	380-440
52	600-680	15	380-440
51	610-670	14	370-430
50	600-660	13	360-420
49	590-650	12	350-410
48	580-640	11	350-410
47	580-640	10	340-400
46	570-630	9	330-390
45	560-620	8	310-390
44	560-620	7	300-380
43	550-610	6	290-370
42	550-610	5	270-370
41	540-600	4	260-360
40	530-590	3	250-350
39	530-590	2	230-330
38	520-580	1	220-320
37	510-570	0	200-290
36	510-570	-1	200-290
35	500-560	-2	200-270
34	500-560	-3	200-250
33	490-550	-4	200-230
32	480-540	-5	200-210
31	480-540	-6 and below	200

Table 3 Writing Score Conversion

Raw Score	Scaled Score	Raw Score	Scaled Score
49	750-800	21	460-590
48	720-800	20	460-580
47	700-800	19	450-580
46	680-800	18	440-570
45	670-800	17	430-560
44	660-790	16	420-550
43	640-780	15	410-540
42	630-770	14	400-530
41	620-760	13	390-520
40	620-750	12	390-510
39	610-740	11	380-510
38	600-730	10	370-500
37	590-720	9	360-490
36	580-720	8	350-480
35	570-710	7	340-470
34	570-700	6	330-460
33	560-690	5	320-460
32	550-680	4	320-450
31	540-670	3	310-440
30	530-660	2	300-430
29	520-650	1	280-410
28	520-650	0	270-410
27	510-640	-1	250-390
26	500-630	-2	240-370
25	490-620	-3	240-360
24	480-610	-4	220-340
23	470-600	-5	200-320
22	460-590	-6 and below	200

Answer Key and Explanations

Section 1

Because grading the essay is subjective, we've chosen not to include any "graded" essays here. Your best bet is to have someone you trust, such as your personal tutor, read your essays and give you an honest critique. Make the grading criteria mentioned in Chapter 5, "SAT/PSAT Verbal," available to whomever grades your essays. If you plan on grading your own essays, review the grading criteria and be as honest as possible regarding the structure, development, organization, technique, and appropriateness of your writing. Focus on your weak areas and continue to practice to improve your writing skills.

Section 2

1. **The best answer is D.** The word "benign" can mean "harmless." Identifying the employee's motives as such in the introductory clause makes the main clause logical; because the employee's motives were "harmless," no disciplinary action would be taken. The other answer choices do not fit the context of the sentence.

2. **The best answer is E.** "Conspicuous" means "visible," so it makes sense that the burglar would choose to enter by the least "visible" window. It is important to notice modifiers such as "least," which can serve as clues to locating the best word for the blanks. In addition, it makes sense that the burglar would choose the least "conspicuous" window, if both doors were "observed" by cameras.

3. **The best answer is A.** Petals and leaves are appreciated by the eye, so both "visual" and "aesthetic" are appropriate for the first blank. The transition word *but* divides two clauses that address a parallel topic but give opposing details. Jennifer loves roses for a certain reason, so the second clause must describe something related to the love of roses. "Enthralled" best fits the context of the sentence, so it fits best in the second blank.

4. **The best answer is B.** "Entrancement" means "the act of placing (something) in a trance," which provides the most logical explanation for the mysterious behavior mentioned in the sentence. The other answer choices do not fit the context of the sentence.

5. **The best answer is C.** You can infer from the context of the sentence that the students wanted the professor to stick to the focus of the lecture and would most likely be disappointed if he "strayed from" the focus. It is unlikely that the students would be disappointed if the professor "adhered to" the focus of the lecture, so answer choice A is incorrect. Likewise, the other answer choices do not fit the context of the sentence.

6. **The best answer is D.** A day on horseback can make a rider's legs uncomfortable, so "labored" make the most sense. An important clue, too, is the modifier *long*, which emphasizes the extent of the horseback riding, and thus the impact on Jonathan's stride.

7. **The best answer is C.** A large metropolis is often "organized" into a system of smaller governmental bodies to improve communication with its citizens. The other answer choices do not make sense based on the context of the sentence.

8. **The best answer is C.** The word "transpire" can sometimes mean to "come about." Because Christine's hairstyle was not to her liking, it makes sense that she would not make a return visit to that stylist. The other answer choices do not fit the context of the sentence.

9. **The best answer is D.** The author of Passage 1 does not agree with the restrictiveness of fad diets and suggests that such diets might be dangerous. Therefore, the author would most likely assert that not indulging, at least occasionally, is not natural and is too restrictive.

10. **The best answer is C.** The last sentence in Passage 1 suggests that people might never learn to live a healthy lifestyle because they choose, instead, to follow fad diets, despite the disadvantages of such diets. The author of Passage 2 might suggest that being aware of these disadvantages is what encourages people to abandon fad diets and embrace a healthy lifestyle. Passage 2 states that "…a growing number of people are realizing that dieting is not the key to long-term weight loss."

11. **The best answer is B.** Passage 1 states that "Losing weight the disciplined way seems to have fallen out of fashion. Many people in the U.S. will probably never achieve a healthy lifestyle, one in which they eat a variety of healthy foods, moderate their food intake, and exercise regularly." This suggests that the author of Passage 1 believes that fad diets are an inevitable part of American culture.

12. **The best answer is D.** Both passages include statements suggesting that the keys to a healthy lifestyle include good eating and exercise habits. Passage 1 states, "Many people in the U.S. will probably never achieve a healthy lifestyle, one in which they eat a variety of healthy foods, moderate their food intake, and exercise regularly." Passage 2 states, "It is becoming increasingly hard to ignore the evidence that a lifestyle of sensible eating and exercise is the path to health."

13. **The best answer is E.** The word "germane" means "relevant or pertinent." It makes sense that the author would suggest that satellite data is more "relevant" because it is not affected by the heat effect.

14. **The best answer is B.** The word "debunk" means to "expose the falseness of a statement." The passage states that satellite data is more accurate because "it is not affected by the heat island effect near major cities, which could alter the readings of ground-based thermometers used by Accu-Weather." This suggests that ground-level temperature data should not be used in determining whether or not global temperatures are rising.

15. **The best answer is C.** The passage states that "any small change in temperature is unlikely to have the catastrophic repercussions that the media likes to foretell." This suggests that the media tends to sensationalize, or exaggerate, the problems of global warming. The other answer choices are not supported by the passage.

16. **The best answer is E.** The passage states that "Even if we are responsible, any small change in temperature is unlikely to have the catastrophic repercussions that the media likes to foretell. The ice caps will not melt as the result of a very minor increase in temperature…" The word "catastrophic" refers to something that is extremely serious or ruinous.

17. **The best answer is A.** According to the passage, "at one point in the past the Vikings were able to farm the now icy continent of Greenland as a result of higher temperatures." This supports the idea that a certain amount of global warming could lead to increase vegetation, which could be a good thing.

18. **The best answer is B.** The word "dissenting" refers to "a difference of opinion." The passage supports the notion that many scientists have differing opinions regarding the impact of increasing global temperatures.

19. **The best answer is A.** A "theory" is an assumption that is often made based on limited knowledge. By making that statement, the author of the passage is suggesting that a reduction in CO_2 levels might not actually have any effect on global temperatures, despite what some scientists are reporting.

20. **The best answer is C.** The word "although" indicates an alternative or suggests that even though one thing might occur, the results might be unexpected. The passage states that "Although perhaps a shift away from fossil fuels is forthcoming (they will eventually run out), a sudden, forced decrease in their use, as proposed by some international coalitions, is not the answer. It would instead be far more beneficial to the planet to increase reforestation efforts and attempt to limit the clear-cutting of valuable rainforest lands."

21. **The best answer is C.** A "coalition" refers to an "alliance" between certain groups. In this case, the "international coalitions" refer to specific countries that have come together to support "a shift away from fossil fuels."

22. **The best answer is C.** The passage states that "Holding off destruction in the tropics would be just as effective in decreasing greenhouse-gas emissions world-wide as would a dramatic decrease in fossil fuel use. In addition, biomass could potentially be converted into materials to replace cement, steel, and plastic, which take large amounts of energy to create and do little to store energy themselves." This best supports answer choice C.

23. **The best answer is B.** According to the passage, "Even making these changes, no one can be sure that the apparent global warming trend will change. There are indeed sustainable practices which we can adopt to improve our situation world-wide…" This statement suggests that the sustainable practices can improve the situation, but they might not actually alter the trend of increasing worldwide temperatures. This best supports answer choice B.

24. **The best answer is D.** The reference to "Mother Nature's hands" indicates that, even though humans might be able to make some changes to reduce CO_2 emissions or end destruction of the rainforests, the fate of the planet is ultimately not dependent upon us.

Section 3

1. **The correct answer is C.** To solve this problem, you must recall the associative property of addition:

   $(x - 4) + 4$

   $= (x + -4) + 4$

   $= x + (-4 + 4)$

   $= x$

   Therefore, $x = 17$.

2. **The correct answer is D.** To solve this problem, you must remember that if you start at the decimal point and count to the right, the place values are tenths, hundredths, thousandths, ten-thousandths, and so on. Therefore, the decimal 0.005 has the digit 5 in the thousandths place.

3. **The correct answer is C.** To solve this problem, first solve the first equation for b, as follows:

   $3a + b = 7$

   $b = 7 - 3a$

   Now substitute $(7 - 3a)$ for b in the second equation, as follows:

   $5a + 2(7 - 3a)$

   $5a + 14 - 6a$

   $14 - a$

   You know that you should solve for b in the first equation because all of the answer choices include the variable a.

4. **The correct answer is D.** To solve this problem, you must write an equation for the price of all of the notebooks and then solve for the price of one notebook. Make N the price of notebooks and B the price of binders purchased by Mandy and Jordan. If Mandy paid \$5.85 for three notebooks and one binder, the result is $3N + B = 5.85$. Likewise for Jordan, \$4.65 for two notebooks and one binder can be represented in the equation $2N + B = 4.65$.

   You can use substitution to solve these equations. Solving Jordan's equation for B yields $B = 4.65 - 2N$. If you substitute $4.65 - 2N$ as B into Mandy's equation, the result is $3N + (4.65 - 2N) = 5.85$. Combining like terms yields $N + 4.65 = 5.85$. If you subtract 4.65 from both sides of the equation, you find that $N = 1.20$. Therefore, the price of one notebook is \$1.20.

5. **The correct answer is A.** To solve this problem, it is critical that you remember that the three angles within a triangle must add up to exactly 180°. In the top triangle with angles 40° and 25°, the unknown angle has a measure of 180° − (40° + 25°) = 115°. You must remember that vertical angles are congruent, and therefore the top angle in the bottom triangle (with angles 50° and $a°$) also has a measure of 115°. Finally, you can find angle a by remembering that the angles 50°, 115°, and $a°$ must add up to 180°. Thus $a = 180° − (115° + 50°) = 15°$.

6. **The correct answer is E.** To solve this problem, realize that because $3^{x-1} = 243$ and $243 = 3^5$, $x − 1 = 5$. Thus $x = 6$.

   Always look for a simple relationship between the base and the exponent. In this case, you know that 3 to some power is equal to 243, so try raising 3 to sequential powers until you get 243.

7. **The correct answer is D.** To find what percent of 5 the number 7 is, you can simply divide 7 by 5 and multiply by 100%, as follows:

   $$\frac{7}{5} = 1.4$$

   $$(1.4)(100) = 140\%$$

8. **The correct answer is B.** To solve this problem, you must realize that because $XY = YZ$, the triangle is isosceles. Because the triangle is isosceles, you know that angles X and Z are congruent and have equal measures. If $a = 40°$, then $180° = 40° + x° + y°$ or $x° + y° = 140°$. Because $x = y$, both angles equal 70°. In triangles, sides have lengths that are proportional to their opposite angles. Because you know that the length of XZ is 5, and XZ is opposite the 40° angle, you can set up a proportion to find the length of side XY using its opposite angle, 70°. Thus $\frac{5}{40} = \frac{XY}{70}$. Therefore, $XY = \frac{(5 \times 70)}{40}$, or 8.75.

9. **The correct answer is C.** To solve this problem, you must recall that the formula for finding the slope of a line between the two points (x_1, y_1) and (x_2, y_2) is $\frac{(y_2 − y_1)}{(x_2 − x_1)}$. You must also recall that the origin lies at point (0, 0). Therefore, in this problem the points are (-6, 2) and (0, 0). You can use either set of points as (x_1, x_2) and (y_1, y_2), as long as you use them consistently within the formula. Therefore, the slope is $\frac{(2 − 0)}{(-6 − 0)} = \frac{2}{-6}$, or $-\frac{1}{3}$.

10. **The correct answer is B.** You can express that the length, l, is 3 times the width, w, as $l = 3w$. If the area is 48, you know that $lw = 48$. If you substitute $3w$ for l, you arrive at $(3w)w = 48$. Dividing by 3 yields $w^2 = 16$, and therefore $w = 4$. Because the length is 3 times the width, the length is 3(4), or 12.

11. **The correct answer is A.** You are given that x divided by 7 leaves a remainder of 4. The easiest approach to this problem is to assume that 7 goes into x one time with a remainder of 4. Therefore, x is equal to 11. If $x = 11$, then $2x = 22$. When 22 is divided by 7, the remainder is 1.

12. **The correct answer is C.** To solve this problem, you must realize that the number of pets that Gary has is determined through relationships between the quantities of the different types of pets: turtles (t), cats (c), and birds (b). Because the number of birds, b, is 4 more than the number of turtles, t, this can be expressed as $b = t + 4$. Also, because the number of cats, c, is 2 times the number of birds, this can be expressed as $c = 2b$. You might want to use a table (like the one below) to show the numerical relationship between the numbers of each pet and the total number of pets:

Numerical Relationships					
Number of turtles (t)	0	1	2	3	4
Number of birds ($b = t + 4$)	4	5	6	7	8
Number of cats ($c = 2b$)	8	10	12	14	16
TOTAL	**12**	**16**	**20**	**24**	**28**

According to this table, Gary *could* have a total of 20 pets, but he could not have a total of 14, 18, 22, or 26 pets.

13. **The correct answer is D.** To solve this problem, you must realize that if g is an integer, $\sqrt{g^2}$ would also have to be an integer. Of the answer choices, only $\sqrt{8}$ is not an integer; in fact, it is an irrational number.

14. **The correct answer is C.** To solve this problem you must realize that Set B contains all of the integers that result from *adding* 4 to each of the integers in Set A, as well as all of the integers that result from *subtracting* 4 from each of the integers in Set A. This results in Set B having twice as many integers as Set A. Therefore, Set B has 10 integers, which is 5 more integers than Set A.

15. **The correct answer is E.** You are given that the smaller circle has a radius of 3, and the larger circle has radius 3 + 5, or 8. To solve this problem, you must recognize that the ratio of areas is equal to the ratio of the squares of the radii because the formula for area is directly related to the square of the radius. Thus the ratio is $8^2 : 3^2$, or 64:9.

16. **The correct answer is D.** To solve this problem, substitute the answer choices in place of x in the equation. Only when $x = 2$ is the equation satisfied:

$$\frac{[7(2) + 6]}{5^2} =$$
$$\frac{20}{25} = \frac{4}{5}$$

17. **The correct answer is B.** To solve this problem, you can follow the instructions step by step, using parentheses to avoid any possible confusion.

Instruction	Result
Multiply x by 3.	$3x$
Add 4 to this product.	$3x + 4$
Divide this sum by 2.	$\frac{(3x + 4)}{2}$

18. **The correct answer is E.** To solve this problem, factor 56 as $28 \times 2 \times 1 = 56$. The numbers 28, 2, and 1 satisfy the requirement of $28 > 2 > 1$. Therefore, $r = 28$.

19. **The correct answer is C.** If you solve the equation $a + b = 3a + 6$ for b, you find that $b = 2a + 6$. By definition, an even number is any number that can be represented as the product $2n$, where n is any integer. Therefore, you can see that b must be even because it is the sum of two even numbers. The integer a is also even because it can be written as $a = (b - 6)/2$. Because b is even, the difference $b - 6$ is also even. Further, because this equation is divided by 2 and a and b are both integers, the quotient will be even. It is impossible to tell whether $a^2 = b^2$.

20. **The correct answer is C.** To solve this problem, you must realize that reducing the price by 20% each time is equivalent to multiplying the price by 0.8 every time it is reduced. Between May and August, the markdown would have occurred 3 times—June, July, and August. If the original price was d, you can conclude that the price in August would be $(0.8)(0.8)(0.8)d$, which equals $.8^3d$, or $.512d$.

Section 4

1. **The best answer is D.** The word "denoted" means "indicated"; therefore, it best fits in the blank.

2. **The best answer is B.** It is likely that Principal Warner would not be happy by John's tardiness. Therefore, John probably wants either to "avoid" or "escape" seeing Principal Warner. Because Principal Warner is most likely displeased, "cutting" is the best adjective to describe his glances.

3. **The best answer is C.** The context of the sentence indicates that squirrels hoard nuts so that they can eat, or "consume," them during the winter. None of the other answer choices make sense based on the context of the sentence.

4. **The best answer is C.** The context of the sentence indicates that quilting is a way to salvage, or preserve, old items of clothing that would probably have been thrown out. It is unlikely that "valuable," "expensive," or "useful" clothes would be thrown out, so eliminate answer choices A, B, and D. The words in answer choice C make the most sense when inserted into the blanks.

5. **The best answer is C.** The word "saturated" means to "fill to capacity" and best fits the context of the sentence. The remaining answer choices do not make sense when inserted into the blank.

6. **The best answer is B.** The word "fittingly" suggests that an action is "appropriate to the situation." The passage indicates that Rembrandt's use of light to illuminate his subjects is appropriate to how he feels about his subjects.

7. **The best answer is E.** According to the passage, "In Rembrandt's day, many of his fellow painters portrayed their characters much like the idealized gods of Greek and Roman mythology. Rembrandt differed by painting people in a more realistic and humble manner." This best supports answer choice E.

8. **The best answer is C.** A "simile" is a comparison of essentially unlike objects using the words "like" or "as." The author compares Wally to an overstuffed envelope, suggesting that he was about to burst and could no longer contain his secret. An "analogy" is a comparison that is made to show some kind of similarity or relationship but generally does not use "like" or "as." A "hyperbole" is an exaggeration; a "metaphor" is a figure of speech that makes an implicit comparison without using "like" or "as"; a "personification" applies human qualities to non-human objects.

9. **The best answer is B.** The passage states that "…she pulled a wrinkly old bag out of the cupboard. From this unassuming bag, she produced a huge wad of cash, and exclaimed, 'We can buy a really big house now!'" This clearly indicates that Ruth was also saving money for a down payment on a house.

10. **The best answer is D.** According to the passage, "Most people in the world today follow the Gregorian calendar, which is based on the solar cycle and keeps track of approximately 365.24 days each year." The passage also states that "In ancient China, the calendar was based on the lunar cycle and consisted of years represented by a cycle of 12 animals." This best supports answer choice D. The other answer choices cannot be supported by information in the passage.

11. **The best answer is C.** The passage states that "The origins of the 12 animals are deeply mythological, with the story being passed down for countless generations. A common telling of the tale includes a celebration to honor the Jade Emperor…" This suggests that there is more than one story regarding the origin of the Chinese calendar and that the source of the mythology cannot be precisely determined. While more than one of the answer choices could be true, only answer choice C is supported by the passage.

12. **The best answer is D.** The purpose of the second paragraph is to introduce the story that is recounted in the third paragraph. The other answer choices are not supported by the passage.

13. **The best answer is A.** The passage states, "Next came the mighty and majestic dragon, who flew across the river; when asked why he was not first, he replied that he needed to make rain for the people of Earth and was thus delayed. His kindness earned him the fifth place in the cycle." The word "benevolent" indicates kindness, so answer choice A is correct.

14. **The best answer is A.** The word "chastity" refers to the condition of being "pure." None of the animals exhibited this quality, whereas the remaining qualities—"industriousness," "teamwork," "dexterity," and "altruism"—were all exhibited by one or more of the animals in the passage.

15. **The best answer is D.** According to the passage, each year of the Chinese calendar is represented by a different animal. The passage states that "The origins of the 12 animals are deeply mythological, with the story being passed down for countless generations. A common telling of the tale includes a celebration to honor the Jade Emperor, with all the animals expected to pay tribute to him on the night of the new year. The first 12 to arrive would be held in high esteem." This best supports answer choice D.

16. **The best answer is D.** The passage indicates that, in addition to the 12 animals, the Chinese calendar also relies on five elements (water, wood, fire, metal, and earth) and two governing forces (Yin and Yang), suggesting that it is quite complicated. This best supports answer choice D.

17. **The best answer is C.** The passage indicates that the Chinese calendar is still used by people today but that it is quite complex and perhaps not clearly understood. The word "opaque" means "obscure, or unclear." Therefore, the Chinese zodiac can best be described as common but opaque.

18. **The best answer is E.** The purpose of the passage is to relay a story regarding the origins of the Chinese calendar, the details of which are not known by many people. Nothing in the passage suggests that the Chinese calendar is better than the Gregorian calendar, so answer choice A is incorrect. Likewise, the author does not assert anything about the precision of the Chinese calendar or correct any misconceptions about the Chinese calendar, so answer choices B and C are incorrect. Although the story might be considered humorous, the purpose of the passage is not to entertain the reader with a humorous anecdote, so answer choice D is incorrect.

19. **The best answer is D.** The passage focuses on the similarities in the eating habits of humans and chimpanzees and states "Scientists know very little about the eating habits of our ancestors from over two and a half million years ago. To solve this problem, scientists have started examining chimpanzees' hunting behavior and diet to find clues about our own prehistoric past. Studying chimpanzees might be beneficial because modern humans and chimpanzees are very closely related." This best supports answer choice D.

20. **The best answer is D.** Because the passage indicates that humans and chimpanzees have very similar DNA, it makes sense that any research findings involving chimpanzees would also hold true for humans.

21. **The best answer is E.** According to the passage, before Jane Goodall reported her findings, "scientists believed that chimpanzees were strict vegetarians." The fact that Dr. Goodall found chimpanzees were "actually very proficient hunters" suggests that true chimpanzee habits had never been observed prior to her work with the creatures.

22. **The best answer is A.** The passage states that "Despite these findings, scientists still maintain that chimpanzees are mostly fruit-eating creatures." As it is used in this context, "maintain" most nearly means "assert."

23. **The best answer is E.** Based on the context of the passage, you can infer that the phrase "truly carnivorous" indicates a dependence on meat. The passage states that "…like chimpanzees, humans are not truly carnivorous creatures. In fact, most ancient humans ate a diet composed primarily of plants, and even modern humans are considered omnivores because they eat fruits, vegetables, and meat."

24. **The best answer is B.** According to the passage, "Experts believe that chimpanzees share about 98.5% of the human DNA sequence. If this is true, humans are more closely related to chimpanzees than to any other animal species." The passage concludes by stating, "The information that scientists have been able to gather regarding chimpanzee hunting behavior is shedding some light on the eating habits of our ancestors." This best supports answer choice B.

Section 5

1. **The correct answer is C.** You are given that $a = 4$, so you can see that $a^3 = 4 \times 4 \times 4$, or 64. Because $a^3 = b^2$, $b^2 = 64$. Therefore, $b = 8$ or $b = -8$.

2. **The correct answer is D.** To solve this problem, you must realize that in order for angles to be supplementary, their sum must equal 180°. In the figure, you can see that adjacent angles that are formed by an intersection, such as angles 5 and 6, are supplementary. Because you know that lines l and m are parallel, alternate interior angles, such as angles 3 and 6, are also congruent. In addition, vertical angles, such as angles 2 and 3, are congruent. This means that angle 2 is congruent to angle 6. Therefore, you can conclude that angles 2 and 5 are supplementary.

3. **The correct answer is B.** You can find the number of unregistered male voters by finding the number of registered male voters and subtracting that quantity from the total number of men. Because you are given that there are 45,000 registered voters and that 26,000 of them are women, you can see that the number of male voters is 45,000 – 26,000 or 19,000. Further, because there are 31,000 men total and 19,000 of them are known to be registered voters, those not registered must number 31,000 – 19,000 or 12,000.

4. **The correct answer is C.** You are given that the net amount raised was $125. To solve the problem, plug $125 into the given equation and solve for l, as follows:

    $125 = 5l - 45$

    $170 = 5l$

    $\dfrac{170}{5} = 34$

5. **The correct answer is E.** If $mn = k$ and $k = x^2n$, you can combine the equations into $mn = x^2n$. Dividing both sides by n yields $m = x^2$.

6. **The correct answer is D.** To solve this equation, you must realize that if the number of total candies is expressed in thirds, the total number of candies must be divisible by 3. The number 20 does not break evenly into thirds. However, every other answer choice *does* break evenly into thirds.

7. **The correct answer is C.** To solve this problem, you must further break down $32\sqrt{32}$ so that it is easier to work with. For example, if you break 32 down into 16(2), the quantity under the radical is reduced to (16)(2). Therefore, $32\sqrt{16}\sqrt{2}$ = $32(4)\sqrt{2}$, which equals $128\sqrt{2}$. You can see that possible values for a and b are 128 and 2, respectively. A possible value for ab, then, is 128(2), or 256.

8. **The correct answer is E.** The formula for the circumference of a circle is $C = 2\pi r$. Given the circumference is $\frac{3}{4}\pi$, solve for r, as follows:

$$\frac{3}{4}\pi = 2\pi r$$

$$\frac{3}{4} = 2r$$

$$\frac{3}{8} = r$$

Now, using the radius, find the area of the circle. The formula for the area of a circle is $A = \pi r^2$; therefore, the area of the circle is $\pi(\frac{3}{8})^2$, or $\frac{9}{64}\pi$.

9. **The correct answer is 114.** You are given that $r^3 = 38$. Therefore, you can conclude that $3r^3 = 3(38)$, or 114.

10. **The correct answer is 55.5.** To solve this problem, you can simply take the average of the two points to determine the point that lies exactly halfway between them; $\frac{(47 + 64)}{2} = \frac{111}{2}$, which is 55.5.

11. **The correct answer is 40.** In triangles, the lengths of sides are proportional to the angles opposite them. Therefore, you know that if two angles in a triangle are equal, the sides opposite each of those two angles will also be equal. If you know that the lengths of two of the sides of the triangle are 10 and 15, the greatest possible perimeter would occur if each of the two sides opposite the congruent angles measures 15 and the other side measures 10. You can conclude that the greatest possible perimeter is thus 15 + 15 + 10, or 40.

12. **The correct answer is 7.** To solve this problem, you must use substitution. Given that $x + y = 9$, you can solve for y, as follows:

$$y = 9 - x$$

You can then substitute $9 - x$ for y in the equation $x^2 - y^2 = 45$, as follows:

$$x^2 - (9 - x)^2 = 45$$

$$x^2 - (81 - 18x + x^2) = 45$$

$$18x - 81 = 45$$

$$18x = 126$$

Therefore, $x = \frac{126}{18}$, or 7.

13. **The correct answer is 285.** To solve, set up three other variables, x, y, and z. Let x be the supplement of angle p. Let y be the supplement of angle q. Let z be the angle opposite of the 105° angle, so $z = 105°$. With these new variables, you know that $p = 180 - x$ and $q = 180 - y$. This means that $p + q = (180 - x) + (180 - y)$, which simplifies to $360 - (x + y)$. You can see that the three lines form a triangle and that one of the angles is 105°. That means that the other two angles, x and y, must have a sum of $180 - 105$, or 75°. Thus, if $x + y = 75°$, then $p + q = 360 - (x + y)$, or $360 - 75$, which is 285°.

14. **The correct answer is 9.** To solve this problem, you must recognize that if each term in the sequence is twice the preceding term, the sum of the first 5 terms would be $n + 2n + 2(2n) + 2(2(2n)) + 2(2(2(2n)))$. Using the associative property of multiplication, you get the following:

    $n + 2n + (2 \times 2)n + (2 \times 2 \times 2)n + (2 \times 2 \times 2 \times 2)n$, which results in $n + 2n + 2^2n + 2^3n + 2^4n$

    This can be simplified as follows:

    $n + 2n + 4n + 8n + 16n = 31n$

    Because the sum of the first 5 terms is 279, then $31n = 279$. Therefore, you can conclude that $n = \frac{279}{31}$, or 9.

15. **The correct answer is 7.** In a rectangle with a length (l) that is 5 inches longer than the width (w), the relation between the sides is $l = w + 5$. Since the perimeter, which is the distance around, can be written as twice the length plus twice the width, $38 = 2l + 2w$. In order to solve for width w, use the equation $l = w + 5$ to substitute into the perimeter equation, as follows:

    $38 = 2(w + 5) + 2w$

    $38 = 2w + 10 + 2w$

    $28 = 4w$

    $7 = w$

16. **The correct answer is 2 or 5.** Given the function $g(x) = 10 + \frac{x^2}{9}$, if $g(3k) = 7k$, then $10 + (3k)^2/9 = 7k$. To solve this problem, you must square the term $3k$ and then factor the resulting quadratic equation, as follows:

    $10 + 9k^2/9 = 7k$

    $10 + k^2 = 7k$

    $k^2 - 7k + 10 = 0$

    $(k - 5)(k - 2) = 0$

    Therefore, you can conclude that $k = 5$ or $k = 2$.

17. **The correct answer is .75 or $\frac{3}{4}$.** To solve this problem, you must set up an equation relating the individual averages to the combined average. The quantities $76n$ and $90p$ represent the total number of points the each class earned, which you would then divide by the number of students to determine the average in each class. One way you could find the combined average would be to take the sum of the total points earned in both classes, $76n + 90p$, and divide that quantity by the total number of students, $n + p$. Therefore, $84 = \frac{(76n + 90p)}{(n + p)}$. To find the ratio of $\frac{p}{n}$, multiply the entire equation by the quantity $n + p$, then combine like terms, as follows:

$$84(n + p) = (76n + 90p)$$

$$84n + 84p = 76n + 90p$$

$$6p = 8n$$

Thus $\frac{n}{p} = \frac{6}{8}$, which is equivalent to $\frac{3}{4}$ or 0.75.

18. **The correct answer is 5.** You are given that $2x - 3y = 9$; subsittute 9 for $2x - 3y$ in the first equation and solve, as follows:

$$3(9)(x + 3) = 162$$

$$27(x + 3) - 162$$

$$27x + 81 = 162$$

$$27x = 81$$

$$x = 3$$

Section 6

1. **The best answer is C.** Because the action taking place in the sentence took place in the past, you must use the past tense verbs "did" and "consisted." Therefore, answer choices A and E are incorrect. The helping verb "had" indicates the past perfect tense, which is not appropriate in this sentence, so answer choices B and D are incorrect.

2. **The best answer is D.** The participle "reducing" is not appropriate in this sentence. To maintain parallelism, you must use the verb "reduce;" the diet "advocates" the limited use of utensils to "reduce" the amount of food eaten.

3. **The best answer is E.** Because the action taking place in the sentence took place in the past, you must use the past tense verbs "nodded" and "caused." The helping verb "had" indicates the past perfect tense, which is not appropriate in this sentence. Answer choice C includes a comma splice, and answer choice D has an incomplete clause following a semicolon, neither of which is correct. Answer choice B is awkward and wordy. Only answer choice E effectively conveys the intended idea using correct grammar and punctuation.

4. **The best answer is B.** The phrase that begins with "such as" is a non-essential clause, which must be preceded by a comma. Although answer choice C includes the correct punctuation, it is wordy and awkward.

5. **The best answer is E.** The superlative "most" should be used to indicate the greatest in degree; according to the sentence, the first step often has the greatest degree of difficulty; therefore, "most" should be used. Answer choices A, C, and D are incorrect because the word "more" suggests a direct comparison, which the sentence does not indicate. Although answer choice B uses "most," it is awkwardly constructed.

6. **The best answer is E.** It is idiomatic to use the word "with" to indicate that you should keep your growing season in mind while you are purchasing plant material. In addition, answer choice E is in the active voice, as opposed to the passive voice, and most clearly and directly conveys the intended idea.

7. **The best answer is A.** This sentence is best as it is written. It effectively expresses the idea and is free from ambiguity. Answer choices B, C, D, and E are awkward and unclear.

8. **The best answer is C.** In the sentence as it is written, it is unclear as to whom the pronoun "they" refers. Pronouns must have clear antecedents. While answer choice E correctly uses "you," it is somewhat awkward.

9. **The best answer is A.** This sentence is best as it is written. The semicolon correctly joins two related sentences. Answer choices B, C, D, and E are awkward and unclear.

10. **The best answer is D.** It is necessary to include punctuation both before the word "therefore" or any coordinating conjunctions in this sentence because the sentence conveys two separate but related ideas. While answer choices C, D, and E are all correctly punctuated, only answer choice D correctly attributes the "loud gasp" to the crowd and uses the simple past tense.

11. **The best answer is A.** This sentence is best as it is written. It effectively expresses the idea and is free from ambiguity. Answer choices B, C, D, and E are awkward and unclear.

12. **The best answer is C.** It is necessary to use the adverb "peacefully" to modify the verb "lived." The remaining underlined portions are correct.

13. **The best answer is C.** The modifier "20-minute" should modify the best noun form of "discuss," which is "discussion," no the gerund "discussing."

14. **The best answer is B.** A gerund cannot be a verb form for the relative subject "who." The best change would be to use the infinitive verb form "to preside."

15. **The best answer is C.** You must use the plural verb "are" to match the plural noun "rules." The sentence indicates that the "rules" regarding negotiation are simple, *not* that the "negotiation" itself is simple. The remaining underlined portions are correct.

16. **The best answer is D.** It is necessary to include a comma after "smoke" because the phrase "not flames" is non-essential. The remaining underlined portions are correct.

17. **The best answer is A.** It is necessary to use the adjective "wise" instead of the adverb "wisely" to describe Thomas Jefferson. The remaining underlined portions are correct.

18. **The best answer is B.** Because the sentence indicates that Carl Rakeman died in 1965, it is necessary to use the simple past tense verb "captured" instead of the future perfect tense verb "will have captured." The remaining underlined portions are correct.

19. **The best answer is E.** This sentence does not contain any errors. It is correct to use the adverb "seemingly" to modify the adjectives "innocent" and "passive." Likewise, the singular nouns "appearance" and "job" are appropriate. It is also correct to use the phrase "contrast to" to indicate the difference between the goalie's appearance and what the goalie does.

20. **The best answer is A.** The sentence as it is written is incomplete—it lacks an inflected verb. It is necessary to use the verb "developed" to create a complete sentence and to indicate past tense. The remaining underlined portions are correct.

21. **The best answer is C.** It is necessary to use the singular verb "generates" to match the singular noun "movement." The sentence indicates that the "movement" of the charges, not the "charges" themselves, "generates" the high temperatures. The remaining underlined portions are correct.

22. **The best answer is E.** This sentence does not contain any errors. It is appropriate to use the simple past tense verbs "noticed," "put," and "was." The phrase "during the night" effectively describes when Dave put logs on the fire.

23. **The best answer is B.** It is necessary to use the word "neither" in conjunction with the word "nor." The remaining underlined portions are correct.

24. **The best answer is D.** It is necessary to use the nominative case of a personal pronoun with a compound subject; therefore, you should replace "him" with "he." The remaining underlined portions are correct.

25. **The best answer is B.** You should use the infinitive verb "fail" after the particle "to." The remaining underlined portions are correct.

26. **The best answer is A.** The apostrophe before the "s" in "American's" indicates possession, which is not appropriate in this sentence. The word "American" should be used to describe the "colonists." The remaining underlined portions are correct.

27. **The best answer is E.** This sentence does not contain any errors. It is clear and concise as it is written.

28. **The best answer is A.** The singular verb "appears" should be used to match the singular noun "link." The remaining underlined portions are correct.

29. **The best answer is D.** The sentence indicates that the planets were identified in the past. Therefore, it is appropriate to use the past tense verb "had been." The remaining underlined portions are correct.

30. **The best answer is C.** The sentence in answer choice C clearly and effectively combines the two ideas presented in Sentences 1 and 2. Answer choice A is incorrect because it is not clear to whom or what the weather patterns belong. Answer choice B is incorrect because it uses the phrase "up to" instead of the word "on" to clearly indicate that the ocean currents have an impact on weather patterns. In addition, the word "ultimately" is placed awkwardly in the sentence. Answer choice D is simply not as clear and direct as answer choice C. Answer choice E is incorrect because it is awkward and uses the passive voice.

31. **The best answer is E.** The sentence as it is written includes the phrase "influencing of producing," which is ungrammatical. Answer choice B is incorrect for the same reasons. Answer choice C is incorrect because the phrase "both of them" is placed in the sentence. Answer choice D is incorrect because it is awkward and uses the passive voice.

32. **The best answer is B.** When talking about speed, it is more appropriate to use the word "increased" than to use the word "arisen" or the phrases "gone up," "speeded up," "jumped up," or "taken off."

33. **The best answer is D.** The "greenhouse effect" is not discussed until the third paragraph, so it is not appropriate to mention it in the second paragraph, which discusses ocean currents.

34. **The best answer is C.** "Impact" is used correctly as a verb, and "degree" is used appropriately in the singular to mean "extent."

35. **The best answer is E.** The essay focuses primarily on weather patterns. The first and second paragraphs include discussions of ocean currents. The third paragraph begins a discussion of the "greenhouse effect," which is a new element of the main topic. The other answer choices are not supported by the passage.

Section 7

1. **The best answer is D.** Because the first words in answer choices A, B, C, and D all suggest that forest fires have a negative impact, it might be best to start with the second blank. You can eliminate answer choice E, which indicates that fires are believed to be "auspicious," or "favorable." The structure of the sentence requires something in the second clause that is unpredicted by the first clause, so "dispersion," or "scattering," of seedpods, an example of life after so much death from the fire suits the sentence construction.

2. **The best answer is A.** "Pretentious" means "vain" or "showing excessive pride in one's merits." Such food critics would most likely not show their approval of unsophisticated restaurants and "withhold" praise. The other answer choices do not fit the context of the sentence.

3. **The best answer is B.** "Liberal," as it is used here, means "based on the traditional arts and sciences of a college curriculum." Liberal studies vary greatly in subject matter and are meant to enrich and "broaden" students' diversity of academic interests. The other answer choices do not fit the context of the sentence.

4. **The best answer is B.** The word "despite" at the beginning of the sentence indicates a contrast. It is likely that because the Mauros spent a large amount of money on the cruise, they would expect the food and the entertainment to be worthy of the expense. However, the context of the sentence indicates that the Mauros were disappointed, so the best words to insert into the blanks should have negative connotations. Eliminate answer choices A and C because the first words have positive connotations. Likewise, eliminate answer choice D, which indicates that there were many entertainment options. Answer choice B is best, because the Mauros would most likely be more disappointed with "limited" entertainment options than they would be with "local" entertainment options.

5. **The best answer is D.** The sentence defines a hypothetical cause-effect relationship. Disease might rise or fall, causing a corresponding rise or fall in beef supply. Therefore, the best words to insert into the blank will indicate a cause-effect relationship. Answer choice D is best because a "swelling" of the disease might "pose" a risk to the beef supply. None of the other answer choices make sense based on the context of the sentence.

6. **The best answer is E.** Snow is frozen water crystals. "Conducive" means "favorable," and it makes sense that snow would form under conditions that are "favorable" to snow formation. The other choices would mean nearly the opposite.

7. **The best answer is E.** Passage 1 states that "All at once, our smooth trip turned into complete pandemonium as the captain at the wheel began yelling directions to his first mate who quickly began struggling with the sails and rigging. Generally, the wind continued offering resistance." Likewise, Passage 2 states that "…it seems that a person has a bit more control over a motorized vehicle than one powered by nature," and the boat "…also needs to be big enough to be capable of staving off a sudden storm or high winds that often present themselves on a large lake. I don't want a sailboat but rather a vessel that relies on a large motor." These statements best support answer choice E.

8. **The best answer is D.** The narrator uses the phrase "A spell is set upon the soul and a euphoric swell rises to push up the corners of the mouth" to show that the narrator was smiling and happy to be relaxing on the boat. The word "euphoric" indicates a feeling of great happiness.

9. **The best answer is C.** The passage states that "All at once, our smooth trip turned into complete pandemonium as the captain at the wheel began yelling directions to his first mate who quickly began struggling with the sails and rigging." This points to a contrast with the calm, "euphoric" feeling that the narrator expresses in the first paragraph.

10. **The best answer is C.** The word "impedance" reflects apparent opposition. The context of Passage 1 indicates that the wind was preventing the crew from getting the sails in order. The other answer choices are not supported by the context of the passage.

11. **The best answer is A.** Passage 1 states "We passengers, however, were still recovering from our terror and wondering to ourselves, 'Was all that supposed to happen? And they think this is fun?'" to illustrate the confusion and fear that the passengers were feeling following the tacking incident. The other answer choices are not supported by the context of the passage.

12. **The best answer is B.** According to the passage, "It was late afternoon when I began to work on the panic that was rising in my throat." This suggests that the narrator was getting nervous about the lateness of the hour and was perhaps wondering if they would make it back to shore at all. The passage goes on to state "From the shore, we may have looked as if we were actually sailing. I know better now and admit I was thrilled to see that the beautiful wind-powered craft could run on a motor in a pinch." This statement resolves the apprehension introduced by the sentence in question.

13. **The best answer is D.** Passage 2 begins with the statement that "It isn't so much the potential speed of a powerboat that attracts me. Perhaps it's like choosing a car over a horse. Certainly a car can break down at any time, but it seems that a person has a bit more control over a motorized vehicle than one powered by nature. This was the premise I operated under when I began talking about purchasing a boat for my lakefront vacation home." Clearly, the author is interested in purchasing a powerboat, which suggests that he or she finds powerboats "appealing."

14. **The best answer is D.** Passage 2 opens by stating that "It isn't so much the potential speed of a powerboat that attracts me. Perhaps it's like choosing a car over a horse. Certainly a car can break down at any time, but it seems that a person has a bit more control over a motorized vehicle than one powered by nature." This statement, along with others made throughout the passage, best support answer choice D.

15. **The best answer is A.** According to Passage 2, the process of elimination involves examining "the unfavorable aspects as well as the positive ones." The passage also states that "it's important to weigh them all before making such a big decision." These statements suggest that the author believes that discovering any negative characteristics ahead of time can ensure that the right decision is made. The other answer choices either focus only on the positive aspects or are not supported by the passage.

16. **The best answer is A.** Passage 2 states that "When purchasing a used boat, it is important to know what questions to ask the seller: 'How old can a boat be before I should question its seaworthiness? How many are too many engine hours?' Because I have never owned a boat before, feeling well informed is a challenge." This indicates that the author does not know very much about purchasing or owning a boat. The other answer choices are not supported by the passage.

17. **The best answer is E.** Both passages include statements that indicate that boating can be dangerous. The second paragraph of Passage 1 details the skill required to engage in the process of tacking and suggests that it can be frightening to those who do not understand the process. Likewise, Passage 2 states that any boat purchased by the author "needs to be big enough to be capable of staving off a sudden storm or high winds that often present themselves on a large lake. I don't want a sailboat but rather a vessel that relies on a large motor." These statements indicate that the author understands the potential dangers of boating and that he or she must ask the right questions to purchase the right boat.

18. **The best answer is D.** The author of Passage 2 states that "...it seems that a person has a bit more control over a motorized vehicle than one powered by nature." Therefore, it is likely that the author of Passage 2 would make the claim that controlled power boating is favorable to hectic sailing. The other answer choices are not supported by the passages.

19. **The best answer is D.** Passage 1 states that "Tacking when sailing is often a harrowing experience for those onboard. All at once, our smooth trip turned into complete pandemonium as the captain at the wheel began yelling directions to his first mate who quickly began struggling with the sails and rigging" and that "This mad yelling and steering, along with the raucous flapping of the sails, went on for several minutes before all was right again and the boat settled in to its new course." These statements suggest that only skilled and prepared sailboat operators can handle certain aspects of boating. Likewise, Passage 2 states that "When purchasing a used boat, it is important to know what questions to ask the seller: 'How old can a boat be before I should question its seaworthiness? How many are too many engine hours?' Because I have never owned a boat before, feeling well informed is a challenge. I have very little idea of what to inquire about, so the danger is buying a watercraft only to spend more in repairs than I would have spent on a brand new boat," which also suggests that one must be prepared to safely undertake the sport of boating.

Section 8

1. **The correct answer is D.** To solve this problem, you must recognize that there are 60 minutes per hour, and therefore there are 45 minutes in three quarters of an hour. If the object is traveling at 4 feet per minute for 45 minutes, the object travels 4×45, or 180 feet.

2. **The correct answer is C.** If the pet store sells only parakeets and finches, then the bird Allayne bought must *either* a parakeet *or* a finch. The problem does not specify which breed of bird Allayne bought, but it must be a parakeet or a finch. Thus answer choice C is correct; the bird Allayne bought must not be a canary.

3. **The correct answer is C.** If Carrie spends $4.65 on lunch for 21 work days, she will spend a total of 4.65×21, or $97.65. Answer choice C is the closest approximation to this, because $4.00 \times 25 = 100$.

4. **The correct answer is C.** Dividing 2,187.5 by 437.5, you see that 2,187.5 is exactly 5 times larger than 437.5. Thus, you know that n is nine times larger than 437.5; $437.5 \times 9 = 3,937.5$.

5. **The correct answer is A.** For the product of two integers to lie between 137 and 149, a multiple of both integers must lie between 137 and 149. Of the answer choices, 15 is the only number without a multiple that lies between 137 and 149; $15 \times 9 = 135$, and $15 \times 10 = 150$. Thus, the only number that cannot be one of the integers is 15.

6. **The correct answer is C.** The median of a list of values is the middle value when the list is in chronological order and there are an odd number of values. In this case, if we include Ryan and his 75 coins, there are now 19 coin collectors. List the number of coins for each collector in chronological order as follows.

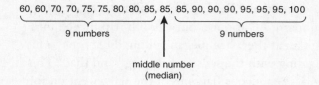

7. **The correct answer is C.** To solve this problem, simply count the numbers that appear both in set M and in set R. Sets M and R share the following numbers: 16, 17, 18, 19, and 20. Therefore, five numbers in set M are also in Set R.

8. **The correct answer is B.** To solve this problem, you must recognize that the triangle is a "special triangle." A right triangle in which the length of the longer leg is $\sqrt{3}$ times the length of the shorter leg is a $30°$-$60°$-$90°$ right triangle. Another property of this type of right triangle is that the hypotenuse is 2 times the length of the shorter leg. So this right triangle has lengths x, $x\sqrt{3}$, and $2x$. The perimeter is the sum of the lengths of the sides. You are given that the perimeter equals $12 + 4\sqrt{3}$.

$$12 + 4\sqrt{3} = x + x\sqrt{3} + 2x$$

$$12 + 4\sqrt{3} = 3x + x\sqrt{3}$$

For the right side of the equation to equal the left side of the equation, x must be equal to 4 because the left side is greater than the right side by a factor of 4.

9. **The correct answer is D.** To solve this equation, you must first calculate how many $\frac{1}{4}$-inch segments there are. Dividing 66 by 12, you can see that there are 5.5 $\frac{1}{4}$-inch segments. Thus, the road's length in inches is $\frac{1}{4} + \frac{1}{4} + \frac{1}{4} + \frac{1}{4} + \frac{1}{4} + \frac{1}{8}$ (which is half of $\frac{1}{4}$). This equals $1\frac{3}{8}$.

10. **The correct answer is D.** To solve this problem, you must remember, when multiplying the same base number raised to any power, to add the exponents. Thus, if $n^x \times n^8 = n^{24}$, $x + 8 = 24$, and x equals 16. Also when raising an exponential expression to a power, remember to multiply the exponent and power. So in $(n^6)^y = n^{18}$, $6y = 18$, and $y = 3$. Therefore, $x + y = 18 + 3$, or 21.

11. **The correct answer is A.** To solve this problem, you must realize that the volume of a cube is equal to (length)(width)(height) or simply (side)^3 because all sides of a cube are equivalent in length. To find the length of one side, find the cube root of 64, which is 4 ($4^3 = 64$). Because all sides of a cube are equal, the shortest distance from the center of the cube to the base of the cube equals the midpoint of the length of the cube, which is $\frac{4}{2}$, or 2.

12. **The correct answer is C.** To correctly answer this question, you must remember that the area of a triangle is calculated using the formula $A = \frac{1}{2}(bh)$, where b is the base of the triangle and h is the height of the triangle. The base of the triangle extends from the origin in the (x, y) coordinate plane $(0, 0)$ to the point $(5, 0)$. This means that the base is 5. The height of the triangle extends from the origin in the (x, y) coordinate plane, $(0, 0)$ to $(0, 4)$. The height of the triangle is 4. Plug these values into the formula:

$A = \frac{1}{2}(bh)$

$A = \frac{1}{2}(5 \times 4)$

$A = \frac{1}{2}(20)$

$A = 10$

13. **The correct answer is E.** To answer this question, you must recognize that any number with a hundreds digit of 8 and a units digit of 2 will appear as 8_2. You can easily enumerate the possibilities of this combination: 802, 812, 822, 832, 842, 852, 862, 872, 882, and 892. Ten three-digit numbers fit the criteria of the question.

14. **The correct answer is B**. The best way to approach this question is to apply reason and eliminate the Roman numerals that cannot be true. For example, x^2 must be a positive number because any non-zero number squared is positive. Therefore, Roman numeral I cannot be true. At this point, you can eliminate answer choices A, D, and E, which all contain Roman numeral I. Now look at Roman numeral III because it is an easier number to work with. Substitute 1 for x in the given equation:

$\frac{x}{5} = x^2$

$\frac{1}{5}$ does not equal 1^2

Now you can eliminate answer choice C, which leaves answer choice B as the only possible correct answer. To check the math, substitute $\frac{1}{5}$ for x in the given equation:

$$\frac{\frac{1}{5}}{5} = 5^2$$

$\frac{1}{5}$ divided by 5 is the same as 5 times 5, which equals 25. 5^2 also equals 25. Because the equation is satisfied, one possible value of x is $\frac{1}{5}$.

15. **The correct answer is C.** If 1 ounce of flavored syrup produces b bottles of soda pop, 20 ounces of syrup will produce a total of $20 \times b$ bottles of soda. $20b$ represents the total number of bottles of soda pop produced from 20 ounces of syrup. The cost of 20 ounces of syrup is d dollars. Therefore, to determine the cost of one bottle of soda pop, divide the total cost by the total number of bottles of pop produced. This is represented by the formula $\frac{d}{(20b)}$, answer choice C.

16. **The correct answer is C.** To solve this problem, you must recognize that the $39 price of the sneakers is 30% *more than* the amount it costs the store to purchase one pair of the sneakers. This can be represented as 130%, or 1.3. Thus, the price that the store pays for the sneakers is $\frac{\$39}{1.3}$, or $30. At the end of the year, sales associates get 20% off of this $30 price, therefore paying 80% of the price the shoe store pays. The cost to the employees is $30 × 0.80, or $24.

Section 9

1. **The best answer is A.** This sentence is best as it is written. It effectively expresses the idea and is free from ambiguity. Answer choices B, C, D, and E are awkward and unclear.

2. **The best answer is B.** The sentence as it is written suggests that Italy visited museums in France. To improve this sentence, use the parallel phrase "in Italy." Answer choices C and E do not maintain parallelism in the sentence, and answer choice D creates ambiguity in the role of "Italy."

3. **The best answer is C.** As it is written, the sentence is a fragment missing an inflected verb. Answer choice C corrects this problem and expresses the meaning of the sentence in a clear and concise manner.

4. **The best answer is B.** Answer choice B uses "older than" to make it clear that the South African bones are older than the age of their supposed Arab ancestors. The phrase "3,000 years" indicates the degree of difference.

5. **The best answer is C.** To maintain parallelism in the sentence, the singular possessive pronoun "its" must be changed to the plural pronoun "their." In addition, to clearly convey the idea that elephants were plentiful prior to being harvested for their trunks, it is necessary to use the word "until."

6. **The best answer is D.** Answer choice D completes the sentence in the most clear and effective manner and uses the common phrase "ever since" to refer to a period of time. Answer choice A includes unnecessary punctuation and is awkward and unclear. Answer choice B correctly eliminates "he" but is unclear. "Whereas" shows contrast, which is unnecessary in this sentence, so answer choice C is incorrect. Answer choice E creates a comma splice, which is not acceptable.

7. **The best answer is C.** Answer choice C correctly describes the rough equivalence between the area of Maine and the area overseen by the ranch-management companies. Answer choice B might appear to be correct. However, answer choice B uses the plural verb "have," which does not agree with the singular subject "number."

8. **The best answer is C.** The sentence as it is written uses the passive voice, which makes it awkward. Answer choice C clearly and effectively indicates who reached the finish line by using the pronoun "they" to refer to the antecedent "runners" and clearly conveys the proper sense of time by using "when."

9. **The best answer is A.** This sentence is best as it is written. It effectively expresses the idea, contains an inflected verb, and is free from ambiguity. Answer choices B, C, D, and E are awkward and unclear.

10. **The best answer is A.** This sentence is best as it is written. It effectively expresses the idea and is free from ambiguity. The remaining answer choices include ambiguous pronoun references and are awkwardly constructed.

11. **The best answer is D.** The phrase "a traumatic incident that occurred when they were adolescents" uses the relative clause "that occurred" to modify "a traumatic incident" and uses "they were" to refer to adult men and women. Answer choice A erroneously introduces the phrase "when an adolescent" with "occurring." This makes "traumatic incident" the grammatical referent of "when an adolescent." In addition, the singular "adolescent" does not correctly agree with the plural "adult men and women" mentioned in the passage.

12. **The best answer is C.** The sentence as it is written is incomplete—it lacks a main verb. To correct this problem, it is necessary to delete the pronoun "who" from before the verb "takes," thereby eliminating the parenthetical expression from the sentence and creating a complete sentence with a subject (artist) and a main verb (takes).

13. **The best answer is D.** The sentence as it is written incorrectly refers to the singular noun "production company" with the plural pronoun "their." Likewise, answer choices B and C, in addition to being awkward, incorrectly use "their." Answer choice E is awkward and uses the passive voice. Only answer choice D clearly and effectively conveys the intended meaning of the sentence, correctly using "on opening night" to refer to "attendance."

14. **The best answer is B.** Answer choice B correctly parallels the "the amount of energy used by" with "the amount used by." The other answer choices are either awkward or contain grammatical errors.

CHAPTER TEN

Practice Test 2 with Answers and Explanations

There are nine separate sections on this simulated test, including:

- ► One 25-minute Essay

- ► Five other 25-minute Verbal and Math Sections

- ► Two 20-minute Verbal and Math Sections

- ► One 10-minute Verbal Section

Work on only one section at a time and make every attempt to complete each section in the time allowed for that particular section. Carefully mark only one answer on your answer sheet for each question. Remember that you can and should write on the test itself to help you to correctly answer the questions.

Tear out pages 272–277 before you begin the test.

SECTION 1

Begin your essay on this page. If you need more space, continue on the next page. Do not write outside of the essay box.

Start with number 1 for each new section. If a section has fewer questions than answer spaces, leave the extra answer spaces blank. Be sure to erase any errors or stray marks completely.

SECTION 2

1 Ⓐ Ⓑ Ⓒ Ⓓ Ⓔ	11 Ⓐ Ⓑ Ⓒ Ⓓ Ⓔ	21 Ⓐ Ⓑ Ⓒ Ⓓ Ⓔ	31 Ⓐ Ⓑ Ⓒ Ⓓ Ⓔ
2 Ⓐ Ⓑ Ⓒ Ⓓ Ⓔ	12 Ⓐ Ⓑ Ⓒ Ⓓ Ⓔ	22 Ⓐ Ⓑ Ⓒ Ⓓ Ⓔ	32 Ⓐ Ⓑ Ⓒ Ⓓ Ⓔ
3 Ⓐ Ⓑ Ⓒ Ⓓ Ⓔ	13 Ⓐ Ⓑ Ⓒ Ⓓ Ⓔ	23 Ⓐ Ⓑ Ⓒ Ⓓ Ⓔ	33 Ⓐ Ⓑ Ⓒ Ⓓ Ⓔ
4 Ⓐ Ⓑ Ⓒ Ⓓ Ⓔ	14 Ⓐ Ⓑ Ⓒ Ⓓ Ⓔ	24 Ⓐ Ⓑ Ⓒ Ⓓ Ⓔ	34 Ⓐ Ⓑ Ⓒ Ⓓ Ⓔ
5 Ⓐ Ⓑ Ⓒ Ⓓ Ⓔ	15 Ⓐ Ⓑ Ⓒ Ⓓ Ⓔ	25 Ⓐ Ⓑ Ⓒ Ⓓ Ⓔ	35 Ⓐ Ⓑ Ⓒ Ⓓ Ⓔ
6 Ⓐ Ⓑ Ⓒ Ⓓ Ⓔ	16 Ⓐ Ⓑ Ⓒ Ⓓ Ⓔ	26 Ⓐ Ⓑ Ⓒ Ⓓ Ⓔ	36 Ⓐ Ⓑ Ⓒ Ⓓ Ⓔ
7 Ⓐ Ⓑ Ⓒ Ⓓ Ⓔ	17 Ⓐ Ⓑ Ⓒ Ⓓ Ⓔ	27 Ⓐ Ⓑ Ⓒ Ⓓ Ⓔ	37 Ⓐ Ⓑ Ⓒ Ⓓ Ⓔ
8 Ⓐ Ⓑ Ⓒ Ⓓ Ⓔ	18 Ⓐ Ⓑ Ⓒ Ⓓ Ⓔ	28 Ⓐ Ⓑ Ⓒ Ⓓ Ⓔ	38 Ⓐ Ⓑ Ⓒ Ⓓ Ⓔ
9 Ⓐ Ⓑ Ⓒ Ⓓ Ⓔ	19 Ⓐ Ⓑ Ⓒ Ⓓ Ⓔ	29 Ⓐ Ⓑ Ⓒ Ⓓ Ⓔ	39 Ⓐ Ⓑ Ⓒ Ⓓ Ⓔ
10 Ⓐ Ⓑ Ⓒ Ⓓ Ⓔ	20 Ⓐ Ⓑ Ⓒ Ⓓ Ⓔ	30 Ⓐ Ⓑ Ⓒ Ⓓ Ⓔ	40 Ⓐ Ⓑ Ⓒ Ⓓ Ⓔ

SECTION 3

1 Ⓐ Ⓑ Ⓒ Ⓓ Ⓔ	11 Ⓐ Ⓑ Ⓒ Ⓓ Ⓔ	21 Ⓐ Ⓑ Ⓒ Ⓓ Ⓔ	31 Ⓐ Ⓑ Ⓒ Ⓓ Ⓔ
2 Ⓐ Ⓑ Ⓒ Ⓓ Ⓔ	12 Ⓐ Ⓑ Ⓒ Ⓓ Ⓔ	22 Ⓐ Ⓑ Ⓒ Ⓓ Ⓔ	32 Ⓐ Ⓑ Ⓒ Ⓓ Ⓔ
3 Ⓐ Ⓑ Ⓒ Ⓓ Ⓔ	13 Ⓐ Ⓑ Ⓒ Ⓓ Ⓔ	23 Ⓐ Ⓑ Ⓒ Ⓓ Ⓔ	33 Ⓐ Ⓑ Ⓒ Ⓓ Ⓔ
4 Ⓐ Ⓑ Ⓒ Ⓓ Ⓔ	14 Ⓐ Ⓑ Ⓒ Ⓓ Ⓔ	24 Ⓐ Ⓑ Ⓒ Ⓓ Ⓔ	34 Ⓐ Ⓑ Ⓒ Ⓓ Ⓔ
5 Ⓐ Ⓑ Ⓒ Ⓓ Ⓔ	15 Ⓐ Ⓑ Ⓒ Ⓓ Ⓔ	25 Ⓐ Ⓑ Ⓒ Ⓓ Ⓔ	35 Ⓐ Ⓑ Ⓒ Ⓓ Ⓔ
6 Ⓐ Ⓑ Ⓒ Ⓓ Ⓔ	16 Ⓐ Ⓑ Ⓒ Ⓓ Ⓔ	26 Ⓐ Ⓑ Ⓒ Ⓓ Ⓔ	36 Ⓐ Ⓑ Ⓒ Ⓓ Ⓔ
7 Ⓐ Ⓑ Ⓒ Ⓓ Ⓔ	17 Ⓐ Ⓑ Ⓒ Ⓓ Ⓔ	27 Ⓐ Ⓑ Ⓒ Ⓓ Ⓔ	37 Ⓐ Ⓑ Ⓒ Ⓓ Ⓔ
8 Ⓐ Ⓑ Ⓒ Ⓓ Ⓔ	18 Ⓐ Ⓑ Ⓒ Ⓓ Ⓔ	28 Ⓐ Ⓑ Ⓒ Ⓓ Ⓔ	38 Ⓐ Ⓑ Ⓒ Ⓓ Ⓔ
9 Ⓐ Ⓑ Ⓒ Ⓓ Ⓔ	19 Ⓐ Ⓑ Ⓒ Ⓓ Ⓔ	29 Ⓐ Ⓑ Ⓒ Ⓓ Ⓔ	39 Ⓐ Ⓑ Ⓒ Ⓓ Ⓔ
10 Ⓐ Ⓑ Ⓒ Ⓓ Ⓔ	20 Ⓐ Ⓑ Ⓒ Ⓓ Ⓔ	30 Ⓐ Ⓑ Ⓒ Ⓓ Ⓔ	40 Ⓐ Ⓑ Ⓒ Ⓓ Ⓔ

CAUTION Use the answer spaces in the grids below for Section 2 or Section 3 only if you are told to do so in your test book.

Student-Produced Responses ONLY ANSWERS ENTERED IN THE CIRCLES IN EACH GRID WILL BE SCORED. YOU WILL NOT RECEIVE CREDIT FOR ANYTHING WRITTEN IN THE BOXES ABOVE THE CIRCLES.

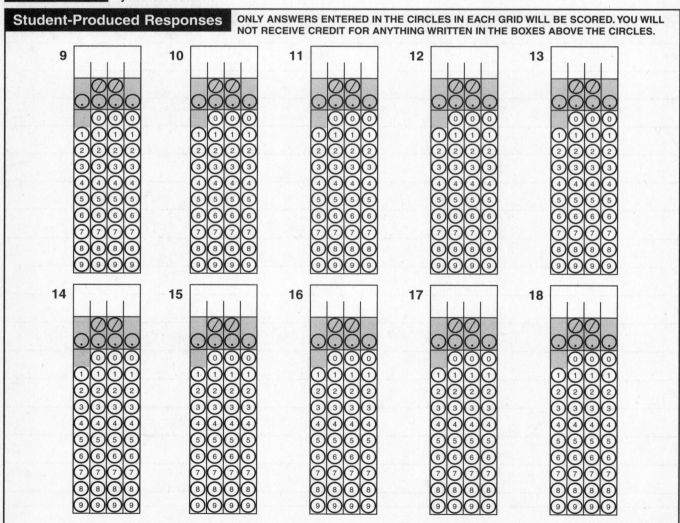

Start with number 1 for each new section. If a section has fewer questions than answer spaces, leave the extra answer spaces blank. Be sure to erase any errors or stray marks completely.

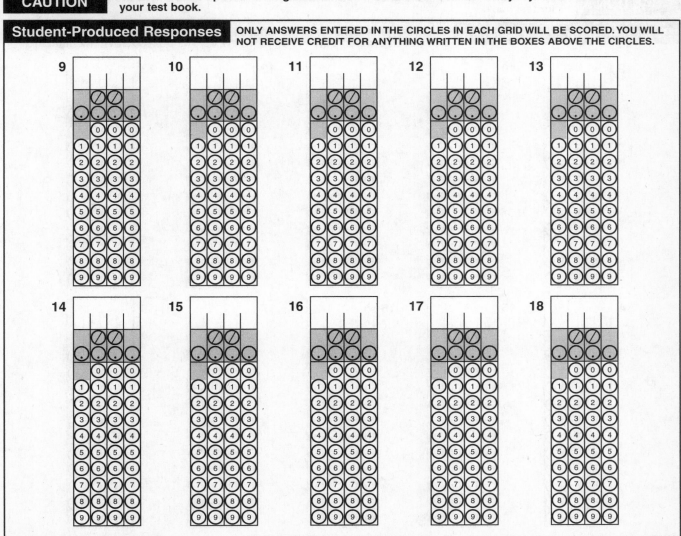

SECTION 4

1 Ⓐ Ⓑ Ⓒ Ⓓ Ⓔ   11 Ⓐ Ⓑ Ⓒ Ⓓ Ⓔ   21 Ⓐ Ⓑ Ⓒ Ⓓ Ⓔ   31 Ⓐ Ⓑ Ⓒ Ⓓ Ⓔ
2 Ⓐ Ⓑ Ⓒ Ⓓ Ⓔ   12 Ⓐ Ⓑ Ⓒ Ⓓ Ⓔ   22 Ⓐ Ⓑ Ⓒ Ⓓ Ⓔ   32 Ⓐ Ⓑ Ⓒ Ⓓ Ⓔ
3 Ⓐ Ⓑ Ⓒ Ⓓ Ⓔ   13 Ⓐ Ⓑ Ⓒ Ⓓ Ⓔ   23 Ⓐ Ⓑ Ⓒ Ⓓ Ⓔ   33 Ⓐ Ⓑ Ⓒ Ⓓ Ⓔ
4 Ⓐ Ⓑ Ⓒ Ⓓ Ⓔ   14 Ⓐ Ⓑ Ⓒ Ⓓ Ⓔ   24 Ⓐ Ⓑ Ⓒ Ⓓ Ⓔ   34 Ⓐ Ⓑ Ⓒ Ⓓ Ⓔ
5 Ⓐ Ⓑ Ⓒ Ⓓ Ⓔ   15 Ⓐ Ⓑ Ⓒ Ⓓ Ⓔ   25 Ⓐ Ⓑ Ⓒ Ⓓ Ⓔ   35 Ⓐ Ⓑ Ⓒ Ⓓ Ⓔ
6 Ⓐ Ⓑ Ⓒ Ⓓ Ⓔ   16 Ⓐ Ⓑ Ⓒ Ⓓ Ⓔ   26 Ⓐ Ⓑ Ⓒ Ⓓ Ⓔ   36 Ⓐ Ⓑ Ⓒ Ⓓ Ⓔ
7 Ⓐ Ⓑ Ⓒ Ⓓ Ⓔ   17 Ⓐ Ⓑ Ⓒ Ⓓ Ⓔ   27 Ⓐ Ⓑ Ⓒ Ⓓ Ⓔ   37 Ⓐ Ⓑ Ⓒ Ⓓ Ⓔ
8 Ⓐ Ⓑ Ⓒ Ⓓ Ⓔ   18 Ⓐ Ⓑ Ⓒ Ⓓ Ⓔ   28 Ⓐ Ⓑ Ⓒ Ⓓ Ⓔ   38 Ⓐ Ⓑ Ⓒ Ⓓ Ⓔ
9 Ⓐ Ⓑ Ⓒ Ⓓ Ⓔ   19 Ⓐ Ⓑ Ⓒ Ⓓ Ⓔ   29 Ⓐ Ⓑ Ⓒ Ⓓ Ⓔ   39 Ⓐ Ⓑ Ⓒ Ⓓ Ⓔ
10 Ⓐ Ⓑ Ⓒ Ⓓ Ⓔ   20 Ⓐ Ⓑ Ⓒ Ⓓ Ⓔ   30 Ⓐ Ⓑ Ⓒ Ⓓ Ⓔ   40 Ⓐ Ⓑ Ⓒ Ⓓ Ⓔ

SECTION 5

1 Ⓐ Ⓑ Ⓒ Ⓓ Ⓔ   11 Ⓐ Ⓑ Ⓒ Ⓓ Ⓔ   21 Ⓐ Ⓑ Ⓒ Ⓓ Ⓔ   31 Ⓐ Ⓑ Ⓒ Ⓓ Ⓔ
2 Ⓐ Ⓑ Ⓒ Ⓓ Ⓔ   12 Ⓐ Ⓑ Ⓒ Ⓓ Ⓔ   22 Ⓐ Ⓑ Ⓒ Ⓓ Ⓔ   32 Ⓐ Ⓑ Ⓒ Ⓓ Ⓔ
3 Ⓐ Ⓑ Ⓒ Ⓓ Ⓔ   13 Ⓐ Ⓑ Ⓒ Ⓓ Ⓔ   23 Ⓐ Ⓑ Ⓒ Ⓓ Ⓔ   33 Ⓐ Ⓑ Ⓒ Ⓓ Ⓔ
4 Ⓐ Ⓑ Ⓒ Ⓓ Ⓔ   14 Ⓐ Ⓑ Ⓒ Ⓓ Ⓔ   24 Ⓐ Ⓑ Ⓒ Ⓓ Ⓔ   34 Ⓐ Ⓑ Ⓒ Ⓓ Ⓔ
5 Ⓐ Ⓑ Ⓒ Ⓓ Ⓔ   15 Ⓐ Ⓑ Ⓒ Ⓓ Ⓔ   25 Ⓐ Ⓑ Ⓒ Ⓓ Ⓔ   35 Ⓐ Ⓑ Ⓒ Ⓓ Ⓔ
6 Ⓐ Ⓑ Ⓒ Ⓓ Ⓔ   16 Ⓐ Ⓑ Ⓒ Ⓓ Ⓔ   26 Ⓐ Ⓑ Ⓒ Ⓓ Ⓔ   36 Ⓐ Ⓑ Ⓒ Ⓓ Ⓔ
7 Ⓐ Ⓑ Ⓒ Ⓓ Ⓔ   17 Ⓐ Ⓑ Ⓒ Ⓓ Ⓔ   27 Ⓐ Ⓑ Ⓒ Ⓓ Ⓔ   37 Ⓐ Ⓑ Ⓒ Ⓓ Ⓔ
8 Ⓐ Ⓑ Ⓒ Ⓓ Ⓔ   18 Ⓐ Ⓑ Ⓒ Ⓓ Ⓔ   28 Ⓐ Ⓑ Ⓒ Ⓓ Ⓔ   38 Ⓐ Ⓑ Ⓒ Ⓓ Ⓔ
9 Ⓐ Ⓑ Ⓒ Ⓓ Ⓔ   19 Ⓐ Ⓑ Ⓒ Ⓓ Ⓔ   29 Ⓐ Ⓑ Ⓒ Ⓓ Ⓔ   39 Ⓐ Ⓑ Ⓒ Ⓓ Ⓔ
10 Ⓐ Ⓑ Ⓒ Ⓓ Ⓔ   20 Ⓐ Ⓑ Ⓒ Ⓓ Ⓔ   30 Ⓐ Ⓑ Ⓒ Ⓓ Ⓔ   40 Ⓐ Ⓑ Ⓒ Ⓓ Ⓔ

CAUTION   Use the answer spaces in the grids below for Section 4 or Section 5 only if you are told to do so in your test book.

Student-Produced Responses   ONLY ANSWERS ENTERED IN THE CIRCLES IN EACH GRID WILL BE SCORED. YOU WILL NOT RECEIVE CREDIT FOR ANYTHING WRITTEN IN THE BOXES ABOVE THE CIRCLES.

Start with number 1 for each new section. If a section has fewer questions than answer spaces, leave the extra answer spaces blank. Be sure to erase any errors or stray marks completely.

SECTION 6

1 Ⓐ Ⓑ Ⓒ Ⓓ Ⓔ	11 Ⓐ Ⓑ Ⓒ Ⓓ Ⓔ	21 Ⓐ Ⓑ Ⓒ Ⓓ Ⓔ	31 Ⓐ Ⓑ Ⓒ Ⓓ Ⓔ
2 Ⓐ Ⓑ Ⓒ Ⓓ Ⓔ	12 Ⓐ Ⓑ Ⓒ Ⓓ Ⓔ	22 Ⓐ Ⓑ Ⓒ Ⓓ Ⓔ	32 Ⓐ Ⓑ Ⓒ Ⓓ Ⓔ
3 Ⓐ Ⓑ Ⓒ Ⓓ Ⓔ	13 Ⓐ Ⓑ Ⓒ Ⓓ Ⓔ	23 Ⓐ Ⓑ Ⓒ Ⓓ Ⓔ	33 Ⓐ Ⓑ Ⓒ Ⓓ Ⓔ
4 Ⓐ Ⓑ Ⓒ Ⓓ Ⓔ	14 Ⓐ Ⓑ Ⓒ Ⓓ Ⓔ	24 Ⓐ Ⓑ Ⓒ Ⓓ Ⓔ	34 Ⓐ Ⓑ Ⓒ Ⓓ Ⓔ
5 Ⓐ Ⓑ Ⓒ Ⓓ Ⓔ	15 Ⓐ Ⓑ Ⓒ Ⓓ Ⓔ	25 Ⓐ Ⓑ Ⓒ Ⓓ Ⓔ	35 Ⓐ Ⓑ Ⓒ Ⓓ Ⓔ
6 Ⓐ Ⓑ Ⓒ Ⓓ Ⓔ	16 Ⓐ Ⓑ Ⓒ Ⓓ Ⓔ	26 Ⓐ Ⓑ Ⓒ Ⓓ Ⓔ	36 Ⓐ Ⓑ Ⓒ Ⓓ Ⓔ
7 Ⓐ Ⓑ Ⓒ Ⓓ Ⓔ	17 Ⓐ Ⓑ Ⓒ Ⓓ Ⓔ	27 Ⓐ Ⓑ Ⓒ Ⓓ Ⓔ	37 Ⓐ Ⓑ Ⓒ Ⓓ Ⓔ
8 Ⓐ Ⓑ Ⓒ Ⓓ Ⓔ	18 Ⓐ Ⓑ Ⓒ Ⓓ Ⓔ	28 Ⓐ Ⓑ Ⓒ Ⓓ Ⓔ	38 Ⓐ Ⓑ Ⓒ Ⓓ Ⓔ
9 Ⓐ Ⓑ Ⓒ Ⓓ Ⓔ	19 Ⓐ Ⓑ Ⓒ Ⓓ Ⓔ	29 Ⓐ Ⓑ Ⓒ Ⓓ Ⓔ	39 Ⓐ Ⓑ Ⓒ Ⓓ Ⓔ
10 Ⓐ Ⓑ Ⓒ Ⓓ Ⓔ	20 Ⓐ Ⓑ Ⓒ Ⓓ Ⓔ	30 Ⓐ Ⓑ Ⓒ Ⓓ Ⓔ	40 Ⓐ Ⓑ Ⓒ Ⓓ Ⓔ

SECTION 7

1 Ⓐ Ⓑ Ⓒ Ⓓ Ⓔ	11 Ⓐ Ⓑ Ⓒ Ⓓ Ⓔ	21 Ⓐ Ⓑ Ⓒ Ⓓ Ⓔ	31 Ⓐ Ⓑ Ⓒ Ⓓ Ⓔ
2 Ⓐ Ⓑ Ⓒ Ⓓ Ⓔ	12 Ⓐ Ⓑ Ⓒ Ⓓ Ⓔ	22 Ⓐ Ⓑ Ⓒ Ⓓ Ⓔ	32 Ⓐ Ⓑ Ⓒ Ⓓ Ⓔ
3 Ⓐ Ⓑ Ⓒ Ⓓ Ⓔ	13 Ⓐ Ⓑ Ⓒ Ⓓ Ⓔ	23 Ⓐ Ⓑ Ⓒ Ⓓ Ⓔ	33 Ⓐ Ⓑ Ⓒ Ⓓ Ⓔ
4 Ⓐ Ⓑ Ⓒ Ⓓ Ⓔ	14 Ⓐ Ⓑ Ⓒ Ⓓ Ⓔ	24 Ⓐ Ⓑ Ⓒ Ⓓ Ⓔ	34 Ⓐ Ⓑ Ⓒ Ⓓ Ⓔ
5 Ⓐ Ⓑ Ⓒ Ⓓ Ⓔ	15 Ⓐ Ⓑ Ⓒ Ⓓ Ⓔ	25 Ⓐ Ⓑ Ⓒ Ⓓ Ⓔ	35 Ⓐ Ⓑ Ⓒ Ⓓ Ⓔ
6 Ⓐ Ⓑ Ⓒ Ⓓ Ⓔ	16 Ⓐ Ⓑ Ⓒ Ⓓ Ⓔ	26 Ⓐ Ⓑ Ⓒ Ⓓ Ⓔ	36 Ⓐ Ⓑ Ⓒ Ⓓ Ⓔ
7 Ⓐ Ⓑ Ⓒ Ⓓ Ⓔ	17 Ⓐ Ⓑ Ⓒ Ⓓ Ⓔ	27 Ⓐ Ⓑ Ⓒ Ⓓ Ⓔ	37 Ⓐ Ⓑ Ⓒ Ⓓ Ⓔ
8 Ⓐ Ⓑ Ⓒ Ⓓ Ⓔ	18 Ⓐ Ⓑ Ⓒ Ⓓ Ⓔ	28 Ⓐ Ⓑ Ⓒ Ⓓ Ⓔ	38 Ⓐ Ⓑ Ⓒ Ⓓ Ⓔ
9 Ⓐ Ⓑ Ⓒ Ⓓ Ⓔ	19 Ⓐ Ⓑ Ⓒ Ⓓ Ⓔ	29 Ⓐ Ⓑ Ⓒ Ⓓ Ⓔ	39 Ⓐ Ⓑ Ⓒ Ⓓ Ⓔ
10 Ⓐ Ⓑ Ⓒ Ⓓ Ⓔ	20 Ⓐ Ⓑ Ⓒ Ⓓ Ⓔ	30 Ⓐ Ⓑ Ⓒ Ⓓ Ⓔ	40 Ⓐ Ⓑ Ⓒ Ⓓ Ⓔ

CAUTION Use the answer spaces in the grids below for Section 6 or Section 7 only if you are told to do so in your test book.

Student-Produced Responses ONLY ANSWERS ENTERED IN THE CIRCLES IN EACH GRID WILL BE SCORED. YOU WILL NOT RECEIVE CREDIT FOR ANYTHING WRITTEN IN THE BOXES ABOVE THE CIRCLES.

9 10 11 12 13

14 15 16 17 18

Start with number 1 for each new section. If a section has fewer questions than answer spaces, leave the extra answer spaces blank. Be sure to erase any errors or stray marks completely.

SECTION 8

1 Ⓐ Ⓑ Ⓒ Ⓓ Ⓔ	11 Ⓐ Ⓑ Ⓒ Ⓓ Ⓔ	21 Ⓐ Ⓑ Ⓒ Ⓓ Ⓔ	31 Ⓐ Ⓑ Ⓒ Ⓓ Ⓔ
2 Ⓐ Ⓑ Ⓒ Ⓓ Ⓔ	12 Ⓐ Ⓑ Ⓒ Ⓓ Ⓔ	22 Ⓐ Ⓑ Ⓒ Ⓓ Ⓔ	32 Ⓐ Ⓑ Ⓒ Ⓓ Ⓔ
3 Ⓐ Ⓑ Ⓒ Ⓓ Ⓔ	13 Ⓐ Ⓑ Ⓒ Ⓓ Ⓔ	23 Ⓐ Ⓑ Ⓒ Ⓓ Ⓔ	33 Ⓐ Ⓑ Ⓒ Ⓓ Ⓔ
4 Ⓐ Ⓑ Ⓒ Ⓓ Ⓔ	14 Ⓐ Ⓑ Ⓒ Ⓓ Ⓔ	24 Ⓐ Ⓑ Ⓒ Ⓓ Ⓔ	34 Ⓐ Ⓑ Ⓒ Ⓓ Ⓔ
5 Ⓐ Ⓑ Ⓒ Ⓓ Ⓔ	15 Ⓐ Ⓑ Ⓒ Ⓓ Ⓔ	25 Ⓐ Ⓑ Ⓒ Ⓓ Ⓔ	35 Ⓐ Ⓑ Ⓒ Ⓓ Ⓔ
6 Ⓐ Ⓑ Ⓒ Ⓓ Ⓔ	16 Ⓐ Ⓑ Ⓒ Ⓓ Ⓔ	26 Ⓐ Ⓑ Ⓒ Ⓓ Ⓔ	36 Ⓐ Ⓑ Ⓒ Ⓓ Ⓔ
7 Ⓐ Ⓑ Ⓒ Ⓓ Ⓔ	17 Ⓐ Ⓑ Ⓒ Ⓓ Ⓔ	27 Ⓐ Ⓑ Ⓒ Ⓓ Ⓔ	37 Ⓐ Ⓑ Ⓒ Ⓓ Ⓔ
8 Ⓐ Ⓑ Ⓒ Ⓓ Ⓔ	18 Ⓐ Ⓑ Ⓒ Ⓓ Ⓔ	28 Ⓐ Ⓑ Ⓒ Ⓓ Ⓔ	38 Ⓐ Ⓑ Ⓒ Ⓓ Ⓔ
9 Ⓐ Ⓑ Ⓒ Ⓓ Ⓔ	19 Ⓐ Ⓑ Ⓒ Ⓓ Ⓔ	29 Ⓐ Ⓑ Ⓒ Ⓓ Ⓔ	39 Ⓐ Ⓑ Ⓒ Ⓓ Ⓔ
10 Ⓐ Ⓑ Ⓒ Ⓓ Ⓔ	20 Ⓐ Ⓑ Ⓒ Ⓓ Ⓔ	30 Ⓐ Ⓑ Ⓒ Ⓓ Ⓔ	40 Ⓐ Ⓑ Ⓒ Ⓓ Ⓔ

SECTION 9

1 Ⓐ Ⓑ Ⓒ Ⓓ Ⓔ	11 Ⓐ Ⓑ Ⓒ Ⓓ Ⓔ	21 Ⓐ Ⓑ Ⓒ Ⓓ Ⓔ	31 Ⓐ Ⓑ Ⓒ Ⓓ Ⓔ
2 Ⓐ Ⓑ Ⓒ Ⓓ Ⓔ	12 Ⓐ Ⓑ Ⓒ Ⓓ Ⓔ	22 Ⓐ Ⓑ Ⓒ Ⓓ Ⓔ	32 Ⓐ Ⓑ Ⓒ Ⓓ Ⓔ
3 Ⓐ Ⓑ Ⓒ Ⓓ Ⓔ	13 Ⓐ Ⓑ Ⓒ Ⓓ Ⓔ	23 Ⓐ Ⓑ Ⓒ Ⓓ Ⓔ	33 Ⓐ Ⓑ Ⓒ Ⓓ Ⓔ
4 Ⓐ Ⓑ Ⓒ Ⓓ Ⓔ	14 Ⓐ Ⓑ Ⓒ Ⓓ Ⓔ	24 Ⓐ Ⓑ Ⓒ Ⓓ Ⓔ	34 Ⓐ Ⓑ Ⓒ Ⓓ Ⓔ
5 Ⓐ Ⓑ Ⓒ Ⓓ Ⓔ	15 Ⓐ Ⓑ Ⓒ Ⓓ Ⓔ	25 Ⓐ Ⓑ Ⓒ Ⓓ Ⓔ	35 Ⓐ Ⓑ Ⓒ Ⓓ Ⓔ
6 Ⓐ Ⓑ Ⓒ Ⓓ Ⓔ	16 Ⓐ Ⓑ Ⓒ Ⓓ Ⓔ	26 Ⓐ Ⓑ Ⓒ Ⓓ Ⓔ	36 Ⓐ Ⓑ Ⓒ Ⓓ Ⓔ
7 Ⓐ Ⓑ Ⓒ Ⓓ Ⓔ	17 Ⓐ Ⓑ Ⓒ Ⓓ Ⓔ	27 Ⓐ Ⓑ Ⓒ Ⓓ Ⓔ	37 Ⓐ Ⓑ Ⓒ Ⓓ Ⓔ
8 Ⓐ Ⓑ Ⓒ Ⓓ Ⓔ	18 Ⓐ Ⓑ Ⓒ Ⓓ Ⓔ	28 Ⓐ Ⓑ Ⓒ Ⓓ Ⓔ	38 Ⓐ Ⓑ Ⓒ Ⓓ Ⓔ
9 Ⓐ Ⓑ Ⓒ Ⓓ Ⓔ	19 Ⓐ Ⓑ Ⓒ Ⓓ Ⓔ	29 Ⓐ Ⓑ Ⓒ Ⓓ Ⓔ	39 Ⓐ Ⓑ Ⓒ Ⓓ Ⓔ
10 Ⓐ Ⓑ Ⓒ Ⓓ Ⓔ	20 Ⓐ Ⓑ Ⓒ Ⓓ Ⓔ	30 Ⓐ Ⓑ Ⓒ Ⓓ Ⓔ	40 Ⓐ Ⓑ Ⓒ Ⓓ Ⓔ

ESSAY
Time—25 minutes

You have 25 minutes to write an essay based on the topic presented below. Do not write on another topic. Your essay should be written on the lined pages provided. For the best results, write on every line and keep your handwriting to a reasonable, legible size. Be sure to fully develop your point of view, present your ideas clearly and logically, and use the English language precisely.

Think carefully about the following issue and assignment:

> It can be said that there is an intrinsic benefit in helping another human being—it makes both people involved feel good. It could also be said that the spirit of volunteerism is lacking in the world. People the world over will come together in times of crisis, pulling together their collective talents to enact real change in the world, yet this behavior is rare in the intervening periods.

Assignment: Should we find ways to stimulate volunteerism outside of times of crisis? Plan and write an essay in which you develop your point of view on this topic. Support your position with reasoning and solid examples taken from your personal experience, observations, reading, or studies.

WRITE YOUR ESSAY ON PAGES 272 AND 273.

If you finish writing before your time is called, check your work on this section only. Do not turn to any other section in the test.

SECTION 2
Time—25 minutes
24 Questions

Directions: For each of the questions in this section, choose the best answer and fill in the corresponding circle on your answer sheet.

Each sentence that follows has either one or two blanks. Each blank indicates that a word has been omitted from the sentence. Following each sentence are five words or sets of words. Select the word or set of words that, when inserted into the sentence in place of the blank(s), best fits the context of the sentence as a whole.

1. Joanna's ------- lack of enthusiasm about the job made the interviewer extremely apprehensive to hire her; the company was searching for motivated employees who enjoyed what they did.

   (A) covert
   (B) manifest
   (C) furtive
   (D) feigned
   (E) deceptive

2. The Eiffel Tower, today considered to be one of the most ------- pieces of architectural art in the world, was initially met with much resistance from the public, many people thinking it was simply -------.

   (A) noisome . . an eyesore
   (B) resplendent . . an inspiration
   (C) unseemly . . a stunner
   (D) striking . . a monstrosity
   (E) appalling . . a calamity

3. Completing a triathlon is a demanding task, taking months of both physical and mental preparation and training before ------- the swimming, biking, and running courses.

   (A) attempting
   (B) insinuating
   (C) convincing
   (D) depleting
   (E) alleviating

4. Because of Aishah's ------- study habits, her test scores were extremely high.

   (A) obsolete
   (B) inconspicuous
   (C) exemplary
   (D) disdainful
   (E) mediocre

5. The teacher's directions regarding how to write our research paper were very ------- and vague, so when she returned the papers and had graded them all quite harshly, the class was ------- that she hadn't given us a better understanding of her expectations.

   (A) meticulous . . indignant
   (B) ambiguous . . agitated
   (C) indefinite . . fortuitous
   (D) explicit . . blithe
   (E) equivocal . . exhilarated

6. The charity ball was ------- affair with a vast array of magnificent food, flowing drinks, and an orchestra playing melodies all evening.

   (A) a scant
   (B) a moderate
   (C) an austere
   (D) a lavish
   (E) a customary

GO ON TO THE NEXT PAGE

7. Sarah's husband planned their entire vacation ------; he had an itinerary broken down into 30-minute increments of what they would be doing at precisely what time for the eight days that they would be gone.

   (A) meticulously
   (B) impetuously
   (C) tenuously
   (D) tumultuously
   (E) imperceptibly

8. Water sports are extremely popular in New Zealand because of the ------- of beaches surrounding Auckland and the year-round moderate temperatures.

   (A) opacity
   (B) scarcity
   (C) jumble
   (D) dearth
   (E) abundance

Each passage that follows is accompanied by several questions based on the content of the passage. Answer the questions based on what is either stated or implied in each passage. Be sure to read any introductory material that is provided.

Questions 9 and 10 are based on the following passage.

In England in the early 1800s, women were jailed simply because their husbands died and left them with debt that they had no means of paying. Prison conditions were appalling, and the injustice was heightened by the fact that the women often had to take their children with them. Elizabeth Fry was determined to make a difference for these women and children. She organized a team of women to visit the prisoners and teach them to sew, which enabled them to earn some money and drastically improve their lives. Fry never gave up on prison reform, and she spearheaded many efforts that had lasting effects.

Line
5

10

9. The author mentions the fact that women often had to bring their children to prison with them in order to

   (A) explain that Fry's initial interest in prison reform could be attributed to children
   (B) call attention to the fact that children were often the cause of the women's debt
   (C) emphasize to the reader the focal point of Fry's prison-reform efforts
   (D) further highlight the bigotry experienced by the women who were jailed
   (E) imply that the injustice children felt was far greater than that felt by their mothers

GO ON TO THE NEXT PAGE ⟩

10. The author's attitude towards the plight faced by the many women jailed in England in the early nineteenth century can best be described as

(A) apathetic
(B) impassioned
(C) exalted
(D) serene
(E) cordial

Questions 11 and 12 are based on the following passage.

It has been said that a picture is worth a thousand words, but does this axiom hold true even for a cartoon? For Thomas Nast, a political cartoonist of the late nineteenth century, it *Line* was indeed true. One cartoon was so powerful 5 that it resulted in the arrest of the corrupt "Boss" Tweed. Tweed was hiding out in Spain when a policeman recognized him from a drawing by Nast. "Boss" Tweed may not be a 10 relevant figure today, but several of Nast's doodles live on. They are the Democratic donkey, the Republican elephant, and the nonpartisan "Uncle Sam."

11. Why does the author begin this passage with the saying "A picture is worth a thousand words"?

(A) The author is implying that political cartoons can often irrevocably impact a politician's election campaign.
(B) The author is questioning whether or not this saying was valid in the late nineteenth century.
(C) The author is demonstrating that because Nast's cartoons resulted in an arrest and that some of his drawings are still very famous, his cartoons were quite salient.
(D) The author is implying that Nast was illiterate and could only communicate with his cartoons.
(E) The author is stating that pictures are more valuable than literature.

GO ON TO THE NEXT PAGE

12. The author likely informs the reader that "several of Nast's doodles live on" in lines 10–11 in order to

(A) demean political cartoons as relatively worthless drawings done while daydreaming

(B) emphasize the point that art visual is time-less and can have influence long after the artist's death

(C) imply that drawing cartoons came so easily to Nast that he did not have to spend much time or effort working on his cartoons

(D) suggest that at times cartoons can be even more important than law enforcement

(E) cause the reader to question whether a picture is more valuable than a cartoon

GO ON TO THE NEXT PAGE

Questions 13–24 are based on the following passages.

The following two passages consider whether or not to continue manned missions into space.

Passage 1

A robot sent into space to gather information is certainly a valuable tool but should only be regarded in that light. Even the most technologically advanced robots cannot and should not replace manned missions to outer space.

Certainly it is cheaper and less dangerous to launch a computer probe that can gather reams of data, but often the information obtained by a machine serves to produce more questions than answers. The space program would be far better off allowing manned missions to follow up on those initial information-gathering robotic ventures.

While manned missions are more costly than unmanned, they are also more successful. Robots and astronauts use much of the same equipment in space, but a human is more capable of calibrating sensitive instruments correctly and placing them in appropriate and useful positions. A computer is often neither as precise nor as accurate as a human managing the same terrain or environmental factors. Robots are also not as well equipped as humans to solve problems as they arise, and robots often collect data that is unhelpful or irrelevant. A human, on the other hand, can make instant decisions about what to explore further and what to ignore.

While technological advances have allowed mankind to make incredible strides in space exploration, they still cannot match the power and intelligence of the human mind. On-site presence of this biological "supercomputer" is necessary to maintain a space program that truly advances to the next level.

So what is that next level? The vast majority of Americans support governmental funding of manned space flight, though probably for a variety of reasons. The bottom line is that most of us view outer space as the next great scientific and exploratory frontier. Some

even believe that soon humans will need another place to live besides Earth.

Passage 2

The end of the twentieth century saw many changes in America's space program, probably due in large part to the Challenger and Columbia Space Shuttle disasters. The tragic deaths of innocent space explorers have shaken support for these endeavors and have caused citizens to question, and some even to reject, the validity of manned space flight. This, coupled with the incredible advances in technological devices, has probably signaled the end of manned space exploration as we know it.

We have no reason, however, to lament the end of this chapter of the space program or to assume that the worlds beyond our Earth will remain unknown and undeveloped. Robotic computers and similar devices continue to evolve and improve. The Mars Pathfinder and rovers have exceeded expectations in providing scientists with important data. With each robot sent into space, not only is valuable information collected, but also the problems the robot encounters are revealed and improvements made for future launches.

One must admit that humans are hardly suited for life away from planet Earth. People need food, water, and oxygen-rich air, all of which appear to be absent in the broader solar system. This means these necessities would fill a large part of the payload of any manned mission, occupying a great deal of the limited space and restricted weight of any space ship. Once the necessary equipment is on board, the tremendous weight alone becomes a hazard to all of the flight's passengers. It's like loading a boat so full of cargo that it sinks to the bottom of the ocean before it ever leaves port.

There is also the cost to consider. It is estimated that for every shuttle launched, two or three unmanned missions could have taken place. In 1999, a single shuttle flight had a price tag of $420 million! When considering that this money primarily comes from tax

GO ON TO THE NEXT PAGE ➡

dollars, it is no wonder that the public has
lost its enthusiasm for manned space
missions.

90   With the rapid improvements in technology, maybe the astronaut is becoming
outdated and should be replaced by the robot.
After all, no one cries when a computer-driven
hunk of metal blows up or disappears. If one
95 more person can be spared from harm by
employing a technological alternative to
manned space flight, how could we not embrace
that technology?

13. The authors of both passages agree that

   (A) too much money is being spent on
       space exploration
   (B) manned space flight is a thing of the
       past
   (C) space exploration will continue in
       some form
   (D) robotics are not yet reliable enough
       to be used in the space program
   (E) the government is not doing enough
       to keep the space program going

14. In line 7, the author of Passage 1 uses the
    word "Certainly" to indicate

   (A) an emphatic statement of fact
   (B) assurance that the statement is accu-
       rate
   (C) a rebuttal to the previous statement
   (D) the potential for a counterargument
   (E) an opinion over a factual statement

15. In line 19, "calibrating" most nearly
    means

   (A) orbiting
   (B) collecting
   (C) operating
   (D) sharing
   (E) adjusting

16. The question in line 37, ("So what...level?"),
    chiefly serves to

   (A) introduce a philosophical aspect of space
       exploration
   (B) describe the historical stages of the space
       program
   (C) argue in favor of private funding of the
       space program
   (D) warn of the dangers of space exploration
   (E) decrease public enthusiasm for manned
       space flight

17. The author mentions the space shuttle disasters
    most likely to

   (A) promote the idea of continued space explo-
       ration
   (B) dismiss the fears held by the public
       regarding space exploration
   (C) emphasize the serious ramifications of
       manned space exploration
   (D) defend the notion of sending innocent civil-
       ians into space
   (E) deny the problems associated with
       unmanned space exploration

18. In line 56, "lament" most nearly means

   (A) agree with
   (B) argue with
   (C) regret
   (D) oppose
   (E) support

19. In lines 68–72, "One must admit, ...the broader
    solar system" emphasizes that which of the
    following is particularly important to consider in
    regard to the space program?

   (A) cost
   (B) reliability
   (C) knowledge
   (D) safety
   (E) desire

GO ON TO THE NEXT PAGE

20. The question at the end of Passage 2 primarily draws attention to

   (A) the hazards involved with manned space travel

   (B) the knowledge that can be obtained by continuing space exploration

   (C) the beauty of life on other planets

   (D) the growing limitations of life on Earth

   (E) space exploration as a public entity

21. Both passages base their arguments on the unstated assumption that

   (A) technology is the way of the future

   (B) fewer and fewer scientists continue to be interested in space exploration

   (C) humans and technology are on a collision course

   (D) human interest in potential life beyond Earth will continue

   (E) human has already conquered the "great frontier"

22. What aspect of manned space flight seems to matter a great deal in Passage 1 but not in Passage 2?

   (A) its high cost

   (B) its marred safety record

   (C) its compatibility with sensitive instruments and large amounts of data

   (D) its powerful images showing intrepid explorers expanding human frontiers

   (E) its requirement of life-sustaining provisions like food and water

23. The last sentence of Passage 1 ("Some even...Earth.") suggests that

   (A) Earth's population is growing to such an extent that the planet might no longer be able to accommodate all of the humans

   (B) Earth's population growth will increase exponentially because of continued space exploration

   (C) scientists are unable to account for the public's reluctance to embrace unmanned space technology, despite the population explosion

   (D) Earth's environment is rapidly becoming inhospitable

   (E) manned space flight is creating a difficult living situation for most humans

24. The author uses the phrase "computer-driven hunk of metal" (lines 93–94) to

   (A) decry the value of machines in space missions

   (B) emphasize the lower risk of unmanned space flight

   (C) foster debate over the role of machines in manned space missions

   (D) question hastily prepared, unmanned space missions

   (E) suggest the limits of scientific machinery

STOP

If you finish before your time is up, check your work on this section only.
You may not turn to any other section in the test.

SECTION 3
Time—25 minutes
20 Questions

Directions: Solve each problem and determine which is the best of the answer choices given. Fill in the corresponding circle on your answer sheet. Use any available space to solve the problems.

Notes

1. The use of a calculator is permitted.
2. All numbers are real numbers.
3. Figures that accompany problems in this test are intended to provide information useful in solving the problems. They are drawn as accurately as possible EXCEPT when it is stated in a specific problem that the figure is not drawn to scale. All figures lie in a plane unless otherwise indicated.
4. Unless otherwise specified, the domain of any function f is assumed to be the set of all real numbers x for which $f(x)$ is a real number.

Reference Information

 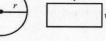

$A = \Pi r^2$
$C = 2\Pi r$ $A = lw$ $A = \frac{1}{2}bh$ $V = lwh$ $V = \Pi r^2 h$ $c^2 = a^2 + b^2$ Special Right Triangles

The number of degrees of arc in a circle is 360.
The sum of the measures in degrees of the angles of a triangle is 180.

---

1. If $5x - 3 = 3x + 11$, what is the value of x?

   (A) 1
   (B) 4
   (C) 5
   (D) 7
   (E) 8

2, 7, 22, 67

2. The first term in the sequence above is 2, and each term after is determined by multiplying the preceding term by a and then adding b. What is the value of a?

   (A) 13
   (B) 8
   (C) 5
   (D) 3
   (E) 1

---

3. The greatest number of diagonals that can be drawn from one vertex of a regular 8-sided polygon is

   (A) 2
   (B) 3
   (C) 4
   (D) 5
   (E) 6

GO ON TO THE NEXT PAGE

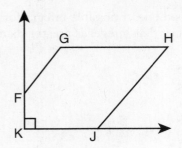

4. In the preceding figure, which two sides of polygon *FGHJK* have the same slope?

(A) *FK* and *KJ*
(B) *FG* and *GH*
(C) *GH* and *KJ*
(D) *FG* and *KJ*
(E) *GH* and *HJ*

5. If *x* is an odd integer greater than 5, what is the next greater odd integer in terms of *x*?

(A) $x + 2$
(B) $x + 3$
(C) $x + 5$
(D) $3x$
(E) x^2

6. A piece of string *s* inches in length is cut into exactly 8 pieces, each $3\frac{1}{2}$ inches in length. What is the value of *s*?

(A) $11\frac{1}{2}$
(B) 24
(C) $24\frac{1}{2}$
(D) 28
(E) 35

7. For any $x < -2$, which of the following values is the <u>least</u>?

(A) x^4
(B) x^3
(C) x^2
(D) $x - 1$
(E) $2x$

8. Three business associates agree to share profits of $46,000 in the ratio of 2:3:5. What is the amount of the largest share?

(A) $9,200
(B) $13,800
(C) $15,300
(D) $18,000
(E) $23,000

9. In an office supply store, pens that normally sell for 89¢ each are on sale at 2 for $1.29. How much can be saved by purchasing 12 of these pens at the sale price?

(A) $2.40
(B) $2.94
(C) $3.04
(D) $4.80
(E) $7.74

GO ON TO THE NEXT PAGE

10. If the average (arithmetic mean) of 7 consecutive numbers is 16, what is the sum of the least and greatest of the 7 integers?

(A) 13
(B) 14
(C) 16
(D) 19
(E) 32

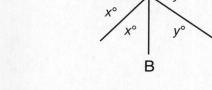

11. In the figure above, AB is a line segment. What is the value of $\frac{(y-x)}{(y+x)}$?

(A) $\frac{1}{3}$
(B) $\frac{1}{4}$
(C) $\frac{1}{5}$
(D) $\frac{1}{6}$
(E) $\frac{1}{7}$

12. The number 0.001 is how many times greater than the number $(0.0001)^2$?

(A) 10
(B) 10^3
(C) 10^5
(D) 10^7
(E) 10^9

13. What is the least possible integer for which 15 percent of that integer is greater than 2.3?

(A) 3
(B) 12
(C) 15
(D) 16
(E) 18

Subtract 4 from n.

Multiply this sum by 2.

Divide this product by 3.

14. Which of the following is the result obtained by performing the operations described above?

(A) $\frac{4n}{6}$
(B) $\frac{(2n-4)}{3}$
(C) $\frac{(2n-8)}{3}$
(D) $\frac{(4n-4)}{3}$
(E) $\frac{(4n-8)}{6}$

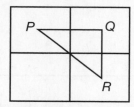

Note: Figure not drawn to scale.

15. In the above figure, each of the four squares has sides of length $2x$. If triangle PQR is formed by joining the centers of three of the squares, what is the perimeter of triangle PQR in terms of x?

(A) $4x\sqrt{2}$
(B) $2x\sqrt{2}$
(C) $4x + \sqrt{2}$
(D) $4x + 2x\sqrt{2}$
(E) $4 + 2x\sqrt{2}$

GO ON TO THE NEXT PAGE ⇒

16. If $m^2 + 9 = 32$, then $m^2 - 9 =$

- (A) 14
- (B) 23
- (C) 41
- (D) 105
- (E) 113

17. The total sum of a list of expenses incurred is divided by the average (arithmetic mean) of the amount of each expense, resulting in the number m. What does m represent?

- (A) the number of expenses incurred
- (B) half of the number of expenses incurred
- (C) the average of the expenses
- (D) the sum of the expenses
- (E) half of the sum of the expenses

18. If $x + y = 23$ and $y < 7$, then which of the following must be true?

- (A) $y > 1$
- (B) $y \neq 0$
- (C) $x < 16$
- (D) $x = 16$
- (E) $x > 16$

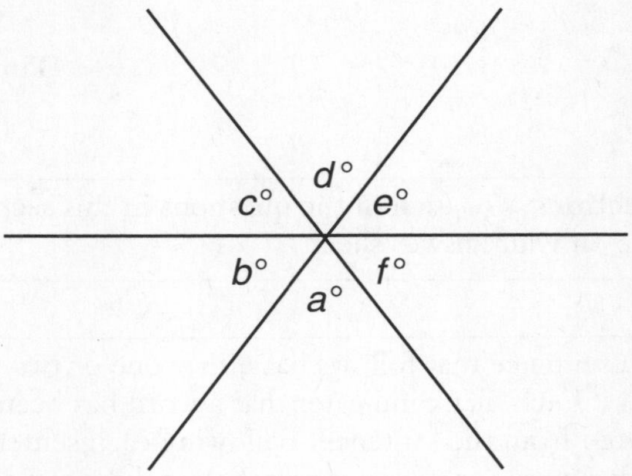

19. Three lines intersect at a point as shown in the figure above. Which of the following pairs of angle measures is NOT sufficient for determining all of the angle measures?

- (A) d and f
- (B) d and a
- (C) c and e
- (D) b and d
- (E) b and c

20. If n is a prime number greater than 3, which of the following could be a prime number?

- (A) n^2
- (B) $\frac{n}{2}$
- (C) $3n$
- (D) $n - 6$
- (E) $n^2 + 1$

STOP

**If you finish before your time is up, check your work on this section only.
You may not turn to any other section in the test.**

SECTION 4
Time —25 minutes
24 Questions

Directions: For each of the questions in this section, choose the best answer and fill in the corresponding circle on your answer sheet.

Each sentence that follows has either one or two blanks. Each blank indicates that a word has been omitted from the sentence. Following each sentence are five words or sets of words. Select the word or set of words that, when inserted into the sentence in place of the blank(s), best fits the context of the sentence as a whole.

1. Apple pie, baseball, rock and roll music, and the stars and stripes of the United States flag are all thought to ------- American popular culture.

    (A) satirize
    (B) embody
    (C) imitate
    (D) affront
    (E) ensconce

2. When the CEO announced the he was ------- after 25 years in the business, there was quite a bit of ------- in the office about who would take his place—no one would be able to match his experience or his enthusiasm.

    (A) commencing . . anticipation
    (B) procuring . . aversion
    (C) vacating . . apathy
    (D) concurring . . trepidation
    (E) resigning . . apprehension

3. Fear inspired by the media's coverage of unprovoked shark attacks is -------; more fatalities actually occur each year from lightning strikes than from shark attacks.

    (A) pompous
    (B) amplified
    (C) candid
    (D) subdued
    (E) veritable

4. Jonathan came to regret his general ------- of schoolwork when it came time to apply to college; his grade point average was not high enough to get him into any of his universities of choice.

    (A) negligence
    (B) prudence
    (C) heedfulness
    (D) solicitousness
    (E) diligence

5. The Great Wall of China stretches over a ------- 3,948 miles, but the proclamation that it is visible all the way from the moon is ------- that was popularized before manned space travel disproved the theory.

    (A) mere . . an actuality
    (B) monumental . . a certainty
    (C) diminutive . . an allegory
    (D) formidable . . a myth
    (E) negligible . . a fabrication

GO ON TO THE NEXT PAGE

Each passage that follows is accompanied by several questions based on the content of the passage. Answer the questions based on what is either stated or implied in each passage. Be sure to read any introductory material that is provided.

Questions 6–9 are based on the following passages.

Passage 1

The minimum wage is insufficient to meet basic costs of living and should be raised. Profit-hungry corporations and greedy business owners are victimizing the working poor.
Line
5 Corporations seem more interested in making money than in providing a living wage to their employees. A full-time worker earning just the minimum wage earns well below the poverty line. It is impossible to provide for a family,
10 much less have any personal dignity or enjoy the benefits of living in America.

Passage 2

Proponents of higher minimum wages should be prepared for higher unemployment of unskilled and low-skilled workers. The
Line
5 problem with raising the minimum wage boils down to simple economics; whenever the price of something goes up and supply remains the same, demand goes down. This is just as true of labor as anything else. If government mandates rather than market forces raise the price of
10 labor, wage controls act as a price floor. If the economic benefit that a worker provides an employer is less than the minimum required wage, that employer will simply do without the services of the worker. So raising the minimum
15 wage also raises unemployment.

6. The author of Passage 2 would most likely respond to the third sentence of Passage 1 by

(A) questioning the objectivity of the author and the author's sources of information
(B) noting the fact that to stay in business, all companies must yield a profit
(C) arguing that if demand suggested it, companies would ideally pay their employees even less
(D) suggesting that workers should increase their level of skill if they are inclined to increase their wages
(E) contending that if the minimum wage were to increase, the demand for unskilled workers would also increase

7. The two passages differ in their views of minimum wage in that Passage 1 states that minimum wage problems

(A) are effects of the poverty line, while Passage 2 suggests that minimum wage problems are caused by variances in supply and demand
(B) are attributable to the owners of corporations and businesses, while Passage 2 advocates that minimum wage problems are due to unemployment levels
(C) can be attributed to businesses and corporations, while Passage 2 suggests that minimum wage problems are a product of the economy
(D) would be less alarming if people did not have families, while Passage 2 suggests that minimum wage problems would be less of a problem if there were more skilled workers in the labor force
(E) would be completely eliminated if the minimum wage was raised, while Passage 2 suggests that minimum wage problems would be eliminated if the price floor on wages was altered

GO ON TO THE NEXT PAGE

8. The author of Passage 1 would most likely assert which of the following about Passage 2 as a whole?

   (A) The author of Passage 2 is most likely a greedy business owner or a part of a profit-hungry corporation.
   (B) The author of Passage 2 used inconsistent assumptions and unclear leaps of logic throughout the passage, making it sound implausible.
   (C) The author of Passage 2 would become more credible if he or she took on a more subjective tone.
   (D) The author of passage 2 probably has beliefs about minimum-wage issues that are analogous to those of the author of Passage 1.
   (E) The author of Passage 2 looks at the issue from on objective point of view, without any regard or compassion for the working poor.

9. Unlike the author of Passage 2, the author of Passage 1 uses which of the following?

   (A) Non-partisan analysis
   (B) Compelling descriptions
   (C) Impassive vocabulary
   (D) A callous tone
   (E) Direct citations

GO ON TO THE NEXT PAGE

Questions 10–15 are based on the following passage.

In this passage, the legal concept of eminent domain is discussed.

Eminent domain is the power of a government to take, or condemn, privately owned property. This power of condemnation
Line is part of the fundamental authority of a
5 governmental entity. Indeed, in 1879, in *Boom Co v Patterson*, the United States Supreme Court explained that eminent domain is "an attribute of sovereignty." However, this power is not without its limitations.

10 The Fifth Amendment to the United States Constitution provides that the federal government may not take private property unless for a public use and unless the owner is reimbursed with just compensation. Just
15 compensation is a monetary amount that will make the owner whole again for the loss and is generally measured in relation to the fair market value of the property, which is the amount of money a reasonable purchaser would
20 pay for the property. Almost all state constitutions contain similar clauses requiring just compensation when a state governmental agency takes private property for public use. Some states, like Alabama, Oklahoma, and
25 South Carolina, allow property to be taken for a private use if the owner consents. Arizona, Washington, and Wyoming even allow their governments to take private property for specific, limited private uses.

30 "Public use" has traditionally meant that the government could take private land only if it could demonstrate that the land was necessary to develop a project that had a valid public purpose and would be used by the public. The
35 most common example of such a use is a new road or highway. Other examples include public utilities, public buildings, public parks, railroads, and bridges. In 1954, in *Berman v Parker*, the United States Supreme Court
40 expanded the scope of the government's taking power when it affirmed the taking of a blighted area, or slum, for redevelopment by a private enterprise. The Court reasoned that the rede-

veloped property would be beneficial to the
45 public welfare of the community.

In June 2005, the United States Supreme Court broadened even further the scope of what type of use constitutes a "public use." In *Kelo v New London*, the Court held that private
50 land can be taken for the purpose of economic development even when the land taken does not qualify as blighted but merely economically depressed. In that case, private homes and businesses in a desirable waterfront locale were
55 taken for the development of new residences, hotels, and retail and office space, which the city contended would create new jobs and increase tax revenues. Opponents of such acquisitions argue that merely incidental benefits to
60 the state are not enough to justify the exercise of the power of condemnation. Many are troubled by the potential abuses that may result from interpreting "public use" so broadly. For example, as Justice Sandra Day O'Connor
65 suggested in her dissenting opinion, the power would very likely be most beneficial to those citizens "with disproportionate influence and power in the political process" to the detriment of residents of poorer sectors of the community
70 or neighborhoods inhabited primarily by minorities. But supporters of the *Kelo* decision emphasize the potential appreciable benefit to the community at large, citing that the needs of the many often outweigh the needs of the few.
75 They also point out that Justice John Paul Stevens expressly recommended that the states are free to impose limitations on the use of such power by local governmental authorities.

10. The second and third sentences (lines 3–8) are characterized, respectively, by

   (A) warning and justification
   (B) assertion and confirmation
   (C) invocation and definition
   (D) authority and reverence
   (E) confession and resolution

GO ON TO THE NEXT PAGE ➡

11. As used in line 11, "provides" most nearly means

  (A) declares
  (B) supplies
  (C) gives
  (D) believes
  (E) infers

12. According to the passage, eminent domain does all of the following, EXCEPT

  (A) allows for condemnation of private property
  (B) provides for just compensation, which is usually based on fair market value
  (C) encourages private takings of public property for private use
  (D) allows for redevelopment of blighted areas
  (E) transfers all decisions regarding fair market value solely to the states

13. The passage suggests that those who disapprove of the *Kelo* ruling and those who support it differ the most in

  (A) their level of respect for the United States Supreme Court
  (B) their belief in the free enterprise system
  (C) their views regarding the definition of public use
  (D) their confidence in the public's ability to decide what purposes to support
  (E) their acceptance of the influence of special interests of the government

14. The author suggests which of the following about "a new road or highway" (lines 35–36)?

  (A) It would be planned to avoid as much private property as possible.
  (B) It is an exemplary public use of land.
  (C) Private ownership rights outweigh governmental rights to seize land on which to build it.
  (D) Private landowners do not benefit from constructing it.
  (E) It would be of greater public good than a new park.

15. The author included discussion of two Supreme Court justices' decisions (lines 63–78) in order to

  (A) suggest that the Supreme Court maintains unlimited control over eminent domain rights
  (B) assert that the debate over eminent domain is fractious and stagnating
  (C) claim that eminent domain rights are fundamentally wrong for democracy
  (D) show that expansion of eminent domain rights is effected in a balanced manner
  (E) expose the corruptibility of the political process

GO ON TO THE NEXT PAGE →

Questions 16–24 are based on the following passage.

In the following passage the origin of and some of the variations in individual languages are examined.

The history of human language is as
much a story of human expansion and interaction as it is one of political turmoil and cultural
oppression. Careful analysis of language variation must seek evidence not just in the flow of
people and information across physical barriers
such as oceans and mountain ranges, but also
across political barriers such as borders, battlefields, and occupied lands. Too often are the
natural, peaceful integration and disintegration
of cultures emphasized over the oppression and
racism in human history that molds what we
call individual languages today. This begs the
question, what is the difference between a
language and a dialect or vernacular? For better
or worse, the answer lies in the seemingly
unshakeable tendency of humans to assert the
dominance of their own culture over those of
other people less capable of resistance.

The first assumption that must be made is
that the concept of individual languages—
English, French, Spanish, and so on—is
commonly misunderstood. In countries with a
dominant national language, children are
taught to speak and write in a standard way.
This is called *prescriptive language instruction*,
meaning teaching a standard usage of the
language. In England, people refer to this standard usage as The King's English; in the
United States, many terms exist to describe this
idealized form of the English language, such as
standard American English, standard written
English, or even Newscaster English, after the
accent and grammar achieved by major national
broadcasters who strive to remove the regional
markers in their mother tongue. Speakers of
the prescriptive norm are often perceived to be
well educated, intelligent, or of the upper
classes.

So what does this reveal about language in
general? First, the idea of well-defined
languages is false and stems from the tradition
of teaching a prescriptive grammar. Linguists
avoid making value judgments based on these
differences; there is no such thing as American
English but rather an indeterminable number
of varied speech patterns that resemble each
other closely enough to be considered part of a
common group. We call this a language. For
example, though many prominent journalists
come from the American South, the typical
listener would be shocked to hear these professionals use *y'all* instead of the standard pronoun
you. The common response to an example like
this is rejection of *y'all* as "correct" English.
The question has little merit because again it
presupposes a higher value placed on Standard
American English. One can narrow down the
divisions of such languages into groups called
dialects, though this term is controversial. What
separates dialects from languages and languages
from each other is better defined in political
history.

A clear example of the problem of labeling
speech is in the Romance Languages, a term
describing those forms of speech descended
from Vulgar Latin, the language of the soldiers,
slaves, and commoners of the Roman Empire.
As the Empire fell and its far-reaching posses-
sions became more fractured and independent,
Vulgar Latin took on unique traits in every
separate area of Europe where it was spoken.
With enough time, clear differences emerged
within different groups' usage of Vulgar Latin.
Today, Portuguese, French, Spanish, Italian,
and Romanian are treated as separate languages,
though Occitan, Catalan, Sardinian and other
lesser known languages are often called dialects.
The key features that separate each of these are
not in the grammar or lexicon, but instead in
the political history behind them. Only recently
have efforts been made to preserve what
language diversity Western Europe has left. It is
a case study in minority discrimination, clearly
manifest in a mistaken view of language.

16. The tone of lines 1–4 ("The…oppres-
sion") is

(A) confiding
(B) skeptical
(C) resigned
(D) defiant
(E) reproaching

GO ON TO THE NEXT PAGE

17. The purpose of lines 4–13 ("Careful...today") is to

    (A) defend diverse perspectives on language change
    (B) support the views held by professional linguists
    (C) introduce a topic of interest to most speakers of English
    (D) object to certain conceptions of language change
    (E) present a sample of the mechanisms of language change

18. The sentence in lines 15–19 ("For...resistance") is best described as

    (A) a decision
    (B) a plea
    (C) an apology
    (D) a concession
    (E) a claim

19. The rhetorical question in lines 14–15 ("what...vernacular") is used to

    (A) characterize the challenges faced by learners of a second language
    (B) illustrate the connection between social injustice and language learning
    (C) identify an ambiguity in defining languages
    (D) suggest the way that terminology can help clarify a difficult distinction
    (E) define the racism mentioned earlier in the paragraph

20. The author suggests that the method of "prescriptive language instruction" described in lines 23–28 ("In...tongue") is one of

    (A) deliberate racism
    (B) genuine empathy
    (C) uncommon effectiveness
    (D) traditional ethnocentrism
    (E) advanced pedagogy

21. One can reasonably infer from the passage that the explanation for "Newscaster English" (line 33) suggests the

    (A) concern over the intelligibility of regional vernaculars
    (B) resistance that most people exhibit toward rural dialects
    (C) fear that most people feel about not speaking well in public
    (D) importance of appearing intelligent and, therefore, credible
    (E) blending of multiple regional dialects

22. The example of "y'all," described in the third paragraph, emphasizes

    (A) social discrimination
    (B) mutual respect
    (C) journalistic ethics
    (D) dialectical uniformity
    (E) editorial bias

23. The word "Vulgar" (line 67) most likely refers to

    (A) the rich vocabulary of expletives and insults in Latin
    (B) the simplistic grammar of Latin
    (C) the lower classes of the Roman Empire
    (D) the formal style of Roman academia
    (E) the wide range of cultures within the Roman Empire

24. The word "lexicon" (line 80) most nearly means

    (A) library
    (B) vocabulary
    (C) differences
    (D) leaders
    (E) politics

STOP

**If you finish before your time is up, check your work on this section only.
You may not turn to any other section in the test.**

SECTION 5
Time—25 minutes
18 Questions

Directions: This section includes two types of questions. For questions 1–8, solve each problem and determine which is the best of the answer choices given. Fill in the corresponding circle on your answer sheet. Use any available space to solve the problems. For questions 9–18, solve each problem and fill in your answer on the answer sheet.

Reference Information

   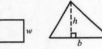 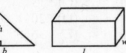 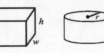

$A = \Pi r^2$
$C = 2\Pi r$ $A = lw$ $A = \frac{1}{2}bh$ $V = lwh$ $V = \Pi r^2 h$ $c^2 = a^2 + b^2$ Special Right Triangles

The number of degrees of arc in a circle is 360.
The sum of the measures in degrees of the angles of a triangle is 180.

1. What is the units digit of $(11)^4(22)^3(36)^2$?

  (A)   1
  (B)   4
  (C)   6
  (D)   8
  (E)   9

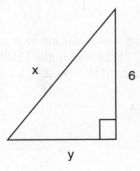

2. In the right triangle above, if $y = 4$, what is the value of x?

  (A)   2
  (B) $2\sqrt{5}$
  (C) $2\sqrt{6}$
  (D) $2\sqrt{13}$
  (E)   4

GO ON TO THE NEXT PAGE ⇨

All numbers that are divisible by both 3 and 9 are also divisible by 6.

3. Which one of the following numbers can be used to show that the statement above is FALSE?

(A) 3
(B) 6
(C) 18
(D) 27
(E) 36

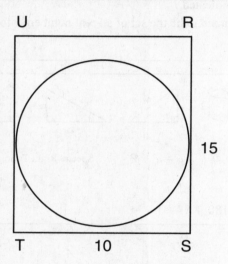

U   R

15

T   10   S

4. In the figure above, the circle is tangent to sides *RS* and *TU* of the rectangle *TURS*. What is the circumference of the circle?

(A) 10π
(B) 15π
(C) 20π
(D) 25π
(E) 50π

5. If $ft = b$, $b = mt$, and $tb \neq 0$, then which of the following is equal to f?

(A) $m + 1$
(B) m
(C) $m - 1$
(D) $\frac{1}{m}$
(E) 1

6. The socks in a drawer are either gray or brown. If the ratio of gray socks to the number of brown socks is $\frac{1}{3}$, each of the following could be the number of socks in the drawer EXCEPT:

(A) 8
(B) 12
(C) 15
(D) 20
(E) 36

7. If Jane traveled 30 miles in 6 hours and Betty traveled 3 times as far in half the time, what was Betty's average speed in miles per hour?

(A) 5
(B) 15
(C) 30
(D) 45
(E) 90

8. $5^x + 5^x + 5^x + 5^x + 5^x =$

(A) 5^{x+1}
(B) 5^{x+2}
(C) 5^{x+5}
(D) 5^{5x}
(E) 5^{25x}

GO ON TO THE NEXT PAGE ⇨

Directions: For Student-Produced Response questions 9-18, use the grids at the bottom of the answer sheet page on which you have answered questions 1-8.

Each of the remaining 10 questions requires you to solve the problem and enter your answer by marking the circles in the special grid, as shown in the examples below. You may use any available space for scratchwork.

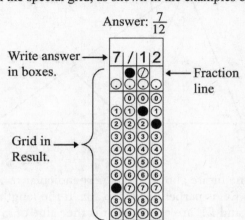

Answer: $\frac{7}{12}$

Write answer in boxes. → Fraction line

Grid in Result.

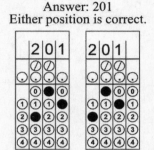

Answer: 2.5 ← Decimal point

Answer: 201
Either position is correct.

Note: You may start your answers in any column, space permitting. Columns not needed should be left blank.

- Mark no more than one circle in any column.

- Because the answer sheet will be machine-scored, **you will receive credit only if the circles are filled in correctly**.

- Although not required, it is suggested that you write your answer in the boxes at the top of the columns to help you fill in the circles accurately.

- Some problems may have more than one correct answer. In such cases, grid only one answer.

- No question has a negative answer.

- **Mixed numbers** such as $3\frac{1}{2}$ must be gridded as 3.5 or 7/2. (If ⎡3 1 / 2⎤ is gridded, it will be

interpreted as $\frac{31}{2}$, not $3\frac{1}{2}$.)

Decimal Answers: If you obtain a decimal answer with more digits than the grid can accomodate, it may be either rounded or truncated, but it must fill the entire grid. enter the most accurate value the grid will accommodate. For example, if you obtain an answer such as 0.6666..., you should record your result as .666 or .667. **A less accurate value such as .66 or .67 will be scored as incorrect.**

Acceptable ways to grid $\frac{2}{3}$ are:

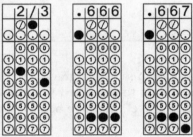

9. What is the decimal equivalent of $(\frac{2}{5})^4$?

10. What is the coordinate of the point on a number line that is exactly halfway between the points with the coordinates (-9, 12)?

GO ON TO THE NEXT PAGE ⟩

11. A certain triangle has two angles that are equal in measure. If the lengths of two of the sides of the triangle are 25 and 40, what is the LEAST possible value for the perimeter of the triangle?

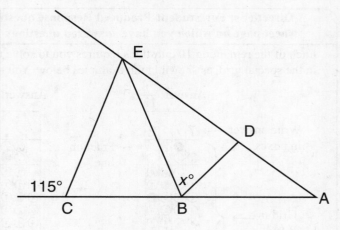

14. In the figure above, DB is perpendicular to AE and EC is perpendicular to AE. If the lengths of EC and BE are equal, what is the value of x?

12. If $x - y = 85$ and $x + y = 5$, what is the value of x?

13. In a mixture of sand and gravel, the ratio by weight of sand to gravel is 3 to 2. How many pounds of gravel will there be in 120 pounds of this mixture?

15. There are 5 more boys than girls on Hortonville High School's chess team. If there are 21 members on the chess team, how many are boys?

GO ON TO THE NEXT PAGE

16. If $r + 3s$ is equal to 150 percent of $8s$, what is the value of $\frac{r}{s}$?

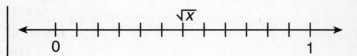

18. On the number line above, there are 12 equal intervals between 0 and 1. What is the value of x?

17. In the xy-coordinate plane, the distance between point $L(8, 12)$ and point $M(x, 4)$ is 10. What is one possible value of x?

STOP

If you finish before your time is up, check your work on this section only.
You may not turn to any other section in the test.

SECTION 6
Time—25 minutes
35 Questions

Directions: For each question, select the best answer from among the choices listed. Fill in the corresponding circle on your answer sheet.

The following questions test the correct and effective use of standard written English in expressing an idea. Part of each sentence (or the entire sentence) is underlined. Following each sentence are five different ways of phrasing the underlined portion. Answer choice A repeats the original phrasing. If you think that the original phrasing is best, select answer choice A. Otherwise, select from the remaining four choices. Your selection should result in the most effective, clear sentence, free from awkwardness or ambiguity.

1. The United States Supreme Court is made up of the Chief Justice and eight associate justices <u>who are all appointed by the president for life</u>.

   (A) who are all appointed by the president for life
   (B) who all are appointed, for life, by the president
   (C) who, all appointed by the president, for life
   (D) whom by the president are all appointed for life
   (E) who are all appointed for life by the president

2. World War II submarines are <u>more accurate called *submersibles*</u> because they could stay submerged for only brief periods of time.

   (A) more accurate called *submersibles*
   (B) more accurate to call them *submersibles*
   (C) called *submersibles* more accurately
   (D) more accurately called *submersibles*
   (E) called *submersibles* to be more accurate

3. Andrea couldn't decide if covering her hideous haircut with a hat was a good solution or if she was <u>lesser conspicuous without the hat</u>.

   (A) lesser conspicuous without the hat
   (B) not as conspicuous, without the hat
   (C) less conspicuous without the hat
   (D) less conspicuous, without the hat
   (E) less conspicuous; without the hat

4. Even though <u>we have immediately seen the distinctive white head</u> and tail of the bald eagle, its presence just above startled us into silence.

   (A) we have immediately seen the distinctive white head
   (B) we immediately saw the distinctive white head
   (C) its distinctive white head had been immediately seen
   (D) its white distinctive head was immediately seen
   (E) we saw immediately the white distinction of its head

5. Astrologers from ancient times believed that the celestial bodies <u>influence over</u> specific parts of the human body.

   (A) influence over
   (B) influenced upon
   (C) had been influenced on
   (D) influenced
   (E) have influenced

6. Throughout the Ming Dynasty, <u>a Chinese navigator by the name of Zheng Ho</u> searched for trade routes in the South Seas.

   (A) a Chinese navigator by the name of Zheng Ho
   (B) Zheng Ho, Chinese navigator
   (C) Chinese navigator Zheng Ho
   (D) Zheng Ho who was a Chinese navigator
   (E) Zheng Ho, the Chinese navigator who

GO ON TO THE NEXT PAGE

7. When Andrew Jackson was sworn in as president, rowdy American frontiersmen <u>stormed</u> the White House and caused general pandemonium.

   (A) stormed
   (B) storming
   (C) had stormed
   (D) were storming
   (E) had been storming

8. During the Great Depression, at least 13 million people <u>lost them jobs</u>.

   (A) lost them jobs
   (B) lost his or her jobs
   (C) lost his jobs
   (D) lost their job
   (E) lost their jobs

9. Maggie, a 9,200-pound African elephant, needs to lose <u>weight, scientists hope that a specially designed</u> treadmill will be beneficial.

   (A) weight, scientists hope that a specially designed
   (B) weight; scientists hope that a specially designed
   (C) weight; scientists hope that and so a specially designed
   (D) weight, scientists hope that specially designed
   (E) weight however a specially designed

10. The tsunami tore through the small oceanside town, hurling boats and cars, engulfing farmlands, and <u>houses were swept away</u>.

    (A) houses were swept away
    (B) houses sweeping away
    (C) houses swept away
    (D) sweeping away houses
    (E) swept away houses

11. Moving to a new location often causes anxiety; <u>fear of the unknown</u> can be unsettling.

    (A) fear of the unknown
    (B) fear of that which is unknown
    (C) unknown fear
    (D) fear that is not known
    (E) fear to be unknown

GO ON TO THE NEXT PAGE

The following questions test your ability to recognize grammar and usage errors in standard written English. Each sentence contains either a single error or no error at all. Refer to the underlined, lettered portions of each sentence. If the sentence contains no error, select answer choice E. If the sentence contains an error, select the one underlined and lettered portion (A, B, C, or D) that is incorrect.

12. One of the most <u>obviously</u> signs of an

                  A

<u>allergic reaction</u> to a bee sting is having

     B

<u>difficulty</u> <u>breathing</u>. <u>No error</u>.

    C   D   E

13. William Butler <u>Yeats' poetry</u> was greatly

                 A

influenced by <u>Irish history</u> and folklore as

             B

<u>to be found</u> in <u>his poem</u> "The Lake Isle of

    C   D

Innisfree." <u>No error</u>.

           E

14. Insects and rodents <u>can be</u> particularly <u>damaging</u>

                A   B

to items that <u>people enjoy</u> collecting, <u>such as</u>

          C   D

photographs and old books. <u>No error</u>.

                   E

15. The works of <u>writer</u> Langston Hughes <u>continues</u>

            A   B

to inspire and instruct <u>readers</u> in <u>understanding</u>

             C   D

racial segregation. <u>No error</u>.

            E

16. When the American flag <u>is flown</u> at <u>half-staff</u>, or

                  A   B

<u>halfway up the flagpole</u> that is a sign of

        C

<u>mourning</u>. <u>No error</u>.

    D   E

17. While <u>high achievers</u> do not <u>necessary</u> feel better

       A   B

than other <u>people, they</u> often do not feel

            C

inferior <u>either</u>. <u>No error</u>.

       D   E

18. <u>People suffering</u> from rheumatoid arthritis

       A

<u>can often use</u> self-help <u>techniques</u> to

       B   C

slow <u>it's</u> pain and progression. <u>No error</u>.

      D   E

19. There are <u>hundreds</u> of clubs and organizations

        A

people <u>can join</u> for <u>fun</u> and entertainment,

       B   C

<u>such as</u> the Wizard of Oz Club or Roller

  D

Sports USA. <u>No error</u>.

          E

20. <u>One</u> of Daniel Boone's most <u>well-known</u>

   A   B

accomplishments <u>were</u> the expansion of <u>the</u>

           C   D

Appalachian Mountains' Cumberland Gap.

<u>No error</u>.

  E

GO ON TO THE NEXT PAGE ⟩

21. Fleas and froghoppers are alike in their <u>abilities</u>
                                              A
to jump, but a <u>froghopper</u> can <u>outdistance</u>
                B   C
a flea by <u>nearly</u> a foot. <u>No error</u>.
           D   E

22. Somehow the hunting dog knew the tree
<u>was hollow</u>, <u>even though</u> the opening in the trunk
    A   B
<u>was</u> way above the dog's <u>eye level</u>. <u>No error</u>.
 C   D   E

23. My two choices <u>were</u> either to take care of the
                    A
<u>trash now</u> or <u>to being</u> behind on all the
    B   C
<u>other chores</u> I had to do. <u>No error</u>.
    D   E

24. The surprise <u>came</u> when Jackie learned that <u>her</u>
                 A   B
and her sister had <u>won</u> shopping <u>sprees</u>
                    C   D
at the mall. <u>No error</u>.
              E

25. The <u>highly acclaimed</u> chef had a <u>propensity</u>
         A   B
<u>of</u> tomato and pasta dishes, <u>most likely</u> because
 C   D
of his Italian upbringing. <u>No error</u>.
                            E

26. All financial <u>institution</u> will assess <u>finance charges</u>
                  A   B
on overdue loans and <u>negligent</u> accounts unless
                      C
other <u>arrangements</u> for payment are made.
       D
<u>No error</u>.
 E

27. As we <u>listened</u> to the dogs <u>barking</u> next door, it
          A   B
<u>suddenly</u> occurred to us that there <u>maybe</u> an
 C   D
intruder in the area. <u>No error</u>.
                       E

28. <u>The bobbing</u> for apples on Halloween <u>probably</u>
     A   B
comes from the Roman festival <u>honoring</u>
                               C
Pomona, the goddess of fruit <u>orchards</u>. <u>No error</u>.
                              D   E

29. Rosie the Riveter, a <u>symbol</u> of <u>womens</u>
                         A   B
involvement during World War II, <u>appeared</u>
                                  C
on posters <u>with the</u> caption, "We Can Do It!"
            D
<u>No error</u>.
 E

GO ON TO THE NEXT PAGE

Directions: The following passage is a rough draft of a student essay. Some parts of the passage need to be rewritten in order to improve the essay.

Read the passage and select the best answer for each question that follows. Some questions ask you to improve the structure or word choice of specific sentences or parts of sentences, while others ask you to consider the organization and development of the essay. Follow the requirements of standard written English.

Questions 30–35 are based on the following passage.

(1)We had assembled all our gear, especially remembering the camera, and were ready to head out. (2)We were finally going to take that ghost town tour. (3)To Rhyolite, Nevada, we were going. (4)Rhyolite, once a thriving gold-mining center, was now a small set of abandoned buildings and ruins. (5)We loaded up the dog and backpack into the car and happily set off with smiles on our faces.

(6) Driving up into the foothills where Rhyolite is situated, a visitor can immediately spot one of the few intact structures. (7)This is the Tom Kelly house, built of nearly 50,000 beer and medicine bottles stuck into clay. (8) It is clear that this home was once considered to be a rather magnificent edifice with its glass windows and wide-sweeping front porch. (9)Out in the expansive yard are fine displays of rusted farm tools. (10)Crude glass mosaic art forms are scattered about. (11)A curator of sorts sits on a chair just outside the bottle house, with a cat in her lap, just waiting to enlighten the next visitor about Rhyolite's many charms. (12)The scruffy cat does not like laying on the lady's lap. (13)The house itself is locked tight, due to what the cat lady describes as "pilferers."

(14)I take my tiny new digital camera out of the backpack, longing to capture Rhyolite's quaintness forever, only to discover the camera's battery pack is dead. (15)This angers my father, who has been looking forward to a bit of Rhyolite on his computer desktop. (16)Unfortunately, driving the two miles into Beatty to purchase new batteries is not a solution; this camera is outfitted with a battery *pack* that requires

recharging with its special recharger. (17)My father is further incensed. (18)We spend only a few more minutes exploring the other Rhyolite foundations and then silently get back into the car. (19)We will return to this ghost town another time, and you can be sure we will be carrying two cameras, both freshly charged!

30. Of the following, which is the best way to revise and combine sentences 2 and 3 (reproduced below)?

    We were finally going to take that ghost town tour. To Rhyolite, Nevada, we were going.

    (A) We were finally going to Rhyolite, Nevada, to take that tour of a ghost town.
    (B) We were finally going to take that tour of the ghost town, Rhyolite, Nevada.
    (C) Finally we were going to Rhyolite, Nevada, and take that ghost town tour.
    (D) We were finally going to go to Rhyolite, Nevada to take that tour of the ghost town.
    (E) That ghost town of Rhyolite, Nevada, was finally going to be taken as a tour.

31. Of the following, which is the best way to phrase Sentence 5 (reproduced below)?

    We loaded up the dog and backpack into the car and happily set off with smiles on our faces.

    (A) (As it is now)
    (B) We loaded up the dog and the backpack and happily set off in the car with smiles on our faces.
    (C) We had smiles on our faces as we loaded up the dog and the backpack into the car and set off happily.
    (D) As we loaded up the dog and backpack into the car, we had smiles on our faces and happily set off.
    (E) We loaded the dog and backpack into the car and happily set off.

GO ON TO THE NEXT PAGE ➡

32. In Sentence 7, the phrase *stuck into clay* is best replaced by

(A) surrounded by clay
(B) clay embedded
(C) that were stuck into clay
(D) that had been put into clay
(E) embedded in clay

33. Which of the following should be omitted to improve the unity of the second paragraph?

(A) Sentence 9
(B) Sentence 10
(C) Sentence 11
(D) Sentence 12
(E) Sentence 13

34. In context, which of the following is the best way to phrase the underlined portion of sentence 15 (reproduced below)?

This angers my father, who has been looking forward to a bit of Rhyolite on his computer desktop.

(A) (As it is now)
(B) who had been really looking forward to
(C) as he had been looking forward to
(D) who has for a long time been looking forward to
(E) as he will be looking forward to

35. A strategy that the writer uses within the second paragraph is to

(A) use physical details to describe the main topic
(B) refer back to the beginning of the essay
(C) try to dissuade the reader from being interested in the topic
(D) use exaggeration to make a point
(E) ask leading questions

STOP

If you finish before your time is up, check your work on this section only.
You may not turn to any other section in the test.

SECTION 7
Time—20 minutes
19 Questions

Directions: For each of the questions in this section, choose the best answer and fill in the corresponding circle on your answer sheet.

Each sentence that follows has either one or two blanks. Each blank indicates that a word has been omitted from the sentence. Following each sentence are five words or sets of words. Select the word or set of words that, when inserted into the sentence in place of the blank(s), best fits the context of the sentence as a whole.

1. Instead of relying entirely upon circumstantial evidence, the prosecutor sought to gather more ------- proof prior to the trial.

   (A) abstract
   (B) contiguous
   (C) tangible
   (D) benign
   (E) peripheral

2. Modern trends toward organically produced fruits and vegetables that lack preservatives have meant produce -------- must make more -------- deliveries of a variety of products in smaller quantities.

   (A) vendors . . labored
   (B) distributors . . greater
   (C) suppliers . . cargo
   (D) wholesalers . . diverse
   (E) farmers . . frequent

3. Exploring the ancient catacombs beneath Paris is today illegal because the layout of the underground system of tunnels is quite -------- and poorly -------, leading to many visitors' disappearance.

   (A) haphazard . . sealed
   (B) unpredictable . . mapped
   (C) patterned . . maintained
   (D) irrational . . ventilated
   (E) repetitious . . decanted

4. More than ever are Wisconsin's dairy farms forced to -------- with those from California for share of the national cheese market.

   (A) argue
   (B) litigate
   (C) bargain
   (D) compete
   (E) react

5. Mary told the sheriff's deputy that her assailant had -------- from the scene of the crime with two other men in an old, gray pick-up truck.

   (A) absconded
   (B) halted
   (C) loitered
   (D) stricken
   (E) deliberated

6. The local animal shelter is funded completely by the -------- donations of the community; without the financial aid of the public, it is -------- that the shelter would be forced to shut down.

   (A) affluent . . conjectural
   (B) generous . . inevitable
   (C) frugal . . destined
   (D) charitable . . wanton
   (E) frivolous . . foreordained

GO ON TO THE NEXT PAGE

The passage that follows is accompanied by several questions based on the content of the passage. Answer the questions based on what is either stated or implied in the passage. Be sure to read any introductory material that is provided.

Questions 7—19 are based on the following passage.

In the following passage, Abraham Lincoln's work to end slavery is discussed and analyzed.

Throughout the Abraham Lincoln-Stephen Douglas debates of 1858, Douglas repeatedly criticized Lincoln's "House Divided"
Line speech. In it, Lincoln argues that the "Spirit of
5 Nebraska," the alleged right of a state to allow slavery, had invaded the country and divided it. The North and the South were no longer working together to put slavery on the road to extinction. In fact, by the late 1850s, the South
10 had fully embraced slavery and wanted to expand it. This new attitude towards slavery promoted by Southerners and some Northern Democrats led Lincoln to believe that they wanted to nationalize slavery.
15 In the Lincoln-Douglas debates, Lincoln stated that the nation was too divided to continue compromising on slavery. Lincoln began his defense by referring to the actions of the Founding Fathers, who had tried to eradi-
20 cate slavery. He mentioned the unanimous abolition of the African slave trade and the lack of the word "slave" in the Constitution. He proposed that the Fathers desired to abolish slavery but could not arrive at a means to do so.
25 In addition, he spoke on the Northwest Ordinance of 1787, an act of the Continental Congress establishing the Northwest Territory in the Great Lakes Region. Slavery is explicitly forbidden in the language of the Ordinance,
30 showing that the Founding Fathers intended slavery to be eradicated. Lincoln argued that the South had moved away from this course of ending slavery. He also stated that the federal government, through the Missouri
35 Compromise and the Compromise of 1850, had always regulated slavery in the territories.
These Compromises, however, were at odds with the new Dred Scott decision of the Supreme Court, which denied that Congress
40 had a right to forbid slavery in the states. The decision also reinforced the idea that African

Americans were not citizens and that slaves could be brought into the North without gaining their freedom. The Dred Scott decision
45 had the effect of undermining Lincoln's Republican platform that fought the Kansas-Nebraska Act, a law separating the two territories to bring slavery where it was previously forbidden.
50 Both in the debates and the "House Divided" speech, Lincoln repeatedly questioned the Democrats' involvement in the Dred Scott decision. Lincoln suggested that a conspiracy might have taken place among
55 President Buchanan, President Pierce, sitting Judge Taney, and other Democrats, such as Stephen Douglas. Lincoln used evidence to show that the Democrats seemed to have known that the Dred Scott decision was
60 coming. A key piece of evidence was that the Dred Scott decision was pushed back until after the election of 1856. In addition, the Democrats had drafted legislation in 1850 and 1854 containing language that seemed to
65 predict that Congress would not be able to exclude slavery in the territories because of Constitutional constraints. The Dred Scott decision cast doubts on the Democrats, whose platform of popular sovereignty sought to leave
70 the decision on slavery to the individual states and territories. The Dred Scott decision reaffirmed for the South that slaves were considered property, and because America's Constitution protects property, exclusion of
75 slavery through unfriendly legislation was unconstitutional.
Lincoln spoke throughout the debates about the Kansas-Nebraska Act and his opinion on the repeal of the Missouri Compromise. He
80 believed that popular sovereignty was contrary to the principle that valued freedom over slavery. The "Spirit of Nebraska" prompted Northerners like Douglas to fashion the

GO ON TO THE NEXT PAGE

Kansas-Nebraska Act contrary to the "Spirit of
85 '76," the hope of the Founding Fathers that
slavery would eventually be purged from the
original Southern states. Without the majority
of public opinion standing firm against slavery,
Lincoln realized that the battle over forced
90 labor could not be won at the rostrum.

7. According to the passage, Lincoln's position on slavery was that

(A) the states should enjoy popular sovereignty and make their own policy decisions
(B) the system was declining and would go away if left undisturbed
(C) the Founding Fathers had wisely begun its abolition
(D) the Southern states should secede if they retained it
(E) the economy would falter without it

8. Lines 11–14 ("This...slavery") imply that

(A) the Northern non-Democrats were generally opposed to slavery
(B) the South had been generally opposed to slavery before 1858
(C) the slave trade was increasing in 1858
(D) Lincoln was deluded to think that slavery posed a threat
(E) a clandestine conspiracy existed to undermine Lincoln

9. What is the relationship between the first paragraph (lines 1–14) and the "Dred Scott decision" discussed in the rest of the passage?

(A) The decision left the states unable to authorize slavery.
(B) The decision opposed Lincoln's aim to end slavery.
(C) The decision weakened the position of popular sovereignty advocates.
(D) The "Spirit of Nebraska" refers to the issues at stake in the Scott case.
(E) The "House Divided" speech carefully avoided addressing the Scott case.

10. The second paragraph (lines 15–36) contributes to the development of the passage primarily by

(A) indicating some of Lincoln's opinions that are later shown to change
(B) showing the necessity of open discourse
(C) describing an alternate path toward the abolition of slavery
(D) supporting a theory that slavery is unsustainable
(E) detailing evidence given to support an assertion

11. In the debate, Lincoln supported the opinion that the Founding Fathers "tried to eradicate slavery" (lines 19–20) with all of the following EXCEPT

(A) stating that importation of slaves had already been banned
(B) showing that federal law forbade slavery in certain lands
(C) pointing out that slaves are not addressed in the language of the Constitution
(D) claiming that the Founding Fathers lacked a way, but not a desire, to end slavery
(E) declaring that several Founding Fathers belonged to abolitionist groups

12. Which of the following statements, if true, would likely undercut Lincoln's argument in lines 31–33 ("Lincoln...slavery")?

(A) The plantation-based economy of the South relied exclusively on forced, or slave, labor.
(B) Northern Democrats, though not slave owners, fought abolitionism.
(C) Congress banned the international slave trade decades earlier.
(D) Bloody slave revolts were becoming more frequent.
(E) Southern plantation owners learned that sharecropping was a more efficient use of labor than was slavery.

GO ON TO THE NEXT PAGE

13. In line 41, "decision" most nearly means

(A) choice
(B) consideration
(C) resolution
(D) settlement
(E) commendation

14. The facts described in the passage provide evidence that most directly supports the conclusion that Lincoln

(A) was highly adaptable to changing arguments
(B) responded cautiously to harsh attacks from his opponents
(C) held a strong abolitionist ethic
(D) eagerly touted the Republican Party platform
(E) regretted the disparity between North and South

15. In line 69, "popular" most nearly means

(A) celebrated
(B) busy
(C) favored
(D) prevailing
(E) modern

16. The author's reaction to the Dred Scott decision in lines 71–76 ("The…unconstitutional") is best characterized as

(A) offended, because it violated legal precedent
(B) respectful, because the author reveres the Supreme Court
(C) receptive, because it quieted the debate over freed slaves
(D) skeptical, because it disregarded the abolitionist movement
(E) objective, because the author explains the impact of it without bias

17. The final sentence of the passage ("Without…rostrum") primarily serves to

(A) surprise the reader with the fact that Lincoln failed in the debates
(B) warn the reader about the importance of public support
(C) foreshadow the armed conflict that arose over slavery
(D) offer sympathy for Lincoln
(E) expose a vulnerable side of Lincoln

18. The passage creates an impression of Lincoln as a person who is

(A) timid and indecisive
(B) bitter and scornful
(C) headstrong and impetuous
(D) thoughtful and empathetic
(E) jocular and gregarious

19. The author uses the Lincoln-Douglas debates to convey which point about slavery in the United States?

(A) It was the most egregious social ill.
(B) It was a divisive issue that prompted much political action.
(C) Lincoln opposed it.
(D) Granting citizenship to former slaves was the only solution to the slavery question.
(E) Public debates on such delicate topics are challenging and require quick thinking.

STOP

**If you finish before your time is up, check your work on this section only.
You may not turn to any other section in the test.**

SECTION 8
Time—20 minutes
16 Questions

Directions: Solve each problem and determine which is the best of the answer choices given. Fill in the corresponding circle on your answer sheet. Use any available space to solve the problems.

Notes

1. The use of a calculator is permitted.
2. All numbers are real numbers.
3. Figures that accompany problems in this test are intended to provide information useful in solving the problems. They are drawn as accurately as possible EXCEPT when it is stated in a specific problem that the figure is not drawn to scale. All figures lie in a plane unless otherwise indicated.
4. Unless otherwise specified, the domain of any function f is assumed to be the set of all real numbers x for which $f(x)$ is a real number.

Reference Information

  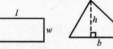

$A = \Pi r^2$ $\quad A = lw \quad A = \frac{1}{2}bh \quad V = lwh \quad V = \Pi r^2 h \quad c^2 = a^2 + b^2 \quad$ **Special Right Triangles**
$C = 2\Pi r$

The number of degrees of arc in a circle is 360.
The sum of the measures in degrees of the angles of a triangle is 180.

---

1. R, S, and T are points on a line, in that order. If $RS = 21$ and $ST = 15$ more than RS, what does RT equal?

   (A) 72
   (B) 57
   (C) 51
   (D) 36
   (E) 21

2. If $4x + 7 = 19$, what is the value of $6x - 3$?

   (A) 10
   (B) 12
   (C) 15
   (D) 18
   (E) 21

GO ON TO THE NEXT PAGE

Athletes At North
High School By Sport

= 15 athletes

Football	
Basketball	
Soccer	
Volleyball	

3. If the four sports shown in the graph above are the only sports played at North High School, the total of which two sports accounts for exactly 60% of all athletes at North High School?

(A)　Football and basketball
(B)　Football and soccer
(C)　Basketball and soccer
(D)　Basketball and volleyball
(E)　Soccer and volleyball

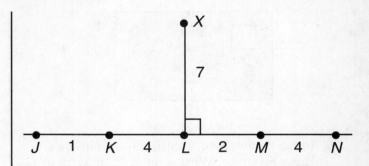

4. In the figure above, XL is perpendicular to JN. Which of the following line segments (not shown) has the greatest length?

(A)　XJ
(B)　XK
(C)　XL
(D)　XM
(E)　XN

5. For which of the following functions is $f(-5) > f(5)$?

(A)　$f(x) = 6x^2$

(B)　$f(x) = 6$

(C)　$f(x) = \dfrac{6}{x}$

(D)　$f(x) = 6 - x^3$

(E)　$f(x) = x^6 + 6$

GO ON TO THE NEXT PAGE

313

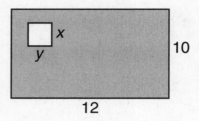

6. In the figure above, a small square is inside a larger rectangle. What is the area, in terms of x, of the shaded region?

(A) $120 - x^2$
(B) $x^2 - 120$
(C) $120 - 2x$
(D) $22 - 2x$
(E) $2x - 22$

7. If $4a = 6b$ and $6b = 12c$, what does a equal in terms of c?

(A) $\dfrac{12}{16c}$

(B) $\dfrac{4}{3c}$

(C) $3c$

(D) $24c$

(E) $28c$

8. A total of f men went on a fishing trip. Each of the r boats that were used to carry the fishermen could accommodate a maximum number of m passengers. If one boat had five open spots and the remaining boats were filled to capacity, which of the following expresses the relationship among f, r, and m?

(A) $rm + 5 = f$
(B) $rm - 5 = f$
(C) $r + m + 5 = f$
(D) $rf = m + 5$
(E) $rf = m - 5$

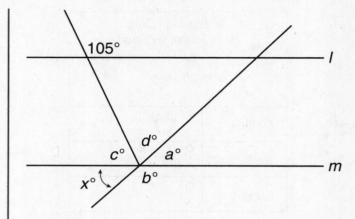

9. In the figure above, line l is parallel to line m. If angle d is $40°$, what is the value of x?

(A) 25
(B) 65
(C) 75
(D) 105
(E) 115

10. If $3^{3x} = 9^{x+2}$, what is the value of x?

(A) 2
(B) 3
(C) 4
(D) 5
(E) 6

11. Rectangle $LMNO$ lies in the xy-coordinate plane so that its sides are *not* parallel to the axes. What is the product of the slopes of all four sides of rectangle $LMNO$?

(A) -2
(B) -1
(C) 0
(D) 1
(E) 2

GO ON TO THE NEXT PAGE

314

12. In the *xy*-plane, the line with equation $y = 4x - 12$ crosses the *x*-axis at the point with coordinates (a, b). What is the value of *a*?

    (A) -12
    (B) -3
    (C) 0
    (D) 3
    (E) 4

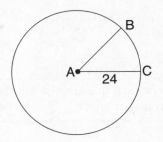

14. In the figure above, *BC* is the arc of a circle with center *A*. If the length of *BC* is 8π, what is the area of sector *ABC*?

    (A) 96π
    (B) 48π
    (C) 24π
    (D) 16π
    (E) 12π

Price by Brand of Dog Food

Brand	Price Per Ounce (Dollars)
A	$2.72
B	$3.08
C	$2.11
D	*b*
E	$1.89
F	$2.94
G	$2.49

13. The table above shows the price per ounce for seven brands of dog food designated A through G. If the median price per ounce of these dog foods is $2.49, then the price per ounce for brand D could be any of the following EXCEPT:

    (A) $1.75
    (B) $1.99
    (C) $2.32
    (D) $2.49
    (E) $2.80

15. If $m + 4(n - 2) = p$, what is $n - 2$, in terms of *m* and *p*?

    (A) $\dfrac{p}{4 + m}$
    (B) $\dfrac{p}{4 - m}$
    (C) $\dfrac{p + m}{4}$
    (D) $\dfrac{p - m}{4}$
    (E) $\dfrac{p}{4m}$

16. If *x* is the greatest prime factor of 34, and *y* is the greatest prime factor of 75, what is the value of $x + y$?

    (A) 7
    (B) 12
    (C) 22
    (D) 24
    (E) 27

STOP

If you finish before your time is up, check your work on this section only.
You may not turn to any other section in the test.

SECTION 9
Time—10 minutes
14 Questions

Directions: For each question, select the best answer from among the choices listed. Fill in the corresponding circle on your answer sheet.

The following questions test the correct and effective use of standard written English in expressing an idea. Part of each sentence (or the entire sentence) is underlined. Following each sentence are five different ways of phrasing the underlined portion. Answer choice A repeats the original phrasing. If you think that the original phrasing is best, select answer choice A. Otherwise, select from the remaining four choices. Your selection should result in the most effective, clear sentence, free from awkwardness or ambiguity.

1. Mr. Jones had just gotten into the classroom <u>when it was told to him</u> that his students were going on a field trip that day with their chemistry teacher.

   (A) when it was told to him
   (B) and then he learned
   (C) and that was when he was told
   (D) when he learned
   (E) and then they told him

2. Laden with eight shopping bags full of new clothing, <u>Megan's frantic search was for her car keys</u>.

   (A) Megan's frantic search was for her car keys
   (B) car keys were what Megan frantically searched for
   (C) Megan searched frantically for her car keys
   (D) Megan's search for her car keys was frantic
   (E) car keys for which Megan frantically searched

3. Archaeological research often requires expeditions called "digs" <u>where they</u> can excavate and study ancient remains.

   (A) where they
   (B) during which the archaeologist
   (C) which they
   (D) through which they
   (E) and the archaeologist

4. In a recent survey, 51% of the public favored <u>laws as strong or stronger than</u> the present laws protecting the environment.

   (A) laws as strong or stronger than
   (B) laws that are stronger; or at least so strong as,
   (C) at least as strong laws as
   (D) laws as strong or stronger than is
   (E) laws at least as strong as

5. Elaine has learned more about George Orwell's writings than the rest of <u>us have since Orwell is her favorite as an author</u>.

   (A) us have since Orwell is her favorite as an author
   (B) us have as a result of Orwell's being her favorite author
   (C) us have; this is a result of Orwell's being her favorite author
   (D) us have because Orwell is her favorite author
   (E) us have because of being her favorite author

6. Some of the British Museum's most valued exhibits, from the Magna Carta to the Rosetta Stone, <u>came from</u> charitable contributions.

   (A) came from
   (B) they come from
   (C) which came from
   (D) they have come from
   (E) coming from

GO ON TO THE NEXT PAGE

7. Grant Wood is best known for his idealized portrayals of farms in America's heartland, and he spent the majority of his time painting in Europe.

(A) Grant Wood is best known for his idealized portrayals of farms in America's heartland, and

(B) Grant Wood is best known for his idealized portrayals of farms in America's heartland,

(C) Although Grant Wood is best known for his idealized portrayals of farms in America's heartland,

(D) Inasmuch as Grant Wood is best known for his idealized portrayals of farms in America's heartland,

(E) Grant Wood is best known for his idealized portrayals of farms in America's heartland, since

8. To warm up before running any race, my mother stretches her muscles, my father jogs in place for several minutes.

(A) To warm up before running any race, my mother stretches her muscles, my father jogs in place for several minutes.

(B) To warm up before running any race, my mother stretches her muscles; my father jogs in place for several minutes.

(C) To warm up before running any race, my mother stretches her muscles so my father jogs in place for several minutes first.

(D) My father jogs in place for several minutes first with my mother stretching her muscles to warm up before running any race.

(E) My mother stretches her muscles to warm up before running any race and my father, he jogs in place for several minutes.

9. McMillan's, an advertising and public relations firm, is obtaining TechNet, it writes and publishes computer software.

(A) TechNet, it writes and publishes

(B) TechNet, writing and publishing

(C) TechNet, which writes and publishes

(D) TechNet; it is writing and publishing

(E) TechNet; for the writing and publishing of

10. The Sears Tower is lauded not only as being among the tallest buildings in North America, but also as having the most breathtaking views of the city of Chicago.

(A) as having the most breathtaking views

(B) having the most breathtaking views

(C) being the building with the most breathtaking views

(D) it has the most breathtaking views

(E) it is lauded for having the most breathtaking views

11. Joanie Laurer, one of the few women ever to compete in the men's division of professional wrestling, and eventually to win the second largest championship title in wrestling.

(A) and eventually to win the second largest championship title in wrestling

(B) she eventually had the second largest championship title in wrestling that she won

(C) she eventually won the second largest championship title in wrestling

(D) having eventually won the second largest championship title in wrestling

(E) eventually won the second largest championship title in wrestling

12. Switzerland is populated by many people who, although their common language is English, the languages at home range from speaking German to Italian to French.

(A) the languages at home range from speaking German to Italian to French

(B) speaking at home is in languages ranging from German to Italian to French

(C) they are speaking languages at home ranging from German to Italian to French

(D) the languages range from German to Italian to French at home

(E) speak languages at home that range from German to Italian to French

GO ON TO THE NEXT PAGE ⟩

13. The new <u>museum, consisting of hundreds of exhibits from the medieval time period, and is subsidized by the state's board of tourism</u>.

   (A) museum, consisting of hundreds of exhibits from the medieval time period, and is subsidized by the state's board of tourism
   (B) museum is subsidized by the state's board of tourism, it consists of hundreds of exhibits from the medieval time period
   (C) museum to consist of hundreds of exhibits from the medieval time period and to be subsidized by the state's board of tourism
   (D) museum, consisting of hundreds of exhibits from the medieval time period, is subsidized by the state's board of tourism
   (E) museum is subsidized by the state's board of tourism consisting of hundreds of exhibits from the medieval time period

14. <u>Many recent law school graduates interviewed for positions in the state's largest law firm, so only a few were selected.</u>

   (A) Many recent law school graduates interviewed for positions in the law firm, so only a few were selected.
   (B) Many recent law school graduates interviewed for positions in the state's largest law firm, but only a few were selected.
   (C) After many recent law school graduates interviewed for positions in the state's largest law firm, only a few being selected.
   (D) Many recent law school graduates, having interviewed for positions in the state's largest law firm, only a few were selected.
   (E) Only a few were selected, many recent law school graduates having interviewed for positions in the state's largest law firm.

STOP

**If you finish before your time is up, check your work on this section only.
You may not turn to any other section in the test.**

Answer Key

Section 1

Because grading the essay is subjective, we've chosen not to include any "graded" essays here. Your best bet is to have someone you trust, such as your personal tutor, read your essays and give you an honest critique. Make the grading criteria mentioned in Chapter 5 available to whomever grades your essays. If you plan on grading your own essays, review the grading criteria and be as honest as possible regarding the structure, development, organization, technique, and appropriateness of your writing. Focus on your weak areas and continue to practice in order to improve your writing skills.

Section 2

1. B	17. C
2. D	18. C
3. A	19. D
4. C	20. A
5. B	21. D
6. D	22. C
7. A	23. A
8. E	24. B
9. D	
10. B	
11. C	
12. B	
13. C	
14. D	
15. E	
16. A	

Section 3

1. D	17. A
2. D	18. E
3. D	19. B
4. C	20. D
5. A	
6. D	
7. B	
8. E	
9. B	
10. E	
11. E	
12. C	
13. D	
14. C	
15. D	
16. A	

Section 4

1. B	19. C
2. E	20. D
3. B	21. D
4. A	22. A
5. D	23. C
6. C	24. B
7. C	
8. E	
9. B	
10. B	
11. A	
12. C	
13. C	
14. B	
15. D	
16. E	
17. D	
18. E	

Section 5

Multiple Choice	Student Produced Response
1. D	
2. D	
3. D	9. .025 or .026
4. A	10. 1.5
5. B	11. 90
6. C	12. 45
7. C	13. 48
8. A	14. 50
	15. 13
	16. 9
	17. 2 or 14
	18. $\frac{1}{4}$

Section 6

1. E	20. C
2. D	21. A
3. C	22. E
4. B	23. C
5. D	24. B
6. C	25. C
7. A	26. A
8. E	27. D
9. B	28. A
10. D	29. B
11. A	30. B
12. A	31. E
13. C	32. E
14. E	33. D
15. B	34. A
16. C	35. A
17. B	
18. D	
19. E	

Section 7

1. C
2. E
3. B
4. D
5. A
6. B
7. C
8. A
9. B
10. E
11. E
12. E
13. C
14. C
15. D
16. E
17. C
18. D
19. B

Section 8

1. B
2. C
3. D
4. E
5. D
6. A
7. C
8. B
9. B
10. C
11. D
12. D
13. E
14. A
15. D
16. C

Section 9

1. D
2. C
3. B
4. E
5. D
6. A
7. C
8. B
9. C
10. A
11. E
12. E
13. D
14. B

Scoring Practice Test 2

Check your responses with the Answer Key. Fill in the blanks below and do the calculations to get your math, critical reading, and writing raw scores. Use the tables on the next pages find your scaled scores.

Remember that this is a simulated test and that the score should only be used to estimate your score on the actual SAT.

Get Your Math Raw Score:

	Number Correct	**Number Incorrect**
Section 3:	_____	_____
Section 5: (#1 – #8)	_____	_____
(#9 – #18)	_____	
Section 8:	_____	_____
Totals:	_____	_____

Divide the total Number Incorrect by 4 and subtract the result from the total Number Correct. This is your Raw Score: _____

Round Raw Score to the nearest whole number. Use Table 1 to find Scaled Score range.

Math Scaled Score Range: _____ - _____

Get Your Critical Reading Raw Score:

	Number Correct	**Number Incorrect**
Section 2:	_____	_____
Section 4:	_____	_____
Section 7:	_____	_____
Totals:	_____	_____

Divide the total Number Incorrect by 4 and subtract the result from the total Number Correct. This is your Raw Score: _____

Round Raw Score to the nearest whole number. Use Table 2 to find Scaled Score range.

Critical Reading Scaled Score Range: _____ - _____

Get Your Writing Raw Score:

	Number Correct	Number Incorrect
Section 6:	_____	_____
Section 9:	_____	_____
Totals:	_____	_____

Divide the total Number Incorrect by 4 and subtract the result from the total Number Correct. This is your Raw Score: _____

Round Raw Score to the nearest whole number. Use Table 3 to find Scaled Score range.

Writing Score Range: _____ - _____

Note that your Writing Score assumes an Essay score of 4. If you believe that your Essay warrants a score of 5 or 6, your Writing Score would increase by an average of 30 to 50 points. Likewise, if your Essay is in the 1 to 3 range, your Writing Score would decrease by an average of 30 to 50 points.

Get Your Composite Score:

To calculate your Composite Score Range, simply add the 3 sub-score ranges (Math, Critical Reading, and Writing).

Composite Score Range: _____ - _____

Table 1 Math Score Conversion

Raw Score	Scaled Score	Raw Score	Scaled Score
54	800	23	460-520
53	750-800	22	450-510
52	720-800	21	440-500
51	700-780	20	430-490
50	690-770	19	430-490
49	680-740	18	420-480
48	670-730	17	410-470
47	660-720	16	400-460
46	640-700	15	400-460
45	630-690	14	390-450
44	620-680	13	380-440
43	620-680	12	360-440
42	610-670	11	350-430
41	600-660	10	340-420
40	580-660	9	330-430
39	570-650	8	320-420
38	560-640	7	310-410
37	550-630	6	290-390
36	550-630	5	280-380
35	540-620	4	270-370
34	530-610	3	260-360
33	520-600	2	240-340
32	520-600	1	230-330
31	520-580	0	210-310
30	510-570	-1	200-290
29	500-560	-2	200-270
28	490-550	-3	200-250
27	490-550	-4	200-230
26	480-540	-5	200-210
25	470-530	-6 and below	200
24	460-520		

Table 2 Critical Reading Score Conversion

Raw Score	Scaled Score	Raw Score	Scaled Score
67	800	30	470-530
66	770-800	29	470-530
65	740-800	28	460-520
64	720-800	27	450-510
63	700-800	26	450-510
62	690-790	25	440-500
61	670-770	24	440-500
60	660-760	23	430-490
59	660-740	22	420-480
58	650-730	21	420-480
57	640-720	20	410-470
56	630-710	19	400-460
55	630-710	18	400-460
54	620-700	17	390-450
53	610-690	16	380-440
52	600-680	15	380-440
51	610-670	14	370-430
50	600-660	13	360-420
49	590-650	12	350-410
48	580-640	11	350-410
47	580-640	10	340-400
46	570-630	9	330-390
45	560-620	8	310-390
44	560-620	7	300-380
43	550-610	6	290-370
42	550-610	5	270-370
41	540-600	4	260-360
40	530-590	3	250-350
39	530-590	2	230-330
38	520-580	1	220-320
37	510-570	0	200-290
36	510-570	-1	200-290
35	500-560	-2	200-270
34	500-560	-3	200-250
33	490-550	-4	200-230
32	480-540	-5	200-210
31	480-540	-6 and below	200

Table 3 Writing Score Conversion

Raw Score	Scaled Score	Raw Score	Scaled Score
49	750-800	21	460-590
48	720-800	20	460-580
47	700-800	19	450-580
46	680-800	18	440-570
45	670-800	17	430-560
44	660-790	16	420-550
43	640-780	15	410-540
42	630-770	14	400-530
41	620-760	13	390-520
40	620-750	12	390-510
39	610-740	11	380-510
38	600-730	10	370-500
37	590-720	9	360-490
36	580-720	8	350-480
35	570-710	7	340-470
34	570-700	6	330-460
33	560-690	5	320-460
32	550-680	4	320-450
31	540-670	3	310-440
30	530-660	2	300-430
29	520-650	1	280-410
28	520-650	0	270-410
27	510-640	-1	250-390
26	500-630	-2	240-370
25	490-620	-3	240-360
24	480-610	-4	220-340
23	470-600	-5	200-320
22	460-590	-6 and below	200

Answers and Explanations

Section 1

Because grading the essay is subjective, we've chosen not to include any "graded" essays here. Your best bet is to have someone you trust, such as your personal tutor, read your essays and give you an honest critique. Make the grading criteria mentioned in Chapter 5, "SAT/PSAT Verbal Sections," available to whomever grades your essays. If you plan on grading your own essays, review the grading criteria and be as honest as possible regarding the structure, development, organization, technique, and appropriateness of your writing. Focus on your weak areas and continue to practice to improve your writing skills.

Section 2

1. **The best answer is B.** The company was searching for motivated and happy employees. The interviewer would be apprehensive, or nervous, to hire Joanna if she showed a "manifest," or "obvious," lack of enthusiasm. Answer choices A and C mean "hidden," or "secretive," and are the opposite of "manifest." Answer choices D and E infer that Joanna was pretending to be unenthusiastic about the job, which does not fit the context of the sentence.

2. **The best answer is D.** The sentence suggests a contrast between how the Eiffel Tower is seen today and how it was seen when it was first constructed; therefore, the answer choices must be contrasting. The words in answer choices A and E both have similar negative meanings, and the words in answer choice B both have similar positive meanings. Because the Tower was met with resistance from the public at first, this suggests that the public first saw the Eiffel Tower as an unattractive addition to the Paris skyline. Answer choice C says that the tower is now considered to be one of the most "ugly" pieces of architectural art in the world and that the public initially thought that it was a "beauty" or "triumph." Answer choice D correctly associates the words that best fit into the blanks; "striking" most closely means "attractive," and "monstrosity" most closely means "eyesore."

3. **The best answer is A.** The sentence indicates that completing a marathon is demanding; therefore, many months of preparation and training are necessary before "attempting" the different segments of a triathlon. The other answer choices do not fit the context of the sentence.

4. **The best answer is C.** According to the sentence, Aishah's high grades were the result of her study habits. It makes sense that Aishah had good study habits, so the best answer will be a synonym of "good." The word "exemplary" means "worthy of imitation" or "commendable," so it best fits the context of the sentence.

5. **The best answer is B.** The adjective describing the teacher's directions must be related to the word "vague." "Meticulous" and "explicit" are antonyms of "vague"; answer choices A and D can be eliminated. Answer choices C and E do not make sense in the context of the sentence; the class would not be "fortuitous" or "lucky" that the teacher graded harshly; nor would the class be "exhilarated" or "excited" that the teacher graded harshly.

6. **The best answer is D.** The context of this sentence indicates that the charity ball was a very fancy and luxurious affair. Based on the context, the word that best describes the ball is the word "lavish," which means "characterized by extravagance." Answer choices A and B have meanings opposite to "lavish," and answer choices C and E do not fit the context of the sentence.

7. **The best answer is A.** The choice that best complete this sentence is the one that best describes the fact that Sarah's husband planned their vacation with extreme detail. To be "meticulous" is to "devote a high amount attention to detail"; thus answer choice A is the best answer choice. Answer choices B and D are the opposite of "meticulous," and answer choices C and E do not fit the context of the sentence.

8. **The best answer is E.** Because you know that water sports are extremely popular, you can conclude that there are many beaches. The word "abundance" means "a great amount," which best fits the context of the sentence. Answer choice D is incorrect because "dearth" refers to a "scarce" number of something. The other answer choices do not fit the context of the sentence.

9. **The best answer is D.** The passage focuses on the unfair imprisonment of women in the early 1800s. It is most likely that the author included the detail regarding women being forced to bring their children to prison with them to further highlight this unfair treatment. The other answer choices are not supported by the passage.

10. **The best answer is B.** The tone of the passage indicates that the author is angry about the plight of women who suffered needlessly in prison. Words such as "appalling" and "injustice" support this notion. Therefore, the author's attitude can best be described as "impassioned."

11. **The best answer is C.** The passage indicates that Nast's cartoons were very powerful and suggests that Nast's ideas were better represented through his drawings than through his words. In fact, according to the passage, many of Nast's nineteenth century drawings are still relevant today. This best supports answer choice C.

12. **The best answer is B.** The passage indicates that Nast's cartoons were very powerful, and the fact that some of them "live on today" shows that they are still relevant and influential, long after his death. The other answer choices are not supported by the passage.

13. **The best answer is C.** Passage 1 states that "While technological advances have allowed mankind to make incredible strides in space exploration, they still cannot match the power and intelligence of the human brain. On-site presence of this biological 'supercomputer' is necessary to maintain a space program that truly advances to the next level." Passage 2 states that "We have no reason, however, to lament the end of this chapter of the space program or to assume that the world beyond our Earth will remain unknown and undeveloped. Robotic computers and similar devices continue to evolve and improve." These statements suggest that the authors of both passages agree that space exploration will continue in some form.

14. **The best answer is D.** Passage 1 states that "Certainly it is cheaper and less dangerous to launch a computer probe that can gather reams of data, but often the information obtained by a machine serves to produce more questions than answers." The word "certainly" makes a statement regarding an advantage of computer probes, while the rest of the sentence offers an argument countering the stated advantage. The other answer choices are not supported by the passage.

15. **The best answer is E.** According to Passage 1, "a human is more capable of calibrating (these instruments) correctly," which suggests that humans are better at making any necessary "adjustments" to the instruments. The other answer choices are not supported by details in this part of the passage.

16. **The best answer is A.** Based on the context of the last paragraph of Passage 1, it is most likely that the author poses the question about the next level of space exploration to force the reader to think about the future. Now that man has produced such advanced technology, what is the best use for it? Also, what should humans do with the data that is collected? The passage suggests that these and other philosophical aspects of space exploration now need to be considered.

17. **The best answer is C.** Passage 2 states that "The tragic deaths of innocent space explorers have shaken support for these endeavors and have caused citizens to question, and some even to reject, the validity of manned space flight. This, coupled with the incredible advances in technological devices, has probably signaled the end of manned space exploration as we know it." This information highlights the inherent dangers involved with manned space flight, which best supports answer choice C. The word "ramifications" means "consequences."

18. **The best answer is C.** Following a discussion regarding the impending end of manned space exploration, Passage 2 states, "We have no reason, however, to lament the end of this chapter of the space program or to assume that the worlds beyond our Earth will remain unknown and undeveloped." The word "lament" means "regret" or "mourn." The context of the passage indicates that, even if manned space exploration comes to an end, we have other means—such as robotics—by which to explore "the worlds beyond our earth." The other answer choices are not supported by the passage.

19. **The best answer is D.** Passage 2 states that "One must admit that humans are hardly suited for life away from planet Earth. People need food, water, and oxygen-rich air, all of which appear to be absent in the broader solar system." Clearly, care must be taken to ensure that humans can remain alive in space. It is true that "knowledge" is an important component to space exploration, but this particular part of the passage more directly emphasizes "safety."

20. **The best answer is A.** The last sentence of Passage 2 states, "If one more person can be spared from harm in space by applying a technological alternative, how could we not embrace that technology?" This sentence serves to emphasize how important it is to use technology to keep humans safe during manned space exploration, thereby drawing attention to the fact that manned space exploration is dangerous. The other answer choices are not supported by the passage.

21. **The best answer is D.** Both passages focus on continued space exploration, whether manned or unmanned. Such a discussion must be based on the assumption that humans will remain interested in learning about the possible existence of life beyond Earth. If answer choice B were assumed, it is unlikely that space exploration would continue. Likewise, the remaining answer choices are either beyond the scope of or not supported by the passage.

22. **The best answer is C.** According to Passage 1, "...often the information obtained by a machine serves to produce more questions than answers. The space program would be far better off allowing manned missions to follow up on those initial information-gathering robotic ventures." In addition, the passage states that "a human is more capable of calibrating sensitive instruments correctly and placing them in appropriate and useful positions. A computer is often neither as precise nor as accurate as a human managing the same terrain or environmental factors." These and other statements contained in Passage 1 indicate that the author of this passage is more concerned with a human's ability to better manage sensitive instruments and large amounts of data. Such a discussion is not made in Passage 2. Both passages address the high cost of manned space flight, so answer choice A is incorrect. Likewise, the remaining answer choices are either primarily discussed in Passage 1 or are beyond the scope of both passages.

23. **The best answer is A.** The last sentence of Passage 1 states that "Some even believe that soon humans will need another place to live besides Earth." This suggests that something must be occurring to make people believe that humans will no longer be able to live on Earth. Of the answer choices listed, only answer choice A provides a valid reason for the possibility of humans seeking out other planets on which to live.

24. **The best answer is B.** The author of Passage 2 says, "After all, no one cries when a computer-driven hunk of metal blows up or disappears." This suggests that unmanned space flights pose a much lower risk to humans than do manned space flights. The context of the passage indicates that the loss of human life is very probable when it comes to manned missions into space. The other answer choices are not supported by the passage.

Section 3

1. **The correct answer is D.** To solve $5x - 3 = 3x + 11$ for x, add 3 and subtract $3x$ from both sides. The resulting equation is $2x = 14$. After dividing by 2, the answer is $x = 7$.

2. **The correct answer is D.** Each term after 2 can be calculated by multiplying the preceding term by 3 and adding 1. For example, $7 = (2)(3) + 1$. Therefore, value of a must be 3.

3. **The correct answer is D.** If you draw a regular octagon (8-sided polygon), you can make only 5 diagonals from one vertex, as shown below:

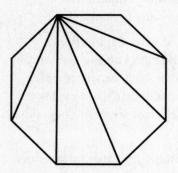

4. **The correct answer is C.** Lines or segments with the same slope are parallel. Polygon *FGHJK* has two pairs of parallel sides; thus, two pairs of sides have the same slope: *GH* and *KJ* and *FG* and *HJ*. However, the only pair available as an answer choice is *GH* and *KJ*.

5. **The correct answer is A.** Recall that the sum of an even and an odd number is always odd. Because x is an odd number, adding any even number to x results in an odd number. To find the next odd number after x, simply take the sum of x and the smallest even number, 2, $(x + 2)$.

6. **The correct answer is D.** Because the string is cut into 8 pieces, each $3\frac{1}{2}$ inches in length, the total length of the string is $8(3\frac{1}{2})$, or 28 inches.

7. **The correct answer is B.** To solve this problem, recall that even powers of a negative number are positive numbers, while odd powers of a negative number are negative numbers. Thus, answer choice A (x^4) and answer choice C (x^2) can be eliminated as possible answer choices because they will be positive. Consider answer choice B: if $x < -2$, then $x^3 < -8$. Pick a value for x that is less than -2, such as -3, and substitute it in the remaining answer choices, as follows:

   $-3 - 1 = -4$. This is greater than -8, so eliminate answer choice D.

   $2(-3) = -6$. This is greater than -8, so eliminate answer choice E.

8. **The correct answer is E.** Because the three associates are sharing profits of $46,000 in the ratio of 2:3:5, you can think of each of them as getting a piece of 2 + 3 + 5, or 10 equal portions. The largest piece of the profit will be $\frac{5}{10}$, or $\frac{1}{2}$ of the total, which is $23,000.

9. **The correct answer is B.** Prior to the sale, 12 pens would have cost 12($0.89), or $10.68. During the sale, a set of 2 pens sells for $1.29; thus the cost is 6($1.29), or $7.74 (note: because the pens are sold in pairs during the sale, only 6 pairs are needed to get 12 pens). Therefore, you can save $10.68 – $7.74, or $2.94, if you purchase the pens at the sale price.

10. **The correct answer is E.** You can apply common sense to solve this problem. If the average of 7 consecutive integers is 16, it would make sense that the middle number is 16 (this assumption only holds because you have an odd number of integers and because the integers are consecutive). Thus, the list of consecutive integers is 13, 14, 15, <u>16</u>, 17, 18, 19. The sum of the first and last integers on the list is 13 + 19, or 32.

11. **The correct answer is E.** The best way to solve this problem is to set up a proportion. If a circle were drawn around this figure, each angle y would represent $\frac{1}{6}$ of the whole circle, and each angle x would constitute $\frac{1}{8}$ of the whole circle. Substituting these values into the equation, you arrive at the following:

$$\frac{(\frac{1}{6} - \frac{1}{8})}{(\frac{1}{6} + \frac{1}{8})}$$

Find the least common denominator and convert fractions:

$$\frac{(\frac{4}{24} - \frac{3}{24})}{(\frac{4}{24} + \frac{3}{24})}$$

$$\frac{(\frac{1}{24})}{(\frac{7}{24})}$$

To divide, multiply the first fraction by the reciprocal of the second fraction, as follows:

$$(\frac{1}{24}) \times (\frac{24}{7}) = \frac{1}{7}$$

12. **The correct answer is C.** To solve this problem, first square 0.0001, which gives you 0.00000001. Because the number 1 is 5 more places to the right in this number, you know that 0.001 is 10^5 times greater than 0.00000001.

13. **The correct answer is D.** If x is the least possible integer for which 15% of x is greater than 2.3, then $0.15x > 2.3$. Dividing both sides by 0.15 yields $x > 15.333$, repeating. The smallest integer greater than 15.333 repeating is 16.

14. **The correct answer is C.** To solve this problem, you can follow the instructions step-by-step, using parentheses to avoid any possible confusion.

Instruction	Result
Subtract 4 from n.	$n - 4$
Multiply this sum by 2.	$2(n - 4)$ or $2n - 8$
Divide this product by 3.	$\frac{(2n-8)}{3}$

15. **The correct answer is D.** Because the length of each side of the square is $2x$, the lengths of PQ and QR are also $2x$. To find PR, use the Pythagorean Theorem, which states that $a^2 + b^2 = c^2$:

$(2x)^2 + (2x)^2 = (PR)^2$

$4x^2 + 4x^2 = (PR)^2$

$8x^2 = (PR)^2$

$x\sqrt{8} = PR$

$2x\sqrt{2} = PR$

Thus, the perimeter of $PQR = 2x + 2x + 2x\sqrt{2}$, or $4x + 2x\sqrt{2}$, which cannot be further simplified.

16. **The correct answer is A.** To solve this problem, begin by solving for m^2, as follows:

$m^2 = 32 - 9$, or 23

It might appear that you need to calculate the square root of 23; however, the problem simply asks you to compute $m^2 - 9$. Because you know that m^2 is 23, simply subtract 9 from 23. $23 - 9 = 14$, answer choice A.

17. **The correct answer is A.** To solve this problem, think critically about what is implied by the problem. The average amount of each expense must be multiplied by some variable to find the total sum of the list of expenses. Multiplying the average amount of each expense by the number of expenses incurred would yield the total sum of the expenses. The other answer choices do not make sense logically.

18. **The correct answer is E.** One way to solve this problem is to substitute a number into the equation for y and solve for x. If $y = 3$ and $x + 3 = 23$, x would equal 20. If $x = 20$, answer choices C and D can immediately be eliminated. Nothing states that y has to be greater than 1 or that y could not equal 0; therefore, answer choice E is correct.

19. **The correct answer is B.** All of the angle measures in this problem can be determined if the measure of two angles that are not vertical angles is known. You must first recognize that there are 180° in a line. Therefore, any three adjacent angles in this problem add up to 180° (for example, a, f, and e). Also, remember that vertical angles, such as b and e, are congruent. If two non-vertical angle measures are known, you will know the measure of the vertical angles respective to the non-vertical angles, and the measure of the unknown angles can be determined by the measure of their adjacent angles. Answer choice B is the only answer choice that does not include two non-vertical angles.

20. **The correct answer is D.** The easiest way to solve this problem is to pick a number for *n*, based on the information given in the question. You know that 7 is a prime number greater than 3, so substitute 7 for *n* in the answer choices until the result is a prime number:

Answer choice A: $7^2 = 49$, which is not a prime number.

Answer choice B: $\frac{7}{2} = 3.5$, which is not a prime number.

Answer choice C: $3(7) = 21$, which is not a prime number.

Answer choice D: $7 - 6 = 1$, which is a prime number, so $n - 6$ could be a prime number, and this is the correct answer.

Section 4

1. **The best answer is B.** To "embody" is to "represent a quality or idea." In this instance, the items listed represent American popular culture. To "satirize" is to "criticize in a humorous way"; to "imitate" is to "behave in a way similar to something else"; to "affront" is to "insult or offend"; and to "ensconce" is to "secure or conceal." Answer choice B is the only choice that fits within the context of the sentence.

2. **The best answer is E.** The context of the sentence indicates that the CEO was leaving the company and that the office was worried about who would take his place. Look at each answer choice and fill in the blanks in the sentence. "Resigning" refers to "giving up" or "quitting," and "apprehension" refers to "anxiety" or "uneasiness." These words complete the sentence effectively and make sense based on the context. Answer choices A, B, C, and D do not make sense when inserted into the sentence.

3. **The best answer is B.** The context of the sentence indicates that the media's coverage of shark attacks might be more than what is warranted because more fatalities occur from lightning strikes than occur from shark attacks. Answer choice B fits into the context of the sentence because one definition of "amplified" is "exaggerated."

4. **The best answer is A.** The context of the sentence indicates that Jonathan did not work as hard as he could have in school. Answer choices B, C, and E do not fit into the context because they imply hard work and forethought. The word "negligence" means "carelessness" or "an inclination to neglect." The word "solicitousness" means "anxiety or concern." The best fit for this sentence is answer choice A because "negligence" would stress that Jonathan was careless or neglectful of his schoolwork, which could result in a low grade point average.

5. **The best answer is D.** The context of the sentence suggests that even though the Great Wall is quite large, the idea that it is visible from the moon is untrue. The sentence stresses that the Great Wall is a massive object, and only the words "monumental" or "formidable" have the same meaning. Of those two choices (B or D), only choice D fits into the context that the wall is not visible from the moon, as it labels the proclamation "a myth."

6. **The best answer is C.** According to Passage 2, companies only employ someone if the economic benefit that a worker provides to the employer is greater than the required minimum wage. In addition, Passage 2 states that "whenever the price of something goes up and supply remains the same, demand goes down." Therefore, it is likely that, if the minimum wage increased and the number of workers remained the same, fewer people would be hired. Likewise, if the minimum wage decreased, the demand for workers might go up because employers could pay the workers less. This best supports answer choice C as a counter to the statement made in Passage 1 regarding corporations being more interested in making a profit than providing a living wage for their employees.

7. **The best answer is C.** Passage 1 states that "Profit-hungry corporations and greedy business owners are victimizing the working poor. Corporations seem more interested in making money than in providing a living wage to their employees." On the other hand, Passage 2 states that "The problem with raising the minimum wage boils down to simple economics; whenever the price of something goes up and supply remains the same, demand goes down.... If the economic benefit that a worker provides an employer is less than the minimum required wage, that employer will simply do without the services of the worker." This best supports answer choice C.

8. **The best answer is E.** While the author of Passage 1 uses phrases such as "victimizing the working poor" to indicate his or her compassion for those people who are living in poverty, the author of Passage 2 uses a more objective tone, citing "simple economics" as a reason to maintain the current minimum wage.

9. **The best answer is B.** The word "compelling" means "to exert a strong force upon." In Passage 1, the author uses strong language, such as "profit-hungry corporations" and "victimizing the working poor" to describe his or her feelings about the current status of the minimum wage. The remaining answer choices do not describe a method used by the author of Passage 1 in conveying his or her opinion.

10. **The best answer is B.** The first sentence makes an "assertion," or a "claim," regarding the legal concept of eminent domain: "Eminent domain is the power of a government to take, or condemn, privately owned property." The third sentence confirms this assertion: "Indeed, in 1879, in *Boom Co v Patterson*, the United States Supreme Court explained that eminent domain is 'an attribute of sovereignty.'" The word "sovereignty" refers to the "authority" of the government. The other answer choices are not supported by the passage.

11. **The best answer is A.** The passage states that "The Fifth Amendment to the United States Constitution *provides* that the federal government may not take private property…" As it is used here, the word "provides" most nearly means "declares," or "states."

12. **The best answer is C.** Each of the other choices contains concepts that were covered in the passage. However, answer choice C is not mentioned. Note that it reads, "encourages private takings of *public* property for private use."

13. **The best answer is C.** The passage discusses the fact that the reason the *Kelo* decision is controversial is because of disagreement regarding the purposes for which private property is taken. Not everyone agrees that economic development of land that does not qualify as blighted justifies the government's taking of such land. No evidence in the passage supports disagreement on the topics mentioned in the other answer choices.

14. **The best answer is B.** According to the passage, the term "public use" has generally "…meant that the government could take private land only if it could demonstrate that the land was necessary to develop a project that had a valid public purpose, that it would be used by the public. The most common example of such a use is a new road or highway." This best supports answer choice B.

15. **The best answer is D.** The passage states that "…Justice Sandra Day O'Connor suggested in her dissenting opinion the power would very likely be most beneficial to those citizens 'with disproportionate influence and power in the political process' to the detriment of residents of poorer sectors of the community or neighborhoods inhabited primarily by minorities." This is an argument *against* the governmental taking of private land for the purposes of economic development. The passage also states that "…supporters of the *Kelo* decision emphasize the potential appreciable benefit to the community at large, citing that the needs of the many often outweigh the needs of the few. They also point out that Justice Paul Stevens expressly recommended that the states are free to impose limitations on the use of such power by local governmental authorities." This represents an argument *supporting* the government taking of private land for the purposes of economic development. This discussion was included to show that any expansion of eminent domain rights is being discussed by both opponents and proponents to ensure that such expansion is effected in a balanced manner.

16. **The best answer is E.** The passage states that "The history of human language is as much a story of human expansion and interaction as it is one of political turmoil and cultural oppression. Careful analysis of language variation must seek evidence not just in the flow of people and information across physical barriers such as oceans and mountain ranges but also across political barriers such as borders, battlefields, and occupied lands. Too often are the natural, peaceful integration and disintegration of cultures emphasized over the oppression and racism in human history that molds what we call individual languages today." These sentences indicate that the author is not satisfied with the more commonly held belief that language evolution is simply the result of natural and peaceful integration of cultures. The author appears "reproachful," or "disapproving," of this particular theory of the history of language.

17. **The best answer is D.** According to the passage, "Careful analysis of language variation must seek evidence not just in the flow of people and information across physical barriers such as oceans and mountain ranges, but also across political barriers such as borders, battlefields, and occupied lands. Too often are the natural, peaceful integration and disintegration of cultures emphasized over the oppression and racism in human history that molds what we call individual languages today." The author implies that not enough attention is paid to the political concepts that contribute to language development and objects to the notion that language evolution is simply the result of natural and peaceful integration of cultures.

18. **The best answer is E.** The passage states that "For better or worse, the answer lies in the seemingly unshakeable tendency of humans to assert the dominance of their own culture over those of other people less capable of resistance." This represents a "claim" made by the author regarding language variations. None of the other answer choices are supported by this statement.

19. **The best answer is C.** The passage states that "Careful analysis of language variation must seek evidence not just in the flow of people and information across physical barriers such as oceans and mountain ranges but also across political barriers such as borders, battlefields, and occupied lands.... This begs the question, what is the difference between a language and a dialect or vernacular?" This suggests that there is a certain ambiguity or uncertainty about the true definition of a language. The passage indicates that it is sometimes difficult to tell the difference between a language and a dialect, which refers to a regional variation of a language.

20. **The best answer is D.** According to the passage, "In countries with a dominant national language, children are taught to speak and write in a standard way. This is called *prescriptive language instruction*, meaning teaching a standard usage of the language. In England, people refer to this standard usage as The King's English; in the United States, many terms exist to describe this idealized form of the English language, such as Standard American English, standard written English, or even Newscaster English, after the accent and grammar achieved by major national broadcasters who strive to remove the regional markers in their mother tongue." This suggests that "prescriptive language instruction" marks a traditional, or standard, method of learning and speaking a language and that such instruction is governed by a country's desire for everyone to speak the same language.

21. **The best answer is D.** The passage defines "prescriptive language" as the "standard usage of the language." According to the passage, one term used to describe this usage is "...Newscaster English, after the accent and grammar achieved by major national broadcasters who strive to remove the regional markers in their mother tongue. Speakers of the prescriptive norm are often perceived to be well educated, intelligent, or of the upper classes." It is likely that "Newscaster English" evolved as a means to indicate the intelligence and credibility of national broadcasters. The other answer choices are not supported by the passage.

22. **The best answer is A.** The third paragraph begins a discussion of language as an indicator of education or intelligence. According to the passage, "...though many prominent journalists come from the American South, the typical listener would be shocked to hear these professionals use *y'all* instead of the standard pronoun *you*. The common response to an example like this is rejection of *y'all* as "correct' English." This best supports answer choice A.

23. **The best answer is C.** The passage states that "A clear example of the problem of labeling speech is in the Romance Languages, a term describing those forms of speech descended from Vulgar Latin, the language of the soldiers, slaves, and commoners of the Roman Empire." This best supports answer choice C.

24. **The best answer is B.** The word "lexicon" often refers to "the vocabulary of a language." According to the passage, "...other lesser known languages are often called dialects. The key features that separate each of these are not in the grammar or *lexicon*..." Because the passage focuses on a discussion of words and language, answer choice B is best.

Section 5

1. **The correct answer is D.** To solve this problem, first find the units, or "ones," digit of each of the separate elements of the expression, as follows:

The units digit of $(11)^4$ is 1 because $1 \times 1 \times 1 \times 1 = 1$.

The units digit of $(22)^3$ is 8 because $2 \times 2 \times 2 = 8$.

The units digit of $(36)^2$ is 6 because $6 \times 6 = 36$, and the units digit of 36 is 6.

Therefore, the units digit of $(11)^4(22)^3(36)^2$ is 8 because $1 \times 8 \times 6 = 48$, and the units digit of 48 is 8.

2. **The correct answer is D.** To solve this problem, use the Pythagorean Theorem, which states that $a^2 + b^2 = c^2$, as follows:

$6^2 + 4^2 = x^2$

$36 + 16 = x^2$

$52 = x^2$

To solve for the value of x, find the square root of 52, as follows:

$\sqrt{52} = \sqrt{13} \times \sqrt{4}$, which is equivalent to $2\sqrt{13}$.

3. **The correct answer is D.** To solve this problem, evaluate each answer choice, as follows:

Answer choice A is incorrect because 3 is not divisible by both 3 and 9.

Answer choice B is incorrect because 6 is not divisible by both 3 and 9.

Answer choice C is incorrect because 18 is divisible by 3, 6, and 9, so it proves that the statement is true.

Answer choice D is correct because 27 is divisible by both 3 and 9 but not by 6.

Answer choice E is incorrect because 36 is divisible by 3, 6, and 9, so it proves that the statement is true.

4. **The correct answer is A.** The circumference of a circle is equal to π times the diameter (πd). In this case, the diameter of the circle is equal to one side of the rectangle that it is contained within, as shown by the figure. Therefore, the circumference of the circle is 10π.

5. **The correct answer is B.** You are given that $ft = b$ and $b = mt$; therefore, $ft = mt$. Dividing both sides by t, you see that $f = m$.

6. **The correct answer is C.** If the ratio of gray socks to brown socks is $\frac{1}{3}$, you have 1 gray sock for every 3 brown socks. In other words, if you have only 1 gray sock, you have 3 brown socks, for a total of 4 socks. Therefore, the total number of socks in the sock drawer is a multiple of 4. Answer choice C (15) is the only number that is not a multiple of 4.

7. **The correct answer is C.** You are given that Jane traveled 30 miles in 6 hours and that Betty traveled 3 times as far in half the time. That means that Jane traveled 30(3), or 90 miles in $6 \times \frac{1}{2}$, or 3 hours. Therefore, Betty traveled $\frac{90}{3}$, or 30 miles per hour.

8. **The correct answer is A.** To solve this problem, you must recall the rules governing exponents. First, simplify the equation, as shown below:

$5^x + 5^x + 5^x + 5^x + 5^x = 5(5^x)$

5 is equivalent to 5^1, and when you multiply like coefficients with exponents, remember that you must add the exponents.

Therefore, $5^1(5^x) = 5^{x+1}$

9. **The correct answer is .025 or .026.** To solve, first convert $\frac{2}{5}$ to 0.40, its decimal equivalent. Then consider the exponent, as follows:

   $0.40^4 = (0.40)(0.40)(0.40)(0.40) = 0.0256$ (remember there are only four spaces on the answer sheet, so you can either round up or down).

   You also could have simply calculated 4^4 and moved the decimal point accordingly.

10. **The correct answer is 1.5.** To solve this problem, first find the difference between -9 and 12, as follows:

    $12 - (-9) = 21$

    Half of this distance is $\frac{21}{2}$, or 10.5. The point lying halfway between -9 and 12 can be found by adding 10.5 to -9 or subtracting 10.5 from 12. The halfway point is thus 1.5.

11. **The correct answer is 90.** Triangles with two equal angles are isosceles triangles, which means that two sides of the triangle are congruent, or equal. To find the perimeter of a triangle, add the length of the three sides. To find the least possible value for the perimeter of the triangle in question, you should assume that the two equal sides are the shortest sides. Therefore, the least possible perimeter for this triangle would be 25 + 25 + 40, or 90.

12. **The correct answer is 45.** You are given that $x - y = 85$ and $x + y = 5$. To solve for x, set up a system of equations and use substitution, as follows:

    $x + y = 5$

    $y = 5 - x$

    Substitute $5 - x$ for y in the equation $x - y = 85$, and solve for y:

    $x - (5 - x) = 85$

    $2x - 5 = 85$

    $2x = 90$

    $x = 45$

13. **The correct answer is 48.** To answer this question, first recognize that you are asked to compare a part (the number of pounds of gravel) to the whole (the number of pounds of the mixture.) The ratio of gravel to the mixture is 2:5; you know this because you are given that the mixture contains 2 parts gravel to 3 parts sand (2 + 3 = 5). You are also given that the mixture weighs 100 pounds. Now, set up a proportion, as follows:

    2 is to 5 as x (pounds of gravel) is to 120.

    Cross-multiply and solve for x:

    $\frac{2}{5} = \frac{x}{120}$

    $5x = 240$

    $x = 48$

    There will be 48 pounds of gravel in a mixture of gravel and sand that weighs a total of 120 pounds.

14. **The correct answer is 50.** According to the figure, 115° plus the measure of angle BCE = 180°. Thus, the measure of angle BCE = 180 − 115, or 65°. Also because it is given that $CE = CB$, ¢BCE is isosceles, and the measure of angle BCE and the measure of angle CBE are equal. Using the fact that the sum of angles in a triangle is 180°, if the measure of angles BCE or EBC is found, then the measure of angle BEC can be calculated as follows:

(180 − 2(measure of angle BCE))

BEC = 180 − 2(65)

BEC = 50°

Because BD is perpendicular to AE and CE is perpendicular to AE, BD and CE are parallel and are cut by the transversal BE. Angles BEC and DBE are alternate interior angles and thus have the same measure of 50°. Because x represents the measure of angle DBE, $x = 50°$.

15. **The correct answer is 13.** To solve this problem, set the number of boys on the team to b and the number of girls on the team to g. Because the number of boys on the team is 5 more than the number of girls on the team, $b = g + 5$. Further, because the total number on the team is 21, $b + g = 21$. Substitute the first equation into the second and solve for g, as follows:

$(g + 5) + g = 21$

$2g + 5 = 21$

$2g = 16$

$g = 8$

Because $b + g = 21$, and $g = 8$, $b + 8 = 21$ and $b = 13$.

16. **The correct answer is 9.** If $r + 3s$ is equal to 150% of $8s$, then $r + 3s = 1.5(8s)$. To solve, multiply the quantities $1.5(8s)$ to get $r + 3s = 12s$. Subtracting $3s$ from both sides yields $r = 9s$. To find the value of r/s, divide both sides of $r = 9s$ by s to get $r/s = 9$.

17. **The correct answer is 2 or 14.** To solve this problem, use the distance formula, which states that the distance, d, between two points (x_1, y_1) and (x_2, y_2) is $d = \sqrt{[(x_2 - x_1)^2 + (y_2 - y_1)^2]}$. If the distance between point $L(8, 12)$ and point $M(x, 4)$ is 10, then $10 = \sqrt{[(x - 8)^2 + (4 - 12)^2]}$, or $\sqrt{[(x - 8)^2 + 64]}$. To solve for x, first square both sides to eliminate the square root to get $100 = (x - 8)^2 + 64$. Subtracting 64 from both sides yields $36 = (x - 8)^2$. If the square root of both sides is taken, the result is $x - 8 = \pm 6$. When $x - 8 = -6$, adding 8 to both sides yields $x = 2$. When $x - 8 = 6$, adding 8 to both sides yields $x = 14$. Thus two possible values for x are 2 and 14.

18. **The correct answer is .25 or $\frac{1}{4}$.** According to the number line shown, $\sqrt{x}$ is located at the sixth of 12 intervals, making it equal to $\frac{6}{12}$, or $\frac{1}{2}$. Because $\sqrt{x} = \frac{1}{2}$, $x = (\frac{1}{2})^2$, or $\frac{1}{4}$.

Section 6

1. **The best answer is E.** The phrase "for life" is intended to modify "appointed" and not the "president"; thus, it should immediately follow the word "appointed" instead of the word "president." Answer choice B is incorrect because it includes extraneous punctuation and is more awkwardly constructed.

2. **The best answer is D.** You should use the adverb "accurately" to modify the verb "be called." The two answer choices using "accurately" are C and D. Of those two, answer choice D is the best answer because it more concisely orders the words such that the verb and its modifier are not separated by the noun "submersibles."

3. **The best answer is C.** A person can be either "more" or "less" conspicuous; thus, "lesser" conspicuous is not correct because "lesser" is a noun. Usually the best way to express an idea is the simplest way. In this case, the remaining choice with no comma or semicolon separating the phrase is the best choice.

4. **The best answer is B.** The correct answer choice must match the rest of the sentence context in both topic and tense. Because the people in this sentence were "startled" by the presence of the eagle, the proper form of "to see" is the past tense, "saw." Only answer choice B matches in tense with the rest of the sentence and flows smoothly.

5. **The best answer is D.** Because the astrologers were from the past, the supposed influence that celestial bodies had on humans should be expressed in the past tense. Thus, the clearest way to express the idea would be "the celestial bodies *influenced* specific parts of the human body."

6. **The best answer is C.** Answer choice C clearly and concisely indicates that Zheng Ho is the Chinese navigator who searched for trade routes. The remaining answer choices are not grammatically correct.

7. **The best answer is A.** To maintain parallelism in the sentence, it is necessary to use the simple past tense verb "stormed" to match the simple past tense verb "caused." Answer choice C is incorrect because it unnecessarily includes the helping verb "had."

8. **The best answer is E.** The subject of the sentence is "13 million people," so you must use the plural possessive pronoun "their." Also, when talking about employment, 13 million people cannot share one job, so you must use the plural noun "jobs."

9. **The best answer is B.** The sentence contains two complete phrases that could stand alone as separate sentences. However, because they are so closely related, it is appropriate to join them using a semicolon.

10. **The best answer is D.** To maintain parallelism in the sentence, it is necessary to match the verb forms. The sentence includes the gerunds "hurling" and "engulfing" in a series; therefore, the underlined portion should also include the verb "sweeping." Answer choice B is incorrect because it implies that the houses were sweeping, which does not fit the context of the sentence.

11. **The best answer is A.** The context of the sentence indicates that the fear is related to moving to an unfamiliar situation in a new location. The best way to express that fear is "fear of the unknown." The rest of the answer choices either do not express the same idea or are not as clear and simple.

12. **The best answer is A.** The word "obviously" is an adverb and should not be used to directly describe the noun "signs." An appropriate word to describe signs is the adjective "obvious."

13. **The best answer is C.** The phrase "to be found" indicates the future tense, while the rest of the sentence is written in a manner indicating that the poem has already been written and is available to be read.

14. **The best answer is E.** This sentence does not contain any errors. It is clear and concise as written.

15. **The best answer is B.** Because the simple subject of the sentence is the plural noun "works," you must use the plural verb "continue."

16. **The best answer is C.** The phrase "or halfway up the flagpole" is parenthetical, meaning that it is extra information inserted into the sentence and should be set off by commas.

17. **The best answer is B.** To correct this sentence, is necessary to use the adverb "necessarily" to modify the verb "feel" in the sentence.

18. **The best answer is D.** The contraction "it's" *always* means "it is." In this sentence, "it" is being used as a possessive pronoun before the noun "progression" you should therefore use the possessive form, "its."

19. **The best answer is E.** This sentence does not contain any errors. It is clear and concise as written.

20. **The best answer is C.** The subject and verb must agree in number. Because the sentence refers to "one" of Daniel Boone's accomplishments, you should use the singular verb "was."

21. **The best answer is A.** Because only one ability is discussed in the sentence (the ability to jump), replace the plural noun "abilities" with the singular noun "ability."

22. **The best answer is E.** This sentence does not contain any errors. It is clear and concise as written.

23. **The best answer is C.** To maintain parallelism in the sentence, "to being" should be replaced with the infinitive form "to take" in order to match.

24. The best answer is B. To replace the subject, Jackie, it is necessary to use the *nominative pronoun* "she." The pronoun "her" is the *objective pronoun* and can be used only as the object of a verb, sentence, or preposition.

25. The best answer is C. A "propensity" is a preference or inclination for something. As a matter of idiom (common usage), someone has a propensity *for* something, not *of* something.

26. The best answer is A. Because the adjective "all" modifies the subject "financial institution," there needs to be agreement in number. The subject should be the plural "financial institutions."

27. The best answer is D. The context of the sentence indicates that a possibility an intruder is in the area. The word "maybe" means "uncertainty" and is an adverb. Instead, the verb phrase "may be" is required in the clause.

28. The best answer is A. It is not necessary to include "the" before a gerund acting as a noun, as in this sentence.

29. The best answer is B. Because the sentence is talking about the involvement of women during World War II, you should use the plural possessive "women's." Furthermore, "womens" is not a word.

30. The best answer is B. The context of the passage indicates that Rhyolite, Nevada, is the ghost town, so it is best to place the modifying phrase (the ghost town) directly before the noun that it modifies (Rhyolite, Nevada). Only answer choice B creates a sentence that best places the modifier and is free from grammatical errors.

31. The best answer is E. It is not necessary to include both the word "happily" and the phrase "with smiles on our faces"; one implies the other. Therefore, the most clear and concise way to express the intended idea of the sentence is to include either "happily" or "smiles on our faces," as in answer choice E.

32. The best answer is E. The word "embedded" means "layed in surrounding matter." The phrase "embedded in clay" is a better way of saying "stuck in clay."

33. The best answer is D. Because the second paragraph deals with the appearance of the ghost town upon the author's arrival, the image of the curator is important; however, the actions of the cat in her lap do not add to the paragraph. Because Sentence 12 only talks about the cat, it distracts from the paragraph, and removing it would improve the unity of the paragraph.

34. The best answer is A. The sentence as it is written is clear, concise, and effectively expresses the author's intended meaning. The remaining answer choices are unnecessarily awkward and wordy.

35. The best answer is A. The second paragraph contains many descriptive, physical details that the author uses to present the reader with a vivid picture of the ghost town. The other answer choices are not supported by the paragraph.

Section 7

1. **The best answer is C.** To answer this question, you do not need to know the exact definition of "circumstantial evidence." You should, however, understand that "circumstantial" describes something that is "dependent on other events and conditions" and "indirect." Hence, the prosecutor is probably looking for "real" or "physical" evidence because "circumstantial" evidence might not be very convincing. "Tangible" is a synonym of "real" and "physical," so answer choice C is correct.

2. **The best answer is E.** In each choice, the first word is plausible; however, only "frequent" fits the context of the sentence. Answer choice B is incorrect because "more greater" is redundant and ungrammatical.

3. **The best answer is B.** Unpredictable space combined with poor maps would lead to getting lost. The fact that the ancient catacombs are "poorly mapped" might logically predict people's disappearances.

4. **The best answer is D.** In an open market, firms "compete" against one another for market share, that is, a proportion of the consumers of a certain product, such as cheese. None of the other answer choices make sense based on the context of the sentence.

5. **The best answer is A.** "Absconded" is an intransitive verb that means to "leave quickly, often to avoid arrest." This best fits the context of the sentence.

6. **The best answer is B.** The context of the sentence indicates that the shelter will shut down without the donations, so you can assume that the donations are a good thing. Both "generous" and "charitable" would fit in the first blank, but only "inevitable" indicates the certainty of the shelter shutting down if it does not receive the donations. Both "affluent" and "frugal" are associated with money, but they do not fit the context of the sentence.

7. **The best answer is C.** The context of the passage indicates that Lincoln was opposed to slavery and pushed for its end in both the North and the South. According to the passage, "…Lincoln stated that the nation was too divided to continue compromising on slavery. Lincoln began his defense by referring to the actions of the Founding Fathers, who had tried to eradicate slavery. He mentioned the unanimous abolition of the African slave trade and the lack of the word 'slave' in the Constitution. He proposed that the Fathers desired to abolish slavery…." This best supports answer choice C.

8. **The best answer is A.** The passage states that "This new attitude towards slavery promoted by Southerners and some Northern Democrats led Lincoln to believe that they wanted to nationalize slavery." One conclusion that can be drawn from this statement is that the Northern *non*-Democrats were opposed to slavery because they did not share the same attitude regarding slavery.

9. **The best answer is B.** The first paragraph indicates that Lincoln was opposed to slavery because during the debates, his position against the right of a state to allow slavery was criticized by his opponent. Because the Dred Scott decision denied the right of Congress to forbid slavery in the states, it is clear that this decision opposed Lincoln's aim to end slavery.

10. **The best answer is E.** The first paragraph outlines Lincoln's position against slavery and indicates that Lincoln did not agree with the attitude towards slavery that was being promoted by Southerners and some Northerners. The second paragraph offers support for and additional details regarding Lincoln's position. The other answer choices are not supported by the passage.

11. **The best answer is E.** The passage explicitly mentions the statements made in answer choices A, B, C, and D but does not indicate that several of the Founding Fathers belonged to abolitionist groups. The passage only states that the Founding Fathers worked toward abolishing slavery, not that they belonged to any specific groups.

12. **The best answer is E.** The passage states that "Lincoln argued that the South had moved away from this course of ending slavery." If southern plantation owners learned that sharecropping was more efficient than slavery, the plantation owners would likely be in favor of ending slavery, and Lincoln's argument would be weakened. The other answer choices are not supported by the passage.

13. **The best answer is C.** According to the passage, "These Compromises, however, were at odds with the new Dred Scott *decision* of the Supreme Court, which denied that Congress had a right to forbid slavery in the states." As it is used in this context, the word "decision" most nearly means "resolution," or "decision made by a court of law."

14. **The best answer is C.** Many statements throughout the passage point to Lincoln's position against slavery and his desire to abolish it from the states. These facts best support answer choice C.

15. **The best answer is E.** The passage states that Lincoln "believed that *popular* sovereignty was contrary to the principle that valued freedom over slavery." This statement, along with additional context, indicates that the "prevailing" governmental rulings, such as the Kansas-Nebraska Act, placed more value on slavery than they did on freedom. In this context, "popular" and "prevailing" mean "common among the people."

16. **The best answer is D.** The passage states that "The Dred Scott decision reaffirmed for the South that slaves were considered property, and because America's Constitution protects property, exclusion of slavery through unfriendly legislation was unconstitutional." Although the passage indicates that Lincoln was opposed to the Dred Scott decision, the author is objective in his or her commentary of the resolution in the passage. Answer choices A, B, C, and D include language in which the connotation is either too positive or too negative.

17. **The best answer is C.** The final sentence of the passage states that "Without the majority of public opinion standing firm against slavery, Lincoln realized that the battle over forced labor could not be won at the rostrum." The word "rostrum," meaning "podium," refers to Lincoln's political platform. This sentence indicates that Lincoln did not believe that the battle over slavery could be won by simply debating the issue; it was more likely that the conflict would continue and would quite likely be elevated to an armed conflict, which was, in fact, the ultimate result.

18. **The best answer is D.** Throughout the passage, Lincoln expresses concern and compassion for the slaves and seeks to abolish the practice of slavery, which prevented certain people from living free lives. The words "thoughtful" and "empathetic" most accurately describe Lincoln as he is portrayed in the passage.

19. **The best answer is B.** The passage discusses at great length the controversy surrounding whether to abolish slavery. The country was so divided over the issue that several acts and decisions resulted from the divergent opinions. According to the passage, "In the Lincoln-Douglas debates, Lincoln stated that the nation was too divided to continue compromising on slavery." This best supports answer choice B.

Section 8

1. **The correct answer is B.** If $RS = 21$ and ST is 15 more than RS, then $ST = RS + 15$, or $21 + 15$, which is 36. Because R, S, and T are points on a line in that order, $RT = RS + ST$, which equals $21 + 36$, or 57.

2. **The correct answer is C.** To solve this problem, first find the value of x in the equation $4x + 7 = 19$, as follows:

$4x + 7 = 19$

$4x = 12$

$x = 3$

When $x = 3$, $6x - 3 = 18 - 3$, or 15.

3. **The best answer is D.** To solve this problem, first count the total number of athletes. Each figure represents 15 athletes, so you have 15×10 or 150 athletes total. 60% of 150 is equal to 150×0.60, or 90 athletes. Because $\frac{90}{15} = 6$, a total of 6 groups of athletes represents 60% of all athletes at North High School. Basketball and volleyball are the only two sports whose combined total is 90, or 60% of 150.

4. **The correct answer is E.** To solve this problem, first realize that the line segments in question form right triangles (with the exception of line segment XL), and thus, their lengths can be computed using the Pythagorean Theorem. Line segment XJ is equal to the square root of $7^2 + 5^2$, or approximately 8.6. Likewise, line segment XK is approximately equal to 8.1, line segment XM is approximately equal to 7.3, line segment XN is approximately equal to 9.3, and line segment XM is simply equal to 7. Thus, line segment XN has the greatest length, answer choice E.

5. **The correct answer is D.** To solve this problem, first eliminate answer choices that yield equal values for f(-5) and f(5). These include answer choices in which the functions have even powers of x, such as answer choice A, where $f(x) = 6x^2$; answer choice B, where $f(x) = 6$; and answer choice E, where $f(x) = x^6 + 6$. Now, substitute -5 and 5 into the remaining answer choices:

Answer choice C: $f(x) = \frac{6}{x}$. When x is -5, $f(x) = -\frac{6}{5}$, and when x is 5, $f(x) = \frac{6}{5}$. Therefore, f(5) is greater than f(-5) and answer choice C is incorrect.

Answer choice D: $f(x) = 6 - x^3$. When $x = -5$, $f(x) = 6 - (-125)$ or 131, and when x is 5, $f(x) = 6 - 125$, or -116. Therefore, f(-5) is greater than f(5) .

6. **The correct answer is A.** To solve this problem, first find the area of the larger rectangle. The formula for the area of a rectangle is $A = length \times width$. The length of the sides given are 10 and 12, so the area is $A = 10 \times 12$, or 120. The area of the smaller square is $A = (x)(x)$, or x^2. Because you are asked for the area of the shaded region, subtract the area of the small square (x^2) from the area of the larger rectangle (120). Thus, the area of the shaded region is $120 - x^2$, answer choice A.

7. **The correct answer is C.** Because $6b = 12c$, $b = 2c$. Substitute $2c$ for b in the equation and solve for a, as follows:

$4a = 6b$

$4a = 6(2c)$

$4a = 12c$

$a = 3c$

8. **The correct answer is B.** If each of the r boats that were used to carry the fishermen could accommodate a maximum number of m passengers, the total capacity of fisherman is rm. Because only one boat had five open spots and the remaining boats were filled to capacity, the number of fishermen (f) was 5 less than the total capacity, or $rm - 5$. Thus $f = rm - 5$.

9. **The correct answer is B.** Remember, when two parallel lines are cut by a transversal, or intersecting line, the angles created are matched in measure and position with a counterpart at the other parallel line. Angles d and a together form a corresponding angle with the angle measuring 105°. Therefore, the sum of angles d and a equals 105°. The measure of angle a is 105° − 40°, or 65°. Vertical angles are congruent, so angle x has the same measure as angle a. Thus, angle x equals 65°, answer choice B.

10. **The correct answer is C.** To solve this problem, first recall that $9 = 3^2$. It follows that $9^{x+2} = (3^2)^{x+2}$ and that $3^{2(x+2)} = 3^{2x+4}$. Because $3^{3x} = 9^{x+2}$ and $3^{3x} = 3^{2x+4}$, then $3x = 2x + 4$. Subtracting $2x$ from both sides yields $x = 4$.

11. **The correct answer is D.** Because the figure is a rectangle, the adjacent sides are perpendicular. Perpendicular lines have slopes that are negative reciprocals of each other, meaning that the product of their slopes is -1. Because you have four lines and four perpendicular angles, the product of the slopes is (-1)(-1)(-1)(-1), or 1.

12. **The correct answer is D.** To solve this problem, remember the standard form for the equation of a line: $y = mx + b$, where b is the y-intercept. In the (x,y) coordinate place, a line crosses the x-axis when $y = 0$. Set y equal to 0 in the equation, and solve for x, which results in the value of point a:

$0 = 4x - 12$

$12 = 4x$

$3 = x$

13. **The correct answer is E.** To solve this problem, put the known prices in order from smallest to greatest: $1.89, $2.11, $2.49, $2.72, $2.94, $3.08. Because it is given in the problem that $2.49 is the median price, it should fall exactly in the center of the list once b is taken into account. That would only occur if b were less than or equal to 2.49. Thus, b cannot equal $2.80.

14. **The correct answer is A.** Because the radius of the circle is 24, the circumference is $2\pi r = 2\pi(24)$, or 48π. Because the length of arc BC is 8π, it constitutes $\frac{8\pi}{48\pi}$, or $\frac{1}{6}$ of the circle. Thus, the area of sector ABC also makes up $\frac{1}{6}$ of the entire area of the circle. The area of the circle is $\pi r^2 = \pi(24)^2$, or 576π. The area of the sector ABC is then $\frac{576\pi}{6}$, or 96π.

15. **The correct answer is D.** Given that $m + 4(n - 2) = p$, $n - 2$ can be found by subtracting m from both sides and dividing by 4 to get $n - 2 = \frac{(p - m)}{4}$.

16. **The correct answer is C.** Given that x is the greatest prime factor of 34 and y is the greatest prime factor of 75, to calculate $x + y$, list the factors of 34 and 75 to find the largest factor that is prime (meaning that it is only divisible by 1 and itself). The factors of 34 are 1, 2, 17, and 34, making the greatest prime factor 17. The factors of 75 are 1, 3, 5, 15, 25, and 75, making 5 the greatest prime factor. Thus $x + y = 17 + 5$, or 22.

Section 9

1. **The best answer is D.** It is better to use the active voice than it is to use the passive voice. Because Mr. Jones is the subject of the sentence, he should be performing an action. Thus, it is better to say "when he learned" than to say "when it was told to him."

2. **The best answer is C.** It is better to use the active voice than it is to use the passive voice. Because Megan is the subject of the sentence, it is better to say that she "searched frantically" than to say that her "frantic search was for her car keys," which is awkward.

3. **The best answer is B.** In the initial sentence, the pronoun "they" is ambiguous because it has no clear antecedent. It is better to restate the noun to ensure that the sentence is free from ambiguity.

4. **The best answer is E.** Answer choice E is the most clear and concise selection, as it does away with repeating "strong."

5. **The best answer is D.** Only answer choice D clearly and effectively conveys the intended meaning of the sentence—that is, that George Orwell is Elaine's favorite author. In addition, it is correctly punctuated.

6. **The best answer is A.** This sentence is best as written. It uses an inflected verb, effectively expresses the idea, and is free from ambiguity. Answer choices B, C, D, and E are awkward and unclear.

7. **The best answer is C.** The context of the sentence reveals a conflict between what Grant Wood painted and where he spent most of his time. It is logical, then, to use words that suggest contrast, such as "although" or "however."

8. **The best answer is B.** The sentence as it is written includes a comma splice, which is not grammatically correct. Answer choices C, D, and E are awkwardly constructed. Only answer choice B correctly uses a semicolon to separate two distinct yet related clauses.

9. **The best answer is C.** The information after "is obtaining TechNet" is extra descriptive information not crucial to the sentence. As such, it should be grammatically set off with a comma and the word "which." While answer choice B uses a comma, the gerund "writing" is incorrect.

10. **The best answer is A.** This sentence is best as written. It effectively expresses the idea and is free from ambiguity. Answer choices B, C, D, and E are awkward and unclear.

11. **The best answer is E.** The phrase "one of the few women ever to compete in the men's division of professional wrestling" is a parenthetical clause. If this extra information is removed, the rest of the sentence should be able to stand alone as a complete sentence. Only answer choice E passes this test.

12. **The best answer is E.** The phrase "although their common language is English" is a parenthetical clause. If this extra information is removed, the rest of the sentence should be able to stand alone as a complete sentence. Only answer choice E passes this test.

13. **The best answer is D.** This sentence is intended to describe how the state's board of tourism subsidizes the museum and that it consists of hundreds of exhibits from the medieval time period. The phrase "consisting of hundreds of exhibits from the medieval time period" should be set off as a parenthetical, using a comma before and after the phrase. If this extra information is removed, the rest of the sentence should be able to stand alone as a complete. Only answer choice D passes this test.

14. **The best answer is B.** Answer choice B most clearly indicates that, despite the fact that many graduates interviewed for the position, only a few were selected. Answer choice A indicates that the few graduates selected were the *result of* many graduates being interviewed; thus, answer choice A is incorrect. Answer choices C and D are incorrect because they are not complete sentences, and answer choice E is ungrammatical. (Note: "interviewed" is used here as a simple past tense intransitive verb. It is not used as an adjective.)

CHAPTER ELEVEN

Practice Test 3 with Answers and Explanations

There are nine separate sections on this simulated test, including:

- ▸ One 25-minute Essay
- ▸ Five other 25-minute Verbal and Math Sections
- ▸ Two 20-minute Verbal and Math Sections
- ▸ One 10-minute Verbal Section

Work on only one section at a time and make every attempt to complete each section in the time allowed for that particular section. Carefully mark only one answer on your answer sheet for each question. Remember that you can and should write on the test itself to help you to correctly answer the questions.

Tear out pages 352–357 before you begin the test.

Begin your essay on this page. If you need more space, continue on the next page. Do not write outside of the essay box.

Start with number 1 for each new section. If a section has fewer questions than answer spaces, leave the extra answer spaces blank. Be sure to erase any errors or stray marks completely.

SECTION 2

1 Ⓐ Ⓑ Ⓒ Ⓓ Ⓔ　　11 Ⓐ Ⓑ Ⓒ Ⓓ Ⓔ　　21 Ⓐ Ⓑ Ⓒ Ⓓ Ⓔ　　31 Ⓐ Ⓑ Ⓒ Ⓓ Ⓔ
2 Ⓐ Ⓑ Ⓒ Ⓓ Ⓔ　　12 Ⓐ Ⓑ Ⓒ Ⓓ Ⓔ　　22 Ⓐ Ⓑ Ⓒ Ⓓ Ⓔ　　32 Ⓐ Ⓑ Ⓒ Ⓓ Ⓔ
3 Ⓐ Ⓑ Ⓒ Ⓓ Ⓔ　　13 Ⓐ Ⓑ Ⓒ Ⓓ Ⓔ　　23 Ⓐ Ⓑ Ⓒ Ⓓ Ⓔ　　33 Ⓐ Ⓑ Ⓒ Ⓓ Ⓔ
4 Ⓐ Ⓑ Ⓒ Ⓓ Ⓔ　　14 Ⓐ Ⓑ Ⓒ Ⓓ Ⓔ　　24 Ⓐ Ⓑ Ⓒ Ⓓ Ⓔ　　34 Ⓐ Ⓑ Ⓒ Ⓓ Ⓔ
5 Ⓐ Ⓑ Ⓒ Ⓓ Ⓔ　　15 Ⓐ Ⓑ Ⓒ Ⓓ Ⓔ　　25 Ⓐ Ⓑ Ⓒ Ⓓ Ⓔ　　35 Ⓐ Ⓑ Ⓒ Ⓓ Ⓔ
6 Ⓐ Ⓑ Ⓒ Ⓓ Ⓔ　　16 Ⓐ Ⓑ Ⓒ Ⓓ Ⓔ　　26 Ⓐ Ⓑ Ⓒ Ⓓ Ⓔ　　36 Ⓐ Ⓑ Ⓒ Ⓓ Ⓔ
7 Ⓐ Ⓑ Ⓒ Ⓓ Ⓔ　　17 Ⓐ Ⓑ Ⓒ Ⓓ Ⓔ　　27 Ⓐ Ⓑ Ⓒ Ⓓ Ⓔ　　37 Ⓐ Ⓑ Ⓒ Ⓓ Ⓔ
8 Ⓐ Ⓑ Ⓒ Ⓓ Ⓔ　　18 Ⓐ Ⓑ Ⓒ Ⓓ Ⓔ　　28 Ⓐ Ⓑ Ⓒ Ⓓ Ⓔ　　38 Ⓐ Ⓑ Ⓒ Ⓓ Ⓔ
9 Ⓐ Ⓑ Ⓒ Ⓓ Ⓔ　　19 Ⓐ Ⓑ Ⓒ Ⓓ Ⓔ　　29 Ⓐ Ⓑ Ⓒ Ⓓ Ⓔ　　39 Ⓐ Ⓑ Ⓒ Ⓓ Ⓔ
10 Ⓐ Ⓑ Ⓒ Ⓓ Ⓔ　　20 Ⓐ Ⓑ Ⓒ Ⓓ Ⓔ　　30 Ⓐ Ⓑ Ⓒ Ⓓ Ⓔ　　40 Ⓐ Ⓑ Ⓒ Ⓓ Ⓔ

SECTION 3

1 Ⓐ Ⓑ Ⓒ Ⓓ Ⓔ　　11 Ⓐ Ⓑ Ⓒ Ⓓ Ⓔ　　21 Ⓐ Ⓑ Ⓒ Ⓓ Ⓔ　　31 Ⓐ Ⓑ Ⓒ Ⓓ Ⓔ
2 Ⓐ Ⓑ Ⓒ Ⓓ Ⓔ　　12 Ⓐ Ⓑ Ⓒ Ⓓ Ⓔ　　22 Ⓐ Ⓑ Ⓒ Ⓓ Ⓔ　　32 Ⓐ Ⓑ Ⓒ Ⓓ Ⓔ
3 Ⓐ Ⓑ Ⓒ Ⓓ Ⓔ　　13 Ⓐ Ⓑ Ⓒ Ⓓ Ⓔ　　23 Ⓐ Ⓑ Ⓒ Ⓓ Ⓔ　　33 Ⓐ Ⓑ Ⓒ Ⓓ Ⓔ
4 Ⓐ Ⓑ Ⓒ Ⓓ Ⓔ　　14 Ⓐ Ⓑ Ⓒ Ⓓ Ⓔ　　24 Ⓐ Ⓑ Ⓒ Ⓓ Ⓔ　　34 Ⓐ Ⓑ Ⓒ Ⓓ Ⓔ
5 Ⓐ Ⓑ Ⓒ Ⓓ Ⓔ　　15 Ⓐ Ⓑ Ⓒ Ⓓ Ⓔ　　25 Ⓐ Ⓑ Ⓒ Ⓓ Ⓔ　　35 Ⓐ Ⓑ Ⓒ Ⓓ Ⓔ
6 Ⓐ Ⓑ Ⓒ Ⓓ Ⓔ　　16 Ⓐ Ⓑ Ⓒ Ⓓ Ⓔ　　26 Ⓐ Ⓑ Ⓒ Ⓓ Ⓔ　　36 Ⓐ Ⓑ Ⓒ Ⓓ Ⓔ
7 Ⓐ Ⓑ Ⓒ Ⓓ Ⓔ　　17 Ⓐ Ⓑ Ⓒ Ⓓ Ⓔ　　27 Ⓐ Ⓑ Ⓒ Ⓓ Ⓔ　　37 Ⓐ Ⓑ Ⓒ Ⓓ Ⓔ
8 Ⓐ Ⓑ Ⓒ Ⓓ Ⓔ　　18 Ⓐ Ⓑ Ⓒ Ⓓ Ⓔ　　28 Ⓐ Ⓑ Ⓒ Ⓓ Ⓔ　　38 Ⓐ Ⓑ Ⓒ Ⓓ Ⓔ
9 Ⓐ Ⓑ Ⓒ Ⓓ Ⓔ　　19 Ⓐ Ⓑ Ⓒ Ⓓ Ⓔ　　29 Ⓐ Ⓑ Ⓒ Ⓓ Ⓔ　　39 Ⓐ Ⓑ Ⓒ Ⓓ Ⓔ
10 Ⓐ Ⓑ Ⓒ Ⓓ Ⓔ　　20 Ⓐ Ⓑ Ⓒ Ⓓ Ⓔ　　30 Ⓐ Ⓑ Ⓒ Ⓓ Ⓔ　　40 Ⓐ Ⓑ Ⓒ Ⓓ Ⓔ

CAUTION Use the answer spaces in the grids below for Section 2 or Section 3 only if you are told to do so in your test book.

Student-Produced Responses ONLY ANSWERS ENTERED IN THE CIRCLES IN EACH GRID WILL BE SCORED. YOU WILL NOT RECEIVE CREDIT FOR ANYTHING WRITTEN IN THE BOXES ABOVE THE CIRCLES.

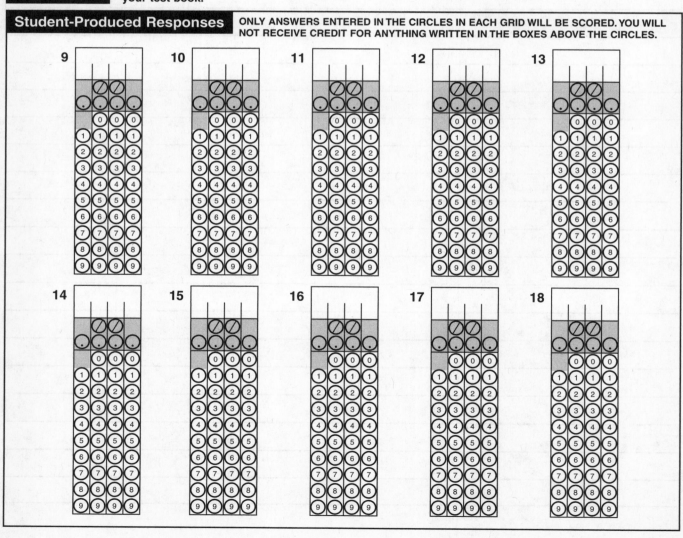

Start with number 1 for each new section. If a section has fewer questions than answer spaces, leave the extra answer spaces blank. Be sure to erase any errors or stray marks completely.

SECTION 4

1 Ⓐ Ⓑ Ⓒ Ⓓ Ⓔ	11 Ⓐ Ⓑ Ⓒ Ⓓ Ⓔ	21 Ⓐ Ⓑ Ⓒ Ⓓ Ⓔ	31 Ⓐ Ⓑ Ⓒ Ⓓ Ⓔ
2 Ⓐ Ⓑ Ⓒ Ⓓ Ⓔ	12 Ⓐ Ⓑ Ⓒ Ⓓ Ⓔ	22 Ⓐ Ⓑ Ⓒ Ⓓ Ⓔ	32 Ⓐ Ⓑ Ⓒ Ⓓ Ⓔ
3 Ⓐ Ⓑ Ⓒ Ⓓ Ⓔ	13 Ⓐ Ⓑ Ⓒ Ⓓ Ⓔ	23 Ⓐ Ⓑ Ⓒ Ⓓ Ⓔ	33 Ⓐ Ⓑ Ⓒ Ⓓ Ⓔ
4 Ⓐ Ⓑ Ⓒ Ⓓ Ⓔ	14 Ⓐ Ⓑ Ⓒ Ⓓ Ⓔ	24 Ⓐ Ⓑ Ⓒ Ⓓ Ⓔ	34 Ⓐ Ⓑ Ⓒ Ⓓ Ⓔ
5 Ⓐ Ⓑ Ⓒ Ⓓ Ⓔ	15 Ⓐ Ⓑ Ⓒ Ⓓ Ⓔ	25 Ⓐ Ⓑ Ⓒ Ⓓ Ⓔ	35 Ⓐ Ⓑ Ⓒ Ⓓ Ⓔ
6 Ⓐ Ⓑ Ⓒ Ⓓ Ⓔ	16 Ⓐ Ⓑ Ⓒ Ⓓ Ⓔ	26 Ⓐ Ⓑ Ⓒ Ⓓ Ⓔ	36 Ⓐ Ⓑ Ⓒ Ⓓ Ⓔ
7 Ⓐ Ⓑ Ⓒ Ⓓ Ⓔ	17 Ⓐ Ⓑ Ⓒ Ⓓ Ⓔ	27 Ⓐ Ⓑ Ⓒ Ⓓ Ⓔ	37 Ⓐ Ⓑ Ⓒ Ⓓ Ⓔ
8 Ⓐ Ⓑ Ⓒ Ⓓ Ⓔ	18 Ⓐ Ⓑ Ⓒ Ⓓ Ⓔ	28 Ⓐ Ⓑ Ⓒ Ⓓ Ⓔ	38 Ⓐ Ⓑ Ⓒ Ⓓ Ⓔ
9 Ⓐ Ⓑ Ⓒ Ⓓ Ⓔ	19 Ⓐ Ⓑ Ⓒ Ⓓ Ⓔ	29 Ⓐ Ⓑ Ⓒ Ⓓ Ⓔ	39 Ⓐ Ⓑ Ⓒ Ⓓ Ⓔ
10 Ⓐ Ⓑ Ⓒ Ⓓ Ⓔ	20 Ⓐ Ⓑ Ⓒ Ⓓ Ⓔ	30 Ⓐ Ⓑ Ⓒ Ⓓ Ⓔ	40 Ⓐ Ⓑ Ⓒ Ⓓ Ⓔ

SECTION 5

1 Ⓐ Ⓑ Ⓒ Ⓓ Ⓔ	11 Ⓐ Ⓑ Ⓒ Ⓓ Ⓔ	21 Ⓐ Ⓑ Ⓒ Ⓓ Ⓔ	31 Ⓐ Ⓑ Ⓒ Ⓓ Ⓔ
2 Ⓐ Ⓑ Ⓒ Ⓓ Ⓔ	12 Ⓐ Ⓑ Ⓒ Ⓓ Ⓔ	22 Ⓐ Ⓑ Ⓒ Ⓓ Ⓔ	32 Ⓐ Ⓑ Ⓒ Ⓓ Ⓔ
3 Ⓐ Ⓑ Ⓒ Ⓓ Ⓔ	13 Ⓐ Ⓑ Ⓒ Ⓓ Ⓔ	23 Ⓐ Ⓑ Ⓒ Ⓓ Ⓔ	33 Ⓐ Ⓑ Ⓒ Ⓓ Ⓔ
4 Ⓐ Ⓑ Ⓒ Ⓓ Ⓔ	14 Ⓐ Ⓑ Ⓒ Ⓓ Ⓔ	24 Ⓐ Ⓑ Ⓒ Ⓓ Ⓔ	34 Ⓐ Ⓑ Ⓒ Ⓓ Ⓔ
5 Ⓐ Ⓑ Ⓒ Ⓓ Ⓔ	15 Ⓐ Ⓑ Ⓒ Ⓓ Ⓔ	25 Ⓐ Ⓑ Ⓒ Ⓓ Ⓔ	35 Ⓐ Ⓑ Ⓒ Ⓓ Ⓔ
6 Ⓐ Ⓑ Ⓒ Ⓓ Ⓔ	16 Ⓐ Ⓑ Ⓒ Ⓓ Ⓔ	26 Ⓐ Ⓑ Ⓒ Ⓓ Ⓔ	36 Ⓐ Ⓑ Ⓒ Ⓓ Ⓔ
7 Ⓐ Ⓑ Ⓒ Ⓓ Ⓔ	17 Ⓐ Ⓑ Ⓒ Ⓓ Ⓔ	27 Ⓐ Ⓑ Ⓒ Ⓓ Ⓔ	37 Ⓐ Ⓑ Ⓒ Ⓓ Ⓔ
8 Ⓐ Ⓑ Ⓒ Ⓓ Ⓔ	18 Ⓐ Ⓑ Ⓒ Ⓓ Ⓔ	28 Ⓐ Ⓑ Ⓒ Ⓓ Ⓔ	38 Ⓐ Ⓑ Ⓒ Ⓓ Ⓔ
9 Ⓐ Ⓑ Ⓒ Ⓓ Ⓔ	19 Ⓐ Ⓑ Ⓒ Ⓓ Ⓔ	29 Ⓐ Ⓑ Ⓒ Ⓓ Ⓔ	39 Ⓐ Ⓑ Ⓒ Ⓓ Ⓔ
10 Ⓐ Ⓑ Ⓒ Ⓓ Ⓔ	20 Ⓐ Ⓑ Ⓒ Ⓓ Ⓔ	30 Ⓐ Ⓑ Ⓒ Ⓓ Ⓔ	40 Ⓐ Ⓑ Ⓒ Ⓓ Ⓔ

CAUTION Use the answer spaces in the grids below for Section 4 or Section 5 only if you are told to do so in your test book.

Student-Produced Responses ONLY ANSWERS ENTERED IN THE CIRCLES IN EACH GRID WILL BE SCORED. YOU WILL NOT RECEIVE CREDIT FOR ANYTHING WRITTEN IN THE BOXES ABOVE THE CIRCLES.

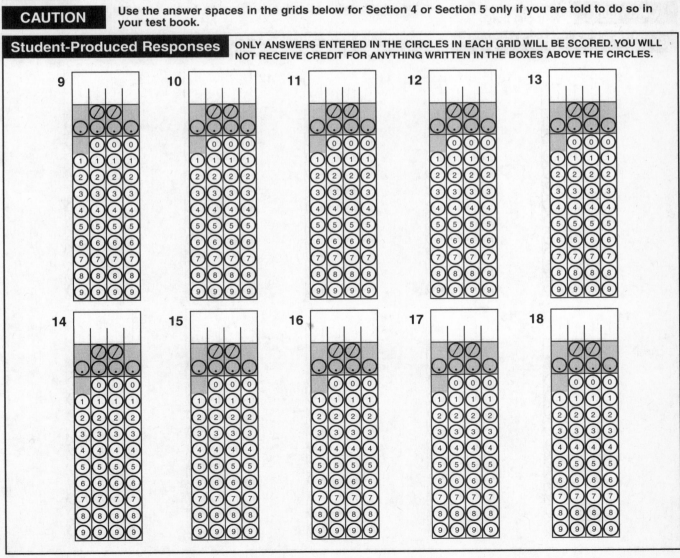

Start with number 1 for each new section. If a section has fewer questions than answer spaces, leave the extra answer spaces blank. Be sure to erase any errors or stray marks completely.

SECTION 6

1 Ⓐ Ⓑ Ⓒ Ⓓ Ⓔ	11 Ⓐ Ⓑ Ⓒ Ⓓ Ⓔ	21 Ⓐ Ⓑ Ⓒ Ⓓ Ⓔ	31 Ⓐ Ⓑ Ⓒ Ⓓ Ⓔ
2 Ⓐ Ⓑ Ⓒ Ⓓ Ⓔ	12 Ⓐ Ⓑ Ⓒ Ⓓ Ⓔ	22 Ⓐ Ⓑ Ⓒ Ⓓ Ⓔ	32 Ⓐ Ⓑ Ⓒ Ⓓ Ⓔ
3 Ⓐ Ⓑ Ⓒ Ⓓ Ⓔ	13 Ⓐ Ⓑ Ⓒ Ⓓ Ⓔ	23 Ⓐ Ⓑ Ⓒ Ⓓ Ⓔ	33 Ⓐ Ⓑ Ⓒ Ⓓ Ⓔ
4 Ⓐ Ⓑ Ⓒ Ⓓ Ⓔ	14 Ⓐ Ⓑ Ⓒ Ⓓ Ⓔ	24 Ⓐ Ⓑ Ⓒ Ⓓ Ⓔ	34 Ⓐ Ⓑ Ⓒ Ⓓ Ⓔ
5 Ⓐ Ⓑ Ⓒ Ⓓ Ⓔ	15 Ⓐ Ⓑ Ⓒ Ⓓ Ⓔ	25 Ⓐ Ⓑ Ⓒ Ⓓ Ⓔ	35 Ⓐ Ⓑ Ⓒ Ⓓ Ⓔ
6 Ⓐ Ⓑ Ⓒ Ⓓ Ⓔ	16 Ⓐ Ⓑ Ⓒ Ⓓ Ⓔ	26 Ⓐ Ⓑ Ⓒ Ⓓ Ⓔ	36 Ⓐ Ⓑ Ⓒ Ⓓ Ⓔ
7 Ⓐ Ⓑ Ⓒ Ⓓ Ⓔ	17 Ⓐ Ⓑ Ⓒ Ⓓ Ⓔ	27 Ⓐ Ⓑ Ⓒ Ⓓ Ⓔ	37 Ⓐ Ⓑ Ⓒ Ⓓ Ⓔ
8 Ⓐ Ⓑ Ⓒ Ⓓ Ⓔ	18 Ⓐ Ⓑ Ⓒ Ⓓ Ⓔ	28 Ⓐ Ⓑ Ⓒ Ⓓ Ⓔ	38 Ⓐ Ⓑ Ⓒ Ⓓ Ⓔ
9 Ⓐ Ⓑ Ⓒ Ⓓ Ⓔ	19 Ⓐ Ⓑ Ⓒ Ⓓ Ⓔ	29 Ⓐ Ⓑ Ⓒ Ⓓ Ⓔ	39 Ⓐ Ⓑ Ⓒ Ⓓ Ⓔ
10 Ⓐ Ⓑ Ⓒ Ⓓ Ⓔ	20 Ⓐ Ⓑ Ⓒ Ⓓ Ⓔ	30 Ⓐ Ⓑ Ⓒ Ⓓ Ⓔ	40 Ⓐ Ⓑ Ⓒ Ⓓ Ⓔ

SECTION 7

1 Ⓐ Ⓑ Ⓒ Ⓓ Ⓔ	11 Ⓐ Ⓑ Ⓒ Ⓓ Ⓔ	21 Ⓐ Ⓑ Ⓒ Ⓓ Ⓔ	31 Ⓐ Ⓑ Ⓒ Ⓓ Ⓔ
2 Ⓐ Ⓑ Ⓒ Ⓓ Ⓔ	12 Ⓐ Ⓑ Ⓒ Ⓓ Ⓔ	22 Ⓐ Ⓑ Ⓒ Ⓓ Ⓔ	32 Ⓐ Ⓑ Ⓒ Ⓓ Ⓔ
3 Ⓐ Ⓑ Ⓒ Ⓓ Ⓔ	13 Ⓐ Ⓑ Ⓒ Ⓓ Ⓔ	23 Ⓐ Ⓑ Ⓒ Ⓓ Ⓔ	33 Ⓐ Ⓑ Ⓒ Ⓓ Ⓔ
4 Ⓐ Ⓑ Ⓒ Ⓓ Ⓔ	14 Ⓐ Ⓑ Ⓒ Ⓓ Ⓔ	24 Ⓐ Ⓑ Ⓒ Ⓓ Ⓔ	34 Ⓐ Ⓑ Ⓒ Ⓓ Ⓔ
5 Ⓐ Ⓑ Ⓒ Ⓓ Ⓔ	15 Ⓐ Ⓑ Ⓒ Ⓓ Ⓔ	25 Ⓐ Ⓑ Ⓒ Ⓓ Ⓔ	35 Ⓐ Ⓑ Ⓒ Ⓓ Ⓔ
6 Ⓐ Ⓑ Ⓒ Ⓓ Ⓔ	16 Ⓐ Ⓑ Ⓒ Ⓓ Ⓔ	26 Ⓐ Ⓑ Ⓒ Ⓓ Ⓔ	36 Ⓐ Ⓑ Ⓒ Ⓓ Ⓔ
7 Ⓐ Ⓑ Ⓒ Ⓓ Ⓔ	17 Ⓐ Ⓑ Ⓒ Ⓓ Ⓔ	27 Ⓐ Ⓑ Ⓒ Ⓓ Ⓔ	37 Ⓐ Ⓑ Ⓒ Ⓓ Ⓔ
8 Ⓐ Ⓑ Ⓒ Ⓓ Ⓔ	18 Ⓐ Ⓑ Ⓒ Ⓓ Ⓔ	28 Ⓐ Ⓑ Ⓒ Ⓓ Ⓔ	38 Ⓐ Ⓑ Ⓒ Ⓓ Ⓔ
9 Ⓐ Ⓑ Ⓒ Ⓓ Ⓔ	19 Ⓐ Ⓑ Ⓒ Ⓓ Ⓔ	29 Ⓐ Ⓑ Ⓒ Ⓓ Ⓔ	39 Ⓐ Ⓑ Ⓒ Ⓓ Ⓔ
10 Ⓐ Ⓑ Ⓒ Ⓓ Ⓔ	20 Ⓐ Ⓑ Ⓒ Ⓓ Ⓔ	30 Ⓐ Ⓑ Ⓒ Ⓓ Ⓔ	40 Ⓐ Ⓑ Ⓒ Ⓓ Ⓔ

CAUTION Use the answer spaces in the grids below for Section 6 or Section 7 only if you are told to do so in your test book.

Student-Produced Responses ONLY ANSWERS ENTERED IN THE CIRCLES IN EACH GRID WILL BE SCORED. YOU WILL NOT RECEIVE CREDIT FOR ANYTHING WRITTEN IN THE BOXES ABOVE THE CIRCLES.

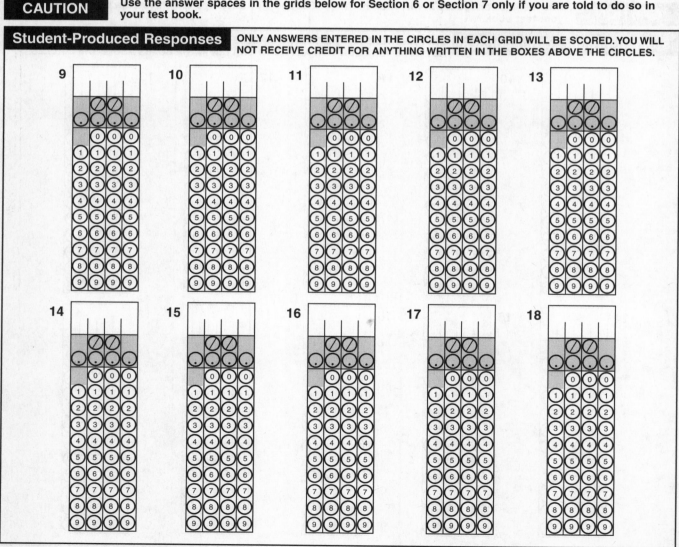

Start with number 1 for each new section. If a section has fewer questions than answer spaces, leave the extra answer spaces blank. Be sure to erase any errors or stray marks completely.

SECTION 8

1 Ⓐ Ⓑ Ⓒ Ⓓ Ⓔ
2 Ⓐ Ⓑ Ⓒ Ⓓ Ⓔ
3 Ⓐ Ⓑ Ⓒ Ⓓ Ⓔ
4 Ⓐ Ⓑ Ⓒ Ⓓ Ⓔ
5 Ⓐ Ⓑ Ⓒ Ⓓ Ⓔ
6 Ⓐ Ⓑ Ⓒ Ⓓ Ⓔ
7 Ⓐ Ⓑ Ⓒ Ⓓ Ⓔ
8 Ⓐ Ⓑ Ⓒ Ⓓ Ⓔ
9 Ⓐ Ⓑ Ⓒ Ⓓ Ⓔ
10 Ⓐ Ⓑ Ⓒ Ⓓ Ⓔ

11 Ⓐ Ⓑ Ⓒ Ⓓ Ⓔ
12 Ⓐ Ⓑ Ⓒ Ⓓ Ⓔ
13 Ⓐ Ⓑ Ⓒ Ⓓ Ⓔ
14 Ⓐ Ⓑ Ⓒ Ⓓ Ⓔ
15 Ⓐ Ⓑ Ⓒ Ⓓ Ⓔ
16 Ⓐ Ⓑ Ⓒ Ⓓ Ⓔ
17 Ⓐ Ⓑ Ⓒ Ⓓ Ⓔ
18 Ⓐ Ⓑ Ⓒ Ⓓ Ⓔ
19 Ⓐ Ⓑ Ⓒ Ⓓ Ⓔ
20 Ⓐ Ⓑ Ⓒ Ⓓ Ⓔ

21 Ⓐ Ⓑ Ⓒ Ⓓ Ⓔ
22 Ⓐ Ⓑ Ⓒ Ⓓ Ⓔ
23 Ⓐ Ⓑ Ⓒ Ⓓ Ⓔ
24 Ⓐ Ⓑ Ⓒ Ⓓ Ⓔ
25 Ⓐ Ⓑ Ⓒ Ⓓ Ⓔ
26 Ⓐ Ⓑ Ⓒ Ⓓ Ⓔ
27 Ⓐ Ⓑ Ⓒ Ⓓ Ⓔ
28 Ⓐ Ⓑ Ⓒ Ⓓ Ⓔ
29 Ⓐ Ⓑ Ⓒ Ⓓ Ⓔ
30 Ⓐ Ⓑ Ⓒ Ⓓ Ⓔ

31 Ⓐ Ⓑ Ⓒ Ⓓ Ⓔ
32 Ⓐ Ⓑ Ⓒ Ⓓ Ⓔ
33 Ⓐ Ⓑ Ⓒ Ⓓ Ⓔ
34 Ⓐ Ⓑ Ⓒ Ⓓ Ⓔ
35 Ⓐ Ⓑ Ⓒ Ⓓ Ⓔ
36 Ⓐ Ⓑ Ⓒ Ⓓ Ⓔ
37 Ⓐ Ⓑ Ⓒ Ⓓ Ⓔ
38 Ⓐ Ⓑ Ⓒ Ⓓ Ⓔ
39 Ⓐ Ⓑ Ⓒ Ⓓ Ⓔ
40 Ⓐ Ⓑ Ⓒ Ⓓ Ⓔ

SECTION 9

1 Ⓐ Ⓑ Ⓒ Ⓓ Ⓔ
2 Ⓐ Ⓑ Ⓒ Ⓓ Ⓔ
3 Ⓐ Ⓑ Ⓒ Ⓓ Ⓔ
4 Ⓐ Ⓑ Ⓒ Ⓓ Ⓔ
5 Ⓐ Ⓑ Ⓒ Ⓓ Ⓔ
6 Ⓐ Ⓑ Ⓒ Ⓓ Ⓔ
7 Ⓐ Ⓑ Ⓒ Ⓓ Ⓔ
8 Ⓐ Ⓑ Ⓒ Ⓓ Ⓔ
9 Ⓐ Ⓑ Ⓒ Ⓓ Ⓔ
10 Ⓐ Ⓑ Ⓒ Ⓓ Ⓔ

11 Ⓐ Ⓑ Ⓒ Ⓓ Ⓔ
12 Ⓐ Ⓑ Ⓒ Ⓓ Ⓔ
13 Ⓐ Ⓑ Ⓒ Ⓓ Ⓔ
14 Ⓐ Ⓑ Ⓒ Ⓓ Ⓔ
15 Ⓐ Ⓑ Ⓒ Ⓓ Ⓔ
16 Ⓐ Ⓑ Ⓒ Ⓓ Ⓔ
17 Ⓐ Ⓑ Ⓒ Ⓓ Ⓔ
18 Ⓐ Ⓑ Ⓒ Ⓓ Ⓔ
19 Ⓐ Ⓑ Ⓒ Ⓓ Ⓔ
20 Ⓐ Ⓑ Ⓒ Ⓓ Ⓔ

21 Ⓐ Ⓑ Ⓒ Ⓓ Ⓔ
22 Ⓐ Ⓑ Ⓒ Ⓓ Ⓔ
23 Ⓐ Ⓑ Ⓒ Ⓓ Ⓔ
24 Ⓐ Ⓑ Ⓒ Ⓓ Ⓔ
25 Ⓐ Ⓑ Ⓒ Ⓓ Ⓔ
26 Ⓐ Ⓑ Ⓒ Ⓓ Ⓔ
27 Ⓐ Ⓑ Ⓒ Ⓓ Ⓔ
28 Ⓐ Ⓑ Ⓒ Ⓓ Ⓔ
29 Ⓐ Ⓑ Ⓒ Ⓓ Ⓔ
30 Ⓐ Ⓑ Ⓒ Ⓓ Ⓔ

31 Ⓐ Ⓑ Ⓒ Ⓓ Ⓔ
32 Ⓐ Ⓑ Ⓒ Ⓓ Ⓔ
33 Ⓐ Ⓑ Ⓒ Ⓓ Ⓔ
34 Ⓐ Ⓑ Ⓒ Ⓓ Ⓔ
35 Ⓐ Ⓑ Ⓒ Ⓓ Ⓔ
36 Ⓐ Ⓑ Ⓒ Ⓓ Ⓔ
37 Ⓐ Ⓑ Ⓒ Ⓓ Ⓔ
38 Ⓐ Ⓑ Ⓒ Ⓓ Ⓔ
39 Ⓐ Ⓑ Ⓒ Ⓓ Ⓔ
40 Ⓐ Ⓑ Ⓒ Ⓓ Ⓔ

ESSAY

Time—25 minutes

You have 25 minutes to write an essay based on the topic presented as follows. Do not write on another topic. Your essay should be written on the lined pages provided. For the best results, write on every line, and keep your handwriting to a reasonable, legible size. Be sure to fully develop your point of view, present your ideas clearly and logically, and use the English language precisely.

Think carefully about the following issue and assignment:

> Fruits and vegetables at the grocery store are fresher and more appealing than ever before. To some degree, this is because of genetic engineering processes developed to create "better produce." Although not entirely natural, some of these processes dramatically increase crop yield by making plants impervious to various diseases and blights, by and stimulating increased plant growth. One concern, however, is that we cannot be certain that these processes are 100% safe, with no potential to cause undesirable side effects in humans.

Assignment: Should farmers be encouraged to continue growing genetically engineered crops? Plan and write an essay in which you develop your point of view on this topic. Support your position with reasoning and solid examples taken from your personal experience, observations, reading, or studies.

WRITE YOUR ESSAY ON PAGES 352 AND 353.

If you finish writing before your time is called, check your work on this section only. Do not turn to any other section in the test.

SECTION 2
Time—25 minutes
20 Questions

Directions: Solve each problem and determine which is the best of the answer choices given. Fill in the corresponding circle on your answer sheet. Use any available space to solve the problems.

Notes

1. The use of a calculator is permitted.
2. All numbers are real numbers.
3. Figures that accompany problems in this test are intended to provide information useful in solving the problems. They are drawn as accurately as possible EXCEPT when it is stated in a specific problem that the figure is not drawn to scale. All figures lie in a plane unless otherwise indicated.
4. Unless otherwise specified, the domain of any function f is assumed to be the set of all real numbers x for which $f(x)$ is a real number.

Reference Information

    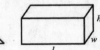

$A = \Pi r^2$
$C = 2\Pi r$ $A = lw$ $A = \frac{1}{2}bh$ $V = lwh$ $V = \Pi r^2 h$ $c^2 = a^2 + b^2$ Special Right Triangles

The number of degrees of arc in a circle is 360.
The sum of the measures in degrees of the angles of a triangle is 180.

1. According to the motorcycle's manual, 15 gallons of gasoline are required to travel 180 miles. At this rate, how many gallons of gasoline are needed to travel 60 miles?

   (A) 3
   (B) 4
   (C) 5
   (D) 6
   (E) 7

2. For $m \times n = m$ for all values of m, what is the value of n?

   (A) $-m$
   (B) -1
   (C) 0
   (D) 1
   (E) m

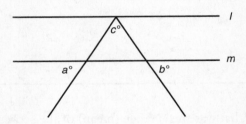

3. In the figure above, line l is parallel to line m. If $a = 65$ and $b = 60$, what is the value of c?

   (A) 55
   (B) 75
   (C) 90
   (D) 120
   (E) 125

GO ON TO THE NEXT PAGE

Questions 4 and 5 refer to the following graph.

TEST SCORES OF 5 STUDENTS (A, B, C, D, E)

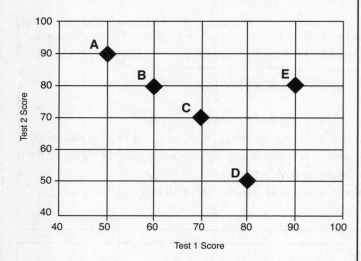

4. For which student was the change in scores from Test 1 to Test 2 the greatest?

(A) A
(B) B
(C) C
(D) D
(E) E

5. What was the average (mean) of the scores of the five students for Test 1 and Test 2 combined?

(A) 144
(B) 80
(C) 72
(D) 70
(E) 50

6. For a certain air conditioner, the increase in monthly cooling expenses is directly proportional to the increase in outdoor temperature. If monthly air conditioning expenses increase by $35 when the outdoor temperature increases by 25° Fahrenheit, by how much will monthly air conditioning expenses increase when the outdoor temperature is increased by 15° Fahrenheit?

(A) $18.00
(B) $21.00
(C) $23.50
(D) $25.00
(E) $30.00

7. If $x = \frac{2}{3}$, what is the value of $\frac{1}{x} + \frac{1}{x-1}$

(A) $\frac{3}{2}$

(B) $\frac{1}{3}$

(C) 0

(D) $-\frac{1}{3}$

(E) $-\frac{3}{2}$

8. If x, x^3, and x^6 lie on a number line in the order shown above, which of the following could be a value of x?

(A) -3

(B) $-\frac{1}{3}$

(C) $\frac{2}{3}$

(D) 1

(E) $\frac{5}{3}$

GO ON TO THE NEXT PAGE

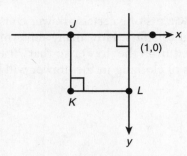

Note: Figure not drawn to scale.

9. In the figure above, $JK = KL$ and the coordinates of K are $(b, -5)$. What is the value of b?

(A) 5
(B) $\sqrt{5}$
(C) 0
(D) $-\sqrt{5}$
(E) -5

$$|a - 8| = 11$$
$$|b + 6| = 9$$

10. In the equations above, $a < 0$ and $b < 0$. What is the value of $a - b$?

(A) -12
(B) 0
(C) 4
(D) 12
(E) 16

11. In the xy-coordinate plane, line p is the reflection of line q about the x-axis. If the slope of line p is $\frac{5}{3}$, what is the slope of line q?

(A) $\frac{5}{3}$
(B) $\frac{3}{5}$
(C) $\frac{1}{3}$
(D) $\frac{3}{5}$
(E) $\frac{5}{3}$

12. How many cubical blocks, each with edges 3 inches in length, are needed to fill a rectangular box that has inside dimensions of 27 inches by 24 inches by 15 inches?

(A) 405
(B) 360
(C) 180
(D) 120
(E) 99

13. If $\frac{(7 + g)}{4}$ is an integer, then g must be

(A) a negative integer
(B) a positive integer
(C) a multiple of 4
(D) an even integer
(E) an odd integer

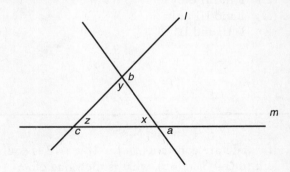

Note: Figure not drawn to scale.

14. In the figure above, if $a = 140$, what is the value of $b + c$?

(A) 320°
(B) 220°
(C) 180°
(D) 140°
(E) 50°

GO ON TO THE NEXT PAGE

15. When it is noon central standard time (CST) in Chicago, it is 9:00 a.m. Alaska standard time (AST) in Anchorage. A plane took off from Chicago at 2:00 p.m. CST and arrived in Anchorage at 6:00 p.m. AST on the same day. If a second plane left Anchorage at 2:00 p.m. AST and took exactly the same amount of time for the trip, what was the plane's arrival time (CST) in Chicago?

(A) 9:00 p.m.
(B) 10:00 p.m.
(C) 11:00 p.m.
(D) 12:00 a.m.
(E) 1:00 a.m.

16. If x is divisible by 7 and y is divisible by 9, which of the following must be divisible by 63?

  I. xy
 II. $7x + 9y$
III. $9x + 7y$

(A) I only
(B) II only
(C) I and II only
(D) I and III only
(E) I, II, and III

17. If r and s are constants and $x^2 + rx + 12$ is equivalent to $(x + 3)(x + s)$, what is the value of r?

(A) 3
(B) 4
(C) 7
(D) 12
(E) It cannot be determined from the information given.

18. The contents of a certain drawer consist of 14 ties and 23 shirts. How many shirts must be removed from the drawer so that 70% of the articles of clothing in the drawer will be ties?

(A) 3
(B) 6
(C) 14
(D) 17
(E) 20

19. The total weekly profit p, in dollars, from producing and selling x units of a certain product is given by the function $p(x) = 225x - (165x + c)$, where c is a constant. If 75 units were produced and sold last week for a profit of $3,365, what is the value of c?

(A) -1,135
(B) -745
(C) 1,135
(D) 4,500
(E) 9,010

20. What is the x-coordinate of the point in the standard (x,y) coordinate plane at which the two lines $y = -2x + 7$ and $y = 3x - 3$ intersect?

(A) 10
(B) 5
(C) 3
(D) 2
(E) 1

STOP

**If you finish before your time is up, check your work on this section only.
You may not turn to any other section in the test.**

SECTION 3
Time—25 minutes
24 Questions

Directions: For each of the questions in this section, choose the best answer and fill in the corresponding circle on your answer sheet.

Each sentence that follows has either one or two blanks. Each blank indicates that a word has been omitted from the sentence. Following each sentence are five words or sets of words. Select the word or set of words that, when inserted into the sentence in place of the blank(s), best fits the context of the sentence as a whole.

1. Kristine fiercely objected to her brother's ------- act; she did not approve of such awful behavior.

   (A) propitious
   (B) reprehensible
   (C) sanctified
   (D) consumptive
   (E) succinct

2. The storm crossed the bay with unrelenting -------, forcing hundreds of islanders to gather their families and evacuate.

   (A) moderation
   (B) ferocity
   (C) zeal
   (D) acrimony
   (E) acquiescence

3. He entered his supervisor's office with an ------- sense of doom; his misdeeds at the office party would certainly cause him to be fired.

   (A) elemental
   (B) impractical
   (C) inadvertent
   (D) inexorable
   (E) assiduous

4. Although sometimes extremely ------- of automobile repair shops as a whole, people are unwilling to treat their own mechanics with equal criticism.

   (A) reverential
   (B) deferential
   (C) contemptuous
   (D) redemptive
   (E) trusting

5. Tatsuro was surprised at the ------- of the crowd at the golf tournament because he had believed the sport to be popular with many different kinds of people.

   (A) dominance
   (B) maturity
   (C) abrasion
   (D) fortitude
   (E) homogeneity

GO ON TO THE NEXT PAGE

Each passage that follows is accompanied by several questions based on the content of the passage. Answer the questions based on what is either stated or implied in each passage. Be sure to read any introductory material that is provided.

Questions 6 and 7 are based on the following passage.

"Joy is the holy fire that keeps our purpose warm and our intelligence aglow. Work without joy shall be as nothing. Resolve to keep happy, and your joy and you shall form an invincible host against difficulties." This quote becomes yet more inspirational upon learning it comes from Helen Keller, a remarkable woman who overcame both blindness and deafness. Her decision to be joyful despite adversity no doubt contributed to her many impressive accomplishments. She succeeded in learning to communicate and reached out to others with her meaningful speeches and writings.

Line
5

10

6. The author mentions Keller's speeches and writings primarily in order to

(A) emphasize the formidable challenges of disability that she overcame
(B) celebrate the achievements of a young woman author
(C) demonstrate the expressiveness of an author who was rarely in a bad mood
(D) confirm that authors with disabilities explore many different creative media
(E) illustrate a dilemma that women authors often face

7. Which of the following statements is most analogous to the quotation presented in the passage?

(A) Fire is an essential tool when respected and attended, but it's a massive destructive force if allowed to spread out of control.
(B) A child's mind is absorptive like the driest sponge, so great care must be taken to keep poisonous notions from infiltrating it.
(C) Sorrowful resignation remains the genius' malady, for truth and knowledge weigh heavy on the heart.
(D) Find your true purpose in life and your days will be filled with peace and harmony, and your troubles will be few.
(E) Enthusiasm raises the sunken spirit and fosters creativity in even the most hardened heart.

Questions 8 and 9 are based on the following passage.

On October 3, 1965, President Lyndon B. Johnson signed a law that sought to overturn four decades of discrimination. The National Origins Quota System, which had been in effect since 1924, determined which immigrants should be allowed to come to the United States based solely on their national origin. The 1965 Immigration Act changed all this by making individual work skills and relationships with current U.S. citizens the criteria for immigration. President Johnson captured the essence of this exciting change by declaring that "those who can contribute most to this country—to its growth, to its strength, to its spirit—will be the first that are admitted to this land."

Line
5

10

15

8. The author's attitude toward the "Act" (line 8) is best characterized as one of

(A) resentment
(B) derision
(C) appreciation
(D) wonder
(E) confusion

9. In the last sentence, the quotation supports the author's assertion that

(A) unskilled laborers should not be allowed to immigrate to the U.S.
(B) reformed immigration law rightly assesses the applicants' merits
(C) individual ethnic groups were denied immigration for more than 40 years
(D) President Johnson led the effort to reexamine immigration policy
(E) people immigrating since 1965 are generally highly skilled workers

GO ON TO THE NEXT PAGE ➔

Questions 10–18 are based on the following passage.

The following passage examines the attempt in 1605 to destroy the English king and Parliament.

> *Remember, remember the 5th of November,*
> *The gunpowder treason and plot.*
> *I know of no reason why gunpowder treason*
> *Should ever be forgot.*

Line
5   This famous children's poem speaks
directly to the Gunpowder Plot of 1605 in
which a group of Roman Catholic coconspirators attempted to blow up Westminster Palace
during the formal opening of Parliament. King
10   James I of England was in attendance to
address the joint assembly of the House of
Lords and the House of Commons. The failed
bomb plot could certainly have killed the King
and potentially the rest of the English
15   Legislature; it would have been a near-
complete removal of the aristocracy. Guy
Fawkes was instrumental in the final stages of
the plot but was apprehended just prior to
completing his work. Shortly thereafter,
20   Fawkes and his coconspirators were put to
death for treason and attempted murder. It has
been said by many—quite tongue-in-cheek—
that Guy Fawkes was the only man ever to
enter Parliament with honest intentions.
25   The plot, masterminded by Robert
Catesby, had surprising origins. He and Guy
Fawkes, along with several other Roman
Catholics, were thought to be denouncers of the
Church of England. Consequently, they risked
30   civil and criminal penalties. In realizing that
Spain, at the time a great Catholic world power,
was involved in too many wars to help the cause
of their brethren in England, Catesby decided
that unless something was done from within,
35   nothing would likely change.
        Luck smiled upon the plotters when they
stumbled upon a cellar for rent beneath the
House of Lords; the original plan, to dig a
mineshaft beneath Westminster, proved
40   remarkably difficult, the rock and debris
requiring removal in secret. Being able to rent
a cellar under Parliament expedited their
efforts immensely, allowing them to fill the
cellar with 1,800 pounds of gunpowder.
45   The one crucial flaw in the plot, though,
was that several conspirators had scruples over

the potential harm to other Catholics who
would likely attend the opening address. One
of the men wrote a letter of warning to
50   William Parker, Fourth Baron Monteagle, a
fellow Catholic, who received it on October 26.
Learning about the letter the following day,
several conspirators wished to abort the plan,
yet the decision was made to continue when
55   Guy Fawkes confirmed that nothing within the
cellar had been discovered. Despite Fawkes'
confidence, Lord Monteagle took the letter
seriously and tasked the secretary of state with
completing a search of all spaces beneath
60   Westminster. Early in the morning on
November 5, Fawkes was apprehended in the
cellar. Over the next few days, he was tortured
until he confessed the identities of the other
individuals who had contributed to the plot.
65   On January 31, 1606, each man convicted of
treason was taken to Old Palace Yard to be
hanged, drawn, and quartered—this most
heinous form of execution was intended as a
lesson to the public: Treason would not be
70   tolerated under any circumstances.
        Currently, on November 5 of each year,
British children burn effigies of Fawkes and
recite the renowned poem as a way of remembering this influential figure of the past. Guy
75   Fawkes Day serves as a chilling reminder to
everyone, not just the British, that if pressed
hard enough, an individual will press back. No
brutal threat can stop the most committed
believer from rising in defense of his beliefs.

10. The author most likely includes the children's poem in lines 1–4 in order to

(A) illustrate the comedy of the
     Gunpowder Plot
(B) lighten the tone of the passage
(C) juxtapose childhood innocence with
     the violence of the Gunpowder
     Plot
(D) suggest the traditional significance
     of the Gunpowder Plot
(E) show how parents teach history to
     their young children

GO ON TO THE NEXT PAGE

11. The author specifies "a near-complete removal of the aristocracy" in lines 15–16 in order to

(A) prove that the bomb plot was indeed treasonous
(B) demonstrate how unusual it was to have so many important figures closely gathered
(C) suggest that some of the non-governmental aristocracy would have survived
(D) illustrate the depravity of the perpetrators' actions
(E) explain how destructive gunpowder explosions can be

12. The author mentions "honest intentions" (line 24) to assert that

(A) some modern English citizens are skeptical of parliamentarians' intentions
(B) the conspirators were committed to blowing up the king and Parliament
(C) the conspirators were dishonest in their attempt to blow up Westminster Palace
(D) some modern English citizens regard parts of their history as frivolous
(E) some modern English citizens are in quiet agreement with the plotters' motives

13. In line 28, "denouncers" is closest in meaning to

(A) cohorts
(B) conformists
(C) rejecters
(D) supporters
(E) disciples

14. The author uses the phrase "Luck smiled" (line 36) in order to

(A) show outrage at the opportunity that the men had to prepare an explosion
(B) point out the ease by which the plot was hatched
(C) express approval of the sordid details of the Gunpowder Plot story
(D) indicate the rarity of the opportunity that the conspirators were granted
(E) suggest that criminals escape justice for their crimes far too easily

15. The author describes some of the conspirators as having "scruples" in line 40 to point out that

(A) they discovered that they disagreed on some fundamental political issues
(B) their moral dilemma caused the plot to fail
(C) the group had no choice but to commit an act of violence
(D) contrary to popular belief, the conspirators were compassionate men
(E) most surprise bomb attacks are perpetrated by conflicted individuals

16. The author mentions "Fawkes' confidence" (lines 56–57) to show that

(A) Fawkes was aware that other Catholics would likely be injured in the impending explosion
(B) even though it would be difficult to dig a mineshaft beneath Westminster, Fawkes and his cohorts intended to proceed
(C) neither Baron Monteagle nor Guy Fawkes believed that the secretary of state would find the hidden explosives
(D) Fawkes was not afraid of being tortured for his beliefs
(E) despite the fact that Fawkes knew that his plan had been compromised, he was still willing to move forward

17. In line 68, "heinous" is closest in meaning to

(A) enlightened
(B) dreadful
(C) lawful
(D) common
(E) well-known

18. In the final sentence, the author's characterization of the challenge of social repression serves to

(A) suggest that the establishment is always at risk for another uprising from an affronted citizen
(B) express ambivalence toward the gory details of archaic punishments
(C) indicate that citizens of the era were especially outspoken in their ideas
(D) show the author's disapproval of torture and capital punishment, regardless of the severity of the crime
(E) point out the risk of injury and death inherent in positions of power

GO ON TO THE NEXT PAGE

Questions 19–24 are based on the following passage.

The following passage is adapted from The American Republic: Constitution, Tendencies, and Destiny *by O.A. Brownson © 1866.*

The ancients summed up the whole of human wisdom in the maxim "Know Thyself," and certainly there is for an individual no more
Line
5   important as there is no more difficult knowledge, than knowledge of himself, what he is, what he is for, what he can do, what he ought to do, and what are his means of doing it. Nations are only individuals on a larger scale. They have a life, an individuality, a reason, a
10   conscience, and instincts of their own, and have the same general laws of development and growth, and, perhaps, of decay, as the individual man. Equally important, and no less difficult than for the individual, is it for a
15   nation to know itself, understand its own existence, its own powers and faculties, rights and duties, constitution, instincts, tendencies, and destiny. A nation has a spiritual as well as a material, a moral as well as a physical existence,
20   and is subjected to internal as well as external conditions of health and virtue, greatness and grandeur, which it must in some measure understand and observe, or become lethargic and infirm, stunted in its growth, and end in
25   premature decay and death.

Among nations, no one has more need of full knowledge of itself than the United States, and no one has hitherto had less. It has hardly had a distinct consciousness of its own national
30   existence, and has lived the naive life of the child, with no severe trial, till the recent rebellion, to throw it back on itself and compel it to reflect on its own constitution, its own separate existence, individuality, tendencies, and end.
35   The defection of the slaveholding States, and the fearful struggle that has followed for national unity and integrity, have brought it at once to a distinct recognition of itself, and forced it to pass from thoughtless, careless,
40   heedless, reckless adolescence to grave and reflecting manhood. The nation has been suddenly compelled to study itself, and henceforth must act from reflection, understanding, science, statesmanship, not from instinct,
45   impulse, passion, or caprice, knowing well what

it does, and why it does it. The change which four years of civil war have wrought in the nation is great, and is sure to give it the seriousness, the gravity, the dignity, the manliness
50   it has heretofore lacked.

Though the nation has been brought to a consciousness of its own existence, it has not, even yet, attained a full and clear understanding of its own national constitution. Its
55   vision is still obscured by the floating mists of its earlier morning, and its judgment rendered indistinct and indecisive by the wild theories and fancies of its childhood. The national mind has been quickened, the national heart has been
60   opened, the national disposition prepared, but there remains the important work of dissipating the mists that still linger, of brushing away these wild theories and fancies, and of enabling it to form a clear and intelligent judgment of
65   itself and a true and just appreciation of its own constitution tendencies; or, in other words, of enabling the nation to understand its own idea and the means of its actualization in space and time.

70   As the states have vindicated their national unity and integrity and are preparing to take a new start in history, nothing is more important than that they should take that new start with a clear and definite view of their
75   national constitution, with a distinct understanding of their political mission in the future of the world. The citizen who can help his countrymen to do this will render them an important service and deserve well of his
80   country, though he may have been unable to serve in her armies and defend her on the battlefield. The work now to be done by American statesmen is even more difficult and more delicate than that which has been accom-
85   plished by our brave armies. As yet the people are hardly better prepared for the political work to be done than they were at the outbreak of the civil war for the military work they have so nobly achieved. But, with time, patience, and
90   good will, the difficulties may be overcome, the errors of the past corrected, and the government placed on the right track for the future.

GO ON TO THE NEXT PAGE ⟩

19. The passage is primarily concerned with the

    (A) deleterious effects of the Civil War
    (B) coming-of-age of the United States
    (C) nature of conflict in society
    (D) lives lost in battle after diplomacy fails
    (E) wide variety of opinions in American politics

20. As used in line 17, "constitution" most nearly means

    (A) charter
    (B) codex
    (C) character
    (D) build
    (E) chassis

21. It is most likely that "the recent rebellion" (lines 31–32) refers to

    (A) a fruitless quarrel, as with a child
    (B) a typical reaction to divisive politics
    (C) an alternative viewpoint on the maturity of a nation
    (D) a conflict the author will proceed to address
    (E) a cryptic representation of bygone political wrangling

22. The author suggests that work remains following the Civil War because

    (A) people retain pre-war judgments
    (B) original illusions are stripped away
    (C) infrastructure is devastated
    (D) opposing forces preserve their mutual hatred
    (E) citizens' loyalty is tested

23. The author's attitude toward the post-war United States can best be characterized as

    (A) condescendingly tolerant
    (B) aggressively hostile
    (C) thoroughly puzzled
    (D) genuinely hopeful
    (E) solemnly regretful

24. The author's assumption in the final paragraph (lines 70–92) is that

    (A) government is best reestablished with the help of former soldiers
    (B) government inherently corrupts and so requires constant oversight
    (C) war is an ineffective and costly means to effect change
    (D) the nation can not fully return to its former glory after so much fighting
    (E) the nation and its unity might be resurrected with the help of the people

STOP

If you finish before your time is up, check your work on this section only.
You may not turn to any other section in the test.

SECTION 4
Time—25 minutes
18 Questions

Directions: This section includes two types of questions. For questions 1–8, solve each problem and determine which is the best of the answer choices given. Fill in the corresponding circle on your answer sheet. Use any available space to solve the problems. For questions 9–18, solve each problem and fill in your answer on the answer sheet.

Notes

1. The use of a calculator is permitted.
2. All numbers are real numbers.
3. Figures that accompany problems in this test are intended to provide information useful in solving the problems. They are drawn as accurately as possible EXCEPT when it is stated in a specific problem that the figure is not drawn to scale. All figures lie in a plane unless otherwise indicated.
4. Unless otherwise specified, the domain of any function f is assumed to be the set of all real numbers x for which $f(x)$ is a real number.

Reference Information

   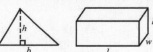

$A = \Pi r^2$
$C = 2\Pi r$

$A = lw$

$A = \frac{1}{2}bh$

$V = lwh$

$V = \Pi r^2 h$

$c^2 = a^2 + b^2$

Special Right Triangles

The number of degrees of arc in a circle is 360.
The sum of the measures in degrees of the angles of a triangle is 180.

1. Which of the following numbers is between $\frac{5}{8}$ and $\frac{2}{3}$?

(A) 0.58
(B) 0.60
(C) 0.62
(D) 0.64
(E) 0.68

2. If Ryan traveled 20 miles in 4 hours and Jeff traveled twice as far in half the time, what was Jeff's average speed, in miles per hour?

(A) 60
(B) 40
(C) 20
(D) 10
(E) 5

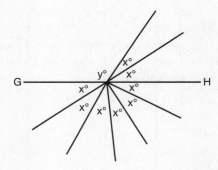

3. In the figure above, if *GH* is a line segment, what is the value of *y*?

(A) 110
(B) 117
(C) 120
(D) 135
(E) 150

GO ON TO THE NEXT PAGE

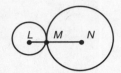

4. In the figure above, the two circles are tangent at point M and $LN = 42$. If the circumference of the circle with center L is half that of the circle with center N, what is the length of MN?

(A) 12
(B) 21
(C) 28
(D) 30
(E) 42

SURVEY RESULTS	
$x < 5$	25%
$5 \leq x < 10$	15%
$10 \leq x < 15$	30%
$15 \leq x \leq 20$	20%
$x \geq 20$	10%

5. The chart above shows the results when 1,500 people were asked, "How many hours of television do you watch per week?" The number of hours they gave is represented by x. How many people said they watch fewer than 15 hours of television each week?

(A) 1,050
(B) 975
(C) 900
(D) 600
(E) 375

6. In the figure above, the perimeter of the triangle is $6 + 3\sqrt{2}$. What is the value of x?

(A) 3
(B) 6
(C) $\sqrt{2}$
(D) $3\sqrt{2}$
(E) $3 + \sqrt{2}$

7. If a is inversely proportional to b and $a = 36$ when $b = 12$, what is the value of a when $b = 48$?

(A) 0
(B) $\frac{1}{3}$
(C) $\frac{1}{4}$
(D) 4
(E) 9

8. If $3x + y = 2z$ and $-6x + 4z + 2y = 36$, what is the value of y?

(A) 12
(B) 9
(C) 6
(D) 3
(E) It cannot be determined from the information given.

GO ON TO THE NEXT PAGE

Directions: For Student-Produced Response questions 9-18, use the grids at the bottom of the answer sheet page on which you have answered questions 1-8.

Each of the remaining 10 questions requires you to solve the problem and enter your answer by marking the circles in the special grid, as shown in the examples below. You may use any available space for scratchwork.

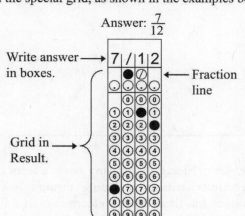

Answer: $\frac{7}{12}$

Write answer in boxes. → Fraction line

Grid in Result.

Answer: 2.5

← Decimal point

Answer: 201
Either position is correct.

Note: You may start your answers in any column, space permitting. Columns not needed should be left blank.

• Mark no more than one circle in any column.

• Because the answer sheet will be machine-scored, **you will receive credit only if the circles are filled in correctly**.

• Although not required, it is suggested that you write your answer in the boxes at the top of the columns to help you fill in the circles accurately.

• Some problems may have more than one correct answer. In such cases, grid only one answer.

• No question has a negative answer.

• **Mixed numbers** such as $3\frac{1}{2}$ must be gridded as

3.5 or 7/2. (If ⊞ is gridded, it will be

interpreted as $\frac{31}{2}$, not $3\frac{1}{2}$.)

Decimal Answers: If you obtain a decimal answer with more digits than the grid can accomodate, it may be either rounded or truncated, but it must fill the entire grid. enter the most accurate value the grid will accommodate. For example, if you obtain an answer such as 0.6666..., you should record your result as .666 or .667. **A less accurate value such as .66 or .67 will be scored as incorrect.**

Acceptable ways to grid $\frac{2}{3}$ are:

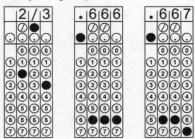

9. A 2-hour long graduation ceremony included 40 minutes of speeches from the principal and class president. What fraction of the graduation ceremony was comprised of speeches?

896, 112, 14...

10. Following the pattern of the sequence above, what will the fifth term of the sequence be?

GO ON TO THE NEXT PAGE →

371

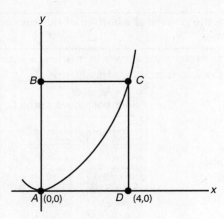

11. In the figure above, *ABCD* is a rectangle, and points *A* and *C* lie on the graph of $y = ax^2$, where *a* is a constant. If the area of *ABCD* is 24, what is the value of *a*?

12. If $xy + z = y + 3z$, what is the value of *y* when $x = 5$ and $z = 2$?

13. The median of a set of 7 consecutive odd integers is 23. What is the greatest of these 7 integers?

14. If the degree measures of the angles of a triangle are in the ratio 2:3:4, what is the degree measure of the smallest angle?

15. The Acme Electric Company sends a team of three electricians to work on a certain job. The company has three master electricians and five apprentice electricians. If a team consists of one master electrician and two apprentice electricians, how many different such teams are possible.

16. If $a + 2b$ is equal to 80% of $5b$, what is the value of $\frac{a}{b}$?

GO ON TO THE NEXT PAGE

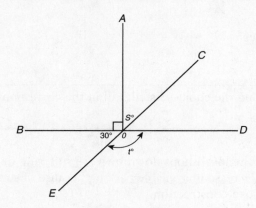

17. In the figure above, line *EC* and line *BD* intersect at *O*. If *OA* is perpendicular to *BD*, what is the value of *t* − *s*?

18. In the *xy*-coordinate plane, the distance between point *B* (15, 7) and point *A* (*x*, 15) is 17. What is one possible value of *x*?

STOP

If you finish before your time is up, check your work on this section only.
You may not turn to any other section in the test.

SECTION 5
Time—25 minutes
35 Questions

Directions: For each question, select the best answer from among the choices listed. Fill in the corresponding circle on your answer sheet.

The following questions test the correct and effective use of standard written English in expressing an idea. Part of each sentence (or the entire sentence) is underlined. Following each sentence are five different ways of phrasing the underlined portion. Answer choice A repeats the original phrasing. If you think that the original phrasing is best, select answer choice A. Otherwise, select from the remaining four choices. Your selection should result in the most effective, clear sentence, free from awkwardness or ambiguity.

1. Although the Royalist Party entered this election season with far more endorsements than they had in their previous campaigns, it had endorsements from only two well-known entertainers.

   (A) they had in their previous campaigns
   (B) their previous campaigns had had
   (C) they had for any previous campaign
   (D) in their previous campaigns
   (E) for any previous campaign

2. One old-time remedy for a flesh wound was generally to pack it with fresh mud and let the mud dry over the wound.

   (A) was generally to pack it
   (B) was to generally pack it
   (C) was to pack it in general
   (D) was packing it
   (E) was to pack it

3. The local shops downtown are suffering due to a decrease in available parking because of summer road construction.

   (A) are suffering due to a decrease in available parking
   (B) are suffering a parking decrease due to availability
   (C) are suffering, from a decrease in the availability of parking spaces to the general public
   (D) have suffered recently, decreasing parking,
   (E) have recently suffered decreased parking availability

4. When a city faces high rates of unemployment, people often blame government officials for its lack of leadership.

   (A) for its lack of leadership
   (B) the leadership of which is lacking
   (C) the lack of leadership of them
   (D) of leadership that is lacking
   (E) for their lack of leadership

5. A major cause of World War I was the rise of militant nationalism, which goaded the general populace to support going to war.

   (A) which goaded the general populace to support going to war
   (B) which to support going to war the general populace was goaded
   (C) in which goaded the general populace to support going to war
   (D) which goaded the general populace to supporting to go to war
   (E) which goading the general populace, supported going to war

GO ON TO THE NEXT PAGE

6. The company did not pay annual bonuses to some managers because it believed that <u>to do it rewards</u> them for cutting essential staff.

   (A) to do it rewards
   (B) doing so would reward
   (C) to do this would reward
   (D) doing it rewards
   (E) to do it would reward

7. Today, snowshoeing is mostly a form of entertainment and exercise, but <u>they began as</u> a mode of transportation.

   (A) they began as
   (B) it began as
   (C) it had begun as
   (D) they had their beginnings as
   (E) they begun as

8. Dogs may love to chew on bones, but pet owners need to be mindful of <u>his or her chewing habits</u> to avoid digestive obstructions.

   (A) his or her chewing habits
   (B) its chewing habits
   (C) their dog's chewing habits
   (D) their chewing habits
   (E) his or her habits of chewing

9. Although the term "nimrod" is popularly applied to an especially foolish or hapless character, in mythology <u>it is someone who is</u> a skilled hunter and outdoorsman.

   (A) it is someone who is
   (B) it is a person
   (C) they are people who are
   (D) it refers to someone who is
   (E) it is in reference to people

10. Most news stories, whether in print, broadcast on television, or posted on the Web, are created by individuals responsible for a series of different tasks such as <u>sorting through press releases and to determine which are newsworthy</u>, deciding which facts to use, preparing the actual story, and creating an appropriate headline.

    (A) to sort through press releases and determine which are newsworthy
    (B) to sort through press releases determining which are newsworthy
    (C) to sort through and determine which press releases are newsworthy
    (D) sorting through press releases and to determine which are newsworthy
    (E) sorting through press releases and determining which are newsworthy

11. Teachers at this high school, <u>one who</u> holds a Ph.D., are known for encouraging students to look at college as preparation for graduate school.

    (A) one who
    (B) one of them who
    (C) and one of them who
    (D) one of whom
    (E) one of which

GO ON TO THE NEXT PAGE ▷

The following questions test your ability to recognize grammar and usage errors in standard written English. Each sentence contains either a single error or no error at all. Refer to the underlined, lettered portions of each sentence. If the sentence contains no error, select answer choice E. If the sentence contains an error, select the one underlined and lettered portion (A, B, C, or D) that is incorrect.

12. <u>Their</u> new home was <u>elegant</u> <u>decorated</u> in the
    A   B   C

    <u>style of</u> a Tuscan villa. <u>No error</u>.
    D   E

13. Alfred B. Nobel <u>bequeathed</u> $9,000,000 for
                 A

    <u>annual</u> prizes to be awarded to <u>those people</u>
    B   C

    who <u>they contributed</u> to society. <u>No error</u>.
          D   E

14. The university's School of Music <u>require</u> <u>each</u>
                        A   B

    prospective student <u>to perform</u> an <u>audition</u>.
                 C   D

    <u>No error</u>.
    E

15. <u>Although</u> the wilderness preserve <u>continues</u> to
    A   B

    exist because of money <u>generated with</u> tourists,
                      C

    the <u>increasing amount</u> of foot traffic in the
          D

    preserve worries some conservation experts.
    <u>No error</u>.
    E

16. <u>Many</u> people are afraid of spiders because of
    A

    <u>their</u> legs and <u>the way</u> those legs <u>make</u>
    B   C   D

    the spiders move and jump. <u>No error</u>.
                           E

17. <u>Whereas</u> most students value <u>their</u> education
    A   B

    and <u>work diligently</u> to earn their grades, others
            C

    <u>attempting to</u> cheat because they simply do not
    D

    care. <u>No error</u>.
         E

18. Studies <u>have</u> shown that <u>an auto</u> mechanic with a
         A   B

    tidy tool box <u>will make</u> more reliable <u>repairs</u>.
              C   D

    <u>No error</u>.
    E

19. <u>Thus far</u> in the ceremony, <u>only</u> the actors in the
    A   B

    movie, not the director, <u>has received</u> any awards
                     C

    for <u>their</u> accomplishments. <u>No error</u>.
        D   E

20. Professor Hornbuckle is always <u>in high demand</u>
                           A

    as a public speaker; <u>in fact</u>, he <u>has</u> never been
                  B   C

    <u>more busier</u> than he is this semester. <u>No error</u>.
    D   E

GO ON TO THE NEXT PAGE →

21. <u>Although</u> a popular and prodigious composer,
   A

   Mozart <u>has not lived</u> to see his final composition
                    B

   <u>performed</u>, and died penniless at <u>an early age</u>.
   C   D

   <u>No error</u>.
   E

22. <u>Though</u> the <u>blacksmith's</u> shop was slowly
    A   B

   becoming run down, the proprietor <u>continued</u>
                                       C

   to work over his hot forge <u>every day</u>. <u>No error</u>.
                                D   E

23. <u>Whether</u> a person <u>liked</u> a piece of artwork
    A   B

   generally depends on <u>his or her</u> <u>initial</u>
                          C   D

   reaction to it. <u>No error</u>.
                    E

24. Angie was <u>pleasantly</u> surprised to <u>find</u> that her
                A   B

   dog and <u>their</u> cat <u>were able</u> to get along well
            C   D

   together. <u>No error</u>.
              E

25. The suspect <u>claimed that</u> the statement he made
                 A

   to the first detective <u>was</u> neither accurate, <u>nor</u>
                           B   C

   <u>could it be</u> interpreted as an admission of guilt.
    D

   <u>No error</u>.
   E

26. People who admire horses <u>often praise</u> them for
                               A

   <u>their</u> strength and <u>power; people</u> who fear horses
    B   C

   often condemn them for the same <u>reasons</u>.
                                     D

   <u>No error</u>.
   E

27. The casting announcement, <u>previously scheduled</u>
                                A

   for 1:00 P.M. today, <u>would</u> be postponed because
                         B

   the director cannot choose <u>between</u> the two
                                C

   actors <u>vying for</u> the lead role. <u>No error</u>.
           D   E

28. The relationship between environment and

   personal harmony <u>are often</u> striking, as
                      A

   <u>disorganization</u> often <u>causes</u> stress and <u>anxiety</u>.
    B   C   D

   <u>No error</u>.
   E

29. In <u>determining</u> the economic health of the
        A

   country, many factors <u>is examined,</u> such as
                           B

   <u>stock prices</u> and interest <u>rates</u>. <u>No error</u>.
    C   D   E

GO ON TO THE NEXT PAGE ⟩

Directions: The following passage is a rough draft of a student essay. Some parts of the passage need to be rewritten to improve the essay.

Read the passage and select the best answer for each question that follows. Some questions ask you to improve the structure or word choice of specific sentences or parts of sentences, while others ask you to consider the organization and development of the essay. Follow the requirements of standard written English.

Questions 30–35 are based on the following passage.

(1)Robert Frost is perhaps one of America's best poets. (2)Maybe the most beloved poet of all time. (3)While Frost is clearly known as a New Englander, he lived his first 11 years in California. (4)Born in 1874, Frost moved east after the death of his father. (5)He attended high school in Massachusetts where he became an avid writer. (6)Though he continued to write during his college years, he never earned a college degree nor did he find much success with publishing his poetry. (7)At the age of 38, Frost moved to England where he quickly joined the literary circles of English writers. (8)A year later, Frost's first book of poetry, *A Boy's Will*, was successfully published and sold. (9)This started the beginning of Frost's acceptance as a literary giant. (10)Prior to this, Frost had been working at mills and grammar schools; he also ran a farm. (11)Shortly after the publication of Frost's second anthology, *North of Boston*, he and his family reestablished their home in the states.

(12)Frost's literary talent met with great success back in the United States. (13)While Frost maintained the family's New Hampshire farm, he also wrote and published prolifically. (14)In 1923, Frost earned the first of his four Pulitzer Prizes for his work and was the first poet to read at a presidential inauguration in 1961. (15)Probably one of Robert Frost's best known and most often quoted poems is "The Road Not Taken", particularly the last lines: "Two roads diverged in a wood, and I—, I took the one less traveled by, And that has made all the difference."

30. Of the following, which is the best way to revise and combine sentences 1 and 2 (reproduced below)?

Robert Frost is perhaps one of America's best poets. Maybe the most beloved poet of all time.

(A) Perhaps Robert Frost is one of America's most beloved poets for all time.
(B) Robert Frost is perhaps one of America's best and most beloved poets.
(C) One of America's best and most beloved poets is perhaps Robert Frost.
(D) Robert Frost, one of America's best poets, is perhaps the most beloved.
(E) The beloved American poet Robert Frost is perhaps the best of all times.

31. Of the following, which is the best way to phrase Sentence 6 (reproduced below)?

Though he continued to write during his college years, he never earned a college degree nor did he find much success in publishing his poetry.

(A) (As it is now)
(B) He continued to write during college while he never earned a degree and didn't publish his poetry.
(C) While he wrote during his college years, he wasn't published and received no degree.
(D) Going to college did not earn him a degree nor did he get his writings published.
(E) Although he continued to attend college and write, he did not earn a degree, and his works were not published.

32. In Sentence 9, the phrase *started the beginning* is best replaced by

(A) started the beginnings
(B) marked the starting
(C) marks the start
(D) starts the marking
(E) marked the beginning

GO ON TO THE NEXT PAGE ⟩

33. Which of the following sentences should be omitted to improve the unity of the second paragraph?

    (A) Sentence 7
    (B) Sentence 8
    (C) Sentence 9
    (D) Sentence 10
    (E) Sentence 11

34. In context, which of the following is the best way to phrase the underlined portion of sentence 12 (reproduced below)?

    Frost's <u>literary talent met with great success</u> back in the United States.

    (A) (As it is now)
    (B) talent literally met with great success
    (C) literary talent meeting with great success
    (D) great success with literary talents
    (E) talents became a great literary success

35. A strategy the writer uses within the third paragraph is to

    (A) write a poem about the essay's subject
    (B) use poetic vocabulary to enhance the essay
    (C) quote directly from the work being discussed
    (D) contrast the works of two American authors
    (E) make an emotional plea

STOP

**If you finish before your time is up, check your work on this section only.
You may not turn to any other section in the test.**

SECTION 6
Time—25 minutes
24 Questions

Directions: For each of the questions in this section, choose the best answer and fill in the corresponding circle on your answer sheet.

Each sentence that follows has either one or two blanks. Each blank indicates that a word has been omitted from the sentence. Following each sentence are five words or sets of words. Select the word or set of words that, when inserted into the sentence in place of the blank(s), best fits the context of the sentence as a whole.

1. Onlookers considered Justin a ------- after watching him eat; however, little did they know that he was ------- following a week-long hunger strike.

   (A) miser . . parched
   (B) glutton . . famished
   (C) madman . . angry
   (D) thief . . tired
   (E) hoarder . . starved

2. Garbanzo beans, also called chickpeas, are the ------- ingredient in hummus, a paste eaten as a dip or a sandwich spread.

   (A) implicit
   (B) teeming
   (C) producing
   (D) chief
   (E) supine

3. Although he appeared to be very ------- at the meeting with his investors, Ryan was actually ------- of participating in such a daunting venture.

   (A) acute . . culpable
   (B) complacent . . hesitant
   (C) collected . . assured
   (D) confident . . terrified
   (E) deferential . . bereft

4. The music store attracts an ------- group of customers; people with varied interests and lifestyles congregate there.

   (A) irate
   (B) optimum
   (C) apprehensive
   (D) aberrant
   (E) eclectic

5. The depiction of the ------- koala bear is largely a misconception: koalas can be very ------- creatures that should never be approached in the wild.

   (A) ferocious . . affable
   (B) tame . . esoteric
   (C) easygoing . . vicious
   (D) volatile . . hysterical
   (E) aggressive . . fierce

6. Linda exposed the illegal actions of her company and was, unfortunately, ------- by her peers for her ethical actions.

   (A) adored
   (B) admired
   (C) ostracized
   (D) relieved
   (E) celebrated

7. Aberrant results in scientific experiments should not be -------; on the contrary, such findings can often be credited as significant breakthroughs.

   (A) abraded
   (B) extolled
   (C) predicted
   (D) discounted
   (E) regulated

GO ON TO THE NEXT PAGE

8. Because the media corporation owned such a large portion of the news channels, it enjoyed a high degree of ------- in the news market.

(A) hegemony
(B) discretion
(C) atonement
(D) monotony
(E) zeal

GO ON TO THE NEXT PAGE ⟩

Each passage that follows is accompanied by several questions based on the content of the passage. Answer the questions based on what is either stated or implied in each passage. Be sure to read any introductory material that is provided.

Questions 9–12 are based on the following passages.

The following passages discuss two women poets.

Passage 1

    English poet Elizabeth Barrett Browning is probably best known for her collection of poems titled *Sonnets from the Portuguese*. By title
Line alone, one might assume that these poems are
5 either translated from Portuguese or written from a Portuguese point of view. In understanding Barrett Browning's poetry, however, it comes as little surprise that the book's title merely reflects the love and devotion of Robert
10 Browning for his wife, whom he called "my little Portuguese" because of her dark complexion.
    Indeed, it was Robert Browning who secured his wife's fame as a literary figure long
15 before her death. While the poems presented in *Sonnets from the Portuguese* were personally written for him, he simply could not keep their beauty to himself and had them published in 1850. Elizabeth died in his arms 11 years later.

Passage 2

20   Sylvia Plath, American author of the tragic story *The Bell Jar*, lived a real-life tragedy bearing many similarities to her fictional story. Like the main character in the story, Plath committed suicide shortly after the dissolution
25 of her marriage to Ted Hughes, an English poet.
    Even as a young child, Plath's life was wrought with melancholy and emotional distress. When she was just 8 years old, Plath's
30 father passed away. Years later, while a junior at Smith College, Plath attempted suicide for the first time and failed.
    Her marriage to Ted Hughes was a tumultuous one, as the two literary geniuses
35 struggled to meld their intense personalities into a normal family life. Just prior to his death,

Hughes published a collection of poems about Plath and their years together, titled *Birthday Letters*. It is largely this legacy that has become
40 Hughes' most popular and well-known book.

9. Which statement best characterizes the relationship between Passage 1 and Passage 2?

  (A) Passage 1 tells the story of a happy marriage, while Passage 2 tells of a tragic one.
  (B) Passage 1 discusses the effects of marriage on a writer's success, and Passage 2 shows another aspect of the same theme.
  (C) Passage 1 describes the personal lives of English writers, while Passage 2 focuses on American literature.
  (D) Passage 1 relates the story of a successful writer, whereas Passage 2 tells about a writer who never found success.
  (E) Passage 1 uses humor to make its point, while Passage 2 has a dark, humorless tone.

10. Unlike Passage 1, Passage 2 primarily focuses on

  (A) ethics in writing
  (B) environmental influences
  (C) natural talent
  (D) moral issues
  (E) tragic life circumstances

11. The author of Passage 1 would most likely characterize the "poems" mentioned in line 3 as

  (A) mediocre
  (B) disrespectful
  (C) informative
  (D) emotional
  (E) religious

12. The authors of both passages would most likely agree that a writer's emotional condition can often affect his or her

  (A) writing style
  (B) popularity
  (C) natural talent
  (D) ability
  (E) personality

GO ON TO THE NEXT PAGE ⇨

382

Questions 13–24 are based on the following passages.

These two passages discuss different points of view on whether Pluto is a planet.

Passage 1

Since its discovery, Pluto has been considered a planet. Some astronomers, however, have suggested lately that Pluto be stripped of its planetary status, arguing that it is more accurately categorized as an asteroid or comet.

The solar system's asteroid belt is a remnant of the *proplyd*, or protoplanetary disk, that preceded the planets. Gravitational interference by Jupiter prevented some material from consolidating in the process that created the planets. Included in the leftover material are asteroids, solid objects much smaller than any planet, with masses that vary considerably. The largest of the known asteroids are found in the main asteroid belt between the orbits of Mars and Jupiter, and not at the fringe of the inner solar system where Pluto resides.

Another example of non-planetary objects, comets, are thought to originate in the Oort cloud, a massive area of comet nuclei occupying the outer reaches of the solar system. It is theorized to have formed following the collapse of the original nebula that formed the sun five billion years ago. According to the hypothesis, comet nuclei are stable at the outer reaches of the solar system until interaction with planetary gravitation—usually Pluto's—causes a comet to enter a highly elliptical orbit around the sun. As a comet nears the sun, a tail becomes visible as light reflects off the trail of ice particles and dust it leaves behind. Several passes through the solar system destroys the comet, which is replaced by another of the billions of comets orbiting in the Oort cloud. Pluto shows no tail at any point in its circuit.

With a diameter of over 1,400 miles, Pluto is almost 1,000 times bigger than an average comet and more than twice the size of 1 Ceres, the largest of the asteroids, which comprises nearly a third of the total mass of the asteroid belt.

A planet can be described as a non-moon, sun-orbiting object that does not generate nuclear fusion and is large enough to be pulled into a spherical shape by its own gravity. Pluto is not a moon, as it does not orbit another planet. Although Pluto's orbital path is irregular compared to the other planets of the solar system, it undisputedly orbits the sun. Even by strict definition alone, Pluto is a planet and assuredly neither an asteroid nor a comet.

Passage 2

Many facts about Pluto suggest that it is actually a member of the Kuiper Belt, a group of substantial comets at the edge of the solar system, and not a planet. Kuiper belt, scattered disk, and Oort cloud objects together comprise the trans-Neptunian objects, which are the least understood celestial bodies in the solar system. As such, much care must be taken in the classification of phenomena in distant orbits of the sun. Calling Pluto a planet—on par with the other eight planets in our solar system—is an ideal example of jumping to unfounded conclusions because of erroneous or incomplete science.

First, Pluto is composed of icy material, as are the comets in the Kuiper Belt, while the other planets of the solar system are either rocky or gaseous. Mercury, Venus, Earth, and Mars are small, rocky, and near the sun. Jupiter, Saturn, Uranus, and Neptune are larger, gaseous, and more distant from the sun. As a small, solid body farthest from the sun, Pluto seems to violate the natural order obeyed by the eight true planets.

The discovery of trans-Neptunian object (TNO) 2003 UB_{313} shows Pluto is unlike the other planets. This celestial body, which orbits the sun beyond Neptune, is more massive than Pluto and is similar in composition and orbit. Why Pluto, discovered in 1930, is called a planet and 2003 UB_{313} a TNO is simply a matter of advancement in science. Astronomers from decades past were not equipped with the knowledge and technology required to make the distinction. The planet is so far away that no exploratory spacecraft have visited it to gather data. NASA's *New Horizons* mission launched a probe toward Pluto in 2006. Traveling at speeds in excess of 40,000 miles per hour, the craft will require over 9 years to arrive within sensor range

GO ON TO THE NEXT PAGE ⟩

of Pluto and its moons. Only then will humanity
90 enjoy an adequate survey of Pluto and, provi-
sionally, a Kuiper belt object for comparison.
    Contemporary observations show that
Pluto is much too small to be a planet. It is less
than half the diameter of the next smallest
95 planet, Mercury. Seven moons, including
Earth's, are larger than Pluto. The body is so
small, in fact, that all of its own moons have
likely yet to be discovered. The latest two were
found in 2005, only after reexamining Hubble
100 Space Telescope imagery from 2002 and 2003
in which the moons were overlooked.
    Finally, the eccentricity of Pluto's orbit
indicates that it is not a planet. While
commonly considered the ninth planet, for 20
105 years of its 249-year orbit, Pluto is actually
closer to the sun than is Neptune, placing it in
eighth position. Over 70 Kuiper Belt comets
share this irregular orbit, proving Pluto is more
similar to them than to proper planets.

13. Both authors agree that Pluto

    (A) is too massive to be considered a
        comet
    (B) has an irregular orbit around the sun
    (C) comprises expansive ice formations
    (D) formed in the Kuiper Belt
    (E) fails to meet the criteria required to
        be considered a planet

14. Lines 24–35 suggest that for defenders of
Pluto's planetary status, "a highly elliptical
orbit" and "a tail" are held to be

    (A) mutually exclusive
    (B) unpredictably variable
    (C) crucial comet features
    (D) essential planet attributes
    (E) highly perceptible

15. In line 35, "circuit" most nearly means

    (A) series of venues
    (B) electrical path
    (C) association
    (D) cyclic motion
    (E) cycle of competitions

16. The author of Passage 1 considers Pluto's size
(lines 36–40) as evidence for its being a planet
because

    (A) planets vary greatly by mass
    (B) very few large comets and asteroids have
        been discovered
    (C) no non-planetary objects come near its size
    (D) it is sufficient to retain a moon
    (E) its gravitation perturbs Oort cloud comets

17. All of the following are referred to in Passage 1
as evidence of Pluto's planetary status EXCEPT
the

    (A) position of Pluto relative to the sun
    (B) destruction of comets in the inner solar
        system
    (C) size of Pluto compared with that of comets
        and asteroids
    (D) significantly oblong orbit of Pluto
    (E) orbit of Pluto exclusively around the sun

18. Which statement about Pluto, if true, would
most directly support the view described in lines
51–54?

    (A) Kuiper belt objects share many characteris-
        tics of the inner, rocky planets of the solar
        system.
    (B) Kuiper belt objects are distinctive in that
        they never reach such size as Pluto.
    (C) The practice of analyzing telescope imagery
        to determine composition of celestial
        bodies is unlikely to distinguish between
        ice and certain types rock.
    (D) A planet is discovered beyond Pluto that has
        similar composition but a stable, circular
        orbit.
    (E) Detailed imagery of Pluto reveals that it
        sheds fine particulate matter as it orbits
        the sun.

GO ON TO THE NEXT PAGE →

19. In context, "substantial" (line 53) most nearly means

(A) immense
(B) valid
(C) corporal
(D) influential
(E) durable

20. The tone of Passage 2 suggests that the author believes

(A) supporters of Pluto's planetary status might be justified in their belief
(B) the *New Horizons* mission holds promise for preserving Pluto's planetary status
(C) astronomy is corrupted by biased researchers
(D) little but tradition reinforces Pluto's planetary status
(E) whether Pluto is a planet is of little long-term consequence

21. According to Passage 2, Pluto is commonly considered a planet because of which of the following?

   I. Vague meaning of the term "planet"
  II. Inadequate science in the past
 III. Ignorance of modern discoveries

(A) I only
(B) II only
(C) I and II only
(D) I and III only
(E) II and III only

22. Which research outcome would best illustrate the argument made in Passage 2?

(A) Telescope surveys of the Oort Cloud reveal that trans-Neptunian objects do not reach the size of Pluto.
(B) The *New Horizons* probe discovers three rocky moons of Pluto, each a different size.
(C) Detailed analysis of Pluto's orbit reveals that it is gradually becoming round.
(D) Trans-Neptunian object 2003 UB_{313} is found to have formed millions of years after the eight undisputed planets.
(E) Pluto's gravitation perturbs the orbit of comets more significantly than previously believed.

23. Passage 1 and Passage 2 share a general tone of

(A) unflinching certitude
(B) affectionate nostalgia
(C) analytical neutrality
(D) sorrowful regret
(E) open hostility

24. The information in Passage 2 supports which assumption about Pluto as described in Passage 1?

(A) Its small size does not preclude it from being a planet.
(B) Its icy composition reveals it is more like a comet than a planet.
(C) It has a highly elliptical orbit like that of comets passing through the inner solar system.
(D) Being so far from the sun keeps its icy surface from disintegrating.
(E) The discovery of additional moons would support Pluto's planetary status.

S T O P

**If you finish before your time is up, check your work on this section only.
You may not turn to any other section in the test.**

SECTION 7
Time—20 minutes
16 Questions

Directions: Solve each problem and determine which is the best of the answer choices given. Fill in the corresponding circle on your answer sheet. Use any available space to solve the problems.

Notes

1. The use of a calculator is permitted.
2. All numbers are real numbers.
3. Figures that accompany problems in this test are intended to provide information useful in solving the problems. They are drawn as accurately as possible EXCEPT when it is stated in a specific problem that the figure is not drawn to scale. All figures lie in a plane unless otherwise indicated.
4. Unless otherwise specified, the domain of any function f is assumed to be the set of all real numbers x for which $f(x)$ is a real number.

Reference Information

$A = \Pi r^2$
$C = 2\Pi r$
$A = lw$
$A = \frac{1}{2}bh$
$V = lwh$
$V = \Pi r^2 h$
$c^2 = a^2 + b^2$
Special Right Triangles

The number of degrees of arc in a circle is 360.
The sum of the measures in degrees of the angles of a triangle is 180.

1. If E is the set of even integers, N is the set of negative integers, and F is the set of integers less than 5, which of the following integers is in all three sets?

   (A) 6
   (B) 3
   (C) -3
   (D) -6
   (E) -9

2. If $4 + \sqrt{k} = 13$, then $k = ?$

   (A) 9
   (B) 81
   (C) 289
   (D) $\sqrt{9}$
   (E) $\sqrt{81}$

GO ON TO THE NEXT PAGE

3. In a poll, 44 people were in favor of constructing a new high school, 58 were against it, and 8 people had no opinion. What fraction of those polled were in favor of constructing a new high school?

   (A) $\frac{1}{9}$

   (B) $\frac{1}{5}$

   (C) $\frac{2}{5}$

   (D) $\frac{3}{5}$

   (E) $\frac{4}{9}$

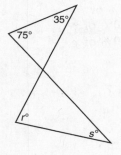

4. In the figure above, what is the value of $r + s$?

   (A) 80
   (B) 90
   (C) 100
   (D) 110
   (E) 120

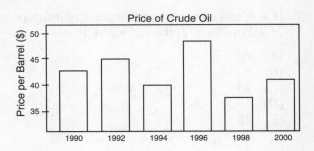

5. According to the graph above, between which two consecutive 2-year periods was there the greatest change in the price of crude oil?

   (A) 1990 and 1992
   (B) 1992 and 1994
   (C) 1994 and 1996
   (D) 1996 and 1998
   (E) 1998 and 2000

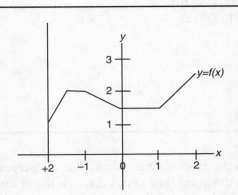

6. The graph of $y = f(x)$ is shown above. If $f(k) = 2$, which of the following is a possible value of k?

   (A) 1.5
   (B) 1.0
   (C) 0.5
   (D) -0.5
   (E) -2

GO ON TO THE NEXT PAGE

7. If a, b, and c are consecutive positive integers and $2^a \times 2^b \times 2^c = 512$, then $2^a + 2^b + 2^c = ?$

   (A) 6
   (B) 9
   (C) 14
   (D) 16
   (E) 28

8. In the xy-coordinate plane, the center of a circle has coordinates (-3, 2). If one endpoint of a diameter of the circle is (-3, -4), what are the coordinates of the other endpoint of this diameter?

   (A) (3, 2)
   (B) (-3, 6)
   (C) (-3, 8)
   (D) (-3, 10)
   (E) (-9, 8)

9. In the xy-coordinate plane, line l is perpendicular to the x-axis and passes through the point (-4, 7). Which of the following is an equation of line l?

   (A) $x = -4$
   (B) $x = 4$
   (C) $y = -4$
   (D) $y = 7$
   (E) $y - 7 = x + 4$

10. A right circular cylinder with a radius of 2 and a height of 6 has a volume of v. In terms of v, what is the volume of a right circular cylinder with a radius of 4 and a height of 6?

    (A) $v + 2$
    (B) $8v^2$
    (C) $4v^2$
    (D) $2v$
    (E) $4v$

11. If 30% of x equals 60% of y, which of the following expresses y in terms of x?

    (A) $y = 33\%$ of x
    (B) $y = 50\%$ of x
    (C) $y = 66\%$ of x
    (D) $y = 150\%$ of x
    (E) $y = 200\%$ of x

12. If m, n, and p are positive integers such that $m + n$ is even and the value of $(m + n)^2 + n + p$ is odd, which of the following must be true?

    (A) m is odd
    (B) n is even
    (C) p is odd
    (D) If n is even, p is odd
    (E) If p is odd, n is odd

GO ON TO THE NEXT PAGE ⇨

13. When the sum of a list of integers is divided by the average (arithmetic mean) of the integers, the result is k. What does k represent?

    (A)   The sum of the integers
    (B)   Half of the sum of the integers
    (C)   The number of integers
    (D)   Half of the number of integers
    (E)   The average of the integers

14. If $-3 < x < 5$ and $0 < y < 12$, which of the following gives the set of all possible values of xy?

    (A) $xy = 6$
    (B) $0 < xy < 60$
    (C) $-3 < xy < 17$
    (D) $-3 < xy < 60$
    (E) $-36 < xy < 60$

15. In the xy-coordinate system, if (r, s) and $(r + 2, s + t)$ are two points on the line defined by the equation $y = 4x + 5$, then $t =$

    (A)   4
    (B)   5
    (C)   8
    (D)   9
    (E)   11

16. After the first term, each term in a sequence is 2 greater than $\frac{1}{4}$ of the preceding term. If t is the first term of the sequence and $t \neq 0$, what is the ratio of the second term to the first term?

    (A) $\dfrac{t}{4 + 2}$
    (B) $\dfrac{t + 2}{4}$
    (C) $\dfrac{t + 8}{4}$
    (D) $\dfrac{t + 2}{4t}$
    (E) $\dfrac{t + 8}{4t}$

STOP

**If you finish before your time is up, check your work on this section only.
You may not turn to any other section in the test.**

SECTION 8
Time—20 minutes
19 Questions

Directions: For each of the questions in this section, choose the best answer and fill in the corresponding circle on your answer sheet.

Each sentence that follows has either one or two blanks. Each blank indicates that a word has been omitted from the sentence. Following each sentence are five words or sets of words. Select the word or set of words that, when inserted into the sentence in place of the blank(s), best fits the context of the sentence as a whole.

1. For some time now, the dissenters have been held in -------; they have suspended their activities.

   (A) contempt
   (B) obscurity
   (C) contrast
   (D) awe
   (E) abeyance

2. Although the production and sale of alcohol was ------- during prohibition, it was readily available illegally.

   (A) permissible
   (B) encouraged
   (C) proscribed
   (D) reconciled
   (E) unobjectionable

3. Residents of the small town enjoyed their serene lifestyle; they calmly went about their daily business without the ------- often associated with a large city.

   (A) peace
   (B) perceptions
   (C) ethics
   (D) chaos
   (E) apathy

4. The largest lake in the world by both surface area and water volume is the Caspian Sea, whose name ------- its complete lack of salt water.

   (A) elucidates
   (B) emphasizes
   (C) belies
   (D) accuses
   (E) confuses

5. It is surprising to observe that Jill's performances have recently been criticized as ------- because her advocates have been touting her great -------.

   (A) ambiguous . . uncertainty
   (B) exceptional . . fidelity
   (C) feckless . . incompetence
   (D) banal . . imagination
   (E) placid . . serenity

6. The movie mogul was known throughout the industry as a ------- man due to his charitable policies towards the needy.

   (A) magnanimous
   (B) tyrannical
   (C) false
   (D) shrewd
   (E) dubious

GO ON TO THE NEXT PAGE

The passage that follows is followed by several questions based on the content of the passage. Answer the questions based on what is either stated or implied in the passage. Be sure to read any introductory material that is provided.

Questions 7–19 are based on the following passage.

In the following passage, the life of an international art critic is discussed.

My first brush with the international artist and critic Fairfield Porter was actually through the poetry of his wife, Anne Channing Porter.
Line While both grew to become quite celebrated in
5 each one's own craft, Fairfield's story is unique.

Born into an affluent, artistic family in 1907, the boy who would one day become a renowned artist and critic showed the least artistic ability among the Porter children.
10 While his older brother Eliot took to photography, Fairfield, despite being remarkably intelligent, appeared to lack such natural talents. It seemed although artists surrounded him, his true talent was in critiquing others' work. He
15 was accepted to the art history program at Harvard, where he studied under archaeologist-scholar Arthur Pope. Eventually, he moved to Europe to continue his studies. Upon his return to the United States, Fairfield enrolled in the
20 Art Students League of New York and became acquainted with the famed photographer Alfred Stieglitz, whose work greatly influenced Porter's broadening art scholarship.

Between the years 1931 and 1932, Fairfield
25 spent the majority of his time in Italy learning to appreciate and critique the works of the great Renaissance painters. He trained under world-famous art historian Bernard Berenson and spent countless hours in museums and galleries.
30 Upon his return from Italy, he married Anne Channing and spent two decades developing his painting skills. During this period, Fairfield Porter's meetings with the French Intimist painter Willem De Kooning
35 profoundly steered Porter's work. Porter would be the first to acclaim de Kooning's tableaux.

Porter's renown as an art critic is due in part to his knack for responding directly to an artist's work. He found fault with the common
40 talk-based criticism that spoke of art only in reference to its past or to some vague theoretical framework; such criticism attempted to shape the future of art and was far too biased for Porter. His time as an art critic for such publications as *Art
45 News* and *The Nation* ended, nevertheless, in 1961, when he decided to pursue a full-time painting career.

The other side of his career, his uncommon approach to painting, is just as
50 important to understanding Fairfield Porter's contributions to the world of art. His personal philosophy comes from blending two views: first, that art should be personal, emotional, and representative of its subject; second, that it
55 should be boldly colorful, expressive, and generally abstract. Drawing on his vast knowledge of art history, and especially the styles of French Intimism, Porter fused these two feelings to create a powerful, emotive body of work with
60 themes of family, the individual, the home, and also nature, as in *The Door to the Woods* (1971) and *Maine—Toward the Harbor* (1967).

Porter died in 1975 on a morning walk at the seaside, depriving the world of one of the
65 century's most important critics. As an artist, his work remains for the art community an amazingly distinctive and especially representative exposition on his life. It is sad to say that now, some 30 years after his death, Porter is still virtually unknown
70 outside of art circles. This remarkably insightful, articulate, creative individual should be fixed in public consciousness and revered for his continuing influence on artists today.

7. The passage is narrated from the point of view of

(A) Fairfield Porter
(B) an observer who knows all about Porter and his career
(C) an observer who has only partial knowledge of Porter
(D) an observer who does not know Porter initially but who learns about him during the course of the passage
(E) a friend of Fairfield Porter

GO ON TO THE NEXT PAGE ⇨

8. The passage can primarily be described as

(A) critical evidence used to refute an established impression
(B) lighthearted anecdotes tempered with
profound observations
(C) skeptical commentary building to a significant conclusion
(D) a brief profile leading to a deferential assertion
(E) a case study followed by a chastening
remark

9. In line 1, the term "brush" most nearly means

(A) sweeper
(B) clash
(C) thicket
(D) encounter
(E) instrument

10. The reference to Fairfield Porter's artistic abilities in lines 10–14 conveys what impression about
artistic sensibilities?

(A) Producing art is the only means to understand it.
(B) Art is unassailable except by the artist.
(C) Perception of art can be enriched through
exposure to art.
(D) The best artists are raised in the company
of other artists.
(E) Most children do not receive the art education afforded affluent families.

11. The author describes Porter's scholarship as
"broadening" (line 23) because

(A) art skills require many years of study to
develop
(B) artistic judgments are subjective and
demand rigorous scrutiny
(C) he attended a prestigious university
(D) he primarily studied painting
(E) he was involved in varied aspects of art as a
student

12. The author refers to Willem de Kooning (lines
32–36) in order to

(A) point out Porter's privileged upbringing
(B) underscore the importance of the appren-
tice system in art
(C) emphasize Porter's natural ability to
critique art
(D) expose a critical accomplishment important
to Porter's career
(E) attack the weakness of criticism unlike
Porter's

13. In lines 41–42, "theoretical framework" most
likely refers to

(A) the system of studs and joists supporting a
structure
(B) the organization of a work process
(C) a common prototypical set of features
(D) a peripheral understanding of an aspect of
history
(E) a concrete representation of an obscure
subject

14. The passage characterizes Porter's painting (line
49) as a

(A) facet of his career worthy of praise
(B) more skilled enterprise than his art criti-
cism
(C) lesser accomplishment than his art criticism
(D) brief exploration that never flourished
(E) difficult part of his career to describe

15. The phrase "blending two views" (line 52) refers
to Porter's style of painting that

(A) remains politically centrist
(B) is characterized by stylized realism
(C) conveys a feeling of conflict and detach-
ment
(D) was developed from two disparate sources
of inspiration
(E) represented a compromise between his
roles as critic and creator

GO ON TO THE NEXT PAGE ⟩

16. The author's remarks in lines 56–62 ("Drawing…(1967)") suggests that

(A) family troubles moved Porter to paint
(B) knowledge of history causes artists to produce dull work
(C) Porter's nature scenes are his most important works
(D) Porter's paintings belong to French Intimism
(E) Porter's experience as a critic directly influenced his painting

17. Why does the author mention that Porter died while on a walk (lines 63–65)?

(A) To emphasize the shock of his death
(B) To maintain the positive tone of the passage
(C) To suggest that his death was hard on his family
(D) To dispel any doubt about his heartiness
(E) To illustrate the unpredictability of life

18. In line 70, the word "circles" most nearly means

(A) cycles
(B) rounds
(C) wheels
(D) groups
(E) domains

19. The passage suggests that Porter's acclaim is

(A) solidly excellent
(B) constantly debated
(C) isolated to certain crowds
(D) subject to renewed criticism
(E) unlikely to improve

STOP

**If you finish before your time is up, check your work on this section only.
You may not turn to any other section in the test.**

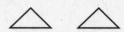
SECTION 9
Time—10 minutes
14 Questions

Directions: For each question, select the best answer from among the choices listed. Fill in the corresponding circle on your answer sheet.

The following questions test the correct and effective use of standard written English in expressing an idea. Part of each sentence (or the entire sentence) is underlined. Following each sentence are five different ways of phrasing the underlined portion. Answer choice A repeats the original phrasing. If you think that the original phrasing is best, select answer choice A. Otherwise, select from the remaining four choices. Your selection should result in the most effective, clear sentence, free from awkwardness or ambiguity.

1. <u>For as many as 30 years and more</u> Ernest Hemingway resided in Key West, Florida.

   (A) For as many as 30 years and more
   (B) For not much more than about 30 years
   (C) For a little over 30 years and more
   (D) For more than 30 years
   (E) For 30 years and then some

2. The first FIFA World Cup, held in Uruguay, was won by the Uruguayan soccer <u>team; it was won by four victories and no defeats.</u>

   (A) team; it was won by four victories and no defeats
   (B) team, which had four victories and no defeats
   (C) team, and there were four Uruguayan victories and no defeats
   (D) team, which was victorious four times and no defeats
   (E) team, having four victories and with no defeats

3. Although Jessica is keenly interested in Italian culture, <u>she has never visited Italy and she does not speak Italian.</u>

   (A) she has never visited Italy and she does not speak Italian
   (B) it is without being able to speak Italian or visit Italy
   (C) she does not speak Italian and has never visited there
   (D) she does not speak Italian nor has she ever visited there
   (E) it is without speaking Italian nor having visited there

4. *The Jazz Singer* was the first successful full-length film to appear <u>with sound, and included lengthy dialogue.</u>

   (A) with sound, and included lengthy dialogue
   (B) with sound, and had lengthy dialogue
   (C) sound and including lengthy dialogue
   (D) having sound, and the film included lengthy dialogue
   (E) included sound and lengthy dialogue

GO ON TO THE NEXT PAGE

5. The escalating <u>rate for tuition is keeping many students from attending college</u>; some blame the school administrators for poor allocation of funds, but the administrators themselves blame the lack of state and private funding.

   (A) rate for tuition is keeping many students from attending college
   (B) rate in tuition is rising and keeps many students from attending college
   (C) rate on tuition has risen to keep many students from attending college
   (D) tuition rates is keeping many students from attending college
   (E) tuition rate is rising and many students are kept from attending college

6. In the late 1400s, the <u>discovery of the New World, development of European interest in Africa, and India, and the emergence of opportunities to generate great wealth suddenly begins to transform</u> the traditional ways of life.

   (A) discovery of the New World, the development of European interest in Africa, and India, and the emergence of opportunities to generate great wealth suddenly begins to transform
   (B) discovery of the New World, development of European interest in Africa, India, and the emergence of opportunities, to generate great wealth, suddenly transforming
   (C) discovery, the New World, the development of European, interest in Africa and India, emergence of opportunities to generate great wealth, and suddenly began to transforms
   (D) discovery for the New World, development for European interest in Africa and India, and the emergence for opportunities to generate great wealth was suddenly transforming
   (E) discovery of the New World, the development of European interest in Africa and India, and the emergence of opportunities to generate great wealth suddenly began to transform

7. Geoffrey Chaucer is credited <u>as having</u> introduced vernacular English literature—most famously with the Canterbury Tales.

   (A) as having
   (B) as being that who
   (C) with having
   (D) for having been the one that
   (E) having been the one who

8. <u>Found high in the Himalayan Mountains, giant hornets</u> have been known to viciously attack humans.

   (A) Found high in the Himalayan Mountains, giant hornets
   (B) Giant hornets, they are found high in the Himalayan Mountains,
   (C) Highly found in the Himalayan Mountains, giant hornets
   (D) High in the Himalayan Mountains are found these giant hornets that
   (E) Hornets that are giant and found high in the Himalayan Mountains

9. Ryan liked to read a lot of <u>books, of which he found mystery and detective novels especially fascinating</u>.

   (A) books, of which he found mystery and detective novels especially fascinating
   (B) books, especially fascinating to him were mystery and detective novels
   (C) books; the fascination of mystery and detective novels especially
   (D) books; he found mystery and detective novels especially fascinating
   (E) books, and it was especially the mystery and detective novels that were of fascination

10. Concern for the well-being of young children <u>has led many states to enacting laws</u> requiring the use of child safety seats.

   (A) has led many states to enacting laws
   (B) has led many states enacting laws to
   (C) has led many states to enact laws
   (D) has many states leading to enact laws
   (E) has, in many states, let to the enacting of laws

GO ON TO THE NEXT PAGE

11. From 1861 on, the separate states of Italy were officially united under one king; however, there was a definite contrast <u>between those who lived in the more wealthy, industrialized North with those who lived in the more poor, rural South</u>.

- (A) between those who lived in the more wealthy, industrialized North with those who lived in the more poor, rural South
- (B) between those living in the wealthier, industrialized North or those living in the poorer, rural South
- (C) between those who lived in the more wealthy, industrialized North and those who lived in the more poor, rural South
- (D) among those who lived in the more wealthy, industrialized North and those who lived in the more poor, rural South
- (E) among those who lived in the more wealthy, industrialized North with those who lived in the more poor, rural South

12. <u>Although only</u> 1 or 2 inches long, the bumblebee bat is a mammal and, therefore, akin to elephants and whales.

- (A) Although only
- (B) Since it is
- (C) Because it is
- (D) Despite a size of
- (E) While its size is

13. In 2004, Pablo Picasso's painting, *Boy with a Pipe*, <u>sold for over $100 million and it was</u> the highest price ever paid for one of his paintings.

- (A) sold for over $100 million and it was
- (B) which sold for over $100 million, being
- (C) and was sold for over $100 million, becoming
- (D) sold for over $100 million, which was
- (E) sold for over $100 million, and that being

14. The U.S. Navy sometimes uses <u>dolphins, and can be trained</u> to conduct dangerous underwater tasks.

- (A) dolphins, and can be trained
- (B) dolphins, after undergoing training,
- (C) the training of dolphins
- (D) dolphins which have been
- (E) trained dolphins

STOP

If you finish before your time is up, check your work on this section only.
You may not turn to any other section in the test.

Answer Key

Section 1

Because grading the essay is subjective, we've chosen not to include any "graded" essays here. Your best bet is to have someone you trust, such as your personal tutor, read your essays and give you an honest critique. Make the grading criteria mentioned in Chapter 5 available to whomever grades your essays. If you plan on grading your own essays, review the grading criteria and be as honest as possible regarding the structure, development, organization, technique, and appropriateness of your writing. Focus on your weak areas and continue to practice in order to improve your writing skills.

Section 2

1. C
2. D
3. A
4. A
5. C
6. B
7. E
8. C
9. E
10. D
11. A
12. B
13. E
14. A
15. D
16. D
17. C
18. D
19. C

Section 3

1. B
2. B
3. D
4. C
5. E
6. A
7. D
8. C
9. B
10. D
11. C
12. A
13. C
14. D
15. B
16. E
17. B
18. A
19. B
20. C
21. D
22. A
23. D
24. E

Section 4

Multiple Choice

1. D
2. C
3. C
4. C
5. A
6. A
7. E
8. B

Student Produced Response

9. $\frac{1}{3}$ or .333

10. $\frac{7}{32}$, .218, or .219

11. $\frac{3}{8}$ or .375

12. 1

13. 29

14. 40

15. 30

16. 2

17. 90

18. 0 or 30

Section 5

1. E
2. E
3. A
4. E
5. A
6. B
7. B
8. C
9. D
10. E
11. D
12. B
13. D
14. A
15. C
16. B
17. D
18. E
19. C
20. D
21. B
22. E
23. B
24. C
25. E
26. E
27. B
28. A
29. B
30. B
31. A
32. E
33. D
34. A
35. C

Section 6

1. B	17. D
2. D	18. E
3. D	19. A
4. E	20. D
5. C	21. E
6. C	22. D
7. D	23. A
8. A	24. C
9. B	
10. E	
11. D	
12. A	
13. B	
14. C	
15. D	
16. C	

Section 7

1. D
2. B
3. C
4. D
5. D
6. A
7. E
8. C
9. A
10. E
11. B
12. D
13. C
14. E
15. C
16. E

Section 8

1. E
2. C
3. D
4. C
5. D
6. A
7. B
8. D
9. D
10. C
11. E
12. D
13. C
14. A
15. B
16. E
17. B
18. D
19. C

Section 9

1. D
2. B
3. A
4. A
5. A
6. E
7. C
8. A
9. D
10. C
11. C
12. A
13. D
14. E

Scoring Practice Test 3

Check your responses with the Answer Key. Fill in the blanks below and do the calculations to get your math, critical reading, and writing raw scores. Use the tables on the next pages find your scaled scores.

Remember that this is a simulated test and that the score should only be used to estimate your score on the actual SAT.

Get Your Math Raw Score:

	Number Correct	**Number Incorrect**
Section 2:	_____	_____
Section 4:		
(#1 – #8)	_____	_____
(#9 – #18)	_____	
Section 7:	_____	_____
Totals:	_____	_____

Divide the total Number Incorrect by 4 and subtract the result from the total Number Correct. This is your Raw Score: _____

Round Raw Score to the nearest whole number. Use Table 1 to find Scaled Score range.

Math Scaled Score Range: _____ - _____

Get Your Critical Reading Raw Score:

	Number Correct	**Number Incorrect**
Section 3:	_____	_____
Section 6:	_____	_____
Section 8:	_____	_____
Totals:	_____	_____

Divide the total Number Incorrect by 4 and subtract the result from the total Number Correct. This is your Raw Score: _____

Round Raw Score to the nearest whole number. Use Table 2 to find Scaled Score range.

Critical Reading Scaled Score Range: _____ - _____

Get Your Writing Raw Score:

	Number Correct	Number Incorrect
Section 5:	_____	_____
Section 9:	_____	_____
Totals:	_____	_____

Divide the total Number Incorrect by 4 and subtract the result from the total Number Correct. This is your Raw Score: _____

Round Raw Score to the nearest whole number. Use Table 3 to find Scaled Score range.

Writing Score Range: _____ - _____

Note that your Writing Score assumes an Essay score of 4. If you believe that your Essay warrants a score of 5 or 6, your Writing Score would increase by an average of 30 to 50 points. Likewise, if your Essay is in the 1 to 3 range, your Writing Score would decrease by an average of 30 to 50 points.

Get Your Composite Score:

To calculate your Composite Score Range, simply add the 3 sub-score ranges (Math, Critical Reading, and Writing).

Composite Score Range: _____ - _____

Table 1   Math Score Conversion

Raw Score	Scaled Score	Raw Score	Scaled Score
54	800	23	460-520
53	750-800	22	450-510
52	720-800	21	440-500
51	700-780	20	430-490
50	690-770	19	430-490
49	680-740	18	420-480
48	670-730	17	410-470
47	660-720	16	400-460
46	640-700	15	400-460
45	630-690	14	390-450
44	620-680	13	380-440
43	620-680	12	360-440
42	610-670	11	350-430
41	600-660	10	340-420
40	580-660	9	330-430
39	570-650	8	320-420
38	560-640	7	310-410
37	550-630	6	290-390
36	550-630	5	280-380
35	540-620	4	270-370
34	530-610	3	260-360
33	520-600	2	240-340
32	520-600	1	230-330
31	520-580	0	210-310
30	510-570	-1	200-290
29	500-560	-2	200-270
28	490-550	-3	200-250
27	490-550	-4	200-230
26	480-540	-5	200-210
25	470-530	-6 and below	200
24	460-520		

Table 2   Critical Reading Score Conversion

Raw Score	Scaled Score	Raw Score	Scaled Score
67	800	30	470-530
66	770-800	29	470-530
65	740-800	28	460-520
64	720-800	27	450-510
63	700-800	26	450-510
62	690-790	25	440-500
61	670-770	24	440-500
60	660-760	23	430-490
59	660-740	22	420-480
58	650-730	21	420-480
57	640-720	20	410-470
56	630-710	19	400-460
55	630-710	18	400-460
54	620-700	17	390-450
53	610-690	16	380-440
52	600-680	15	380-440
51	610-670	14	370-430
50	600-660	13	360-420
49	590-650	12	350-410
48	580-640	11	350-410
47	580-640	10	340-400
46	570-630	9	330-390
45	560-620	8	310-390
44	560-620	7	300-380
43	550-610	6	290-370
42	550-610	5	270-370
41	540-600	4	260-360
40	530-590	3	250-350
39	530-590	2	230-330
38	520-580	1	220-320
37	510-570	0	200-290
36	510-570	-1	200-290
35	500-560	-2	200-270
34	500-560	-3	200-250
33	490-550	-4	200-230
32	480-540	-5	200-210
31	480-540	-6 and below	200

Table 3   Writing Score Conversion

Raw Score	Scaled Score	Raw Score	Scaled Score
49	750-800	21	460-590
48	720-800	20	460-580
47	700-800	19	450-580
46	680-800	18	440-570
45	670-800	17	430-560
44	660-790	16	420-550
43	640-780	15	410-540
42	630-770	14	400-530
41	620-760	13	390-520
40	620-750	12	390-510
39	610-740	11	380-510
38	600-730	10	370-500
37	590-720	9	360-490
36	580-720	8	350-480
35	570-710	7	340-470
34	570-700	6	330-460
33	560-690	5	320-460
32	550-680	4	320-450
31	540-670	3	310-440
30	530-660	2	300-430
29	520-650	1	280-410
28	520-650	0	270-410
27	510-640	-1	250-390
26	500-630	-2	240-370
25	490-620	-3	240-360
24	480-610	-4	220-340
23	470-600	-5	200-320
22	460-590	-6 and below	200

Answers and Explanations

Section 1

Because grading the essay is subjective, we've chosen not to include any "graded" essays here. Your best bet is to have someone you trust, such as your personal tutor, read your essays and give you an honest critique. Make the grading criteria mentioned in Chapter 5, "SAT/PSAT Verbal," available to whomever grades your essays. If you plan on grading your own essays, review the grading criteria and be as honest as possible regarding the structure, development, organization, technique, and appropriateness of your writing. Focus on your weak areas and continue to practice to improve your writing skills.

Section 2

1. **The correct answer is C.** To solve this problem, set up a proportion between the gallons of gasoline required and the miles driven. You are given that the motor-cycle requires 15 gallons to travel 180 miles. Set the number of gallons required to travel 60 miles to x, and solve for x, as shown in the following:

   15 is to 180 as x is to 60

   $$\frac{15}{180} = \frac{x}{60}$$
   $$180x = 900$$

   $$x = 5$$

2. **The correct answer is D.** Because $m \times n = m$, no matter the value of m, n functions as the multiplicative identity, which is 1. In other words, because $m \times n$ always equals m, n must equal 1.

3. **The correct answer is A.** To solve, use the fact that vertical angles are congruent. The angle vertical to a also has the angle measure of a, and the angle vertical to b also has the angle measure of b. Now that all of the measures of the angles inside the triangle are known, use the fact that the angles of triangles always sum 180°. Therefore $a + b + c = 180$. Solving for c yields $c = 180 - a - b$.

4. **The correct answer is A.** To solve this problem, calculate the difference between the test scores for each student as represented in the graph. Student A had the greatest difference, 40 points (90 − 50).

5. **The correct answer is C.** To solve this problem, add both scores from each student as shown in the graph, then divide by 10 (the total number of test scores): $(90 + 50 + 80 + 60 + 70 + 70 + 50 + 80 + 80 + 90) \div 10 = 720 \div 10$, or 72.

6. **The correct answer is B.** To solve this problem, set up a proportion between the increase in expenses and the increase in outside temperature. According to the question, expenses increase by \$35 when the temperature increases by 25°. You are asked to calculate the increase in expenses, (set expenses equal to x) when the temperature increases by 15°:

35 is to 25 as x is to 15

$$\frac{35}{25} = \frac{x}{15}$$

$$25x = 525$$

$$x = 21$$

7. **The correct answer is E.** To solve this problem, substitute the value $\frac{2}{3}$ for x in the equation $\frac{1}{x} + \frac{1}{x-1}$ as follows:

$$\frac{\frac{1}{2}}{\frac{2}{3}} + \frac{1}{\frac{2}{3} - 1}$$

$$\frac{3}{2} + \frac{1}{\frac{1}{3}}$$

$$\frac{3}{2} - \frac{3}{1} = \frac{-3}{2}$$

8. **The correct answer is C.** To solve this problem, recall that when numbers greater than 1 are raised to powers greater than 1, the original numbers always increase. However, when numbers that are between 1 and 0 are raised to powers greater than 1, they approach 0 (think about what happens when you multiply any number by a fraction—the product is closer to 0). On the number line, $x^6 < x^3 < x$, they are all greater than 0 (positive). Because the numbers are greater than 0, any negative answer choice can be eliminated. Also because greater powers of x are less than x, x must be less than 1. Therefore, the only logical answer choice is $\frac{2}{3}$.

You could also solve this problem by replacing x with each of the answer choices and using the process of elimination.

9. **The correct answer is E.** Because the y-coordinate of point K is -5 and line segment JK begins at the x-axis, you know that the length of line segment JK is 5. The length of segment KL is equal to the length of segment JK; thus, segment KL is also 5 units long. If KL is 5 units long, originating at the y-axis and in Quadrant III of the plane, the coordinates of point K must be (-5, -5). Therefore, the value of b is -5, answer choice E.

10. **The correct answer is D.** When solving equations that involve absolute values, you always have two solutions. When solving for a, the equation $|a - 8| = 11$ is equivalent to $a - 8 = 11$ and $a - 8 = -11$. Solving these two equations yields $a = 19$ or $a = -3$. However, the problem states that $a < 0$; thus, the only acceptable answer is $a = -3$.

Likewise, when solving for b, the equation $|b + 6| = 9$ is equivalent to $b + 6 = 9$ and $b + 6 = -9$. Solving these two equations yields $b = 3$ or $b = -15$. However, the problem states that $b < 0$, thus the only acceptable answer is $b = -15$. The value of $a - b$ is, therefore, $-3 - (-15)$, or $-3 + 15$, which is 12.

11. **The correct answer is A.** In the xy-coordinate plane, a reflection about the x-axis has the property of changing the y-coordinates only (in fact, the reflection has the effect of multiplying every y-coordinate by -1). Because slope can be defined as rise/run, line p rises (y-coordinate) 5 units for every 3 units of run (x-coordinate). Rise is related to the change in y-coordinates, and multiplying them by -1 would yield a rise of -5 for every 3 units of run. Thus, line q has a slope of $-\frac{5}{3}$.

12. **The correct answer is B.** To solve this problem, first calculate the total volume of the box and divide it by the volume of a single cube. This yields the number of cubes necessary to fill the box. Because the box has the dimensions 27 inches by 24 inches by 15 inches, the volume is $27 \times 24 \times 15$, or 9,720 cubic inches. Each cube has the dimensions $3 \times 3 \times 3$ inches, so the volume of each cube is 27 cubic inches. Thus, the total number of cubic blocks needed is $9,720 \div 27$, or 360.

13. **The correct answer is E.** To solve this problem, recall that the definition of integers is the set of the positive natural numbers and their negatives (…-3, -2, -1, 1, 2, 3,…) and the number zero. Therefore, for $\frac{(7 + g)}{4}$ to be an integer, the quantity 7 + g must be evenly divided by 4. For that to happen, the sum of 7 + g must be a multiple of 4, and, therefore, 7 + g must be even. The sum of two numbers is even only when they are both even or both odd. Therefore, because 7 is odd, g must also be odd.

14. **The correct answer is A.** To solve this problem, use the fact that supplementary angles add to 180. In the figure shown, x, y, and z form relationships with a, b, and c, respectively. Because a and x are vertical angles, they have the same measure. Angles b and y are supplementary, so they add to 180, making $y = 180 - b$. Likewise, $z = 180 - c$. Therefore, the sum of the angles within the triangle is $180 = x + y + z$, which is equivalent to $a + (180 - b) + (180 - c)$. You are given that $a = 140$, so substitute 140 for a, as follows:

$180 = 140 + (180 - b) + (180 - c)$

$180 = 140 + 180 + 180 - b - c$

$180 = 500 - b - c$

$-320 = -b - c$

$320 = b + c$

15. **The correct answer is D.** When the plane landed in Alaska, it was 6 p.m. AST, which is equivalent to 9 p.m. CST. Thus, the flight was $9 - 2$, or 7 hours long. A plane leaving Anchorage at 2 p.m. AST would arrive in Chicago 7 hours later, 9 p.m. AST, which is equivalent to 12 a.m. CST.

16. **The correct answer is D.** This is a *must be* question, so you should evaluate each Roman numeral and eliminate those that either simply *could be* true or are false.

    Because x is divisible by 7, you know that x is a multiple of 7. Likewise, because y is divisible by 9, y is a multiple of 9. Therefore, the product xy is a multiple of both 9 and 7, and because 63 is the least common multiple of 9 and 7, xy must be a multiple of 6; therefore, xy must be divisible by 63. Eliminate answer choice B because it does not include Roman numeral I.

    Because you know that x is a multiple of 7, one value of x is 7. Likewise, one value of y is 9 because y is a multiple of 9. The quantity $7x + 9y$ is not divisible by 63 because 49 + 81 is not divisible by 63. Eliminate answer choices B, C, and E because they include Roman numeral II.

    The quantity $9x + 7y$ is divisible by 63 because $9x$ is divisible by 7, 9, and their least common multiple, 63, and $7y$ is divisible by 7, 9, and their least common multiple, 63. Therefore, both Roman numeral I and Roman numeral III must be divisible by 63.

17. **The correct answer is C.** To solve this problem, multiply the expression $(x + 3)$ by $(x + s)$ to get $x^2 + 3x + sx + 3s$. You are given that $x^2 + rx + 12$ is equivalent to $x^2 + 3x + sx + 3s$. Therefore, $3s$ is equal to 12, making s equal to 4. It is also apparent that $3x + sx$ is equivalent to rx. Set the quantities as equal and solve for r, as follows:

    $rx = 3x + sx$

    $rx = x(3 + s)$

    $r = 3 + s$

    Because $s = 4$, r must equal 7.

18. **The correct answer is D.** You have a total of 37 articles of clothing in the drawer (14 + 23 = 37). If x shirts must be removed from the drawer, leaving $37 - x$ articles of clothing, then the 14 ties would constitute 70% of $37 - x$. Set up a proportion, and calculate this value as follows:

    14 is to $37 - x$ as 70% is to 100%

    $14/(37 - x) = 0.70$

    $14 = .70(37 - x)$

    $14 = 25.9 - 0.7x$

    $-11.9 = -0.7x$

    $17 = x$

19. **The correct answer is C.** To solve this problem, substitute the given values into the given equation:

$$3,365 = 225(x) - (165x + c)$$

You know that 75 units were sold, so set x equal to 75 and solve for c:

$$3,365 = 225(75) - (165(75) + c)$$

$$3,365 = 16,875 - (12,375 + c)$$

$$3,365 = 16,875 - 12,375 - c$$

$$3,365 = 4,500 - c$$

$$1,135 = c$$

20. **The correct answer is D.** To find the x-coordinate where the lines with equations $y = -2x + 7$ and $y = 3x - 3$ intersect, set $-2x + 7$ equal to $3x - 3$ and solve for x:

$$-2x + 7 = 3x - 3$$

$$-5x + 7 = -3$$

$$-5x = -10$$

$$x = 2$$

Section 3

1. **The best answer is B.** The context of the sentence indicates that Kristine's brother behaved badly and that she objected to such behavior. "Reprehensible" means "deserving of blame," which best fits the context of the sentence.

2. **The best answer is B.** The word "ferocity" denotes "fierceness" or "turbulence," which best fits the context of the sentence; it makes sense that the islanders would have to evacuate if the storm was "fierce." The other answer choices do not fit the context of the sentence.

3. **The answer is D.** The context of the sentence indicates that the employee was certain that his misdeeds would most likely yield negative consequences. Therefore, it makes sense that his sense of doom in approaching his supervisor's office would not be changed. "Inexorable" means "relentless" or "not likely to be diverted." None of the other words fit the context of the sentence.

4. **The best answer is C.** The preposition "although" indicates a contradiction; people believe one thing about automobile repair shops as a whole, but they believe another thing about their own mechanics. Because they are unwilling to criticize their own mechanics, they must be critical of automobile repair shops as a whole. You should look for a synonym of "critical." The word "contemptuous" means "scornful," which best fits the context of the sentence.

5. **The best answer is E.** "Homogeneity" is the quality of "being uniform throughout." The context of the passage indicates that Tatsuro was expecting the crowd to be comprised of different kinds of people, so the fact that the crowd was "homogeneous" would certainly surprise him. The other answer choices do not fit the context of the sentence.

6. **The best answer is A.** The author emphasizes the fact that Helen Keller overcame adversity in the forms of both blindness and deafness and the point that Keller did not let her disadvantages hold her back from being successful. This most closely correlates with answer choice A. Answer choice B might appear to be correct, but this choice ignores the obstacles that Helen Keller had to overcome to be successful, a central theme in this passage. Answer choices C, D, and E are not supported by the context of the passage.

7. **The best answer is D.** According to the passage, "Joy is the holy fire that keeps our purpose warm and our intelligence aglow. Work without joy shall be as nothing. Resolve to keep happy, and your joy and you shall form an invincible host against difficulties." This statement is most like the statement in answer choice D because both express the theme that focusing on being happy will ensure that you lead a fulfilling life.

8. **The best answer is C.** The author describes the Immigration Act as an "exciting change." This indicates that the author felt positively about the Act and the effects it would have on immigration for the U.S. Answer choice D might appear to be correct, but "wonder" indicates astonishment or surprise, neither of which is indicated by the tone of this passage. Answer choices A, B, and E are not supported by the context of the passage.

9. **The best answer is B.** The author states that the Immigration Act made "individual work skills and relationships with current U.S. citizens the criteria for immigration." Answer choices A and E might appear to be correct, but both of these answer choices indicate that work skills are the sole standard upon which immigrants are allowed into the United States. The author implies that the altered immigration laws now assessed immigration applicants fairly and correctly, which best correlates with answer choice B. Answer choices C and D are beyond the scope of the passage.

10. **The best answer is D.** The children's poem speaks of remembering the Gunpowder Plot and never forgetting it. This, coupled with the fact that the passage goes on to mention that the poem is famed, suggests that the Gunpowder Plot is a significant part of British history. The rest of the answer choices are beyond the scope of the passage.

11. **The best answer is C.** The author states "The failed bomb plot could certainly have killed the King and potentially the rest of the English Legislature." It was uncertain whom exactly the blast would have harmed, but it certainly did not have the power to wipe out the entire aristocracy. Answer choice A is incorrect because there is no doubt that the Gunpowder Plot was treasonous. Likewise, answer choice D is incorrect because it is quite clear that the perpetrator's actions were depraved, or corrupt and immoral. Answer choices B and E are beyond the scope of the passage.

12. **The best answer is A.** In saying "It has been said by many…that Guy Fawkes was the only man ever to enter Parliament with honest intentions," the author implies that many people are not convinced that the members of Parliament are fully trustworthy and have an honorable purpose. The rest of the answer choices are not supported by information found in the passage.

13. **The best answer is C.** The group behind the Gunpowder Plot was fighting in the name of the Catholic Church and worried only about protecting fellow Catholics from harm. Thus, this group was not supportive of other religions, such as that of the Church of England. The only word that correctly fits this use of the word "denouncers" is answer choice C, "rejecters."

14. **The best answer is D.** The passage describes the difficulty that the conspirators had when trying to dig a mineshaft beneath Westminster and that "Luck smiled upon the plotters when they stumbled upon a cellar for rent beneath the House of Lords." This was a rare, unexpected opportunity for the plotters that is best expressed in answer choice D. Answer choices A and C are incorrect because the author writes the passage from an unbiased point of view and does not express his opinion, positive or negative, towards the conspirators. Answer choice B is incorrect because the passage describes the difficulty that the men had in finding a place in which the gunpowder could be placed. Answer choice E is incorrect because the phrase "Luck smiled…" has nothing to do with the criminals escaping justice.

15. **The best answer is B.** "Scruples" are "feelings arising from morals or conscience that tend to hinder actions." Ultimately, the plotters failed because they felt obligated to warn other Catholics of the events that were about to happen. Answer choice A might appear to be correct because according to the passage, "Learning about the letter the following day, several conspirators wished to abort the plan"; however, this indicates no disagreement on fundamental political issues but rather disagreement over whether the plan was still safe to continue on with. Answer choice D might also appear to be correct if one assumes that the men wrote the letter out of compassion. However, compassionate men would most likely not plan a bombing intended to murder a large number of people. Answer choices C and E are not supported by information found in the passage.

16. **The best answer is E.** The statement regarding Fawke's confidence is intended to show that despite the fact he knew his plan had been exposed, he still felt that the mission could be completed because no one had yet discovered the explosives in the cellar. The other answer choices include details in the passage, but they are not relevant to the statement regarding Fawke's continued confidence.

17. **The best answer is B.** Because the execution was intended to be a lesson to others to deter them from committing treason, a most notorious crime against the nation, it is fitting that the execution be particularly gruesome and degrading. In this context, "heinous" most closely means "dreadful" or "terrible," and such an execution would certainly send a message to others.

18. **The best answer is A.** The author comments on the hazards of social repression saying, "No brutal threat can stop the most committed believer from rising in defense of his beliefs." This is most closely linked to answer choice A, the statement that the establishment is always at risk for another uprising from an affronted, or angry and impassioned, citizen. Answer choices B and D are incorrect because the author writes in a neutral tone and does not express any opinion either way on the issue. Answer choice C is incorrect because the statement in question is written in the present tense and is not discussing the citizens of the era of Guy Fawkes. Answer choice E is not supported by the context of the passage.

19. **The best answer is B.** As stated in the passage, the United States was forced to "pass from thoughtless, careless, heedless, reckless adolescence to grave and reflecting manhood." This best supports answer choice B. Although the passage discusses the Civil War, it discusses the maturing effects the war had on the United States rather than the harmful effects; therefore, answer choice A is incorrect. Answer choices C, D, and E are not supported by information found in the passage.

20. **The best answer is C.** The third paragraph states that the nation has not yet attained "a full and clear understanding of its own national constitution" and goes on to make statements regarding the nations obscured "vision" and "judgment" that is indistinct and indecisive. The nation is described as having human-like qualities. So in this context the "constitution" of the nation must refer to some human-like quality, such as "character," answer choice C. Answer choices A, B, and E do not refer to human-like qualities and are thus incorrect.

21. **The best answer is D.** The author discusses the fact that the United States had not experienced any severe test until "the recent rebellion, to throw it back on itself and compel it to reflect on its own constitution, its own separate existence, individuality, tendencies, and end." This statement indicates that the United States was struggling with internal conflict and revolution. Answer choices A, B, C, and E are not supported by the context of the passage.

22. **The best answer is A.** As stated by the author, "but there remains the important work of dissipating the mists that still linger, of brushing away these wild theories and fancies, and of enabling it to form a clear and intelligent judgment of itself." By indicating that there are "mists that still linger," the author indicated that pre-war sentiments still exist. The other answer choices are not supported by the passage.

23. **The best answer is D.** The passage considers the rebirth of the United States following the Civil War. The concluding sentence of the passage provides an excellent example of the positive tone of the passage: "…the difficulties may be over come, the errors of the past corrected, and the government placed on the right track…" This best supports answer choice D.

24. **The best answer is E.** The necessity of "the help of the people" is emphasized in the second sentence of the final paragraph: "The citizen who can help his countrymen to do this will render them an important service and deserve well of his country…" The next clause of that sentence shows that answer choice A is incorrect. Answer choices B, C, and D can be dismissed for their negativity, which does not reflect the spirit of the passage.

Section 4

1. **The correct answer is D.** To solve this problem, convert $\frac{5}{8}$ and $\frac{2}{3}$ to decimals and compare the possible answer choices. The fraction $\frac{5}{8}$ is equivalent to 0.625, and $\frac{2}{3}$ is equivalent to 0.666, repeating. Thus, the only value that is between the two values is 0.64.

2. **The correct answer is C.** Because Jeff traveled twice as far as Ryan in half the time, Jeff traveled 40 miles in 2 hours. Jeff's average speed is equivalent to 40 miles ÷ 2 hours, or 20 miles per hour.

3. **The correct answer is C.** If GH is a line, then $y + 2x = 180°$ because y and $2x$ are supplementary angles. As shown in the figure, it is also clear that $6x = 180$ because 6 angles of measure x are on one side of line GH (remember, there are 180° in a line). Therefore, $x = \frac{180}{6}$, or 30, making $y + 2x = y + 60 = 180$. Thus, $y = 180 - 60$, or 120°.

4. **The correct answer is C.** If L and N are the centers of their respective circles, line segments LM and MN represent the radii of the circles. You are given that the circumference of the circle with center L is half that of the circle with center N. Circumference is equal to πd, or $\pi(2r)$; thus, the circumference is in direct proportion to the radius. The sum of the radii of LM and MN is 42, and MN is double LM. Therefore, MN is equal to $\frac{2}{3}$ of 42, which is 28, answer choice C.

5. **The correct answer is A.** To solve this problem, find the sum of the percentages in the rows that represent fewer than 15 hours, and then take that percentage of the total number of people surveyed. The total percent of the people surveyed who watch less than 15 hours per week is 25% + 15% + 30%, or 70%. The number of people can be calculated by taking 70% of the total surveyed: (1,500)(0.7) = 1,050 people.

6. **The correct answer is A.** The perimeter of the triangle shown equals the sum of the two legs, both with length x, and the hypotenuse. The hypotenuse can be found using the Pythagorean Theorem ($c^2 = a^2 + b^2$). Because both legs are x, $c^2 = 2x^2$, and $c = x\sqrt{2}$. Thus, the perimeter of the triangle is $x + x + x\sqrt{2}$, or $2x + x\sqrt{2}$. Given that the perimeter is $6 + 3\sqrt{2}$, you know that $6 + 3\sqrt{2} = 2(3) + 3\sqrt{2}$, and $x = 3$.

7. **The correct answer is E.** If a and b are inversely proportional, then $a_1 b_1 = a_2 b_2$. In the case of this problem, $(36)(12) = (48)a$. Solve for a as follows:

$(36)(12) = (48)a$

$432 = 48a$

$9 = a$

8. **The correct answer is B.** Given that $3x + y = 2z$, it follows that $2(3x + y) = 2(2z)$, or $6x + 2y = 4z$. From there, substitute $6x + 2y$ for $4z$ in the equation $-6x + 4z + 2y = 36$, and solve for y as follows:

$-6x + (6x + 2y) + 2y =$

$4y = 36$

$y = 9$

9. **The correct answer is $\frac{1}{3}$ or .333.** To solve this problem, divide the total number of minutes devoted to speeches by the total number of minutes in the ceremony. Because the ceremony took 2 hours, there were $2(60)$, or 120 minutes, in the ceremony. Thus, the fraction comprised of speeches was $\frac{40}{120}$, or $\frac{1}{3}$.

10. **The correct answer is $\frac{7}{32}$, .218, or .219.** To solve this problem, first determine the pattern of the sequence. You will likely need to employ some trial-and-error, but you should also use common sense. The best approach is to decide if 14 is a multiple of 112; when you divide 112 by 14, you get 8, and when you multiply 112 by 8, you get 896. So, the fourth term will be equivalent to 14 divided by 8, or 1.75. Finally, the fifth term will be equivalent to 1.75 divided by 8, or .219.

11. **The correct answer is $\frac{3}{8}$ or .375.** Recall that the area of a rectangle is length times width. According to the figure, the length of the side AD is 4. Thus, the length of the side BC is also 4. The lengths of AB and CD can be calculated by dividing the area by the length of the known sides; $\frac{24}{4} = 6$. Thus, point C has coordinates $(4, 6)$. Because it is known that the graph of $y = ax^2$ passes through C, you can substitute the coordinates into the equation and solve for a, as follows:

$6 = a(4)^2$

$6 = 16a$

$a = \frac{6}{16}$, or $\frac{3}{8}$

12. **The correct answer is 1.** To solve this problem, substitute the number values given in the problem for x and z, as follows:

$xy + z = y + 3z$

$5y + 2 = y + 6$

$4y = 4$

$y = 1$

13. **The correct answer is 29.** To solve this problem, recall that the median is the middle number of a set when the set is arranged in ascending or descending order. In a set of 7 consecutive odd integers, the middle number has 3 numbers before it and 3 numbers after it. To find the largest of the integers in the set, count up from 23: 25, 27, 29. Thus, 29 is the greatest of the 7 integers.

14. **The correct answer is 40.** If the degree measures of the angles of a triangle are in the ratio 2:3:4, then the smallest angle constitutes $\frac{2}{(2 + 3 + 4)}$, or $\frac{2}{9}$, of the sum of the three angles of the triangle. Because all triangles are composed of three angles whose sum is 180°, the degree measure of the smallest angle is $\frac{2}{9}$ of 180°, or 40°.

15. **The correct answer is 30.** To solve this problem, multiply the number of different combinations that can be made when 1 in 3 master electricians is on a team by the number of different combinations that can be formed when 2 of 5 apprentices are on a team. Because you have 3 master electricians and only one is on a team, you can have 3 different combinations of masters. If the 5 apprentices are A, B, C, D, and E, the pairs that can be formed are as follows: AB, AC, AD, AE, BC, BD, BE, CD, CE, and DE, for a total of 10 possible combinations. Thus, the total number of different teams that can be assembled is 3(10), or 30.

16. **The correct answer is 2.** To solve this problem, express the question mathematically, as follows:

$a + 2b$ is equal to 80% of $5b$ can be written as $a + 2b = 0.80(5b)$

To find $\frac{a}{b}$, simplify the equation $a + 2b = 0.80(5b)$ by distributing and combining like terms, as follows:

$a + 2b = 0.80(5b)$

$a + 2b = 4b$

$a = 2b$

$\frac{a}{b} = 2$

17. **The correct answer is 90.** You are given that angle BOE is 30°, which means that its vertical angle COD is also 30°. This means that angle s must equal 60°. In addition, because angle BOE is 30°, angle t must be 150°. The value of $t - s$, or $150 - 60$, is 90.

18. **The correct answer is 0 or 30.** Using the distance formula, the distance, d, between 2 points (x_1, y_1) and (x_2, y_2) is $d^2 = (x_2 - x_1)^2 + (y_2 - y_1)^2$. Substitute the points given in the problem and solve for x, as follows:

$17^2 = (x - 15)^2 + (15 - 7)^2$

$289 = (x - 15)^2 + 64$

$225 = (x - 15)^2$

$(x - 15) = \pm 15$

For $x - 15 = 15$, $x = 30$; for $x - 15 = -15$, $x = 0$.

Section 5

1. **The best answer is E.** The word "than" is followed by a clause referring to the singular subject "Royalist Party"; therefore, the clause should contain the singular pronoun "it," not the plural pronoun "they." Answer choices A, B, C, and D are incorrect because each contains a form of the plural pronoun "they."

2. **The best answer is E.** It is necessary to maintain parallel construction among the verb forms in a sentence. Therefore, "to pack" is correct because it matches "to let." Only answer choice E uses the correct verb forms and expresses the idea clearly and simply.

3. **The best answer is A.** As it is written, this sentence clearly expresses the intended idea that the summer construction has reduced the number of available parking spaces, thereby hurting local downtown shops. Answer choices B, C, D, and E are awkward and wordy and do not effectively convey the main idea of the sentence.

4. **The best answer is E.** Because "government officials" is plural, it is necessary to use the plural possessive pronoun, "their." It is correct to say that people often blame government officials for their lack of leadership.

5. **The best answer is A.** This sentence is best as it is written. It effectively expresses the idea and is free from ambiguity. Answer choices B, C, D, and E are awkward and unclear.

6. **The best answer is B.** Answer choice B appropriately uses the adverb "so" to refer back to the verb phrase "pay annual bonuses to some managers." The other answer choices are not as clear and concise.

7. **The best answer is B.** Based on the context of the sentence, the underlined portion refers to snowshoeing as an activity. The pronoun used to replace the noun "snowshoeing" must agree in number; because "snowshoeing" is a singular noun, the correct pronoun is "it." Answer choice C should be eliminated because the past perfect tense is not appropriate.

8. **The best answer is C.** The context of the sentence indicates that owners should monitor the habits of their dogs. Answer choice C best expresses that the owners need to be mindful of "their dog's" habits, and not their own, with respect to chewing on bones.

9. **The best answer is D.** This is the clearest and most concise of the answer choices. It is not necessary to include "people," "person," or "someone."

10. **The best answer is E.** The verb phrases listed in the sentence must be parallel in form. The remaining verbs "deciding," "preparing," and "creating" are gerunds. Therefore, the verbs in the underlined portion must be "sorting" and "determining." Answer choice E is the only selection that is parallel to the rest of the sentence.

11. **The best answer is D.** The object pronoun "whom" is used correclty after the preposition "of" to refer to a group of people: "teachers."

12. **The best answer is B.** The adjective "elegant" should be replaced with the adverb "elegantly" for this sentence to be correct. An adverb may modify an adjective. In this sentence, the adjective is "decorated."

13. **The best answer is D.** It is incorrect to include the pronoun "they" between the relative pronoun "who" and the verb "contributed."

14. **The best answer is A.** The subject of this sentence, "The university's School of Music," is singular. Therefore, the plural verb form "require" should be changed to the singular verb "requires."

15. **The best answer is C.** The preposition "with" is not correct after the verb "generated." (The prepositions "by" and "from" would be acceptable.) The adverb "although" is appropriate for introducing the contrast within the sentence. The form of the verb "continues" agrees with the singular noun "preserve." The word "increasing" correctly describes how the "amount of foot traffic" is changing.

16. **The best answer is B.** In the sentence the way it is written, the pronoun "their" is ambiguous; it is unclear whether the pronoun refers to the people or to the spiders. Therefore, the pronoun "their" should be replaced with the noun phrase "the spiders'."

17. **The best answer is D.** The progressive verb "attempting" suggests an ongoing action. The context of this sentence requires that all verbs be in present tense and refer to the plural noun "students"; therefore, "attempting to" should be "attempt to." "Whereas" is effective in introducing the direct contrast within the sentence, the possessive pronoun "their" agrees with the plural noun "the students," and "diligently" correctly modifies the verb "work."

18. **The best answer is E.** There are no errors in this sentence. The plural verb "have" is used correctly with the plural subject "studies"; the context of the sentence clearly indicates a singular auto mechanic, so it is correct to say "an auto"; the context of the sentence indicates a future action, so the verb phrase "will make" is correct; it is logical to assume that an auto mechanic will make numerous "repairs," so the plural form of that verb is correct.

19. **The best answer is C.** In this sentence, "has received" should be "have received" because the plural subject of the sentence, "the actors," requires a plural verb. "Thus far" is an appropriate way to refer to the amount of time that has elapsed, "only" correctly indicates to whom the sentence is referring, and "their" matches the plural noun "the actors."

20. **The best answer is D.** The comparative "more" must be followed by the verb "busy." It would also be correct to simply say "busier." "In" is an appropriate preposition to precede "high demand." "In fact" effectively introduces the descriptive information in the rest of the sentence. "Has" agrees with the singular subject of the sentence, "he," or "Professor Hornbuckle," and is also in the correct verb tense; "has never been" implies that the event began at some point in the past, is occurring in the present, and will continue to occur until some point in the future.

21. **The best answer is B.** The phrase "has not lived" is in present tense. This sentence describes events that occurred in the past and requires the simple past tense form: "did not live." The adverb "although" is appropriate for introducing the contrast within the sentence. "Performed" agrees with the verb tense of the sentence, and the phrase "an early age" is correctly used.

22. **The best answer is E.** There are no errors in this sentence. The preposition "though" correctly introduces the contrast that is apparent in the sentence; the possessive "blacksmith's" is correct because the shop belongs to the blacksmith; the past tense verb "continued" matches the past tense verb "was"; and the phrase "every day" is appropriate to the context of the sentence.

23. **The best answer is B.** To maintain parallelism among the verbs in this sentence, the past tense verb "liked" should be changed to the present tense verb "like." The context of the sentence indicates the present tense.

24. **The best answer is C.** Because Angie is one person, the plural pronoun "their" should be changed to the singular pronoun "her." (The cat belongs to Angie, not to Angie and her dog.) In this sentence, the pronoun could simply be omitted.

25. **The best answer is E.** There are no errors in this sentence. "Claimed" agrees with the verb tense of rest of the sentence, and "that" correctly introduces an essential clause of the sentence. "Was" agrees with the singular noun "statement" and is also in the proper verb tense. "Nor" is the correct coordinating conjunction to use with "neither." The pronoun "it" in the phrase "could it be" correctly refers to the suspect's "statement." The phrase also maintains parallelism within the sentence.

26. **The best answer is E.** There are no errors in this sentence. "Often" correctly modifies the verb "praise." The possessive pronoun "their" agrees with the plural noun "horses." A semicolon is appropriate between "power" and "people" because it separates two related clauses. "Power" is an appropriate noun used to describe "horses," and "people" correctly precedes the pronoun "who." The plural noun "reasons" agrees with "strength and power."

27. **The best answer is B.** The word "because" indicates a cause-and-effect relationship. In this sentence, an event will occur in the future as a result of an event that occurs in the present; therefore, the past tense verb "would" should be replaced with the present tense verb "will." "Previously scheduled" begins an interrupting phrase that is appropriate for this sentence. "Between" is an appropriate preposition to use after "choose." The gerund "vying" effectively describes an event that is ongoing, and "for" is an appropriate preposition to follow "vying."

28. **The best answer is A.** The simple subject of this sentence is the singular noun "relationship." Therefore, the plural verb form "are" should be changed to the singular verb form "is."

29. **The best answer is B.** The singular verb form "is" should be changed to the plural verb form "are" to correctly parallel the plural subject "factors."

30. **The best answer is B.** The revision in answer choice B simply and clearly combines the two sentences. There is no ambiguity or awkwardness. Answer choice A is incorrect because it says nothing about the quality of Frost's work, which is stated in sentence 1. Answer choices C, D, and E are awkwardly constructed.

31. **The best answer is A.** The sentence is best as it is written and requires no revision. It follows logically from the topic of the preceding sentence.

32. **The best answer is E.** The phrase "started the beginning" is redundant and not idiomatic. It is better to say "marked the beginning" to clearly indicate that the publication of Frost's book of poetry initiated his success as a writer. Answer choice A is incorrect because it is redundant and includes the plural noun "beginnings." Answer choice B, while it appropriately uses the word "marked," is not idiomatic. Answer choice C is incorrect primarily because it is in the present tense, and answer choice D is incorrect because it is not idiomatic.

33. **The best answer is D.** The primary focus of the second paragraph is Frost's literary beginnings and his acceptance as a legitimate author. Sentence 10 has nothing to do with the topic of the paragraph and should be deleted.

34. **The best answer is A.** The sentence is best as it is written and requires no revision. The adjective "literary" effectively describes Frost's "talent." Answer choice B is incorrect because it replaces "literary" with "literally." Both answer choices C and D create incomplete sentences. Answer choice E is incorrect because it indicates that Frost's talent, not Frost himself, became a great literary success.

35. **The best answer is C.** The third paragraph includes direct quotes from Frost's work "The Road Not Taken." None of the other answer choices is supported by the third paragraph.

Section 6

1. **The best answer is B.** Following a week-long hunger strike, it is likely that Justin would be either "famished" or "starved." Someone in that state might be eating vast quantities of food in a hurried, frantic manner could be labeled a "glutton," which refers to someone who overindulges in food or drink.

2. **The best answer is D.** "Chief," used as an adjective, means "major" or "principal." This best fits the context of the sentence.

3. **The best answer is D.** The word "although" at the beginning of the sentence suggests that Ryan appeared to be one way but actually felt another way. To determine the correct answer, look at the second blank, which is followed by descriptive information. A "daunting venture" would most likely make someone "terrified," and "confident" appropriately contrasts "terrified." Answer choice A does not fit the context of the sentence. Answer choice B could work in this sentence, but "complacent" and "hesitant" are not as effective. Answer choices C and E do not fit the context of the sentence.

4. **The best answer is E.** The phrase "people with varied interests and lifestyles" helps to define the missing word. The context of the sentence indicates that many different types of people gather at the music store. "Eclectic" is an adjective that describes a combination of things (in this case, people) "from a variety of different sources." An "eclectic" group of people would likely include people from many different backgrounds and walks of life.

5. **The best answer is C.** According to the context of the sentence, the noun "misconception" indicates that the information before the colon contradicts the information after the colon. In addition, the phrase "should never be approached…" indicates that the word in the second blank must suggest danger. "Easygoing," which means "calm," and "vicious," which means "violent" or "aggressive," are opposites and fit the context of the sentence.

6. **The best answer is C.** The word "ostracized" means "banished" or "shunned." This might be an unfortunate reaction to Linda's exposure of her company's illegal actions. The other answer choices all indicate a positive reaction, which does not fit the context of the sentence.

7. **The best answer is D.** The phrase "on the contrary" indicates that a contrast exists between the word in the blank and the information following the semicolon. Because the information following the semicolon states that aberrant results can be credited, the word that best fits in the blank should be an antonym of "credited." "Discount" means to "disregard" or "underestimate the value of" of something. Therefore, "discounted" is the best choice.

8. **The best answer is A.** "Hegemony" means "domination over others." A company with a large market share is said to exert dominance in the market. The other answer choices do not fit the context of the sentence.

9. **The best answer is B.** Both passages focus on a particular author's writing and how it was affected by the author's marriage. While answer choice A correctly notes the difference in the quality of the marriages, it is not correct because the passages do not go into detail about the relationships.

10. **The best answer is E.** The focus of Passage 2 is the tragedy of Sylvia Plath's life story, which includes her failed marriage and subsequent suicide.

11. **The best answer is D.** The passage states that the title of the book of poetry in question "reflects the love and devotion of Robert Browning for his wife." Such language eliminates choices A and B and makes C and E quite unlikely to be correct. The poems would best be characterized as "emotional."

12. **The best answer is A.** Passage 1 mentions the "beauty" of poetry inspired by a successful marriage. Passage 2 describes a sorrowful life that begot a "tragic story." This best supports answer choice A.

13. **The best answer is B.** Passage 1 states "Pluto's orbital path is irregular," and Passage 2 cites "the eccentricity of Pluto's orbit," suggesting that both authors would agree that Pluto has an irregular orbit around the sun. The other answer choices are not supported by the passages.

14. **The best answer is C.** The passage states that "...comet nuclei are stable at the outer reaches of the solar system until interaction with planetary gravitation—usually Pluto's—causes a comet to enter a highly elliptical orbit around the sun. As a comet nears the sun, a tail becomes visible as light reflects off the trail of ice particles and dust it leaves behind." The lines indicated detail the formation of comets and their behavior in the solar system.

15. **The best answer is D.** One definition of the word "circuit" is "revolution about a point," which describes the cyclic movement of a celestial body relative to the sun. This is clearly supported by the passage.

16. **The best answer is C.** According to Passage 1, "With a diameter of over 1,400 miles, Pluto is almost 1,000 times bigger than an average comet and more than twice the size of 1 Ceres, the largest of the asteroids, which comprises nearly a third of the total mass of the asteroid belt." If another non-planetary object were found to be near Pluto's size, then the conclusion that Pluto's size makes it a planet would be severely undermined. None of the other answer choices is supported by the passage.

17. **The best answer is D.** A clue to the answer of this question is the qualifying word "Although" in line 46, which serves to inform the reader that the author foresees some evidence for a counterargument. Furthermore, an oblong, or elliptical, orbit is declared a characteristic feature of comets, not of planets. The other answer choices are specifically mentioned in Passage 1 as evidence of Pluto's planetary status.

18. **The best answer is E.** Passage 2 states that "Many facts about Pluto suggest that it is actually a member of the Kuiper Belt, a group of substantial comets at the edge of the solar system, and not a planet." A tail of particulate matter is mentioned in Passage 1 as a phenomenon of comets: "As one nears the sun, a tail becomes visible..." Therefore, if detailed imagery revealed that Pluto had a tail, the view detailed in Passage 2 would be supported.

19. **The best answer is A.** Both passages raise the issue of Pluto's size: if it is indeed big enough to be a planet, too big to be a comet, or the right size for either. The first sentence of Passage 2 implies that there might be reason to think that Pluto is not a planet but a member of a group of comets. The word "substantial" helps to support this claim, as it relates to the large size of Pluto, because if the other relevant comets were close in size to Pluto, Pluto's inclusion in the Kuiper Belt is more plausible.

20. **The best answer is D.** Answer choices A and B are incorrect because the author does not support and makes no claim to the future preservation of Pluto's planetary status. Answer choice C is incorrect because the author concentrates on contradictory science and not what originally supported Pluto being called a planet. Because the author is strong in his opinion and supports it with thorough evidence, answer choice E should be eliminated. Only answer choice D is supported by the tone of Passage 2.

21. **The best answer is E.** The author makes no qualifications about the meaning of the word "planet." Therefore, you can eliminate answer choices A, C, and D because they include Roman numeral I. Bad science is cited in the third paragraph ("Astronomers…distinction") as a reason for Pluto being a planet. "Ignorance of modern discoveries" includes the little-known facts of "trans-Neptunian object (TNO) 2003 UB_{313}," which the author feels contradict the claim of Pluto being a planet. Both Roman numeral II and Roman numeral III are mentioned in Passage 2.

22. **The best answer is D.** As the author of Passage 2 states, 2003 UB_{313} "has similar composition and orbit" to Pluto. Therefore, it can be inferred that the author believes the two are closely related. If research found a discrepancy between the formation of 2003 UB_{313} and the rest of the proper planets, then the case for including Pluto among the planets would be weakened. The other answer choices are not supported by the passage.

23. **The best answer is A.** The passages are written to be persuasive and hold firm to their arguments. (The word "unflinching" means "determined" or "unwavering.") The other answer choices do not accurately reflect the tone of the passages.

24. **The best answer is C.** The only point on which the two passages agree is the fact that Pluto orbits the sun more like a comet than a planet. The other answer choices are either points of contention between the authors or are beyond the scope of the passages.

Section 7

1. **The correct answer is D.** Of the answer choices, only 6 and -6 are even. Of those two possibilities, only -6 is both less than 5 and negative. Therefore, -6 will be in all three sets.

2. **The correct answer is B.** To solve this problem, first subtract 4 from both sides of the equation to get $\sqrt{k} = 9$. Squaring both sides yields $k = 81$.

3. **The correct answer is C.** To solve this problem, divide the number of those in favor of constructing a new high school by the total number polled:

   $44 \div (44 + 58 + 8) = \frac{44}{110}$, or $\frac{2}{5}$

4. **The correct answer is D.** As shown in the figure, the center angles are vertical angles, meaning they have equal measures. Thus, $75° + 35° = r° + s° = 110°$.

5. **The correct answer is D.** To solve this problem, find the 2-year interval in which there is the greatest difference in the height of the bars on the graph. On the graph, this occurs between years 1996 and 1998.

6. **The correct answer is A.** As shown in the graph, the possible values of k for which f(k) = 2 are as follows: $k = 1.5$ and $-1.5 \leq k \leq -1$. However, only 1.5 is among the answer choices.

7. **The correct answer is E.** To solve this problem, it might be helpful to make a list of the powers of 2: $2^1 = 2$, $2^2 = 4$, $2^3 = 8$, $2^4 = 16$, $2^5 = 32$, and so on. Select values from this list and multiply them, starting with the values that make the most sense. For example, you know that $2 \times 4 \times 8$ is less than 512, so try $4 \times 8 \times 16$, which does equal 512. Now, add those same terms: $4 + 8 + 16 = 28$.

8. **The correct answer is C.** The best approach to answering this question is to draw a diagram. Below is a drawing of the circle with center (-3, 2). One endpoint of a diameter is shown at (-3, -4). Along this diameter, it is clear that the radius of the circle is 6, and 6 units above the center along the diameter is the point (-3, 8).

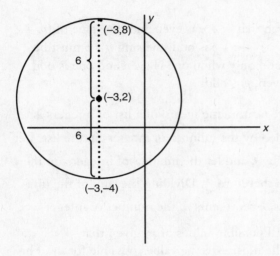

9. **The correct answer is A.** A line perpendicular to the x-axis is parallel to the y-axis, and thus is vertical. Vertical lines are sets of points that share the same x-coordinates, and the equations are in the form $x = \dots$. Because this line passes through the point (-4, 7), its equation is $x = -4$. Refer to the drawing below to help you visualize the answer to this problem.

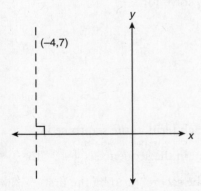

10. **The correct answer is E.** The volume, v, of a circular cylinder is given by the formula $V = \pi r^2 h$, where r is the radius and h is the height. If a right circular cylinder has a volume of v with a radius of 2 and a height of 6, then a cylinder with a radius of 4 and a height of 6 has a radius twice that of the smaller cylinder. From the formula, the volume of the cylinder is proportional to the square of the radius. So the volume of the larger cylinder is $2^2 = 4$ times larger than that of the smaller cylinder; it has a volume of $4v$.

11. **The correct answer is B.** Given that 30% of x equals 60% of y, $.3x = 0.6y$. To express y in terms of x, solve for y by dividing by 0.6. The result is $y = 0.5x$, which is the same as saying that $y = 50\%$ of x.

12. **The correct answer is D.** You are given that $m + n$ is even and the value of $(m + n)^2$ is also even. However, because $(m + n)^2 + n + p$ is odd, the sum $n + p$ must be odd. A sum of two positive integers is odd only when one is even and one is odd. Therefore, it must be true that if n is even, p is odd.

13. **The correct answer is C.** The average (arithmetic mean) of a list of integers is defined as the sum of the integers divided by the number of integers in the list. Let the sum of the integers be represented by s, and let the number of integers on the list be represented by n. The average is therefore $\frac{s}{n}$. Dividing the sum of the integers by the average yields $\frac{s}{\frac{s}{n}} = n$. Thus, k represents n, the number of integers.

14. **The correct answer is E.** The set of all possible values of xy given that $-3 < x < 5$ and $0 < y < 12$ is the interval between the most extreme values possible for xy. The lower bound for xy is $(-3)(12)$, or -36. The upper bound is given by $(5)(12)$, or 60. Thus, the set of possible values of xy is $-36 < xy < 60$.

15. **The correct answer is C.** To solve this problem, you need to recognize that the slope of the line is equal to 4. In the standard equation for a line, $y = mx + b$, m is equivalent to the slope. The slope is equal to the change in y-values over the change in x-values; set up the following equation to solve for t:

$$\text{slope} = \frac{(s + t) - s}{(r + 2) - r}$$

$$4 = \frac{t}{2}$$

$$8 = t$$

16. **The correct answer is E.** If the first term is t and each term in the sequence is 2 greater than $\frac{1}{4}$ of the preceding term, the second term in the sequence is $\frac{t}{4} + 2$. To find the ratio of the second term to the first, divide the second term by the first term to get $\frac{(\frac{t}{4} + 2)}{t}$. To simplify, multiply the top and bottom of the fraction by 4 to get $\frac{(\frac{4t}{4} + 4 \times 2)}{4t}$, which equals $\frac{(t + 8)}{4t}$.

Section 8

1. **The answer is E.** In this sentence, the phrase "activities have been suspended" defines the missing word. An "abeyance" is a "suspension," so answer choice E is correct. "Contempt" has several meanings that fit the context of the first portion of the sentence, but none of the meanings relate to "suspension," so answer choice A is incorrect. Likewise, "obscurity," "contrast," and "awe" do not have meanings that relate to "suspension," so answer choices B, C, and D are incorrect.

2. **The best answer is C.** The context of the sentence suggests that the production and sale of alcohol was illegal during prohibition. The word "proscribed" means "condemned or outlawed" and conveys that the production and sale of alcohol would not have been legal.

3. **The best answer is D.** The word "serene" means "calm," while "chaos" refers to a condition of "great disorder" and is the only answer choice that reflects the contrast between living in a small town and living in a large city.

4. **The best answer is C.** "Belies" means "presents an appearance not in agreement with." The word "sea" is generally reserved for saltwater bodies, so the name might lead to some confusion about the actual characteristics of the Caspian Sea. The other answer choices do not fit the context of the sentence.

5. **The answer is D.** The context of the sentence indicates a contrast between the words that best fit the two blanks. On one hand, Jill's performances have been criticized for being a certain way; on the other hand, her advocates have been "touting," or "publicly promoting," Jill for a certain quality. "Banal" means "boring or ordinary," so a "banal" performance would not be expected from a person with great "imagination." "Ambiguous" means "uncertain," "feckless" means "incompetent," and "placid" means "serene," so answer choices A, C and E are incorrect. Answer choice B is incorrect because the words do not contradict each other, and "fidelity" does not fit within the context of the sentence.

6. **The best answer is A.** Because the movie mogul is known for his charitable policies, it can be assumed that he is generous. The word "magnanimous" means "noble or generous" and is the best choice. The other answer choices do not fit the context of the sentence.

7. **The best answer is B.** According to the first sentence, the passage is written from the point of view of someone who learned of Porter by reading the poetry of Porter's wife. This eliminates answer choices A and E. Because the whole passage provides a rather detailed account of Porter's life, answer choice C can be dismissed. Answer choice D is not supported by the passage, which ignores personal details about the narrator.

8. **The best answer is D.** A "profile" is a description of a particular person, much like a "biography." "Deferential" means "showing respect," which is supported by the opinion expressed in the final paragraph on the passage, especially the last sentence: "This remarkable insightful, articulate, creative individual should be fixed in public consciousness…" None of the other choices accurately describe the passage.

9. **The best answer is D.** Because "brush" is followed by "the international artist and critic Fairfield Porter," only answer choices B and D make sense. The narrator never admits to meeting the man, especially not to "clash" with him, so answer choice B is wrong.

10. **The best answer is C.** The passage states that, "…by being surrounded by artists, his true talent was in critiquing others' work." This best supports answer choice C.

11. **The best answer is E.** The paragraph mentions Porter's enrollment in an art history program, as well as his study under an archaeologist and a photographer, supporting the claim he was "involved in varied aspects of art." Although the passage indicates that Porter did attend a prestigious university, this is not relevant to a discussion of Porter's "broadening" scholarship, so answer choice C is incorrect. The other answer choices are not supported by the passage.

12. **The best answer is D.** The last sentence of the fourth paragraph and the beginning of the fifth paragraph support the conclusion that Porter's career was bolstered by his notable first acclamation of a now-famous artist, de Kooning. The other answer choices are not supported by the passage.

13. **The best answer is C.** Art is subject to categorization, which is sorting based on some kind of common set of features. The word "framework" refers to "a supporting structure." The narrator asserts that Porter found fault with criticism that he felt was pigeonholing artwork. The other answer choices are not supported by the passage.

14. **The best answer is A.** The first sentence of the sixth paragraph states that Porter's painting is "just as important to understanding [his] contributions to the world of art" as Porter's career in criticism described in preceding paragraphs. This best supports answer choice A.

15. **The best answer is B.** Art that juxtaposes, or blends, "personal, emotional, and representative" treatment of the subject with "boldly colorful, expressive, and generally abstract" aesthetics could be called "stylized realism." The "realism" comes into play with the "personal, emotional, and representative" treatment, while the terms "boldly colorful, expressive, and generally abstract" reflect a stylized representation. This best supports answer choice B.

16. **The best answer is E.** The passage declares that Porter drew "on his vast knowledge of art history, and especially the styles of French Intimism" in his painting. These are subjects Porter explored as an art critic, which directly influenced his painting. The other answer choices are not supported by the passage.

17. **The best answer is B.** The passage has a continuously positive tone, so the bittersweet detail about the artist's death preserves the uplifting tenor of the piece. Answer choices A and C are wrong because no further detail is given about Porter's death. Answer choices D and E are irrelevant and would distract from the purpose of the passage.

18. **The best answer is D.** Groups of people who share a common interest or vocation can be called "circles," as in "legal circles," which could be a group of lawyers, judges, and interested journalists, for example. The art circle referenced in the passage might contain artists, critics, museum curators, as well as admirers, patrons, and other benefactors of the arts. The other answer choices are synonyms of "circles" but do not fit the context of the passage.

19. **The best answer is C.** The last paragraph asserts, "It is sad to say that…Porter is still virtually unknown outside of art circles." This suggests that Porter's acclaim, or success, is limited to certain groups of people. The other answer choices are not supported by the passage.

Section 9

1. **The best answer is D.** Use the phrase "For more than 30 years" to effectively and concisely express the intended idea of the sentence. The other answer choices are wordy and awkward.

2. **The best answer is B.** Answer choice B effectively indicates that the Uruguayan soccer team had four victories and no defeats. Answer choices A, C, D, and E are awkwardly constructed and do not effectively convey the intended meaning of the sentence.

3. **The best answer is A.** The sentence is best as written. Answer choice B creates an incomplete sentence. Answer choices C, D, and E suggest that Jessica visited "Italian," which does not make sense.

4. **The best answer is A.** It is clear and concise. The other answer choices are awkward. Answer choices B and D are grammatical but wordy. Answer choices C and E do not use the correct form of "include."

5. **The best answer is A.** The sentence is best as written. "For" is an appropriate preposition to follow "rate." Any mention of "rising" is redundant with "escalating," so answer choices B, D, and E may be eliminated. Answer choice D may be eliminated because the singular verb form "is" does not agree with the plural simple subject "rates."

6. **The best answer is E.** As it is written, the elements in the series are poorly separated. In addition, the phrase "in the late 1400s" indicates that the sentence refers to an event that occurred in the past, which makes the correct verb form "began," not "begins." Answer choice E is the only selection that clearly separates the elements of the list with commas, maintains parallel construction of the elements in the list, and uses the correct verb tense.

7. **The best answer is C.** It is idiomatic to "credit" someone "with having" done something rather than "as having" done something. Therefore, answer choice C is the best answer.

8. **The best answer is A.** This sentence is best as it is written. It clearly conveys the intended idea and is grammatically correct. The other answer choices are awkward, wordy, or contain errors in grammar or punctuation.

9. **The best answer is D.** This sentence includes two independent but related clauses. The best way to separate these clauses is with a semicolon. Only answer choice D effectively uses a semicolon to separate two independent clauses.

10. **The best answer is C.** The sentence as it is written incorrectly uses the verb "enacting;" the correct verb form to use in this sentence is the infinitive "enact." Answer choice D is incorrect because, although it uses the correct verb, it is awkwardly constructed.

11. **The best answer is C.** The use of the preposition "between" requires the conjunction "and" rather than the conjunction "with." Answer choice C corrects this error without changing the rest of the sentence.

12. **The best answer is A.** The sentence is best as written. Answer choices B and C are incorrect because they suggest that the fact that the bumblebee bat is only 1 or 2 inches long is the reason that it is a mammal. Of the remaining answer choices, only answer choice A clearly and concisely indicates the contradictory nature of the bumblebee bat.

13. **The best answer is D.** The phrase "the highest price ever paid for one of his paintings" is not essential to the meaning of the sentence. Therefore, it should be set off with the word "which." Answer choice B correctly uses "which" but incorrectly uses the gerund "being." The other answer choices are wordy and awkward.

14. **The best answer is E.** The most clear and direct way to express the idea in the sentence is to simply say that the "Navy sometimes uses trained dolphins to conduct dangerous underwater tasks." The sentence as it is written suggests that the U.S. Navy, not the dolphins, can be trained. Answer choice B is incorrect for the same reason. Answer choice C is incorrect because it indicates that the training of dolphins, and not the dolphins themselves, is used to conduct dangerous underwater tasks. Answer choice D is incorrect because you must use a comma before "which" to set off a non-essential clause; the fact that trained dolphins are used to conduct dangerous underwater tasks is essential to the sentence.

12

Practice Test 4 with Answers and Explanations

There are nine separate sections on this simulated test, including:

- ▶ One 25-minute Essay
- ▶ Five other 25-minute Verbal and Math Sections
- ▶ Two 20-minute Verbal and Math Sections
- ▶ One 10-minute Verbal Section

Work on only one section at a time and make every attempt to complete each section in the time allowed for that particular section. Carefully mark only one answer on your answer sheet for each question. Remember that you can and should write on the test itself to help you to correctly answer the questions.

Tear out pages 430–435 before you begin the test.

Begin your essay on this page. If you need more space, continue on the next page. Do not write outside of the essay box.

Start with number 1 for each new section. If a section has fewer questions than answer spaces, leave the extra answer spaces blank. Be sure to erase any errors or stray marks completely.

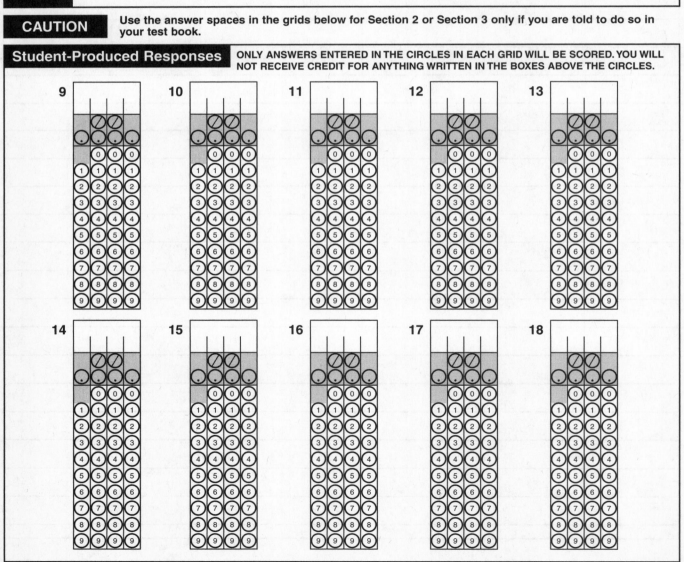

SECTION 2

1 Ⓐ Ⓑ Ⓒ Ⓓ Ⓔ   11 Ⓐ Ⓑ Ⓒ Ⓓ Ⓔ   21 Ⓐ Ⓑ Ⓒ Ⓓ Ⓔ   31 Ⓐ Ⓑ Ⓒ Ⓓ Ⓔ
2 Ⓐ Ⓑ Ⓒ Ⓓ Ⓔ   12 Ⓐ Ⓑ Ⓒ Ⓓ Ⓔ   22 Ⓐ Ⓑ Ⓒ Ⓓ Ⓔ   32 Ⓐ Ⓑ Ⓒ Ⓓ Ⓔ
3 Ⓐ Ⓑ Ⓒ Ⓓ Ⓔ   13 Ⓐ Ⓑ Ⓒ Ⓓ Ⓔ   23 Ⓐ Ⓑ Ⓒ Ⓓ Ⓔ   33 Ⓐ Ⓑ Ⓒ Ⓓ Ⓔ
4 Ⓐ Ⓑ Ⓒ Ⓓ Ⓔ   14 Ⓐ Ⓑ Ⓒ Ⓓ Ⓔ   24 Ⓐ Ⓑ Ⓒ Ⓓ Ⓔ   34 Ⓐ Ⓑ Ⓒ Ⓓ Ⓔ
5 Ⓐ Ⓑ Ⓒ Ⓓ Ⓔ   15 Ⓐ Ⓑ Ⓒ Ⓓ Ⓔ   25 Ⓐ Ⓑ Ⓒ Ⓓ Ⓔ   35 Ⓐ Ⓑ Ⓒ Ⓓ Ⓔ
6 Ⓐ Ⓑ Ⓒ Ⓓ Ⓔ   16 Ⓐ Ⓑ Ⓒ Ⓓ Ⓔ   26 Ⓐ Ⓑ Ⓒ Ⓓ Ⓔ   36 Ⓐ Ⓑ Ⓒ Ⓓ Ⓔ
7 Ⓐ Ⓑ Ⓒ Ⓓ Ⓔ   17 Ⓐ Ⓑ Ⓒ Ⓓ Ⓔ   27 Ⓐ Ⓑ Ⓒ Ⓓ Ⓔ   37 Ⓐ Ⓑ Ⓒ Ⓓ Ⓔ
8 Ⓐ Ⓑ Ⓒ Ⓓ Ⓔ   18 Ⓐ Ⓑ Ⓒ Ⓓ Ⓔ   28 Ⓐ Ⓑ Ⓒ Ⓓ Ⓔ   38 Ⓐ Ⓑ Ⓒ Ⓓ Ⓔ
9 Ⓐ Ⓑ Ⓒ Ⓓ Ⓔ   19 Ⓐ Ⓑ Ⓒ Ⓓ Ⓔ   29 Ⓐ Ⓑ Ⓒ Ⓓ Ⓔ   39 Ⓐ Ⓑ Ⓒ Ⓓ Ⓔ
10 Ⓐ Ⓑ Ⓒ Ⓓ Ⓔ   20 Ⓐ Ⓑ Ⓒ Ⓓ Ⓔ   30 Ⓐ Ⓑ Ⓒ Ⓓ Ⓔ   40 Ⓐ Ⓑ Ⓒ Ⓓ Ⓔ

SECTION 3

1 Ⓐ Ⓑ Ⓒ Ⓓ Ⓔ   11 Ⓐ Ⓑ Ⓒ Ⓓ Ⓔ   21 Ⓐ Ⓑ Ⓒ Ⓓ Ⓔ   31 Ⓐ Ⓑ Ⓒ Ⓓ Ⓔ
2 Ⓐ Ⓑ Ⓒ Ⓓ Ⓔ   12 Ⓐ Ⓑ Ⓒ Ⓓ Ⓔ   22 Ⓐ Ⓑ Ⓒ Ⓓ Ⓔ   32 Ⓐ Ⓑ Ⓒ Ⓓ Ⓔ
3 Ⓐ Ⓑ Ⓒ Ⓓ Ⓔ   13 Ⓐ Ⓑ Ⓒ Ⓓ Ⓔ   23 Ⓐ Ⓑ Ⓒ Ⓓ Ⓔ   33 Ⓐ Ⓑ Ⓒ Ⓓ Ⓔ
4 Ⓐ Ⓑ Ⓒ Ⓓ Ⓔ   14 Ⓐ Ⓑ Ⓒ Ⓓ Ⓔ   24 Ⓐ Ⓑ Ⓒ Ⓓ Ⓔ   34 Ⓐ Ⓑ Ⓒ Ⓓ Ⓔ
5 Ⓐ Ⓑ Ⓒ Ⓓ Ⓔ   15 Ⓐ Ⓑ Ⓒ Ⓓ Ⓔ   25 Ⓐ Ⓑ Ⓒ Ⓓ Ⓔ   35 Ⓐ Ⓑ Ⓒ Ⓓ Ⓔ
6 Ⓐ Ⓑ Ⓒ Ⓓ Ⓔ   16 Ⓐ Ⓑ Ⓒ Ⓓ Ⓔ   26 Ⓐ Ⓑ Ⓒ Ⓓ Ⓔ   36 Ⓐ Ⓑ Ⓒ Ⓓ Ⓔ
7 Ⓐ Ⓑ Ⓒ Ⓓ Ⓔ   17 Ⓐ Ⓑ Ⓒ Ⓓ Ⓔ   27 Ⓐ Ⓑ Ⓒ Ⓓ Ⓔ   37 Ⓐ Ⓑ Ⓒ Ⓓ Ⓔ
8 Ⓐ Ⓑ Ⓒ Ⓓ Ⓔ   18 Ⓐ Ⓑ Ⓒ Ⓓ Ⓔ   28 Ⓐ Ⓑ Ⓒ Ⓓ Ⓔ   38 Ⓐ Ⓑ Ⓒ Ⓓ Ⓔ
9 Ⓐ Ⓑ Ⓒ Ⓓ Ⓔ   19 Ⓐ Ⓑ Ⓒ Ⓓ Ⓔ   29 Ⓐ Ⓑ Ⓒ Ⓓ Ⓔ   39 Ⓐ Ⓑ Ⓒ Ⓓ Ⓔ
10 Ⓐ Ⓑ Ⓒ Ⓓ Ⓔ   20 Ⓐ Ⓑ Ⓒ Ⓓ Ⓔ   30 Ⓐ Ⓑ Ⓒ Ⓓ Ⓔ   40 Ⓐ Ⓑ Ⓒ Ⓓ Ⓔ

CAUTION Use the answer spaces in the grids below for Section 2 or Section 3 only if you are told to do so in your test book.

Student-Produced Responses ONLY ANSWERS ENTERED IN THE CIRCLES IN EACH GRID WILL BE SCORED. YOU WILL NOT RECEIVE CREDIT FOR ANYTHING WRITTEN IN THE BOXES ABOVE THE CIRCLES.

Start with number 1 for each new section. If a section has fewer questions than answer spaces, leave the extra answer spaces blank. Be sure to erase any errors or stray marks completely.

SECTION 4

1 Ⓐ Ⓑ Ⓒ Ⓓ Ⓔ	11 Ⓐ Ⓑ Ⓒ Ⓓ Ⓔ	21 Ⓐ Ⓑ Ⓒ Ⓓ Ⓔ	31 Ⓐ Ⓑ Ⓒ Ⓓ Ⓔ
2 Ⓐ Ⓑ Ⓒ Ⓓ Ⓔ	12 Ⓐ Ⓑ Ⓒ Ⓓ Ⓔ	22 Ⓐ Ⓑ Ⓒ Ⓓ Ⓔ	32 Ⓐ Ⓑ Ⓒ Ⓓ Ⓔ
3 Ⓐ Ⓑ Ⓒ Ⓓ Ⓔ	13 Ⓐ Ⓑ Ⓒ Ⓓ Ⓔ	23 Ⓐ Ⓑ Ⓒ Ⓓ Ⓔ	33 Ⓐ Ⓑ Ⓒ Ⓓ Ⓔ
4 Ⓐ Ⓑ Ⓒ Ⓓ Ⓔ	14 Ⓐ Ⓑ Ⓒ Ⓓ Ⓔ	24 Ⓐ Ⓑ Ⓒ Ⓓ Ⓔ	34 Ⓐ Ⓑ Ⓒ Ⓓ Ⓔ
5 Ⓐ Ⓑ Ⓒ Ⓓ Ⓔ	15 Ⓐ Ⓑ Ⓒ Ⓓ Ⓔ	25 Ⓐ Ⓑ Ⓒ Ⓓ Ⓔ	35 Ⓐ Ⓑ Ⓒ Ⓓ Ⓔ
6 Ⓐ Ⓑ Ⓒ Ⓓ Ⓔ	16 Ⓐ Ⓑ Ⓒ Ⓓ Ⓔ	26 Ⓐ Ⓑ Ⓒ Ⓓ Ⓔ	36 Ⓐ Ⓑ Ⓒ Ⓓ Ⓔ
7 Ⓐ Ⓑ Ⓒ Ⓓ Ⓔ	17 Ⓐ Ⓑ Ⓒ Ⓓ Ⓔ	27 Ⓐ Ⓑ Ⓒ Ⓓ Ⓔ	37 Ⓐ Ⓑ Ⓒ Ⓓ Ⓔ
8 Ⓐ Ⓑ Ⓒ Ⓓ Ⓔ	18 Ⓐ Ⓑ Ⓒ Ⓓ Ⓔ	28 Ⓐ Ⓑ Ⓒ Ⓓ Ⓔ	38 Ⓐ Ⓑ Ⓒ Ⓓ Ⓔ
9 Ⓐ Ⓑ Ⓒ Ⓓ Ⓔ	19 Ⓐ Ⓑ Ⓒ Ⓓ Ⓔ	29 Ⓐ Ⓑ Ⓒ Ⓓ Ⓔ	39 Ⓐ Ⓑ Ⓒ Ⓓ Ⓔ
10 Ⓐ Ⓑ Ⓒ Ⓓ Ⓔ	20 Ⓐ Ⓑ Ⓒ Ⓓ Ⓔ	30 Ⓐ Ⓑ Ⓒ Ⓓ Ⓔ	40 Ⓐ Ⓑ Ⓒ Ⓓ Ⓔ

SECTION 5

1 Ⓐ Ⓑ Ⓒ Ⓓ Ⓔ	11 Ⓐ Ⓑ Ⓒ Ⓓ Ⓔ	21 Ⓐ Ⓑ Ⓒ Ⓓ Ⓔ	31 Ⓐ Ⓑ Ⓒ Ⓓ Ⓔ
2 Ⓐ Ⓑ Ⓒ Ⓓ Ⓔ	12 Ⓐ Ⓑ Ⓒ Ⓓ Ⓔ	22 Ⓐ Ⓑ Ⓒ Ⓓ Ⓔ	32 Ⓐ Ⓑ Ⓒ Ⓓ Ⓔ
3 Ⓐ Ⓑ Ⓒ Ⓓ Ⓔ	13 Ⓐ Ⓑ Ⓒ Ⓓ Ⓔ	23 Ⓐ Ⓑ Ⓒ Ⓓ Ⓔ	33 Ⓐ Ⓑ Ⓒ Ⓓ Ⓔ
4 Ⓐ Ⓑ Ⓒ Ⓓ Ⓔ	14 Ⓐ Ⓑ Ⓒ Ⓓ Ⓔ	24 Ⓐ Ⓑ Ⓒ Ⓓ Ⓔ	34 Ⓐ Ⓑ Ⓒ Ⓓ Ⓔ
5 Ⓐ Ⓑ Ⓒ Ⓓ Ⓔ	15 Ⓐ Ⓑ Ⓒ Ⓓ Ⓔ	25 Ⓐ Ⓑ Ⓒ Ⓓ Ⓔ	35 Ⓐ Ⓑ Ⓒ Ⓓ Ⓔ
6 Ⓐ Ⓑ Ⓒ Ⓓ Ⓔ	16 Ⓐ Ⓑ Ⓒ Ⓓ Ⓔ	26 Ⓐ Ⓑ Ⓒ Ⓓ Ⓔ	36 Ⓐ Ⓑ Ⓒ Ⓓ Ⓔ
7 Ⓐ Ⓑ Ⓒ Ⓓ Ⓔ	17 Ⓐ Ⓑ Ⓒ Ⓓ Ⓔ	27 Ⓐ Ⓑ Ⓒ Ⓓ Ⓔ	37 Ⓐ Ⓑ Ⓒ Ⓓ Ⓔ
8 Ⓐ Ⓑ Ⓒ Ⓓ Ⓔ	18 Ⓐ Ⓑ Ⓒ Ⓓ Ⓔ	28 Ⓐ Ⓑ Ⓒ Ⓓ Ⓔ	38 Ⓐ Ⓑ Ⓒ Ⓓ Ⓔ
9 Ⓐ Ⓑ Ⓒ Ⓓ Ⓔ	19 Ⓐ Ⓑ Ⓒ Ⓓ Ⓔ	29 Ⓐ Ⓑ Ⓒ Ⓓ Ⓔ	39 Ⓐ Ⓑ Ⓒ Ⓓ Ⓔ
10 Ⓐ Ⓑ Ⓒ Ⓓ Ⓔ	20 Ⓐ Ⓑ Ⓒ Ⓓ Ⓔ	30 Ⓐ Ⓑ Ⓒ Ⓓ Ⓔ	40 Ⓐ Ⓑ Ⓒ Ⓓ Ⓔ

CAUTION Use the answer spaces in the grids below for Section 4 or Section 5 only if you are told to do so in your test book.

Student-Produced Responses ONLY ANSWERS ENTERED IN THE CIRCLES IN EACH GRID WILL BE SCORED. YOU WILL NOT RECEIVE CREDIT FOR ANYTHING WRITTEN IN THE BOXES ABOVE THE CIRCLES.

9   10   11   12   13

14   15   16   17   18

Start with number 1 for each new section. If a section has fewer questions than answer spaces, leave the extra answer spaces blank. Be sure to erase any errors or stray marks completely.

SECTION 6

1 Ⓐ Ⓑ Ⓒ Ⓓ Ⓔ	11 Ⓐ Ⓑ Ⓒ Ⓓ Ⓔ	21 Ⓐ Ⓑ Ⓒ Ⓓ Ⓔ	31 Ⓐ Ⓑ Ⓒ Ⓓ Ⓔ
2 Ⓐ Ⓑ Ⓒ Ⓓ Ⓔ	12 Ⓐ Ⓑ Ⓒ Ⓓ Ⓔ	22 Ⓐ Ⓑ Ⓒ Ⓓ Ⓔ	32 Ⓐ Ⓑ Ⓒ Ⓓ Ⓔ
3 Ⓐ Ⓑ Ⓒ Ⓓ Ⓔ	13 Ⓐ Ⓑ Ⓒ Ⓓ Ⓔ	23 Ⓐ Ⓑ Ⓒ Ⓓ Ⓔ	33 Ⓐ Ⓑ Ⓒ Ⓓ Ⓔ
4 Ⓐ Ⓑ Ⓒ Ⓓ Ⓔ	14 Ⓐ Ⓑ Ⓒ Ⓓ Ⓔ	24 Ⓐ Ⓑ Ⓒ Ⓓ Ⓔ	34 Ⓐ Ⓑ Ⓒ Ⓓ Ⓔ
5 Ⓐ Ⓑ Ⓒ Ⓓ Ⓔ	15 Ⓐ Ⓑ Ⓒ Ⓓ Ⓔ	25 Ⓐ Ⓑ Ⓒ Ⓓ Ⓔ	35 Ⓐ Ⓑ Ⓒ Ⓓ Ⓔ
6 Ⓐ Ⓑ Ⓒ Ⓓ Ⓔ	16 Ⓐ Ⓑ Ⓒ Ⓓ Ⓔ	26 Ⓐ Ⓑ Ⓒ Ⓓ Ⓔ	36 Ⓐ Ⓑ Ⓒ Ⓓ Ⓔ
7 Ⓐ Ⓑ Ⓒ Ⓓ Ⓔ	17 Ⓐ Ⓑ Ⓒ Ⓓ Ⓔ	27 Ⓐ Ⓑ Ⓒ Ⓓ Ⓔ	37 Ⓐ Ⓑ Ⓒ Ⓓ Ⓔ
8 Ⓐ Ⓑ Ⓒ Ⓓ Ⓔ	18 Ⓐ Ⓑ Ⓒ Ⓓ Ⓔ	28 Ⓐ Ⓑ Ⓒ Ⓓ Ⓔ	38 Ⓐ Ⓑ Ⓒ Ⓓ Ⓔ
9 Ⓐ Ⓑ Ⓒ Ⓓ Ⓔ	19 Ⓐ Ⓑ Ⓒ Ⓓ Ⓔ	29 Ⓐ Ⓑ Ⓒ Ⓓ Ⓔ	39 Ⓐ Ⓑ Ⓒ Ⓓ Ⓔ
10 Ⓐ Ⓑ Ⓒ Ⓓ Ⓔ	20 Ⓐ Ⓑ Ⓒ Ⓓ Ⓔ	30 Ⓐ Ⓑ Ⓒ Ⓓ Ⓔ	40 Ⓐ Ⓑ Ⓒ Ⓓ Ⓔ

SECTION 7

1 Ⓐ Ⓑ Ⓒ Ⓓ Ⓔ	11 Ⓐ Ⓑ Ⓒ Ⓓ Ⓔ	21 Ⓐ Ⓑ Ⓒ Ⓓ Ⓔ	31 Ⓐ Ⓑ Ⓒ Ⓓ Ⓔ
2 Ⓐ Ⓑ Ⓒ Ⓓ Ⓔ	12 Ⓐ Ⓑ Ⓒ Ⓓ Ⓔ	22 Ⓐ Ⓑ Ⓒ Ⓓ Ⓔ	32 Ⓐ Ⓑ Ⓒ Ⓓ Ⓔ
3 Ⓐ Ⓑ Ⓒ Ⓓ Ⓔ	13 Ⓐ Ⓑ Ⓒ Ⓓ Ⓔ	23 Ⓐ Ⓑ Ⓒ Ⓓ Ⓔ	33 Ⓐ Ⓑ Ⓒ Ⓓ Ⓔ
4 Ⓐ Ⓑ Ⓒ Ⓓ Ⓔ	14 Ⓐ Ⓑ Ⓒ Ⓓ Ⓔ	24 Ⓐ Ⓑ Ⓒ Ⓓ Ⓔ	34 Ⓐ Ⓑ Ⓒ Ⓓ Ⓔ
5 Ⓐ Ⓑ Ⓒ Ⓓ Ⓔ	15 Ⓐ Ⓑ Ⓒ Ⓓ Ⓔ	25 Ⓐ Ⓑ Ⓒ Ⓓ Ⓔ	35 Ⓐ Ⓑ Ⓒ Ⓓ Ⓔ
6 Ⓐ Ⓑ Ⓒ Ⓓ Ⓔ	16 Ⓐ Ⓑ Ⓒ Ⓓ Ⓔ	26 Ⓐ Ⓑ Ⓒ Ⓓ Ⓔ	36 Ⓐ Ⓑ Ⓒ Ⓓ Ⓔ
7 Ⓐ Ⓑ Ⓒ Ⓓ Ⓔ	17 Ⓐ Ⓑ Ⓒ Ⓓ Ⓔ	27 Ⓐ Ⓑ Ⓒ Ⓓ Ⓔ	37 Ⓐ Ⓑ Ⓒ Ⓓ Ⓔ
8 Ⓐ Ⓑ Ⓒ Ⓓ Ⓔ	18 Ⓐ Ⓑ Ⓒ Ⓓ Ⓔ	28 Ⓐ Ⓑ Ⓒ Ⓓ Ⓔ	38 Ⓐ Ⓑ Ⓒ Ⓓ Ⓔ
9 Ⓐ Ⓑ Ⓒ Ⓓ Ⓔ	19 Ⓐ Ⓑ Ⓒ Ⓓ Ⓔ	29 Ⓐ Ⓑ Ⓒ Ⓓ Ⓔ	39 Ⓐ Ⓑ Ⓒ Ⓓ Ⓔ
10 Ⓐ Ⓑ Ⓒ Ⓓ Ⓔ	20 Ⓐ Ⓑ Ⓒ Ⓓ Ⓔ	30 Ⓐ Ⓑ Ⓒ Ⓓ Ⓔ	40 Ⓐ Ⓑ Ⓒ Ⓓ Ⓔ

CAUTION Use the answer spaces in the grids below for Section 6 or Section 7 only if you are told to do so in your test book.

Student-Produced Responses ONLY ANSWERS ENTERED IN THE CIRCLES IN EACH GRID WILL BE SCORED. YOU WILL NOT RECEIVE CREDIT FOR ANYTHING WRITTEN IN THE BOXES ABOVE THE CIRCLES.

9, 10, 11, 12, 13 — answer grids

14, 15, 16, 17, 18 — answer grids

Start with number 1 for each new section. If a section has fewer questions than answer spaces, leave the extra answer spaces blank. Be sure to erase any errors or stray marks completely.

SECTION 8

1 Ⓐ Ⓑ Ⓒ Ⓓ Ⓔ	11 Ⓐ Ⓑ Ⓒ Ⓓ Ⓔ	21 Ⓐ Ⓑ Ⓒ Ⓓ Ⓔ	31 Ⓐ Ⓑ Ⓒ Ⓓ Ⓔ
2 Ⓐ Ⓑ Ⓒ Ⓓ Ⓔ	12 Ⓐ Ⓑ Ⓒ Ⓓ Ⓔ	22 Ⓐ Ⓑ Ⓒ Ⓓ Ⓔ	32 Ⓐ Ⓑ Ⓒ Ⓓ Ⓔ
3 Ⓐ Ⓑ Ⓒ Ⓓ Ⓔ	13 Ⓐ Ⓑ Ⓒ Ⓓ Ⓔ	23 Ⓐ Ⓑ Ⓒ Ⓓ Ⓔ	33 Ⓐ Ⓑ Ⓒ Ⓓ Ⓔ
4 Ⓐ Ⓑ Ⓒ Ⓓ Ⓔ	14 Ⓐ Ⓑ Ⓒ Ⓓ Ⓔ	24 Ⓐ Ⓑ Ⓒ Ⓓ Ⓔ	34 Ⓐ Ⓑ Ⓒ Ⓓ Ⓔ
5 Ⓐ Ⓑ Ⓒ Ⓓ Ⓔ	15 Ⓐ Ⓑ Ⓒ Ⓓ Ⓔ	25 Ⓐ Ⓑ Ⓒ Ⓓ Ⓔ	35 Ⓐ Ⓑ Ⓒ Ⓓ Ⓔ
6 Ⓐ Ⓑ Ⓒ Ⓓ Ⓔ	16 Ⓐ Ⓑ Ⓒ Ⓓ Ⓔ	26 Ⓐ Ⓑ Ⓒ Ⓓ Ⓔ	36 Ⓐ Ⓑ Ⓒ Ⓓ Ⓔ
7 Ⓐ Ⓑ Ⓒ Ⓓ Ⓔ	17 Ⓐ Ⓑ Ⓒ Ⓓ Ⓔ	27 Ⓐ Ⓑ Ⓒ Ⓓ Ⓔ	37 Ⓐ Ⓑ Ⓒ Ⓓ Ⓔ
8 Ⓐ Ⓑ Ⓒ Ⓓ Ⓔ	18 Ⓐ Ⓑ Ⓒ Ⓓ Ⓔ	28 Ⓐ Ⓑ Ⓒ Ⓓ Ⓔ	38 Ⓐ Ⓑ Ⓒ Ⓓ Ⓔ
9 Ⓐ Ⓑ Ⓒ Ⓓ Ⓔ	19 Ⓐ Ⓑ Ⓒ Ⓓ Ⓔ	29 Ⓐ Ⓑ Ⓒ Ⓓ Ⓔ	39 Ⓐ Ⓑ Ⓒ Ⓓ Ⓔ
10 Ⓐ Ⓑ Ⓒ Ⓓ Ⓔ	20 Ⓐ Ⓑ Ⓒ Ⓓ Ⓔ	30 Ⓐ Ⓑ Ⓒ Ⓓ Ⓔ	40 Ⓐ Ⓑ Ⓒ Ⓓ Ⓔ

SECTION 9

1 Ⓐ Ⓑ Ⓒ Ⓓ Ⓔ	11 Ⓐ Ⓑ Ⓒ Ⓓ Ⓔ	21 Ⓐ Ⓑ Ⓒ Ⓓ Ⓔ	31 Ⓐ Ⓑ Ⓒ Ⓓ Ⓔ
2 Ⓐ Ⓑ Ⓒ Ⓓ Ⓔ	12 Ⓐ Ⓑ Ⓒ Ⓓ Ⓔ	22 Ⓐ Ⓑ Ⓒ Ⓓ Ⓔ	32 Ⓐ Ⓑ Ⓒ Ⓓ Ⓔ
3 Ⓐ Ⓑ Ⓒ Ⓓ Ⓔ	13 Ⓐ Ⓑ Ⓒ Ⓓ Ⓔ	23 Ⓐ Ⓑ Ⓒ Ⓓ Ⓔ	33 Ⓐ Ⓑ Ⓒ Ⓓ Ⓔ
4 Ⓐ Ⓑ Ⓒ Ⓓ Ⓔ	14 Ⓐ Ⓑ Ⓒ Ⓓ Ⓔ	24 Ⓐ Ⓑ Ⓒ Ⓓ Ⓔ	34 Ⓐ Ⓑ Ⓒ Ⓓ Ⓔ
5 Ⓐ Ⓑ Ⓒ Ⓓ Ⓔ	15 Ⓐ Ⓑ Ⓒ Ⓓ Ⓔ	25 Ⓐ Ⓑ Ⓒ Ⓓ Ⓔ	35 Ⓐ Ⓑ Ⓒ Ⓓ Ⓔ
6 Ⓐ Ⓑ Ⓒ Ⓓ Ⓔ	16 Ⓐ Ⓑ Ⓒ Ⓓ Ⓔ	26 Ⓐ Ⓑ Ⓒ Ⓓ Ⓔ	36 Ⓐ Ⓑ Ⓒ Ⓓ Ⓔ
7 Ⓐ Ⓑ Ⓒ Ⓓ Ⓔ	17 Ⓐ Ⓑ Ⓒ Ⓓ Ⓔ	27 Ⓐ Ⓑ Ⓒ Ⓓ Ⓔ	37 Ⓐ Ⓑ Ⓒ Ⓓ Ⓔ
8 Ⓐ Ⓑ Ⓒ Ⓓ Ⓔ	18 Ⓐ Ⓑ Ⓒ Ⓓ Ⓔ	28 Ⓐ Ⓑ Ⓒ Ⓓ Ⓔ	38 Ⓐ Ⓑ Ⓒ Ⓓ Ⓔ
9 Ⓐ Ⓑ Ⓒ Ⓓ Ⓔ	19 Ⓐ Ⓑ Ⓒ Ⓓ Ⓔ	29 Ⓐ Ⓑ Ⓒ Ⓓ Ⓔ	39 Ⓐ Ⓑ Ⓒ Ⓓ Ⓔ
10 Ⓐ Ⓑ Ⓒ Ⓓ Ⓔ	20 Ⓐ Ⓑ Ⓒ Ⓓ Ⓔ	30 Ⓐ Ⓑ Ⓒ Ⓓ Ⓔ	40 Ⓐ Ⓑ Ⓒ Ⓓ Ⓔ

ESSAY

Time—25 minutes

You have 25 minutes to write an essay based on the topic presented as follows. Do not write on another topic. Your essay should be written on the lined pages provided. For the best results, write on every line, and keep your handwriting to a reasonable, legible size. Be sure to fully develop your point of view, present your ideas clearly and logically, and use the English language precisely.

Think carefully about the following issue and assignment:

> Caution is essential to security. Individuals should carefully consider the impact of their actions and proceed only after a thorough analysis of possible negative outcomes. Those who rush to act often create unintended consequences that far outweigh any benefits of immediate action.

Assignment: Is haste more dangerous than delay? Plan and write an essay in which you develop your point of view on this topic. Support your position with reasoning and solid examples taken from your personal experience, observations, reading, or studies.

WRITE YOUR ESSAY ON PAGES 430 AND 431.

If you finish writing before your time is called, check your work on this section only.
Do not turn to any other section in the test.

SECTION 2
Time—25 minutes
20 Questions

Directions: Solve each problem and determine which is the best of the answer choices given. Fill in the corresponding circle on your answer sheet. Use any available space to solve the problems.

Notes

1. The use of a calculator is permitted.
2. All numbers are real numbers.
3. Figures that accompany problems in this test are intended to provide information useful in solving the problems. They are drawn as accurately as possible EXCEPT when it is stated in a specific problem that the figure is not drawn to scale. All figures lie in a plane unless otherwise indicated.
4. Unless otherwise specified, the domain of any function f is assumed to be the set of all real numbers x for which $f(x)$ is a real number.

Reference Information

$A = \prod r^2$
$C = 2 \prod r$

$A = lw$

$A = \frac{1}{2}bh$

$V = lwh$

$V = \prod r^2 h$

$c^2 = a^2 + b^2$

Special Right Triangles

The number of degrees of arc in a circle is 360.
The sum of the measures in degrees of the angles of a triangle is 180.

1. When Roger went to the store to buy cola, only 5 packages of cola were left on the shelf. Two packages contained 12 cans of cola, and each of the others contained 6 cans of cola. If Roger bought all 5 packages, how many cans of cola did he purchase at the store?

(A) 60
(B) 48
(C) 42
(D) 36
(E) 30

2. P, Q, and R are points on a line in that order. If $PQ = 12$ and QR is 8 more than PQ, what does PR equal?

(A) 12
(B) 20
(C) 24
(D) 32
(E) 40

GO ON TO THE NEXT PAGE

3. If $a(m + n) = 24$ and $am = 8$, what is the value of an?

(A) 2
(B) 6
(C) 8
(D) 12
(E) 16

4. How many positive four-digit integers can be formed if the four digits 2, 3, 4, and 5 must be used in each of the integers?

(A) 4
(B) 10
(C) 16
(D) 24
(E) 32

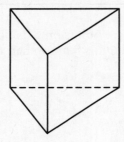

5. The three-dimensional figure represented above consists of rectangular and triangular faces. Each rectangular face has area a, and each triangular face has area b. What is the total surface area of the figure, in terms of a and b?

(A) a^3b^2
(B) $9a^2 + 4b^2$
(C) $3a + 2b$
(D) $2a + 3b$
(E) $5ab$

6. If k is a positive integer and $\frac{(k + 1)}{3^k} = \frac{1}{3}$, then $k =$

(A) 1
(B) 2
(C) 3
(D) 4
(E) 5

7. What is the smallest positive integer that is divisible by each of the integers 1 through 6, inclusive?

(A) 30
(B) 60
(C) 120
(D) 360
(E) 720

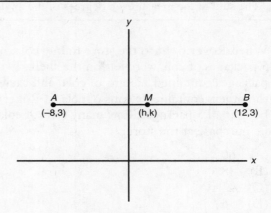

8. Point M is the midpoint of segment AB in the figure above. What is the value of h?

(A) 2
(B) 3
(C) 4
(D) 6
(E) 10

GO ON TO THE NEXT PAGE

9. If $c(4x + 3)(x - 1) = 22$ when $x = 2$, what is the value of c?

(A) 0
(B) 1
(C) 2
(D) 3
(E) 4

10. If all men in the Hernandez family weigh less than 175 pounds, which of the following statements must be true?

(A) All men weighing less than 175 pounds are members of the Hernandez family.
(B) No man weighing over 175 pounds is a member of the Hernandez family.
(C) All men who are not members of the Hernandez family weigh over 175 pounds.
(D) Every member of the Hernandez family weighs less than 175 pounds.
(E) One man in the Hernandez family weighs less than 175 pounds.

11. What is the area of a circle that has the circumference of π?

(A) $\frac{1}{2}$

(B) $\frac{1}{4}$

(C) $\frac{\pi}{2}$

(D) $\frac{\pi}{4}$

(E) π^2

12. If r is an even integer and s is an odd integer, which of the following must be an even integer?

(A) $\frac{s}{r}$

(B) $r + s$

(C) $2(r + s)$

(D) $\frac{3s}{r}$

(E) $3(r + s)$

13. Let the function g be defined by $g(x) = 3(x^2 - 2)$. When $g(x) = 69$, what is a possible value of $2x - 3$?

(A) -7
(B) -5
(C) 2
(D) 5
(E) 7

14. If a soccer team scores an average (arithmetic mean) of x goals per game for y games and then scores z goals in its next game, what it is the team's average score for the $y + 1$ games?

(A) $\frac{xy + z}{y + 1}$

(B) $\frac{x}{y + z}$

(C) $xyz(y + 1)$

(D) $y + 1(xy + z)$

(E) $y + 1 \frac{(xy)}{z}$

GO ON TO THE NEXT PAGE

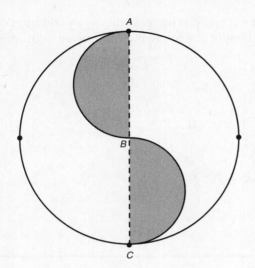

15. The circle above has center B and diameter AC. The two semicircles have diameters AB and BC. If the circumference of the circle is 12π, what is the area of the shaded regions?

(A) 3π
(B) 6π
(C) 9π
(D) 12π
(E) 36π

16. In the xy-plane, the equation of line l is $y = \frac{3x}{2} + 6$. If line m is the refection of line l about the y-axis, what is the equation of line m?

(A) $y = -\frac{2x}{3} + 6$

(B) $y = -\frac{3x}{2} + 6$

(C) $y = \frac{3x}{2} - 6$

(D) $y = \frac{3x}{2} + 6$

(E) $y = \frac{2x}{3} - 6$

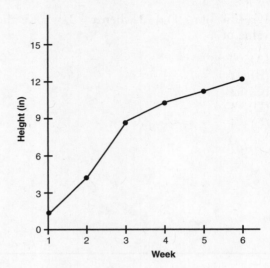

17. The graph above shows the height of a plant in inches from week 1 to week 6. The plant's height at week 6 is approximately what percent greater than its height at week 3?

(A) 75%

(B) $66\frac{2}{3}\%$

(C) 50%

(D) $33\frac{1}{3}\%$

(E) 25%

18. The least integer in a set of consecutive integers is -12. If the sum of these integers is 13, how many integers are in this set?

(A) 12
(B) 13
(C) 24
(D) 25
(E) 26

GO ON TO THE NEXT PAGE

19. The McCallister family vacations every year at the same resort. The cost of the vacation increases each year by 5%. The McCallisters paid $900 this year for their vacation. If the cost, c, of the vacation x years from now is given by the function $c(x) = 900r^x$, what is the value of r?

    (A) .05
    (B) .45
    (C) 1.05
    (D) 1.45
    (E) 45

20. At the Acme Widget Company, machine A cuts widget stock into smaller pieces, and machine B accepts the pieces only if the widths are between $3\frac{11}{12}$ and $4\frac{1}{12}$ inches. If machine B accepts a widget with a width of n inches, which of the following describes all possible values of n?

    (A) $|n - 4| < \frac{1}{12}$
    (B) $|n + 4| < \frac{1}{12}$
    (C) $|n - 4| > \frac{1}{12}$
    (D) $|n - 4| = \frac{1}{12}$
    (E) $|n + 4| = \frac{1}{12}$

STOP

**If you finish before your time is up, check your work on this section only.
You may not turn to any other section in the test.**

SECTION 3
Time—25 minutes
24 Questions

Directions: For each of the questions in this section, choose the best answer and fill in the corresponding circle on your answer sheet.

Each sentence that follows has either one or two blanks. Each blank indicates that a word has been omitted from the sentence. Beneath each sentence are five words or sets of words. Select the word or set of words that, when inserted into the sentence in place of the blank(s), best fits the context of the sentence as a whole.

1. When the journalist suggested an article on the benefits of exercise, her callous boss ------- her for a lack of creativity.

    (A) commended
    (B) ridiculed
    (C) sanctioned
    (D) ratified
    (E) esteemed

2. We needed to find ------- hiking boots for our -------; we planned to cover nearly 200 miles in only one week!

    (A) substandard . . outing
    (B) formidable . . saunter
    (C) shoddy . . excursion
    (D) robust . . gait
    (E) sturdy . . expedition

3. What was supposed to be the summer's biggest blockbuster movie turned into the summer's biggest -------; the lead actor was far too ------- for the serious role he was intended to play.

    (A) debacle . . melodramatic
    (B) triumph . . exaggerated
    (C) fiasco . . sincere
    (D) failure . . representational
    (E) sensation . . original

4. The student's essay lacked -------; her teacher found it difficult to follow and thought that the argument was rather unclear.

    (A) entitlement
    (B) references
    (C) coherence
    (D) discrepancies
    (E) incongruity

5. Agriculturists have traditionally considered crop rotation to be -------; it helps to preserve soil nutrients, control disease, and deter weed growth.

    (A) aesthetic
    (B) insolvent
    (C) pedantic
    (D) incidental
    (E) crucial

GO ON TO THE NEXT PAGE

Each passage that follows is accompanied by several questions based on the content of the passage. Answer the questions based on what is either stated or implied in each passage. Be sure to read any introductory material that is provided.

Questions 6–9 are based on the following passages.

Passage 1

After reading Betty Smith's *A Tree Grows in Brooklyn* for the third time, it occurred to me why I so enjoy that story. It begins when the main character, Francie Nolan, is an 11-year-old girl living in tenement housing in Brooklyn, New York, in the early 1900s. The story tells of both her struggles and her dreams, painting a picture of both sadness and elation.

This is a girl, and then a woman, who faces life's obstacles, endures them, and comes out stronger because of them. It is nearly impossible to read the story at any time in your life and not feel that life truly is worth living. Through Francie, the reader can feel a great sense of hope when considering the many disparaging and discouraging situations that many people experience. Francie *is* the "Tree of Heaven," growing strong amidst the poverty and despair of urban life.

Line 5

Line 10

Line 15

Passage 2

The very first line of the lengthy saga *Anna Karenina* gives the reader an immediate sense of Leo Tolstoy's main theme: "Happy families are all alike; every unhappy family is unhappy in its own way." Obvious at the start is that Tolstoy's characters are probably not going to be bland or stereotypical. Throughout the novel, Tolstoy depicts the ambiguities and ambivalences felt by real people in real-life situations.

The main character, Anna Karenina, seems to have a tragic undertone throughout the story. The reader first meets her when she visits her sister-in-law in an attempt to talk her out of leaving Anna's cavorting brother. Even in this scene, Anna seems to be missing a part of herself though she pretends to be happy and content. Tolstoy continues to weave Anna's sad story until she finally throws herself in front of a train and is killed.

Anna's pursuit of happiness only leads her to more unhappiness, leaving the reader with a sense of despair and hopelessness. It is difficult, if not impossible, to feel uplifted after reading Tolstoy's long narrative *Anna Karenina*.

Line 5

Line 10

Line 15

Line 20

6. Which statement best characterizes the relationship between Passage 1 and Passage 2?

   (A) Passage 1 presents a moral tale that is absent in Passage 2.
   (B) Passage 1 describes a story's setting while Passage 2 focuses strictly on character development.
   (C) Passage 1 relates to a time period that is far removed from that in Passage 2.
   (D) Passage 1 describes a novel with a positive tone while Passage 2 describes a more dire one.
   (E) Passage 1 tells a story in factual terms while Passage 2 uses innuendo.

7. Unlike Passage 1, Passage 2 focuses primarily on a novel's

   (A) underlying message
   (B) negativism
   (C) author
   (D) time period
   (E) reader

8. The author of Passage 2 would most likely describe the "characters" mentioned in line 6 as

   (A) uneducated
   (B) charming
   (C) emotional
   (D) spiritual
   (E) unnecessary

9. The authors of both passages would most likely agree that a novel should be

   (A) inspiring
   (B) informative
   (C) factual
   (D) creative
   (E) challenging

GO ON TO THE NEXT PAGE

Questions 10–15 are based on the following passage.

The following passage discusses an important American inventor.

Eli Whitney (1765–1825) invented the cotton gin, an innovative machine that effectively ended the laborious process of removing cotton seeds by hand, enabling farmers of the American South to harvest the crop en masse. Without a cotton gin, even the most experienced worker could process only one pound of cotton per day. Whitney's machine could screen 50 times as much, making the fiber profitable for the first time.

Although Whitney's cotton-cleaning machine was the first of its kind in America, simple devices had been used around the world for centuries to perform the job. For example, over a millennium ago in India, a device called a *charka* was invented to separate cotton seeds from lint by pulling the crude fibers through a spinning wheel. The machine was not adaptable, however, to the short-staple cotton produced in North America. In order to process the specific type of cotton fiber grown in the American South, a new apparatus had to be constructed.

Whitney recognized the need for a specialized device to separate cotton's sticky seeds from its desirable fibers. He had already designed many useful items during his lifetime (including muskets and the machines to manufacture them), but none impacted the lives of people as dramatically as the cotton gin did. Some credit it alone for transforming the Southern economy. Even small farms could benefit from a hand-cranked gin; larger versions could be tied to a horse or a water wheel. Large cotton plantations throughout the southern states displaced farmers of other crops. Cotton production was so profitable, in fact, that food crops fell by the wayside, having a marked effect on every Southern family's larder.

The cotton gin has to its credit the boost to the cotton industry and the resultant expansion of slavery in Southern plantations. A rush of new immigrants to the United States was making labor inexpensive enough that slavery was an increasingly unprofitable undertaking. Enormous cotton plantations tipped the balance, though, by quickly requiring a massive labor force to work land that had theretofore been unplanted. Plantation owners became fierce advocates for slavery. While immigrants wanted work, many were unwilling to perform the arduous tasks of cotton production. Plantation owners relied almost solely on slave labor until its abolition at the end of the Civil War.

Whitney's cotton gin revolutionized agriculture in the United States. The weight of his invention notwithstanding, he struggled to make a profit from it. After receiving a patent for his invention, Whitney and a partner opted to produce as many cotton gins as possible and charge farmers a steep fee to use them. Farmers considered this fee unnecessary and exorbitant and began manufacturing copies of the cotton gin instead, claiming that their inventions were unique. Because of a loophole in the patent law, the many lawsuits brought by Whitney and his partner against the farmers were fruitless. The duo finally agreed to license their cotton gins at a reasonable price, preventing the windfall that Whitney had foreseen.

10. According to the passage, which one of the following was an obstacle to Whitney earning a profit on the cotton gin?

(A) Whitney's reluctance to seek a patent for his cotton gin

(B) The high fees being charged to farmers for the use of Whitney's cotton gin

(C) The negative impact of Whitney's cotton gin on the economy of the south

(D) Whitney's inability to distribute cotton gins fast enough

(E) Whitney's reliance on slave labor in the production of his cotton gin

GO ON TO THE NEXT PAGE

11. The author of the passage would most probably agree with which one of the following statements about slave labor?

    (A) The Civil War caused plantation owners to rely more heavily on slave labor.
    (B) Slave labor was a positive result of improved farming methods in the South.
    (C) A decrease in the availability of slave labor would have ultimately led to the demise of large cotton plantations.
    (D) Increased slave labor was a consequence of the invention of an innovative device.
    (E) Slave labor was justified by the burgeoning Southern economy.

12. The author of the passage would most probably agree with which one of the following statements about the "the Southern economy" (line 32)?

    (A) Prior to the invention of the cotton gin, the Southern economy was suffering.
    (B) The Southern economy declined significantly with the advent of large cotton plantations.
    (C) Expanded cotton production allowed Southern farmers to hire more immigrant workers, thereby improving the Southern economy.
    (D) The invention of the cotton gin had little effect on the Southern economy.
    (E) As a result of slow economic growth in the South, many farmers were unable to produce large cotton crops.

13. The author cites all of the following as advantages of Whitney's cotton gin EXCEPT

    (A) it allowed small farms to produce larger quantities of cotton
    (B) it efficiently processed short-staple cotton
    (C) it increased the profitability of many farms throughout the South
    (D) it could be adapted for both large and small cotton farms
    (E) it created jobs for immigrant farm workers

14. As used in line 57, "weight" most nearly means

    (A) heaviness
    (B) burden
    (C) importance
    (D) consideration
    (E) potency

15. Which one of the following titles most accurately describes the contents of the passage?

    (A) "Eli Whitney: Father of the Deep South"
    (B) "The Cotton Gin: Economic Savior of the South and Inadvertent Stimulus of Slavery"
    (C) "An Impetus for Social Change: The Advent of the Cotton Plantation in the American South"
    (D) "Innovative Inventions: Mass Production in the Eighteenth Century"
    (E) "American Ingenuity: One Man's Struggle"

GO ON TO THE NEXT PAGE

Questions 16–24 are based on the following passage.

This passage was written by a public health officer for a community newspaper.

Fear is a normal, legitimate response to genuine danger. However, when fear spirals out of control, becoming persistent and irrational,
Line
5 it constitutes a phobia. Phobias affect a significant portion of the American population. Some experts believe that nearly 25 percent of Americans live with irrational fears that prevent them from performing everyday activities. Phobias, like other anxiety disorders, can
10 greatly affect quality of life. Generally defined as an unrelenting, anomalous, and unfounded fear of an object or situation, a phobia is normally developed from a past negative experience or encounter. Children might adopt
15 phobias by observing a family member's reaction to specific stimuli. There is also data to suggest genetic factors linked to phobias.

    Phobias come in three distinct classes: agoraphobia, social phobia, and specific phobia.
20 Agoraphobics have an intense fear of leaving a safe place, such as their homes, or being in certain wide-open or crowded spaces, essentially any place where a means of escape is not easily identifiable. Agoraphobia is the most
25 disabling type of phobia, and treatment is generally complicated by the many associated fears a patient might have. The fear of panic attacks caused by agoraphobia is common. Social phobias are fears related to people or
30 social situations. Social phobias can greatly interfere with work responsibilities and personal relationships. Specific phobia is a general category for any phobia other than agoraphobia and social phobia. This class
35 contains the most recognizable set of symptoms and is often the easiest class of phobias to treat.

    Under the heading of specific phobia, there are four categories: situational, environmental, animal, and medical phobias. Over 350
40 different phobias have been identified across these 4 categories. Observers often notice symptoms of a person experiencing intense fear. In many cases, a person facing a phobia will show signs of panic, trepidation, and terror. He
45 or she may also exhibit physical signs including

rapid heartbeat, shortness of breath, and trembling. Often one begins to fear a phobic attack and will experience symptoms without the presence of any external stimuli.

50   Once a person has been diagnosed with agoraphobia, social phobia, or specific phobia, there is a wide range of treatment options available. Recent medical advances have allowed researchers to identify the parts of the
55 brain associated with phobias. The *amygdala* is one such area of the brain under intense study. This almond-shaped bundle of nerve cells located deep within the brain releases excitatory hormones into the bloodstream and is
60 involved in normal fear conditioning; however, if the amygdala becomes over-active, normal fear responses are heightened. The brain chemical *oxytocin* has been found to quell activity in the amygdala, thereby weakening the produc-
65 tion of the excitatory hormones and limiting the amygdala's communication with other areas of the brain that telegraph the fear response. This relationship between *oxytocin* and the amygdala indicates a potentially powerful treat-
70 ment for phobias.

    Prior to the development of medical treatments, many people suffering from extreme phobias were often forced to meet with behavioral specialists. These specialists
75 believe that the exaggerated fear experienced is an acquired reflex to some benign stimulus. For example, a normal fear resulting from a dangerous stimulus, such as being bitten by a dog, can turn into an irrational fear of all
80 animals. Behavioral specialists attempt to combat irrational fears through repeated exposure to the phobic stimulus. For example, a *cynophobic* person might be introduced first to a small, non-threatening dog and then be repeat-
85 edly exposed to larger dogs in controlled situations until the fear eventually disappears. These behavioral approaches are still very common and show some positive results. One key to the success of behavioral therapy is the emphasis
90 that therapists place on ensuring that their patients know there indeed are others afflicted with the same disorder. Just knowing that they

GO ON TO THE NEXT PAGE ➔

do not suffer alone helps patients to focus on their treatment and reap the rewards of the
95 therapy.

Any acute fear that hampers daily living and causes great emotional and physical stress should be treated. The vast majority of patients respond to treatment, overcoming their fears to enjoy
100 symptom-free lives. Effective and often permanent relief can come from behavior therapy, medication, or a combination of the two.

16. Which one of the following most accurately summarizes the main point of the passage?

(A) Legitimate fears often become debilitating phobias.
(B) Phobias can and should be diagnosed and treated.
(C) Phobias are just one of many treatable anxiety disorders.
(D) Specific phobias are typically easy to identify.
(E) Phobias often run in families and can be learned.

17. Which one of the following most likely reflects the author's views on recent medical research into the treatment of phobias?

(A) Recent medical advances will provide relief for people who suffer from social phobias but might not help those suffering from specific phobias.
(B) Although the *amygdala* has been identified as the source of fear responses, it is unlikely that further research will be beneficial.
(C) It is likely that additional research will show that medical treatment of phobias is less effective than are behavioral approaches.
(D) Recent medical advances undermine all of the previous results of research conducted in the treatment of phobias.
(E) The identification of specific areas in the brain that are associated with phobias allow for more, and perhaps better, treatment options.

18. The author's primary purpose in writing the passage is to

(A) defend recent medical advances in identifying and treating phobias
(B) criticize the medical community's current views on treating phobias
(C) advocate behavioral therapy over medication as a treatment for phobias
(D) evaluate each of the various options for treating phobias
(E) identify the seriousness of phobias and suggest possible treatment options

19. According to the passage, behavioral specialists advance which one of the following claims to support their theory?

(A) While their origins are unknown, every phobia is exorable.
(B) Fear is a detrimental response to dangerous stimuli.
(C) Phobias are a learned response and, thus, reversible.
(D) Altering brain chemicals can effectively treat phobias.
(E) Dog attacks on humans do not cause fear of all dogs.

20. The author most probably mentions the function of the *amygdala* in order to

(A) illustrate how far medical research has come
(B) establish a direct link between the biological source of fear and the treatment of phobias
(C) provide evidence for the existence of specific brain chemicals
(D) cast doubt on the behavioral approach to the treatment of phobias
(E) suggest an alternative to the current method of identifying and treating phobias

GO ON TO THE NEXT PAGE

21. According to the passage, all of the following could be classified as a specific phobia EXCEPT:

    (A) fear of public places
    (B) fear of surgery
    (C) fear of foreigners
    (D) fear of heights
    (E) fear of large dogs

22. The author implies that which one of the following was true prior to the advent of medical treatments for phobias?

    (A) Many phobias were incorrectly identified, resulting in improper treatments.
    (B) Because there were no other viable options, many people were forced to undergo an emotional form of treatment that might have been unpleasant.
    (C) There was a limited number of behavioral therapists trained to diagnose and treat most social and specific phobias.
    (D) In spite of the efforts of well-trained behavioral therapists, many people diagnosed with a specific phobia failed to respond to treatment.
    (E) Most phobias remained undetected and, therefore, untreated.

23. Which one of the following is most analogous to the treatment described in the example given by the author in the fifth paragraph?

    (A) A farmer seeking water drills twelve holes before discovering a suitable aquifer.
    (B) Cows have multiple stomachs, which allow for thorough digestion of fibrous plants.
    (C) Flow within a siphon can be initiated with a relatively low amount of suction.
    (D) Every layer of plaster on a wall must be solid before it can support additional layers.
    (E) A grocery saves money by stocking pre-cut meats instead of maintaining a butcher shop.

24. As used in line 96, "acute" most nearly means

    (A) astute
    (B) intense
    (C) local
    (D) sensitive
    (E) crucial

STOP

**If you finish before your time is up, check your work on this section only.
You may not turn to any other section in the test.**

SECTION 4
Time—25 minutes
18 Questions

Directions: This section includes two types of questions. For questions 1–8, solve each problem and determine which is the best of the answer choices given. Fill in the corresponding circle on your answer sheet. Use any available space to solve the problems. For questions 9–18, solve each problem and fill in your answer on the answer sheet.

Notes

1. The use of a calculator is permitted.
2. All numbers are real numbers.
3. Figures that accompany problems in this test are intended to provide information useful in solving the problems. They are drawn as accurately as possible EXCEPT when it is stated in a specific problem that the figure is not drawn to scale. All figures lie in a plane unless otherwise indicated.
4. Unless otherwise specified, the domain of any function f is assumed to be the set of all real numbers x for which $f(x)$ is a real number.

Reference Information

   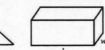

$A = \Pi r^2$
$C = 2\Pi r$ $A = lw$ $A = \frac{1}{2}bh$ $V = lwh$ $V = \Pi r^2 h$ $c^2 = a^2 + b^2$ Special Right Triangles

The number of degrees of arc in a circle is 360.
The sum of the measures in degrees of the angles of a triangle is 180.

1. According to a certain formula, 250 mg of dry concentrate is needed to make 20 L of solution. At this rate, how many mg of dry concentrate are needed to make 4 L of solution?

   (A) 12
   (B) 25
   (C) 50
   (D) 75
   (E) 100

2. If $xy = 12$, what is the value of $3\left(\frac{x}{y}\right)y^2$?

   (A) 3
   (B) 6
   (C) 12
   (D) 24
   (E) 36

GO ON TO THE NEXT PAGE

3. If $x + y = 25$ and $x < 12$, then which of the following must be true?

(A) $y > 0$
(B) $y < 13$
(C) $y = 13$
(D) $y > 13$
(E) $x > 0$

$A(3, 6)\ B(7, 6)\ C(7, 9)$

4. The coordinates of A, B, and C in the xy-plane are given above. What is the perimeter of triangle ABC?

(A) 10
(B) 12
(C) 13
(D) 15
(E) 17

13, 20, 27, 34, 41, …

5. The first five terms in a sequence are shown above. Each term after the first is found by adding 7 to the term immediately preceding it. Which term in this sequence is equal to $13 + 7(32 - 1)$?

(A) The 7th
(B) The 8th
(C) The 31st
(D) The 32nd
(E) The 33rd

6. If $|\,4 - 3x\,| < 5$, which of the following is a possible value of x?

(A) 2
(B) 3
(C) 4
(D) 5
(E) 6

7. The sum of two numbers that differ by 2 is m. In terms of m, what is the value of the greater of the two numbers?

(A) $\dfrac{(m + 1)}{2}$

(B) $\dfrac{(m + 2)}{2}$

(C) $\dfrac{(m - 1)}{2}$

(D) $\dfrac{m}{(2 + 2)}$

(E) $\dfrac{(2m - 1)}{2}$

Number of Gaming Consoles Owned	Number of Members
1	8
2	1
3	3
4	2

8. The table above shows the number of gaming consoles owned by each of the 14 members of the video game club. A new member joined the club, and the average (arithmetic mean) number of gaming consoles per member became equal to twice the median number of consoles owned per member. How many consoles did the new member have?

(A) 0
(B) 1
(C) 2
(D) 3
(E) 4

GO ON TO THE NEXT PAGE

Directions: For Student-Produced Response questions 9-18, use the grids at the bottom of the answer sheet page on which you have answered questions 1-8.

Each of the remaining 10 questions requires you to solve the problem and enter your answer by marking the circles in the special grid, as shown in the examples below. You may use any available space for scratchwork.

Answer: $\frac{7}{12}$

Answer: 2.5

Answer: 201
Either position is correct.

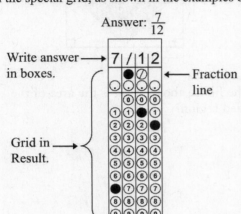

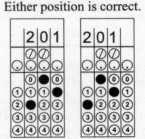

Write answer in boxes.

Fraction line

Decimal point

Grid in Result.

Note: You may start your answers in any column, space permitting. Columns not needed should be left blank.

- Mark no more than one circle in any column.

- Because the answer sheet will be machine-scored, **you will receive credit only if the circles are filled in correctly**.

- Although not required, it is suggested that you write your answer in the boxes at the top of the columns to help you fill in the circles accurately.

- Some problems may have more than one correct answer. In such cases, grid only one answer.

- No question has a negative answer.

- **Mixed numbers** such as $3\frac{1}{2}$ must be gridded as

3.5 or 7/2. (If ☐ is gridded, it will be

interpreted as $\frac{31}{2}$, not $3\frac{1}{2}$.)

Decimal Answers: If you obtain a decimal answer with more digits than the grid can accomodate, it may be either rounded or truncated, but it must fill the entire grid. enter the most accurate value the grid will accommodate. For example, if you obtain an answer such as 0.6666..., you should record your result as .666 or .667. **A less accurate value such as .66 or .67 will be scored as incorrect.**

Acceptable ways to grid $\frac{2}{3}$ are:

9. If $3(x-4) = 24$, what does $\frac{(x-4)}{(x+4)}$ equal?

10. When three times a number is increased by 7, the result is 109. What is the number?

GO ON TO THE NEXT PAGE

Car Production for May

	Cassette Player	CD Player	Total
Standard Speakers		1,450	
Premium Speakers	250		
Total	1,000		4,750

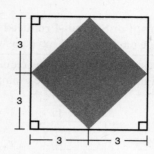

11. A certain auto manufacturer installs two types of audio players in its cars, both of which are available with a standard or premium speaker system. On the basis of the information in the table above, how many cars were produced with a CD player *and* premium speakers in May?

12. Five points, *P*, *Q*, *R*, *S*, and *T*, lie on a line, not necessarily in that order. Segment *PQ* has a length of 16. Point *R* is the midpoint of segment *PQ*, and point *S* is the midpoint of segment *PR*. If the distance between *S* and *T* is 7, what is one possible distance between *P* and *T*?

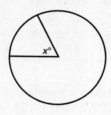

13. A certain delicatessen sells portions of cheese wheels by weight. Each portion is wedge shaped and makes an angle at the center of the wheel, as shown above. If the wheel of cheese weighs 64 ounces and the weight is uniformly distributed, what would the value of *x* be if the wedge weighed 8 ounces?

14. In the figure above, what is the area of the shaded region?

15. If $x^2 - y^2 = 18$ and $x + y = 6$, what is the value of $x - y$?

16. The greatest integer of a set of consecutive even integers is 12. If the sum of these integers is 40, how many integers are in this set?

GO ON TO THE NEXT PAGE

17. If $3^x + 3^x + 3^x = 3^6$, what is the value of x?

$$h(t) = -16t^2 + dt + c$$

18. At time $t = 0$, a rocket was launched upward from an initial height of 6 feet. Until the rocket hit the ground, its height, in feet, after t seconds was given by the function h above, in which c and d are positive constants. If the rocket reached its maximum height of 350 feet at time $t = 4$, what was the height, in feet, of the rocket after time $t = 1$?

STOP

**If you finish before your time is up, check your work on this section only.
You may not turn to any other section in the test.**

SECTION 5
Time—25 minutes
35 Questions

> **Directions:** For each question, select the best answer from among the choices listed. Fill in the corresponding circle on your answer sheet.

> The following questions test the correct and effective use of standard written English in expressing an idea. Part of each sentence (or the entire sentence) is underlined. Beneath each sentence are five different ways of phrasing the underlined portion. Answer choice A repeats the original phrasing. If you think that the original phrasing is best, select answer choice A. Otherwise, select from the remaining four choices. Your selection should result in the most effective, clear sentence, free from awkwardness or ambiguity.

1. French impressionist Claude Monet began his career drawing caricatures, which became wildly popular, so making him a tidy living.

   (A) which became wildly popular, so making him a tidy living
   (B) which became wildly popular, making him a tidy living
   (C) which had become wildly popular and made him a tidy living
   (D) becoming wildly popular to make him a tidy living
   (E) and they became wildly popular and made him a tidy living

2. The U.S. Department of Labor has proposed legislation requiring that employers should retain all employee records indefinitely or for at least 10 years after termination of the employee.

   (A) that employers should retain all employee records
   (B) that all employee records be retained by employers
   (C) employers to retain all employee records
   (D) employers' retention of all employee records
   (E) the retaining by employers of all employee records

3. June 24 is still considered Midsummer Day, marking the halfway point that is between planting and harvesting of summer crops.

   (A) halfway point that is between
   (B) halfway point; that is between
   (C) halfway point, that is between
   (D) halfway point between
   (E) point that is halfway between

4. Van Cliburn began learning to play the piano at age three and was only 24 when he won the first International Tchaikovsky Competition in Moscow.

   (A) began learning to play the piano
   (B) had begun to learn to play the piano
   (C) began to learn how to play the piano
   (D) had begun learning to play the piano
   (E) begun to play the piano by learning

5. Scientists believe that, unlike most of the 2,500 mosquito species, females of one species in the Florida Keys are restricted to a nectar diet, but not a blood meal, and it lays eggs in the soil, rather than in standing water.

   (A) but not a blood meal, and it lays
   (B) instead of a blood meal, and laying
   (C) not a blood meal, and are laying
   (D) rather than a blood meal, and lay
   (E) but not a blood meal, laying

GO ON TO THE NEXT PAGE

6. During the Revolutionary War, the Quartering Act was passed, <u>which this required</u> the colonists to house British troops.

    (A) which this required
    (B) which required
    (C) and requiring
    (D) thus requiring that
    (E) which then required

7. The speed at which the Earth and other planets such as Mars, Saturn, and Pluto <u>revolves are determined from</u> eccentricity and distance.

    (A) revolves are determined from
    (B) revolves are determined because of
    (C) revolve was determined through
    (D) revolve is determined by
    (E) revolve is determined as a result of

8. Citizens of Denver cater to their canine friends <u>as is evidenced by its</u> water bowls and doggie parks present throughout the business districts.

    (A) as is evidenced by its
    (B) as evidenced by the
    (C) as evident in
    (D) as is evidenced by their
    (E) as it is evidenced by its

9. Thousands of people must leave their homes each year because of local <u>flooding, hepatitis can often develop</u> in these situations.

    (A) flooding, hepatitis can often develop
    (B) flooding because of the fact that hepatitis can often develop
    (C) flooding, however hepatitis is often developed
    (D) flooding; hepatitis can often develop
    (E) flooding whereas hepatitis can often be developed

10. By offering lower prices, outstanding customer service, and the latest merchandise, the sporting goods company <u>has not only captured customers from other sporting goods companies but also forced them</u> to offer competitive prices and a better selection of merchandise.

    (A) has not only captured customers from other sporting goods companies but also forced them
    (B) has not only captured customers from other sporting goods companies, but it also forced them, the companies,
    (C) has not only captured customers from other sporting goods companies but also forced these companies
    (D) not only has captured customers from other sporting goods companies, but it also has forced them
    (E) not only captured customers from other sporting goods companies, but it also has forced them

11. Some analysts have been critical of the research studies conducted by the university because the figures <u>far exceeds those that were previously published</u>.

    (A) far exceeds those that were previously published
    (B) exceeds by far those previously published
    (C) far exceeds those previously published
    (D) exceed by far those published previous to this
    (E) far exceed those previously published

GO ON TO THE NEXT PAGE

The following questions test your ability to recognize grammar and usage errors in standard written English. Each sentence contains either a single error or no error at all. Refer to the underlined, lettered portions of each sentence. If the sentence contains no error, select answer choice E. If the sentence contains an error, select the one underlined and lettered portion (A, B, C, or D) that is incorrect.

12. Suzanne was treated <u>stern</u> by her doctor who
         A
<u>had advised</u> her <u>earlier</u> to rest more <u>often</u>.
         B   C   D
<u>No error</u>.
   E

13. Because I <u>rarely watch</u> football, the conflicting
              A
predictions of the announcers <u>make</u> it more
                                B
difficult for me to decide which of the teams <u>are</u>
                                                C
<u>most likely</u> to win the game. <u>No error</u>.
      D   E

14. <u>In 1964</u>, Thurgood Marshall <u>had became</u> the
      A   B
first black <u>justice</u> of the United States
              C
<u>Supreme Court</u>. <u>No error</u>.
      D   E

15. Today, <u>more than</u> half a century after his death,
            A
Elvis <u>Presley's</u> work still <u>intrigued</u> music
        B   C
<u>aficionados</u> around the world. <u>No error</u>.
      D   E

16. Winter <u>temperatures</u> will be <u>close to</u> normal in
            A   B
the <u>north</u> and <u>slightly below</u> normal in the
      C   D
South. <u>No error</u>.
         E

17. While <u>snowy roads</u> can <u>make</u> driving
           A   B
<u>treacherous</u>, <u>partial</u> frozen rain can create even
      C   D
more difficulties. <u>No error</u>.
                     E

18. When <u>visiting</u> any national park, <u>its</u> a good idea
           A   B
to <u>obtain</u> a trail map at the <u>visitor</u> center.
     C   D
<u>No error</u>.
   E

19. Formaldehyde is a <u>likely</u> carcinogen that is
                        A
difficult <u>to detect</u> but can be <u>found</u> in many
            B   C
common household <u>products</u>. <u>No error</u>.
                    D   E

GO ON TO THE NEXT PAGE

20. The <u>reason</u> people <u>are</u> advised to stay low to the
       A   B

ground <u>in</u> a fire is because smoke <u>tends</u> to rise.
     C   D

<u>No error</u>.
  E

21. <u>Entomologist</u> Thomas Say and Thaddeus Harris
     A

are <u>both considered</u> fathers of the study of
        B

insects, but Harris <u>focused</u> mostly on insects
              C

<u>that are</u> harmful to crops. <u>No error</u>.
  D   E

22. The emphasis in French Rococo <u>paintings</u> <u>are on</u>
                      A   B

more carefree and restful subject <u>matter</u> than
                    C

<u>previously</u> seen. <u>No error</u>.
  D   E

23. Of the two choices, <u>neither</u> the remodeling job
            A

<u>nor</u> the new home <u>purchase</u> <u>are</u> currently
 B   C   D

obtainable. <u>No error</u>.
        E

24. The hunting dog was <u>happiest</u> when <u>him</u>
            A   B

and his master <u>went out</u> to the woods <u>early</u> in the
         C   D

evening. <u>No error</u>.
      E

25. Rigorous preparation <u>is</u> considered
            A

<u>necessary</u> <u>for</u> the amateur runner <u>who expects</u>
 B C   D

to finish a full marathon. <u>No error</u>.
           E

26. Pierre Corneille and Moliere both <u>wrote</u> during
                  A

the Age of <u>Reason; so</u> Corneille wrote <u>tragedies</u>,
        B   C

while Moliere is <u>best known</u> for his comedies.
           D

<u>No error</u>.
  E

27. As summer approached, the students <u>grew</u>
                  A

<u>increasingly</u> unruly, forcing Miss Kern <u>to be</u>
 B   C

<u>more stricter</u> with her punishments. <u>No error</u>.
 D   E

28. Vitamins and minerals are <u>equally</u> important to
                A

the health of the human body, and <u>it</u> can be
                  B

<u>obtained</u> through <u>proper</u> foods. <u>No error</u>.
 C   D   E

29. Helen Frankenthaler, <u>unlike</u> many abstract
         A

<u>expressionists</u>, used <u>rich, strong</u> colors on
 B   C

large <u>canvasses</u>. <u>No error</u>.
    D   E

GO ON TO THE NEXT PAGE →

Directions: The following passage is a rough draft of a student essay. Some parts of the passage need to be rewritten in order to improve the essay.

Read the passage and select the best answer for each question that follows. Some questions ask you to improve the structure or word choice of specific sentences or parts of sentences, while others ask you to consider the organization and development of the essay. Follow the requirements of standard written English.

Questions 30–35 are based on the following passage.

(1)I remember when my sister told me she had to attend a night class. (2)It was an exercise class on Pilates. (3)When she said the word "Pilates," I had no idea what she was saying. (4)It sounded like gobbledygook, and I made no effort to have her repeat it to me. (5)All I could think was, "What's wrong with biking or swimming or plain ol' walking? (6)Why would anyone be drawn to this fancy Pilates, or whatever it is?"

(7)Then winter came and I found myself unwilling to venture onto the snowy, icy, slushy roads for my daily walk. (8)I already had about eight exercise DVDs, yet they were getting boring. (9)When people get bored with their exercise routines, they often abandon them. (10)Lo and behold, my sister presented me with two brand new exercise DVDs at Christmas. (11)And there it was, that strange word, printed across both covers—Pilates!

(12)Even though I was skeptical, I chose the DVD that looked like the least intimidating and loaded it into the player. (13)Fortunately, my sister had chosen a very entertaining exercise guru to teach me these new Pilates gyrations. (14)I knew if I could do it at all, it would be through her cheery, can-do approach. (15)Surprisingly, 3 months later, I have become a Pilates queen of sorts, stretching and sucking in my central core with the best of them! (16)And now, even that funny word rolls right off my tongue!

30. Of the following, which is the best way to revise and combine sentences 1 and 2 (reproduced below)?

I remember when my sister told me she had to attend a night class. It was an exercise class on Pilates.

(A) I remember when my sister told me she had to attend a night Pilates class.

(B) When my sister told me she had to attend a night class, she said it was a Pilates class.

(C) I remember my sister telling me she had to attend a night class; it was a Pilates exercise class.

(D) My sister had told me, I remembered, that she had to attend a night class that was for Pilates exercise.

(E) I remember when my sister told me she had to attend a night class for Pilates exercise.

31. Of the following, which is the best way to phrase Sentence 7 (reproduced below)?

Then winter came and I found myself unwilling to venture onto the snowy, icy, slushy roads for my daily walk.

(A) (As it is now)

(B) Then winter came, and I found that I was no longer excited about the prospect of venturing out for my daily walk.

(C) Once winter came, I felt I didn't want to venture out onto the dangerous roads anymore for my daily walk.

(D) Then once the winter came, venturing out onto the snowy, icy, and slushy roads was not something I wanted to do anymore.

(E) Then winter came and the roads were snowy, icy and slushy; I found that I didn't want to venture out anymore for my daily walk.

GO ON TO THE NEXT PAGE

32. In Sentence 8, the phrase *yet they were getting boring* is best replaced by

(A)   however I found them to be getting boring
(B)   nevertheless they had been getting boring
(C)   yet I was getting them boring
(D)   but they were getting boring
(E)   and yet they were getting boring

33. Which of the following sentences should be omitted to improve the unity of the second paragraph?

(A)   Sentence 7
(B)   Sentence 8
(C)   Sentence 9
(D)   Sentence 10
(E)   Sentence 11

34. In context, which of the following is the best way to phrase the underlined portion of Sentence 12 (reproduced below)?

Even though I was skeptical, I chose the DVD that looked like the least intimidating and loaded it into the player.

(A)   (As it is now)
(B)   looked like it was the least intimidating
(C)   looked to be like the least intimidating
(D)   was looking like the least intimidating
(E)   looked the least intimidating

35. A strategy that the writer uses within the third paragraph is to

(A)   refer to unfamiliar vocabulary
(B)   intimidate the reader
(C)   abandon the main topic
(D)   foreshadow her final statement
(E)   use humor to make her point

STOP

**If you finish before your time is up, check your work on this section only.
You may not turn to any other section in the test.**

SECTION 6
Time—25 minutes
24 Questions

Directions: For each of the questions in this section, choose the best answer and fill in the corresponding circle on your answer sheet.

Each sentence that follows has either one or two blanks. Each blank indicates that a word has been omitted from the sentence. Following each sentence are five words or sets of words. Select the word or set of words that, when inserted into the sentence in place of the blank(s), best fits the context of the sentence as a whole.

1. Though the author writes with -------, his short narratives and anecdotes always have meaning that goes far beyond the surface story line.

   (A) diffuseness
   (B) empathy
   (C) intricacy
   (D) brevity
   (E) rapture

2. Industrial manufacturers trying to obtain permission to build factories near residential areas argued that the effects of pollution in the vicinity of factories in comparable areas have been -------.

   (A) tumultuous
   (B) detrimental
   (C) inconsequential
   (D) pivotal
   (E) benevolent

3. Advancements in technology in the twentieth century greatly ------- the ------- of families and friends around the globe to keep in touch with each other.

   (A) impeded . . capability
   (B) accelerated . . deficiency
   (C) tapered . . savvy
   (D) abated . . capacity
   (E) enhanced . . facility

4. To avoid being ------- a typical teenybopper actress, the young star took a role in a dark satire that was completely different than any of the movies on which she had previously worked.

   (A) devised
   (B) deemed
   (C) dabbled
   (D) dissipated
   (E) imbued

5. Many ------- Elvis fans make ------- to his gravesite in Memphis, Tennessee, at least once a year, regardless of where they are from or how far the trip is.

   (A) scanty . . a crusade
   (B) obstinate . . an evasion
   (C) irresolute . . a venture
   (D) dedicated . . a pilgrimage
   (E) passionate . . a shirking

6. A ------- glance at the plethora of red marks ------- the rough draft of my essay told me that my professor had not liked what I had written at all.

   (A) cursory . . traversing
   (B) banal . . obscuring
   (C) meticulous . . crossing
   (D) fleeting . . annulling
   (E) hasty . . accommodating

GO ON TO THE NEXT PAGE

7. Although the church was considered to be one of the most beautiful in Europe, visitors complained that scaffolding ------- most of the church from sight.

   (A) exalted
   (B) shrouded
   (C) yielded
   (D) resolved
   (E) snared

8. Because of reports of forgeries, the coin collector ------- the rare quarter before agreeing to purchase it.

   (A) glanced at
   (B) perused
   (C) sauntered
   (D) scrutinized
   (E) admitted to

GO ON TO THE NEXT PAGE ▷

Each passage that follows is accompanied by several questions based on the content of the passage. Answer the questions based on what is either stated or implied in each passage. Be sure to read any introductory material that is provided.

Questions 9–10 are based on the following passage.

Anna watched languidly as her mom sorted through the box of secondhand clothing sent by their wealthy relatives. Anna didn't
Line expect much for herself, as these boxes typically
5 only contained items for her brothers and her mom. Still, she felt a thrill of excitement when her mom pulled out a fur coat worthy of a catalog. Looking wistfully at these catalogs was the nearest Anna had come to fashion since the
10 stock market had crashed in 1929. Anna's mother perceived the tiny spark of hope in her daughter's eyes and tossed the coat to her with a knowing smile.

9. Why does the author use the word "languidly" in line 1?

(A) The author wants to emphasize that Anna has a certain degree of apathy about the activity she is witnessing.
(B) The author means to imply that Anna is lazy and ungrateful.
(C) The author is foreshadowing that Anna's family is going through difficult financial times.
(D) The author is suggesting that Anna is still able to get excited about small things.
(E) The author is criticizing Anna for being concerned about fashion when her family is so poor.

10. Based on the information in the passage, Anna and her mother can best be described as

(A) affluent
(B) critical
(C) poor
(D) witty
(E) spontaneous

Questions 11–12 are based on the following passage.

Soothing a fussy crying baby is an important step in learning to respond to your baby's needs and in establishing a system of communi-
Line cation. Most babies cry because they are in
5 need; something is not right in their world. Feeding, burping, and changing diapers are among the basic duties involved in caring for babies. Sometimes, however, problems beyond these need attention, and a baby will continue
10 to cry, despite your best efforts.
Maybe the baby is having some kind of intestinal pain. A tooth might be emerging. Perhaps the baby simply wants the comfort of being held. Most infants respond favorably to
15 motion because that is what they experienced inside their mother's womb. Walking, riding in a car or baby sling, gently bouncing—these can all serve to pacify the infant so he or she stops crying and perhaps even falls asleep. Sucking
20 on something also calms babies, so even after a feeding there is nothing wrong with offering a pacifier.

11. The passage implies that the crying of babies is

(A) highly indecipherable
(B) deeply complex
(C) especially irresolvable
(D) easily mitigable
(E) normally reproachable

12. The author's attitude toward the "pacifier" (line 22) can best be characterized as one of

(A) confusion
(B) awe
(C) derision
(D) resentment
(E) approval

GO ON TO THE NEXT PAGE

Questions 13–24 are based on the following passages.

The following passages address two specific battles of the Civil War.

Passage 1

Nine times as many Americans fell in the farmlands near Antietam Creek in the fall of 1862 than fell on the beaches of Normandy on D-Day, the so-called longest day of World War
Line
5 II. The bloodiest single day of war in the nation's history came when General Robert E. Lee's Confederate Army undertook its first engagement on northern soil. According to the Antietam National Battlefield, when the
10 fighting had subsided, more than 23,000 soldiers lay dead or wounded, more than all of the dead or wounded Americans in the Revolutionary War, War of 1812, Mexican War, and Spanish-American War combined.
15 Just a week after his army's victory in the Second Battle of Bull Run, Lee resolved to advance the front into Northern territory. The vast farm fields of western Maryland were ready for harvest, and Lee saw in them an
20 opportunity to nourish his soldiers, replenish his supplies, and turn the residents of the unde-cided border state to his cause.

Lee's grander vision sought a victory in the North to legitimize his army in the eyes of
25 France and England, whom he could subse-quently solicit for aid. Their pressure could turn public opinion against President Lincoln and intensify calls for peace, solidifying the division between Union and Confederacy.
30 So with great fanfare, Lee and fellow General "Stonewall" Jackson marched their ragged Army of Northern Virginia across the Potomac River and straight through the Frederick town square. Lee issued the
35 *Proclamation to the People of Maryland* to invite the citizens to join the Southern movement. Soldiers obeyed Lee's order to refrain from violence and pillaging, so for several days the townspeople maintained tacit compliance and
40 sold food, clothes, and shoes to Southern troops. Lee keenly observed, however, that while pleasant, the people of Maryland reserved no sympathy for the Confederate side, so he needed a revised plan.
45 Forces would divide to take western Maryland and then reform to advance along the railroad toward Harrisburg, Pennsylvania, a crucial Union transport hub. General Jackson led 22,000 troops southwest to Harpers Ferry
50 to engage the 12,000-man Federal fortification. Lee's remaining 18,000 soldiers would march over the mountains 25 miles to Hagerstown and wait for the others. On September 10, 1862, all began their march. No one knew how fateful it
55 would be.

Lee soon realized that the Union was a step ahead. Their Army of the Potomac was reassembled in days instead of the weeks Lee had forecast. In addition, the Harpers Ferry
60 garrison had remained instead of fleeing, as Lee imagined it would upon learning of his advance. Lastly, an enlisted man searching a recently abandoned Confederate camp recovered a copy of Lee's order detailing the siege of Maryland.
65 Union General George McClellan moved his forces west through Frederick, and Lee caught word of it. Knowing the peril his divided troops were in, he ordered men to fortify the paths across the mountains, granting sufficient
70 time to the majority of his soldiers to establish a defensive position near Sharpsburg. Simultaneously, McClellan and his 85,000 men waited along Antietam Creek outside town. By nightfall on September 16, the stage was set for
75 the devastating Battle of Antietam, which would begin at sunrise.

Passage 2

The three days of the Battle of Gettysburg, Pennsylvania, constitute the blood-iest fight of the Civil War—50,000 combatants
80 falling dead or wounded or disappearing. Gettysburg is often cited as the last crucial battle of the war before the Confederate surrender. In the intervening two years, the Confederate Army would never again attempt
85 such a grand offensive in the North. On the last day of battle, Union forces anticipated and

GO ON TO THE NEXT PAGE

defused what is now known as Pickett's Charge, the final assault ordered by General Robert E. Lee, leaving Confederate forces in tatters.

90   Lee approached the third day of Gettysburg with the same strategy as he had the day before. He would divide his forces to attack Federal positions from both the east and the west. Troops under General James Longstreet
95 were to take up the assault on Culp's Hill. However, standing by at dawn, Longstreet and his men unexpectedly suffered a devastating artillery bombardment from Union troops intent on reclaiming the previous day's losses.

100   Lee hastened to revise his plan of attack. Nine brigades were set to attack Federal positions in the center of the line on Cemetery Ridge. The selection of troops for this mission was the first of many Confederate blunders that
105 doomed Pickett's Charge. Confederate General A.P. Hill was ill, so responsibility for his men was passed to General George Pickett, who failed to distinguish between Hill's well-rested men and those who had recently fought in
110 battle. Indeed the battle-fatigued soldiers that made the charge fell into ranks in a thicket behind the cannons.

In advance of the infantry assault, Confederate artillery pieces launched the Civil
115 War's largest bombardment against Union emplacements. Initially, Union artillery held its fire to save precious ammunition. Soon enough, though, scores of Federal cannons joined the fray, exchanging two hours of volleys with the
120 Confederate Army, who fell gravely low on ammunition. Overall, the barrage was ineffective. Shells often overshot Union positions, a fact lost on Confederate commanders blinded by thick smoke that blanketed the battlefield. At times,
125 Union officers ordered cease fire to conserve powder and balls, which Confederate artillery chief Colonel Edward Alexander erroneously took to mean his assaults were destroying Union batteries. Union cannoneers overshot targets,
130 too, but in their case, balls regularly fell on soldiers holed up in the woods waiting to advance. The Confederacy suffered shocking casualties even before involvement of riflemen.

Longstreet initiated the infantry assault
135 under orders from General Lee. The southern force numbered over 12,000 men across nine brigades to form a mile-long offensive front. The thousand-yard march to within musket range of the Union fortifications was peppered
140 with harrowing artillery fire. When cannonade became fusillade, the mile of men had narrowed to nearly half. Flanking fire from the left decimated an entire brigade. Forces in the center wheeled to support them but were met with a
145 musket attack from the Eighth Ohio Infantry regiment, which had unexpectedly moved to ambush the Confederate soldiers. The Virginians under General Pickett brought up the rear and retook the fight to the left. Soon,
150 their right flank was exposed to calamitous enfilade fire from the Vermont Brigade. Remaining Confederates succeeded in a partial breech of the center Union line, but reinforcements from the right quickly put down the
155 southern offensive.

The charge was a massacre. Pickett's brigade commanders, each of his 13 regiment leaders, and nearly half his 12,000 enlisted men fell during the assault. Union dead or wounded
160 numbered fewer than 2,000. Today at Gettysburg, a monument commemorates the "high water mark" of the Confederacy along Cemetery Ridge, for after Pickett's Charge on July 3, 1863, the Army of the South never fully
165 recovered and began the series of retreats and surrenders that concluded the Civil War.

13. The author of Passage 1 uses D-Day (lines 4–5) as evidence of the brutality of the Battle of Antietam because D-Day

(A) involved large-scale infantry deployments

(B) is known as a terrifying battle but resulted in fewer casualties

(C) occurred over a similar extended period of time as Antietam

(D) was a large invasion of enemy territory

(E) was a mission to regain lost territory of great strategic importance

GO ON TO THE NEXT PAGE ⟩

14. In line 8, the word "engagement" most nearly means

(A) match
(B) betrothal
(C) confrontation
(D) arrangement
(E) commitment

15. Lines 17–22 ("The…cause") suggest that Lee's army was

(A) eager for another fight
(B) satisfied with their progress
(C) fatigued from recent battle
(D) broken and despondent
(E) callous and terrifying

16. Which statement about the Army of Northern Virginia, if true, would most directly support the view described in lines 30–41?

(A) Soldiers were difficult to control in times of great privation.
(B) Soldiers took great pains to keep their uniforms and equipment tidy.
(C) General Lee was a powerful but often barbaric man.
(D) A rigid chain of command maintained strict order throughout the ranks.
(E) During the Civil War, the homes of dissenting townspeople were often fired on by soldiers.

17. In context, "grand" (line 85) most nearly means

(A) massive
(B) extravagant
(C) wonderful
(D) haughty
(E) beautiful

18. In Passage 2, the author's attitude toward Confederate preparations for the charge (lines 90–112) suggests

(A) a single-minded commitment to decry the Confederate cause
(B) a way in which an overabundance of leaders can cause confusion over mission objectives
(C) a striking inconsistency between the quality of the plan and its execution
(D) an understanding of the link between hurried planning and defeat in battle
(E) a contradiction between the author's personal beliefs and those espoused in popular history

19. According to Passage 2, Confederate troops on Pickett's Charge were attacked with which of the following?

I. Amphibious vehicles
II. Artillery fire
III. Infantry charges

(A) I only
(B) II only
(C) I and II
(D) I and III
(E) II and III

20. In the context of Passage 2, the statement "When cannonade became fusillade" (lines 140–141) suggests that the Confederate line

(A) was suffering massive losses
(B) moved within firearms range
(C) made very slow progress across the field
(D) was easy for Union soldiers to target
(E) stopped shooting to make a bayonet charge

GO ON TO THE NEXT PAGE

21. In line 162, the quotation marks around the phrase "high water mark" serve to

(A) emphasize the uniqueness of the author's writing
(B) criticize the human preoccupation with expansion
(C) emphasize the limitations of military conquest
(D) indicate that this word is used allegorically
(E) demonstrate the author's disagreement with the choice of phrase

22. Unlike the author of Passage 1, the author of Passage 2 does which of the following?

(A) Explains a war strategy
(B) Questions an officer's decision
(C) Details a battle
(D) Offers an alternative interpretation
(E) Quotes a historical authority

23. Passage 1 and Passage 2 share a general tone of

(A) respectful acknowledgement
(B) analytical detachment
(C) righteous indignation
(D) affectionate nostalgia
(E) personal regret

24. The information in Passage 1 supports which assumption about the Battle of Gettysburg described in Passage 2?

(A) It could be called the bloodiest battle of the Civil War because it lasted for several days.
(B) It was a crucial battle for the Confederates because they were drawing near to the Union capital.
(C) It left more dead and wounded soldiers than any other single-day battle in recorded history.
(D) It was foolish of General Lee to attempt a fight in northern territory.
(E) It was essential for winning the state of Pennsylvania to the southern cause.

STOP

**If you finish before your time is up, check your work on this section only.
You may not turn to any other section in the test.**

SECTION 7
Time—20 minutes
16 Questions

Directions: Solve each problem and determine which is the best of the answer choices given. Fill in the corresponding circle on your answer sheet. Use any available space to solve the problems.

Notes

1. The use of a calculator is permitted.
2. All numbers are real numbers.
3. Figures that accompany problems in this test are intended to provide information useful in solving the problems. They are drawn as accurately as possible EXCEPT when it is stated in a specific problem that the figure is not drawn to scale. All figures lie in a plane unless otherwise indicated.
4. Unless otherwise specified, the domain of any function f is assumed to be the set of all real numbers x for which $f(x)$ is a real number.

Reference Information

    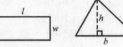 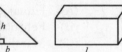

$A = \Pi r^2$

$C = 2\Pi r$

$A = lw$

$A = \frac{1}{2}bh$

$V = lwh$

$V = \Pi r^2 h$

$c^2 = a^2 + b^2$

Special Right Triangles

The number of degrees of arc in a circle is 360.

The sum of the measures in degrees of the angles of a triangle is 180.

1. If $(x - 1)^2 = 1,600$, which of the following could be the value of $x - 7$?

(A) 9
(B) 32
(C) 34
(D) 41
(E) 48

The sum of $4x$ and 6 is equal to
the product of x and $\frac{1}{4}$.

2. Which of the following equations gives the relationship stated in the problem above?

(A) $4x = (\frac{1}{4})x + 6$

(B) $6(4x) = x + \frac{1}{4}$

(C) $4x + 6 = (\frac{1}{4})x$

(D) $4x + 6 = \frac{x}{(\frac{1}{4})}$

(E) $6(4x) = (\frac{1}{4})x$

GO ON TO THE NEXT PAGE

3. If 7 and 13 are the lengths of two sides of a triangle, which of the following can be the length of the third side?

   I.   7
   II. 17
   III. 21

   (A) I only
   (B) II only
   (C) I and II only
   (D) II and III only
   (E) I, II, and III

4. A particular grocery store has 120 shopping carts, 20 of which are blue. What is the probability that a shopping cart selected at random will be blue?

   (A) $\frac{1}{120}$
   (B) $\frac{1}{20}$
   (C) $\frac{1}{12}$
   (D) $\frac{1}{6}$
   (E) $\frac{1}{4}$

Jefferson Family Electricity Use by Month

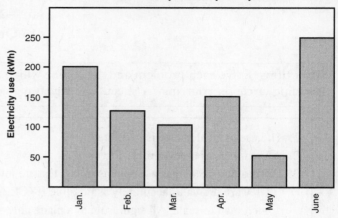

5. According to the graph above, during which of the following two-month periods did the Jefferson family use the most electricity?

   (A) January and February
   (B) February and March
   (C) March and April
   (D) April and May
   (E) May and June

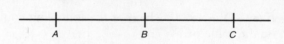

6. In the figure above, $AC = 32$ and $AB = BC$. Point D (not shown) is on the line between B and C such that $BD = DC$. What does AD equal?

   (A) 32
   (B) 24
   (C) 16
   (D) 8
   (E) 4

GO ON TO THE NEXT PAGE

7. If k is a positive integer, then $(7 \times 10^{-k}) + (2 \times 10^{-k})$ must equal

   (A) $\dfrac{9}{10}$

   (B) $\dfrac{9}{10^{-k}}$

   (C) $\dfrac{9}{10^{k}}$

   (D) $\dfrac{9}{10^{2k}}\approx$

   (E) $\dfrac{7}{20^{k}}$

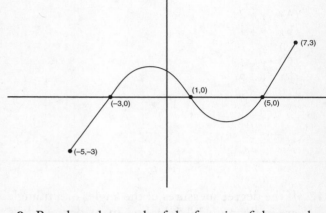

9. Based on the graph of the function f above, what are the values of x for which $f(x)$ is positive?

   (A) $-3 < x < 1$
   (B) $1 < x < 5$
   (C) $-3 < x < 1$ and $1 < x < 5$
   (D) $-3 < x < 1$ and $5 < x < 7$
   (E) $-5 < x < -3$ and $1 < x < 5$

8. How many more degrees of arc are there in $\frac{1}{5}$ of a circle than in $\frac{1}{6}$ of a circle?

   (A) $6°$
   (B) $12°$
   (C) $24°$
   (D) $60°$
   (E) $72°$

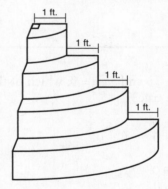

10. The figure above shows the dimensions of an object constructed of 4 layers of wood. Each layer is $\frac{1}{4}$ of a right circular cylindrical solid that is 1 foot high. How many cubic feet of wood make up the object?

   (A) $\dfrac{15}{2}$

   (B) 30

   (C) 30π

   (D) 15π

   (E) $\dfrac{15\pi}{2}$

GO ON TO THE NEXT PAGE ⟹

11. If x and y are positive integers and $9(3^x) = 3^y$, what is x in terms of y?

  (A) $y + 2$
  (B) $y + 1$
  (C) y
  (D) $y - 1$
  (E) $y - 2$

12. If the degree measures of the angles of a triangle are in the ratio 3:4:5, by how many degrees does the measure of the largest angle exceed the measure of the smallest angle?

  (A) $15°$
  (B) $20°$
  (C) $30°$
  (D) $45°$
  (E) $60°$

13. If $abcd = 36$ and $abde = 0$, which of the following must be true?

  (A) $a > 0$
  (B) $b > 0$
  (C) $c = 0$
  (D) $d = 0$
  (E) $e = 0$

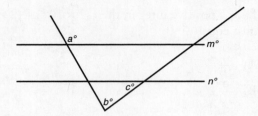

14. In the figure above, if m is parallel to n, what does c equal in terms of a and b?

  (A) $180 - a - b$
  (B) $180 - a + b$
  (C) $180 + a - b$
  (D) $a - b$
  (E) $a + b$

15. $(3^2 + 1)(3^2 - 1)(2^2 + 1)(2^3 - 1) =$

  (A) 750
  (B) 1,200
  (C) 2,800
  (D) 4,000
  (E) 5,600

16. To gain membership into a certain organization, a candidate must receive the votes of at least $\frac{2}{3}$ of the group's 267 members. What is the least number of votes the candidate must receive to become a member?

  (A) 207
  (B) 178
  (C) 89
  (D) 66
  (E) 23

STOP

**If you finish before your time is up, check your work on this section only.
You may not turn to any other section in the test.**

SECTION 8
Time—20 minutes
19 Questions

> **Directions:** For each of the questions in this section, choose the best answer and fill in the corresponding circle on your answer sheet.

Each sentence that follows has either one or two blanks. Each blank indicates that a word has been omitted from the sentence. Following each sentence are five words or sets of words. Select the word or set of words that, when inserted into the sentence in place of the blank(s), best fits the context of the sentence as a whole.

1. Fans of the director's latest movie were disappointed by the film's ------- action sequences; viewers have come to expect non-stop excitement from his movies.

   (A) attention to
   (B) lack of
   (C) speculation about
   (D) sympathy for
   (E) parody of

2. The ------- task of negotiating a peace agreement between the warring countries was quite lengthy; finding points that the two parties would ------- proved to be nearly impossible.

   (A) inane . . assent to
   (B) insidious . . disagree with
   (C) onerous . . agree to
   (D) tranquil . . condescend to
   (E) merciless . . admit to

3. During periods of protracted drought, many plants ------- water by temporarily shutting down their respiratory systems.

   (A) pursue
   (B) lose
   (C) conserve
   (D) regain
   (E) locate

4. Despite Kathy's ------- to perform on stage, she received a standing ovation for her rendition of the popular song.

   (A) desire
   (B) reluctance
   (C) ability
   (D) tendency
   (E) attraction

5. The minimum wage is ------- to meet the basic costs of living; many people who work for the minimum wage cannot afford to pay their bills.

   (A) imperceptible
   (B) inherent
   (C) invaluable
   (D) implicit
   (E) insufficient

6. The students watched the chemistry professor with ------- attention, astonished by the results of each experiment.

   (A) rapt
   (B) indifferent
   (C) plausible
   (D) naive
   (E) mundane

GO ON TO THE NEXT PAGE

The passage that follows is accompanied by several questions based on the content of the passage. Answer the questions based on what is either stated or implied in the passage. Be sure to read any introductory material that is provided.

Questions 7–19 are based on the following passage.

This passage is adapted from a book titled Prehistoric World: or, Vanished Races, *written by E. A. Allen in 1885.*

For a clear understanding of questions relating to the beginnings of early man, a casual acquaintance with geology is required. To see
Line
5 where in this strange unfolding of life the first faint, indecisive traces of man's presence are to be found and to learn what great changes in climate, in geography, and in life had occurred before man's appearance, let us pass in brief review the history of early geological periods.
10 There must have been a very long period of time during which no life was possible on the globe. As to the extent of time during which there was no life, we have no means of determining. Toward the close of this extended
15 period of time, faint traces of life appear, though not as we are apt to think of it today. No nodding flowers were kissed by the sunshine of this early time. The earliest forms of flowerless plants, such as seaweeds, and in
20 dry places possibly lichens covering the rocks, were the highest forms of vegetable life. Animal life, if present, occurs in the very lowest form, merely structureless bodies, their motion consisting simply in protruding and with-
25 drawing hair-like processes. Such was the beginning of life. This vast period of time is known among geologists as Achaean time and is considered, by geologists, as extending from 3,800 million years ago (mya) to 543 mya.
30 The period following Achaean time is called, by geologists, Paleozoic time (543 mya–248 mya), meaning "early life forms." During the course of this age, the forms of life present wide differences from those of modern
35 time. The vegetation commenced with the lowest orders of flowerless plants, such as seaweeds, but, before it was brought to a close, there was a wonderful variety and richness of

plants of the *Cryptogamic* division. In some of
40 the warmest portions of the globe today, we have ferns growing four or five feet high. During the end of the Paleozoic time, ferns 30 feet or so in height were growing. Near the close of the Paleozoic era, vegetation assumed
45 a higher form of life. Flowering plants were represented. Pines were growing in the coal measures. In animal life a similar advance is noted. The class of animals having no backbone, or invertebrate animals, were largely
50 represented, and, toward the close of the Paleozoic time, we meet with representatives of the vertebrate family. The waters swarmed with fishes. Besides these, there were amphibians and reptiles in the closing portions of this time
55 period.
The time at last came for the dawning of a new era. Vast changes had been taking place in the geography of the continents; thus, old forms of life died away and were succeeded by
60 creatures more similar to those of our own times. The name of this period is the Mesozoic time (248 mya–65 mya). The abundant flowerless vegetation of the preceding epoch dwindles away. The flowering trees increase in number
65 and importance until, in the closing period of Mesozoic time, we have trees with deciduous leaves.
In the animal world there were many strange forms. This was the age of reptiles.
70 They dominated on the land, in the air, and in the sea. On the land huge reptiles 50 and 60 feet long stalked, and, when standing upright, at least 30 feet tall. Some of these huge creatures were carnivorous, living on other animals.
75 Others fed on the foliage of trees. In the air, huge reptilian bats, veritable flying dragons with a spread of wings from 10 to 20 feet, disported themselves. In the sea swam great reptilian whales, seals, and walruses. At the
80 present day, not more than six species of

GO ON TO THE NEXT PAGE ⟹

reptiles in the whole world have a length of over 15 feet, and not more than 18 species exceed 10 feet in length. But from one limited locality, representing but one era of this age in
85 England, there have been discovered 4 or 5 species of carnivorous reptiles 20 to 50 feet long, 10 or 12 species of crocodiles, lizards, and swimming reptiles from 10 to 60 feet long.

Birds made their first appearance during
90 the Mesozoic time. There is little doubt among archaeologists that birds were just modified, more highly adapted reptiles. The first bird had a long jointed tail and a bill well supplied with formidable teeth. It is also during this time that
95 we meet with the first members of the class *Mammalia*; the remains of marsupials, the lowest form of mammal, can be found in the rocks of the Mesozoic age. These marsupials are the first representatives of the class
100 *Mammalia*, the class to which man belongs. Because of their more highly evolved nature, mammals have been the rulers of the animal kingdom since their appearance.

The last great division of time is called
105 Cenozoic (65 mya–present). This means "new life forms." In this age, the forms of life are much nearer to those of present day. It was at some time during this epoch when man made his appearance.

7. The author's main point in the passage is that

(A) geologic changes spurred the emergence of new life forms
(B) humans have always been the dominant life form on earth
(C) different life forms developed over millions of years
(D) fossil records reveal many primitive life forms
(E) life first emerged on earth a tremendously long time ago

8. As used in line 3, "acquaintance" most nearly means

(A) friendship
(B) colleague
(C) familiarity
(D) affiliation
(E) companion

9. The discussion of the earliest life forms in the second paragraph (lines 18–29) primarily suggests that

(A) conditions on earth so long ago were suitable for modern life forms
(B) the earth was an ugly place before modern plants
(C) lichen dominant in the Archaean period is extinct today
(D) the earliest life forms existed longer than any life form that has emerged since
(E) ancient life forms were undetectably small and formless

10. Which of the following assertions detracts LEAST from the author's statements in the second paragraph?

(A) Multicellular organisms might have been present in the deep sea during the Achaean period.
(B) All species of seaweed throughout earth's history have had a distinct form.
(C) Early plant life was abundant on earth and gave the planet its oxygen-rich atmosphere.
(D) Fossils of low-growing leafy plants can be found in Achaean rocks.
(E) Life was always possible on earth but for a long time lacked the crucial electrochemical reaction.

11. The author develops the third paragraph (lines 30–55) by presenting

(A) a common argument followed by a repudiation of it
(B) a common opinion and the reasons it is held
(C) different sides of a single issue
(D) details that culminate in truth
(E) a thesis followed by specific illustrations

GO ON TO THE NEXT PAGE

12. In line 32, the quotation marks around the phrase "early life forms" serve to

    (A) emphasize the inadequacy of the description
    (B) indicate that the phrase is the definition of a word
    (C) emphasize the vagueness of the description
    (D) criticize the opaqueness of scientific jargon
    (E) demonstrate the author's agreement with the description

13. The author cites the example of ferns (lines 39–43) to substantiate which of the following claims?

    (A) Modern vegetation is little changed from its Paleozoic form.
    (B) Single-celled organisms no longer dominated the earth in the Paleozoic.
    (C) Similar plants flourished more in the Paleozoic than they do today.
    (D) Flowering plants had not yet appeared on earth.
    (E) More advanced plants appeared by the end of the Paleozoic.

14. As used in line 59, "succeeded" most nearly means

    (A) displaced
    (B) thrived
    (C) accomplished
    (D) bequeathed
    (E) ascended

15. In lines 64–67, the author implies that deciduous trees

    (A) emerged before flowering species
    (B) did not exist prior to the Mesozoic
    (C) spread across all the diverging continents
    (D) died off from the increase in flowering species
    (E) are the most important of the plant species

16. The examples cited in the fifth paragraph (lines 68–88) are primarily drawn from

    (A) paleontology
    (B) botany
    (C) fiction
    (D) geology
    (E) geography

17. The author mentions birds and reptiles (lines 89–92) in order to

    (A) demonstrate the vast differences between life forms
    (B) explain the geographic significance of flying organisms
    (C) emphasize the period of time between the domination of reptiles and the emergence of birds
    (D) suggest that birds derived from reptilian ancestors
    (E) conjure up the image of a ferocious, toothed bird

18. Which of the following, if true, would undermine the validity of the author's assumption about the dominance of mammals ("Because of…since their appearance") in lines 101–103?

    (A) The mongoose of the Indian subcontinent is ideally suited to repelling cobra attacks.
    (B) The grizzly bear is the top predator in the forest except when humans are permitted to hunt them.
    (C) The deadliest venom in the world flows from the fangs of a tropical spider.
    (D) Sharks in a North American bay are skilled hunters of seals and walruses and have no natural enemies.
    (E) Acorns are food for chipmunks, which are food for the red-tailed hawk.

19. Which of the following statements is supported by the passage?

    (A) All species descend from earlier life forms.
    (B) The Paleozoic era was characterized by climate conditions that encouraged greater plant growth than is possible today.
    (C) Over millions of years, a vast number of species go extinct as others take their place.
    (D) Flowers mark the most advanced of plant species.
    (E) The start of life on earth can be attributed to a highly improbable chemical reaction.

STOP

**If you finish before your time is up, check your work on this section only.
You may not turn to any other section in the test.**

SECTION 9
Time—10 minutes
14 Questions

Directions: For each question, select the best answer from among the choices listed. Fill in the corresponding circle on your answer sheet.

The following questions test the correct and effective use of standard written English in expressing an idea. Part of each sentence (or the entire sentence) is underlined. Following each sentence are five different ways of phrasing the underlined portion. Answer choice A repeats the original phrasing. If you think that the original phrasing is best, select answer choice A. Otherwise, select from the remaining four choices. Your selection should result in the most effective, clear sentence, free from awkwardness or ambiguity.

1. Willa Cather wrote her first novel in 1911 at age thirty-eight years old.

   (A) at age thirty-eight years old
   (B) and she was thirty-eight years old then
   (C) when she was thirty-eight
   (D) at the time when she was thirty-eight
   (E) upon reaching the age of thirty-eight

2. Tracy, Kate, and Ryan were skiing and, since Kate has hit an icy patch, she fell down and lost one of her skis.

   (A) and, since Kate has hit an icy patch, she fell down and lost one of her skis
   (B) and then she fell down and lost one of her skis after she hit an icy patch
   (C) when Kate fell down and lost one of her skis, since she hit an icy patch
   (D) when, hitting an icy patch, she fell down and lost one of her skis
   (E) when Kate hit an icy patch and fell down, losing one of her skis

3. A levee constructed along the banks of the river kept the townspeople safe from flooding, because many citizens had feared a catastrophe.

   (A) because many citizens had feared a catastrophe
   (B) a catastrophe that many citizens had feared
   (C) this was a catastrophe many citizens had feared
   (D) it was feared by many citizens as disaster
   (E) the fear many citizens had would be a disaster

4. Urban sprawl can be characterized not only by the larger scale developments but also by the low-density use of land.

   (A) also by the
   (B) also the
   (C) it has a
   (D) in the way of having a
   (E) as well in the

5. Doctors claim that patients typically either ignore the symptoms of anemia and mistake the symptoms as those of other conditions.

   (A) ignore the symptoms of anemia and mistake the symptoms as those of other conditions
   (B) ignores the symptoms for anemia or will mistake these for other conditions
   (C) ignore the symptoms of anemia or mistake the symptoms for those of other conditions
   (D) ignore the symptoms for anemia or mistake it for symptoms of other conditions
   (E) ignore the symptoms of anemia and mistake the symptoms for those of other conditions

GO ON TO THE NEXT PAGE

6. The term "metaphor" <u>which refers to directly comparing</u> between two seemingly unrelated things, as when one says "you are my sunshine" or "I'm feeling blue."

(A) which refers to directly comparing
(B) referring to comparing directly
(C) is when it refers to comparisons made directly
(D) refers to a direct comparison
(E) referring to a comparison which is made directly

7. In 1908, Henry Ford, one of the pioneering automotive engineers, transformed personal transportation by introducing the Model T, <u>a vehicle that was easy to operate, maintain, and handle</u> on rough roads.

(A) a vehicle that was easy to operate, maintain, and handle
(B) creating a vehicle more easier to operate, maintain, and handle
(C) and creates a vehicle easy to operate, maintain, and handle
(D) and created a vehicle, easy to operate, maintain, and handle
(E) and he created the easier to operate, maintain, and handle

8. <u>Prized for its rarity, jewelry collectors will spend a small fortune on platinum rather than settle for common silver or white gold.</u>

(A) Prized for its rarity, jewelry collectors will spend a small fortune on platinum rather than settle for common silver or white gold.
(B) Prized for its rarity, platinum demands a small fortune among jewelry collectors unwilling to settle for common silver or white gold.
(C) Prized as rare, jewelry collectors will spend a small fortune on platinum as opposed to settling for demands silver or white gold.
(D) Platinum, prized for its rarity by jewelry collectors who will spend a small fortune, but not to settle for common silver or white gold.
(E) As prized for rarity, platinum, being costly, demands a small fortune for jewelry collectors unwilling to settle for common silver or white gold.

9. Evidence from research and long-term use <u>show lead-acid rechargeable batteries tend to last</u> longer than nickel-cadmium rechargeable batteries.

(A) show lead-acid rechargeable batteries tend to last
(B) shows lead-acid rechargeable batteries tends to last
(C) shows that lead-acid rechargeable batteries tend to last
(D) show lead-acid rechargeable batteries that tend to last
(E) is showing lead-acid rechargeable batteries tending to last

10. A recent publication estimated that, over the working lives of adults in a household, the average income of a household of two college graduates is $1.8 million more than <u>where there are two high school graduates</u>.

(A) where there are two high school graduates
(B) of a household where both are high school graduates
(C) a household in which two are high school graduates
(D) those households of two who are high school graduates
(E) that of a household of two high school graduates

11. Because they were raised in a household where laughter was constant and practical jokes were a daily occurrence, Jeremiah and John both firmly resolved <u>of becoming comedic pairs</u> known around the world.

(A) of becoming comedic pairs
(B) of becoming a comedic pair
(C) that they would become comedic pairs
(D) to become a comedic pair
(E) to become comedic pairs

GO ON TO THE NEXT PAGE ➡

12. The local news station does not broadcast as many international stories <u>compared to what the national does</u>.

    (A)   compared to what the national does
    (B)   as does the national
    (C)   as does the national news station
    (D)   like the national news station does
    (E)   like the one that is national does

13. <u>As well as hydration, water is a source of</u> essential vitamins and minerals.

    (A)   As well as hydration, water is a source of
    (B)   Besides hydration, also water is a source of
    (C)   Besides hydration, water is also a source of
    (D)   Water is a source not only of hydration but also of
    (E)   Water is a source of not only hydration but, as well, of

14. Franz Josef Gall, one of the pioneering phrenologists, was the first to consider the brain <u>to be an organ of mental function and to identify what regions</u> are responsible for different mental functions.

    (A)   to be an organ of mental function and to identify what regions
    (B)   an organ of mental function and to identify which regions
    (C)   as being an organ of mental function and to identify what regions
    (D)   as if it was an organ of mental function and identified what regions
    (E)   organs of mental function and identifying which regions

STOP

**If you finish before your time is up, check your work on this section only.
You may not turn to any other section in the test.**

Answer Key

Section 1

Because grading the essay is subjective, we've chosen not to include any "graded" essays here. Your best bet is to have someone you trust, such as your personal tutor, read your essays and give you an honest critique. Make the grading criteria mentioned in Chapter 5 available to whomever grades your essays. If you plan on grading your own essays, review the grading criteria and be as honest as possible regarding the structure, development, organization, technique, and appropriateness of your writing. Focus on your weak areas and continue to practice in order to improve your writing skills.

Section 2

1. C	17. D
2. D	18. E
3. E	19. C
4. D	20. A
5. C	
6. B	
7. B	
8. A	
9. C	
10. B	
11. D	
12. C	
13. E	
14. A	
15. C	
16. B	

Section 3

1. B	17. E
2. E	18. E
3. A	19. C
4. C	20. B
5. E	21. A
6. D	22. B
7. B	23. D
8. C	24. B
9. A	
10. B	
11. D	
12. A	
13. E	
14. C	
15. B	
16. B	

Section 4

Multiple Choice

1. C
2. E
3. D
4. B
5. D
6. A
7. B
8. D

Student Produced Response

9. $\frac{1}{2}$ or .5
10. 34
11. 2300
12. 3 or 11
13. 45
14. 18
15. 3
16. 5
17. 5
18. 140

Section 5

1. B
2. C
3. D
4. A
5. D
6. B
7. D
8. B
9. D
10. C
11. E
12. A
13. C
14. B
15. C
16. C
17. D
18. B
19. E
20. E
21. A
22. B
23. D
24. B
25. E
26. B
27. D
28. B
29. E
30. A
31. A
32. D
33. C
34. E
35. E

Section 6

1. D	19. E
2. C	20. B
3. E	21. D
4. B	22. C
5. D	23. A
6. A	24. A
7. B	
8. D	
9. A	
10. C	
11. D	
12. E	
13. B	
14. C	
15. C	
16. D	
17. A	
18. D	

Section 7

1. C
2. C
3. C
4. D
5. A
6. B
7. C
8. B
9. D
10. E
11. E
12. C
13. E
14. D
15. C
16. B

Section 8

1. B
2. C
3. C
4. B
5. E
6. A
7. C
8. C
9. D
10. B
11. E
12. B
13. C
14. A
15. B
16. A
17. D
18. D
19. C

Section 9

1. C
2. E
3. B
4. A
5. C
6. D
7. A
8. B
9. C
10. E
11. D
12. C
13. D
14. B

Scoring Practice Test 4

Check your responses with the Answer Key. Fill in the blanks below and do the calculations to get your math, critical reading, and writing raw scores. Use the tables on the next pages find your scaled scores.

Remember that this is a simulated test and that the score should only be used to estimate your score on the actual SAT.

Get Your Math Raw Score:

	Number Correct	**Number Incorrect**
Section 2:	_____	_____
Section 4:		
(#1 – #8)	_____	_____
(#9 – #18)	_____	
Section 7:	_____	_____
Totals:	_____	_____

Divide the total Number Incorrect by 4 and subtract the result from the total Number Correct. This is your Raw Score: _____

Round Raw Score to the nearest whole number. Use Table 1 to find Scaled Score range.

Math Scaled Score Range: _____ - _____

Get Your Critical Reading Raw Score:

	Number Correct	**Number Incorrect**
Section 3:	_____	_____
Section 6:	_____	_____
Section 8:	_____	_____
Totals:	_____	_____

Divide the total Number Incorrect by 4 and subtract the result from the total Number Correct. This is your Raw Score: _____

Round Raw Score to the nearest whole number. Use Table 2 to find Scaled Score range.

Critical Reading Scaled Score Range: _____ - _____

Get Your Writing Raw Score:

	Number Correct	**Number Incorrect**
Section 5:	_____	_____
Section 9:	_____	_____
Totals:	_____	_____

Divide the total Number Incorrect by 4 and subtract the result from the total Number Correct. This is your Raw Score: _____

Round Raw Score to the nearest whole number. Use Table 3 to find Scaled Score range.

Writing Score Range: _____ - _____

Note that your Writing Score assumes an Essay score of 4. If you believe that your Essay warrants a score of 5 or 6, your Writing Score would increase by an average of 30 to 50 points. Likewise, if your Essay is in the 1 to 3 range, your Writing Score would decrease by an average of 30 to 50 points.

Get Your Composite Score:

To calculate your Composite Score Range, simply add the 3 sub-score ranges (Math, Critical Reading, and Writing).

Composite Score Range: _____ - _____

Table 1 Math Score Conversion

Raw Score	Scaled Score	Raw Score	Scaled Score
54	800	23	460-520
53	750-800	22	450-510
52	720-800	21	440-500
51	700-780	20	430-490
50	690-770	19	430-490
49	680-740	18	420-480
48	670-730	17	410-470
47	660-720	16	400-460
46	640-700	15	400-460
45	630-690	14	390-450
44	620-680	13	380-440
43	620-680	12	360-440
42	610-670	11	350-430
41	600-660	10	340-420
40	580-660	9	330-430
39	570-650	8	320-420
38	560-640	7	310-410
37	550-630	6	290-390
36	550-630	5	280-380
35	540-620	4	270-370
34	530-610	3	260-360
33	520-600	2	240-340
32	520-600	1	230-330
31	520-580	0	210-310
30	510-570	-1	200-290
29	500-560	-2	200-270
28	490-550	-3	200-250
27	490-550	-4	200-230
26	480-540	-5	200-210
25	470-530	-6 and below	200
24	460-520		

Table 2 Critical Reading Score Conversion

Raw Score	Scaled Score	Raw Score	Scaled Score
67	800	30	470-530
66	770-800	29	470-530
65	740-800	28	460-520
64	720-800	27	450-510
63	700-800	26	450-510
62	690-790	25	440-500
61	670-770	24	440-500
60	660-760	23	430-490
59	660-740	22	420-480
58	650-730	21	420-480
57	640-720	20	410-470
56	630-710	19	400-460
55	630-710	18	400-460
54	620-700	17	390-450
53	610-690	16	380-440
52	600-680	15	380-440
51	610-670	14	370-430
50	600-660	13	360-420
49	590-650	12	350-410
48	580-640	11	350-410
47	580-640	10	340-400
46	570-630	9	330-390
45	560-620	8	310-390
44	560-620	7	300-380
43	550-610	6	290-370
42	550-610	5	270-370
41	540-600	4	260-360
40	530-590	3	250-350
39	530-590	2	230-330
38	520-580	1	220-320
37	510-570	0	200-290
36	510-570	-1	200-290
35	500-560	-2	200-270
34	500-560	-3	200-250
33	490-550	-4	200-230
32	480-540	-5	200-210
31	480-540	-6 and below	200

Table 3 Writing Score Conversion

Raw Score	Scaled Score	Raw Score	Scaled Score
49	750-800	21	460-590
48	720-800	20	460-580
47	700-800	19	450-580
46	680-800	18	440-570
45	670-800	17	430-560
44	660-790	16	420-550
43	640-780	15	410-540
42	630-770	14	400-530
41	620-760	13	390-520
40	620-750	12	390-510
39	610-740	11	380-510
38	600-730	10	370-500
37	590-720	9	360-490
36	580-720	8	350-480
35	570-710	7	340-470
34	570-700	6	330-460
33	560-690	5	320-460
32	550-680	4	320-450
31	540-670	3	310-440
30	530-660	2	300-430
29	520-650	1	280-410
28	520-650	0	270-410
27	510-640	-1	250-390
26	500-630	-2	240-370
25	490-620	-3	240-360
24	480-610	-4	220-340
23	470-600	-5	200-320
22	460-590	-6 and below	200

Answers and Explanations

Section 1

Because grading the essay is subjective, we've chosen not to include any "graded" essays here. Your best bet is to have someone you trust, such as your personal tutor, read your essays and give you an honest critique. Make the grading criteria mentioned in Chapter 5, "SAT/PSAT Verbal," available to whomever grades your essays. If you plan on grading your own essays, review the grading criteria and be as honest as possible regarding the structure, development, organization, technique, and appropriateness of your writing. Focus on your weak areas and continue to practice to improve your writing skills.

Section 2

1. **The correct answer is C.** Because there were 2 packages that contained 12 cans of cola, Roger must have bought 2(12), or 24, cans in the 12-can packages. Likewise, there were 3 packages that contained 6 cans of cola so he bought 3(6), or 18, cans in the 6-can packages. Therefore, the total Roger purchased was 2(12) + 3(6), or 24 + 18, which is 42 cans.

2. **The correct answer is D.** Because P, Q, and R are points on a line in that order, Q is between P and R. To find PR, add PQ and QR. It is given that $PQ = 12$ and QR is 8 more than PQ; therefore, $QR = PQ + 8$, or $12 + 8$, which is 20. Finally, using the fact that $PR = PQ + QR$, PR must equal $12 + 20$, or 32.

3. **The correct answer is E.** To solve this problem, distribute the a in $a(m + n) = 24$ to get $am + an = 24$. It is given in the problem that $am = 8$. Substituting that into the equation yields $8 + an = 24$. Subtracting 8 from both sides of the equation results in $an = 24 - 8$, or 16.

4. **The correct answer is D.** If the four digits must be used to create a four-digit number, the number of combinations that result can be found by diagramming the situation. In a four-digit number, you have four possible locations for each digit: ___ ___ ___ ___. In the first location, you have four possibilities; in the second location, because one digit has already been used, you have three possibilities. Similarly, you have two possibilities in the third location, and one in the fourth. Thus, the total number of four-digit numbers possible is: $\underline{4} \times \underline{3} \times \underline{2} \times \underline{1}$, or 4!, which is equivalent to 24 possibilities.

5. **The correct answer is C.** In the figure shown, you have 2 triangular faces and 3 rectangular faces. You are given that each rectangular face has an area of a and each triangular face has an area of b; therefore, the total surface area can be represented as $3a + 2b$.

6. **The correct answer is B.** The best approach to solving this problem is to try test values for k. Because k is a positive integer, try values $k = 1, 2, 3, \ldots$. For $k = 1$, $\frac{(k+1)}{3^k} = \frac{2}{3}$. For $k = 2$, $\frac{(k+1)}{3^k} = \frac{3}{3^2}$, or $\frac{3}{9}$, which can be reduced to $\frac{1}{3}$. Therefore k must equal 2.

7. **The correct answer is B.** The smallest positive integer that is divisible by each of the integers 1 through 6, inclusive, can be found by multiplying some of the integers between 1 and 6 together. First, however, notice that from the integers 1, 2, 3, 4, 5, and 6, if an integer is divisible by 6, it is also divisible by 3. Also, if an integer is divisible by 4 it is also divisible by 2. Thus a reasonable starting point would be to multiply $(4)(5)(6) = 120$. To check whether 120 is the smallest integer, divide by 2 and then check the result: $\frac{120}{2} = 60$. The integer 60 is also divisible by all of the integers 1 through 6. Checking $\frac{60}{2} = 30$ yields the result that 30 is not divisible by 4. Thus the smallest positive integer that is divisible by each of the integers 1 through 6, inclusive, is 60.

8. **The correct answer is A.** As the figure shows, h is the x-coordinate of the midpoint of segment AB. To solve this problem, take the average of the x-coordinates of points A and B. The average is $\frac{(-8 + 12)}{2}$, or $\frac{4}{2}$, which can be reduced to 2.

9. **The correct answer is C.** To solve this problem, substitute $x = 2$ into the equation $c(4x + 3)(x - 1) = 22$ as follows:

$c(4(2) + 3)((2) - 1) = 22$

$11c = 22$

$c = 2$

10. **The correct answer is B.** Answer choice B must be the correct answer because if a man weighs over 175 pounds and is a member of the Hernandez family, the statement given in the question would be directly contradicted. The other answer choices are not supported by the information given in the question.

11. **The correct answer is D.** Recall that where r is the radius of a circle, the circumference is $2\pi r$ and the area is πr^2. Given that the circumference is π, then $\pi = 2\pi r$. Dividing by 2π yields $r = \frac{1}{2}$. The area is then $\pi(\frac{1}{2})^2$, or $\frac{\pi}{4}$.

12. **The correct answer is C.** The best way to solve this problem is to pick numbers for r and s and substitute those values for r and s in each of the answer choices. If the result is an odd integer, eliminate the answer choice. Pick easy numbers to work with and remember that you might have to pick several numbers, as follows:

Answer choice A: When $r = 2$ and $s = 1, \frac{s}{r} = \frac{1}{2}$, which is not an integer. Eliminate answer choice A.

Answer choice B: When $r = 2$ and $s = 1$, $r + s = 2 + 1$, or 3, which is an odd integer. Eliminate answer choice B.

Answer choice C: Because $r + s$ is in parentheses, the entire quantity is multiplied by 2. Therefore, the result will always be an even number. Answer choice C is correct.

13. **The correct answer is E.** To solve this problem, first find the values of x for which $g(x) = 69$ by solving the equation $69 = 3(x^2 - 2)$, as follows:

$69 = 3(x^2 - 2)$

$23 = x^2 - 2$

$25 = x^2$

$x = 5$ or $x = -5$

The possible values of $2x - 3$ are therefore 7 or -13, of which 7 is the only available answer choice.

14. **The best answer is A.** To answer this question, set up an equation using information in the problem. In this question, the average, or mean, score for the games is calculated by dividing the sum of the goals scored by the number of games $(y + 1)$. Determine the sum of all the goals scored:

$$x = \frac{\text{total goals}}{y \text{ games}}$$

$xy = $ total games

z goals in the next game $= z$

The sum is $xy + z$

Now, set up the mean equation (sum of goals scored ÷ number of games):

$$\frac{xy + z}{y + 1}$$

15. **The correct answer is C.** You are given that the circumference of the circle is 12π; therefore, the diameter is 12 and the radius is 6. The diameters of the semicircles are equal to the radius of the large circle; thus their diameters are 6, making each of their radii 3. Together the two semicircles have the area equal to a whole circle of radius 3. The area of a circle with radius 3 is $\pi 3^2$, or 9π.

16. **The correct answer is B.** A reflection across the *y*-axis results in opposite values of the *x*-coordinates; thus, the slope of the reflected line would be negative the original slope. In this case line *l* had slope $\frac{3}{2}$, making the slope of line $m = \frac{3}{2}$. The *y*-intercept would be the same as the point at which line *l* crosses the *y*-axis would be stationary in a reflection about the *y*-axis. The following drawing illustrates the reflection:

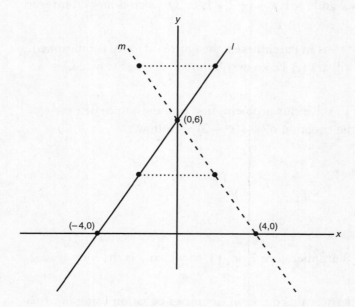

17. **The correct answer is D.** According to the graph, the plant's height at week 3 was about 9 inches, and its height at week 6 was about 12 inches. To calculate what percent greater the height was at week 6 than at week 3, divide the difference in heights by the height at week 3 and then multiply by 100%. The difference is 12 – 9, or 3 inches; 3 inches ÷ 9 inches = $\frac{1}{3}$, or .3333...; multiplying by 100% yields 33.333%, which is approximately equal to $33\frac{1}{3}$%.

18. **The correct answer is E.** If the least integer in a set of consecutive integers is -12, and the sum of these integers is 13, then the set is -12, -11, -10, ... 10, 11, 12, and 13. Each of the negative integers has a positive counterpart, so their sum is equal to zero. The sum of the set, then, is 0 + 13, or 13.

The number of integers in this set can be found by breaking up the set. First, there are 12 integers from -12 to -1; there are also 12 integers from 1 to 12. Remember that 0 is also an integer and 13 must be counted. Therefore, the total number of integers in the set is 12 + 12 + 1 + 1, or 26.

19. **The correct answer is C.** This question describes the concept of simple interest. If the McCallisters paid $900 for their vacation this year, and the cost increases by 5% every year, the cost one year from now will be $900 + 900(0.05)$, or $900(1 + 0.05)$, which equals $900(1.05)$. Two years from now the cost would be $900(1.05)(1.05)$, or $900(1.05)^2$. Similarly, three years from now the cost of the vacation will be $900(1.05)^2(1.05)$, or $900(1.05)^3$. Therefore, x years from now, the cost will be $900(1.05)^x$.

20. **The correct answer is A.** Because the widths of the widgets must be between $3\frac{11}{12}$ and $4\frac{1}{12}$ inches in order for machine B to accept them, the widgets must be $4 \pm \frac{1}{12}$ inches, not inclusive. Taking the absolute value of the difference, $|n - 4|$, shows the degree to which each widget differs from the target of 4 inches. Because the widgets are acceptable only if they differ by *less than* $\frac{1}{12}$ of an inch from a width of 4 inches, $|n - 4| < \frac{1}{12}$.

Section 3

1. **The best answer is B.** The word "callous" means "emotionally hardened," so it makes sense that such a boss would make insensitive remarks to his or her employees. The best choice to insert into the blank is "ridiculed" because it means "mocked or derided."

2. **The best answer is E.** Hiking boots are useful for long trips on foot. Because the sentence states that nearly 200 miles will be covered in one week, the best words to describe the event are "excursion" or "expedition." The best choice is E because "sturdy" means "substantially built or constructed," a desirable property in hiking boots.

3. **The best answer is A.** The context of the sentence indicates that the movie was not a success. Therefore, answer choices B and E can be eliminated because the first word does not fit the context of the sentence. Of the remaining answers, answer choice A is best because "debacle" refers to something that is a "total failure," and "melodramatic" means "artificial, exaggerated, or over dramatic."

4. **The best answer is C.** "Coherence" is the "quality of being logical and clear." If an essay lacked "coherence," it would be unclear and would not progress in a logical manner, making it difficult to follow. The other answer choices are not supported by the context of the sentence.

5. **The best answer is E.** The information following the semicolon indicates that crop rotation is a good and probably necessary thing. Therefore, the best word for the blank is a synonym for "good" or "necessary." "Crucial" means "extremely important," so it is the best choice.

6. **The best answer is D.** Passage 1 describes a girl who succeeds under adverse conditions. Passage 2 also identifies a struggling young girl, but the result is heartbreaking, not uplifting. This best supports answer choice D.

7. **The best answer is B.** Passage 1 focuses on the inspiring story of Francie, while Passage 2 emphasizes Tolstoy's (the author's) intentionally "negative" painting of Anna, the book's tragic figure. Therefore, Passage 2 focuses primarily on a novel's negativism.

8. **The best answer is C.** Passage 2 uses the terms "bland" and "stereotypical," which would describe unappealing characters who fail to inspire the reader. The most effective characters are those to whom the reader can relate and with whom the reader empathizes (or "shares emotion"). According to the passage, Tolstoy's characters were *not* "bland" or "stereotypical," which best supports answer choice C.

9. **The best answer is A.** Passage 1 celebrates its subject novel for the inspirational story it tells. The author of Passage 2 did not appreciate *Anna Karenina* because the story was disheartening. It is reasonable to assume the author would have preferred a novel with a positive message, something "inspiring." This best supports answer choice A.

10. **The best answer is B.** The passage states that the high fees Whitney sought for his cotton gin led farmers to build their own versions of the machine, thereby reducing sales of Whitney's cotton gin. Reduced sales contributed to Whitney's inability to earn a profit on the cotton gin.

11. **The best answer is D.** While the passage contains many details on the positive boon to the economy provided by the cotton gin, it dedicates the fourth paragraph to the legacy of slavery it inadvertently helped to sustain. The author makes no claims as to the validity of slavery and does not elaborate on the practice beyond its link to the cotton gin, so the other answer choices are not correct.

12. **The best answer is A.** The passage states that the cotton gin "impacted the lives of people" and "transformed" the economy, which best supports answer choice A. Answer choice C cannot be correct because most laborers on the plantations were unpaid slaves, not hired immigrants. Likewise, the other answer choices are not supported by the passage.

13. **The best answer is E.** The passage states that, "While immigrants wanted work, many were unwilling to perform the arduous tasks of cotton production. Plantation owners relied almost solely on slave labor until its abolition at the end of the Civil War." Therefore, the passage does not support the statement that Whitney's cotton gin created jobs for immigrant farm workers.

14. **The best answer is C.** According to the passage, "Whitney's cotton gin revolutionized agriculture in the United States. The weight of his invention notwithstanding, he struggled to make a profit from it." The purpose of the passage is to describe the great impact that the cotton gin made on Southern agriculture, that is, the machine's "importance." The context indicates that even though the cotton gin was important, Whitney had a hard time making any money from its use.

15. **The best answer is B.** The best title will reflect the main idea of the passage. Because the passage focuses on the cotton gin and how it affected the economy of the South, answer choice B is best. Answer choices A and E can be eliminated because the passage is concerned with the cotton gin and not its inventor. Answer choices C and D are too vague because they fail to define the central subject of the passage, the cotton gin.

16. **The best answer is B.** An important clue is in the italicized information preceding the passage: a "public health officer" is an advocate for general well-being and would encourage the sick to seek treatment for what ails them. Within the passage, a disorder is defined, as are treatments for it. Furthermore, the author explicitly states in the final paragraph that phobias "should be treated." This best supports answer choice B.

17. **The best answer is E.** The author mentions the correlation between the *amygdala* and the fear response but does not elaborate on the science, saying that the relationship between that part of the brain and the hormone oxytocin "indicates a potentially powerful treatment for phobias." The word "potentially"—and the fact that the paragraph ends there—indicates that such psychiatric care is in an early stage of development but that such treatment could be successful. The other answer choices are either contradicted by details in the passage or are beyond the scope of the passage.

18. **The best answer is E.** The author's goal is to raise awareness of a little-understood medical condition and identify ways to treat it. The passage is not opinionated, so it would not "defend," "criticize," or "advocate," as in answer choices A, B, and C. Answer choice D is incorrect because the author does not evaluate the psychiatric treatment option, choosing only to identify that it might be a powerful therapeutic tool in the future.

19. **The best answer is C.** The repeated exposure of patients to the objects that they fear as a form of therapy presupposes that a phobia can be eliminated, that it is not a fundamental part of the patients' psyche. In this way, if a specific fear can be reduced, it makes sense that it can be increased ("learned"). The example of a traumatizing dog bite is given in the fourth paragraph, which best supports answer choice C.

20. **The best answer is B.** The mention of a specific region of the brain involved in the fear response indicates that researchers have narrowed their search from the brain as a whole. The more specifically the mechanism of fear is defined within the brain, the stronger the causal link becomes between biology and emotions of fear. While the passage indicates that the *amygdala* produces specific brain chemicals, answer choice C is incorrect because it is not specific enough—the passage is about phobias, so it is more likely that the author mentions the *amygdala* to show that it could offer some insight into the treatment of phobias.

21. **The best answer is A.** The passage defines "agoraphobia" as the fear associated with exposure to public spaces, which is not a specific phobia.

22. **The best answer is B.** An important clue from Paragraph 4 is the word "forced," indicating that behavioral therapy was generally undesirable, but no suitable alternatives existed prior to the development of medical treatments. The other answer choices are not supported by the passage.

23. **The best answer is D.** The behavioral therapy described in the passage uses phobic stimuli (such as a dog) to gradually increase the degree of intensity to build up a kind of immunity in the patient. It is not effective to show the patient the most frightening dog at first, just as it is not appropriate to apply all of the plaster to the wall at once; each layer must be stable before the next layer can be applied.

24. **The best answer is B.** Details in the passage indicate that severe or "intense" phobias should be treated because such fears often have a negative impact on a person's daily life. "Acute" is often used to mean "intense," especially with medical conditions, which is most appropriate based on the context.

Section 4

1. **The correct answer is C.** To solve this problem, set up a proportion in which $\frac{250 \text{ mg}}{20 \text{ L}} = \frac{x \text{ mg}}{4 \text{ L}}$, where x is the unknown amount of dry concentrate needed to make 4 L of solution. Multiplying both sides of the equation by 4 L yields $x = \frac{(250)(4)}{20}$, or 50 mg.

2. **The correct answer is E.** To solve this problem, first simplify $3(\frac{x}{y})y^2$ to $\frac{3xy^2}{y}$, which is equivalent to $3xy$. Because you are given that $xy = 12$, it follows that $3xy = 3(12)$, or 36.

3. **The correct answer is D.** You are given that $x < 12$; for $x + y = 25$ to hold true, y would have to be greater than 13. Because $x + y = 25$, $y = 25 - x$. If x approached the largest it could be (close to 12), then y would decrease approaching $25 - 12$, or 13. Therefore, $y > 13$.

4. **The correct answer is B.** To solve this problem, it might be helpful to draw a picture similar to the one below.

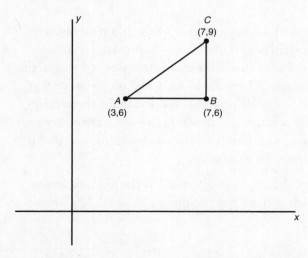

According to the picture it is clear that triangle *ABC* is a right triangle. To find the perimeter, first find the length of each side, and then take the sum of the lengths. Sides *AB* and *BC* are easy to find because you can take the difference between the *x*-coordinates of *B* and *A* for *AB* and the difference between the *y*-coordinates of *C* and *B* for *BC*. Thus, *AB* = 7 − 3, or 4; *BC* = 9 − 6, or 3. To find *CA*, recognize that it is the hypotenuse of a right triangle and use the Pythagorean Theorem, which states that $c^2 = a^2 + b^2$ (or simply recognize that it is a 3-4-5 right triangle). The perimeter is then 3 + 4 + 5, or 12.

5. **The correct answer is D.** To solve this problem, examine the first five terms of the sequence. Because it is given that the first term is 13 and each term after the first is found by adding 7 to the term immediately preceding it, the second term can be written as 13 + 7. The third term would then be 13 + 7 + 7, or 13 + 7(2). Similarly, the fourth term is 13 + 7(2) + 7, or 13 + 7(3), and the fifth term is 13 + 7(3) + 7, or 13 + 7(4). It would be convenient, though, to have a simple formula for the *n*th term of the sequence. Use the following chart to find a pattern:

Term #		
1	13	= 13
2	13 + 7	= 20
3	13 + 7(2)	= 27
4	13 + 7(3)	= 34
5	13 + 7(4)	= 41
⋮		
n	13 + 7(*n*−1)	=

Thus the *n*th term is 13 + 7(*n* − 1). Therefore 13 + 7(32 − 1) represents the 32nd term.

6. **The correct answer is A.** This problem tests your knowledge of absolute values and inequalities. | 4 − 3*x* | < 5 can be written as two separate inequalities: 4 − 3*x* < 5 AND 4 − 3*x* > -5. Because the original inequality was a "less than," the word in between the two new inequalities must be AND. Solve both inequalities as follows:

4 − 3*x* < 5

-3*x* < 1

$-x < \frac{1}{3}$

When you multiply both sides of an inequality by a negative number, you must reverse the inequality sign.

$x > -\frac{1}{3}$

Now move onto the next inequality

$4 - 3x > -5$

$3x > -9$

$x < 3$

Only 2, answer choice A, is less than 3 and greater than $-\frac{1}{3}$.

7. **The correct answer is B.** To solve this problem, let x be the greater number. If the two numbers differ by 2, the lesser number can be written as $x - 2$. Because their sum is given to be m, then $x + (x - 2) = m$. Solve the equation $x + (x - 2) = m$ for x, as follows:

$x + (x - 2) = m$

$2x - 2 = m$

$x = \frac{(m + 2)}{2}$

8. **The correct answer is D.** Because you have 14 members, adding 1 would bring the new total to 15. With 15 members, the median number of gaming consoles occurs at the eighth member, if the members were ordered according to number of consoles owned. The eighth member has only 1 console regardless of what the 15th member owns. For the mean to be twice the median, it would have to equal 2(1), or 2. As it stands, when you include the number of consoles owned by the 15th member, the group has a total of 27 consoles. For the average to be 2 consoles per person, the total would have to be 2(15), or 30 consoles. Thus the 15th member would have to possess 30 – 27, or 3 consoles.

9. **The correct answer is $\frac{1}{2}$ or .5.** First, solve $3(x - 4) = 24$ for x by dividing the entire equation by 3 and adding 4 to get $x = 12$. Then $\frac{(x - 4)}{(x + 4)}$ equals $\frac{(12 - 4)}{(12 + 4)}$, or $\frac{8}{16}$, which can be reduced to $\frac{1}{2}$.

10. **The correct answer is 34.** To solve this problem, convert the words into their mathematical equivalents. The phrase "When three times a number is increased by 7, the result is 109" can be written as $3x + 7 = 109$, where x is the unknown number. To find the number, solve for x, as follows:

$3x + 7 = 109$

$3x = 102$

$x = 34$

11. **The correct answer is 2300.** To solve this problem, complete the necessary squares in the chart using simple arithmetic. For example, the number of cars produced with CD players equals the total number of cars produced, less the number of cars produced with cassette players: 4,750 – 1,000 = 3,750 cars. The total number of cars with both CD players and premium speakers is the total number of cars with CD players, less the number of cars with CD players and standard speakers: 3,750 – 1,450 = 2,300.

12. **The correct answer is 3 or 11.** To solve this problem, it is helpful to draw a picture, as shown below:

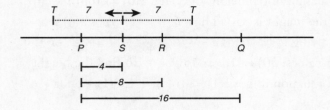

Because R is the midpoint of PQ, $PR = RQ = 8$. Further, because S is the midpoint of PR, S is between P and R, and $PS = SR = 4$. If T is a distance of 7 units from S, it can be to either side of S. Thus the length of PT is either $PS + ST$ or $PS - ST$, resulting in either $4 + 7 = 11$ or $4 - 7 = -3$. Because distance does not depend on direction, the distance between P and T would then be either 3 or 11. Remember that distance refers to the absolute value of a number, which is always positive.

13. **The correct answer is 45.** Because the entire cheese wheel weighs 64 ounces, an 8-ounce wedge of the wheel would be $\frac{8}{64}$, or $\frac{1}{8}$ the weight of the entire wheel. The degree measure of x would then be $\frac{1}{8}$ of the number of degrees in the entire circle, which is 360. Thus $x = 360(\frac{1}{8})$, or 45.

14. **The correct answer is 18.** To solve this problem, find the length of one side of the inner square, which is also the hypotenuse of a right triangle with legs of length 3. You can either use the Pythagorean Theorem or the fact that this is a special right triangle to find the hypotenuse. Because the legs are the same length, the hypotenuse is equal to $\sqrt{2}$ times the length of a leg, so the hypotenuse is equal to $3\sqrt{2}$. Therefore, the area of the shaded region, a square with sides $3\sqrt{2}$, is $(3\sqrt{2})^2$, or $9(2)$, which is 18.

15. **The correct answer is 3.** To solve this problem, recognize that $x^2 - y^2$ can be factored into $(x + y)(x - y)$. Thus $(x + y)(x - y) = 18$. Because it is given that $x + y = 6$, substitute 6 into the equation to get $6(x - y) = 18$. Dividing both sides by 6 yields $x - y = 3$.

16. **The correct answer is 5.** The easiest way to solve this problem is to start with 12 and add each preceding even integer until you get to a sum of 40, and then count the terms:

$12 + 10 + 8 + 6 + 4 = 40$

There are 5 terms.

17. **The correct answer is 5.** To solve this problem, write $3^x + 3^x + 3^x$ as $3(3^x)$, which equals 3^{x+1}. It follows that $3^{x+1} = 3^6$. From there it is apparent that $x + 1 = 6$, and $x = 5$.

18. **The correct answer is 140.** To solve this problem, use the given values for time and height in the problem to solve for the unknown constants, using a function. Because at time $t = 0$ the rocket has an initial height of 6 feet, $h(0) = -16(0)^2 + d(0) + c = 6$, and $c = 6$. At time $t = 4$, the height is 350. Thus, $h(4) = -16(4)^2 + d(4) + 6 = 350$, and $-256 + 4d + 6 = 350$. Solving for d yields $d = \frac{(350 + 256 - 6)}{4} = \frac{600}{4}$, or 150. Replace the constants with their values: $h(t) = -16t^2 + 150t + 6$. To find the height at $t = 1$, simply insert 1 into the equation to get $h(1) = -16(1)^2 + 150(1) + 6$, or $-16 + 150 + 6$, which equals 140 feet.

Section 5

1. **The best answer is B.** As it is written, the sentence contains an unnecessary conjunction, "so." The best answer is B, which omits "so" but keeps the rest of the underlined portion intact. The other answer choices are awkward and do not effectively convey the intended meaning of the sentence.

2. **The best answer is C.** Answer choice C is the clearest, most concise selection and is idiomatically correct. Answer choice A contains "should," which is unnecessary language. Answer choice B is incorrect because it uses the passive voice. Answer choices D and E are awkward.

3. **The best answer is D.** As it is written, the sentence is awkward. To make the sentence more clear and concise, the phrase "that is" should be omitted. Only answer choice D clearly and effectively conveys the intended meaning of the sentence.

4. **The best answer is A.** This sentence is best as it is written. It effectively expresses the idea, is in the simple past tense, and is the most concise. Answer choices B, C, D, and E are awkward and unclear.

5. **The best answer is D.** Answer choice D is correct because it clearly and concisely states the comparisons between one species and most other species. The phrase "but not," used in answer choices A and E, does not clearly convey that other species require a "blood meal." Answer choice D uses the correct simple present tense plural verb form "lay" to match the plural subject "females."

6. **The best answer is B.** As it is written, the sentence is awkward. To make the sentence more clear and concise, the unnecessary pronoun "this" can be omitted without changing the meaning of the sentence. The other answer choices either include incorrect verb forms or are awkwardly constructed.

7. **The best answer is D.** The verbs "is" and "resolve" must agree in number with the subject nouns. "Earth and other planets…" is plural, so the plural verb form "revolve" is correct. "The speed" is singular, so use the singular verb form "is."

8. **The best answer is B.** As it is written, the antecedent of the pronoun "its" in the underlined portion is ambiguous. While answer choice D correctly uses the plural pronoun "their" to refer to "citizens," it includes the unnecessary verb "is." Also, the water bowls and doggie parks do not necessarily belong to the citizens of Denver, so simply using the definite article "the" is sufficient.

9. **The best answer is D.** Because the sentence contains two complete thoughts that could stand on their own as complete sentences, these independent clauses should be separated using a semicolon as in answer choice D. Answer choices A and C include comma splices. Answer choice B is wordy and awkward, and answer choice E incorrectly uses the transition word "whereas," which indicates a contradiction that is not apparent in the sentence.

10. **The best answer is C.** Answer choice C maintains parallelism with the construction of the phrase "has not only captured…but also forced" and clearly refers to "these companies," rather than the ambiguous pronoun "them." Answer choice A uses the ambiguous pronoun "them" to refer to "sporting goods companies." In answer choice B, "but it also" is not parallel with "has not only…". Likewise, answer choices D and E contain the phrase "but it also."

11. **The best answer is E.** As it is written, the singular verb "exceeds" incorrectly refers to the plural noun "figures" and uses the unnecessary phrase "that were." Answer choice E correctly uses the plural verb "exceed" and states the intended meaning of the sentence in the most concise manner. Answer choices B and C incorrectly use the singular verb "exceeds," and answer choice D is awkward.

12. **The best answer is A.** The adjective "stern" is modifying the verb "treated" and thus should be in the adverb form, "sternly."

13. **The best answer is C.** In this sentence, the plural verb "are" should be replaced with the singular verb "is" because the phrase "which of the teams" refers to a single team and, therefore, requires a singular verb. "Rarely watch" effectively expresses the frequency at which the event occurs. The plural verb "make" correctly refers to the plural noun "predictions," and "most likely" appropriately modifies the verb "to win."

14. **The best answer is B.** The sentence improperly uses the helping verb "had" where no helping verb is necessary. The correct verb is simply "became," which indicates the simple past tense.

15. **The best answer is C.** Because the sentence is referring to "today," the verb "intrigued," which is in the past tense, should be written in the present tense, "intrigues."

16. **The best answer is C.** Proper nouns, such as place names, must be capitalized. In this sentence, "north" should be capitalized just as "South" is later in the sentence.

17. **The best answer is D.** Because the adjective "partial" is modifying the adjective "frozen," it should be in the form of the adverb, "partially."

18. **The best answer is B.** The word "its" is the possessive form of "it." The contraction "it's" means "it is" and would be correctly used at this point in the sentence.

19. **The best answer is E.** This sentence does not contain any errors. It is clear and concise as it is written. The adjective "likely" correctly modifies the noun "carcinogen," and the verbs "to detect" and "can be found" both indicate future tense. The plural noun "products" correctly parallels the plural pronoun "many."

20. **The best answer is E.** This sentence does not contain any errors. It is clear and concise as it is written. The sentence indicates only one "reason," so the singular form is correct. The sentence is written in the present tense, so the present tense verb "are advised" is correct. It is idiomatic to say "in a fire." The singular present tense verb "tends to" is appropriate.

21. **The best answer is A.** Because the sentence refers to two people, the singular noun "entomologist" should be plural. No other corrections are necessary.

22. **The best answer is B.** The subject of this sentence is "emphasis," a singular noun. Therefore, it is necessary to use the singular verb "is." No other corrections are necessary.

23. **The best answer is D.** The word "neither" functions as a pronoun for the subject "of the two choices" and refers to one or the other of the choices. The pronoun "neither" is singular, so it is necessary to use the singular verb "is."

24. **The best answer is B.** Because the subject of the sentence is being replaced with a pronoun, the nominative form "he" is correct. The objective form "him" should be used only when the pronoun acts as a direct or indirect object.

25. **The best answer is E.** There are no errors in this sentence. It is clear and concise as written.

26. **The best answer is B.** The best way to correct this sentence would be to remove the coordinating conjunction "so." It is appropriate to separate two independent clauses with a semicolon and no transitional adverb is necessary in this sentence.

27. **The best answer is D.** The comparative "more" must be followed by the adjective "strict." It would also be correct to simply say "stricter." The past progressive verb "grew" correctly refers to an event that occurred in the past along with another event. "Increasingly" correctly modifies "grew." "To be" correctly refers to the verb tense of the sentence and the singular proper noun "Miss Kern."

28. **The best answer is B.** The subject of the sentence, "vitamins and minerals," is plural, so it is necessary to use the plural pronoun "they." The adverb "equally" correctly modifies the verb "important." No other corrections are necessary.

29. **The best answer is E.** This sentence does not contain any errors. It is clear and concise as it is written. The word "unlike" correctly sets up the contradiction that is apparent in the sentence. The noun "expressionists" does not need to be capitalized because it does not refer to a specific person. It is necessary to use a comma between "rich" and "strong," and it is appropriate to use the plural noun "canvasses."

30. **The best answer is A.** The subject "It" of the second sentence refers to "a night class" from the first sentence. The easiest way to combine the sentences is to include the subject of the class ("Pilates") as a modifier of "class" in the first sentence. The word "exercise" is omitted, too, because Pilates is itself a form of exercise (like "aerobics," for example) that does not require the word "exercise" to make sense.

31. **The best answer is A.** As it is written, and compared to the other answer choices, the sentence is clear and succinct. The other choices are wordy and awkward.

32. **The best answer is D.** The fact that the narrator has so many exercise videos would suggest that she has an acceptable variety from which to choose. The context indicates that she is bored by all of them, which contradicts the previous notion, so "but" is the appropriate conjunction.

33. **The best answer is C.** It seems self-evident that anything boring is avoided by people. Sentence 9, therefore, does not provide anything meaningful to the rest of the passage.

34. **The best answer is E.** The verb "look" means "appear" in this case, so it is optimally followed by an adjectival phrase. Including the word "like" signals that a noun should follow. Eliminating the word "like" allows the phrase "the least intimidating" to take its correct place immediately after "looked."

35. **The best answer is E.** The exclamation points and colorful imagery of the last two sentences show that the author is using humor to emphasize her success at Pilates. The other answer choices are not supported by the context of the essay.

Section 6

1. **The best answer is D.** Because the author's works are short stories and have meanings that go beyond what is written, it can be inferred that the author is not wordy. "Brevity" refers to "concise expression," so something written with brevity is short in length yet laden with significance.

2. **The best answer is C.** The context of the sentence indicates that because the factories are attempting to build near residential areas, the industrial manufacturers would want to downplay the effects of pollution. Of the answer choices, "inconsequential" is the best choice because it means "insignificant or negligible."

3. **The best answer is E.** The context of the sentence indicates that because of advancements in technology, global communication has become more prevalent and easier. Of the answer choices, only B and E indicate an improvement. Of the two, answer choice E is the better answer because "facility" in this context means "ease of doing."

4. **The best answer is B.** The context of the sentence indicates that the actress took on a different role to avoid being thought of or labeled as a particular type of actress. "Deemed" means "regarded as" and fits the context the best.

5. **The best answer is D.** The context of the sentence indicates that Elvis fans journey to his gravesite. Of the answer choices, only A, C, and D fit into the context of the sentence because they specify a trip of some sort. Also only truly devoted fans would travel to the gravesite regardless of the distance. Answer choice D is the best answer because "dedicated" means "devoted and committed" and a "pilgrimage" is a journey to a sacred place or shrine.

6. **The best answer is A.** The context indicates that a quick glance at the essay could reveal the extent to which a professor liked the essay depending on how many corrections were made. The word "plethora" refers to a "large number." The best answer is answer choice A because "cursory" means "performed with haste and scant attention to detail" and "traversing" means "crossing and re-crossing," which indicates a large number and correctly corresponds to "plethora."

7. **The best answer is B.** From the context, visitors would only complain about one of the most beautiful churches in Europe if they could not see it. Thus it is reasonable to infer that the scaffolding is hiding or covering the church. The best answer is B because "shrouded" means "masked or covered."

8. **The best answer is D.** The context of the sentence indicates that a coin collector would inspect the quarter carefully to make sure that it was not a forgery. The word "scrutinize" means "to examine closely." The other answer choices do not fit the context of the sentence.

9. **The best answer is A.** "Languidly" means "without spirit or vitality." The passage goes on to explain that the boxes of clothes usually do not contain items for Anna. A normal reaction to seeing others receive gifts while you did not would be one of disinterest, or "apathy."

10. **The best answer is C.** According to the passage, Anna and her mother were sorting through a "box of secondhand clothing sent by their wealthy relatives." In addition, the passage states that "Looking wistfully at these catalogs was the nearest Anna had come to fashion since the stock market had crashed in 1929." This suggests that Anna and her mother were "poor." The other answer choices are not supported by the passage.

11. **The best answer is D.** "Mitigable" means "able to be moderated." The other choices are incorrect because they express either confusion or spite on the part of the author, who actually maintains an even, explanatory tone throughout the passage.

12. **The best answer is E.** The last clause of the passage, "there is nothing wrong with offering a pacifier," indicates the author's "approval" of the pacifier. The other answer choices are not supported by the passage.

13. **The best answer is B.** The first sentence of Passage 1 states, "Nine times as many Americans fell in the farmlands near Antietam Creek in the fall of 1862 than fell on the beaches of Normandy on D-Day, the so-called longest day of World War II." This indicates that there were more American casualties at Antietam than on D-Day. Because D-Day is widely held to be a shockingly violent battle, by comparison, Antietam would be, too.

14. **The best answer is C.** To "engage" something can mean to enter into combat with it. Therefore, in this context, the word "engagement" most nearly means "confrontation." The other answer choices could be used in place of "engagement" in other contexts.

15. **The best answer is C.** The mention of feeding soldiers and replenishing supplies in Passage 1 suggests that the army had worked hard in recent days. The preceding sentence says the troops had fought only a week earlier. This information best supports answer choice C.

16. **The best answer is D.** According to paragraph four in Passage 1, "...with great fanfare, Lee and fellow General 'Stonewall' Jackson marched their ragged Army of Northern Virginia across the Potomac River and straight through the Frederick town square. Lee issued the *Proclamation to the People of Maryland* to invite the citizens to join the Southern movement. Soldiers obeyed Lee's order to refrain from violence and pillaging..." This indicates that, although Lee's army was "ragged," soldiers followed his order calling for good behavior, which best supports answer choice D.

17. **The best answer is A.** "Grand" modifies the noun "offensive," meaning "attack," and because the rest of the paragraph emphasizes the destruction it caused, the best choice is "massive." The other answer choices could be used in place of "grand" in other contexts.

18. **The best answer is D.** Passage 2 indicates that Lee had to change his plans following the surprise attack. The bungled troop selection for the new plan is called the "first of many" mistakes that "doomed" the Confederate assault. This best supports answer choice D.

19. **The best answer is E.** Passage 2 does not include any discussion of attacks by amphibious vehicles, so answer choices A, C, and D should be eliminated because they include Roman numeral I. Passage 2 discusses both artillery fire and infantry charges, using terms such as "cannons," "batteries," and "musket."

20. **The best answer is B.** A cannonade is a series of cannon attacks, which occur at long ranges, and a fusillade is a wave of gunfire, which is less effective over great distances. The statement is a creative way of stating that the Confederate line had moved close enough that the Union used small arms instead of cannons against the Confederate soldiers.

21. **The best answer is D.** An "allegory" is a symbolic representation. The "mark" is the farthest the South succeeded in penetrating Northern soil before being forced to retreat. The other answer choices are not supported by the passage.

22. **The best answer is C.** While Passage 2 describes a raging firefight, Passage 1 only describes the troop movements made in preparation for such a fight. This best supports answer choice C.

23. **The best answer is A.** Both authors show respect by emphasizing the human cost of the fight and each side's dedication to the fight. In other words, both authors indicate a "respectful acknowledgement" of the soldiers described in each passage.

24. **The best answer is A.** While, as stated in Passage 1, Antietam saw the most men fall in a single day, Gettysburg can be called the bloodiest battle because casualties mounted over three days. The other answer choices are not supported by the passage.

Section 7

1. **The best answer is C.** To solve this problem, first solve for x, as follows:

$(x - 1)^2 = 1,600$

$x - 1 = \sqrt{1,600}$

$x - 1 = 40$

$x = 41$

(Note: since no answer choice is negative, you may disregard the negative result of the square root.)

Now, substitute 41 for x in the second equation:

$x - 7 =$

$41 - 7 = 34$

2. **The correct answer is C.** "The sum of $4x$ and 6" can be written as $4x + 6$. "The product of x and $\frac{1}{4}$" can be written as $(\frac{1}{4})x$. Because they are equal, $4x + 6 = (\frac{1}{4})x$.

3. **The best answer is C.** According to the Triangle Inequality rule, the length of any side must be less than the sum of the lengths of the other two sides and greater than the difference of the lengths of the other two sides. Therefore, the length of the third side can be no longer than 20 (or 13 + 7) and no shorter than 6 (or 13 – 7). The length of the third side cannot be 21, so answer choice C is correct.

4. **The correct answer is D.** Because 20 out of 120 shopping carts are blue, the probability of getting a blue cart is $\frac{20}{120}$, or $\frac{1}{6}$.

5. **The correct answer is A.** To solve this problem, compare the total electricity use in each answer choice. During the months of January and February the Jefferson family used 200 + 125, or 325 kilowatts of electricity. The next largest 2-month period was May and June, with 250 + 50, or 300 kilowatts of electricity use.

6. **The correct answer is B.** According to the figure, $AB = BC$, and B is the midpoint of AC. Also because $AC = 32$, $AB = BC = 16$. If point D is on the line between B and C so that $BD = DC$, D is the midpoint of BC and $BD = DC = 8$. Inserting D into the figure makes it clear that $AD = AB + BD$. Thus, $AD = 16 + 8$, or 24.

7. **The correct answer is C.** To solve this problem, use the Distributive Property as follows:

$(7)(10^{-k}) + (2)(10^{-k})$

$(7 + 2)(10^{-k})$

$9(10^{-k})$

Further, using the exponent rule which stats that $n^{-x} = \frac{1}{n^x}$, you know that $9(10^{-k}) = 9(\frac{1}{10^k})$, or $\frac{9}{10^k}$.

8. **The correct answer is B.** To solve this problem, calculate the degrees of arc in $\frac{1}{5}$ of a circle and in $\frac{1}{6}$ of a circle. Because you have $360°$ in a circle, $\frac{1}{5}$ of a circle has $360°(\frac{1}{5})$, or $72°$. Likewise, $\frac{1}{6}$ of a circle has $360°(\frac{1}{6})$, or $60°$. Therefore, you have $72° - 60°$, or $12°$, more in $\frac{1}{5}$ of a circle than in $\frac{1}{6}$ of a circle.

9. **The correct answer is D.** According to the graph, the function f is positive when the graph is above the x-axis. Because we are interested in the values of x, the x-coordinates of the intervals for which the graph is above the x-axis are the answer. The function is positive between $x = -3$ and $x = 1$ and also between $x = 5$ and $x = 7$. Therefore, the correct interval for x is $-3 < x < 1$ and $5 < x < 7$.

10. **The correct answer is E.** To solve this problem, treat each layer as a different right circular cylinder and take the sum of the individual volumes to get the total volume. In order to find the volume of a right circular cylinder, use the formula $V = \pi r^2 h$, which calls for the radius of the circle base and the height of the cylinder. In this problem, the height of each cylinder is 1 foot. The radius of each cylinder is one greater than the radius of the layer above it, making the radii 1, 2, 3, and 4 feet, respectively. In addition, remember that each layer is actually a quarter of a cylinder; thus, divide the volume calculated by 4. Now, insert the values into the equation and solve, as follows:

$$V = \frac{[\pi(1)^2(1) + \pi(2)^2(1) + \pi(3)^2(1) + \pi(4)^2(1)]}{4}$$

$$V = \frac{[\pi + 4\pi + 9\pi + 16\pi]}{4}$$

$$V = \frac{30\pi}{4}$$

$$V = \frac{15\pi}{2}$$

11. **The correct answer is E.** To solve this problem, remember that $9 = 3^2$. The equation $9(3^x) = 3^y$ can then be written as $(3^2)(3^x) = 3^y$, or $3^{x+2} = 3^y$. It follows, then, that $x + 2 = y$, or $x = y - 2$.

12. **The correct answer is C.** If the degree measures of the angles of a triangle are in the ratio 3:4:5, then you can think of there being 3 + 4 + 5, or 12 parts to the degrees in the triangle. Because you always have 180° in a triangle, each of the 12 "parts" has $\frac{180}{12}$, or 15°. The smallest angle, which has $\frac{3}{12}$ of the degree measure is 3(15°), or 45°. The largest angle, which has $\frac{5}{12}$ of the degree measure is 5(15°), or 75°. Thus the largest angle exceeds the smallest by 75° – 45°, or 30°.

13. **The correct answer is E.** Because *abcd* = 36, none of these variables can equal 0. If one of them did equal 0, their product would also be 0. Thus, eliminate answer choices C and D. If *a* and *b* were both negative, *a* times *b* would still be positive, and, therefore, you can eliminate answer choices A and B. Because *abde* = 0 and *a*, *b*, and *d* cannot equal 0, *e* must equal 0.

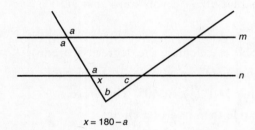

$x = 180 - a$

14. **The correct answer is D.** To solve this problem, use the fact that the sum of angles within a triangle is 180°. In the triangle formed in the picture, *c* equals 180 less the measures of *b* and the unknown angle that we'll call *x*. According to the figure, the angle that is supplementary to *x* (on the other side of line *n*) has the same measure as *a* because they are corresponding angles of an intersection with parallel lines. Therefore *x* = 180 – *a*. Because the sum of the unknown angle *x*, angle *b*, and angle *c* is 180, (180 – *a*) + *b* + *c* = 180. Solving for *c*, *c* = 180 – (180 – *a*) – *b*, which simplifies to *a* – *b*.

15. **The correct answer is C.** To solve this problem, first perform the operations inside each of the parentheses, as follows:

$3^2 + 1 = 9 + 1 = 10$

$3^2 - 1 = 9 - 1 = 8$

$2^2 + 1 = 4 + 1 = 5$

$2^3 - 1 = 8 - 1 = 7$

Now, multiply the results together: 10 × 8 = 80, 80 × 5 = 400, and 400 × 7 = 2,800.

16. **The correct answer is B.** If you recognize that $\frac{2}{3}$ is roughly equivalent to 66%, you can determine that the least number of votes is around 66% of 267. Because 66% is more than half, you can safely eliminate answer choices C, D, and E, which are all less than half of 267. You can now either multiply 267 by 0.66, the decimal equivalent of 66%, to get approximately 176, or you can use logic to make an educated guess; 267 can be rounded up to 270, and 0.66 can be rounded up to 0.70. Because 270×0.70 is 189, answer choice A is clearly more than 66% of 267, so it cannot be correct.

Section 8

1. **The best answer is B.** The context reveals that because viewers expecting excitement were disappointed, the level of action sequences was less than expected, making answer choice B the most logical selection.

2. **The best answer is C.** The context indicates that negotiating the settlement was a rather difficult task. In addition, parties try to compromise and come to agreements during a negotiation. The best answer is C because "onerous" means "arduous or difficult."

3. **The best answer is C.** The word "protracted" means "prolonged." It makes sense that during periods of prolonged drought, plants would "conserve" water because water would not be readily available. The other answer choices do not fit the context of the sentence.

4. **The best answer is B.** The context indicates conflict between how Kathy felt before the performance and how she actually performed. Answer choice B is best because "reluctance" means "unwillingness or disinclination."

5. **The best answer is E.** The context of the sentence indicates that minimum wage is not adequate to meet the basic costs of living. Answer choice E is the best answer because "insufficient" means "inadequate or lacking."

6. **The best answer is A.** The context of the passage indicates that the students paid a high level of attention to the professor's experiments. Of the answer choices, B, C, D, and E do not indicate that the students were particularly interested in the experiments. Answer choice A is the best answer because "rapt" means "completely occupied by or focused on something."

7. **The best answer is C.** The last sentence of the first paragraph clearly defines the purpose of the essay, to "pass in brief review the history of early geological periods." This review describes the general forms of life that occurred over the range of prehistoric time. No details about geology or fossil records are given, and no evidence is given to defend the claim that mammals rule the animal kingdom.

8. **The best answer is C.** The "acquaintance" is with geology, so a sense of the word tied to relationships between people is not appropriate, effectively eliminating answer choices A, B, D, and E. The word "acquaintance" sometimes refers to "knowledge or information about something," which best fits the context.

9. **The best answer is D.** The second paragraph states that life was at its most basic during the "Achaean time." No mention is made of the suitability of condition or the aesthetics of the earth, so answer choices A and B can be eliminated. No claim about the extinction of lichen made, so answer choice C is incorrect. Answer choice E is incorrect because the paragraph cites the examples of lichen-covered rocks and seaweed, which would not be "undetectably small."

10. **The best answer is B.** The "structureless bodies" mentioned in the second paragraph refer to the earliest animals, not plants, so any claim about the form of seaweed is irrelevant and would not detract from the author's statements.

11. **The best answer is E.** The thesis is captured in the second sentence of the paragraph, which states "During the course of this age, the forms of life present wide differences from those of modern time." The "specific illustrations" mentioned in the paragraph are the examples of enormous ferns, invertebrate animals, fishes, amphibians, and reptiles. Answer choices A, B, and C are incorrect because the author does not offer or discuss any opinion. No conclusion or "truth" is asserted by the end of the paragraph, so answer choice D is incorrect.

12. **The best answer is B.** The word "meaning" is the biggest clue here and indicates a definition. It is useful to note, too, that a scientific term like "Paleozoic" could come from ancient Greek or Latin, so a translation of its component parts would appear in quotation marks or italics; for example, "Tyrannosaurus, or 'terrible lizard.'"

13. **The best answer is C.** The author says that even in the warmest parts of the globe today, ferns only grow "4 or 5 feet high." This pales in comparison to the "30 or so" feet high fern of the Paleozoic, which best supports answer choice C.

14. **The best answer is A.** The important clue in the sentence is that something "died away," which suggests room for something to take its place, or "succeed." The other answer choices could be used in place of "succeeded" in a different context.

15. **The best answer is B.** The paragraph states that "in the closing period of Mesozoic time, we have trees with deciduous leaves," indicating that such trees had not been present before. The other answer choices are not supported by the passage.

16. **The best answer is A.** The discussion of dinosaurs and similar creatures falls under the heading of "paleontology," which is the study of prehistoric plants and animals. Although "geology" is mentioned elsewhere in the passage, it is not reflected in the examples cited in the fifth paragraph.

17. **The best answer is D.** The passage states, "There is little doubt among archaeologists that birds were just modified, more highly adapted reptiles." This statement proposes that birds are "modified" reptiles and that they "derived" from their reptilian ancestors. The other answer choices are not supported by the passage.

18. **The best answer is D.** According to the passage, "Because of their more highly evolved nature, mammals have been the rulers of the animal kingdom since their appearance." This statement supports the assumption that mammals are dominant over other creatures on earth. The correct answer choice indicates that the sharks, which are not mammals, prey on "seals and walruses," which are mammals. In this ecosystem, a mammal does not rule the animal kingdom, so the author's assumption about the dominance of mammals is undermined, or weakened.

19. **The best answer is C.** Several times in the passage, the author mentions the disappearance, or extinction, of certain forms of life, which are then replaced by other life forms. In this way, there seems always to be a mixture of life on earth that, piece by piece, joins the uncountable number of species that have gone extinct over millions of years. This best supports answer choice C. Answer choice A is incorrect because the author uses very little language that asserts one species necessarily derives from another. Answer choices B and D are incorrect because the passage does not detail the development of plants, describing only when certain kinds appeared on earth.

Section 9

1. **The best answer is C.** As it is written, the sentence is redundant. The most clear and concise way to phrase the underlined portion is answer choice C. The remaining answer choices are awkward and redundant.

2. **The best answer is E.** Answer choice E is best because it is the clearest way to express the idea, and it places the events in the correct order—first Kate hit an icy patch, then she fell down, and then she lost a ski. The sentence as it is written mixes up verb tenses. Answer choice B mixes up the order of events. Answer choices C and D are awkward.

3. **The best answer is B.** Because the portion of the sentence that is not underlined is a complete thought, the underlined portion should be worded so that it functions as a parenthetical expression, clarifying the writer's train of thought. Only answer choice B clearly and effectively conveys the idea that the "flooding" was the "catastrophe" that the citizens had feared. It is also the only choice that would be appropriate to follow a comma.

4. **The best answer is A.** The sentence is best as written. It effectively expresses the idea and is free from ambiguity. Answer choices B, C, D, and E are awkward and unclear, and do not maintain parallelism with the first part of the sentence.

5. **The best answer is C.** This sentence requires the use of the conjunction "or," not "and," to complete the "either...or" construction. In addition, it is idiomatic to "mistake" something "for those" of another thing, rather than "as those" of another thing. Answer choice C is the only selection that correctly uses the "either...or" construction and the correct idiomatic phrase.

6. **The best answer is D.** As it is written, the sentence lacks a verb in the main clause. Answer choice D is best because it most clearly expresses the idea and contains a clear verb, "refers to."

7. **The best answer is A.** The sentence is best as written. In answer choice A, it is clear that the "Model T" was the vehicle introduced. In addition, the construction of the descriptive phrase that follows is clear and concise and is free from grammatical errors. Answer choice B uses the phrase "more easier," which is redundant. Answer choices C, D, and E fail to clearly convey that one event caused another, and they contain some grammatical errors.

8. **The best answer is B.** It is usually best to not separate a phrase that modifies the subject from the subject. Answer choices A and C are awkward because they separate the modifying phrase from the subject and suggest that the "jewelry collectors" are rare. Answer choices D and E are excessively cut up by commas and are either illogical or unclear. Only answer choice B effectively indicates that "platinum" is "prized for its rarity."

9. **The best answer is C.** Because the subject of the sentence, "evidence," is a singular noun, the verb "show" should be singular "shows" to assure number agreement. Answer choice B is incorrect because it uses the singular verb "tends" with the plural subject "batteries."

10. **The best answer is E.** As it is written, the sentence compares the "average income" of one household to another "household," which does not make sense. Answer choice E correctly uses the singular pronoun "that" to refer to "income," and the prepositions "of" and "with," thus establishing a parallel comparison. The remaining answer choices fail to create a clear and logical comparison between the income of one household and the income of another household.

11. **The best answer is D.** The verb "resolve" takes a verb phrase in the infinitive form as its object ("to become..."). Also, John and Jeremiah can only form one comedic pair, not the plural "pairs." Thus, the best answer is D because it incorporates both corrections.

12. **The best answer is C.** For the sake of clarity in expression, it is best in this case to reiterate that the sentence is referring to the national *news station*. Also because the sentence is a comparison, it takes on the form "*as many _____ as...*" The best answer is C because it addresses both corrections.

13. **The best answer is D.** The most efficient way to express the intended idea of this sentence is with the "not only...but also" construction. Answer choice D correctly uses this construction and clearly expresses the idea of the sentence. As written, answer choices A, B, and C modify "water," which suggests that "hydration," in addition to "water," is a source of "essential vitamins and minerals." Answer choice E uses the "not only...but also" construction but does not maintain parallelism and is awkwardly constructed.

14. **The best answer is B.** The verb "consider" does not require the use of "to be," "as being," or "as if." Therefore, answer choices A, C, and D are incorrect. Answer choice B is correct because it eliminates any unnecessary phrases. In addition, the verb phrase "to identify" is parallel to "to consider." Answer choice E is incorrect because "identifying" is not parallel to "to consider."

PART V
Appendixes

SAT/PSAT Vocabulary List

While this is by no means a comprehensive list, it does contain words that have appeared on actual PSAT and SAT tests, each followed by a sentence or sentences appropriately using the word or a derivation of the word. The words are included here because they have been selected by experienced SAT/PSAT instructors as representative of the vocabulary level that is expected on the PSAT and the SAT.

A

Absurd   Extremely ridiculous or completely lacking reason.

The idea that Samantha would fail her test was completely absurd; she had studied for hours and was completely prepared.

Abundance   Having considerably more than is necessary or adequate; more than enough.

The local car dealership was having an amazing sale because of the abundance of cars on the lot.

Accommodate   To adapt or adjust in a way that makes someone else comfortable; make room.

The Johnsons had to build a nursery to accommodate the new family member they were expecting.

Acrid   Harsh or bitter taste or smell.

Sean immediately turned the engine off when he smelled acrid smoke billowing from beneath the hood of his car.

Acute   Quick and precise, intense; sharp, keen.

The acute pain in Sarah's wrist kept her from performing even the simplest activity.

Henry was an acute observer; he quickly learned the rules of the game.

Adjacent   Close, next to.

Chase took a new job in downtown Chicago but purchased a house in an adjacent suburb.

Aesthetic   Appeals to the senses because it is beautiful.

The aesthetic quality of the painting was more appealing than its historical significance.

Alienate   To isolate oneself from others or another person from oneself.

Gregg often felt <u>alienated</u> from his classmates because of his illness.

Ambiguous   Unclear or capable of having more than one meaning.

The student's <u>ambiguous</u> answer left the professor wondering whether the student had studied the assigned material.

Amiable   Friendly and pleasant.

Joe was very <u>amiable</u>; as a result, he made friends easily at his new school.

Anomaly   Something that is different from the norm.

The botanists were excited when they discovered the unique flower; it was a complete <u>anomaly</u>.

Anticipate   To look forward to or expect.

In light of the difficult subject matter, Mr. Mauro <u>anticipated</u> many questions and concerns from his students.

Apathy   A lack of any emotion or concern.

Mary's <u>apathy</u> was quite evident at her trial; she seemed unconcerned by the jury's guilty verdict.

Articulate   *v.* To clearly explain; *adj.* The quality of being able to speak clearly.

Young children often find it difficult to <u>articulate</u> exactly what they are thinking.

Mayor Smith was quite <u>articulate in his</u> speech at the commencement ceremony.

Assert   To demonstrate power; to defend a statement as true.

It is often necessary for a parent to <u>assert</u> his or her authority over an unruly child.

Tom continues to <u>assert</u> his innocence despite the collapse of his alibi.

Assiduous   Characteristic of careful and persistent effort.

The journey to earning good grades is an <u>assiduous</u> one; consistent effort must be put forth.

Assumption   Something believed to be true without proof; unstated evidence.

Because Jennifer wore glasses every day, we made the <u>assumption</u> that she had poor eyesight.

Aversion   Strong dislike.

Kelly has such an <u>aversion</u> to strenuous exercise that she never goes to the gym.

B

Banish   To force to leave.

The deposed dictator was <u>banished</u> from his native country.

Beneficiary   Recipient of benefits, such as funds or property.

Carol named her husband as her <u>beneficiary</u> so that he would receive her assets after her death.

Benign   Kind, mild, harmless.

Katherine was relieved to discover that her tumor was <u>benign</u>; she would not require surgery after all.

Bereft   Deprived or despondent.

Jill was <u>bereft</u> when she discovered that the coveted role had been offered to another actress.

Burgeoning   Thriving or growing rapidly.

Although it was completely undeveloped a year ago, the vacant land is now home to a <u>burgeoning</u> commercial area, complete with a new shopping mall.

C

Capacity   Maximum amount that an object or area can hold; mental ability.

The Italian restaurant had a <u>capacity</u> of 200 people.

Studies have shown that chimpanzees have the <u>capacity</u> to learn human language.

Capricious   Impulsive; prone to sudden change.

Jill's sudden move to Hollywood was considered <u>capricious</u> by the rest of her family.

Chaos   A state of complete disarray.

Leah lost control of her kindergarten class, and total <u>chaos</u> ensued.

Chronicle   *n.* A detailed narrative; *v.* To document or record.

Several biographers have <u>chronicled</u> the life of Albert Einstein, one of the world's greatest physicists.

Coherent   The quality of being logical and clear.

The essay lacked <u>coherence</u>; it did not flow logically from one concept to the next.

Coincidental   Occurring by chance.

The <u>coincidental</u> meeting of the two old friends was a pleasant surprise for them both.

Commendable   Worthy of praise.

Hank saved three people in the Los Angeles apartment fire; everyone agreed that his actions were <u>commendable</u>.

Competence   The quality of having adequate skill, knowledge, and experience.

Margaret's experience and knowledge of the product increased her <u>competence</u> as a salesperson.

Comprehensive   All-inclusive.

In order to complete her report, Francis required a <u>comprehensive</u> list of books pertaining to plant life.

Concede   To admit or reluctantly yield; to surrender.

The presidential candidate decided to <u>concede</u> defeat based on the latest poll results; he was too far behind to win.

Consequence   Result of an action.

The <u>consequence</u> for cheating was immediate expulsion from school.

Contemporary   Current, modern.

Jon used only <u>contemporary</u> resources in his essay, referring to statistics he discovered in recent newspapers and journals.

Context   Text or spoken words that surround a word or passage and help determine meaning; circumstances that surround an event.

When taken out of <u>context</u>, Sam's statement appeared to be insensitive.

Contradict   To assert the opposite.

Some members of the community believe the mayor is a hypocrite because his actions <u>contradict</u> his words.

Converge   To meet or come together at a common point.

Ambulances, police cars, and fire trucks quickly <u>converged</u> on the scene of the accident.

Cordial   Sincere; courteous.

The doorman at the luxury hotel <u>cordially</u> greeted all arriving guests.

Correlate   To have corresponding characteristics.

Researchers attempted to discover a <u>correlation</u> between the length of time a student studies and the grades that the student receives.

Corroborate   To confirm, to substantiate with evidence.

Further laboratory tests <u>corroborated</u> the scientist's theory that taking vitamins could help to maintain a person's good health.

Crucial   Extremely important.

To get into the university of his choice, it was <u>crucial</u> that David maximize his SAT score.

D

Decipher   To interpret meaning, usually of a code.

Jessica could not <u>decipher</u> her father's handwriting; as a result, his letter did not make sense to her.

Decry   To denounce or criticize.

A loyal fan of classical music, Megan <u>decried</u> all popular rap and hip-hop artists.

Delve   To deeply search through.

Many philosophers and scientists <u>delve</u> into the secrets of the universe.

Derive   To infer certain knowledge; to trace the obtainment or development of something.

Many new scientific hypotheses are <u>derived</u> from existing, proven theories.

Descend   To come from a particular origin; to move down from a higher point.

Both my maternal and my paternal grandfathers <u>descend</u> from British nobility.

The airplane quickly <u>descended</u> for its arrival into sunny Acapulco.

Deter   To prevent from taking a particular course of action.

Many merchants use security guards as a visual <u>deterrent</u> against crime; their presence prevents many thieves from attempting to enter the store.

Diligent   Continuously putting in great effort.

Ben <u>diligently</u> trained for the marathon, running at least 40 miles per week.

Discern   To differentiate or distinguish; to perceive.

The moon's distance from the earth makes it difficult to <u>discern</u> most of the features on the surface of the moon with the naked eye.

Disconcerting   Unsettling.

Linda found the movie <u>disconcerting</u>; there wre too many strange similarities between the plotline and her own life.

Dispel   To rid one's mind of; to drive out.

To <u>dispel</u> any rumors that they had broken up, the celebrity couple began a barrage of public appearances together.

Disperse   To scatter or spread out.

The crowd began to <u>disperse</u> as the concert came to an end.

Docile   Easy to train or teach.

The normally <u>docile</u> students became very rowdy as the day's pep rally drew near.

Drastic   Extreme.

The large budget cuts led to a <u>drastic</u> reduction in the number of workers employed by the company.

Dubious   Unsure, skeptical.

Mike was very <u>dubious</u> when his older brother, infamous for playing pranks, told Mike that he had a surprise for him.

E

Egregious   Noticeably bad or offensive.

William committed an <u>egregious</u> error when he failed to mention his wife during his acceptance speech.

Eloquent Very clear and precise; quality of being skilled in clear and precise speech.

Julie's valedictory speech was quite eloquent; she clearly articulated her hopes and dreams for a prosperous future.

Emit To release or give out.

Environmentalists protested against construction of the new factory, because they feared that the factory would emit too many pollutants into the air.

Empirical Based on or can be proven by observation and experiment.

The hypothesis had to be backed up by empirical evidence in order to be considered credible.

Emulate To follow an admirable example; imitate.

As she entered law school, she hoped to emulate the success of her sister, who was already a prominent partner in a law firm.

Endorse To support or sign.

The sports superstar was paid more than $10 million to endorse the new athletic shoe.

Enigmatic Unexplainable, puzzling.

The Mona Lisa's enigmatic smile is legendary.

Enumerate To state things in a list.

At his performance review, the employee listened to his boss enumerate several ways he could improve his performance in the workplace.

Ephemeral Temporary, fleeting.

Considered a "one-hit wonder," the pop star enjoyed only ephemeral fame.

Ethical In line with the principles of right and wrong.

The attorney was very ethical and refused to allow his client to lie under oath.

Exacerbate To intensify bitterness or violence.

The terrorist attacks exacerbated the already strained relations between the two countries.

Exceptional Having uncommonly great qualities.

Kevin was an exceptional basketball player and received many offers to play at the collegiate level.

Exhort To urge or try to persuade.

After graduating from college, Diana exhorted her parents to lend her the money to start her own business.

Expunge To get rid of or erase.

The speeding infraction would be expunged from John's driving record after he paid a $600 fine and kept a clean record for one year.

Exquisite Characterized by great beauty and intricacy.

The crown jewels were even more <u>exquisite</u> in real life than they appeared to be in photographs.

Extravagant   Lavish beyond the norm.

Jade bought himself the <u>extravagant</u> gift of a new car when he landed the job of his dreams.

Exultant   Gleeful because of success.

The <u>exultant</u> crowd cheered louder than ever when the soccer team won the World Cup.

F

Fabricate   To create or make something up.

The criminal's story was completely <u>fabricated</u>; he lied about every detail of his alibi.

Facilitate   To aid or make easier.

To <u>facilitate</u> good relations between the groups, a meeting was held during which all members had an opportunity to speak.

Feign   To fabricate or deceive.

She <u>feigned</u> astonishment when she walked into her surprise party; her best friend had previously told her about the party.

Fickle   Something that is unpredictable and inconsistent.

The music industry is very <u>fickle</u>, making it difficult to predict who will flourish and who will flop.

Figurative   Using symbolic language or illustrations.

<u>Figuratively</u> speaking, our hockey team was slaughtered in the district championship game.

Flourish   To thrive; a dramatic gesture; a written embellishment.

Orange trees <u>flourish</u> in areas with warm weather.

The orchestra conductor <u>flourished</u> his baton to encourage the wind section to play more loudly.

Forage   To search for food or provisions.

During the cold winter months, many wild animals are forced to <u>forage</u> for scarce food.

Formidable   Capable of arousing fear or awe.

The current championship team was a <u>formidable</u> opponent for the yet unranked team.

Frivolous   Unnecessary and silly.

Dave's mother lectured him constantly about his <u>frivolous</u> spending habits and told him that he needed to start saving for college.

Frugal   Thrifty, not wasteful.

My mother was always very <u>frugal</u>; she saved more money then she spent.

G

Garrulous   Very talkative.

The normally garrulous teenager was very subdued at the party; contrary to her nature, she barely spoke to anyone.

Glib   Doing something with ease and slickness but lacking sincerity.

The president's glib speech about the financial state of the company resulted in a general sense of unease among the members of the staff.

Grandiose   Of great size of magnitude, pompous.

The grandiose palace that the dictator built for himself mirrored his massive ego.

Gratuitous   For no reason and at no cost.

Her gratuitous acts of kindness earned her fondness and respect within the community.

Gullible   Easily tricked.

Internet scams can easily fool gullible people into giving away valuable personal information.

H

Hackneyed   Unoriginal, overused.

The hackneyed plot of the television show led to its cancellation after only three episodes.

Hamper   To prevent from doing something easily.

The lack of a solid business plan often hampers a company's ability to achieve success.

Hierarchy   A way to rank or place things in order.

The business's hierarchy allowed room for all employees to advance within the company if they worked hard enough.

Hostile   Unfriendly, adversarial.

The hostile crowd booed as the opposing team ran out onto the field.

Hypothetical   Based on an assumption or a theory.

The teacher described the hypothetical situation of a person bouncing a ball on a moving train rather than providing an actual example to illustrate Einstein's theory of relativity.

I

Idiosyncrasy   A peculiar characteristic.

One of the most annoying idiosyncrasies of the computer is that it must be completely restarted every 2 hours.

Imminent   Close to happening; impending.

The struggling business is in <u>imminent</u> danger of declaring bankruptcy if sales don't increase soon.

Impartiality   Characterized by fairness.

The court must be convinced of the neutrality and <u>impartiality</u> of any jurors selected for the trial.

Implicit   Implied, not directly expressed.

Although she never voiced her disappointment, it was <u>implicit</u> in her actions.

Imply   To indirectly suggest.

High test scores might <u>imply</u> innate intelligence and good study habits.

Improvise   To do or perform without preparation.

When she won the award, Karen had to <u>improvise</u> an acceptance speech; she hadn't expected to win.

Incarcerate   To put in prison.

Mark was <u>incarcerated</u> in a maximum security prison after being convicted of stealing over $250,000 from the restaurant he managed.

Incorporate   To make a part of.

I tried to <u>incorporate</u> both a sense of nostalgia and a sense of a new beginning into the speech I gave to my high school's graduating class.

Incorrigible   Impossible to change or reform.

The child was <u>incorrigible</u>; he refused to listen when his parents repeatedly told him to stop teasing the dog.

Indifference   Total lack of concern or interest.

The students' <u>indifference</u> frustrated the teacher, who wanted them to be as excited about history as he was.

Indigenous   Native; innate.

The Maori are the <u>indigenous</u> people of New Zealand.

Indignant   Angry because of unfairness.

Leslie became very <u>indignant</u> when her professor refused to change her grade; she felt justified in asking for an A.

Inevitable   Impossible to avoid; predictable.

After spending the weekend doing everything but studying, it was <u>inevitable</u> that she would fail her exam.

Inexplicable   Impossible to give the reason for; unexplainable.

<u>Inexplicably</u>, although he parked in a no-parking zone all day, he did not get a parking ticket.

Infer   To conclude from evidence.

Mr. Mauro was able to <u>infer</u> from his employee's attitude that she was not satisfied with her job.

Infuse   For one substance to penetrate into another.

The steak was <u>infused</u> with garlic, which substantially enhanced its flavor.

Inherent   Naturally occurring.

The risks <u>inherent</u> in driving in a car are surprisingly greater than those associated with riding in an airplane.

Insinuate   To subtly imply or insert.

Andrew attempted to <u>insinuate</u> himself into the conversation by replying to a question that was not directed at him.

Intricate   Highly involved or elaborate.

Despite the difficulties of implementing it, the <u>intricate</u> plan was adopted by the design team.

Invaluable   Priceless.

An <u>invaluable</u> collection of ancient pottery was destroyed when one wing of the museum caught on fire.

Involuntary   An action done without one's consent or free will.

Josh shuddered <u>involuntarily</u> when the door suddenly creaked open and no one was there.

Irony   Use of words to express a meaning that is the opposite of the real meaning; similar to and often confused with sarcasm, which means: words used to insult or scorn.

Noelle's voice was thick with <u>irony</u> as she watched the rain pour down on the beach and commented, "I'm glad the weather is so nice for our vacation!"

Irrevocable   Impossible to reverse.

Tearing down the Victorian-era homes and replacing them with condominiums would <u>irrevocably</u> alter the character of the community.

J

Jeopardize   To endanger.

Eliza knew that letting her grades slip would <u>jeopardize</u> her chances of getting into college, so she continued to study diligently.

Judicious   Sensible, having good judgment.

Kate's decision not to take the job appeared to be quite <u>judicious</u>, considering that she had no previous marketing experience.

Juxtapose   To place things next to each other to compare or contrast.

The artist <u>juxtaposed</u> some of his early sketches with some of his later works to show how much his style had changed over time.

K

Keen   Quick-witted, sharp.

His keen sense of smell allowed him to guess what was for dinner long before he reached the kitchen.

Kudos   Compliments for achievements.

The volunteers all received kudos for their work at the homeless shelter.

L

Languish   To exist in a dreadful or gloomy situation; to become weak.

The convict had been languishing in prison for nearly 20 years.

Lavish   *adj.* Elaborate and luxurious; *v.* To freely and boundlessly bestow.

He showered her with lavish gifts of jewelry and clothes in an attempt to win her over.

He lavished her with compliments throughout their courtship.

Lenient   Easy-going, tolerant.

Sarah's parents were not lenient at all when it came to grades; she was expected to earn straight As.

Listless   Characterized by a lack of energy.

During his long illness, Michael became very listless and spent most of his time in bed.

Lithe   Gracefully slender.

Her lithe, athletic figure helped her to excel as a dancer.

Loathsome   Offensive, disgusting.

His loathsome behavior ultimately resulted in his being fired; his employers had received numerous complaints from his coworkers.

Loquacious   Very talkative or rambling.

My plans for a quiet dinner were disrupted by a loquacious patron seated at the next table.

M

Magnanimous   Courageous, generous, or noble.

Coach Davis was magnanimous in defeat and congratulated the winning team on a game well played.

Malevolent   Purposefully wishing harm on others.

The villain in the movie was a <u>malevolent</u> old man who would stop at nothing to gain power over the citizens in his community.

Manifest   *adj.* Clearly recognizable; *v.* To make clear; *n.* A list of transported goods or passengers used for record keeping.

The airline workers' dissatisfaction with their wages <u>manifested</u> itself as a two-week long strike.

The cruise ship's <u>manifest</u> did not include Jen's name, even though she had purchased her ticket well in advance of the ship's departure.

Melancholy   Glumness; deep contemplative thought.

Reid attributed his <u>melancholy</u> mood to the weather; it had been raining for nearly a week straight.

Melodramatic   Overly emotional or sentimental.

"I'm never talking to you AGAIN!" she exclaimed <u>melodramatically</u> to her sister.

Metamorphosis   A transformation or change.

The new CEO vowed that the struggling business would undergo a complete <u>metamorphosis</u> and that it would soon be thriving and successful.

Meticulous   Devoting a high amount of attention to detail.

Janine was <u>meticulous</u> about her appearance and refused to be seen in public without makeup.

Mollify   To calm down or alleviate, to soften.

The experienced referees attempted to <u>mollify</u> the angry players before a fight broke out.

Monotony   Repetitive, lacking variety.

The <u>monotony</u> of the professor's lecture quickly put many of her students to sleep.

Moral   *adj.* Based on standards of good and bad; *n.* A rule of proper behavior.

Many people blame television and video games for the <u>moral</u> decline of America's youth.

Mundane   Occurring everyday, routine.

In Nancy's opinion, any time spent on <u>mundane</u> tasks such as cleaning the house and cooking meals was time that could be better spent; as a result, Nancy was overweight and lived in a dirty home.

Munificence   The act of liberally giving.

The soup kitchen was able to feed over one thousand homeless people every day, thanks to the <u>munificence</u> of its supporters.

N

Naive   Lacking experience in life or the world.

She was very naive to believe that everything she read in the tabloids was true.

Narcissism   Being conceited or having too much admiration for oneself.

Carrie's extreme narcissism prevented her from having a conversation about anything but herself.

Negligent   Characterized by carelessness and neglectfulness.

His often negligent behavior led to his being replaced by a more diligent manager.

Negligible   Meaningless and insignificant.

The difference between the two brands of baby food was negligible; both offered the same nutritional value at a similar cost to the consumer.

Nonchalant   Behavior that is indifferent or unconcerned.

Libby's nonchalant manner after losing her roommate's cell phone was infuriating.

Noxious   Unwholesome or harmful.

Environmentalists protested the construction of a new factory that would emit large quantities of noxious gases into the atmosphere each day.

Nurture   To support or help in development.

The young parents tried to nurture their toddler's intellectual development by reading five books to him every day.

O

Onerous   Very troublesome or oppressive.

The police had the onerous task of somehow convincing the kidnapper to set his hostages free.

Ostracize   To eliminate from a group.

His friends ostracized him when they found out that Rick had been gossiping about them behind their backs.

Overt   Obvious and clearly shown.

The overt stares Charlie received when he walked into the room made him realize that he had not dressed appropriately for the occasion.

P

Paradox   A self-contradiction; something that appears to be self-contradictory but is nonetheless true.

It was a strange paradox that adding more capacity to the network actually reduced its overall performance.

Penchant   A tendency or fondness.

Her penchant for designer clothes was something that her income could simply not afford her.

Perceive   To become aware of something, usually through the senses.

Perceiving the sadness in his voice, I asked him if anything was wrong.

Periphery   The outermost boundary of an area.

Paul jogged daily along the periphery of the lake, enjoying the view of the water as he worked out.

Peruse   To examine or review something.

Each day Liz perused the want ads in the newspaper, desperately trying to find a job.

Pervasive   Capable of spreading or flowing throughout.

Living on a farm, it was impossible to avoid the pervasive smell of cow manure at certain times during the year.

Phenomenon   Observable fact or event; an unusual, significant, or outstanding occurrence.

Many cosmological phenomena have yet to be fully explained.

Plagiarize   To copy another's work and pretend that it is original.

The journalist was sued for plagiarizing an article from another writer and selling it to a national magazine.

Plausible   Reasonable, likely.

Her reasons seemed highly plausible; nonetheless, her friends found it hard to accept her unusual tardiness.

Pragmatic   Practical.

She was pragmatic in her approach to applying for the job; she thoroughly researched the company prior to her interview.

Predominant   More noticeable, important, or powerful; most common or prominent.

The predominant reason for the huge jump in sales was the millions of dollars pumped into the product's advertising campaign.

Preliminary   Preceding or coming prior to.

Preliminary election polls predict that Grant will win the election, but we'll have to wait until election day to know for sure.

Prerequisite   Required beforehand.

As a <u>prerequisite</u> for the study abroad program in Paris, a student was required to study French for a minimum of three years.

Prestigious   Having honor or respect from others.

Joey won the <u>prestigious</u> "Rookie of the Year" award for posting higher sales than anyone else in his region.

Prevail   To triumph or come out on top.

Much to her surprise, Amy <u>prevailed</u> as the spelling bee champion for the second year in a row.

Prevalent   Widely or commonly occurring or accepted.

Poverty is <u>prevalent</u> in most countries with centrally planned economies.

Procure   To acquire something.

Phoebe managed somehow to <u>procure</u> two tickets to the sold-out concert.

Promulgate   To publicize.

At the township meeting, the mayor <u>promulgated</u> his beliefs that the new governor was unfit for the job.

Prototype   An original form of something.

The <u>prototypes</u> of countless sports cars will be debuted at the auto show next week.

Protracted   Lengthy.

Mr. Miller took a <u>protracted</u> leave of absence from school; his health was failing.

Prowess   Great skill or ability in something.

Chandler's athletic <u>prowess</u> was overshadowed by that of his legendary older brother, who was named MVP all four years of his high school football career.

Q

Querulous   Characterized by constant complaining or whining.

The losing candidate's <u>querulous</u> remarks regarding his opponent were not included in the newspaper article.

Quixotic   Unpredictable and impractical.

The <u>quixotic</u> nature of the weather in April requires that you carry an umbrella with you wherever you go.

R

Rapt   Being completely occupied by or focused on something.

The children watched the magician with <u>rapt</u> attention, enchanted by his illusions.

Reciprocate   To give and take in equal amounts.

After I purchased all of Rachel's groceries for her, it was only fair that she <u>reciprocated</u> by cooking me dinner.

Relevant   Logically connected; pertinent.

The state of a nation's economy is highly <u>relevant</u> to calculating the exchange rates of its currency.

Reluctant   Unwilling; resistant.

The student was <u>reluctant</u> to reveal his poor grades to his mother.

Remedial   Intending to correct or remedy.

Josh's <u>remedial</u> treatment included physical therapy 2 days each week.

Reproach   Expressing disapproval.

Zach's wife <u>reproached</u> him for spending all of his time watching sports on TV.

Resolute   Definite, determined.

Kelly is <u>resolute</u> in her decision to run a marathon this year, despite her current inability to run more than one mile without a break.

Resonant   Strong and deep; lasting.

The <u>resonant</u> voices of the choir rang out through the concert hall.

Rife   Very frequent or common.

During the winter, runny noses and sore throats were <u>rife</u> among the children at the daycare center.

Rudimentary   Relating to basic facts; elementary.

The child's painting was very <u>rudimentary</u>; it did not display the skill of a more accomplished artist.

S

Scrutinize   Closely examine.

Jenna <u>scrutinized</u> her face in the mirror every morning, hoping that she wouldn't find any new wrinkles.

Shrouded   Covered, concealed.

Staci's wedding plans were <u>shrouded</u> in secrecy; she refused to share even the smallest detail.

Simultaneously   Happening or existing at the same time.

When Jane was hired, she felt <u>simultaneously</u> happy and concerned.

Skepticism   An attitude of doubt or disbelief.

Miranda's claims to be a psychic were met with <u>skepticism</u> by her friends and family.

Solace   Comfort, safety.

Paul sought <u>solace</u> from the cold near the roaring fireplace in his living room.

Stagnant   Not moving or changing; stale.

The water in the pond was <u>stagnant</u> and choked with weeds.

Stoic   Indifferent or unaffected.

Kevin's <u>stoic</u> expression gave no clue as to what he was thinking about.

Strident   Offensively harsh and loud.

Many people are repelled by Fran's <u>strident</u> laugh.

Subjective   Depending or based on a person's attitudes or opinions.

I think that my best friend is the greatest actress in the world, but my opinion of her is rather <u>subjective</u>.

Suppress   To restrain or reduce.

Maria couldn't <u>suppress</u> an excited yelp when the recruiter called to inform her that she had gotten the job.

Sustenance   Things that provide nourishment for survival.

Meals from fast food restaurants are high in calories but provide little <u>sustenance</u>.

Synchronized   Occurring at the same time and at the same rate.

The lights in the show were <u>synchronized</u> with the pulsing rhythm of the music.

Synthesize   To combine to form a new, more complex product.

Ideas from all departments were <u>synthesized</u> to create the new operations manual.

T

Tacit   Implied or unspoken.

With a smile, Rob's girlfriend gave <u>tacit</u> approval of his gift of a dozen roses.

Tenuous   Very thin or consisting of little substance.

My sister has a <u>tenuous</u> grasp of physics; she does not completely understand how the physical world works.

Transcend   To go above and beyond; to rise above.

His hard-earned financial success <u>transcended</u> his humble upbringing.

Transgress   To exceed or violate.

Joel was forced to pay for his many <u>transgressions</u> by performing six months of community service.

Translucent   Allowing light to pass through but clouded or frosted in such a way that objects on the other side are not clearly visible; often confused with *transparent*, which means clear.

The Withrows replaced the glass in their bathroom window with a <u>translucent</u> glass pane so that outsiders could not see into the room.

Trivialize   To make something appear insignificant.

She attempted to <u>trivialize</u> her failing grade by telling her parents that the class was not part of her required curriculum.

U

Uniform   Continuing to be the same, consistent; *n.* Identical clothing worn by members of a certain group.

The teacher used a specific grading rubric to score her papers, ensuring that grades were distributed <u>uniformly</u> among the students.

Unprecedented   Having no previous example.

The coffee shop franchise was opening new locations at an <u>unprecedented</u> rate, with an average of eight new stores opening per day across the country.

Utilitarian   Useful or practical.

The workers' coveralls were very <u>utilitarian</u> but had no regard at all for style or looks.

V

Variegated   Having a variety of colors or marks.

Calico cats have <u>variegated</u> coats of many shades of brown, tan, black, and white.

Versatile   Having many uses or a variety of abilities.

She is a very <u>versatile</u> singer and is equally as comfortable singing operatic arias as she is singing country-western ballads.

Vindication   The act of clearing someone or something from blame.

The suspect was <u>vindicated</u> when the person who actually committed the robbery turned himself in.

Virtually   In almost all instances; simulated as by a computer.

The scar from my car accident has <u>virtually</u> disappeared over the past few months.

W

Wane   To gradually decrease.

Randy's interest in his baseball card collection began to <u>wane</u> as he got older.

Wary   Cautious and untrusting.

Emily threw a <u>wary</u> glance at the man who had been following her for nearly five blocks.

Wily   Very sly, deceptive.

The <u>wily</u> politician convinced many voters that he had their best interests at heart, when really he only wanted power for personal gain.

Z

Zealous   Very passionate or enthusiastic.

As a dedicated and honest attorney, Kara remained committed to the <u>zealous</u> pursuit of the truth.

Glossary of SAT/PSAT Math Terms

The reference information included here should serve as a review of the concepts that are commonly tested on both the PSAT and the SAT. Refer to Chapters 6 and 7 for a more in-depth look at the specific math question types and content covered on the tests.

Numbers and Operations

These questions might involve basic arithmetic operations, operations involving exponents, factoring, absolute value, prime numbers, percents, ratios, proportions, sequences, number sets, and number lines.

The Properties of Integers

The following are properties of integers commonly tested on the SAT/PSAT.

▶ Integers include both positive and negative whole numbers.

▶ Zero is considered an integer.

▶ Consecutive integers follow one another and differ by 1.

▶ The value of a number does not change when multiplied by 1.

Order of Operations (PEMDAS)

Following is a description of the correct order in which to perform mathematical operations. The acronym PEMDAS stands for *parentheses*, *exponents*, *multiplication*, *division*, *addition*, *subtraction*. It should help you to remember to do the operations in the correct order, as follows:

1. **P**—First, do the operations within the *parentheses*, if any.

2. **E**—Next, do the *exponents*, if any.

3. **M**—Next, do the *multiplication*, in order from left to right.

4. **D**—Next, do the *division*, in order from left to right.

5. **A**—Next, do the *addition*, in order from left to right.

6. **S**—Finally, do the *subtraction*, in order from left to right.

Fractions and Rational Numbers

The following are properties of fractions and rational numbers that are commonly tested on the SAT/PSAT.

- The reciprocal of any number, n, is expressed as 1 over n, or $1/n$. The product of a number and its reciprocal is always 1. For example, the reciprocal of 3 is $\frac{1}{3}$, and $3 \times \frac{1}{3} = \frac{3}{3}$, which is equivalent to 1.

- To change any fraction to a decimal, divide the numerator by the denominator. For example, $\frac{3}{4}$ is equivalent to $3 \div 4$, or 0.75.

- Multiplying and dividing both the numerator and the denominator of a fraction by the same non-zero number results in an equivalent fraction. For example, $\frac{1}{4} \times \frac{3}{3} = \frac{3}{12}$, which can be reduced to $\frac{1}{4}$.

- When adding and subtracting like fractions, add or subtract the numerators and write the sum or difference over the denominator. So, $\frac{1}{8} + \frac{2}{8} = \frac{3}{8}$, and $\frac{4}{7} - \frac{2}{7} = \frac{2}{7}$.

- To simplify a fraction, find a common factor of both the numerator and the denominator. For example, $\frac{12}{15}$ can be simplified into $\frac{4}{5}$ by dividing both the numerator and the denominator by the common factor 3.

- To convert a mixed number to an improper fraction, multiply the whole number by the denominator in the fraction, add the result to the numerator, and place that value over the original denominator. For example, $3\frac{2}{5}$ is equivalent to $(3 \times 5) + 2$ over 5, or $\frac{17}{5}$.

- When multiplying fractions, multiply the numerators to get the numerator of the product, and multiply the denominators to get the denominator of the product. For example, $\frac{3}{5} \times \frac{7}{8} = \frac{21}{40}$.

- When dividing fractions, multiply the first fraction by the reciprocal of the second fraction. For example, $\frac{1}{3} \div \frac{1}{4} = \frac{1}{3} \times \frac{4}{1}$, which equals $\frac{4}{3}$, or $1\frac{1}{3}$.

- A rational number is a fraction whose numerator and denominator are both integers and the denominator does not equal 0.

- Place value refers to the value of a digit in a number relative to its position. Starting from the left of the decimal point and moving toward the left, the values of the digits are ones, tens, hundreds, and so on. Starting to the right of the decimal point and moving toward the right, the values of the digits are tenths, hundredths, thousandths, and so on.

- When numbers are very large or very small, they are often expressed using scientific notation. Scientific notation is indicated by setting a positive number, n, equal to a number less than 10, then multiplying that number by 10 raised to an integer. The integer depends on the number of places to the left or right that the decimal was moved. For example, 667,000,000 written in scientific notation would be 6.67×10^8, and 0.0000000298 written in scientific notation would be 2.98×10^{-8}.

Ratio, Proportion, and Percent

The following are properties of ratios, proportions, and percents that are commonly tested on the SAT/PSAT.

▶ A ratio expresses a mathematical comparison between two quantities. A ratio of 1 to 5, for example, is written as either $\frac{1}{5}$ or 1:5.

▶ When working with ratios, be sure to differentiate between part-part and part-whole ratios. If two components of a recipe are being compared to each other, for example, this is a part-part ratio (2 cups of flour:1 cup of sugar). If one group of students is being compared to the entire class, for example, this is a part-whole ratio (13 girls:27 students).

▶ A proportion indicates that one ratio is equal to another ratio. For example, $\frac{1}{5} = \frac{x}{20}$ is a proportion.

▶ A percent is a fraction whose denominator is 100. The fraction 25/100 is equal to 25%.

Squares and Square Roots

The following are properties of squares and square roots that are commonly tested on the SAT/PSAT.

▶ Squaring a negative number yields a positive result. For example, $-2^2 = 4$.

▶ The square root of a number, n, is written as $\sqrt{n}$, or the non-negative value a that fulfills the expression $a^2 = n$. For example, the square root of 5 is expressed as $\sqrt{5}$, and $(\sqrt{5})^2 = 5$.

▶ A number is considered a perfect square when the square root of that number is a whole number. The polynomial $a^2 \pm 2ab + b^2$ is also a perfect square because the solution set is $(a \pm b)^2$.

Arithmetic and Geometric Sequences

The following are properties of arithmetic and geometric sequences that are commonly tested on the SAT/PSAT.

▶ An arithmetic sequence is one in which the difference between one term and the next is the same. To find the nth term, use the formula $a_n = a_1 + (n-1)d$, where d is the common difference.

▶ A geometric sequence is one in which the ratio between two terms is constant. For example, $\frac{1}{2}$, 1, 2, 4, 8..., is a geometric sequence where 2 is the constant ratio. To find the nth term, use the formula $a_n = a_1(r)^{n-1}$, where r is the constant ratio.

Sets of Numbers

The following are properties of number sets that are commonly tested on the SAT/PSAT

► A set is a collection of numbers. The numbers are elements or members of the set. For example, {2, 4, 6, 8} is the set of positive, even integers less than 10.

► The *union* of two sets includes all of the elements in each set. For example, if Set A = {2, 4, 6, 8} and Set B = {1, 3, 5, 7, 9}, then {1, 2, 3, 4, 5, 6, 7, 8, 9} is the union of Set A and Set B.

► The *intersection* of two sets identifies the common elements of two sets. For example, if Set A = {1, 2, 3, 4} and Set B = {2, 4, 6, 8}, then {2, 4} is the intersection of Set A and Set B.

Factors and Multiples

The following are properties of factors and multiples that are commonly tested on the SAT/PSAT.

► A prime number is any number that can only be divided by itself and 1. That is, 1 and number itself are the only factors of a prime number. For example, 2, 3, 5, 7, and 11 are prime numbers. (Note that 2 is the only even prime number.)

► Factors are all of the numbers that divide evenly into one number. For example, 1, 2, 4, and 8 are all factors of 8.

► Common factors include all of the factors that two or more numbers share. For example, 1, 2, 4, and 8 are all factors of 8, and 1, 2, 3, and 6 are all factors of 6. Therefore, 8 and 6 have common factors of 1 and 2.

► The Greatest Common Factor (GCF) is the largest number that divides evenly into any 2 or more numbers. For example, 1, 2, 4, and 8 are all factors of 8, and 1, 2, 3, and 6 are all factors of 6. Therefore, the Greatest Common Factor of 8 and 6 is 2.

► A number is a multiple of another number if it can be expressed as the product of that number and a second number. For example, $2 \times 3 = 6$, so 6 is a multiple of both 2 and 3.

► Common multiples include all of the multiples that two or more numbers share. For example:

Multiples of 3 include $3 \times 4 = 12$; $3 \times 8 = 24$; $3 \times 12 = 36$.

Multiples of 4 include $4 \times 3 = 12$; $4 \times 6 = 24$; $4 \times 9 = 36$.

Therefore, 12, 24, and 36 are all common multiples of both 3 and 4.

- ► The Least Common Multiple (LCM) is the smallest number that any two or more numbers divides evenly into. For example, the common multiples of 3 and 4 are 12, 24, and 36; 12 is the smallest multiple, and is, therefore, the Least Common Multiple of 3 and 4.

- ► The Commutative Property of Multiplication is expressed as $a \times b = b \times a$, or $ab = ba$. For example, $2 \times 3 = 3 \times 2$.

- ► The Distributive Property of Multiplication is expressed as $a(b + c) = ab + ac$. For example, $x(x + 3) = x^2 + 3x$.

Mean, Median, and Mode

The following are properties of mean, median, and mode that are commonly tested on the SAT/PSAT.

- ► The arithmetic mean is equivalent to the average of a series of numbers. Calculate the average by dividing the sum of all of the numbers in the series by the total count of numbers in the series. For example, a student received scores of 80%, 85%, and 90% on 3 math tests. The average score received by the student on those tests is 80 + 85 + 90 divided by 3, or 255/3, which is 85%.

- ► The median is the middle value of a series of numbers when those numbers are in either ascending or descending order. In the series (2, 4, 6, 8, 10) the median is 6. To find the median in an even set of data find the average of the middle two numbers. In the series (3, 4, 5, 6) the median is 4.5.

- ► The mode is the number that appears most frequently in a series of numbers. In the series (2, 3, 4, 5, 6, 3, 7) the mode is 3 because 3 appears twice in the series and the other numbers each appear only once in the series.

Outcomes

Following is a property of outcomes and probability that is commonly tested on the SAT/PSAT. Two specific events are considered independent if the outcome of one event has no effect on the outcome of the other event. For example, if you toss a coin, there is a 1 in 2, or $\frac{1}{2}$, chance that it will land on either heads or tails. If you toss the coin again, the outcome will be the same. To find the probability of two or more independent events occurring together, multiply the outcomes of the individual events. For example, the probability that both coin tosses will result in heads is $\frac{1}{2} \times \frac{1}{2}$, or $\frac{1}{4}$.

Algebra and Functions

These questions might involve factoring, rules of exponents, solving equations and inequalities, solving linear and quadratic equations, setting up equations to solve word problems, and working with functions.

Factoring

The following are properties of factoring that are commonly tested on the SAT/PSAT.

- ▶ The standard form of a simple quadratic expression is $ax^2 + bx + c$, where a, b, and c are whole numbers. $2x^2 + 4x + 4$ is a simple quadratic equation.

- ▶ To add or subtract polynomials (expressions consisting of more than two terms), simply combine like terms. For example, $(2x^2 + 4x + 4) + (3x^2 + 5x + 16) = 5x^2 + 9x + 20$.

- ▶ To multiply polynomials, use the distributive property, expressed as $a(b + c) = ab + ac$. Also remember the *FOIL* Method: multiply the *F*irst terms, then the *O*utside terms, then the *I*nside terms, then the *L*ast terms. For example:

  Distributive Property: $2x(4x + 4) = 8x^2 + 8x$

  FOIL Method: $(x + 2)(x - 2) = x^2 - 2x + 2x - 4$, or $x^2 - 4$.

- ▶ You might be required to find the factors or solution sets of certain simple quadratic expressions. A factor or solution set takes the form $(x \pm \text{some number})$. Simple quadratic expressions usually have two of these factors or solution sets. For example, the solution sets of $x^2 - 4$ are $(x + 2)$ and $(x - 2)$.

- ▶ To find the common factor, simply look for the element that two expressions have in common. For example, $x^2 + 3x = x(x + 3)$; the common factor is x.

- ▶ You might be required to find the difference of two squares. For example, $a^2 - b^2 = (a + b)(a - b)$.

Exponents

The following are properties of exponents that are commonly tested on the SAT.

- ▶ $a^m \times a^n = a^{(m+n)}$

  When multiplying the same base number raised to any power, add the exponents. For example: $3^2 \times 3^4 = 3^6$. Likewise, $3^6 = 3^2 \times 3^4$; $3^6 = 3^1 \times 3^5$; and so on.

- ▶ $(a^m)^n = a^{mn}$

  When raising an exponential expression to a power, multiply the exponent and power. For example: $(3^2)^4 = 3^8$. Likewise, $3^8 = (3^2)^4$; $3^8 = (3^4)^2$; and so on.

- ▶ $(ab)^m = a^m \times b^m$

  When multiplying two different base numbers and raising the product to a power, the product is equivalent to raising each number to the power and multiplying the exponential expressions. For example: $(3 \times 2)^2 = 3^2 \times 2^2$, which equals 9×4, or 36. Likewise, $3^2 \times 2^2 = (3 \times 2)^2$, or 6^2, which equals 36.

- $[\frac{a}{b}]^m = \frac{a^m}{b^m}$

  When dividing two different base numbers and raising the quotient to a power, the quotient is equivalent to raising each number to the power and dividing the exponential expressions. For example: $(\frac{2}{3})^2 = \frac{2^2}{3^2}$, or $\frac{4}{9}$.

- $a^0 = 1$, when $a \neq 0$

  When you raise any number to the power of 0, the result is always 1.

- $a^{-m} = \frac{1}{a^m}$, when $a \neq 0$

  When you raise a number to a negative power, the result is equivalent to 1 over the number raised to the same positive power. For example: $3^{-2} = \frac{1}{3}^2$, or $\frac{1}{9}$.

Inequalities

The following are properties of inequalities that are commonly tested on the SAT/PSAT.

- Greater than is expressed with this symbol: >

- Greater than or equal to is expressed with this symbol: ≥

- Less than is expressed with this symbol: <

- Less than or equal to is expressed with this symbol: ≤

- Inequalities can usually be worked with in the same way equations are worked with. For example, to solve for x in the inequality $2x > 8$, simply divide both sides by 2 to get $x > 4$.

- When an inequality is multiplied by a negative number, you must switch the sign.

  For example, follow these steps to solve for x in the inequality $-2x + 2 < 6$:

  $-2x + 2 < 6$

  $-2x < 4$

  $-x < 2$

  $x > -2$

Word Problems

The following are properties of word problems that are commonly tested on the SAT/PSAT.

- When solving word problems, translate the verbal statements into algebraic expressions. For example:

  "greater than," "more than," and "sum of" mean addition (+)

  "less than," "fewer than," and "difference" mean subtraction (–)

"of" and "by" mean multiplication (×)

"per" means division (÷)

▶ Remember, apply logic and critical thinking to more easily solve word problems.

Functions

The following are properties of functions that are commonly tested on the SAT/PSAT.

▶ A function is a set of ordered pairs where no two of the ordered pairs have the same x-value. In a function, each input (x-value) has exactly one output (y-value). For example: $f(x) = 2x + 3$. If $x = 3$, then $f(x) = 9$. For every x, there is only one $f(x)$, or y.

▶ The *domain* of a function refers to the x-values, while the *range* of a function refers to the y-values.

Geometry

These questions might involve parallel and perpendicular lines, triangles, rectangles and other polygons, circles, area, perimeter, volume, and angle measure in degrees.

Coordinate Geometry

The following are properties of coordinate geometry that are commonly tested on the SAT/PSAT. The (x, y) coordinate plane is defined by two axes at right angles to each other. The horizontal axis is the x-axis, and the vertical axis is the y-axis.

The origin is the point (0, 0), where the two axes intersect, as shown in Figure B.1.

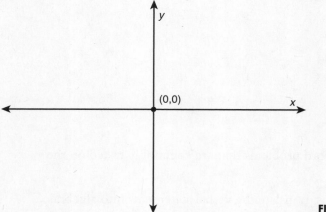

FIGURE B.1 Origin.

The slope of a line is calculated by taking the change in y-coordinates divided by the change in x-coordinates from two given points on a line. The formula for slope is $m = \frac{(y_2 - y_1)}{(x_2 - x_1)}$ where (x_1, y_1) and (x_2, y_2) are the two given points.

A positive slope means the graph of the line goes up and to the right. A negative slope means the graph of the line goes down and to the right. A horizontal line has slope 0, while a vertical line has an undefined slope because it never crosses the y-axis. See Figure B.2.

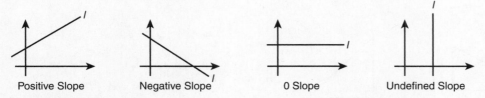

Positive Slope   Negative Slope   0 Slope   Undefined Slope

FIGURE B.2 Different slopes.

The slope-intercept (standard) form of the equation of a line is $y = mx + b$, where m is the slope of the line and b is the y-intercept (that is, the point at which the graph of the line crosses the y-axis).

Two lines are parallel if and only if they have the same slope. For example, the two lines with equations $2y = 3x + 7$ and $y = 3x - 14$ have the same slope (3).

Two lines are perpendicular if and only if the slope of one of the lines is the negative reciprocal of the slope of the other line. In other words, if line a has a slope of 2, and line b has a slope of $\frac{-1}{2}$, the two lines are perpendicular.

To find the distance between two points in the (x, y) coordinate plane, use the formula $\sqrt{(x_2 - x_1)^2 + (y_2 - y_1)^2}$, where (x_1, y_1) and (x_2, y_2) are the two given points.

To find the midpoint of a line given two points on the line, use the formula $(\frac{[x_1 + x_2]}{2}, \frac{[y_1 + y_2]}{2})$.

A translation slides an object in the coordinate plane to the left or right or up or down. The object retains its shape and size and faces in the same direction.

A reflection flips an object in the coordinate plane over either the *x*-axis or the *y*-axis. When a reflection occurs across the *x*-axis, the *x*-coordinate remains the same, but the *y*-coordinate is transformed into its opposite. When a reflection occurs across the *y*-axis, the *y*-coordinate remains the same, but the *x*-coordinate is transformed into its opposite. The object retains its shape and size.

Triangles

The following are properties of triangles that are commonly tested on the SAT/PSAT.

- In an equilateral triangle, all three sides have the same length, and each interior angle measures 60°.

- In an isosceles triangle, two sides have the same length.

- The sum of the interior angles in a triangle is always 180°.

▶ The perimeter (P) of a triangle is the sum of the lengths of the sides.

▶ The area (A) of a triangle is equivalent to $\frac{1}{2}$(base)(height).

▶ The Pythagorean Theorem states that $c^2 = a^2 + b^2$, where c is the hypotenuse (the side opposite the right angle) of a right triangle and a and b are the two other sides of the triangle. You might also see the Pythagorean Theorem written as $a^2 + b^2 = c^2$.

▶ Figure B.3 shows angle measures and side lengths for Special Right Triangles:

30-60-90 Triangle

45-45-90 Triangle   **FIGURE B.3** Special right triangles.

▶ The sides of a 3-4-5 Special Right Triangle have the ratio 3:4:5.

Quadrilaterals, Lines, and Angles

The following are properties of quadrilaterals, lines, and angles that are commonly tested on the SAT/PSAT.

▶ In a parallelogram, the opposite sides are of equal length, and the opposite angles are equal.

▶ The area (A) of a parallelogram is equivalent to (base)(height).

▶ A rectangle is a polygon with four sides (two sets of congruent, or equal sides) and four right angles. All rectangles are parallelograms.

▶ The sum of the angles in a rectangle is always 360°.

▶ The perimeter (P) of both a parallelogram and a rectangle is equivalent to $2l + 2w$, where l is the length and w is the width.

▶ The area (A) of a rectangle is equivalent to $(l)(w)$.

▶ The lengths of the diagonals of a rectangle are congruent, or equal.

▶ A square is a special rectangle where all four sides are of equal length. All squares are rectangles.

▶ The length of the diagonals of a square are equivalent to the length of one side times $\sqrt{2}$.

▶ When two parallel lines are cut by a *transversal*, each parallel line has four angles surrounding the intersection that are matched in measure and position with a counterpart at the other parallel line. The vertical (opposite) angles are congruent, and the adjacent angles are supplementary (they total 180°). See Figure B.4.

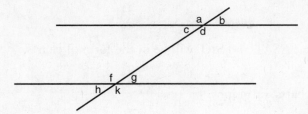

FIGURE B.4 Parallel lines cut by a transversal.

▸ An acute angle is any angle less than 90°.

▸ An obtuse angle is any angle that is greater than 90° and less than 180°.

▸ A right angle is an angle that measures exactly 90°.

Circles

The following are properties of circles that are commonly tested on the SAT/PSAT.

▸ The radius (*r*) of a circle is the distance from the center of the circle to any point on the circle.

▸ The diameter (*d*) of a circle is twice the radius.

▸ The area (A) of a circle is equivalent to πr^2.

▸ The circumference (C) of a circle is equivalent to $2\pi r$ or πd.

▸ The equation of a circle centered at the point (*h*, *k*) is $(x - h)^2 + (y - k)^2 = r^2$, where *r* is the radius of the circle.

▸ The complete arc of a circle has 360°.

▸ A tangent to a circle is a line that touches the circle at exactly one point.

Special Symbols

Special symbols are sometimes defined on the PSAT and SAT. Read the definition carefully and evaluate the mathematical expressions given in the question.

For example:

Let $a \ominus b = \frac{1}{ab}$. What is the value of $2 \ominus 3$?

To solve, simply substitute the numbers given in the problem for *a* and b.

$2 \ominus 3 = \frac{1}{(2)(3)} = \frac{1}{6}$

Data Interpretation

Some of the information presented on the PSAT and SAT will be in the form of charts, tables, and graphs.

Carefully read the labels on the tables, charts, or graphs.

Make sure that you understand the relationships between the data represented in the tables, charts, or graphs before you answer the question. For example:

Price of Computer X, Projected	# of Computers Sold, Projected
$400	250
$600	100

Based on the projections, how much more money would be received from sales of Computer X when the price is $400 than when the price is $600?

(A) $10,000

(B) $40,000

(C) $60,000

(D) $100,000

(E) $250,000

The correct answer is B. To solve this problem, first notice that more computers are projected to be sold for $400 rather than $600. Next, calculate the total projected dollars to be received from sales at $400, as follows:

$250 \times \$400 = \$100,000$

Now, calculate the total projected dollars to be received from sales at $600, as follows:

$100 \times \$600 = \$60,000$

Because you are asked for the difference (how much more money would be received from sales of Computer X when the price is $400 than when the price is $600), subtract $60,000 from $100,000. Based on the information in the table, $40,000 more would be received. The other answer choices could be arrived at if you either misinterpreted the data or performed the wrong mathematical calculations.

APPENDIX C

Additional Resources

The purpose of this book is to help you prepare for both the PSAT and SAT. While this book provides you with helpful information about the tests and realistic practice materials to get you ready for the real thing, the following additional resources might also be useful in your preparation:

The College Board Website

The College Board website (http://www.collegeboard.com) offers a wealth of up-to-date information about the PSAT and SAT. Once you get to the "For Students" area of the website, you can find out when and where the tests are administered, try practice questions from past tests, and even access MyRoad™, an online program designed to help you explore different majors, colleges, and careers.

National Merit Scholarships

The primary purpose of the PSAT is to qualify students for the National Merit Scholarhip. Each year, approximately 10,000 students receive scholarships worth a total of $50 million for college undergraduate study. Find out more about this program by visiting http://www.nationalmerit.org.

The Official SAT Study Guide for the New SAT

The Official SAT Study Guide for the New SAT (ISBN 0-87447-718-2), published by the College Board, is a great source of practice material for both the PSAT and the SAT. This book is usually available at all the major bookstores. Pick one up as a great complement to *SAT/PSAT Exam Prep*. You can order it online at http://AdvantageEd.com/hsbooks.htm.

Advantage Education Programs

Advantage Education offers many programs for college-bound students, including programs that prepare students for the PSAT, SAT, and ACT, as well as admissions counseling and college preparation. To learn about individual tutoring, workshops, courses, and other programs for college-bound students, visit http://AdvantageEd.com.

Sources for Help with Vocabulary

We've discovered two books that take a unique approach to learning vocabulary words that are often tested on both the PSAT and the SAT. These books are designed to make learning vocabulary words fun and interesting by using them in exciting mystery novels. Check out *Tooth and Nail* (ISBN 0-15-601382-7) and *Test of Time* (ISBN 0-15-601137-9), both usually available at major bookstores. Order them online at http://AdvantageEd.com/hsbooks.htm.

School Textbooks

Middle school and high school textbooks are extremely valuable resources. The content areas tested on the PSAT and SAT are the same content areas that you've been studying in school. Hence, textbooks cover many of the relevant skills and subjects you will need for success on the PSAT and SAT. If you do not have your textbooks, your school library should have copies that you can use.

Teachers and Older Students

Don't forget to talk to teachers and older students who have some experience with the PSAT and SAT. They might be able to shed some additional light on getting ready for the test. It is in your best interest to be as well prepared as possible on test day.

Index

A

Q

THIS BOOK IS SAFARI ENABLED

INCLUDES FREE 45-DAY ACCESS TO THE ONLINE EDITION

The Safari® Enabled icon on the cover of your favorite technology book means the book is available through Safari Bookshelf. When you buy this book, you get free access to the online edition for 45 days.

Safari Bookshelf is an electronic reference library that lets you easily search thousands of technical books, find code samples, download chapters, and access technical information whenever and wherever you need it.

TO GAIN 45-DAY SAFARI ENABLED ACCESS TO THIS BOOK:

- Go to **http://www.examcram.com/safarienabled**

- Complete the brief registration form

- Enter the coupon code: **NQEL-481C-1LHT-MICE-8F43**

If you have difficulty registering on Safari Bookshelf or accessing the online edition, please e-mail customer-service@safaribooksonline.com.

Prepare for your tests with products from Pearson Education

The Global Leader in Educational Publishing

Exam Prep books from Pearson Education provide comprehensive preparation tools, from learning the topics, to test-taking strategies, to practice exams for confidence building and self-assessment. The partnership between industry-expert authors and the proven tools and techniques of the Exam Prep line of books creates a unique way for students to learn and prepare at the same time, ensuring test success and knowledge retention.

Visit www.examcram.com to find out more about these and other Exam Prep and Exam Cram titles.

EXAM✓PREP

GRE Exam Prep
ISBN: 0789735946

NCLEX-RN Exam Prep
ISBN: 0789735962

ACT Exam Prep
ISBN: 0789736160

GED Exam Prep
ISBN: 0789736586

LSAT Exam Prep
ISBN: 0789735954